FOURTH EDITION

# HUMANKIND EMERGING

## Bernard G. Campbell

# HUMANKIND
# EMERGING

# HUMANKIND EMERGING

## Fourth Edition

**Bernard G. Campbell,** EDITOR

University of California, Los Angeles

This volume has been adapted in part from materials
published by TIME-LIFE BOOKS in two series:
*The Emergence of Man* and *The LIFE Nature Library*

LITTLE, BROWN AND COMPANY
Boston    Toronto

**Library of Congress Cataloging in Publication Data**

Main entry under title:

Humankind emerging.

"This volume has been adapted in part from materials published by Time-Life Books in two series: The emergence of man, and The life nature library."
Bibliography: p.
Includes index.
1. Human evolution.   2. Man, Prehistoric.
3. Physical anthropology.    I. Campbell, Bernard Grant.
GN281.H85 1984        573        84-27796
ISBN 0-316-12553-9

Library of Congress Catalog Card No. 84-27796


ISBN 0-316-12553-9


9  8  7  6  5  4  3  2  1

MV

Published simultaneously in Canada
by Little, Brown & Company (Canada) Limited

Printed in the United States of America

*Edited portions of the following volumes are included in this text.*
*Cro-Magnon Man* by Tom Prideaux and the Editors of TIME-LIFE BOOKS. © 1973 TIME-LIFE BOOKS Inc. Consultants: Philip E. L. Smith, Richard Klein.
*Early Man* by F. Clark Howell and the Editors of TIME-LIFE BOOKS. © 1965, 1973 TIME-LIFE BOOKS Inc.
*Evolution* by Ruth Moore and the Editors of TIME-LIFE BOOKS. © 1962, 1964 TIME-LIFE BOOKS Inc.
*The First Cities* by Dora Jane Hamblin and the Editors of TIME-LIFE BOOKS. © 1973 TIME-LIFE BOOKS Inc. Consultant: C. C. Lamberg-Karlovsky.
*The First Farmers* by Jonathan Norton Leonard and the Editors of TIME-LIFE BOOKS. © 1973 TIME-LIFE BOOKS Inc. Consultant: Robert H. Dyson, Jr.
*The First Men* by the Editors of TIME-LIFE BOOKS and Edmund White and Dale Brown. © 1973 TIME-LIFE BOOKS Inc. Consultants: Bernard G. Campbell, F. Clark Howell.

*Life Before Man* by the Editors of TIME-LIFE BOOKS and Peter Wood, Louis Vaczek, Dora Jane Hamblin, and Jonathan Norton Leonard. © 1972 TIME-LIFE BOOKS Inc. Consultants: A. W. Crompton, Farish A. Jenkins, Jr., Robert T. Bakker, Theodore Delevoryas, John H. Ostrom, Elwyn L. Simons.
*The Missing Link* by Maitland A. Edey and the Editors of TIME-LIFE BOOKS. © 1972 TIME-LIFE BOOKS Inc. Consultants: Sherwood L. Washburn, Bernard G. Campbell.
*The Neanderthals* by George Constable and the Editors of TIME-LIFE BOOKS. © 1973 TIME-LIFE BOOKS Inc. Consultant: Ralph S. Solecki.
*The Primates* by Sarel Eimerl and Irven DeVore and the Editors of TIME-LIFE BOOKS. © 1965, 1974 TIME-LIFE BOOKS Inc.

**Cover photo**   Gilles Guittard/The Image Bank.
**Title page photo**   Leonard Lee Rue/Animals, Animals.

*(continued on page 515)*

# Preface

In preparing this fourth edition of *Humankind Emerging*, I have tried to strengthen the features that made the earlier editions so popular in introductory anthropology, physical anthropology, and human evolution courses. The book treats all the subdisciplines and relatives of physical anthropology, such as genetics, modern variation and adaptation, and the behavior of nonhuman primates. But it focuses on paleoanthropology, that science that fits together the fossil and cultural evidence of human evolution into a coherent statement. Through the book's eighteen chapters, the reader sees what we know of how, when, and where we came to exist. The investigation of our past is exciting, and *Humankind Emerging* conveys the excitement to students who are studying physical anthropology for the first time. Each short chapter relates a story of discovery while expounding an important topic, with a minimum of technical language.

This edition includes the most recent fossil finds as well as the latest interpretations of both new and older discoveries. As in previous editions, the photographs, drawings, and charts give students visual help in learning where we came from, who we are, and how we know. And I have tried to carry through the spirit of the book's title, emphasizing the complementary and equal roles of the two sexes, by eliminating the use of "man" or "he" to refer to the human species as a whole.

*Humankind Emerging* continues to benefit from material in TIME-LIFE BOOKS' Emergence of Man series and The LIFE Nature Library, from which the text and illustrations were originally developed. My thanks go to the authors, editors, and consultants who worked on those volumes. Teachers and students who used the early editions have provided constructive suggestions for change. Many friends and colleagues were generous with their time and comments. Several anthropologists helped especially by sharing their thoughts in careful and detailed reviews. My special thanks to Peter Andrews, British Museum (Natural History); Peter J. Bertocci, Oakland University; David Carpenter, Oakland Community College; John van Couvering, American Museum of Natural History; David M. Glassman, Southwest Foundation for Research and Education; James D. Loy, University of Rhode Island; and James J. McKenna, Pomona College.

Finally, I want to thank Susan Campbell, who created the delightful environment in which I work, and Brad Gray, Sally Stickney, and Linda Belamarich of Little, Brown, who have made a vital contribution to the book's continuing success.

# Contents

# Introduction

Know then thyself, presume not God to scan;
The proper study of mankind is man.
Placed on this isthmus in a middle state,
A being darkly wise, and rudely great:
With too much knowledge for the sceptic side,
With too much weakness for the Stoic's pride,
He hangs between; in doubt to act or rest;
In doubt to deem himself a God, or beast;
In doubt his mind or body to prefer;
Born but to die; and reas'ning but to err;
Alike in ignorance, his reason such,
Whether he thinks too little or too much;
Chaos of Thought and Passion, all confused;
Still by himself abused, or disabused;
Created half to rise, and half to fall;
Great Lord of all things, yet a prey to all;
Sole judge of truth, in endless error hurled;
The glory, jest, and riddle of the world!

ALEXANDER POPE, 1688–1744.
*Essay on Man*, Ep. ii, 1, 1–18.

These profound and brilliant lines by the English poet and satirist Alexander Pope describe the paradox of human nature. Throughout history, people have been puzzled and exasperated by humankind's strange duality of nature—half animal, half angel—and much of religious and philosophic teaching has been an attempt to understand and integrate these two sides of our being. Neither priest nor philosopher has offered us an explanation that has proved either intellectually satisfactory or (in modern jargon) operationally effective. The writings of wise men through the ages have not enabled most of us to come to terms with our dual nature, however much we may have thought about these things or faced the moral dilemmas that are our inheritance. On the one hand, we carry the marks and needs of an animal, but on the other hand, we find ourselves alienated and unsure in the natural world and in the face of our own biology. In our imagination, we travel far beyond the bounds of our own environment and our biological nature, and yet we still feel rooted to it in a way that seems to constrict the highest reaches of our humanity. Our forces tend to be ranged opposite each other like the poles and we find ourselves torn between them, caught in a conflict that has been cruelly sharpened by the demands of every culture in every age.

Humanity has, quite logically, looked to the past to explain the present and in so doing has developed mythological accounts of human origins. In the Judeo-Christian religions our duality is explained by a story about a stern God, who placed a perfect man and a perfect woman in paradise and then expelled them from it when they disobeyed His commands. This story of humankind's fall from perfection has been used to account for the darker side of human nature.

Today, we have a different story to explain our duality. This story began to be written with the work of Scottish geologist James Hutton, who demonstrated in 1795 that the world was vastly older than anyone had ever supposed. As this remarkable scientific deduction became generally accepted, humanity's short past was stretched a thousandfold, and to the future, present, and immediate past of the historical period was added prehistory. Understanding this new dimension of human history has become a major requirement for understanding our present.

*Humankind Emerging* is about this new dimension. It recounts the extraordinary story about the discovery of, and the evidence for, humanity's long past. It reveals to us the nature of our distant ancestors, who began the long journey from the African forests to Cape Canaveral. It brings prehistory to bear upon present-day human nature and thus gives us an entirely new way of approaching and understanding ourselves. The evolutionary perspective, which we owe to the genius of Charles Darwin and Alfred Russel Wallace, throws light not only on our humanity but on the darker side of our nature which derives from our animal past. But that is not all: this perspective also shows us the integrated and dynamic evolution of both aspects and their essentially interlocking relationship. The evolutionary perspective gives us profound insights into human nature and shows us that its duality arises not from two warring halves but from two interdependent aspects of an integrated whole—or what should and could be an integrated whole if we saw ourselves as we truly are, instead of as we have mistakenly believed ourselves to be.

This new view of human nature is just one small part of the revolution in knowledge and understanding brought about by the work of Charles Darwin and his successors. Our past has created us and influences or determines every part of our lives. Our present condition is a consequence not just of our individual life history, important though it may be, but of the whole history of the human species. We are, in this sense, a product both of our childhood and of our prehistory.

The theory of evolution has now been developed over more than a century by an enormous amount of painstaking research. The evidence that living organisms have evolved over many millions of years is today very strong and convincing. Science builds up such hypotheses or theories on the basis of a vast range of accumulated *evidence* derived from experiment and observation. Each new piece of evidence has corroborated the central theory. No evidence presently known either falsifies or undermines the theory of organic evolution.

Creationism (misnamed "creation-science"), which posits the separate creation of every species, is based on *belief*—a system of belief developed without a scientific assessment of evidence. It is a modern version of traditional beliefs that are based on the Book of Genesis. It claims that the earth and universe are only 6,000 to 10,000 years of age; that the present physical form of the earth can be explained by "catastrophism," including a worldwide flood that covered the highest mountains; and that all living organisms, including humans, were created at one time essentially in the form in which we find them today. To any person who has read widely, travelled, and observed the earth and its creatures, these ideas are incredible. More than one hundred years of objective observation and research show them to have no foundation. Only by selecting a very limited range of evidence can any sort of case be made for creationism. It is therefore not a scientific theory but a statement of religious belief, which for support draws on the Biblical texts and the work of a few biologists where such work can be manipulated to clothe the belief in a pseudoscientific light.

The theory of evolution and a belief in special creation are not rival explanations of organic life that have comparable status as scientific hypotheses; they are quite distinct approaches to the problem of the origin of species.

Although it was seen in the last century as a devastating threat to fundamentalist religious belief, the theory of evolution does not in any way negate the existence of God. It merely describes the mode in which the creation of living species occurred. We are beginning to understand some of the mechanics of this process of creation: it is no less miraculous, no less full of wonder. As Charles Darwin wrote on the last page of *The Origin of Species:*

There is a grandeur in this view of life, with its several powers, having been originally breathed into a few forms or into one; and that . . . from so simple a beginning endless forms most beautiful and most wonderful have been, and are being, evolved.

# PART I
# EVOLUTION

# Chapter 1

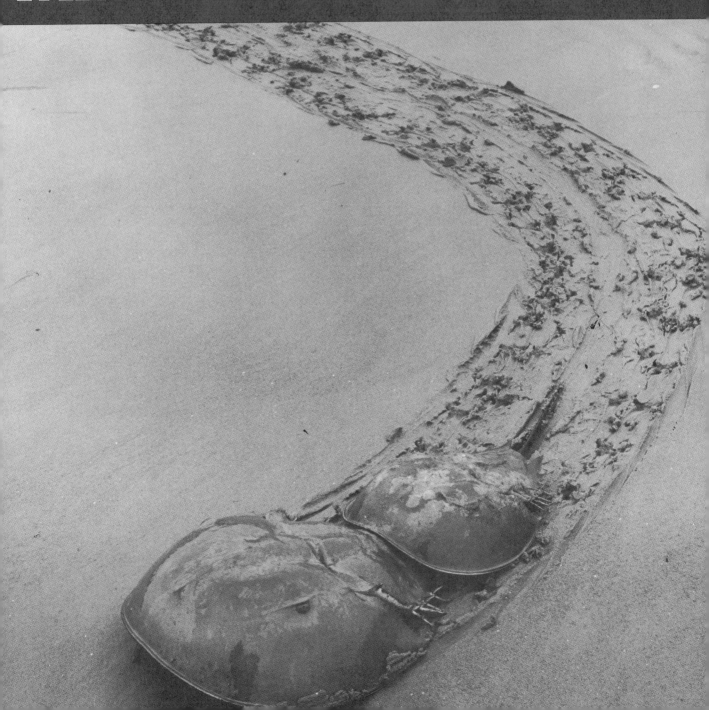

# The Search for Human Origins

I would not be ashamed to have a monkey for my
ancestor, but I would be ashamed to be connected with
a man who used great gifts to obscure the truth.

THOMAS HENRY HUXLEY, 1825–1895.
*Defending Darwin's theory against the attack of Bishop Samuel Wilberforce.*

**EARLY THEORIES OF
HUMAN ORIGINS**

Where did humans come from? The question of our origin has preoccupied human thought for thousands, conceivably for tens of thousands
of years. It is responsible for numerous myths associated with the
world's religions, each myth an attempt to explain the creation of the
earth and of humankind. Many of these explanations are exceedingly
interesting and beautiful, but today much of their detail is no longer
regarded as strictly factual. Instead, they are interpreted as reflections
of a yearning to fathom mysteries not understood, and a fear of the
unknown, and they are seen as poetic attempts to construct a kind of
theological prehistory to satisfy people's curiosity and their need for
meaning.

The story of creation told in the Bible (Genesis 1) is a good case in
point (Figure 1–1). It is seldom taken literally now. Its sweeping concepts are interpreted by most modern Christians and Jews as symbolic
of the spirit and majesty of God. Today the evidence seems unavoidable
that the world was not created in six days as the Bible says it was, but
this discrepancy no longer troubles most devout people. Still, old ideas
die hard; there are men and women in the United States today who
believe that the earth is flat.

FIGURE 1–1  *A woodcut from Schedel's* World Chronicle of 1493 *depicting God's creation of woman from Adam's rib as told in* Genesis.

Three hundred years ago most self-respecting citizens took the Bible literally. Hell was a fiery place beneath their feet; heaven was above them. In the year 1650, Archbishop James Ussher of Armagh, Ireland, making careful calculations based on Biblical references, determined that the year of creation was 4004 B.C. Subsequently this date was inserted in the margins of authorized versions of the Bible, and before long it came to acquire the infallibility of Scripture itself. At about the same time, another cleric working independently of Ussher came up with the exact day and time: the moment of creation was 9 A.M. on October 23.

The Bible also dictated explanations of odd discoveries from within the earth. Along with the shells, petrified wood, and other ancient objects that people had been digging from the earth over the years were some curious things strangely resembling the bones of animals. Though a few authorities held that these objects had been molded into familiar forms by Satan to deceive humankind, the generally accepted notion was that these fossils had been formed by natural forces in chance imitation of life.

## EARLY NATURALISTS

### John Ray

The Reverend John Ray (1627–1705), a Cambridge University lecturer and a great naturalist, recognized that some of the fossilized shells he collected in the mountains were exactly like other shells he gathered on the seashore. The landlocked fossils were obviously the remains of fish and shellfish that must have lived in the ocean deeps. To account for the presence of marine fossils in the mountains, Ray resorted to ingenious interpretations of Old Testament earth history. He concluded after much study that the fossils were washed up to their places of deposit when the Bible's forty days and forty nights of unceasing deluge filled the reservoirs of the world and caused the "Fountains of the Great Deep" to break forth. In the tremendous surge that overflowed the globe, he reasoned, the fish and other creatures of the sea were simply swept up rivers and carried through underground streams, right into the high mountains.

In these early days of prehistoric studies, there was no body of tested scientific knowledge, and outside of a rare genius like Ray, Galileo, or Newton, there were few active scientists. The men who were interested in exploring for and collecting such things as stones and bones were usually antiquarians motivated by their own curiosity. In the seventeenth century one such man, a Frenchman named Isaac de la Peyrère, studied a large collection of oddly chipped stones gathered in the French countryside. He then had the courage to publish a book suggesting that these stones had been shaped by primitive men who lived before the time of Adam. His book was burned publicly in 1655.

**J. F. Esper, John Frere,
P. C. Schmerling**

But odd-shaped stones continued to turn up. So did even odder-shaped bones. Gradually a few skeptical people began to realize that the earth had been inhabited at one time by a great number of creatures that no longer existed—huge mammoths, woolly rhinoceroses, saber-toothed tigers. More digging produced more puzzles. In 1771, human bones were found in association with the remains of extinct cave bears in a site in Germany; these bones suggested not only ancient animals but ancient people, too. Their finder, Johann Friedrich Esper, was flabbergasted. "Did they belong to a Druid, or to an Antediluvian, or to a Mortal Man of more recent times?" he wrote. He would not face the logical answer and concluded that the human and animal fragments must have come together by chance.

Others guessed rightly but could not get a hearing. In 1790 John Frere found unfamiliar stone tools in the same beds with the remains of extinct animals at Hoxne, England. He recognized that they must have been made in "a very remote period indeed; even beyond that of the present world." Working in Belgian caves in 1830, P. C. Schmerling found many stone artifacts associated with the bones of long-since-vanished rhinoceroses and mammoths, and in addition uncovered two human skulls. He, too, recognized the contemporaneity of the human and animal bones. These astonishing finds went generally unnoticed.

**Jacques Boucher de Perthes**

It was difficult even to get anyone to pay serious attention to the idea that stone tools were tools at all. The first person to attempt to prove in a systematic way that ancient worked stones were human artifacts was a French customs official named Jacques Boucher de Perthes (1788–1868). Interested in archaeology, he began poking about in gravel banks near Abbeville in northern France and was perplexed by the number of flint objects that not only did not "belong" in the pits, because they were made of a different kind of stone, but also bore unmistakable signs of human workmanship. Many of them were carefully chipped around the edge and looked enough like axes to set even a less observant person than Boucher de Perthes thinking. He began collecting and organizing his finds, and some years later he had what he considered an overwhelmingly strong case for the existence of human beings far older than any previously known. In 1838 and 1839, his findings were laid before two French learned societies and rejected by both. He published them later in five volumes, but they were ignored for many years.

**Problems of Early Investigators:
J. McEnery**

These early investigators were laboring under two handicaps. The first was the lack of any scientific method in excavating, recording finds, or presenting results. This lack made it easier for critics to argue that tools and human and extinct animal bones had come together by accident

FIGURE 1–2 *Excavation of the cave called Goat Hole in Wales took William Buckland many years. Although one skeleton that he found has since been dated to 18,000 years* B.P. *(before the present), Buckland insisted that the fossils he discovered were remains of the Biblical flood. He described his finds in his book* Reliquiae Diluvianae *(1823), from which this figure comes.*

(or even by the sinister design of the scientist) than for the scientist to prove that they had come to their final resting place by natural means. A Catholic priest, Father J. McEnery, was to suffer from this first handicap. In 1829 he dug his way through an absolutely unbroken layer of stalagmite to find flint tools and ancient bones below a cave floor on the south coast of England. When he reported his discovery, other geologists, led by the Dean of Westminster, William Buckland, insisted that the tools belonged to ancient Britons who had dug ovens in the stalagmite floor of the cave and accidentally dropped some of their stone implements into the holes. Father McEnery's earnest rebuttal that there were no such holes fell on deaf ears; his findings, to which he had devoted some fifteen years, were not published until after his death. Meanwhile, William Buckland was excavating skeletal remains of great age (Figure 1–2) but entirely failed to understand their true significance.

A second and much more serious handicap was that scientists and laymen alike seemed almost instinctively suspicious of stone tools and fossils and, from our viewpoint, were severely limited in their thinking. Most people still had not the faintest notion of how old the earth actually was, nor did they have any way of accurately determining its age. (Bishop Ussher's chronology allowed almost no time for the evolutionary process).

Early geologists had made some progress, however. The great French naturalist Comte de Buffon had published his three-volume *Natural History* in 1749 and included in it an account of the creation of the earth. The earth originally derived, he wrote, from the collision of a comet with the sun and slowly and steadily developed over a very long time—not the six days outlined in Genesis. Such was the response that in 1753 he was forced by theologians to retract in print: the time for such ideas was not yet ripe. However, he was the first to introduce the idea of *uniformitarianism.* This long word embraces a very simple and logical idea: if the earth's mantle is now affected by natural forces—by wind and flowing water, by frost, by volcanic activity, by faulting along lines of crustal weakness, by mountain building—then it stands to reason that such forces also operated in a similar, or uniform, fashion in the past.

This concept was taken up by a few scholars who were beginning to get some alarming ideas about the earth's long history. This they read in the "testimony of the rocks," the various layers of different kinds of sediments—river gravels, sands, and marine limestones—that they encountered, one layer beneath another, some of them dozens of feet thick, indicating that the layers had been laid down over long periods of time. The antiquity of the earth, however, was not effectively documented until the Scotsman James Hutton (1726–1797) developed it fully in his book *Theory of the Earth* (1795). He showed convincingly the immense period of time of which the earth bore witness and he made the remarkable claim that it carried "no vestige of a beginning—no prospect of an end."

Clearly, the passage of immense amounts of time can explain the presence of such diverse strata as exist in the earth's crust. The world is constantly remaking itself, and the only reason we are not aware of the continual reconstruction is that it happens so slowly. Watching a few pebbles fall from a crag, we are watching the disintegration of a mountain. Muddy water flowing down a river can eventually move billions of tons of material from the center of a continent to the bottom of the sea. This immense layer of mud may harden and be covered in turn by other layers in a process extending over great amounts of time. All this, which seems so obvious now, was entirely new thinking at the end of the eighteenth century; it was a new and mechanistic interpretation of earth history and a new key to past and present. And to a society accustomed to believing that the earth was less than 6,000 years old, it was a heretical proposition, a staggering revelation.

**Georges Cuvier, Alexandre Brongniart, William Smith**

Much excitement had been generated in 1796 when Georges Cuvier (1769–1832), professor of natural history at the Collège de France, discovered elephant bones in the soil of the Paris area itself. Soon Cuvier and other diggers were unearthing even stranger inhabitants of an unknown and unsuspected past—reptiles as big as whales, mammoths with long tusks, bears, wolves, and other creatures that bore only a superficial similarity to living species. From a few of their bones Cuvier put the animals back together with such startling realism that the novelist Honoré de Balzac marveled: "Is Cuvier not the greatest poet of our century? Our immortal naturalist has reconstructed worlds from blanched bones. He picks up a piece of gypsum and says to us 'See!' Suddenly stone turns into animals and another world unrolls before our eyes."

Like the living members of the animal kingdom, such collections of ancient animals did not come in a random assortment but could be classified into species and genera. Cuvier counted ninety species, and some whole genera, that had entirely disappeared from the earth. What could have brought about such terrible decimation, he wondered, and how could the lost species have been succeeded by still others before the animals of "the present creation" appeared?

To find the answers to such riddles, Cuvier set out to learn how the fossil creatures had been entombed and to find out all he could about the earth of their distant time. He enlisted the aid of Alexandre Brongniart, a professor of mineralogy and head of the famous Sèvres china factory. For years the two studied the Paris countryside in depth. They discovered that layer was piled upon layer: one stony bed filled with millions of sea shells, and just below it a different formation with a scattering of freshwater or land shells. Other strata were studded with the bones of extinct giant mammals. Still others had no fossils at all.

Cuvier and Brongniart tried to interpret the puzzling succession of vanished worlds. At times, as they explained to rapt Parisian audiences, the seas had flooded into the Paris basin. At other times the salt waters had receded, and the dry land had been dotted with freshwater lakes. Again the seas had returned, and again they had rolled back. In deposits laid down during the marine eras were the shells and bones of ocean life; in sediments marking the bottoms of the freshwater lakes lay freshwater shells and bones of land animals. There was no mixing of the freshwater and seawater deposits; one ended when the other began.

At about the same time as Cuvier was making his studies, an English surveyor named William Smith (1769–1839) was making similar observations in his own country and coming to similar conclusions. "Each stratum contains organized fossils peculiar to itself," he reported. In 1815 Smith published a painstaking geologic map of England, showing the strata that underlie the landscape and proving again that "the same species of fossils are found in the same stratum, even at wide distances."

The implications of these studies were extremely disturbing to the men making them. Cuvier was a scientist intensely devoted to the truth, but even with the succession of species before him he could not admit that one species had arisen from another. The prevalent conception of the earth's age did not allow enough time for such a process of change, and to have made such an admission would have denied his strong Huguenot faith in a special creation. Cuvier preferred another explanation: that a series of vast floods had wiped out the old and cleared the stage for new creations. This theory, which Cuvier first described in 1812 and elaborated in 1825, was called *catastrophism*.

**Charles Lyell**   It remained for another Scotsman, Charles Lyell (1797–1875), to synthesize from the growing avalanche of evidence a more effective statement of the uniformitarian position. His best-known book, *Principles of Geology*, was extremely important because it was published at a time when ideas of organic evolution, or *transformism* as it was often known, were common currency, and it proved to be a major influence on the thinking of Charles Darwin. Lyell's strength lay in the fact that his theory was based on numerous and detailed observations throughout Europe and North America, which enabled him to present a most convincing theory. Unlike Hutton, who was concerned mainly with rock formation and stratification, Lyell also looked at fossils and their succession. At this time Cuvier's doctrine of successive creations was in the ascendancy. Lyell rejected catastrophism on the basis of the evidence he examined and demonstrated that the uniformitarian principle applied to a limited extent, to the organic as well as the inorganic realm. However, he could not accept the idea of organic evolution: the only theory known to him then was that proposed by Lamarck.

**Lamarck**   The French naturalist Jean Baptiste de Monet, Chevalier de Lamarck (1744–1829), was a friend of Buffon and provided the first persuasive theory that could account for the process of organic evolution. In his *Système des Animaux* (1801) and later books, Lamarck developed his theory of the means by which animal species had been transformed. He recognized that animals and plants were finely adapted to their environments and that their relationship was dynamic, with environmental change generating biological change and adaptation. He suggested that in their daily lives animals recognized certain needs and that their inner feelings generated forces that stimulated the development and growth of organs, even completely novel ones. Thus the evolution of the species was a response to need, to use, or to disuse of organs, and the changes produced in each generation were inherited. This theory is sometimes described as that of "the inheritance of acquired characters."

Although Lamarck's ideas were to be discredited, they were extremely important in the early part of the nineteenth century and have a small place in evolutionary biology to this day. The theory, however, is generally discounted because it has not been possible to demonstrate conclusively that characters acquired during the lifetime of an individual are in fact passed on to the succeeding generation.

## Charles Darwin

Lyell's great work, *Principles of Geology*, was published between 1830 and 1833. Among its readers was a young man named Charles Darwin (1809–1882), who in another twenty-six years was to publish his even more revolutionary book. Darwin's student life at Cambridge was undistinguished except in one respect: he was passionately interested in natural history and in collecting birds, butterflies, spiders, flowers, even rocks—there was nothing in nature that did not fascinate him. While a student he became a great friend of Dr. Henslow, the professor of botany, who gave him much encouragement. When he heard of the sailing of one of the navy's survey ships, the H.M.S. *Beagle*, he joined first as the captain's companion, later as the ship's naturalist, and sailed round the world observing and collecting for nearly five years. The *Beagle* left Devonport on December 27, 1831, and returned to Falmouth on October 2, 1836. Three and a half years were spent surveying and collecting along the coasts of South America; five weeks were spent in the Galapagos Islands of Ecuador, and a year was spent returning home via Tahiti, New Zealand, Australia, and South Africa (Figure 1–3). This voyage offered Darwin a priceless opportunity to carry his observations to foreign lands, and it gave him a brilliant panorama of the variety of

FIGURE 1–3   *Charles Darwin left Devonport, England in December 1831 and returned to Falmouth in October 1836. Out of the four and a half years spent on the voyage in HMS* Beagle, *Darwin spent nearly four years in South America and its islands. The voyage was completed with visits to New Zealand, Australia, the Keeling (Cocos) Islands, the Cape of Good Hope, and St. Helena. Darwin's experience on this voyage was a rich and fertile source of observation and inspiration in the development of his ideas.*

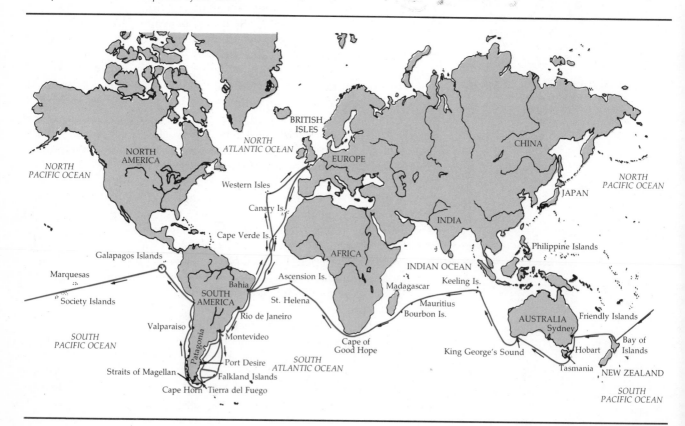

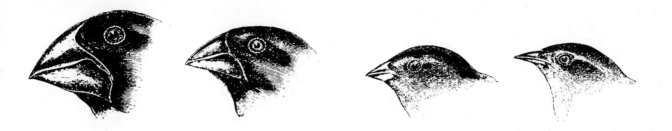

FIGURE 1–4  These four species of Galapagos finch show some of the variety of form into which the beak evolved. The left species is most powerfully equipped and is adapted to crack seeds and nuts. That on the right is adapted to feed from flowers and fruit. These species evolved in isolation on the different islands, with little or no competition.

organic life. Perhaps the most important part of the voyage for the development of Darwin's ideas was the visit to the Galapagos or Enchanted Islands.

Soon after his arrival Darwin wrote in his journal: "Here, both in space and time, we seem to be brought somewhere near to that great fact—that mystery of mysteries—the first appearance of new beings on this earth." Later he wrote: "It was most striking to be surrounded by new birds, new reptiles, new shells, new insects, new plants, and yet by innumerable trifling details of structure, and even by the tones of voice and plumage of the birds, to have the temperate plains of . . . Patagonia, or the hot dry deserts of northern Chile, vividly brought before my eyes." Struck by the basic similarities yet subtle differences that linked the Galapagos fauna to that of the mainland, Darwin also learned that many species differed slightly from island to island even though many of the islands were only fifty or sixty miles apart. Most striking perhaps were the finches, all obviously related yet distinct. On one island they had strong thick beaks used for cracking nuts and seeds; on another the beak was smaller and used for catching insects; on another the beak was elongated for feeding on flowers and fruit (Figure 1–4). One species had learned to use a cactus spine to probe grubs out of holes in tree trunks and branches. Clearly the birds had found different foods on different islands and through successive generations had adapted in some manner so that they were better able to survive in their own particular environments. All this evidence was critically important in the development of Darwin's ideas.

When, in 1859, Charles Darwin published his revolutionary book *On the Origin of Species by Means of Natural Selection*, he presented a theory that was the product of many years of observation. Darwin was encouraged to publish by seeing the work of Alfred Russel Wallace (1823–1913), who, working independently, came to similar conclusions (Figures 1–5 and 1–6). Both men traveled widely and observed in great detail the variation that exists within animal and plant species. Members of species, they noted, are not identical, but vary in size, strength, health, fertility, longevity, behavior, and many other characteristics. Darwin realized that humans use this natural variation when they selectively

FIGURE 1–5  *Charles Darwin as a young man. In his* Autobiography *he wrote: "In September 1858 I set to work by the strong advice of Lyell and Hooker to prepare a volume on the transmutation of species, but was often interrupted by ill-health. . . . [The book] cost me thirteen months and ten days hard labour." Darwin was an intermittent invalid for forty years, but invalidism had some advantages. He wrote: "Even ill-health, though it annihilated several years of my life, has saved me from the distractions of society and amusement." He lived to the age of seventy-three.*

breed plants and animals; a breeder allows only particular individuals possessing desired qualities to interbreed.

Both Darwin and Wallace saw that a kind of natural selection was at work, but they did not know how it worked. An understanding of the means by which selection operates in nature came to both from the same source. The first edition of *An Essay on the Principle of Population* by an English clergyman, T. R. Malthus, appeared in 1798. In his book, Malthus showed that the reproductive potential of humankind far exceeds the natural resources available to nourish an expanding population. In a revised version of his essay, published in 1830, Malthus began: "In taking a view of animated nature, we cannot fail to be struck with the prodigious power of increase in plants and animals . . . their natural tendency must be to increase in a geometrical ratio—that is, by multiplication." He continued by pointing out that, in contrast, subsistence can increase only in an arithmetical ratio. "A slight acquaintance with numbers will shew the immensity of the first power in comparison of the second." And he had written in 1798, "By that law of our nature that makes food necessary to the life of man, the effects of these two unequal powers must be kept equal. This implies a strong and constantly operating check on population from the difficulty of subsistence." As a result he argued that the size of human populations is limited by disease, famine, and war and that, in the absence of "moral restraint," such factors alone appear to check what would otherwise be a rapid growth in population.

Both Darwin and Wallace read Malthus's essay, and, remarkably, both men recorded in their diaries how they realized that in that book lay the key to understanding the evolutionary process. It was clear that what Malthus had discovered for human populations was true for populations of plants and animals: the reproductive potential vastly exceeds the rate necessary to maintain a constant population size. They realized that the individuals that do survive must be in some way better equipped to live in their environment than those that do not survive. It follows that in a natural interbreeding population any variation would most likely be preserved, or passed on to future generations, that increased the organism's ability to produce fertile offspring, while the variations that decreased that ability would most likely be eliminated.

Darwin had carried these ideas for some years, afraid to put pen to paper. He knew he would shock the public and his family; he could hardly face the implications of his thoughts. Wallace was held back by no such inhibitions and early in 1858, after reading Malthus, the idea of natural selection occurred to him and he immediately wrote to Darwin. Darwin received his letter on June 18. He was quite astounded and wrote in his diary, "I never saw a more striking coincidence; if Wallace had my MS sketch written out in 1842, he could not have made a better short abstract."

## THEORY OF EVOLUTION

Around Malthus's ideas Charles Darwin and Alfred Russel Wallace formulated a theory of evolution by natural selection. The theory is not difficult to understand and may be stated as follows:

1. Organisms produce far more offspring than required to maintain their population size, and yet their population size generally remains more or less constant over long periods of time. From this, as well as from observation, it seems clear that there is a high rate of mortality among immature individuals.

2. Individuals in any population show much variation, and those that survive probably do so to some extent because of their particular characteristics. That is, individuals with certain characteristics can be considered better *adapted* to their particular environment.

3. Since offspring resemble their parents closely, though not exactly, successive generations will maintain and improve on the degree of adaptation by gradual changes in every generation.

This process of variation and selection by the environment for better-adapted individuals is called *natural selection,* and the change in the nature of the population that follows upon selection through *differential mortality* is the process of *organic evolution.* The same processes occur among both plants and animals. The process of evolution is extremely slow, and to be accepted, the theory required the earth to be of great age. Darwin's and Wallace's theory could not have been accepted by the generations taught by Bishop Ussher, who believed the earth only 6,000 years old. But Lyell had provided the time dimension required for evolution to work.

The first presentation of their ideas was made at the Linnaean Society in London. On July 1, 1858, a paper entitled "On the tendency of Species to form Varieties; and on the Perpetuation of Varieties and Species by means of Selection" was read before the fellows of the Society. This was the first publication to the world of Darwin's and Wallace's theory, and the world has not been the same since that day. Neither Darwin nor Wallace was present.

It is impossible today to re-create the atmosphere of intellectual and moral shock that swept England when Darwin's book was published the following year (Figure 1–7). It was not that the evolution of plants or animals was so hard to swallow. After all, humans themselves had been responsible, through selective breeding, for the evolution of a number of domestic animals and a great variety of crops. Then there were those peculiar dinosaur bones that people had begun digging up; they had to be explained, as did the growing evidence that the earth was not simply thousands of years old but hundreds of thousands, perhaps hundreds of millions. No, those things were not really the problem. What was so hard to accept was the implied suggestion that

FIGURE 1–6 *Alfred Russel Wallace was a complete contrast to Darwin in both background and character. Whereas Darwin did not need to work for a living, Wallace earned his way by collecting rare tropical plants and animals for private collectors and museums. As a result, he traveled far more widely than Darwin in both South America and Southeast Asia. Later in his life he wrote a number of books on evolution. Although of considerable interest, they do not have the originality and intellectual integrity of Darwin's writings.*

FIGURE 1–7   A cruel caricature of Darwin, which appeared in The Hornet in 1871 (the year of publication of The Descent of Man), labeled him "a venerable orangoutang" and cited his contribution to "unnatural history."

human beings were descended from a bunch of "repulsive, scratching, hairy apes and monkeys."

Those awful monkeys! As one Victorian lady is reported to have said: "My dear, let us hope that it is not true, but if it is, let us pray that it will not become generally known."

Darwin was an extremely cautious scientist, and the evidence he used to support his theory ranged among both plants and animals, but did not include human beings. He mentioned the origin of humans only once in his book *On the Origin of Species*, permitting himself a single timid sentence in his conclusion: "Light will be thrown on the origin of man and his history." But the implication was plain, and nobody missed it.

In 1863 Thomas H. Huxley (1825–1895), a friend of Darwin and an ardent propagandist for his theory, published *Zoological Evidences as to Man's Place in Nature*. This was the first book to address itself in an orderly and scientific way to the problem of human origins. By making many telling anatomical comparisons between humans and the apes, Huxley established that of all animals on earth, the African great apes—the chimpanzee and gorilla—are most closely related to humans (Figure 1–8). He further stated that the evolutionary development of apes and humans had taken place in much the same way and according to the same laws. From this it followed that if prehuman fossils were ever found, older and older humanlike fossils would be found, leading eventually to types that would turn out to be ancestral to both apes and humans. And these common ancestors would probably be found in Africa.

Darwin, confronted by the same relationship of fossil species to living ones, saw that the latter were the modified descendants of the former. Carrying the case to its full conclusion in *The Descent of Man*, published in 1871, Darwin was forced to propound the theory of an unbroken chain of organisms that began with the first forms of life and evolved to humans. Here was a true scientific theory, a theory of evolution subject to proof; but where was the proof? Where were the bones of this multitude of organisms? Surely many of them should have survived in the earth, yet the fossils found up to Darwin's day supplied only the most fragmentary evidence. Where were the missing links? It was a painful time for the evolutionists. Despite all the logic in Huxley's and Darwin's views, they were difficult to support, because in Africa, or indeed anywhere else, there was an embarrassing lack of fossils resembling human beings.

In all the ancient menageries that Georges Cuvier dug out of the Parisian subsoil a century and a half ago, there was not a trace of prehistoric humans. It seemed plain enough to the great paleontologist: "L'homme fossile n'existe pas," fossil man does not exist. This did not stop people from looking. Here and there, in this old cave and that old river bed, excavators ran across chipped flints and polished axes, but the bones mixed in with such finds were those of animals and not humans. It never occurred to the finders that some of the pebble implements they collected might actually be older than modern humans—that tools had been the making of humans as well as humans the makers of tools.

At this turning point in the history of human knowledge, there had emerged two great and related ideas about the origin of nature and of humankind: that the earth is extremely ancient, long populated by many kinds of animals, some of which are no longer living; and that humans themselves, mutable creatures like the animals, have their ancestors far back in time. But how far back and who those ancestors were, nobody had even the slightest notion. Everything we know about our ancestry we have learned in the last century, most of it during the last couple of decades.

Darwin and Wallace had provided a rational and convincing explanation of the diversity and changing nature of species. If humans, too, were products of this process, humankind had to develop a completely new attitude toward the natural world and face an entirely novel view of human origins. This agonizing reappraisal was possible only for those who were capable of rational thought, free from earlier ideas and prejudices. It would not be unreasonable to claim that Darwin's book is the most important book ever published, and the changes that it has brought about in our view of ourselves are only a part of its revolutionary impact. From it derives our modern and extraordinarily fruitful perspective on humankind—evolutionary biology.

Evolution is a creative process and, as the eminent geneticist Theodosius Dobzhansky pointed out, "Any creative process involves a risk

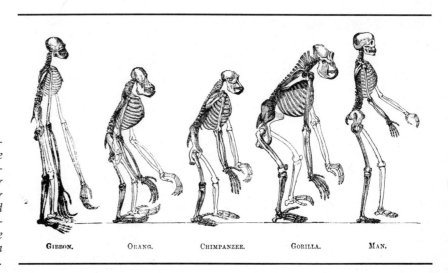

FIGURE 1–8   In 1863, T. H. Huxley published this drawing of the skeletons of the four apes and a human to illustrate their extraordinary similarity. He wrote: "Whatever part of the animal fabric might be selected for comparison, the lower Apes (monkeys) and the Gorilla would differ more than the Gorilla and the Man." All drawings are to the same scale except the gibbon, which is drawn to twice the scale.

GIBBON.     ORANG.     CHIMPANZEE.     GORILLA.     MAN.

*FIGURE 1–9   The human embryo grows in a salty solution called amniotic fluid, which is not greatly different in composition from the ocean. The embryo shows certain characteristics of ancestral forms, some of which are remnants of marine fishlike adaptations of 500 million years ago. At about four weeks gill slits and a tail can be seen, which rapidly develop into other structures.*

of failure, which in biological evolution means extinction. On the other hand, creativity makes possible striking successes and discoveries." In the billions of years of the grand procession of life on earth, there have been both successes and failures. Thousands of forms have arisen to swim, wriggle, crawl, walk, or fly past some immutable reviewing stand and then collapse. Some creatures seemed merely bizarre experiments, and others were successful for varying lengths of time: the dinosaurs ruled the earth for 130 million years before they vanished. Some dropouts were crucial to the development of human beings. The human line can be traced to early vertebrates that first possessed a rudimentary backbone and the beginnings of a brain. The human body is full of traces of ancestors that were very different from us and led wholly different lives: for instance, we have a coccyx—the vestige of a tail—at the end of our spines, and as an embryo (Figure 1–9) we carry ephemeral gill slits, which remind us that our ancestors were once marine creatures. This book is about one experiment in the creation of animal life that, although starting from the same ancestral sources as the dinosaurs, did not end in an evolutionary blind alley. In time it led to modern *Homo sapiens*, a product of variation and selection that began more than 3 billion years ago.

The search for the origin of human beings begins with the very first life on earth, in the primitive sea where living cells first reproduced themselves. There was no hint then, of course, that more than 3 billion years later similar cells multiplied a billion-billionfold would manifest themselves in the complex cellular structure of our bodies. Yet it happened. We are here to prove it. And if we are to gain any real understanding about ourselves, we must learn to recognize the age-old elements from which we have emerged, and discover how and why they go together as they do.

## MODERN STUDY OF HUMAN ORIGINS

*Paleoanthropology* is the branch of science dealing with the study of early humans. It involves connecting human and nonhuman on a chain so long lost that the links we possess almost defied assembly. For those engaged in this science, today is a time of extraordinary interest. Recent discoveries and analysis now begin to make it possible to lay out some of those links next to one another and to look at them closely in relation to one another.

In 1859, when Darwin propounded the theory of evolution, scientists knew of only two fossils that were relevant to the search for our origins: one of an extinct ape and another of the early type of *Homo sapiens* called Neandertal man. Just a little more than a hundred years later, expeditions in East Africa unearthed more than 600 near-human bones in a decade. The discovery and interpretation of such evidence of our ancestors involves many specialists (Table 1–1).

# TABLE 1–1 Special Skills to Study Fossil Sites

## IN THE FIELD

| | |
|---|---|
| Paleoanthropologists | In charge of investigations from start to finish, they must pick the site, get permission to excavate, obtain financial support, hire the labor, and organize, plan, and supervise the work in progress. Finally, they must integrate the data collected by each of the specialists and publish their conclusions. |
| Geologists | Often assist in selecting the site. Their knowledge of the geologic history of the region is indispensable in determining the relative ages of fossils. Their study of the strata at the site determines the natural processes—erosion, volcanic action—that laid the strata down, and the conditions under which fossilization took place. |
| Surveyors | Map the general region of the site and the site itself, plotting it in relation to natural landmarks and making a detailed record of its contours before they are obliterated by digging. |
| Draftsmen | Record the exact position of all fossils, tools, and other artifacts as they are excavated, marking their relationships to each other in both the horizontal and vertical planes. |
| Photographers | Document fossil remains and artifacts and their associations as they are uncovered, record work in progress and the use of special equipment, and provide overall views of the site as well as of personnel at work. |

## IN THE LABORATORY

| | |
|---|---|
| Petrologists | Identify and classify the rocks and minerals found around the site. They can determine the nature of rocks from which tools were made and identify stones that do not occur naturally in the area, which would indicate that the stones were imported by early humans. |
| Palynologists | Specialize in the study and identification of fossil plant pollen, which may shed light on early humankind's environment and diet, and the climate at the time. |
| Pedologists | Experts on soils and their chemical composition, their findings round out the picture of the environment as it once was. |
| Geochemists | With geophysicists, conduct chemical and physical tests in the laboratory to determine the absolute age of material found at the site. They may also study the chemical composition of bones and artifacts. |

## IN THE FIELD AND LABORATORY

| | |
|---|---|
| Preparators | At the site, they preserve and protect fossils and artifacts with various hardening agents, and make plaster casts for particularly fragile bones and other organic remains. In the laboratory, preparators clean and restore the specimens, making them ready for study by various specialists. |
| Paleontologists | Study the fossil animal remains found at the site. From the finds, they can learn much about the ecology and the eating habits of early humans. |
| Physical anthropologists[a] | Specialists in the comparative anatomy of apes and humans, they evaluate the remains found at the site and the evolutionary status of the fossil hominids who lived there. |
| Archaeologists | Study humankind's past material culture: tools of stone, bone, and wood; living sites, settlement patterns, and food remains; art and ritual. |

[a]Physical anthropology is the branch of biology that deals with many aspects of humankind besides our prehistory. It includes the distribution and nature of modern human beings, their racial diversity, their adaptations and their adaptability.

The knowledge and insights of other modern sciences also contribute to attempts to understand our ancestors. Atomic physicists, for example, have determined that certain radioactive elements discharge energy at a constant rate, turning into certain other materials. This knowledge has provided paleontologists with new methods for establishing the age of fossils and interpreting the stages in the evolution of life.

Equally valuable have been the contributions of modern biochemistry. In the past decades biochemists have deciphered the code found in the substance DNA (see Chapter 4) by which instructions for building new cells and new organisms are passed along. Knowledge of this code provides insights into how members of a species reproduce themselves, generation after generation, virtually unchanged; how, on the other hand, minute variations do occur in offspring; and how these variations may accumulate in time. Knowledge of how these variations create differences in the structures of proteins can be used to determine the affinity between different types of organisms. Some scientists believe that these differences accumulate at a steady rate over time, so that this biochemical knowledge can provide yet another method of dating and thus be used to determine when existing species of animals first emerged.

Other clues to the past are coming from studies of a very different kind, involving living animals—the science of animal behavior, called *ethology*. It is a relatively new discipline, but a flourishing one. Studies of the behavior of living animals (for example, the chimpanzees shown in Figure 1–10) have been used to help explain the basis for some human behaviors and to suggest how ancestral humans may have acted and why. We will see the usefulness of animal behavior studies when we discuss the social organization of our ancestors (Chapter 9).

## PALEOANTHROPOLOGY IN PROGRESS

### Scarcity of Human Fossils

Humans are a maddeningly poor source of fossils. In 1956, the paleontologist G. H. R. von Koenigswald calculated that if all the then-known fragments of human beings older than the Neandertal people were gathered together they could be comfortably displayed on a medium-sized table. Although many more fossils of early hominids have been found since then, discoveries are still rare.

Why are human fossils so scarce? Why can one go to good fossil sites almost anywhere in the world and find millions of shell remains or thousands of bones of extinct reptiles and mammals, while peoples earlier than Neandertal are known from only a handful of sites at which investigators, working through tons of deposits, pile up other finds by the bushel basket before recovering a single human tooth?

There are many reasons. First, the commonness of marine fossils is a direct reflection of the abundance of these creatures when they were alive. It also reflects the tremendous span of time during which they

FIGURE 1–10 *The more closely chimpanzees are studied, the more like them we appear to be, especially in the realm of individual relationships and nonverbal communication. Here, an adult chimpanzee stretches out its hand to reassure a young one and to receive a kiss of submission.*

abounded. Many of them swarmed through the waters of the earth for hundreds of millions of years. When they died, they sank and were covered by sediments. Their way of life—their life in the water—preserved them, as did their extremely durable shells, the only parts of them that now remain. Humans, by contrast, have never been as numerous as oysters and clams. They existed in small numbers, reproduced slowly and in small numbers, and lived a relatively long time. They were more intelligent than, for example, dinosaurs and were perhaps less apt to get mired in bogs, marshes, or quicksands. Most important, their way of life was different. They were not sea creatures or riverside browsers but lively, wide-ranging food-gatherers and hunters. They often lived and died in the open, where their bones could be gnawed by scavengers and bleached and decomposed in the sun and rain. In hot climates, particularly in tropical forests and woodlands, the soil is likely to be markedly acid. Bones dissolve in such soils, and early humans who lived and died in such an environment would have had a very poor chance of leaving remains that would last until today. Finally, human ancestors have been on earth only a few million years. There simply has not been as much time for them to scatter their bones about as there has been for some of the more ancient species of animals.

**Fossil Sites**    To catch a glimpse of a clever, elusive, uncommon animal like the early human we need a quiet cave where a corpse can be gently covered by blown-in dust or washed-in soil, or even sand and mud from the rising water level of a river. Or the cave might be a large one with a deep rock fissure at the back serving as a garbage dump into which the dead were once placed along with the bones of game animals, just to get them out of the way. Finally, the cave may simply be one that is occupied steadily for a long time. The dirt and debris of mere living will gradually build up the floor so that it becomes deeper and deeper, and if people live in it long enough, their story will be revealed—from recent times to increasingly primitive ones—just by carefully digging downward from one layer to another.

Not all fossil sites are caves; the earliest known cave occupations are little more than half a million years old. From earlier times we find occupation sites that were in the open, often by a stream or on a lake shore. In these circumstances, evidence is more difficult to come by, but seasonal flooding sometimes leaves deposits of mud and clay on the bones of animals and early humans. In other places, fossils of human ancestors have been found scattered among animal bones without any clear archaeological context; these are the rarest occurrences. Indeed, as we go backward in time the fossil record becomes dimmer, and the specimens scarcer, as might be expected. But where animal bones are found preserved (most commonly near an ancient lake shore or river) there we can reasonably expect to find fossils of early humans, if the geographical area, climate, age, and environment are appropriate.

The gradual revealing of the story of human evolution can be compared to the cleaning of an old tapestry that has been covered with mud and dirt. Let us suppose modern humanity is at the top of the tapestry, and our most primitive ancestors are woven into it near the bottom. The whole tapestry is fragile, increasingly so the nearer one gets to the bottom. It must be cleaned with great care so that it will not be destroyed. There is no assurance the spot one picks to clean will have a meaningful picture on it. It may be bare. It may have a hole in it. It may reveal only a fragment of one of the figures in the design, a fragment so small and mysterious as to be of no value. It may reveal an entire figure, but a totally unexpected one whose presence cannot be explained until further parts are cleaned. But the position of every piece of design on the tapestry—exactly where it is located with respect to all other pieces—is enormously important. In paleontology, deductions can be made about specific fossils and their relationship only when they are evaluated in the light of all other available evidence and knowledge.

**Relative Dating Methods: Earth and Fossils**

To begin to understand our ancestors' fossil remains, we must know how old these bits and pieces are. Strange shapes and sizes may suggest all sorts of intriguing ideas and hypotheses about who descended from whom. But these hypotheses can be nailed down tightly only by reliable dating.

The problem of determining the age of fossils is handled in several ways. The first is through *geology*, the study of the earth itself. This branch of science is concerned with the location, size, and nature of the various layers of clay, silt, sand, lava, limestone, and other kinds of rock that constitute the earth's surface, and with their relationship to one another. It examines certain processes, such as erosion, the accumulation of layers of silt at the bottom of the sea, and their compaction into rock again by heat and pressure; it notes that these processes take place now at measurable rates and assumes that the same processes took place at comparable rates in the past, just as Lyell suggested. Analysis of these layers, or strata—a scientific discipline known as *stratigraphy*—permits the working out of a rough picture of past earth history (Figure 1–11). From this information the fossils found in different rock structures can be arranged in order of age. The deepest strata are the oldest, and the more recent levels are laid down above them. Thus fossils in the upper strata are relatively younger than those in the lower strata. These data, however, do not give us the absolute age of the fossils in years.

The second way to determine relative age is by studying the fossils themselves. Fossil types are usually not the same in different layers. Animals evolved through time and thus their fossils provide clues of

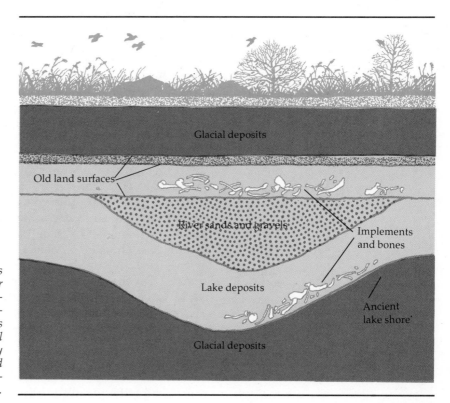

FIGURE 1–11  *Fossils are found in deposits formed by the action of glaciers and rivers or laid down in ancient riverbeds, lakes, estuaries, and seas. Some deposits are windblown and may contain volcanic ash. Fossils are laid down in more or less horizontal beds, or strata, as shown here. Stratigraphy is the science that attempts to understand stratigraphic deposition—its form, its sequence, and its age.*

their own, particularly if the time sequence can be worked out. The evolution of the horse, for example, is very well known through fossils. Over a period of about 60 million years, the creature developed from an animal the size of a dog with four toes on each foot to the modern large animal with one toe per foot; the numerous intermediate fossil stages located in various geological strata tell this story with great clarity. Fossils of ancestral horses become tools for dating, because any other animal or plant fossil that occurs in the same layer as one of the ancestral horses can be considered of the same age. Once relative ages are established, one fossil can help date another. This method is called dating by *faunal correlation*.

One problem paleontologists have had to face is establishing contemporaneity when fossils from the same site are said to be associated but their association is questioned. This problem is now less serious than in earlier days, for two reasons. First, today we can check claims of contemporaneity and association by chemically analyzing the bone: bones of roughly the same age should have roughly the same chemical analyses. The chemicals usually assayed are nitrogen (which occurs in bone in the form of the protein collagen and is lost slowly during fossilization), and uranium and fluorine (both of which frequently enter bone from the surrounding ground water and increase in concentration over a long period). Such analyses can be a very valuable tool in establishing contemporaneity at a site: they are especially valuable if it is suspected that a skeleton has been buried within a deposit that is substantially older than the skeleton itself (as in the famous Piltdown hoax discussed in Chapter 10).

The second reason that contemporaneity can be more clearly established today is that more careful records of excavations are now being kept. Early investigators usually failed to realize the importance of carefully analyzing fossil sites and the position of fossils. Too often they dug with reckless abandon, recovering only the largest bones and major pieces of worked stone. They did not appreciate the information they could get from the position of things relative to one another—and from the surrounding earth itself. Many questions will occur to the curious and well-trained observer. Is there evidence of fire? Was it natural or controlled by humans? Do certain kinds of animal bones predominate at one level and decrease at another, indicating a change of diet or climate? Do the deposits preserve snails, or perhaps pollen grains, which are more sensitive clues to vegetation, and hence climate, than the mineral deposits themselves? With their careful plotting of finds and sites, paleontologists can come closer to answering these questions.

**Chronometric Dating Methods: From Physics and Biochemistry**

Through the constant cross-checking and fitting together of enormous amounts of both rock and fossil evidence, science has been able to construct a rather detailed chronology of the past. But this chronology provides only relative dates: *chronometric,* or absolute dates, are lacking.

Atomic physics provides the finest technique for obtaining chronometric dates. We know that certain radioactive elements discharge energy at a constant rate, known as the decay rate. Radium, for example, turns slowly but steadily into lead. Once this steady decay rate is known, it is only a matter of laboratory technique to determine how old a piece of radium is by measuring how much of it is still radium and how much is lead.

One long-lasting radioactive substance used for chronometric dating is potassium 40. This material breaks down into the gas argon at a constant and known rate. Because it is found in volcanic ash and lava, *potassium-argon* (abbreviated K/Ar) dating can be used to date fossils located in volcanic rock or ash or sandwiched between two layers of volcanic matter. The clock starts as the lava or ash cools (argon produced previously escaped when the potassium was heated in the volcano), and it continues steadily. It takes 1,265 million years for half the potassium 40 in a sample to decay into argon (this period of time is known as potassium 40's *half-life*). The age of the rock can therefore be calculated with remarkable precision by determining the ratio of argon gas to potassium 40. Clearly, argon is produced extremely slowly, and so the method cannot be used with great accuracy for dates of less than 0.5 million years, because very little argon will have been generated. Problems arise when the rock sample containing the potassium also contains air (which itself contains small quantities of argon) or if the rock has been reheated by later volcanic eruptions, which may have driven off the argon already produced by radioactive decay. The other, more general difficulty is that the method can be used to date fossils only from areas where volcanic eruptions occurred at about the same time as the fossils were deposited. Fortunately, many of the most important fossil sites in East Africa are in an area where volcanic activity was widespread (see Chapter 7), but in much of Asia, America, and Europe, this method cannot be used.

An important development that supports this technique involves recognizing tuffs that have been deposited over wide areas. It has been shown by Frank Brown of the University of California at Berkeley that each ash layer can be recognized by a unique analysis of its mineral components—each tuff has its own "chemical signature." Because of this characteristic, dated tuffs can be recognized over very great distances—their spread may be thousands of miles in extent. Thus it is possible to correlate tuffs from sites as far apart as Kenya, Ethiopia, and the Indian Ocean, where they can be recognized in deep-sea cores. In this way, dated tuffs may be widely mapped, and their K/Ar dates in one area checked against their K/Ar dating in another part of Africa.

Another useful radioactive element is carbon 14, which reverts to atmospheric nitrogen (Figure 1–12). Physicist Willard Libby showed that carbon 14 is present in the atmosphere as carbon dioxide ($CO_2$) and is incorporated into all plant material. In the plant, the proportion of carbon

*FIGURE 1–12   Carbon 14 is an unstable form of carbon (the stable form is carbon 12). A certain proportion of C¹⁴ exists in the atmosphere and as $CO_2$ is absorbed and incorporated by plants into their bodies in the form of carbohydrates. Animals absorb C¹⁴ by eating the plants. Thereafter the C¹⁴ disintegrates at a known rate (the half-life), and the extent of this disintegration can be measured and related to the amount of C¹⁴ remaining, and so to the age of the organic material.*

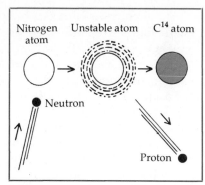

1. Nitrogen atom becomes C¹⁴ atom in the atmosphere.

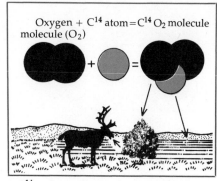

2. C¹⁴ and oxygen enter live organisms.

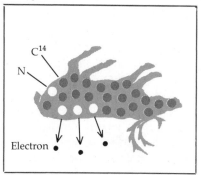

3. C¹⁴ atoms disintegrate.

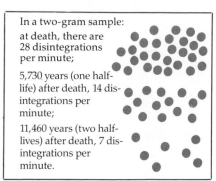

In a two-gram sample: at death, there are 28 disintegrations per minute;

5,730 years (one half-life) after death, 14 disintegrations per minute;

11,460 years (two half-lives) after death, 7 disintegrations per minute.

4. C¹⁴ continues to disintegrate at an orderly, predictable rate.

14 to the stable atom carbon 12 is the same as the proportion of the two in the atmosphere. The clock starts when the $Co_2$ is taken into the plant (which animals may feed on) and is buried as either fiber or wood, or as the collagen in bone, or as charcoal left by a fire (which is found in many archaeological sites). As the organism becomes fossilized, the carbon 14 breaks down, and the proportion of carbon 12 increases. The laboratory technique consists in measuring the ratio of carbon 14 to carbon 12 in these prehistoric samples. Carbon 14 has a half-life of only 5,730 years and therefore measurements of the age of carbon compounds will cover a relatively short period. The method is most useful between 500 and 40,000 years B.P. (before the present), although it can be extended a little.

Errors in this method arise from a number of factors. It was originally supposed that the carbon-14 level in the atmosphere was constant, but we now know that it is not. Volcanoes produce $CO_2$ without carbon 14, which causes local reductions in the level of carbon 14 in the atmosphere. A more serious variation is in the atmospheric level itself, which alters according to variations in the chemical reactions in the upper atmosphere that create the carbon 14 in the first place. Samples can

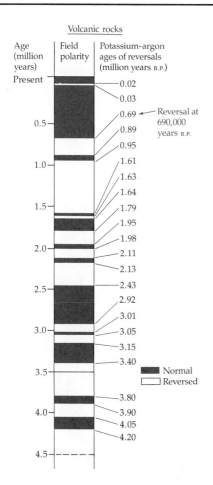

Volcanic rocks

| Age (million years) | Field polarity | Potassium-argon ages of reversals (million years B.P.) |
|---|---|---|

FIGURE 1–13 *This time scale shows known reversals in world magnetic polarity during the last 4.5 million years. The evidence is obtained by measuring the polarity of volcanic lavas, which can also be potassium-argon dated. Deposits that are only roughly dated by relative methods can often be more accurately dated by measuring their magnetic polarity and referring to this chart. For example, fossils in Bed IV at Olduvai Gorge (see Table 9–1) indicate it is less than one million years of age and it is also all of normal polarity. We can therefore conclude that it was laid down after 0.69 and before 0.03 million years B.P. Because Bed III, which underlies it, is of reversed polarity, we can say that the boundary between them is dated approximately 0.69 million years B.P.*

also become contaminated by modern organic compounds (such as the inks with which the fossils are labeled) or by modern $CO_2$ from the atmosphere. Although these factors somewhat limit the value of carbon-14 dating, the method has proved of great value to paleoanthropologists when it is carefully used.

Another dating method that depends in a different way on radioactive decay is the *fission-track* method. The rare radioactive element uranium 238 splits spontaneously to create a minute region of crystal disruption in a mineral. The disruption is called a track. In the laboratory, microscopic examination can determine track densities in mineral crystals containing uranium 238, in proportion to total uranium content. Since the rate of spontaneous fission is known, the age of the crystal can be calculated. However, the clock is started (as with potassium-argon) with the eruption of volcanoes, and so this method has the same geographical limitations as the potassium-argon method.

The main value of the fission-track method at present is as a cross-check on the potassium-argon method. The same volcanic samples can often be used and the comparison aids in detection of errors. The fission-track method itself has other problems. With low uranium content and rather recently formed minerals, the track density will be low. Heating eliminates tracks (as we have seen, heating also causes problems with potassium-argon dating). Fission-track dating, however, has proved of great value in dating samples from the beginning of the earth to about 300,000 years B.P. It is now being used quite widely in dating early periods of human evolution in volcanically active regions.

The value of radioactive dating methods has been greatly increased by using them to date changes that we now know to have occurred in the earth's magnetic field. It appears that the north-south magnetic field of the earth has reversed in direction many times during the earth's history. (On such an occasion, a compass needle would point south instead of north.) The direction of the prehistoric magnetic field can be detected by measuring the "fossilized" direction of the magnetic field in a rock sample in the laboratory and comparing it with the north-south orientation that the sample had at the site. Such measurements of so-called *fossil magnetism* of dated rocks have enabled geophysicists to prepare a chart (Figure 1–13) that indicates past ages of normal and reversed magnetism. The data help to tell us the age of sites for which potassium-argon or fission-track dates are not available. For example, Bed IV at Olduvai Gorge in East Africa does not contain datable volcanic ash deposits, yet we know it is probably much younger than one million years B.P. because it is normal throughout its polarity, but Bed III, which lies below it, is reversed. Looking at Figure 1–13, we can see that the bottom of Bed IV must be about 690,000 years old and that therefore the deposits of the bed postdate this point in time. In this way, magnetism can help paleoanthropologists, in some instances, date deposits in which some general indications of geological age are available but volcanic rocks are not present. Fossil magnetism can also be used to cross-check potassium-argon and fission-track dates at particular sites.

A very different kind of dating method has been developed as a result of the study of the degenerative processes that occur in animal bones after death. Amino acids in solution change the direction of polarized light under the microscope; depending on their effect, they are called left-handed or right-handed compounds. In living plants and animals, all amino acids are right-handed. During the process of decay, amino acids slowly lose this right-handedness and become randomly

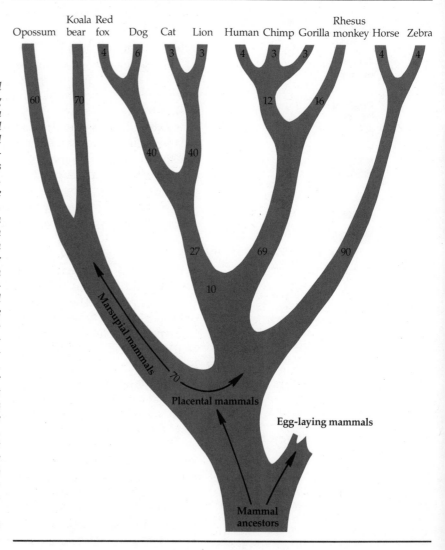

FIGURE 1–14   *The protein molecules of all animals are made up of the same building blocks—twenty amino acids that link to form long chains. It is how the acids are arranged on the chains that determines which animal is which. The more alike the sequences of acids are, the more closely related the animals are; the more different their sequences are, the more distant the relationship, and the longer ago they evolved in different ways. This "family tree" devised by Vincent Sarich and Allan Wilson shows how differences in the proteins of species reflect their evolution since they split from a common ancestor. For instance, analysis shows six differences in one protein (serum albumin) between chimpanzees and gorillas, meaning they evolved differently in relatively recent times (see the small fork at the top of the diagram). Humans show seven differences from both chimpanzees and gorillas. Since the latter are already credited with three differences each, the remaining four go to humans, and their fork can be plotted at about the same point on the tree as the chimp-gorilla fork. Rhesus monkeys, which have about thirty-one serum-albumin differences from humans, chimpanzees, and gorillas, must have split from the others earlier, so the fork is lower on the diagram. Only half the differences go to the rhesus monkeys; the other half are assigned to the apes (for the chimps and gorillas 12 + 3 = 15, for humans 12 + 4 = 16). The forks for the other animals shown are similarly derived.*

**TABLE 1–2  Estimated Times of Evolutionary Divergence Among Higher Primates**

| SPECIES | TIME OF DIVERGENCE BASED ON IMMUNOLOGICAL STUDIES | TIME OF DIVERGENCE ESTIMATED FROM FOSSIL EVIDENCE |
|---|---|---|
| Human and great ape (chimpanzee) | *4 ± 1.5 million years | 5–7 million years |
| Human and lesser ape (gibbon) | *12 ± 3 million years | 12–19 million years |
| Human and rhesus monkey (Old World monkey) | †20–22 million years | 26–40 million years |
| Human and capuchin monkey (New World monkey) | †35–38 million years | 50–60 million years |

* Derived from P. Andrews and J. E. Cronin 1982, *Nature* 297: 541.
† Derived from Vincent M. Sarich and J. E. Cronin 1977, *Nature* 269:354.

oriented to both left and right because of a natural chemical rearrangement of the molecules called *racemization*. The rate of this loss of right-handedness at any particular temperature is known, and when calibrated by carbon-14 tests it can be used to date bone. Thus, in an ideal situation, layers of bone that lie between samples dated with carbon 14 can themselves be dated with some accuracy. The method has the advantage of being direct but the disadvantage of being dependent on temperature. It is valuable only if it can be calibrated in the actual sites in which it is being applied. If it is calibrated by carbon dates at one site, it cannot reliably be applied to another; a different history of temperature variations may seriously affect the accuracy of the dates obtained. The rate of decay limits the time period over which this method is useful, and it tends to be unreliable outside the period of 1,000 to 100,000 years B.P. But racemization has been used with some success in both Africa and North America. In fact, it has indicated a surprisingly early appearance of modern humans in North America (Chapter 16). Better calibration is required, however, before these dates can be finally accepted.

We will see in Chapter 4 that the process of evolution involves slow changes at the biochemical level in every species. Some evidence indicates that various proteins change in time at a roughly constant rate. We can therefore measure the differences between the proteins of different species, and if we know how fast the proteins change, we can calculate the time when the lineages leading to different living species diverged from their common ancestor by counting the changes in the various proteins (Figure 1–14). This calculation generates the scale known as the *protein clock*. It requires very careful calibration and its reliability is still somewhat uncertain and may be limited. But it has been used to indicate the dates of some important events in human evolution (Table 1–2). The dates given in the first column of this table

**TABLE 1–3   Relationships Between Humans and Other Primates Using Biochemical Markers**

| BIOCHEMICAL MARKER | CHIMPANZEE | GORILLA | GIBBON | OLD WORLD MONKEY | NEW WORLD MONKEY | PROSIMIAN | SOURCE |
|---|---|---|---|---|---|---|---|
| Protein immunology | 8 | 8 | 18 | 40 | 70 | 140 | V. M. Sarich and J. E. Cronin, 1976 |
| DNA hybridization | 2.3 | 2.4 | 6.4 | 9 | 15 | — | R. E. Beneviste and G. J. Todaro, 1976 |
| Amino-acid sequencing | 0.3 | 0.6 | 2.4 | 3.8 | 7.5 | 11.3 | M. Goodman, 1975 |

*Note:* The figures in this table indicate the distance of humankind from other primates using various biochemical markers. Protein immunology (line 1) uses several different classes of blood protein and gives a broad indication of immunological distance. The results are roughly comparable to those shown in Figure 1–14 based on a single protein. DNA hybridization results (line 2) are claimed to signify the approximate number of major changes in DNA sequencing that have occurred since the two species separated in evolution. Each change in sequencing represents approximately 17,000 protein substitutions. Amino-acid sequencing work on a number of different proteins shows percentage differences in amino acids between the same pairs of primates (line 3). All these data contrast clearly the close biochemical relationship between humans and the great apes of Africa with the more distant relationship of humans with monkeys and prosimians.

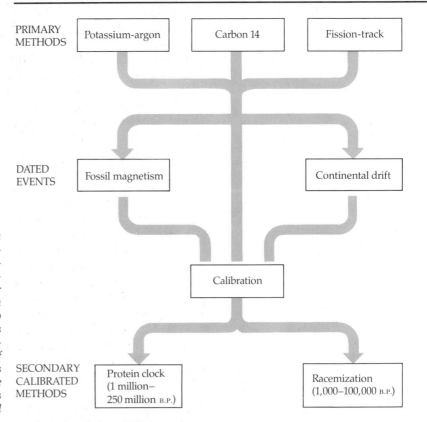

*FIGURE 1–15   All chronometric dating in paleoanthropology depends on the measurement of radioactive decay. The three techniques involved constitute the primary methods of chronometry (top line). Further knowledge of the age of certain deposits can be gained by using the primary methods to date major geological phenomena, such as magnetic reversals and continental movements (especially the splitting and fusing of continental plates). Both primary methods and dated events can be used to calibrate the process of organic change, which themselves can help us to estimate the age of fossils and species divergence (bottom line).*

are based on the two assumptions: (1) that blood-serum-protein evolution is constant and (2) that the divergence between prosimians and Anthropoidea occurred 70–75 million years ago. This is the calibration point and is based on the fossil record of prosimian evolution. Both these assumptions are reasonable and possible, but neither is certain. Nevertheless, biochemists feel that the evidence is so good that there is no possibility of the human-African ape evolutionary divergence predating, say, 8 million years B.P. Paleontologists, in contrast, feel that only the fossil evidence can give us conclusive evidence of the times when these major groups diverged.

Biochemists have studied other biochemical systems besides amino-acid sequences of blood-serum proteins. These systems include hemoglobins, fibrinopeptides, and transferrins—the nonbinding proteins from serum. Also, DNA has been studied for the degree of chemical differences between different but related species. All this evidence points to an extremely close relationship between humankind and the African great apes (Table 1–3).

Further evidence of the age of species divergences can sometimes be gained from our knowledge of *continental drift*, which is calibrated by the potassium-argon method. For example, New World and Old World primates shared a common ancestor (Chapter 5) and did not diverge until the North American and Eurasian land masses separated and the North Atlantic Ocean was formed. This event is now believed to have occurred about 55 million years ago. This date may now be taken as a reasonable estimate of the date at which the two primate groups separated, and it is in striking contrast to the figure of 35–38 million given in the first column of Table 1–2.

Figure 1–15 summarizes the various dating techniques and Table 1–4 summarizes their effective time spans.

TABLE 1–4   Principal Methods of Determining the Chronometric Age of Fossils and Geological Deposits

| TIME PERIOD | MOST EFFECTIVE METHOD OF DATING |
|---|---|
| Modern times–2,500 B.C. | Historical documents; tree-ring chronology; imported objects |
| Recent time–50,000 B.P. | Carbon 14 (half-life: 5,730 years); new techniques under development extend range back to 100,000 years |
| 100,000 B.P.–500,000 B.P. | No reliable method yet available: methods of relative dating used |
| 500,000 B.P.–age of earth | Potassium-argon (potassium 40, half-life: 1,265 million years); fission-track (uranium 238, half-life: $4.5 \times 10^9$ years) |

*Australopithecus*

*Homo habilis*

*Homo erectus*

## Modern Excavations

Modern work at sites occupied by early humans is time-consuming and demanding. The tools of today's field worker are not so much picks and shovels as surveyor's transits, dental instruments, and small camel's-hair brushes. With such tools, it may take two weeks to excavate properly a few square meters. Every scrap of bone that is gently and patiently worked free must be mapped both horizontally and vertically; every-

Early *Homo Sapiens*                Early Modern Human                    Modern Human

*FIGURE 1–16   These reconstructions suggest far more knowledge of human evolution than we actually possess. We do not have a complete skeleton of any fossil older than Neandertal, nor do we have any direct evidence about the extent of hair in these forms. Nevertheless, the drawings give the sequence of our ancestors and some idea of their nature.*

thing recorded, everything labeled. When this kind of study in three dimensions is done, the information compiled from one occupation site can be compared with data gained from another site. There may well be an overlap, permitting the matching-up of several layers from each of the two sites and a better understanding of both than was possible with one alone. Work of this sort is made still more precise when stone tools are brought into the picture, for different cultural phases are known to have had different kinds of tools and different techniques for making them.

Thus the full development of an important site may take many years, and may require many specialists to analyze the findings in different ways, and substantial amounts of money. But the scientist will not select a site haphazardly. Something—bones or tools—must first be exposed by the erosional forces in nature to suggest that a site is worth investigating. Then a series of test trenches are opened to expose the layered deposits and to pinpoint concentrations of interesting material. In these ways paleoanthropologists vastly improve their chances of significant discoveries; otherwise they might dig out an entire hillside, using up much time and large sums of research money, and find nothing at all.

Does this difficulty in finding sites mean that the great, exciting days of paleoanthropology are over? Not at all. It is true that the basic concepts have been established and there can no longer be quite the sense of absolute astonishment that greeted Hutton's concept of geological time and Darwin's theory of evolution, or even the amazed disbelief that greeted the discovery of Java man (see Chapter 10). Nevertheless, these are stirring times for paleoanthropologists. Not only is the body of evidence growing almost faster than it can be analyzed, but there are still surprises in store and problems unsolved. Each fact, each new bit of evidence that is found, speeds up the overall process of coming to an understanding of the story of human evolution.

It is the highlights of that story that we will deal with in this book. After discussing the genetic mechanisms of evolution, we will find out what characteristics of ourselves set us apart from other animals. Then we will learn what is known about fossil apes and their possible connections with our own fossil forerunners. Then will come those predecessors themselves (Figure 1–16): our *Australopithecus* ancestors of 6 to 2 million years ago; *Homo habilis*, the first member of the genus *Homo*; then *Homo erectus*; and finally archaic *Homo sapiens*, the earliest members of our own species; the remarkably well-documented Neandertals—those ice-age hunters of large animals, and the early modern humans, who live just over the hill from us in time and are no different from us physically.

# Chapter 2

# Humans Among the Animals

What a piece of work is a man! How noble in reason!
How infinite in faculties! In form and in moving, how
express and admirable! In action how like an angel! In
apprehension how like a God! The beauty of the world!
The paragon of animals!

WILLIAM SHAKESPEARE, 1564–1616.
*Hamlet*, II, ii.

Before we start examining our past, we must first learn something about
what we are like today. We cannot completely—or even partially—
answer this question until we have answered simpler questions about
our similarities to and differences from other animals.

**CLASSIFICATION OF
*HOMO SAPIENS***

Humankind is biologically classified under the Latin name *Homo sapiens;
Homo* means "man," and *sapiens* "wise." The human has been called
the thinking animal. The human has also been labeled a political animal,
a tool-using animal, a social animal, a speaking animal, and the animal
that is aware of itself. We are all these things, and more.

The Latin name *Homo sapiens* was coined by the great Swedish biologist Carl von Linné (1707–1778) as part of his classification of all plants
and animals. Though a practicing doctor for part of his life, Linnaeus
(the Latinized form of his name, by which he is more commonly known)
collected plants and animals in Europe and received specimens from
collectors throughout the world. He began to develop a system for
naming and classifying most of the then-known living organisms. He
used a binomial (two-name) system to label each one, choosing Latin
for the names because it was a convenient international language. He
published his system of names in his famous book *Systema Naturae*,
which ran for twelve editions between 1735 and 1766.

It was already clear to biologists that some creatures were more similar to each other than to others; they seemed to be created on the same general plan. Linnaeus grouped the similar ones in *classes* and *orders* to form a hierarchic arrangement. In 1735, Linnaeus had put *Homo* in his first class of Quadrupeds in the order Anthropomorpha, with the apes (*Simia*) and the sloth. In the tenth edition (1758) he called humans *Homo sapiens* and placed them with monkeys and apes in the order called *Primates*. Although not based on a theory of evolution, this classification indicated anatomical similarities—similarities that disturbed Linnaeus, among others. In 1766 he wrote: "It is remarkable that the stupidest ape differs so little from the wisest man."

Linnaeus's classification is still used because his method has proved to be of immense value. An international system of *nomenclature* (the rules of naming) has become essential in the development of the biological sciences, and the Linnaean system has survived the development of evolutionary biology since Darwin. The use of a dead language such as Latin means that the terms do not undergo the changes through time that are characteristic of spoken languages. The theory of evolution changed the basis of the system, however, making it clear that the similarities seen by Linnaeus and others were in many cases a result of evolutionary (phylogenetic) relationships. Groups based on anatomical likeness proved to share a common ancestor. The form of the system of classification remained, but its meaning altered. The hierarchy became phylogenetic, and species became variable and adaptable. The species was no longer the expression of an ideal type created by God, which Linnaeus had believed it to be, but the changing product of natural selection. As we will see, the system of classification reflects the evolutionary process, indicates shared common ancestors, and links related species in genera and families.

Linnaeus's grouping of humans, monkeys, and apes in the order Primates was continued at the next highest level, where he grouped the primates with other furry, warm-blooded creatures that suckled their young in the class *Mammalia*. We mammals have backbones and share an even more general structure with such animals as fish and birds, with whom we constitute the *phylum Vertebrata*. Our position in this hierarchic classification, known as *taxonomy*, is summarized in Table 2–1. In the pages that follow, we shall hear much of our *genus, Homo*, of its *species, sapiens, erectus*, and *habilis*, and of our zoological *family*, the *Hominidae*, in which are included humans and their ancestors since their divergence from the lineage leading to the living African apes. Our species *Homo sapiens* can also be subdivided into smaller units—into ancient and modern subspecies such as *Homo sapiens neanderthalensis* and the variety of living races that constitutes *Homo sapiens* today (see Chapter 18).

As we shall see in later chapters of this book, taxonomy presents the physical anthropologist with many problems in classifying new fossil

## TABLE 2–1  Classification of Humankind

| TAXONOMIC CATEGORY | GROUP INCLUDING HUMANS | CHARACTERISTICS | MEMBERS |
|---|---|---|---|
| Kingdom | Animalia | Organisms that move, and feed by the mouth. | Vertebrates and all other animals (e.g., insects) |
| Phylum | Vertebrata | Phylum of the animal kingdom of bilaterally symmetrical animals with flexible internal segmented backbones and other bony skeletal structures. | Mammals and all other animals with backbones (e.g., fish, birds, reptiles) |
| Class | Mammalia | Class of Vertebrates characterized by fur, warm blood, the feeding of live-born young by means of milk glands, and maternal care of young. | Primates and all other warm-blooded furry animals that suckle their young (e.g., dogs, elephants) |
| Order | Primates | Order of Mammals distinguished by adaptations to tree living, such as grasping hands and feet, nails on digits, flexible limbs, and highly developed visual sense. | Anthropoidea and Prosimii (lower primates: tarsiers, lorises, lemurs) |
| Suborder | Anthropoidea | Suborder of the Primates, with evolved social organization, daytime activity, and notable development of intelligence and ability to learn. | Hominoidea, Old World monkeys (e.g., rhesus), and New World monkeys (e.g., spider monkey) |
| Superfamily | Hominoidea | Superfamily of the Anthropoidea characterized by relatively erect posture, loss of tail, development of arms and shoulders for climbing, and (generally) five cusped molars. | Hominidae, Pongidae (orangutans), Panidae (chimpanzees, gorillas), and Hylobatidae (gibbons, siamangs) |
| Family | Hominidae | Family of the Hominoidea characterized by bipedalism, grinding teeth, and a trend toward brain enlargement and tool use. | Humans (*Homo*), and apemen (*Australopithecus*) |
| Genus | *Homo* | Genus of the Hominidae characterized by a relatively large brain, skillful hands, opposable thumb, and evolving traditions of tool use, toolmaking, and culture. | Early humans (*habilis* and *erectus*) and modern humans (*sapiens*) |
| Species | *sapiens* | Species of the genus *Homo* characterized by a large brain, an advanced culture, technology, and language. | Modern humans, including early subspecies (such as *neanderthalensis*) and all living races |

discoveries. Classification is an art and often arouses discussion and disagreement. It is important because names are essential, and the correct use of bionomial names depends on an understanding of the rules of nomenclature and of the relationship between individual fossils, races, and species. This work usually involves painstaking study and interpretation of the fossil evidence and sound knowledge of taxonomic procedures. Some of the problems that arise in the work of classification will be discussed in this book.

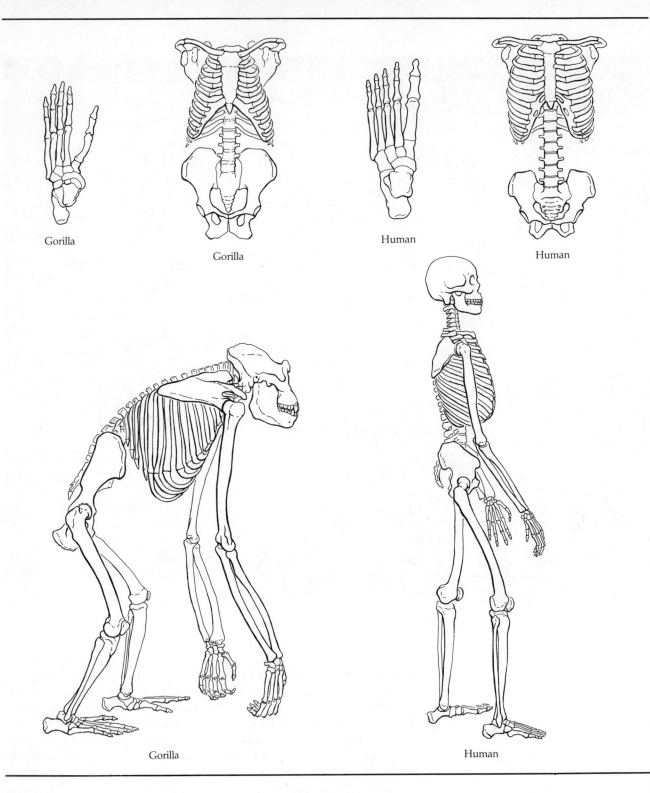

Gorilla

Gorilla

Human

Human

Gorilla

Human

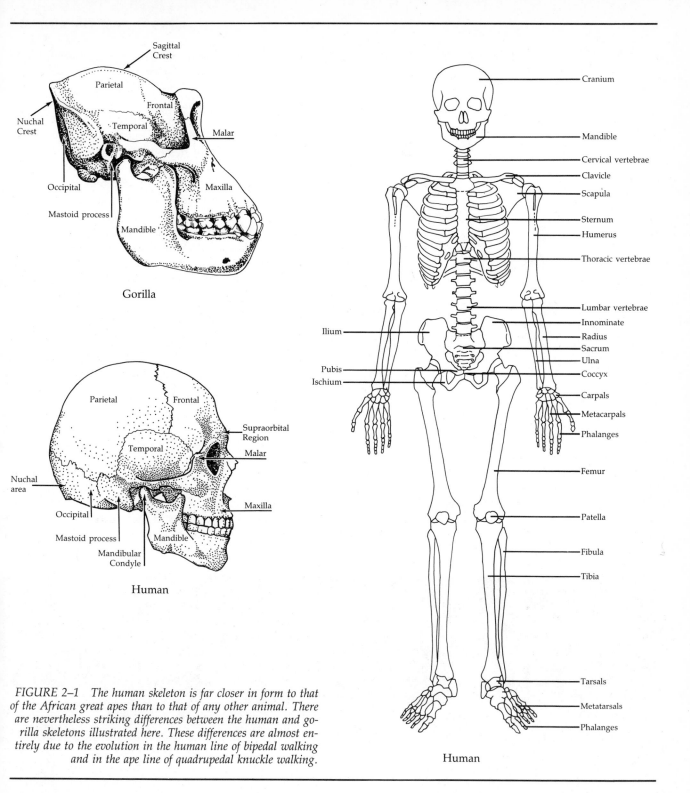

FIGURE 2–1    *The human skeleton is far closer in form to that of the African great apes than to that of any other animal. There are nevertheless striking differences between the human and gorilla skeletons illustrated here. These differences are almost entirely due to the evolution in the human line of bipedal walking and in the ape line of quadrupedal knuckle walking.*

**HUMAN CHARACTERISTICS**  Despite their place in the animal kingdom, humans are unique among animals, and they alone see themselves in command of the planet. Why? What makes them different?

The human mind, to be sure. But our new knowledge makes clear that the mind is not enough. Without a remarkable combination of organic hardware that supports and abets it, the mind would be useless. Humans dominate the animal kingdom not only because they possess a relatively big, complex brain but also because of a special combination of physical characteristics that we often take for granted. When compared with the sleek grace of a jungle cat, the streamlined strength of an 1,800-pound tuna, or the regal bearing of a horse, what is the human's puny body? The answer to that rhetorical question, as a careful examination of our physical adaptations will illustrate, is: everything.

Among the physical traits that, added together, separate all humans from all other animals, three have overwhelming significance: a skeleton built for walking upright (see Figure 2–1); eyes capable of sharp, three-dimensional vision in color; and hands that can both grip powerfully and manipulate things nimbly. These features are found in some degree in many primates; it is their elaboration and special combination with one another that distinguishes us. Controlling and making use of this equipment is the brain—a physical organ itself, but one that introduces the capacity for rational thought and, with the body, makes possible that other most human of all our abilities, speech.

**Locomotion**  The three distinguishing attributes, uniquely combined in humans, interact with one another. It is impossible to say that one led to the next, or that one is necessarily more important than the others. Each reinforces the others and makes improvements in them possible. Nevertheless, one attribute stands out simply because it is so conspicuous: up-

right walking. It is a remarkably effective method of locomotion, and no animal can use it as consistently as humans can.

For all its apparent simplicity, walking is an adaptation as specialized as flying is to a bat or swimming to a seal. True, humans are not the only animal able to stand on their hind legs; birds, bears, and a number of our primate cousins are sometimes *bipedal*, or two-footed. But with the exception of a few flightless birds such as the ostrich, humans are the only animals that depend exclusively on two legs for locomotion. (Kangaroos, which may seem to be bipedal, actually use their tail as a third limb and jump rather than walk.) Using two legs, a human has the endurance to outrun a deer and can carry heavier loads, pound for pound of body weight, than a donkey. (The French-Canadian *voyageurs* who transported trade goods through the American woods routinely backpacked 180 pounds over nine-mile portages, and a legendary hero among them, named La Bonga, is said to have backpacked 450 pounds.) No terrain is totally impossible to humans. They can reach an eagle's nest or a pearl oyster's bed. Only a human, the British scientist J. B. S. Haldane noted, can swim a mile, walk twenty miles, and then climb a tree. Hominid bipedalism is specialized, yet it allows extraordinary versatility in locomotion.

Like horses, human beings have a variety of gaits; they amble, stride, jog, and sprint. The simple stride, though, is at once the most useful and the most peculiarly human way of getting from one place to another. Probably evolved on the African grassland, or *savanna*, where our early ancestors often covered many miles in a day's food-gathering or hunting, the stride has taken us to every corner of the earth. Striding is no minor accomplishment. When compared with the way four-legged animals get about, human walking turns out to be a surprisingly complex feat (see Figure 2–2). "Without split-second timing," says John Napier, a British authority on primates, "man would fall flat on his face; in fact with each step he takes, he teeters on the edge of catastrophe."

*FIGURE 2–2   Bipedalism involves split-second balancing feats with precise muscular control. The right foot pushes off from the toe; the left foot bears the full body weight while the right leg moves ahead to land on the heel; then the left foot thrusts off. To run fast, human beings stay on their toes.*

*FIGURE 2–3  More distant information about its environment is available to an animal with eyes three or four feet above ground level (bottom) than to one of low height (top). These photographs taken from different heights are sharp at all distances, but animals other than primates can usually focus only at certain ranges of distance.*

Human walking is actually a balancing act in which the muscles of the feet, legs, hips, and back are alternately contracted and relaxed according to synchronized orders from the brain and spinal cord.

The human skeleton is closer in form to that of the African great apes than to that of any other animal. There are nevertheless striking differences between the human and chimpanzee skeletons—differences almost entirely due to the evolution in the human line of bipedal walking and in the ape line of quadrupedal knuckle walking. The human foot has lost the ability to grip with the big toe and the toe itself has become long and robust, forming the ball of the foot—an essential pivot for the act of walking. Human arms are short and legs long, in relation to the length of the trunk, while the gorilla has relatively long arms and short legs, indicating that the arms are more important for locomotion. The human knee has been modified for the transmission of weight and can be locked when extended. Fundamental changes have occurred in the pelvis to make the support of the trunk by the legs mechanically more efficient. The broader, shorter pelvis gives greater leverage to the muscles which hold the body erect, and the broad blade of the pelvis, called the ilium, anchors the large buttock muscles, which do most of the work in walking. Almost every bone in the body reflects the remarkable evolution of these two distinct kinds of posture and locomotion.

Balanced bipedalism is uniquely human, and to those who can see it with fresh eyes, it is strangely beautiful in its sheer efficiency and its superb adaptation of bone and muscle, brain and nerve, to the tricky problem of moving about on two legs rather than four. The adaptation was achieved at considerable cost. Back trouble, foot ailments, and difficulty in giving birth—common among humans—result partly from upright posture.

## Vision

Why is it so important to human evolution that we stand erect and walk on two legs? Part of the answer has to do with the human head. The head is where the eyes are, and the taller an animal stands the more it sees. A dog running through tall grass is forced to leap into the air time and again to get its bearings, but even on a smooth surface where no obstacles obstruct vision the advantage of height is marked. Eyes that are two feet above ground level can detect low objects about six miles away; eyes five feet above the ground can see nine miles farther (Figure 2–3).

The advantage of height is especially important because vision is the most important of our five major senses. Scientists estimate that some 90 percent of the information stored in the brain arrives there through the agency of the eyes. Human eyes are attuned precisely to human needs. In general, they are unsurpassed by any other eyes in the world.

A hawk can see more sharply, but cannot move its eyes easily and must move its head to follow its prey. A dragonfly can follow faster movement, but cannot focus a sharp image. A horse can see almost completely behind its head, but has difficulty seeing objects straight ahead at close range. Most important, among higher animals only human beings and their nearest primate relatives have the special combination of full *stereoscopic vision* and *color vision* (Figure 2–4). Human eyes, placed at the front of the head rather than at the sides, can focus together on an object so that it is perceived as a single three-dimensional image in the brain. And within this image, color vision enables us to pick out details by hue as well as by form, relationship, and brightness.

Taken together, color vision and depth perception bring us enormous advantages over most other animals, the majority of which are color-blind and have a relatively poor capacity to judge visual distances and to focus in fine detail upon particular objects. What a hunting dog sees when it looks out over an open field is little more than what a black-and-white movie might show, and the dog's distance focus is limited. The dog is unlikely to spot a rabbit in the field unless the rabbit moves—one reason why rabbits and similar prey react to noises by freezing, which conceals them from their enemies. Human hunters, on the other hand, can scan a scene from their feet to the horizon in a few seconds by focusing sharply and selectively upon a succession of images. And they see more images than any dog does because their eyes are raised at least three feet higher above the ground.

**Hands**  Humans stand up partly in order to see, and stay up partly because they see so well. But the freedom that this posture gives to their arms, and particularly their hands, has proved even more decisive in distinguishing humans from animals. Chimpanzees, among our closest competitors in upright posture and bipedal movement, are quadrupedal animals, and they lack free use of the arms. In an experimental situation they can get around with a bunch of bananas in their arms, but they must always be ready to maintain their balance with the help of a knuckle on the ground. Humans have far less need for caution. Babies may crawl on all fours; old people may rely on canes; but most humans go about with never a thought of support from anything but their two legs. Their hands are free to grab, carry, and manipulate.

Not needing our hands for support, we have been able to use them for more complicated and more creative tasks. With twenty-five joints and fifty-eight distinctly different motions, the human hand is one of the most advanced mechanisms produced by nature. Imagine a single tool that can meet the demands of tasks as varied as gripping a tool, playing a violin, wringing out a towel, holding a pencil, gesturing, and—something we tend to forget—simply feeling. For, in addition to its ability to perform tasks, the hand is our prime organ of touch. In the dark or around corners, it substitutes for sight. In a way, the hand has an advantage over the eye, because it is a sensory and a manipulative organ combined. It can explore the environment by means of touch, and then immediately do something about what it detects. It can feel around on a forest floor for nuts and roots, seize them on contact, and pop them into the mouth; when your eyes read the end of this page, your hand can find the corner of the page and then turn it.

The hand itself may be a marvelous tool, but it is used to full value only when it manipulates still other tools. This capacity is a second-stage benefit of upright walking. With our erect posture, our hands are free; with hands free, we can use tools; with tools we can get food more easily and exploit the environment in other ways to ensure our survival. Humans are not the only animals that employ tools, but they are the only ones that do so to any great extent and with any consistency.

There are two distinct ways of holding and using tools: the *power grip* and the *precision grip,* as John Napier termed them (Figure 2–5). Human infants and children begin with the power grip and progress to the precision grip. Think of how a child holds a spoon: first in the power grip, in its fist or between its fingers and palm, and later between the tips of the thumb and first two fingers, in the precision grip. Many primates have the power grip also. It is the way they get firm hold of a tree branch. But neither a monkey nor an ape has a thumb long enough or flexible enough to be completely *opposable* through rotation at the wrist, able to reach comfortably to the tips of all the other fingers, as is required for our delicate yet strong precision grip (see Figure 2–6). It is the opposability of our thumb and the independent control of our fingers that make possible nearly all the movements necessary to handle tools, to make clothing, to write with a pencil, to play a flute.

If the precision grip required to play a flute can be related to upright walking, the mind required to make such music may be related to the grip. Tools and brain seem to have developed together. The hand carries out some of the most critical and complex orders of the brain, and as the hand grew more skillful so did the brain.

**The Brain**     The human brain is not much to look at. On the dissecting table, it is a "pinkish-gray mass, moist and rubbery to the touch . . . perched like a flower on top of a slender stalk." (The stalk is the spinal cord, which may be considered an extension of the brain.) An ape's brain does not look very different. But there is a difference, and it is crucial. It lies in the extent of the gray layer called the *cortex,* which constitutes the outer layer of the largest part of the brain, the cerebrum. The cortex, scientists now know, plays the major role in reasoned behavior, memory, and abstract thought—and also supervises the delicate and accurate muscular movements that control the precision grip. The cortex is quite thin, but it represents 80 percent of the volume of the human brain. If

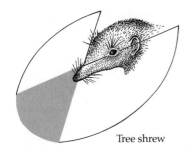

Tree shrew

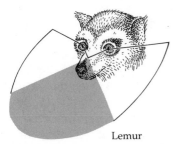

Lemur

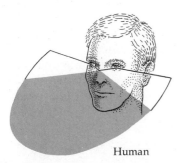

Human

FIGURE 2–4  Stereoscopic vision is of great importance to primates. The ability to judge distances is essential to an arboreal animal, which jumps from branch to branch. The primitive tree shrew's eyes look sideways and the visual fields have small overlap; in the lemur the overlap is greater. In monkeys, apes, and humans the extent of visual field overlap is great. Upright posture permits easy head rotation, which compensates for the loss of backward vision. As the eyes moved to the front of the face in primate evolution and vision became the primary sense, the sense of smell became less important; the snout has been reduced and the face flattened.

spread out flat, it would be about the size of a large newspaper page. It fits inside the head only by being compressed like a crumpled rag (the famous "convolutions" of the brain are mainly the folds and overlaps of the cerebral cortex). This compression demonstrates that the cortex has all but outgrown its allotted space. Somehow, the increase in the size of the cortex has made our brain the uniquely human thing it is (Figure 2–7).

Although many mysteries about the brain remain to be solved, some of its secrets, particularly the importance of the huge cortex, are now well understood. The cortex is not only the seat of intelligence; it is also, and perhaps more significantly, the part of the brain where sense impressions and memories are stored to be called forth and acted upon as circumstances suggest. The working of the human cortex follows no fixed pattern that dictates certain associations between experience and memory, as in some animal brains, and few predetermined responses are generated in the cortex. Among animals, many patterns of action are effectively automatic, performed by inborn programs or through previous conditioning. In humans, these patterns are, to a considerable extent, performed consciously, or refrained from consciously, or replaced by completely new patterns, again consciously. This use of the brain results in what is known as reasoned behavior, a phenomenon typically human and rarely seen in other animals.

The great brain gap between humans and lower animals can be visualized by looking at what happens when a human hand pokes the outspread tentacles of a sea anemone. The anemone will instantly retract its tentacles into its body. The reaction is automatic, since what passes for a brain in the anemone is programmed for only one pattern of action: in response to touch, the tentacles retract. No reasoned behavior is involved. In response to the same contact, humans may pull their hands back, or they may not. Their brains consider options, and their actions will depend on many things—whether they think anemones are dangerous or harmless, whether the contact is pleasing or discomforting, whether they touch the anemone on purpose or accidentally. Most higher animals also can react to a stimulus in a variety of ways, but no other animal has anything like the number or diversity of potential responses available to humans. And humans are alone in their capacity to examine all options in advance, to look inward upon themselves, and to observe the processes of their own minds. Perhaps even more important is that when humans think, they know they are thinking.

Conscious thinking and self-awareness are among our most striking characteristics, yet they remain the most puzzling. We cannot yet explain the operation of brain cells in the way we can analyze the movement of bones and muscles in walking and grasping. But a start has been made. Thinking depends on memory and association in the cortex.

FIGURE 2–5   The power grip (top) and the precision grip are illustrated in these photographs, together with the uniquely human independent control of five fingers.

Ideas, memories, and thoughts are registered in the nerve cells, or *neurons*, somewhat as they are in a man-made computer, in the form of electrical patterns, and they are retrieved and shuffled about by electrical actions. This much is clearly established, since thinking produces measurable electric currents in the brain, and many experiments demonstrate that electric stimulation affects such processes as memory. Electroshock therapy of a schizophrenic patient, for example, can erase some of the patient's recent memories while leaving unchanged memories that date from the more distant past. Like a computer, the brain evidently has two memories: one stores a great deal of information more or less permanently, another temporarily records current data.

The brain's similarities to a computer are remarkable, but they are only coarse similarities. Comparing a brain with a computer is much like comparing an aircraft carrier with a bark canoe. The brain contains an estimated 10 billion nerve cells, each of which may be thought of as a switching point for the electrochemical signals of mental activity. The largest modern computer may contain as many switching points. The system of interconnecting circuits between neurons within the brain is, however, millions of times larger and more complex than that of the most complicated computer, in which the possibility of interconnection is severely limited. As Warren McCulloch, an American student of the brain, has put it, "The brain is like a computing machine, but there is no computing machine like the brain."

If the brain is more than a computing machine, it is also more than a thinking machine. Reasoned behavior itself did not make us the paragon of animals. We rose to dominance through the crucial physical achievements made possible as our extraordinary brain evolved with our body. Both the senses and the skills of humans (as of any animal)

FIGURE 2–6   Though superficially like a human hand, the hand of a chimpanzee has a relatively short thumb and less independent control of the fingers. As the photograph shows, when the chimpanzee picks up an object between finger and thumb it does not (and cannot) oppose the tip of the thumb to the tips of the fingers as humans can. Not only is the chimpanzee's thumb very short, but it cannot be rotated at its base in the way the human thumb rotates to oppose the fingers. Compare Figure 5–5.

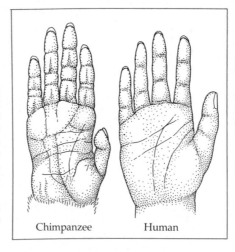

Chimpanzee          Human

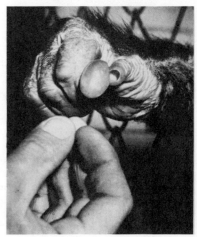

must be attributed to the joint evolution of a highly complex body and brain structures that function in total dependence upon each other. The ceiling of the Sistine Chapel was painted by a precision grip and color-sensitive eyes controlled by Michelangelo's brain. Neither bodily machinery nor creativity alone could have produced this masterpiece; both were needed, working together.

### Language

FIGURE 2–7 *Conscious mental activity takes place at the surface, or cortex, of the cerebral hemispheres, the two halves of the cerebrum. This cortex has evolved so much in primate evolution that, in apes and humans, it is too large to be smooth, as it used to be, but is deeply folded. This series of diagrams illustrates the importance of the cerebrum and its cortex in humans. The photo shows a freshly dissected human brain.*

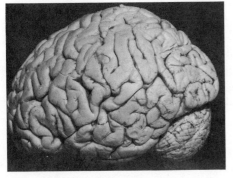

The great significance of this combination of human brain and human body is perhaps best shown by humans' most important innovation: *language*. Although all animals communicate with their fellows, only humans can talk. Bees dance to direct the swarm to food; wolves warn off intruders by marking their territories with scent; one bird calls to announce danger, another to invite courtship. Besides employing these primitive methods of communication, these bodily movements and simple sounds, humans also use language, a repertory of short, contrasting sounds that can be combined in an almost infinite number of ways to express very complex facts and ideas. The prairie dog's quick, high-pitched barks can send up a vague alarm; the animal cannot specify: "Five men armed with shotguns are approaching from the west and will be upon us in half an hour."

Such communications obviously depend on the human brain, for some animals equal humans in vocal performance without mastering language. Myna birds and parrots can mimic a human's voice perfectly; they can even be taught to repeat sentences of several words or more; but they cannot really talk, because their brains are incapable of abstract thought. They cannot combine elements from two different sentences learned by rote and use these elements to construct a third sentence.

Language is so clearly dependent on brainpower that its dependence on the body is often overlooked. The role of the body is most clearly

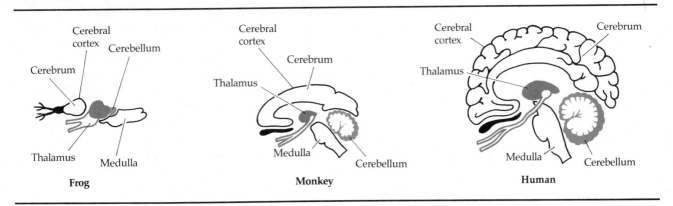

Frog

Cerebral cortex
Cerebellum
Cerebrum
Thalamus
Medulla

Monkey

Cerebral cortex
Cerebrum
Thalamus
Medulla
Cerebellum

Human

Cerebral cortex
Cerebrum
Thalamus
Medulla
Cerebellum

demonstrated by chimpanzees. Chimpanzees have brains that appear to be adequate for some degree of abstract thought. They can stack several boxes on top of one another to reach a bunch of bananas, a simple act to us, but one requiring the imaginative combination of superficially unrelated elements. They can also produce a wide range of sounds. It seems that they ought, then, to be able to talk. Since the turn of the century scientists have been trying to teach chimpanzees to speak. The best anyone has been able to do, after years of patient tutelage, is to get a chimpanzee to say "mama," "papa," and one or two other infant words. Only recently has the reason for this failure been traced. It involves not simply brain size but another aspect of the anatomy. Chimpanzees and gorillas are indeed able to use very simple sentences—but they cannot speak them. These apes lack the kind of pharynx that enables humans to articulate vowels. They can "speak" their sentences not with auditory symbols, but with visual ones—specifically, with the symbols of the American Sign Language, originally designed for the deaf (see Chapter 13). The human remains the only creature that has developed both the physical structures and the powerful, specialized brain needed to produce speech.

## Cultural Adaptation

Language was perhaps the last of our major biological characteristics to evolve. With the gift of speech, we acquired an immensely powerful tool for cultural evolution. Until about a million years ago, the evolution of all animals was a response to the challenge of the environment, and nature alone influenced the developments that eventually provided the human body with its internal skeletal support, its constantly warm temperature, its legs for walking upright, its hands for deft manipulation. If the climate was cold, natural selection favored the development of special biological adaptations such as fur and fat. When supplies of leaves and grass increased and spread, selection favored crunching and grinding teeth. Every animal was at the mercy of its surroundings. If a species suited its environment, it prospered; if it did not, it evolved new adaptations to the environment, moved to an environment more suitable, or became extinct.

This dominance of natural environment over species evolution became profoundly modified in the evolution of humankind. If humans had to find food by preying on other creatures, they did not need to develop fangs and claws; they made weapons of wood and stone. When the climate turned cold, they wrapped themselves in the skins of other animals instead of growing a furry coat. The human acquisition of a material culture and the capacity to adapt culturally was something completely new on earth, enabling humans to insulate themselves from the environment and to exploit that environment (Figure 2–8).

But culture was more than this picture suggests. It not only enabled humans to survive adverse conditions, but allowed them to extend their

*FIGURE 2–8   Manipulation of the environment is not unique to human beings. Nest-building is a common example of it among birds and many other animals. But humans have taken manipulation further. They are not only builders, but toolmakers as well, and this makes possible much more complex structures.*

conquest of nature into unfriendly environments with cold and barren winters. It enabled them to exploit resources that they could not otherwise have attempted to utilize, such as fish. It increased their total resource base many times by making them more effective hunters and more competent gatherers. It finally brought humans control of energy sources through fire and stored fuel, through dams and windbreaks. Culture was not just an accumulation of new materials and technology, but a new way of looking at the world, in which difficulties were no longer just accepted, but often overcome, and in which problems could be solved by knowledge and ingenuity.

The ability to speak facilitated and speeded up this ability for cultural adaptation. Once humankind acquired speech, the members of the hunting-and-gathering bands used their ability to communicate verbally in planning a hunt, passing on information, or agreeing on a rendez-vous. But the greatest benefit humankind gained through language came later, through the ability to learn from the accumulated experience of other people and other groups. Before the birth of language, human experience was pitifully brief and transitory; when a human being died, much of his knowledge died with him. By the gift of language the shared experience of humankind, our cultural heritage, could more readily be preserved and kept accessible over many generations—first through recited lore and legends and later through written words.

Physically, we are hardly distinguishable from humans who lived 30,000 years ago. But socially, human life has been transformed by the accumulation of the experience of millions of human lives over thousands upon thousands of years. This new social world is based entirely on words. Once a species limited to a tropical savanna, humankind now thrives throughout the entire globe. From an estimated population of 10 million as recently as 10,000 years ago, we have multiplied to more than 4 billion today, and now threaten by our very success to exhaust the resources of the earth before the next century is well advanced.

There is nothing like the human body in all the world. Humans are the only organisms that combine the abilities to think about themselves, talk, habitually walk on their hind legs, make things with their hands, and enjoy stereoscopic color vision. No other creature depends on both biological adaptations and cultural adaptations to enable it to survive. Without our culture at the interface of biology and our environment, we would be lost. We created our symbolic culture, and our culture has in turn made us the creatures that we are. The foot that evolved from a branch-gripping prehensile organ to an organ capable of carrying a human steadily over rolling grassland is now found encased in a boot, slogging with its human owner through city slush. The hand that first wielded a stick as a weapon and later chipped flint into a cutting edge today fashions tools that make tools that make more tools that make rocketships that reach other planets. The eye that used to spot a wounded giraffe hiding in a grove of trees now scans this page. And the mind that learned to analyze the migrations of game, to recognize dozens of different animal spoors, to distinguish among hundreds of varieties of plants, now dictates the playing of a game of chess, the writing of a book, the waging of a war.

# Chapter 3

# The Riddle of Heredity

Variety's the very spice of life,
That gives it all its flavour.

**WILLIAM COWPER, 1731–1800.**
*The Task*, Book 2.

It may well be difficult to accept that our unique and miraculous qualities are a product of natural selection. Is Bach's Mass in D Minor merely the result of a lengthy process of chance and change? Organic evolution is a process of change based on chance but more complex than chance alone, and more efficient. Natural selection operates on accumulated variations: as we shall see, selection is not the only creative factor in the evolutionary process.

For decades after the principles of evolution had been formulated, a knotty problem remained: why do living things vary, and how do variations occur? It was clear that evolution functions through the selective preservation or elimination of inherited differences between individuals, yet no one could say how such differences come about in the first place. To complicate the problem, people knew that traits were preserved by inheritance, but did not know how a given trait was handed down from parent to offspring. Black-haired parents could produce a child with red hair, which the child inherited from a grandparent or an even more remote ancestor. Baffled, people fell back on the idea that heredity is somehow transmitted with the blood, and that a child bears a blend of the parents' bloods. So deeply rooted was this idea that it became a part of the language—people spoke of a prince "of royal blood"; a "blooded" mare; "blood will tell."

In Darwin's day, this idea of *blending inheritance* held sway, and yet it introduced a seemingly insurmountable problem. If each child is a blend of the parents' characteristics, the succession of generations must result in a loss of variation. The long-term effect of sexual reproduction within a population would have to be decreasing variability, until all individuals were almost exactly the same. And yet the opposite is true: variability is maintained over time, and often increases.

Darwin was plagued for years by this problem. In an attempt to discover how traits are inherited, he experimented with the garden pea and other plants. For all the care he took, he could never figure out the pattern or order of inheritance that he felt certain must exist. Nor, apparently, could anyone else: Darwin read many scientific journals, but none enlightened him. And yet, by an ironic coincidence, the basic laws of evolution and the fundamentals of heredity were discovered, as we shall see, at about the same time.

## WORK OF GREGOR MENDEL

Just as Darwin was turning at last to the final formulation of the theory of evolution, the Austrian monk Gregor Johann Mendel (1822–1884) (Figure 3–1) launched the first of a series of experiments that were to demonstrate that inheritance, like evolution, is not chaos, chance, or miracle, but a matter of natural law. But Mendel's discoveries were not immediately seized upon and incorporated into the theory of evolution. Darwin never heard of Mendel's work, and the monk's reports lay ignored by the scientific world for more than thirty years.

Mendel was born on July 22, 1822, in a little village in what is now Czechoslovakia. His father, Anton, was known for his fine fruit trees, and he taught young Johann how to improve them with grafts from the orchards of the local manor house. In addition to learning much from his father, Johann did well in his classes, and was recommended for higher schooling, but there was little money to pay for it. By the time he had gone on to a two-year philosophy course at the Olmütz Institute, he knew that he would have to look for a profession in which he would be "spared perpetual anxiety about a means of livelihood." A teacher suggested that he enter the Augustinian monastery at Brünn. When he was accepted in 1843, he gratefully began religious studies there, assuming the name Gregor.

From his youth, as he said, he had been "addicted to the study of Nature." In the monastery, as long as he continued his religious studies, he was free to work on botanical experiments. In a small strip of garden Mendel began experimenting with crossbreeding flowers. He soon discovered that when he crossed certain flower varieties the same characteristics kept appearing with surprising regularity. The books he consulted helped very little. Many people had studied *hybridization*, the crossing of two varieties or species, but no one detected any pattern in the offspring. The varieties that resulted seemed to follow no rule, occurring in all sizes, colors, and forms.

## First Experiments

It struck Mendel, who was remarkably free of preconceptions, that the studies themselves had been chaotic. No one had bred hybrids systematically for generation after generation and recorded exactly what individual characteristics appeared in each plant; no one had even worked out the kinds of experiments that would make this systematic study possible. Mendel decided to develop a workable procedure, realizing as he started that the experiments would have to be done on a large enough scale to rule out small accidents of chance.

To begin with, he needed *true-breeding* plants, plants that showed little variation from generation to generation. He also needed a plant easily protected from all foreign pollen, for if an insect or a breeze should fertilize a plant with pollen from outside his garden, an experiment on the inheritance of some selected character would be ruined. Legumes most nearly fulfilled his needs, and after some testing Mendel chose the common garden pea as the ideal experimental plant. The pea ordinarily fertilizes itself and is easily protected from outside pollen. Mendel ordered thirty-four varieties from seedsmen and subjected the plants to a two-year trial, eventually selecting twenty-two as suitable for his experiments.

One of Mendel's greatest assets was that he worked step by step in patient, well-disciplined ways. Instead of trying to compare plant with plant in all possible respects, a procedure that soon would have led him into difficulties, he decided to study a few easily compared pairs of characteristics of the pea. He selected seven, illustrated in Figure 3–2:

1. The form of the ripe seed—round or wrinkled
2. The color of the peas—yellow or intense green
3. The color of the seed coats—gray or white
4. The form of the ripe pods—inflated or constricted between the seeds
5. The color of the unripe pods—green or vivid yellow
6. The position of the flowers—axial (distributed along the stem) or terminal (bunched at the top of the stem)
7. The length of the stem—long (6 or 7 feet) or short (9 to 18 inches)

Mendel was now ready to produce hybrids, and he decided to start by crossing wrinkled-seed plants with round-seed ones. As soon as buds formed on the vines, Mendel opened those of each wrinkled plant and pinched off the stamens to prevent the pea from producing pollen for its own fertilization. To prevent any outside pollen from being carried in, he tied a little paper or calico bag around each bud. Then he collected pollen from the round-seed plants. This pollen he dusted on

FIGURE 3–1  *Gregor Mendel's country childhood gave him deep knowledge and sympathetic understanding of the plant world. As a monk with some leisure, he took up plant breeding in the monastery garden, with remarkable and brilliant results.*

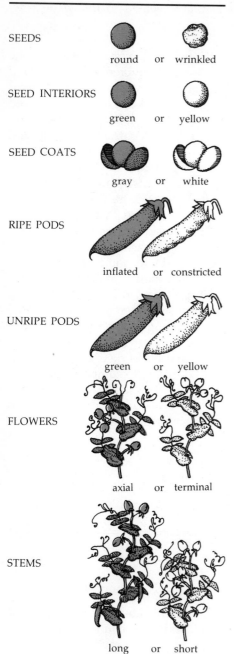

SEEDS

round    or    wrinkled

SEED INTERIORS

green    or    yellow

SEED COATS

gray    or    white

RIPE PODS

inflated    or    constricted

UNRIPE PODS

green    or    yellow

FLOWERS

axial    or    terminal

STEMS

long    or    short

FIGURE 3–2  *Mendel's pioneering observations of the pea plant were based on a comparison of these seven easily identifiable characteristics.*

the stigmas of the wrinkled flowers, removing the protective bags to do so. To settle any doubt that his results might be influenced by the choice of plants to serve as parents, he also reversed the fertilizing process, dusting wrinkled-seed pollen on round-seed stigmas. Mendel then performed the same interchange with each of the other pairs of characteristics he was testing. Altogether he fertilized 287 flowers on seventy plants.

Then he could only wait until time, sun, and rain performed their work. Finally he was able to open the pods of his round-wrinkled hybrids. In them nestled only round peas. The wrinkling, a trait of half of the parents, had disappeared as completely as though it had never existed. So it was with the other six characteristics he tested: although he crossed tall plants with short ones, all the offspring were tall; although he mated yellow peas with green, all the offspring were yellow. In each test plot one characteristic and only one appeared in this first hybrid generation (Figure 3–3).

During the winter, as Mendel worked with his jars of labeled pea seeds, he decided to call the characteristic that prevailed (like roundness or yellowness) *dominant,* and the one that seemingly disappeared (like wrinkledness or greenness) *recessive.* Thanks to his methodical approach, he knew what had gone into his hybrids. The next step was to see whether the recessive characteristics had survived the crossing. To find that out he planned to let the hybrids fertilize themselves in the normal manner of peas. In the spring he planted his hybrid seeds and waited.

Once again the critical time came when the pods could be opened. Mendel broke open the first. Inside lay both round and wrinkled peas, side by side in the same pod! The wrinkling of the wrinkled grandparent, lost in the first generation, had reappeared. Mendel harvested 7,324 peas: 5,474 were round and 1,850 wrinkled; the ratio was nearly three round to one wrinkled.

It was the same for the other characteristics in the second generation. In the experiment on color there were three yellow peas to each green. Overall—ruling out a few small deviations introduced by chance—the ratio was always 3:1. Here was no haphazard recurrence of the traits of the grandparents, but an exact recurrence (Figure 3–4).

What would happen in the third generation? The next year Mendel planted his 3-to-1 group and again permitted each plant to fertilize itself. Now the wrinkled seeds (those showing the recessive characteristic) produced only wrinkled peas, and as long as Mendel continued to plant their descendants (he planted seven generations) they produced only wrinkled peas.

The story was remarkably different with the round seeds, however. In appearance they were all indistinguishable, but internally some were different from others. When Mendel planted them these differences appeared (see Figure 3–5). Two out of three of the plants produced both

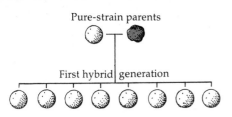

Pure-strain parents

First hybrid generation

*FIGURE 3–3 This diagram shows the results obtained when Mendel crossed a plant produced by round seeds with one produced by wrinkled seeds. The hybrid seeds show the character of only one parent (round); this character Mendel termed dominant. Mendel got similar results with the other six pairs of characteristics.*

round and wrinkled peas, in the ratio of 3:1. One out of three plants bore only round peas. Why did seemingly identical peas produce such varied descendants? With this question, Mendel began to solve the riddle of heredity. The true hereditary nature of the round peas was hidden deep within their cells. Some were truly round and produced only round descendants. Others merely looked round, and produced both wrinkled and round descendants. Which was which could be revealed only by planting them and seeing what kinds of seeds they would produce. This test disclosed that two out of three plants that looked round were actually hybrids containing both the round and the wrinkled trait; only one in three was a true round. (Today, we call the hereditary qualities of a plant or animal its *genotype*, and their physical expression its *phenotype*. A pea whose phenotype is round might have either a round or a round-and-wrinkled genotype.)

Mendel labeled the dominant characteristics *A* and the recessive ones *a*. When *A* and *A* came together it meant two dominants; if these plants self-fertilized, they would produce nothing but round peas. These peas are described as *homozygous*. When *a* and *a* came together it meant two recessives—and as long as the plants self-fertilized, there would be nothing but wrinkled peas, also a homozygous condition. It was only when *A* was combined with *a* to form the *heterozygous* type *Aa* that hybrids occurred. These hybrids could produce different kinds of offspring in future generations (see Figure 3–6).

## Experiments Using Many Characteristics

Mendel had concentrated so far on single contrasting characteristics. What would happen, he next asked, if two or more diverse characteristics were studied together? To see, he crossed round yellow peas (peas showing two dominant characteristics) with wrinkled green peas (two recessive). As he anticipated, all first-generation offspring were round and yellow. But in the next plantings, the round yellows revealed their inner nature—their genotype. As Mendel broke open the pods, he found that some had four kinds of peas: round yellow, wrinkled yellow, round green, and wrinkled green.

Mendel sorted the 556 peas borne by his fifteen double-hybrid plants: 315 were round yellow, 101 wrinkled yellow, 108 round green, and 32 wrinkled green. The ratio was almost exactly 9:3:3:1. Then he went on to the extremely difficult experiment of crossing plants that differed in three characteristics. He crossed round yellow peas having grayish seed coats (*ABC*) with wrinkled green peas having white seed coats (*abc*). It took "time and trouble," Mendel noted, but he obtained all the different varieties and all the proportions his calculations had predicted.

Charles Darwin, in similar experiments, also had obtained the 3:1 division in the hybrids. Being no mathematician, he had failed to understand the significance of what he was seeing. But Mendel grasped it easily. If each trait marked a separate hereditary factor, then he was obtaining every combination that could possibly be formed. Combine

*A* and *a* and only one unit could be formed: *Aa*. But if *Aa* and *Aa* came together, three different combinations could be made: *AA*, *Aa*, and *aa*. Thus from a cross of a pair of hybrids (*Aa* × *Aa*) three kinds of offspring would be produced; from a cross of a pair of double hybrids, in which two kinds of characteristics are studied (*AaBb* × *AaBb*), nine kinds would be produced (as shown in Figure 3–7); from a triple-hybrid cross, twenty-seven. The combinations would pile up three times three times three, in cubic power. In short order the possible variations could reach an astronomical number.

## Principles of Segregation and Independent Assortment

Mendel lacked the microscopic techniques to peer into the inner structure of his peas and search out the physical units of heredity that his experiments told him must exist. His results, however, were explicable in no other way. Mendel proceeded to formulate the biological laws that he saw must underlie his findings:

1. Heredity is transmitted by a large number of independent, heritable units. These occur in pairs in individuals. The pairs are separated during the production of gametes (eggs and sperm) so that a gamete has only one of each kind. This is the *principle of segregation.*

2. When each parent contributes the same kind of factor, a similar characteristic is produced in the progeny. If each furnishes a different kind, a hybrid results, and when the hybrid forms its own reproductive cells the two different units "liberate" themselves again.

3. The hereditary units are unaffected by their long association in an individual. They emerge from any union as distinct as when they entered. This is the *principle of independent assortment.*

Mendel regarded his findings only as hypotheses that required further testing. If he was correct, though, and each hybrid pea was made up of independent hereditary units, it should be possible to prove the point by a different shuffling of the units. Two experiments would suffice.

If Mendel was correct, when he backcrossed the heterozygous hybrid *AaBb,* a pea round and yellow in appearance, with the homozygous parent plant *AABB,* also round and yellow, only four combinations could be formed—*AABb, AaBB, AaBb,* and *AABB.* Since each combination would contain two dominants, all the peas would be round and yellow in appearance. Their true nature would emerge in later generations.

Mendel made this test cross-fertilization. When the pods finally matured they contained ninety-eight peas, every one of them round and yellow.

The same experiment in reverse backcrossed the hybrid *AaBb* with the recessive *aabb,* the green wrinkled plant. It went with equal precision. Mendel's calculations showed that four combinations should be formed—*AaBb* (round yellow), *Aabb* (round green), *aaBb* (wrinkled yel-

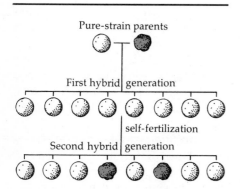

Pure-strain parents

First hybrid generation

self-fertilization

Second hybrid generation

FIGURE 3–4   *Production of a second hybrid generation by self-fertilization of the plants produced by the seeds in Figure 3–3 showed that the first-generation hybrids had carried the characteristics of both their parents, but with the wrinkled characteristic hidden. The new generation of seeds were of both kinds (like the pure-strain parents) but came in the proportion of three round ones to one wrinkled.*

FIGURE 3–5 *Mendel found the explanation of the 3:1 proportion shown in Figure 3–4 when he allowed the second-generation plants to self-pollinate. In the third hybrid generation he found new combinations of characteristics. The wrinkled seeds had bred true (and would always do so); some of the round peas also bred true, while others repeated the 3:1 ratio.*

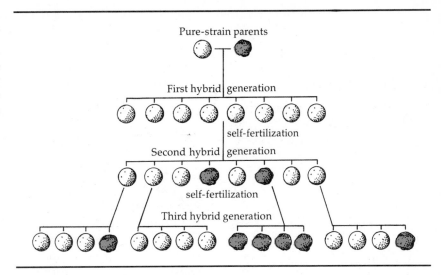

low), and *aabb* (wrinkled green)—and that they should appear in equal numbers. When he harvested his peas he had thirty-one round yellow, twenty-six round green, twenty-seven wrinkled yellow, and twenty-six wrinkled green. As he had predicted, the ratio, allowing for small chance variations, was 1:1:1:1.

"In all experiments," said Mendel with modest understatement, "there appeared all the forms which the proposed theory demands." All the necessary tests had been made. The results had been predicted, and nature had responded with astonishing exactness. The time had come for Mendel to publish a report on his eight years of work. During the fall and winter of 1864 Gregor Mendel wrote the paper that would demonstrate for the first time how individual traits are transmitted from parent to offspring.

On a frosty night in February 1865 Mendel read his paper before the Brünn Society for the Study of Natural Science. The members listened in unbroken silence to his discussion of the unvarying ratios in pea hybrids. At the next meeting Mendel went on to explain what the ratios meant. The combination of mathematics and botany was unheard of, and the idea that lay behind it, a vast shuffling of unseeable, unknown units, ran completely contrary to the belief that heredity was a matter of blending. The minutes of the meetings recorded no questions and no discussion. But Mendel was invited to prepare his paper for publication in the society's proceedings. The monk's monograph, "Experiments in Plant Hybridization," appeared in 1866. Copies of the publication were sent, as usual, to more than 120 other scientific organizations and universities in Europe and America. Once more there was silence. No one praised or disputed Mendel's work, or gave it any attention at all. They probably did not see that it had any significance.

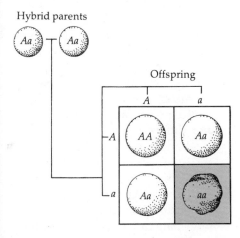

FIGURE 3–6 *The experiment described in Figure 3–4 was explained by Mendel in this way. Using the letters A and a for the characters smooth and wrinkled, he accounted for the 3:1 proportion by proposing that A is always dominant to a in every hybrid.*

## Multiple Independent Characteristics

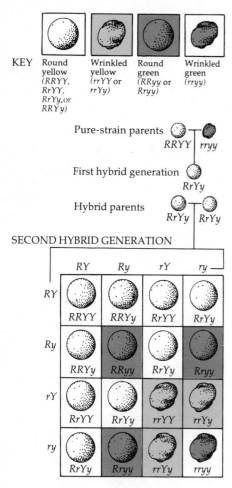

KEY

| Round yellow (RRYY, RrYY, RrYy, or RRYy) | Wrinkled yellow (rrYY or rrYy) | Round green (RRyy or Rryy) | Wrinkled green (rryy) |

Pure-strain parents
RRYY | rryy

First hybrid generation
RrYy

Hybrid parents
RrYy | RrYy

SECOND HYBRID GENERATION

|     | RY   | Ry   | rY   | ry   |
| --- | ---- | ---- | ---- | ---- |
| RY  | RRYY | RRYy | RrYY | RrYy |
| Ry  | RRYy | RRyy | RrYy | Rryy |
| rY  | RrYY | RrYy | rrYY | rrYy |
| ry  | RrYy | Rryy | rrYy | rryy |

FIGURE 3–7  The Punnett square shows Mendel's law of independent assortment. A pea with two dominant characteristics (roundness and yellowness, RR and YY is crossed with a pea having two recessive characteristics (wrinkledness and greenness rr and yy). The hybrid combines all four genes of its parents (RrYy). If these hybrids are crossed, their genes produce the combinations shown: four kinds of peas appearing in a ratio of 9:3:3:1.

Soon after, in an attempt to establish that his results were applicable to other plants, Mendel undertook considerable work with hawkweed, but the plant soon proved unsuitable. He also tried beans. Some upsetting results began to appear. Only in certain characteristics did bean flowers follow the same laws as the peas. When Mendel crossed a white-flowered, white-seeded bean with a bean having reddish-purple flowers and red seeds flecked with black, all of the first generation bore pale red flowers unlike either parent. In the next hybrid generation Mendel was greeted with a range of color, from pure white through a wide spectrum ending in reddish-purple. He saw colors that had not previously appeared in any of his test plants.

Could he have been wrong? Could an error have been made in his first results, which had shown that the first hybrid generation resembled the dominant parent? As Mendel puzzled over the in-betweenness of the pale red flowers of the first generation and the many colors of the second, it occurred to him that the nonconforming results could be explained if color is determined in some species not by a single hereditary unit, but by two units acting together. The two units could produce nine variations of color, as shown in Figure 3–8. Only one-ninth of the plants would bear white flowers, one-ninth would have reddish-purple flowers, and seven-ninths would produce almost exactly the range of color he had observed.

Mendel's explanation for the in-between appearance of many offspring was that more than one hereditary unit enters into the production of certain traits. Though Mendel knew nothing of how the hereditary units might be arranged in the cell, he had come upon yet another of the basic laws of heredity.

The modest monk did not dare to recognize how far he had gone. In his report to the Brünn Society, he said only that anyone studying color in plants "could hardly escape the conviction" that color, too, follows a definite law, but a law that finds "expression in the combination of several independent color characters." He stopped with this statement. Gregor Mendel did not admit that he had rounded out his formulation of the laws of heredity, nor did he realize that the whole basic pattern of inheritance, the understanding the world had sought for centuries, was now laid out.

In 1868 Mendel was elected abbot of the monastery. At first he thought that the new post would afford wider opportunities for his work, but this proved a futile hope. Other duties pressed on him, and soon his experiments with hybridization had to be dropped entirely. Death eventually came to the abbot on January 6, 1884. The townspeople and civil and religious authorities gathered for the funeral of a man they held in the highest esteem. But in all that gathering—and indeed in the world at large—no one realized that a great scientist had gone, or that his fame would be everlasting. Most of Mendel's experimental notes and records were burned by the monks.

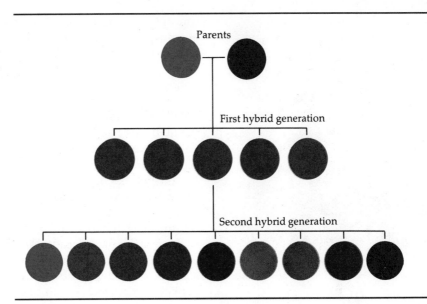

FIGURE 3–8 *The question of flower color in beans proved complex. When red- and white-flowered strains were crossed, the first generation bore flowers of a single intermediate color, whereas the second bore flowers of many intermediate shades. By a brilliant insight, Mendel explained this result by postulating that two hereditary characters are responsible for flower color in this species. This meant that one in nine of the second-generation plants would bear flowers similar to each parent stock and the remainder would be intermediate.*

## MENDEL'S WORK REDISCOVERED

Darwin had died two years before Mendel, never having found the answer to the ever-present problem of the evolutionary base—the causes of the variations on which natural selection acts. With the passing of the years, the problem became increasingly critical; the answer had to be found if the theory of evolution were to be accepted. In the 1880s one of those asking how the variations and modifications of life come about was Hugo De Vries (1848–1935), a botanist at the University of Amsterdam. De Vries (Figure 3–9) accepted Darwin's thesis that descent with modification is the main law of nature in the organic world. But if natural selection has only small, individual variations to act upon, how can wide differences between species be produced?

De Vries knew that breeders could produce only limited changes when they had only small individual differences with which to work. By selecting the redder tulips in their gardens they could breed a more intensely red flower. But for a completely different shade of red they had to wait for nature to produce what De Vries called a *mutation*, a radical change from previously existing qualities. Darwin had used the word "sport" for such suddenly appearing new characteristics, and had emphasized their importance but could offer no conclusive evidence in support of that emphasis. Some of his followers, in their all-out insistence on natural selection, tended to dismiss the effect of these sudden changes.

## De Vries's Work on the Evening Primrose

De Vries decided to watch for the occurrence of mutations. He thought that they would most likely be found in some place where a plant was adapting to new living conditions. One afternoon in 1886, as he walked

*FIGURE 3–9   Hugo De Vries was a Dutch botanist of great distinction. From his observations of the evening primrose,* Oenothera lamarckiana, *De Vries developed a theory of mutation that was to prove very important in our understanding of genetics. He was also the first to recognize the importance of Mendel's observations—thirty-five years after Mendel announced them.*

through the countryside near Hilversum, Holland, a yellow mass of the evening primrose, *Oenothera lamarckiana,* caught his admiring eye. The tall plants with the golden flowers had recently escaped from a nearby park and were multiplying rapidly in a former potato field. De Vries noticed that they varied widely. They differed in the shape of their leaves, in their mode of branching, and in their height.

De Vries found ten specimens of a new type growing in a corner of the field that had not been invaded by any of the other primroses. Their petals were smaller and more oval than the heart-shaped petals typical of *O. lamarckiana* plants. Were they truly a new species, and would they produce others of their kind? To find out, De Vries planted their seeds. The seeds produced new plants with small, oval petals like those of the parent plant—and quite unlike the petals of *O. lamarckiana.* He felt certain that he had a new species, and named it *Oenothera laevifolia.*

During the next decade De Vries raised or observed 53,509 primrose plants. Among them he discovered what he believed to be several new species. The new plants always appeared full-blown: no intermediates between *O. lamarckiana* and the newcomers were found. And once the new plant had appeared it repeated itself; it did not revert to its ancestral form.

De Vries also noticed that the new plants did not change in all their aspects, as he and most naturalists would have expected. On the contrary, they changed in only one or a few characteristics. In *O. rubrinervis* the color of the veins turned red, but there was little other change; the flowers and the general size of the plant were unaffected. Yet it was a different plant. (It was later discovered that *Oenothera* undergoes a complex and rare mixture of various kinds of genetic change.)

If plants and other living things changed in only one or a few aspects, this suggested that the characteristics must be produced by separate hereditary units. If so, then each part could vary separately. Though he was working with segregated characteristics, not mutations, De Vries struck out boldly—and correctly: "Attributes of organisms consist of distinct, separate and independent units. These units can be associated in groups and we find, in allied species, the same units and groups of units. Transitions, such as we so frequently meet with in the external form both of animals and of plants, are as completely absent between these units as they are between the molecules of the chemist."

He was venturing onto new ground and introducing concepts completely at variance with most of the beliefs that had always been accepted. De Vries wanted to find whatever support might be available for so radical a theory. He searched the literature to see if any other naturalist had suggested that heredity is not a whole but a compound of separate units. Turning through a work on plant hybridization by a German scientist, W. O. Focke, De Vries came upon a reference to a hybridization experiment by an Austrian monk, Gregor Mendel. "Mendel believed," said Focke, "he had found constant numerical ratios among the types produced by hybridization."

Constant numerical ratios! This implies separate units. De Vries tracked down the reference and thus—in the year 1900—the world discovered the work Mendel had published in 1866. De Vries knew at once the import of what he was reading. Time and progress had at last caught up with Mendel. Until that moment De Vries had thought that he, and not an unknown monk of an earlier generation, had discovered the long-sought secrets of heredity. But in a paper read before the German Botanical Society on March 24, 1900, the Dutch botanist, describing one of the most momentous discoveries in scientific history, gave full credit to the man to whom it belonged.

Coincidence came into play. On April 24, just a month after De Vries made his disclosure, a German scientist, Karl Correns, went before the same society to tell how he too had recently found the work of Mendel. He too had studied peas and maize, and had encountered constant ratios from generation to generation. He too had believed the discovery was his own.

By further coincidence, a third scientist, Erich Tschermak of Vienna, had made the same discovery at the same time. He had repeated Mendel's experiments with peas, and had found the constant ratios. On June 24, two months after Correns's report and three months after De Vries's, Tschermak reported to the same society that he, too, thought he had happened upon something new until he read the work of Mendel.

The remarkable triple discovery undid the neglect of decades. The simultaneous recovery of Mendel's work by a Dutch, a German, and an Austrian scientist and their joint confirmation of his findings caught the attention of the world. Mendel received the scientific acclaim that had never come in his lifetime. The world, for its part, gained its first true understanding of the most immediate and ancient of mysteries—how the distinctiveness and the very form of all living things are passed down from parents to offspring. The theory of evolution at last had its base.

## MUTATION AND NATURAL SELECTION

It began to seem to Hugo De Vries, once he had studied *Oenothera* and rediscovered Mendel's work, that evolution could never get anywhere by the slow process of natural selection alone. To him the sudden structural novelties that he called mutations (whose products he was overeager to label as new species) were the chief force in evolution. Natural selection, he argued, is not a force of nature but only a sieve that separates which organisms live and which die. It had nothing to do with the single steps of evolution; only after a step has been taken does the sieve act. It was clear to De Vries that novel characteristics—mutants—have to be put in the sieve before it can make a selection.

The Darwinians battled back: natural, gradual selection is everything, they said, and large, sudden mutations in species are meaningless in evolution's long run. De Vries retorted that "the general belief in slow changes has held back science during half a century." The battle became fierce.

## The Case of Mimicry

The mutationists for a time thought they had found incontrovertible proof in the phenomenon of *mimicry* (see Figure 3–10). In the Orient lives a handsomely marked butterfly, *Danaida tytia*. Its grayish upper wings are patterned in a strong tracery of black and its lower wings are etched in brown. In some of *Danaida's* territory, the butterfly *Papilio agestor* also lives. Its wings bear the same coloring and markings as *Danaida's* and are even very nearly the same shape, though they are slightly wider: in every important way *Papilio* is an excellent mimic of *Danaida*. The latter has another mimic in southwest China, *Neptis imitans*, just as close a replica, with the same striking colors and designs. Even a careful observer—or a careless bird—may mistake the mimics for *Danaida*. And this is the point of the mimicry. For all its delicate appearance, *Danaida* is a tough, rubbery insect. Naturalists have seen it flutter away unharmed after being seized by a bird and dropped because of its bad taste. And so birds avoid *Danaida*. On the other hand, *Papilio* and *Neptis* are tender morsels. They have found safety in mimicking the unpalatable *Danaida*: the more they resemble it, the better their chance of not being eaten.

The mutationists decided that such wonderful resemblances could have arisen only by mutation. How else could an elaborate design on the wings of a butterfly come into being? Mimicry, they said, is the outstanding proof of mutation, or the "discontinuous" origin of species (the Darwinians argued for the "continuous" or steady evolution of species caused by natural selection).

## Mathematical Evidence

The dispute was a standoff until such men as Sir Ronald Aylmer Fisher, J. B. S. Haldane, and Sewall Wright entered the fray with a new weapon, mathematics. Such things as hereditary units, change, degrees of difference, and alterations in natural populations are subject to mathematical analysis and test. Fisher, a statistician, mathematician, and later a professor of genetics at Cambridge, brought mathematical analysis to bear on the mutationists' pet phenomenon, mimicry. His calculations showed that only natural selection acting on relatively small variations could bring about such intricate adaptations as the matching of mimic to model. The double occurrence of patterns and shapes by the randomness of mutation is so unlikely as to be mathematically impossible.

Nor could mutation explain the proximity of model and mimic, which are always found in the same regions and in the same season. Often *Danaida* and its imitators are captured flying together. If their similarities had arisen by mutation, why should not the same patterns have occurred in other butterflies in other places? Fisher also pointed out that the mimic resembles the copied species no more than is necessary. Beneath the obvious, eye-deceiving colorings, shapes, and movements, model and mimic are as unlike as any two species.

### Role of Mutations

After additional proofs confirmed Fisher's findings, natural selection was unequivocally assigned the role of evolution's prime agent. Mutation was given a supplementary role. Mutation alone was no longer credited for the amazing adaptations of the natural world, but research showed that it at least supplies raw material for these changes. Mutation is indeed the major source of new genetic material in all organisms. Without the new opportunities produced by mutation, evolution would surely stagnate, its products unable to adapt to such changes in the physical environment as ice ages, long droughts, and the slow elevations and subsidences of the earth's crust, or such changes in the living environment as the appearance of a swifter predator, a deadlier germ, or a new competitor for food.

"The function of a mutation," wrote Fisher, "is to maintain the stock of genetic variance at a high level." If this analysis was right, some seeming contradictions had to be resolved. Work in many laboratories was showing that most mutations are detrimental, and most drastic ones lethal. They are steps in the wrong direction, in the sense that any random change in a smooth-running, well-adjusted organism is likely to be for the worse. Most bearers of radical mutations never survive long enough to pass the changes along to offspring. How then can mutations build up a "stock" for variation?

In fact, whereas a big change in an organism is often fatal, a tiny change or adjustment may be an improvement. A few mutations, generally small ones, may prove beneficial to a species. The next question for geneticists was: How can a rare, tiny, beneficial change—say a minute change in the color or pattern of a butterfly's wing—spread through a species with a large population? Will it not be swamped by the fact that the mutant will be vastly outnumbered by the normal individuals? Not at all, said the mathematicians. Assume a mutation offers an advantage of only one percentage point to the organism in which it arose. That would mean the survival of one hundred mutants as against ninety-nine unmutated individuals. In a short time (as evolution goes), say 200 generations, the mutant would replace the original as the population's normal type. And so even a small change in adaptability spreads relatively quickly throughout the species. Although harmful or useless mutations may crop up, vanish, and reappear, the

FIGURE 3–10 *Mimicry occurs quite widely among animals (and even some plants). In this example, the Danaid butterfly* Danais plexippus *(top) is mimicked by the Nymphalid butterfly* Limenitis archippus. *Both butterflies have an orange ground and black and white markings. Experiments have demonstrated the function and effectiveness of this mimicry: the Danaid butterfly is protected from predators by its unpalatability;* Limenitis *is protected by mimicking it.*

ones that ultimately pervade a species and become part of its normal makeup are either neutral or beneficial.

To Fisher, the great contrast between populous species and unpopulous ones lay in the fact that an abundance of individuals means an abundance of possible mutations—hence, more possibilities for adapting to new conditions. With fewer possible mutants to help it cope with changes in the environment, a small species might eventually dwindle into extinction. But a numerous species, such as humankind, is likely to have a varied enough genetic pool to meet almost any change that might confront it. If a species had only 100 characteristics that could exist in two forms, Fisher computed, more than 1,000,000, 000,000,000,000,000,000,000,000 genetic combinations would be possible when two of its members produced offspring. Mendel's conclusion that the number of combinations would increase in mathematical ratio was amply borne out. Evolution, Fisher realized, could head off in many directions and along tangents no one could conceive. Haldane, from his own calculations, reached conclusions that agreed with Fisher's. Recently it has become clear that natural populations possess an enormous reservoir of genetic variation, much of it not expressed in the phenotype.

"It has not so often been realized," Fisher commented, "how far most species must be from a state of stagnation, or how easily, with no more than one hundred factors, a species may be modified to a condition considerably outside the range of its previous variation." In *The Genetical Theory of Natural Selection* (1930), Fisher proved that this richness of genetic variability is directly related to fitness for survival. What counts is not the single plant surviving the drought or the one rabbit eluding the fox, but the nature and the preservation of the genetic material that makes it possible for the plant species or the rabbit species as a whole to survive. Fisher saw organic evolution as the evolution of the mysterious, almost infinitely variable hereditary units whose existence Mendel had inferred.

Although the question of discontinuous or continuous evolution seemed to be resolved, it has recently been revived in the form of an argument between those who support what is now considered the orthodox view of continuous and gradual evolution of Darwinian theory (*gradualism*) and those who stress the importance of large mutations and periods of very rapid evolution interspersed with periods of no change (stasis). This view is sometimes called the "jump" theory but is better known as the hypothesis of *punctuated equilibrium:* in this case the process of evolution is believed to be discontinuous (Figure 3–11).

The arguments made in the past are still valid: there is no *need* to postulate major mutations to account for rapid evolution. It is worth adding, however, that major mutations *may* have occurred and played a significant part in the process of animal speciation—and probably did

FIGURE 3–11   *The horse has evolved over 60 million years from a creature the size of a fox terrier, with four toes, that lived in North America. But was the process one of continuous gradual change, or of short bursts of rapid change interspersed with long periods of relative evolutionary inactivity? In most instances the fossil record is inadequate to answer this question.*

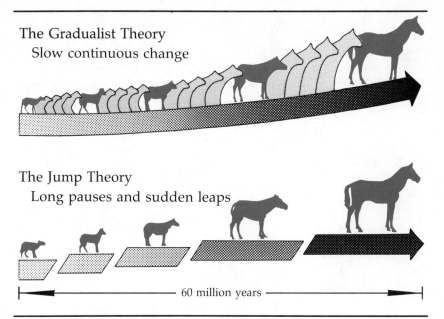

The Gradualist Theory
Slow continuous change

The Jump Theory
Long pauses and sudden leaps

60 million years

in some instances. The rapidity of speciation that the "jumpers" stress is in fact predictable on the basis of orthodox Darwinian theory. It is also quite clear that rates of evolution vary a great deal and that some species undergo very long periods of stasis when almost no change occurs. As might be expected, this situation is commonly seen in deep-sea species, where it is clearly related to the extraordinary constancy of the environment. Hypotheses of gradualism and of punctuated equilibrium are not mutually exclusive. As our knowledge of the fossil record improves, we may eventually be able to pinpoint periods of rapid change and periods of stasis so as to see the part played by each in the evolution of particular species. Such an analysis would, however, require a fossil record with very accurate dating. Although the hominid fossil record is well dated, we do not yet have sufficiently good dates to calculate rates of evolution with any accuracy.

# Chapter 4

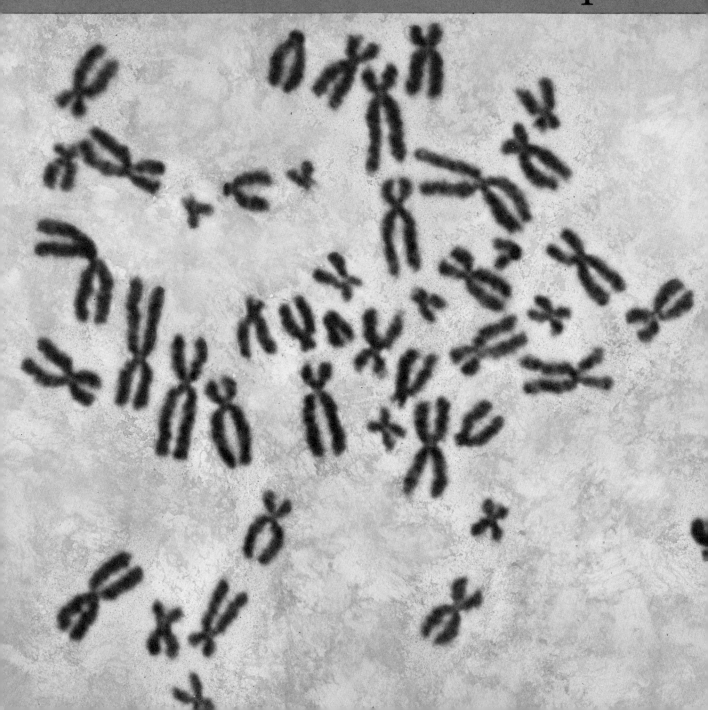

# Genes and Populations

The object is to combine certain ideas derivable from a consideration of . . . a population of organisms, with the concepts of the factorial scheme of inheritance, so as to state the principle of Natural Selection in the form of a rigorous mathematical theorem.

R. A. FISHER, 1890–1962.
*The Genetical Theory of Natural Selection.*

## UNITS OF HEREDITY

### The Chromosomes

In spite of his extraordinary achievement, Gregor Mendel had no way to discover what form the hereditary units that he believed to exist might take, or where they might be located within the living cell. But in the years when his monographs were sitting unread on library shelves, biologists discovered a number of tiny, threadlike structures in the nucleus of each living cell. When stained, these structures could be seen under a microscope, and so were called *chromosomes* (colored bodies). All an organism's cells, except the sex cells, have the same number of chromosomes. There are 20 in the cells of corn, 24 in the tomato, 8 in the fruit fly, 40 in the house mouse, 48 in chimpanzees, and 46 in humans. Close observation revealed that they go through remarkable maneuvers (Figure 4–1). When a normal cell is about to divide, in a process called *mitosis*, the chromosomes split in two and move to opposite ends of the cell. A cell wall grows between them, and in an hour, more or less, there are two cells where there had been only one, each new cell equipped with a full, identical set of these chromosomes (Figure 4–2). But when a new egg or sperm cell is to be formed, the maneuvers differ. In a process called *meiosis*, only half of each set of chromosome pairs goes into each sex cell, which is now described as *haploid*, as shown in Figure 4–3. Thus when a new individual is created by the fertilization of egg by sperm, the full *diploid* chromosome complement is reestablished, half of it coming from each parent.

It was in 1902, two years after the discovery of Mendel's work, that the suggestion was made independently by Walter Sutton in the United States and Theodor Boveri in Germany that chromosomes might be the containers of Mendel's hereditary units. In their coming together and pulling apart, they supplied the kind of mechanism needed to produce Mendel's results.

A few years later William Bateson and R. C. Punnett, experimenting with sweet peas, crossed a purple-flowered plant having a long pollen grain with a red-flowered, round-grained plant. Instead of obtaining the independent segregation of characteristics that Mendel found in garden peas, these English researchers found that the red flower and the round pollen grain tended to stay in constant association. Other investigators came upon the same phenomenon. Certain traits seemed to be coupled; perhaps they were controlled by the same chromosome.

## Morgan's Work on Fruit Flies

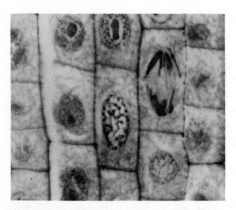

FIGURE 4–1  *A thin section of the growing root tip of an onion shows cell division occurring in many places. The phenomenon is accompanied by remarkable changes in the nucleus (the dark circular zone in each rectangular cell), in which the chromosomes appear as threadlike structures that divide and are pulled apart as though by magnets. This is the process called mitosis, common to plants and animals, which ensures distribution of the entire genetic material to every cell.*

Thomas Hunt Morgan was one of those finding associated characteristics. They kept cropping up in the fruit flies with which he was working. In 1910, about a year after he began studying *Drosophila melanogaster*, the little flies that orbit ripe fruit, a male fly with white eyes appeared in one of the milk bottles he used for incubators. Since the wild flies have red eyes, Morgan felt certain that this was a mutation. He bred the white-eyed male to a red-eyed female and in a short time had hundreds of red-eyed offspring, just as the Mendelian laws would lead him to expect. To bring out their underlying heredity, Morgan then bred red-eyed hybrids to red-eyed hybrids. The matings produced 50 percent red-eyed females, 25 percent red-eyed males, and 25 percent white-eyed males—but not one white-eyed female. By all indications the hereditary unit for white eyes, the mutated unit, was on the same chromosome as the factor that determined sex (assuming, of course, that the chromosomes were the bearers of heredity). White eyes was a *sex-linked* characteristic.

It was obvious to Morgan "that there was one essential requirement for the chromosome view, namely that all factors carried by the same chromosome should tend to remain together." The fruit fly has four pairs of chromosomes. If Morgan was right, it should be possible to map the hereditary factors carried by each, and he set out to do so. It took nearly seventeen years and the breeding of millions of flies, but in the end he found that precise locations on the chromosomes control specific characteristics in a fly. Ultimately, he made actual chromosome maps, long vertical lines on which he marked the sites of "yellow body,

FIGURE 4–2 *Mitosis, or cell division, is the process by which one cell splits into identical twins. It requires an elaborate mechanism for dividing and separating the chromosomes, which results in two identical cells, each with a complete diploid set of chromosomes, its own nucleus, and two centrioles, minute granules just outside the nucleus. (Here, chromosomes are shown in color; the small circles are the centrioles; the larger circle, the nucleus wall.)*

1. Chromosomes become prominent in the nucleus.

2. Chromosomes thicken; the *spindle*, an ellipsoid structure of protein molecules, grows between the centrioles.

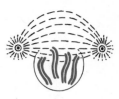

3. Chromosomes divide.

4. Chromosomes align in pairs and attach to the spindle.

5. One of each pair of chromosomes migrates to opposite end of the cell.

6. Spindle disappears; two nuclei appear, each with a complete set of chromosomes.

white eyes, echinus eyes, cross veinless, cut wing, vermilion eyes, miniature wing, sable body, garnet eyes, forked bristles, bar eyes, clipped wing and bobbed bristles." These were the descriptions of the physical characteristics of the different flies, characteristics whose determinant factors had been narrowed down to specific locations on their chromosomes. These determining units were given the name *genes* by Johannsen in 1909. On one chromosome in particular were the factors determining sex differences. In many animals the sex chromosomes are strikingly different in the two sexes, and easily recognizable among the chromosomes of a cell (Figure 4–4).

Often, however, a whole group of genes is involved in producing a single characteristic and such a trait is named *polygenic* ("many-gened"). Examples are numerous and include many characteristics from the color of a plant's stem to the weight of a fowl. In one experiment a race of fowls weighing an average of 1,300 grams was bred to a race of bantams whose weight averaged 750 grams. The offspring tended to split the difference in weight, but when hybrid was bred to hybrid there was a "wild outburst" of variation, ranging from monstrous birds of 1,700 grams down to some that were tinier than the bantam grandparents. J. B. S. Haldane estimated that if ten genes affected weight, they could combine in enough ways to produce 59,049 different weights. In effect, the variation would be continuous: that is, birds would be found in time at all points on a continuum of weight.

1. The chromosomes appear as double-stranded threads and thicken as in the early stages of mitosis, but then they pair up. Here the pairs are lying alongside each other.

2. Where chromosomes happen to cross, an exchange of genetic material occurs, so that the final products of the process have a gene complement different from the parent chromosomes.

3. The pairs are now separated on a spindle, each double-stranded chromosome of a pair moving apart, and the nucleus divides as in mitosis.

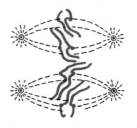

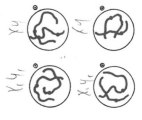

4. A new nuclear wall is formed, but the chromosomes remain distinct. Each nucleus now contains half the number of double-stranded chromosomes as were present in the original cell. A further division immediately follows.

5. Spindle formation again proceeds normally, and the split chromosomes are separated as in mitosis.

6. The final product is four nuclei, but each cell nucleus contains only half the number of chromosomes of the original cell. These are the haploid gametes or sex cells. The full diploid number of chromosomes is achieved again by fertilization.

*FIGURE 4–3  Meiosis, or reduction division, occurs in the formation of sex cells (eggs and sperm). It consists of two rapid cell divisions that bring about a halving of the number of chromosomes in each sex cell. The process is shown here for four chromosomes.*

In all these painstaking research projects, two important principles were established. One was that inheritance is, as Mendel had already claimed, *particulate*—it operates through the transmission of discrete bits of self-reproducing matter. The other was that it is *cooperative*—the genes, being organized in a single functional system (the gene complex), combine or interact to produce their effects (that is, usually more than one gene causes a trait to be expressed). Furthermore, it was clear that Mendel's second principle of independent assortment was true only if the genes were on separate chromosomes. By some strange chance, or possibly as a result of trial and error, Mendel had chosen such independent characters of his pea plants. In reality many genes are linked on particular chromosomes and remain together through meiosis. With these realizations not only did genetics find a firm scientific base, but the relations between genetics and evolution were put on a new and satisfactory footing.

FIGURE 4-4 *Humans have forty-six chro-*
*mosomes as twenty-three matching pairs.*
*The sex chromosomes (labeled X and Y) are*
*indicated in this photograph of male human*
*chromosomes. Only males have the small Y*
*chromosome, and so in this sex the twenty-*
*third pair cannot be matched. Females have*
*two similar X chromosomes.*

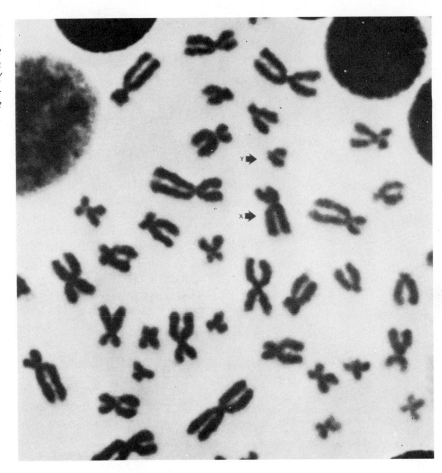

## Muller's Work with X-Rays

But what *was* a gene, and what happened when a gene mutated? Many scientists worked on the problem. In efforts to force changes in these submicroscopic units deep in the nucleus of the cell, they tried heat, cold, drugs, poison, and mutilation. But genes were too tough and stable to be altered by such tampering. Then H. J. Muller, who had begun his work with Morgan, got to wondering if mutation might be brought about by ultramicroscopic forces. In 1927 he put hundreds of fruit flies in gelatin capsules and bombarded them with X-rays. The irradiated flies were then bred to untreated ones. In ten days thousands of their offspring were buzzing around their banana-mash feed, and Muller was looking at an unprecedented variety of mutations. There were flies with bulging eyes, flat eyes, purple, yellow, and brown eyes. Some had curly bristles, some no bristles. There were flies with broad wings or down-turned wings or almost no wings at all. "They were a motley throng," said Muller. "The results of these experiments were startling and unequivocal. The roots of life—the genes—had indeed been struck and they had yielded." Muller's work won him a Nobel Prize.

## Raw Material of Heredity: DNA

Genes had yielded some secrets of their mechanics, but their chemistry remained inscrutable. Through most of the years Morgan and Muller were tracing the effects of heredity's units, and Fisher, Haldane, and Wright were establishing the sum of the continuous changing and recombining of these units as the genetic basis for evolution, bottles of a white powder were sitting on laboratory shelves. The bottles were labeled *nucleic acid*. A Swiss chemist named Friedrich Miescher had discovered this substance in 1869 while breaking down some cells. The cells had disintegrated, but part of their nuclei had remained intact. When analyzed, this remainder was found to differ chemically from all other known cellular material.

In time scientists found that the acid has a threadlike structure and that its molecules are huge. They also learned that it occurs only in chromosomes. When its chemical composition was worked out, the powder was renamed *deoxyribonucleic acid,* or DNA for short. Later a second nucleic acid was found, differing slightly from DNA. It was called RNA, for *ribonucleic acid.* There the matter rested; the bottles continued to sit on laboratory shelves.

By the 1940s it was clear that the answer to the form and functioning of life had to be sought in the materials out of which chromosomes were made. These were essentially two, DNA and protein. A brilliant series of experiments were conducted at the Biological Laboratory, Cold Spring Harbor, New York. The experiments showed that when a virus, acting much like a physician's syringe, shot its DNA into a bacterial cell, the virus DNA took command. In twenty-four minutes it produced complete copies of itself. The virus's protein shell, comparable to the casing of the syringe, was left on the outside of the bacterial cell wall. All that entered the cell was the DNA, which produced not only new virus DNA, but new protein overcoats for the new viruses as well. All the directives for building more DNA and more protein were enclosed in the DNA, or in its near-copy, the RNA. This, then, was the long-sought raw material of heredity, the basic stuff of life and evolution.

Here was a bit of matter too small to be detected in the cell except by the tremendous enlarging power of the electron microscope, yet so powerful as to be the determinant of life, because it contained all the instructions needed for building a virus, a beetle, or a human being. All DNA in all organisms is made of the same materials: *nucleotides* composed of four bases called adenine, thymine, cytosine, and guanine (and known as A, T, C, and G), plus some sugar molecules and a kinked phosphate molecule linking the sugar pieces. Because everything is made of the same basic elements, the secret of DNA's marvels of creative diversity had to be sought not in its composition, but in its structure; something in the way DNA was built had to account for the billions of forms it could command.

In the 1950s at the Cavendish Laboratory at Cambridge University in England, F. H. C. Crick and James D. Watson, a young American working with him, discovered the basic structure. They fashioned a wire model that portrayed DNA as a helix or spiral, looking like a spiral staircase (see Figure 4–5). The sugars and the phosphate made up the framework, and around them were strung the four nucleotide bases, adenine always paired with thymine, cytosine always with guanine, like two kinds of repeated steps. H. J. Muller estimated that the forty-six human chromosomes in combination contain some 4 billion of these bases or steps on the spiral staircase. The order of the bases is different for each living thing. It is the endless variety of that order which explains the limitless variety of the living world.

The long coils of DNA have a second important property—their capacity for reproducing, or *replicating*, themselves. To self-replicate, the helix divides down the middle. From free nucleotide units in the cell nucleus, each base attaches to itself a complementary unit (A with T, C with G), and a new coil is formed (Figure 4–5). Life now was seen to hang by a thread: it appeared to depend on self-replicating strings of DNA. However, DNA does not always replicate itself accurately.

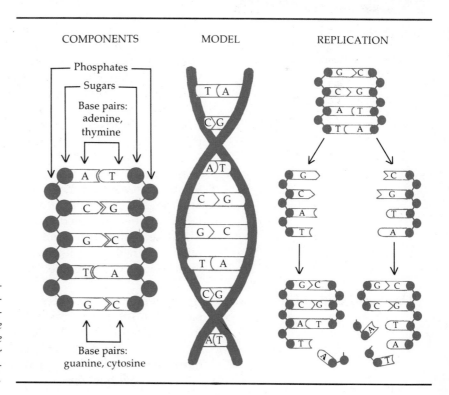

COMPONENTS    MODEL    REPLICATION

FIGURE 4–5    The DNA molecule is a double spiral (or helix) linked by four interlocking chemical subunits—the base pairs. Replication and protein synthesis take place by the splitting of the double helix: each separate strand replicates by synthesizing its mirror image from the unit molecules floating in solution, as shown here.

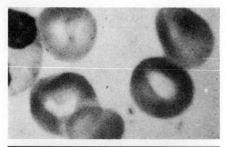

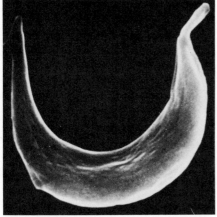

*FIGURE 4–6   The sickle-cell trait is due to an abnormal hemoglobin (S), which differs from normal hemoglobin (A) in only one amino acid out of nearly 300 that constitute the protein. The red blood corpuscles in the top photograph appear normal; the bottom photograph of one of those corpuscles shows the distortion that gives sickle-cell anemia its name.*

When it fails to do so, its coding changes; and these changes are mutations. With a large population and a high reproductive rate, the chances for mutations increase, and the high number of normal and mutant individuals provides a varied population for natural selection.

How fine these DNA variations might be, and how far-reaching their effects, became apparent as research progressed. In the disease called sickle-cell anemia, human red blood cells (shown in Figure 4–6) are twisted into a sickle shape in the person's venous blood (where the cells are low in oxygen), but resume their normal round form when the blood passes through the lungs and becomes replenished with oxygen. A few sickle cells make little difference, but a person who inherits a high percentage gets a serious, sometimes fatal, anemia. Nobel Prize winner Linus Pauling knew that the only parts of the red blood cell that are involved in taking on and giving up oxygen are the 100 million hemoglobin molecules of each cell. "The idea burst upon me," he said, "that the molecules of hemoglobin in the red cells might be responsible for the disease—that the disease might be a molecular one involving an abnormal sort of hemoglobin manufactured by the patient because of the possession of abnormal genes in place of the normal genes that control the manufacture of normal hemoglobin."

Pauling's insight proved correct. Vernon M. Ingram decided to trace the sickle-cell disease back to its DNA source. He had to find what part of hemoglobin, a huge molecule with 8,000 atoms, was altered in a sickle-cell patient. Ingram reported, "The sole chemical difference is that in the abnormal molecule a valine is substituted for glutamic acid at one point. A change of one amino acid in nearly 300 is certainly a very small change indeed, and yet this slight change can be fatal to the unfortunate possessor of the errant hemoglobin."

Such changes are the product of *point mutations* in the DNA of a cell, which may lead to replacement of one amino acid by another in the protein specified by a gene. Other point mutations convert the *codon*, or genetic code for an amino acid, into a "stop" codon: these are called *nonsense mutations* because they result in failure of the full protein synthesis. Other mutations may involve insertion of an extra nucleotide into the DNA molecule or deletion of a nucleotide from it. Segments of DNA may be duplicated and added or simply dropped from the chain. All these changes are random, and a population consisting of several million individuals is likely to have a few mutations per generation in virtually every gene carried by the population.

## Universal Code of Inheritance

All of life, it eventually became apparent, is not only coded by the same basic DNA units, but is assembled by a single kind of code (Table 4–1). In 1961, Dr. Fritz Lipmann, another Nobel Prize winner, replaced RNA in the precursor cells (cells that give rise to other cells) of rabbit red blood cells with RNA from a foreign body—a bacterium found in human intestines—without destroying the normal function of protein formation

## TABLE 4–1  The Genetic Code

| FIRST RNA NUCLEOTIDE BASE | SECOND RNA NUCLEOTIDE BASE | | | | THIRD RNA NUCLEOTIDE BASE |
|---|---|---|---|---|---|
| | U | C | A | G | |
| Uracil (U) | Phenylalanine | Serine | Tyrosine | Cysteine | U |
| | Phenylalanine | Serine | Tyrosine | Cysteine | C |
| | Leucine | Serine | Stop | Stop | A |
| | Leucine | Serine | Stop | Tryptophan | G |
| Cytosine (C) | Leucine | Proline | Histidine | Arginine | U |
| | Leucine | Proline | Histidine | Arginine | C |
| | Leucine | Proline | Glutamine | Arginine | A |
| | Leucine | Proline | Glutamine | Arginine | G |
| Adenine (A) | Isoleucine | Threonine | Asparagine | Serine | U |
| | Isoleucine | Threonine | Asparagine | Serine | C |
| | Isoleucine | Threonine | Lysine | Arginine | A |
| | Start/Methionine | Threonine | Lysine | Arginine | G |
| Guanine (G) | Valine | Alanine | Aspartic acid | Glycine | U |
| | Valine | Alanine | Aspartic acid | Glycine | C |
| | Valine | Alanine | Glutamic acid | Glycine | A |
| | Valine | Alanine | Glutamic acid | Glycine | G |

*Note:* The genetic code is universal, from the lowest bacterium to humankind. In RNA, which carries coded instructions from the cell DNA in order to construct proteins, coding is transcribed by means of the four nucleotide bases uracil (U), cytosine (C), adenine (A), and guanine (G) in units of three. Thus AUG signifies "start" to a coded protein, while UAA, UAG, and UGA signify "stop," meaning "end of transcript" and release the protein from the messenger RNA construction molecule. The three-letter codes, which can be combined in sixty-four ways, specify only the twenty different amino acids found in living animals. The code therefore has much redundancy. Point mutations in a nucleotide base may bring about substitution of one amino acid by another, or substitute a "stop" code for an amino acid that will result in failure of the full protein synthesis. Because of the redundancy, many mutations will be harmless, as we see from the table.

in the rabbit red cells. It would hardly be more amazing for a cat to give birth to a fish, or a plant to puppies. And yet it was not so strange. The common denominator already had been found in the basic units that Mendel had hypothesized and in those units' basic plan of assembly. The code, by all indications, was universal. No more striking proof of the unity of all living forms had been adduced since Darwin provided the living world with one immemorial pedigree. The universality of the self-replicating, self-varying genetic material, DNA, testifies conclusively to the oneness of life and its evolution from a single source.

## POPULATIONS AND SPECIES

### Genotype and Gene Pool

In this short history of the science of genetics, we have dealt mainly with the structures that bring about replication of, and occasional variation in, the genotype, the genetic material of individual organisms. In looking at the process of evolution, we must look beyond the indi-

82

**GENES AND POPULATIONS**

1. The original frogs in this area interbreed with each other and constitute a single species.

2. Changes in the topography and drainage conditions of the region eventually create two distinct regions—swamp and forest—with a barrier between the two that the frogs cannot cross.

3. Over a long period of time, the frogs in the swamp and those in the forest adapt to their different environments. As they adapt and remain isolated from each other, the frogs in the two areas become different.

4. So many differences have now been selected in the two new populations that the frogs do not interbreed even if they meet; they do not recognize foreigners as potential mates.

vidual to the population and the species. Individuals are born, reproduce, and die, yet the population continues, changing and adapting to its environment.

Fisher envisaged a *gene pool* of all the individuals in a species, a pooling of the total genetic material available to a species in adapting to its environment. The concept of the gene pool is an important one: the continuity we see in an evolving species is in truth the continuity and survival of the gene pool. Individuals, in particular their bodies, or phenotypes, are little more than temporary homes of the genes they carry. The phenotype can be seen as the genotype's means of survival in a range of environments over eons of geological time.

When the individuals in a population reproduce sexually, genetic material is sorted, shuffled, and recombined, and so variation among the offspring is increased. This increase in the potential for variation is the primary advantage of sexual reproduction. When species reproduce asexually, the variation available to natural selection is due to mutation alone, making it much more limited in its evolutionary possibilities.

## Gene Flow, Speciation, the Founder Effect, and Genetic Drift

Sexual reproduction has another advantage. If two populations of the same species that have been isolated for some time come into contact, they can hybridize. Genes can pass between them, and their differing characteristics can be combined in future generations. In time, advantageous qualities that had previously been selected in one population only can pass to the other, and so become available to both populations. This phenomenon is called *gene flow;* it allows the maintenance of genetic continuity between neighboring populations. Therefore gene flow increases variation within populations and decreases variation between them.

In contrast, interruption of gene flow by geographical barriers, called *geographical isolation,* may result in *speciation,* the creation of two species where one existed before (Figure 4–7). In this case, the variations accumulated over time in the different populations under the differing pressures of their two environments cause a genetic and phenotypic divergence between the populations. In the absence of gene flow, isolation will eventually allow large enough differences to develop between the two populations that they come to form distinct species. The distinction comes about because mutations will be selected differently in the different environments (and no two environments are *exactly* the same). Should their geographical ranges overlap in the future, no interbreeding would occur. This leads us to the definition of a species: *a group of interbreeding natural populations that are reproductively isolated from other such groups.*

It is important to emphasize the word *natural.* Many closely related populations of animals that fulfill this definition in the wild will interbreed in the zoo or laboratory under special conditions. Such interbreed-

FIGURE 4–7 *A simplified visual description of speciation in an imaginary frog population. In the last stage, two separate and independent gene pools now exist, eventually constituting two species where one existed before.*

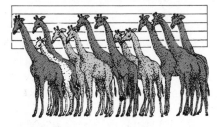

*FIGURE 4–8  Evolution is the change in the average expression of any characteristic in a species. A simple case is the lengthening of the necks of the ancestors of giraffes. Because long-necked giraffes have more reliable and extensive food sources in trees than short-necked ones, they are more successful and have more offspring over time. As a result, the average neck length slowly increases. Eventually all individuals are relatively long-necked. In contrast, Lamarck would have seen this change as a response of the individual to need and to the continual stretching of the neck.*

ing occurs as a result of the breakdown of isolating mechanisms. Geographical isolation is the most common mechanism (it brings about speciation in the first place), but scientists have identified other mechanisms, the most important of which are behavioral. Typical behavioral mechanisms include differences in breeding season and courtship pattern. Courtship often involves complicated ritualistic behavior that is important in species recognition: it helps ensure that individuals do not mate with members of different but related species. Species that are closely related and whose ranges overlap are normally separated by behavioral mechanisms. They are also prevented from interbreeding effectively because they have incompatible sex cells, which fail to fertilize, or because a hybrid that is produced will be sterile, as are mules (the offspring of horses and asses).

What is the actual effect of natural selection on a population? It is to alter the frequency with which different genes occur in the population, to increase beneficial genes (those that promote successful adaptation to the environment) and decrease disadvantageous genes (see Figure 4–8). Evolution, then, is the alteration of *gene frequencies*—the alteration of the proportions in which different genes occur in a species, as a result of natural selection.

It is important to recognize that to bring about evolutionary change, natural selection does not have to destroy less well-adapted individuals before they achieve reproductive age. Natural selection need only bring about a *differential reproductive rate* in the population, so that better-adapted individuals contribute more to the next generation than do the less well adapted. A small difference in the genetic contribution across generations will eventually bring about the adjustment in gene frequencies that constitutes adaptive evolution.

If a very small population becomes isolated from its parent species, various special factors may operate. First, this small *founder population*, as it is called, may not be a typical sample of its parent species. In that case, its successors will, from the very start, carry different gene frequencies from the mother species. These differences, which may to some extent be perpetuated, are ascribed to the *founder effect*.

Another phenomenon, called random *genetic drift*, has been predicted and observed in very small populations. When small populations are subject to low competition and low selection pressure, genetic drift may be expected. That means that random mutation over time leads to the loss or gain of new characteristics, which have not been subjected to the pressures of natural selection. If population size or selection pressure increases, however, as they inevitably will (unless extinction occurs), the random mutations will be eliminated in due course if they are not of positive value, though some neutral traits may remain.

It seems probable that the founder effect has been of some importance in human evolution, especially where small populations have colonized islands or multiplied in isolation. The random effects of ge-

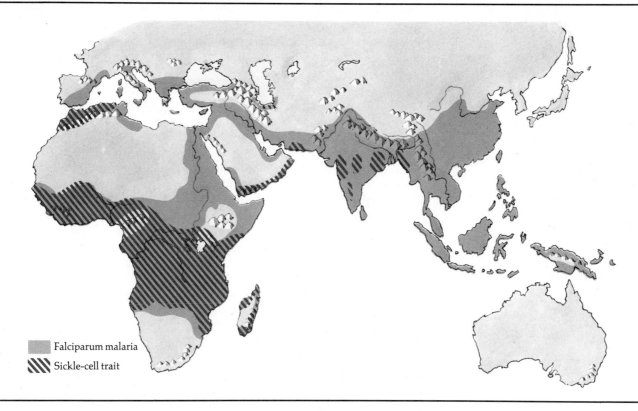

Falciparum malaria

Sickle-cell trait

*FIGURE 4–9   Coincidence of the sickle-cell trait and malaria in parts of the Old World led us to understand why the abnormal hemoglobin S appears in these areas. Though disadvantageous elsewhere, in malarial areas the sickling gene gives considerable protection against the dangerous malarial parasite. The two hemoglobin forms are in balance according to the advantages and disadvantages they offer. Therefore, this instance of the phenomenon of polymorphism is termed balanced polymorphism. Other genes give similar protection in other parts of the world where malaria occurs.*

netic drift have probably played a smaller part in determining the human genotype because small isolated populations would rapidly have expanded and become subject to natural selection.

We can classify the biological processes we have described into those which *increase* genetic variability in a population, and those which *decrease* it. Mutation, sexual recombination, genetic drift, gene flow, and increase in population size all increase population variability. Natural selection and reduction in population size (as in the founder effect) decrease variability. The interplay of all these factors determines the evolutionary potential of an evolving lineage.

## Polymorphism and Genetic Load

All populations of plants and animals appear to carry harmful unexpressed recessive genes. These are termed the *genetic load*. The genes constituting the genetic load are expressed only in the relatively rare recessive homozygote, when they may bring about a physical malformation or a fatal genetic disease. An example of such a phenomenon is sickle-cell anemia. The disease is common in certain regions of West and Central Africa (Figure 4–9). The anemic condition is due to a rare hemoglobin, known as hemoglobin S. The gene for this hemoglobin may be present alongside or in place of the normal gene for hemoglobin A. In many Central African populations, from 20 to 40 percent of individuals are AS heterozygotes; 1 to 2 percent are SS homozygotes, who usually die soon after birth.

Because natural selection would ordinarily select out such an undesirable trait, we have to ask why such a high frequency of the S gene is maintained. In 1954, A. C. Allison, a British doctor, showed that the sickle-cell trait in its heterozygote condition (AS) affords protection against malarial infection, and that the distribution of the S gene coincides with the distribution of the *Anopheles* mosquito, which carries malaria. The S gene was maintained by natural selection according to the balanced advantages and disadvantages that it offered: protection from disease for the AS carrier, death for the SS. This is an example of *balanced polymorphism*. Polymorphism usually refers to the expression of two or more alleles of a single gene in a population in more or less constant proportions. The human blood groups described in Chapter 18 constitute further well-known examples.

Today in the United States we live in an environment free of malaria, yet approximately 10 percent of Americans of African origin still carry the S gene. It has become a liability and in the rare homozygous state is still a serious and often lethal condition. Clearly, a lifesaving adaptation in one environment is part of humankind's genetic load in another without selection against the homozygous. However, normal condition (AA) and for the heterozygote (AS), the frequency of the S allele will decrease in the United States in time.

We can see, then, that genes are neither "good" nor "bad"; their survival value is determined by the environment in which they are expressed. We can see, too, how natural selection acting on genetic variability will often compromise between advantages and disadvantages, so that ordinarily lethal phenotypes are maintained in a population in balance with advantageous phenotypes. Thus it is possible that our genetic load, like that of other species, represents a potential for variability that may in the future be necessary for survival, as it may have been in the past. Natural selection operates on phenotypes—that is, only on the expression of a proportion of the genotype. Hidden genetic variability is, to some extent, our insurance against environmental change.

These genetic phenomena form the groundwork of the evolutionary process. They are the source of the variation on which natural selection operates, and they supply the material from which novelties are selected and incorporated into the succession of diverse species.

## Selection of Inclusive Fitness

In recent years the concept of Darwinian fitness and the way in which natural selection operates has been developed and extended in important ways. Traditionally, fitness has been defined broadly as reproductive success, usually measured in terms of the number of offspring of an individual reared to reproductive age. On the basis of this principle it was not possible, however, to account for the existence of, for example, sterile worker bees and wasps, or similar phenomena in other species that evolved forms of apparently altruistic, selfless behavior not directed to protect an individual's own offspring but to help others. A classic example of such behavior is the warning call given by so many birds and mammals, which, in allowing other members of the social group to take avoidance action, would attract the predator and create a risk for the altruist. Such behavioral traits are individually disadvantageous but socially advantageous.

The science of the biology of social behavior, called *sociobiology*, has developed the concept of *inclusive fitness*, first discussed by the British zoologist W. D. Hamilton in 1964. The concept implies that the fitness of an individual not only includes its own reproductive success but that of its relatives, which share the individual's genes. It is, as it were, the particular packages of genes that are being selected rather than particular individuals. Thus because of the unusual genetics of the social insects such as bees, where the males are haploid (i.e., carry only half the normal diploid gene complement so that the nucleus of the cells does not undergo meiosis in the production of gametes), the daughters inherit a full set of their father's genes compared with the usual 50 percent of their diploid mother's genes. Therefore, because each worker bee shares (on average) 75 percent of its genes with its siblings (50 percent from having the same father and 25 percent from having the same mother), it pays it to work for the survival of its siblings as much as (in fact more than) for its own offspring, were it to have any, who would carry only 50 percent of its genes.

The case of the social insects is an unusual one because the males are haploid. A somewhat similar situation can arise, however, among birds and mammals even though their genetics are normal. For example, if an animal giving a warning cry can thus protect a number of individuals that share its genes, the gain in survival of its genes may be greater than the loss that would occur if it was killed. In practice, the selective advantage of an individual assisting a relative in this or any other way will depend on three factors: the risk to its own fitness, the benefit to the relative or relatives, and the degree of relatedness of each relative. We find that on this basis we can account for the selection of altruistic behavior in close-knit social groups where individuals are closely related. In reality, however, the behavior is not truly altruistic insofar as an individual is protecting its "own" genes. The phenomenon has been termed *kin selection* or *gene selection*. It is not, however, an alternative to natural selection but an extension of it. The term *gene selection* is appropriate in one sense, but it should be recalled that selection always operates on the phenotype and not on the genotype. The best way to describe this phenomenon, therefore, is to see it as a development of the concept of Darwinian fitness that is now extended to include not only the reproductive success of an individual and its offspring but the reproductive success of all individuals in a social group that carry a particular individual's genes. We shall follow the suggestion of Hamilton and refer to the phenomenon as inclusive fitness.

The concept is extremely important in understanding the behavior of individuals in the kinds of social groups that are found among the higher primates. We must conclude that natural selection produces individuals that are adapted to maximize the spread of their own genes through both their own offspring and their relatives.

**Hardy-Weinberg Law**     Assuming that mating is random, we can determine mathematically whether a breeding population is in a period of genetic equilibrium or a period of change. The so-called Hardy-Weinberg Law (actually first formulated by the American geneticist W. Castle) makes it possible to predict gene frequencies in the next generation on the basis of the phenotypes and genotypes of the present generation. It thus allows us to assess whether the population's observed genetic traits are in equilibrium or whether these traits are subject to some disturbance—either natural selection, drift, migration, or mutation.

To understand the Hardy-Weinberg Law, we must recall Mendel's work, and introduce some new terms. *Alleles* are the paired alternative genes that occur on a chromosome, at a single *locus* or location, which bring about alternative phenotypic states (such as a pea's roundness or wrinkledness). A homozygous genotype consists of two like alleles, either both recessive or both dominant, which are both expressed in the organism's phenotype. A heterozygous genotype consists of two different alleles, one dominant (and expressed in the phenotype), the other recessive. According to the Hardy-Weinberg Law, genetic equilibrium exists in a population when the proportion of heterozygotes (mixed dominant and recessive traits) equals twice the square root of the two homozygotes' proportions multiplied together:

$$Aa = 2\sqrt{AA \times aa}$$

Here, *Aa*, *AA*, and *aa* stand for the proportions of the genotypes in the population: *Aa* is heterozygous, *AA* is dominant homozygous, and *aa* is recessive homozygous. This formula is more usually written as

$$p^2 + 2pq + q^2 = 1$$

In this formula, *p* and *q* stand for the alternative alleles ($p = A$ and $q = a$) of a single locus.

A simple and well-known example of the use of this formula is found in the work of the American anthropologist Frederick Hulse. He and a colleague examined the proportions of the M and N blood types among the Quinault Indians of Washington state. The two blood types are alternative alleles at a single locus, and neither is dominant. The data he obtained and the application of the Hardy-Weinberg formula are shown in Figure 4–10. A simple statistical test (Chi-square) tells us whether the differences between the present data and the predictions for the next generation indicate a significant rate of change in the

| GENOTYPE | | ALLELES PRESENT | | | | |
|---|---|---|---|---|---|---|
| Blood type | No. of persons | | | No. of alleles | M | N |
| M | 77 | M homozygotes | $2 \times 77$ | 154 | 154 | |
| N | 23 | N homozygotes | $2 \times 23$ | 46 | | 46 |
| MN | 101 | MN heterozygotes | $2 \times 101$ | 202 | 101 | 101 |
| Population totals | 201 | | | 402 | = 255 | + 147 |

Therefore frequency of allele M $= \dfrac{255}{402} = 63\%$ or 0.63.

and frequency of allele N $= \dfrac{147}{402} = 37\%$ or 0.37.

Is the population in equilibrium with respect to this trait?

Using the formula: $p^2 + 2pq + q^2 = 1$     let $p$ = allele M,
and $q$ = allele N.

Then   $0.63^2 + (2 \times 0.63 \times 0.37) + 0.37^2 = 0.397 + 0.466 + 0.137 = 1.$

The frequency of each allele in the next generation will therefore be:
$0.397 \times 201 = 80$ M
$0.137 \times 201 = 28$ N
$0.466 \times 201 = 94$ MN

Now compare *actual* and *predicted* numbers:

| | M | N | MN |
|---|---|---|---|
| ACTUAL | 77 | 23 | 101 |
| PREDICTED | 80 | 28 | 94 |

The population is in equilibrium.

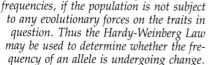

*FIGURE 4–10  The Hardy-Weinberg Law is a probability statement that predicts the gene frequencies in a population given the allele frequencies, if the population is not subject to any evolutionary forces on the traits in question. Thus the Hardy-Weinberg Law may be used to determine whether the frequency of an allele is undergoing change. Here we see the computation of such frequencies based on an actual example published by Frederick Hulse. The M and N blood group genes constitute a simple two-allele trait, neither of which is dominant to the other. Genetic stability in these traits is indicated by the fact that the observed frequencies are not significantly different from those predicted.*

population. For the Quinault Indians, the difference turns out to be trivial: the population is in equilibrium.

The Hardy-Weinberg formula also allows us to calculate allele frequencies if we know the percentage of the homozygotes that carry the allele in question. For example, a rare recessive trait due to a single recessive allele in modern human populations is albinism, a pigment deficiency that usually results in milky skin color, white or colorless hair, and pink or blue eyes with a red pupil. It is expressed (as a homozygote) in one person in 20,000. The square root of 20,000 is 141, so that the allele frequency is $141 \div 20,000 = 0.007$ or 0.7 percent. The frequency of the normal dominant allele is therefore 99.3 percent.

Formulas of this type can be applied to more complicated situations where more than two alleles are being studied (as in the ABO blood groups discussed in Chapter 18), and can be used to establish the genetic status of different populations for a number of traits. What we are seeing is the application of the principles established by Mendel to whole populations. This application, known as population genetics, is the way we approach the mathematics of natural selection.

## Sexual Selection

In discussing the action of selection and the transmission of characteristics in a population, we have assumed that mating occurs randomly between members of the opposite sex of a population or species. Rarely is this so in practice, and a number of mating patterns can often be recognized. When struggle or choice enter into mating, we have what Darwin described as *sexual selection*. In 1871 he defined two kinds of sexual selection. The first kind was the result of competition between members of one sex (usually males) for the opposite sex. Good examples are found among the higher primates such as some multi-male baboon groups (Chapter 6) where the senior male may have sexual access to most females in his troop as they come into estrus. This reproductive pattern of behavior will select the genes of powerful or impressive males (Chapter 7).

Darwin's second kind of sexual selection involves differential choice by members of one sex for members of the opposite sex: this usually takes the form of the female's choice of some males in preference to others and is best illustrated among birds. Both these phenomena are most commonly observed among polygamous species and play a much smaller part in a purely monogamous species in which every individual has a mate.

The importance of sexual selection in human evolution is not yet understood, but it is clearly not a significant factor in a monogamous society with a 50:50 sex ratio. Insofar as human societies permit polygamy (and very many do), it is possible that sexual selection has indeed brought about the evolution of traits which are not the product of natural selection (and which in theory could become nonadaptive if developed to excess). The kind of characteristics in humans that may be a product of sexual selection are those which appear to advertise sex, such as hair patterns and types, breast development in women, and penis size in men. The second type of selection (differential choice of mate) has probably been more important in human evolution than the first. The elucidation of this problem depends on knowledge of the mating pattern of early peoples—information that is probably unobtainable. Were matings a result of free choice or were they arranged by parents or elders for political and economic reasons? The present arrangements may not tell us much about the past.

Another nonrandom mating system found in animals and humans is *inbreeding* and *outbreeding*. Inbreeding occurs in small populations of animals or humans in which mating pairs are likely to share a recent common ancestor. It often results in homozygous pairing of recessive genes, so that the recessive trait becomes expressed in the phenotype. Recessive genes are often harmful, and in due course they will be eliminated by natural selection. Until then, their expression may be accompanied by increased disease and higher mortality rates, both of which have been predicted and observed in inbred animal populations. Outbreeding is characteristic of human groups with extensive incest taboos, such as those groups who insist on marriage with members of other clans for political and economic reasons. Outbreeding has the opposite genetic effect of inbreeding: variation increases, and lethal recessives remain unexpressed, and possibly accumulate, although the population may show improved health and lower mortality.

The mating system is therefore an important characteristic of a species and is a key, not only to the species' social life as a whole, but, as we shall see, to many of its most striking anatomical adaptations.

# PART II

# THE ORIGIN OF HUMANKIND

# Chapter 5

# Back Beyond the Apes

It is an axiom of mine that when you have excluded the impossible, whatever remains, however improbable, must be the truth.

SIR ARTHUR CONAN DOYLE, 1859–1930.
*The Adventures of Sherlock Holmes:* The Beryl Coronet.

The study of prehistoric humans is, of necessity, the study of their fossil remains. To begin to understand who our ancestors were and what they were like, we must be able to interpret the fragments of them that are coming to the surface in increasing numbers. Given fairly reliable methods to determine their age, we can now turn with more confidence to primate fossils for an answer to the all-important question: How do we tell monkeys, apes, and humans apart? For present-day species we have no problem; all have evolved sufficiently so that they no longer resemble one another. But since they all have a common ancestor, the further back we go in time, the more similar their fossils begin to look. There finally comes a point when they are indistinguishable. The construction of a primate fossil family tree is essential if we are ever going to discover the line of descent from early primate to modern human.

We must therefore sort through the teeth and bones that have survived through the ages to see what physical changes took place in our ancestors and how these changes led to modern humans. Each step along the way is equally important. The new developments that characterize each new link of the chain of life that leads to humankind were made possible only by earlier developments. To understand precisely what we are, we must consider the entire chain and look behind apes and monkeys to the earlier animals from which they sprang. Traits that would later emerge as distinctly human had their origins in the anatomy and behavior of these distant creatures, the earliest primates.

**THE EARLIEST PRIMATES**   We must go back about 65 million years to the Paleocene epoch (see Figure 5–1), a time when human ancestors resembled squirrels more than people, and take a look at certain rat-shaped, rat-sized, insect-

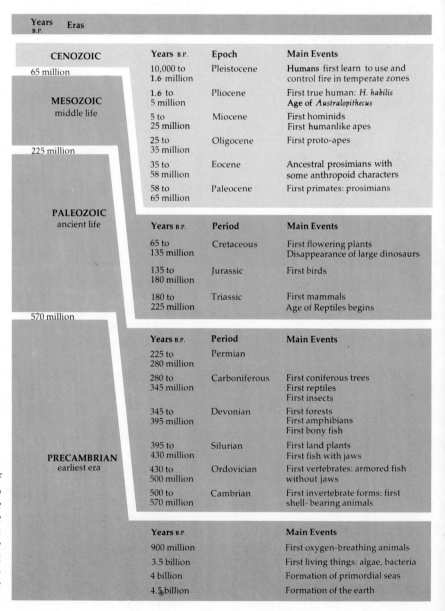

| Years B.P. | Eras | | | |
|---|---|---|---|---|

| CENOZOIC | Years B.P. | Epoch | Main Events |
|---|---|---|---|
| 65 million | 10,000 to 1.6 million | Pleistocene | **Humans** first learn to use and control fire in temperate zones |
| MESOZOIC middle life | 1.6 to 5 million | Pliocene | First true human: *H. habilis* **Age of** *Australopithecus* |
| | 5 to 25 million | Miocene | First hominids First humanlike apes |
| 225 million | 25 to 35 million | Oligocene | First proto-apes |
| | 35 to 58 million | Eocene | Ancestral prosimians with some anthropoid characters |
| | 58 to 65 million | Paleocene | First primates: prosimians |

| PALEOZOIC ancient life | Years B.P. | Period | Main Events |
|---|---|---|---|
| | 65 to 135 million | Cretaceous | First flowering plants Disappearance of large dinosaurs |
| | 135 to 180 million | Jurassic | First birds |
| 570 million | 180 to 225 million | Triassic | First mammals Age of Reptiles begins |

| PRECAMBRIAN earliest era | Years B.P. | Period | Main Events |
|---|---|---|---|
| | 225 to 280 million | Permian | |
| | 280 to 345 million | Carboniferous | First coniferous trees First reptiles First insects |
| | 345 to 395 million | Devonian | First forests First amphibians First bony fish |
| | 395 to 430 million | Silurian | First land plants First fish with jaws |
| | 430 to 500 million | Ordovician | First vertebrates: armored fish without jaws |
| | 500 to 570 million | Cambrian | First invertebrate forms: first shell-bearing animals |

| Years B.P. | | Main Events |
|---|---|---|
| 900 million | | First oxygen-breathing animals |
| 3.5 billion | | First living things: algae, bacteria |
| 4 billion | | Formation of primordial seas |
| 4.5 billion | | Formation of the earth |

FIGURE 5–1   *Geologic time scales are of such immense duration that it is hard to fully comprehend the great period of time during which nature and humankind have evolved. If the almost five hundred million years of vertebrate evolution is symbolized by one hour of time, then primate evolution took seven minutes and human evolution occurred in the last twelve seconds of that hour.*

FIGURE 5–2    The ring-tailed lemur (Lemur catta) is typical of the varied group of prosimian primates (Lemuroidea) from Madagascar. The most striking primate features of lemurs are large forward-looking eyes and long separated fingers on hands and feet. They stand about fifteen inches high.

eating mammals that were scuttling about on the ground. The Paleocene opened on a warm and placid world, with enormous tropical forests spreading much farther north and south from the equator than they do today. France and Germany were moist, humid jungles, as was much of Africa and nearly everywhere in between. Parts of North America were similarly forested, and that continent was joined to Greenland and Europe across the North Atlantic. Among the inhabitants of these immense expanses of forest was a large population of long-tailed, rodentlike mammals. Their closest relatives living today are the insectivores, those small insect- and seed-eating mammals, the voles, moles, hedgehogs, and shrews. Some early mammals began climbing into the trees, presumably because of intense competition on the ground and because there was a rich and untapped source of food up there. They became adept at leaping about in the trees, seeking out fruit and seeds, slow-moving grubs and insects, buds, birds' eggs, and an occasional baby bird. They were the earliest primates. Mammals like them exist today in Africa and Asia and are called *prosimians*—pre-monkeys; the group includes the well-known lemurs (Figure 5–2) and lorises (Figure 5–3), including the bush baby, and the less-known tarsier. Modern tree shrews (Figure 5–4) represent an intermediate group, with some characteristics of insectivores and some of primates. As comparison with fossils of the early forms has shown, some of these creatures have survived with practically no changes in their skeletons. Others did change. They changed so radically that their evolution is hard to believe, because those ancient prosimians were ancestral primates; from them sprang the whole present array of prosimians, monkeys, apes, and humans (Table 5–1).

## Prosimian Adaptation

Primate evolution illustrates very well the competition between the tendency toward stability and the tendency toward change. For 30 million years the prosimian stock was tremendously successful in the tropical forests of the world. Some of the ancestral insect-eating mammals evolved very little and very slowly. Tree shrews exist in their present form because there was little pressure for them to change: their environment remained fairly static, and they still fit in well. Other early prosimians evolved more rapidly. The challenge that spurred their evolution may have been subtle, as subtle as a slightly more intelligent or slightly stronger brother lemur, who was a little better at catching the insect or attracting the female on the next branch. It might have been a very minor change in environment, in climate, or in the evolution of other animals, whether competitors or predators. Over a long time, and in some places, differently adapted populations evolved.

The rapidly changing populations were adapting in response to the evolutionary shaping that an arboreal way of life encouraged. Jumping and clinging was a better way of getting safely and quickly about in the branches than the ratlike scuttling that had preceded it. Hind legs

FIGURE 5–3 *The loris (Loris tardigradus) represents another group of prosimians (Lorisoidea) found in Africa and Asia. Lorises are smaller than lemurs but have very large eyes adapted for hunting insects and other small creatures at night. Their bodies are about ten inches long.*

became longer. Front paws gradually lost their ratlike claws and acquired the flat nails that are a hallmark of primates today (Figure 5–5). Claws are a reasonably effective adaptation for small animals that climb up the trunks of large trees, but they are less good for coming down, as anyone who owns a cat knows. They are also less reliable than grasping hands as a means of hanging on and useless among smaller branches. With the evolution of the grasping hand, the claw became redundant, if not positively inconvenient, and in most species it evolved into a flat nail (structurally not very different) except in some prosimians where a long claw was retained on a toe for grooming. All four paws began to turn into grasping organs. The digits grew longer, more flexible, and capable of grasping, and tactile pads developed throughout their lengths to increase friction. The animals retained their tails as organs of balance or (in the case of New World monkeys) as fifth limbs. They developed upright posture and the ability to rotate their heads extensively. And they evolved special nerve pathways to give precise and rapid control of the muscles, while the cortex of the brain expanded. All these innovations greatly improved the ability of these new-model animals to move rapidly and suddenly in a tree—to grip a branch or to catch and hold a fast-moving insect or small lizard.

As leaping, clinging, and catching became a way of life, dependence on smelling became less important than dependence on seeing. This change was particularly necessary for an animal that lived in a three-dimensional world of trees instead of the two-dimensional world of flat

FIGURE 5–4 *Tree shrews are found in Southeast Asia. They are primitive animals and are probably like the first ancestral primates. Their appearance is similar to the squirrel, but they are quite distinct from any rodent. Their bodies are about five inches long.*

| TABLE 5–1  Classification of Living Primates | |
| --- | --- |
| **ORDER: PRIMATES** | |
| Suborder: Prosimii | |
|   Infraorder: Lemuriformes | Lemurs |
| | Indris |
| | Sifakas |
|           Lorisiformes | Lorises |
| | Bush babies |
|           Tarsiiformes | Tarsiers |
| | |
| Suborder: Anthropoidea | |
|   Infraorder: Platyrrhini | New World monkeys |
|           Catarrhini | Old World monkeys, apes, and humans |
|     Superfamily: Cercopithecoidea | Old World monkeys |
|           Hominoidea | Apes and humans |
|     Family: Hylobatidae | Lesser apes |
|           Pongidae | Orangutans |
|           Panidae | African apes |
|           Hominidae | Humans |

ground, an animal that was constantly called on to make precise judgments about how far away a branch or an insect was. In response to the growing importance of sight over smell, the head of the ancestral primate began to change. Its snout became shorter, its skull rounder (Figure 5–6). The retinas of its eyes became sensitive to low levels of illumination and able to differentiate colors. The eyes themselves enlarged, increasing the amount of light and detail received; a bony protection evolved around them. And they moved gradually toward the front of the head, where vision from one eye could overlap that from the other, giving the animal what is known as binocular (two-eyed) vision, which eventually led to stereoscopic (depth-perceiving) vision.

As we saw in Chapter 2, with stereoscopic vision came a far greater ability to judge distances than is possessed by a creature whose eyes are located on the sides of its head, like a rabbit. Rabbits must be alert to what may be about to attack them from the side or from behind, but they have no need to see what they eat: grass does not move and can be located easily by the mouth and nose. Nor does eating grass require a high degree of intelligence—less, certainly, than does hunting down elusive insect game in the treetops and coping with a dangerous three-dimensional environment. The forest was a more complex environment than the grassland, and the primates' sensory and locomotor adaptations made possible the exploitation of the forest's resources. The primate brain processes information from the senses and brings about movement of the limbs. Thus it, too, was important for adaptation and became larger (in relation to body size) in Primates than in other orders of animals. A summary of the major Primate adaptations is given in Table 5–2.

The simple explanation of the origin of Primate adaptations has been amended by the American anthropologist Matt Cartmill, who has pointed out that many other mammals are arboreally adapted without

*FIGURE 5–5   Hands are one of the most characteristic features of primates. One distinction between the tree shrew (shown in the left drawing) and higher primates is that the former carries claws, the latter only fingernails. Prosimians have some claws, and some nails. The loris has claws only on its second toe: they have been retained as an adaptation for grooming—for scratching. Macaque monkeys have thumbs longer than other higher primates and have a weak precision grip. The thumb, however, is usually pressed against the side of the first finger.*

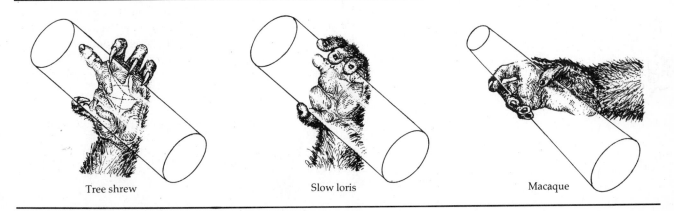

Tree shrew                    Slow loris                    Macaque

FIGURE 5–6   *Apart from the tree shrews (which most scientists do not consider to be primates) the most primitive skull among living primates is the lemur's. As in most primitive mammals, the facial part of the skull is large in relation to the small braincase. The elongated snout lies in front of rather than below the braincase. In the chimpanzee the snout is reduced and the braincase enlarged. The jaws lie at a lower level in relation to the braincase; the eyes are more forward-looking. The scale is approximately 1-1/3 actual size for the lemur and 1/3 actual size for the chimpanzee.*

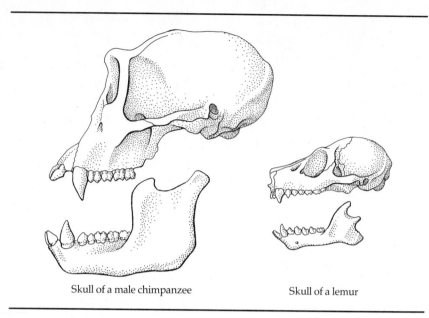

Skull of a male chimpanzee                Skull of a lemur

evolving all these characters. Tree squirrels, for example, have laterally facing eyes, no stereoscopic vision, no significant reduction in the olfactory sense, claws on all digits except the thumb, and no opposability of either thumb or big toe. Nevertheless, they are well-adapted arboreal mammals. For this reason, Cartmill interprets many of the primate visual characteristics as "predatory adaptations comparable to the similar specializations seen in cats and owls and allowing the predator to gauge its victim's distance accurately without having to move its head." He claims that the primate complex of characters is a product of the predation by prosimians on insects in the lower strata of tropical forests.

There is no doubt that many prosimians, such as the loris, are well adapted for insect predation and that the visual characteristics of primates are adaptive for this purpose. We also know that many other prosimians are insectivorous, and being those primates most closely related to the insectivores, all were perhaps descended from insect predators. It is clear, however, that insectivory cannot account for all Primate characteristics and that the best way to view the original members of the Primate order is as arboreal insect predators, many of which later became mainly vegetarian in diet.

In a very real sense, we owe our nature to these primate adaptations, which are all a product of natural selection operating on a primitive mammal in a tropical forest environment. The rich forest niche was almost unexploited until the primates made their world in it. We are a product of the primate arboreal adventure.

## TABLE 5–2 Major Characteristics of Primates

A. Characteristics relating to motor adaptations
1. Retention of ancestral mammalian limb structure, with five digits in hands and feet, and free mobility of limbs with unfused radius and fibula.
2. Evolution of mobile, grasping digits, with sensitive friction pads, and nails replacing claws. Palmar surfaces with friction skin.
3. Retention of tail as an organ of balance (except in apes and a few monkeys) and as a grasping "limb" in some New World monkeys.
4. Evolution of erect posture in many groups with extensive head rotation.
5. Evolution of nervous system to give precise and rapid control of musculature.

B. Characteristics relating to sensory adaptations
1. Enlargement of the eyes, increasing amount of light and detail received.
2. Evolution of retina to increase sensitivity to low levels of illumination and to different frequencies (that is, to color).
3. Eyes that look forward with overlapping visual fields that give stereoscopic vision.
4. Enclosure of eyes in a bony orbit in all living groups.
5. Reduction in olfactory apparatus, especially the snout.
6. Internal ear structures enclosed within petrosal bone.

C. Dental characteristics
1. Simple cusp patterns in molar teeth.
2. In most groups 32 or 36 teeth; all the Anthropoidea have 32 teeth.

D. General characteristics
1. Lengthened period of maturation, of infant dependency, and of gestation, compared with most mammals. Relatively long life span.
2. Low reproductive rate, especially among Hominoidea.
3. Relatively large and complex brain, especially those parts involved with vision, tactile inputs, muscle coordination and control, and memory and learning.

**Prosimians' Competitors**

Within 10 or 15 million years these modifications have become sufficiently advanced that a distinct new group of animals could have been identified had a zoologist been there to observe. Some modern prosimians, particularly some of the larger lemurs, look and act very much like modern monkeys. If this new group, the monkeys, had never evolved, large prosimians might still exist in places where monkeys are now found; they do exist on one island where monkeys never penetrated. This is the island of Madagascar, a large land mass southeast of Africa. The island was too far offshore to be reached by the newly evolved monkeys, so its early prosimian inhabitants faced no competition from these bigger-brained animals. As a result, Madagascar is still the kingdom of the prosimians, in particular of the lemurs. In this isolated land, their evolution has resulted in something like fifteen genera (five of which have been eliminated by humans since they settled there) with nineteen surviving species.

Unfortunately for lemurs elsewhere, monkeys and apes did evolve, establishing a fork in the primate family tree. At first, they could not be called anything more than super prosimians, because the differences between them and the older prosimian species were too small to be significant. But as these differences began to build up, by giving a survival advantage to the individuals that had them, the trees became filled with smarter, swifter, defter, altogether abler animals. The prosimians remained nocturnal or died away in many places because they could not compete. Nevertheless those first primates, the prosimians, do give us the first pieces of the puzzle of humankind's evolution, the pictures at the very bottom edge of our tapestry.

## THE FIRST HIGHER PRIMATES

It was not until the Eocene epoch, about 40 million years ago, that anything at all reminiscent of a monkey or ape showed up. What appeared then were two creatures named *Amphipithecus* and *Pondaungia*, whose existence is known only because of some small pieces of jaw found in the Pondaung Hills of central Burma. Certainty is impossible because of the fossil's fragmentary nature, but the structure of the teeth and the form of the jawbone possibly suggest a very primitive monkey or ape. There is no evidence at present that they either were or were not ancestral to later forms.

### *Apidium* and *Parapithecus*

For a better clue, we must move ahead to the late Eocene epoch (about 38 million years B.P.) (see Figure 5–1), to a spot in the Egyptian desert about sixty miles southwest of Cairo. This is a shallow dip in the landscape known as the Fayum Depression. Today it is one of the driest places on earth, but in Eocene times the southern shore of the Mediterranean reached further inland than it does now, and the Fayum lay on the borderline between sea and forest. Apparently it was heavily wooded in parts and was laced with rivers, features that made it a fine place for proto-monkeys and proto-apes to live and evolve. Evolve they did, and the Fayum proves it, for it contains a rich deposit of primate fossils—not those of little prosimians that were so common elsewhere at that time, but those of creatures that were beginning to look less like prosimians and more like monkeys and apes. Two in particular have caught the scientific eye as among the earliest known candidates for inclusion in the line of Old World monkeys. They bear the names *Apidium* and *Parapithecus*. (Old World monkeys are a distinct group from New World monkeys, those of Central and South America. The New

World monkeys split off from the North American branch of the prosimian line considerably further back—about 55 million years ago. They are not at all closely related to Old World monkeys, though they resemble them considerably in form and habits. Since we know that humans evolved in the Old World, it follows that the New World monkeys played no part in human evolution.)

What makes *Apidium* and *Parapithecus* seem like a monkey instead of a prosimian? Answering this question gives us the first opportunity to observe how paleontologists deduce as much as they do from one piece of fossil evidence. Often that evidence consists mainly of teeth. Teeth are composed of the hardest and longest-lasting substances in the body, so there are more fossils of them than there are of bones, and they have been more intensively studied. *Molars* (the large grinding teeth in the back of the mouth) have small conical *cusps* on their biting surface for chewing food. All chewing and grinding teeth are cusped, and all species have particular cusp patterns. One of these, a design of four cusps connected in pairs by small ridges, is known to occur only in Old World monkeys (though the third molar on the lower jaw has a fifth cusp). So if a fossil molar with that unmistakable four-cusp pattern turns up, logic suggests that it belongs to a monkey or to some creature on the way to becoming a monkey.

*Apidium* and *Parapithecus* have such teeth; prosimians do not (see Figure 5–7). Does that make *Apidium* and *Parapithecus* monkeys? Not necessarily, for elsewhere in their mouths they are more prosimian than monkey.

## Evaluating the Total Morphological Pattern

In determining whether a fossil is a monkey, comparative anatomists do not just look at teeth. They look for other things that all monkeys have in common and that separate monkeys from all other animals. Such a list of features constitutes the *morphological pattern* that characterizes a group of animals. Each genus and species of animals has its own morphological pattern, and how closely one overlaps with others

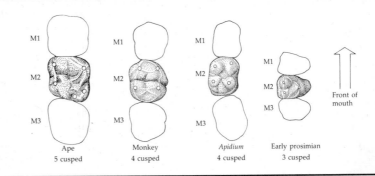

*FIGURE 5–7  Molars are invaluable in identifying the different groups of primates and are frequently preserved as fossils. The main key to identification lies in the arrangement and number of cusps. These teeth are second molars from the right side of the upper jaw. The ape molars are about actual size; the others are twice actual size.*

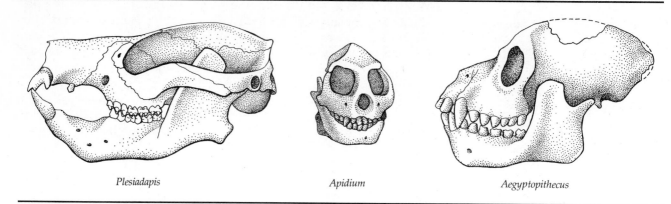

Plesiadapis                          Apidium                          Aegyptopithecus

FIGURE 5–8   *The orbits of living primates are surrounded by a ring of bone that constitutes an extension of the frontal bone joining the cheekbone. This structure protects the large forward-pointing eyes.* Apidium *has these closed orbits, as does the more advanced* Aegyptopithecus. *In more primitive primates such as* Plesiadapis, *the orbit is open at the back to the jawbone and its muscles. Shown 60 percent of actual size.*

determines how closely the genera are related. For example, dogs and wolves share so many structural and behavioral characteristics that even a nonscientist would have no difficulty recognizing that they are very closely related. In the same way, though dogs and wolves share with cats the traits of four legs, warm blood, caring for young, and sharp teeth, among a great many others, it is obvious that they are much less like cats than they are like each other.

It is by systematically and laboriously studying the total morphological pattern of fossil species that the paleontologist begins to establish the relationships between long-extinct species. The evidence may be frustratingly meager, but each added fragment either increases or decreases our knowledge of the similarity of one animal's morphological pattern to another animal's. As the bits of evidence are sorted out, enough characteristics like the four-cusped, ridged molar pattern may finally be established for an expert to state with considerable conviction (even in the absence of other evidence): "This fossil is a monkey, or a direct monkey ancestor, while that one has too many non-monkey characteristics and is something else."

From this kind of detective work it has been concluded that *Parapithecus* and *Apidium* probably lie not far from the main monkey ancestral line. In addition to teeth we have another important piece of "monkey" evidence: an *Apidium* frontal bone. In higher primates, this bone lies above the eyes and comes down around the eye sockets to form a complete circle, like the one that gives the modern human skull its unmistakable vacant stare. Among most lower forms of primates, frontal bones do not complete the circle. But in *Apidium,* as in the more advanced creature shown at the right in Figure 5–8, the frontal bones form a full circle, a condition known as *orbital closure.* Another monkey feature that can easily be detected is the shortened face, indicated by the shape of the jaw.

Aside from these facts we do not know much about either *Parapithecus*

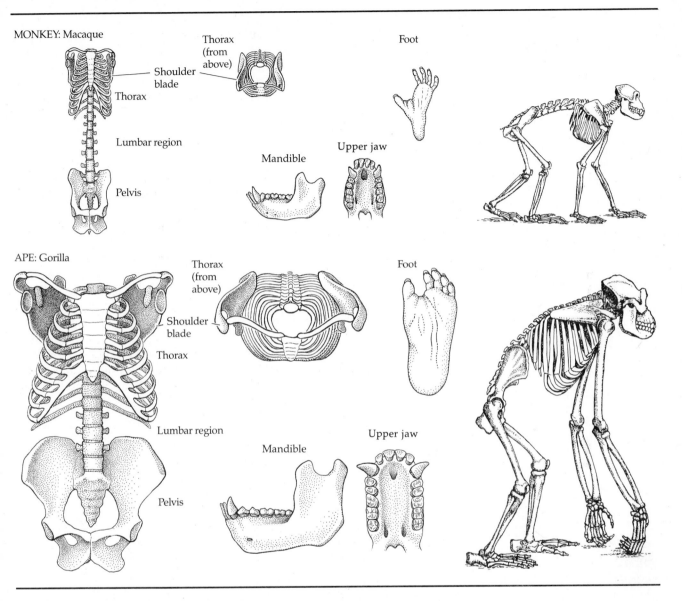

MONKEY: Macaque

Shoulder blade

Thorax

Thorax (from above)

Lumbar region

Pelvis

Mandible

Upper jaw

Foot

APE: Gorilla

Shoulder blade

Thorax

Thorax (from above)

Lumbar region

Mandible

Upper jaw

Pelvis

Foot

*FIGURE 5–9   Ape and monkey skeletons have much in common. Apes are more like humans than like monkeys in skeletal structure. Note the different proportions of limbs, the form of the tail, rib cage, and shoulder blade, and the use of hands in locomotion. Scale is approximately 1/20th actual size.*

or *Apidium.* Each was apparently about a foot high—no bigger than a small cat—and, like many monkeys, quadrupedal, though it has been claimed that *Apidium* leaped, like some prosimians. Was either one a direct ancestor of humankind? Almost certainly not, for they were not the only primates in the forests of the Fayum. There were a great many others, some not so much monkeylike as apelike—which is another way of saying that they were more humanlike, for humans and apes are closer in their total morphological pattern than humans and monkeys.

## THE EARLY APES

### Characteristics of Apes

When the principal differences between apes and monkeys are spelled out (see Figure 5–9), the humanlike nature of apes is unmistakable. Many species of monkeys are built to go on all fours and do so much of the time. Apes, by contrast, normally climb and sit and maintain their trunk semierect except when moving quadrupedally (on all fours), when they are on the ground. Associated with this tendency toward an erect posture, an ape has much more flexible arms and shoulders for hand-over-hand climbing and swinging (see Figure 5–10), and its arms and fingers are longer; the arrangement and proportions of its limb muscles are also different. Its spinal column is shorter and less flexible; its pelvis is broader; it has no tail; its head is better balanced on the spinal column, rather than being thrust forward like a monkey's; and its brain is larger and more complex.

The main characteristics of apes are related to their feeding habits and their size. Most of the food in trees is found among the small branches and twigs at the end of the main limbs, and one of the problems encountered by any primate feeding here is that the branches are too small and frail to bear the weight of any but the smallest animal. But for other reasons it pays to be big: large size gives protection from predators such as eagles and hawks, and a bigger body may mean a bigger brain, to name just two rather obvious advantages. In consequence of this, a new locomotor behavior that was impractical for small prosimians appears among some monkeys and among all apes: they spread their weight through their four limbs and support themselves,

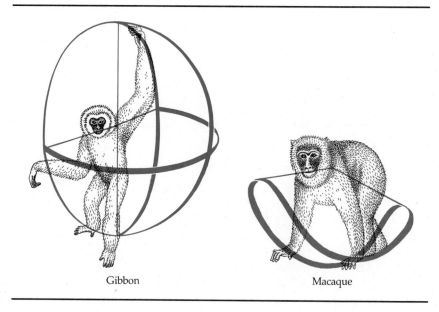

Gibbon                    Macaque

FIGURE 5–10   One of the basic differences between apes and monkeys lies in the greater freedom of movement that the former have in their forelimbs. Apes are climbers; they can swing by their arms in trees and move them freely in all directions (gibbon, left). Most monkeys, by contrast, are true quadrupeds. Since they travel on four limbs, they need only move their front legs backward and forward (macaque, right) and a little to the side. They leap and jump in trees.

not upon a single branch in quadrupedal fashion, but on a number of branches, hanging by their arms from branches above their heads as well as placing their feet on the branches below them (see Figure 5–11). This adaptation has enabled some of the larger monkeys and all the apes to move more freely among smaller branches, and at the same time to increase their size through evolution.

Gorillas, however, have increased in size beyond the point at which they can easily feed among small branches. When adult, they spend much of their time on the ground. In this, gorillas are not typical primates, or even typical apes. The smaller and much more active gibbon probably acts more like the ancestral, arboreal apes that we find in the Eocene and Oligocene fossil record.

*FIGURE 5–11  These photographs show the quadrupedal doglike walk of monkeys in contrast to the hanging locomotion (called brachiation) of gibbons (here photographed brachiating along a rope in a cage).*

*Propliopithecus*    These are some of the major differences that we find today between monkeys and apes. In sorting out the Fayum fossils it would be nice to have some spinal columns and leg bones to tell us if there were any apes or proto-apes among them. Unfortunately we have no such evidence, but we do have teeth. We have seen that certain molars in Old World monkeys have four cusps in a rectangular pattern. In the lower jaw of apes—and in humans—these same molars have five cusps, arranged in a characteristic Y pattern (Figures 5–7 and 5–12) with a different arrangement of connecting ridges. If we can find such five-cusped molars among the Fayum fossils, we can find a hint of apes or their ancestors and, presumably, of human ancestors also. Such molars, with their jaws, have been found; some belong to an animal named *Propliopithecus* (see Figure 5–13). (See also Table 5–3.)

The existence of both monkeylike and apelike molars among the Fayum fossils makes one startling fact plain: as long as 30 to 35 million years ago, the creatures that were becoming monkeys and those that were becoming apes were already different.

*Aegyptopithecus*    In 1966 a magnificent new find of a creature closely related to *Propliopithecus* was made in the Oligocene levels of the Fayum (about 32 million years B.P.) by Elwyn Simons, then at Yale University. The *Aegyptopithecus* fossil, as it was called, consisted of a virtually complete skull: head bones, upper and lower jaw, and an almost full set of teeth. The long canine teeth in the front of the upper jaw fitted the lower jaw to allow the same shearing ability that modern apes have. With this stunning find the promise of apishness made by the cusps in the lower molars of *Propliopithecus* was triumphantly confirmed by the apelike arrange-

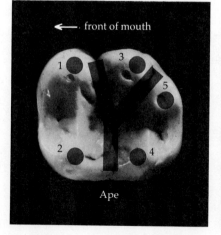
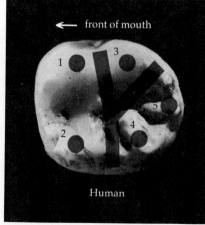

FIGURE 5–12   *The cusp patterns of the lower molars enable us to distinguish apes and monkeys with ease. In contrast, humans are relatively difficult to distinguish from apes on the basis of teeth: both have five cusps following a Y pattern. In some human lower molars, however, the fifth cusp has been lost, and it is commonly much reduced.*

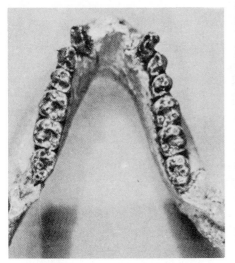

<FIGURE 5-13>*FIGURE 5–13  Propliopithecus has a five-cusped pattern on its lower molars. This early primate appears to be a small ancestral ape, which may have given rise to both living apes and humans.*

## TABLE 5–3   Classification of Fossil Apes

Superfamily: Hominoidea
Family: Propliopithecidae

| | | |
|---|---|---|
| Genus: | *Propliopithecus* } | Africa |
| | *Aegyptopithecus* | |
| Dryopithecidae | *Dryopithecus* | Europe, Asia |
| | *Proconsul* | Africa |
| Sivapithecidae | *Sivapithecus* | Africa, Europe, Asia |
| | *Ramapithecus* | Africa, Europe, Asia |
| | *Gigantopithecus* | Asia |
| Genera of uncertain status: | *Pondaungia* | Asia |
| | *Amphipithecus* | Asia |
| | *Apidium* | Africa |
| | *Parapithecus* | Africa |

ment and fit of all the teeth of *Aegyptopithecus*. *Aegyptopithecus* (Figures 5–8, 5–14, and 5–15) is, in fact, the most primitive ape yet discovered. Spaniel-sized, with a skull shaped very much like that of a monkey, it may have looked more like a monkey than an ape, but the convincing evidence of its jaws and teeth proves that it was already separate from the monkeys and was following a course of its own.

Additional evidence from the Fayum continues to accumulate, indicating not only that monkeys and apes were distinct at a very early date, but, equally significant, that apes were beginning to differentiate among themselves. Of the four modern species of apes—gibbon, orangutan, gorilla, and chimpanzee—the gibbon is considered the least like a human in its morphological pattern, and the chimpanzee is the most like a human. In these early days, however, these distinctions did not exist, and we can logically expect to find ancestral forms that carry the characteristics of all living apes to some degree. *Aegyptopithecus* showed a considerable amount of sexual dimorphism: the males were significantly bigger than the females and had much larger canines. It is from the survivors of these early species that modern apes have descended, and from among them, therefore, that we confidently may begin looking for our direct ancestors.

### *Proconsul* and *Dryopithecus*

Simons himself is convinced that *Aegyptopithecus*, which he calls the "Dawn Ape," was the forebear of another genus that followed in the Miocene and is much better known. *Proconsul* (shown in Figure 5–16) first appears in Africa at the start of the middle Miocene (about 20 million B.P.) and was contemporary with *Dryopithecus* in Europe and

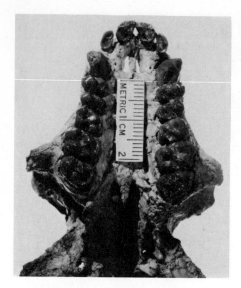

FIGURE 5–14   *The palate of* Aegyptopithecus *shows the apelike dentition and almost rectangular dental arcade. The creature, however, was very small, as indicated
by the scale. This specimen was discovered
by Elwyn Simons in the Fayum region of
Egypt. It is dated about 32 million
years* B.P.

Asia, about 14 million years ago. A number of *Dryopithecus* fossils had
been dug up since as early as 1856 in France. But the extremely limited
knowledge of the times when its first fossils were found, and the
unthinkability at that time of looking for human ancestors further back
than half a million years or so, led *Dryopithecus* to be catalogued as a
fossil ape and more or less forgotten.

*Dryopithecus* was back in the news, though, in the 1930s, when the
African fossil ape called *Proconsul* was discovered on Rusinga Island
in Lake Victoria, in Kenya. Finding the proper pigeonhole for this
animal was difficult. That it closely resembled chimpanzees was quickly
recognized: it was obviously an ape. But then again it wasn't, for it had
monkeylike characteristics. At last, some wondered if this could be the
first faint whisper of humanity. In all the excitement over *Proconsul*, it
occurred to scientists to go back to museum drawers and blow the dust
off *Dryopithecus*. Looked at by modern eyes sharpened by the *Proconsul*
finds, *Dryopithecus* quickly came into new focus. *Proconsul* was closely
related to *Dryopithecus*. Somewhere, a local species of such an ape might
have evolved into humankind.

Now a new puzzle appeared, for more and more *Proconsul* fragments
were being assembled, which indicated that the animal came in more
than one size: some, like *P. africanus*, were as small as pygmy chimpanzees; others were middle-sized; still others were almost as large as
gorillas. The relationship of the *Proconsul* and *Dryopithecus* species to
each other is still unclear, although it is now accepted that they all
belong to the same family.

FIGURE 5–15   *Finds of* Aegyptopithecus
*bones are now so numerous that a full re-
construction is possible. This drawing was
made under the direction of Elwyn Simons,
who described the twelve-pound creature as
"a nasty little thing." Notice that although
it is an ape, it carries a long tail.*

## A HUMAN ANCESTOR?

If you open your mouth wide and stand in front of a mirror, you notice two things. The first is that your hard palate, the roof of your mouth, is arched. The second is that your teeth go back on each side in a broad curve, with the widest part of the curve at the very back. By contrast, the hard palate of an ape is flat, and its jaws are U-shaped. The sides of the U are parallel, meaning that the back molars are no further apart than those nearer the front of the mouth (see Figure 5–17).

*Proconsul* had these apelike parallel rows of molars, so that we might infer that its descendants were apes and not humans. But what if the broadly curving jaw was a later evolutionary development? Digging in the Siwalik Hills of India in 1932, G. E. Lewis discovered a right upper jaw fragment of the late Miocene age, which he believed indicated a wide-curving jaw with an arched palate. He named his find *Ramapithecus* after the Indian god Rama. On the strength of these two features, Lewis wrote in 1937 that his find not only belonged to a different genus from the other apelike Miocene primates, but also was the most humanlike of the lot. This was a pretty optimistic step—too optimistic, many specialists felt, for Lewis's specimen consisted of only part of an upper jaw with four teeth attached. To anchor the entire human line to such a small fragment of fossil seemed to be rushing things.

To appreciate the significance of the *Ramapithecus* finds we need to examine the differences between ape and human teeth. The most striking difference lies in the size and form of the canines (Figure 5–18). Apes have long projecting canines, whereas humans' canines frequently project no farther than the other teeth, and are often flat like the incisors. Apes also have broader incisors than those of humans. The ape's long lower canines are associated with gaps in the upper tooth row, called *diastemata*, which accommodate these large teeth (see Figure 5–17); and a pointed lower first premolar, described as *sectorial*, which forms a cutting edge against the upper canine and thus has only one cusp. The human lower first premolar has two cusps, as you can feel with your tongue. Otherwise, ape molars are not strikingly different from those

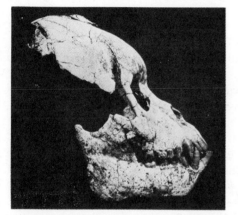

FIGURE 5–16   *The skull of* Proconsul *is a typical ape skull. The ape line evolved relatively slowly after this time—about 15 million years* B.P. *(This photograph is approximately 40 percent of actual size.)*

FIGURE 5–17   *The dentition of the upper jaw of an ape (a chimpanzee) and a human is here compared. Notice the distinct shape of the dental arcade, the large ape canines, and their diastemata.*

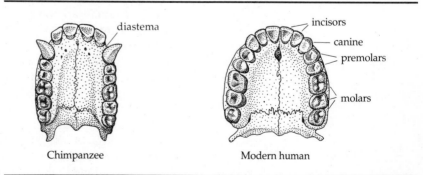

Chimpanzee

Modern human

FIGURE 5–18   *The ape and human skulls are quite distinct. The chimpanzee has a large jaw with large canines, especially in the male skull shown here. In humans the teeth are smaller and the canines often project no farther than the other teeth. The presence of the chin in humans results from the reduction in the size of the dentition, which is carried by smaller jaws. The enlarged braincase of humans brings about a more vertical alignment of the face and jaws. The scale is approximately one-fifth actual size.*

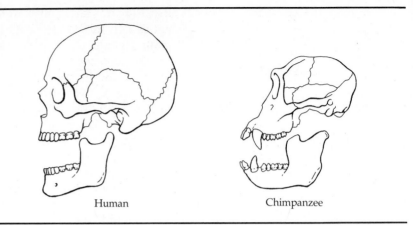

Human                                    Chimpanzee

of human beings, and individual molars cannot easily be attributed to one species or the other.

When the *Ramapithecus* jaw was reconstructed, neither large canines nor wide diastemata were believed to be present. Although the canine was still rather apelike in shape, it did not project much beyond the level (called the *occlusal plane*) of the other teeth. The diastemata and lower incisors appeared to be extremely small, and both jaws were shorter and less outwardly jutting, or *prognathous*, than the jaws of other apes. *Ramapithecus*, then, seemed to be neither ape nor human, but something between the two. The age of these jaw fragments is uncertain: it lies between 8 and 10 million years B.P. There is no convenient layer of volcanic ash in the Siwalik Hills for precise potassium-argon dating; age estimates had to be made by comparing other animal fossils present in these strata with similar fossils in other places and through comparative study of local paleomagnetism.

Recently, the taxonomic status of these fossils has been resolved. After fifty years standing in the wings as the most likely candidate for the proto-human ancestor, new discoveries have at last revealed their nature (Figure 5–19).

Alongside *Ramapithecus* in the Siwaliks is found another genus of fossil ape called *Sivapithecus*. This creature, also known mainly by jaws and teeth, shared many features with *Ramapithecus*, but the evidence seemed to suggest that *Ramapithecus* was distinct in having a number of hominidlike characters. It was only in 1980, when David Pilbeam and his team from Yale University made further discoveries of *Ramapithecus*, including parts of the face, that the true nature of the genus was revealed. The fossils proved surprising: the genus was clearly related not to the Hominidae, but to the orangutan, and was probably ancestral

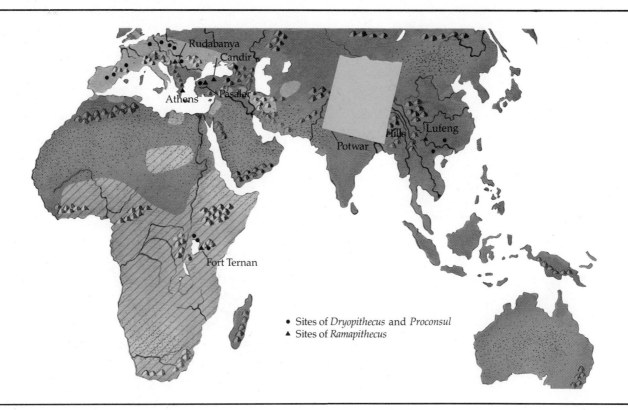

*FIGURE 5–19  This map of the Old World shows sites where fossils of* Ramapithecus, Proconsul, *and* Dryopithecus *have been found.*

to it. Furthermore, its close similarities to *Sivapithecus* meant that the whole *Sivapithecus-Ramapithecus* group of fossils probably belonged to the orang lineage (Pongidae) and bore no close relationship to our own line.

Before these new discoveries, many scholars (including this writer) believed that *Ramapithecus* was a possible ancestor of the Hominidae, and that the human family most probably evolved in Asia at this period of its history, rather than in Africa. We now know that this interpretation was wrong. The human family did indeed arise in Africa (as Darwin so wisely believed) and as we shall see, the earliest known hominids show an extremely close relationship to the central African great apes, the chimpanzee and gorilla.

**Other Apes**  These intensive investigations into the hominoids of the Miocene have yielded one more fascinating piece of information. It now appears that during the late Miocene, the climate in southern Eurasia was becoming drier. This is also the time when *Ramapithecus, Sivapithecus,* and *Dryopithecus* became extinct throughout Europe and Western Asia. Evidently

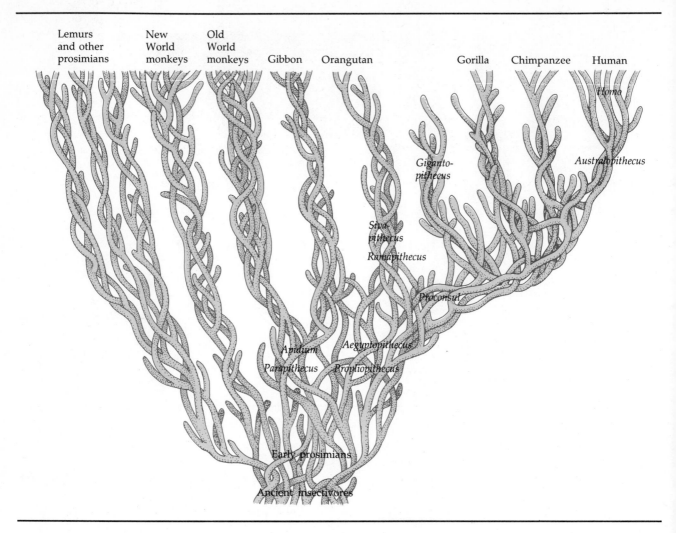

Lemurs and other prosimians

New World monkeys

Old World monkeys

Gibbon

Orangutan

Gorilla

Chimpanzee

Human

*Homo*

*Australopithecus*

*Giganto-pithecus*

*Siva-pithecus*

*Ramapithecus*

*Proconsul*

*Apidium*

*Aegyptopithecus*

*Parapithecus*

*Propliopithecus*

Early prosimians

Ancient insectivores

*FIGURE 5–20   Evolutionary "trees," or dendrograms, are always greatly oversimplified and in certain ways inaccurate, but they nevertheless give a good indication of the relative age and phylogenetic relationships of the species shown. The multiplicity of lines indicates that any evolving lineage contains an unknown number of divergent populations that may or may not be different species. Many such populations become extinct. The chart is highly speculative.*

the almost total disappearance of the forest in the Eurasian land mass defeated these creatures; they became extinct except where the forest remained, in Eastern Asia. There thrived the ancestors of gibbons and orangutans.

One genus, however, survived. This ape was called *Gigantopithecus*, because of its immense size. Rather like a fully terrestrial gorilla, *Gigantopithecus* survived as a successful quadruped in Asia for about 9 million years, and became extinct about 1 million years ago, when its last traces occur in China. It carried immense molars, and a dentition suited to a tough and fibrous vegetable diet. *Gigantopithecus* was the only successful ground-living savanna ape, and may have been a powerful competitor for any hominids that lived in Asia. Indeed, its final extinction was possibly a result of increasing competition from hominids. (That *Gigantopithecus* is in fact extinct has been questioned by those who believe it survives as the Yeti of the Himalayas or the Sasquatch of the Northwest American coast. But the evidence for these creatures, especially the latter, is not convincing.)

**REASSESSING THE FOSSIL PICTURE**

As time goes on, the clouds that have obscured the Miocene primate picture are beginning to thin out. The situation is far more complicated than has been indicated in this necessarily brief chapter. Many forms have not been mentioned at all. Most fossils exist in lamentably small fragments, and how they all relate is a question that is still being worked on. But they make clear that the primate family tree has nothing like a central trunk but is more like a luxuriant vine with many tendrils and shoots that grew side by side, some withering and dying, some branching further (Figure 5–20). One of those branches belongs to extremely ancient prosimian types, another to more advanced monkeylike and apelike types, and one to a group that belongs definitely in the ape line alone. Some of these ape ancestors were more like gibbons. Others, like *Proconsul,* were ancestral to the larger apes and probably to humans.

Much study and reorganization of the Oligocene and Miocene primate fossil record is going on today. We already have a far clearer picture than was possible as recently as five years ago. That it may be turned inside out by other discoveries is always a possibility, but the more evidence that is collected to support the conclusions the more unlikely it becomes that it will be upset.

The Miocene, then, during about 10 million years, saw the development of a number of proto-apes. They were widely distributed through Europe, Asia, and Africa; they were evolving rather rapidly; they may well have been exceedingly numerous. One of these creatures must almost certainly have given rise to the living African apes—the Panidae; and it seems increasingly likely that it also gave rise to the earliest members of the human family—the Hominidae.

| | Cro-Magnon, Neandertal, and *Homo erectus* | YEARS B.P. | FOSSIL RECORD | PRIMATES |
|---|---|---|---|---|
| | | **Pleistocene** | | *HOMO* |
| **CENOZOIC** | | 2 million — | Early *Homo* | *AUSTRALO-PITHECUS* |
| | | **Pliocene** | | |
| 65 million | Early prosimians | 5 million — | Earliest *Australopithecus* ? | |
| | Basic insectivores | | | |
| | | | *Sivapithecus* in Asia and Europe | |
| | | | *Dryopithecus* in Asia | |
| **MESOZOIC** | | **Miocene** | *Dryopithecus* in Europe | |
| | | | *Proconsul* in Africa | *PROCONSUL* |
| | First mammals | | | |
| 225 million | | 25 million — | | |
| | | | | **PROTO-MONKEYS AND PROTO-APES** |
| | | **Oligocene** | | |
| | | | *Propliopithecus* and *Aegyptopithecus* at Fayum | |
| | | 35 million — | *Apidium, Parapithecus* | |
| | | | *Amphipithecus* and *Pondaugia* in Burma | |
| **PALEOZOIC** | | | | |
| | | **Eocene** | | |
| | | | | **EARLY PROSIMIANS** |
| | First vertebrates | 58 million — | | |
| | | **Paleocene** | | |
| 570 million | **PRECAMBRIAN** | 65 million — | | |

## BACK BEYOND THE APES

The time scale of primate evolution is immense. The first half of the 65 million years of primate history was the age of the prosimians, which occupied much of the Old and New Worlds. By 30 million years ago the apes were established in Africa, and for this reason we too find our origin on this continent. By about 15 million years ago the apes had spread into Eurasia.

# Chapter 6

# The Behavior of Living Primates

We love animals, we watch them with delight, we
study their habits with ever-increasing curiosity; and
we destroy them.

KENNETH CLARK, b. 1903.
*Animals and Men*, Ch. 5.

Fossils can provide a very good indication of the course of evolution,
but they are less good at indicating precisely how evolution came about.
This limitation has been a source of frustration to anthropologists for
many years—so much so that many are now looking for answers elsewhere than in the fossil record. One alternative field that is fruitful is
the study of humankind's primate relatives, the monkeys and apes;
closely related to us, they are even more closely related to our ancestors.

**STUDYING PRIMATES**    Recent developments in biochemistry have shown close similarities of
DNA, cell proteins, and blood proteins and hemoglobin between hu-
mans and the other primates. Now, thanks to an upsurge in studies of
monkeys and apes in their natural environment, it is becoming clear
that in their social behavior, too, they stand much closer to us than we
had suspected. Many live in highly organized groups in which following
routines and sharing knowledge permit a relatively stable social organization. Others, like chimpanzees, live in more loosely organized
groups. Whatever the size or structure of the group, some members
will be good friends, others dedicated enemies; some will be collaborators, others rivals; some will be popular, others despised. Infant apes
and monkeys, as they grow up, must learn a code of behavior, much
as a human child has to do; and all the members of a group are linked

119

by an elaborate system of communication that uses both sounds and gestures and shows considerable sophistication.

The comparison of ape and monkey behavior with human behavior, of course, must not be pushed too far. Yet in their daily routine and in many aspects of their relationship with their fellows the nonhuman primates resemble humans in many surprising ways.

**Early Work**  Although new aspects of the connection between us and our primate kin are continually coming to light, the idea of studying primates is by no means a new one. In the parts of the world where humans live in close contact with monkeys or apes, accounts of their primate neighbors have dotted observers' writings for centuries: the Chinese general Wang Jeñ-yü, for instance, mentioned his pet gibbon Yeh-pin in his memoirs written in the tenth century. Western travelers to foreign lands were especially impressed by monkeys and apes, who in many ways were uncannily similar to themselves. In the mid-1800s, while writers like Edgar Allan Poe spun tales emphasizing the eerie aspects of the resemblance between ape and human, others who observed monkeys and apes in their natural habitat were awed by what they saw. In 1840, the English naturalist William Charles Martin, observing a female gibbon, wrote, "It is almost impossible to convey in words an idea of the quickness and graceful address of her movements: they may indeed be termed aerial as she seems merely to touch in her progress the branches along which she exhibits her evolutions."

Early in the twentieth century, casual observation of primates began to give rise to more serious study. In the 1920s, psychobiologist Robert Yerkes observed captive chimpanzees in the United States, and was so impressed by what he saw and so astonished at how little was known about the great apes that he sent two students to Africa to study the chimpanzee and the gorilla. In 1930 he opened the Laboratories of Primate Biology at Orange Park, Florida, which later moved to Emory University in Atlanta, and were renamed the Yerkes Regional Primate Research Center. Behavioral studies, including intelligence tests and other studies on social behavior, as well as studies on stress and other physiological matters, are carried out at the center, which today has the largest collection of apes in the country.

The first systematic investigations of the behavior of apes and monkeys living under natural conditions were made by Dr. C. R. Carpenter. In the early 1930s, Carpenter journeyed to Barro Colorado Island in Panama to study howler monkeys and then traveled to southeast Asia to observe gibbons. Later he set up a colony of rhesus monkeys on an island near Puerto Rico and observed them. Carpenter published some revolutionary findings on monkey behavior. The results he obtained viewing primates in the wild pointed up the limitations of studying primates in captivity, which had been the practice up to that time.

Around the same period, the English zoologist Sir Solly Zuckerman was studying baboons—first, hamadryas baboons in the London Zoo, then, chacma baboons in South Africa. Zuckerman was especially interested in what these creatures' behavior might suggest about that of humans. He concluded that sexual behavior was the original force behind social organization among primates, an idea that has since been alternately discredited and somewhat revived. But he was seriously misled by studying baboons in the zoo: their behavior in captivity was quite different from the way they were later found to behave in the wild.

Psychologists too took an interest in the behavior of nonhuman primates, particularly that of apes. Dr. Wolfgang Kohler conducted experiments investigating chimpanzees' capacity to find solutions to problems, such as stacking boxes or using sticks to reach bundles of bananas. Dr. Harry Harlow studied monkeys' learning ability: learning proved extremely important in the proper social development of a monkey. Harlow's research also demonstrated the power of the mother-infant bond in a young monkey's development. The behavior of adult monkeys that had not had access to their mothers when young was greatly disturbed. Other researchers raised a young chimpanzee or gorilla in their own home, bringing it up much as if it were a human baby, to see how similarly to a human it might grow up.

It is exceedingly difficult to do some kinds of experimental work in an animal's natural habitat—for example, surgery, chemical therapy, and experimental separations of mothers and infants. But however useful for gauging an individual animal's response to a specific stimulus or situation it was, observing apes or monkeys in a small laboratory cage provided little insight into normal primate behavior. The other handy spot for observation was the zoo; but there too the subjects' behavior was distorted by the abnormal environment (Figure 6–1). Small cages provided scant room for movement, there is no need for ordinary activities like seeking food, and the crowding found in many zoos transforms the animals' social relationships. For scientists interested in studying normal primate behavior, the only realistic option was to observe monkeys and apes in their natural setting.

A major development in field research occurred after World War II, when primatologists in Japan established the Primate Research Group to study native Japanese macaques under natural conditions. At Takasakiyama, by setting up feeding stations that a macaque colony with 200-odd members visited regularly, scientists were able to observe one group of monkeys over an extended period. On the island of Koshima, with an isolated macaque population, researchers not only recorded their subjects' customs, but to some extent changed them, thereby gaining numerous insights into the way in which the monkeys' behavior and social structure were determined.

FIGURE 6–1   Zoos are necessarily extremely unnatural environments for primates, which in nature are gregarious, inquisitive and extremely active animals. In these photographs a gorilla attempts to build a nest on a concrete floor out of dry leaves. Neither hard floor nor dry leaves are present in a tropical forest, where nests are built from soft living vegetation folded to make a comfortable bed. Compare Figure 6–8.

**Recent Studies**   The trend toward studying primates in their native habitats really caught hold in the late 1950s. Led by various anthropologists, a large number of young field workers began pouring out all over the world from universities and museums in a dozen countries. In the late 1950s they began by studying langurs and baboons. During the 1960s, they studied rhesus monkeys in India, and gorillas, chimpanzees, and many forest monkeys in Africa. During the 1960s and 1970s, they observed the gibbons and orangutans of southeast Asia. At various times, studies of New World monkeys have been conducted in Central and South America (Figure 6–2).

FIGURE 6–2   Old World monkeys (top), a long-tailed macaque and a mandrill, both adapted to terrestrial quadrupedalism. New World monkeys like the spider monkey (bottom) are highly adapted to an arboreal life. Notice the long arms and long prehensile tail in the New World monkey. Compare the form of the nostrils in the two groups.

Primates turned out to be much harder to study than anyone had imagined. Many, like the mountain gorilla, live in inaccessible places. Many stay in the tops of trees in dense forest, where they are nearly invisible. Others, like the orangutan, are extremely rare. Most are shy. There is also the problem of what to look for, and how to interpret it. Different species act differently in different areas, under different ecological influences, and even under different population densities. Primate behavior is not stereotyped, but complex and highly variable.

Yet, as we shall see, field studies have proven an invaluable source of information. Our knowledge of apes' behavior has greatly increased over the past two decades, thanks to the work of researchers like Vernon and Frances Reynolds, who studied chimpanzees in the Budongo Forest of Uganda; Adrian Kortland, who studied chimpanzees in West Africa; Jane Goodall, who spent decades at the Gombe Stream Chimpanzee Reserve in Tanzania; Toshisada Nishida, who studied chimpanzees in the Mahali Mountains of Tanzania; George Schaller, who observed gorillas on the mountain slopes of central Africa; Biruté Galdikas, who studied orangutans in Kalimantan (Borneo); and Dian Fossey, who carried on Schaller's work. As each new fact is unearthed, old prejudices are dispelled. The gorilla, whose size and appearance cast it for more than a hundred years as a fearsome forest monster, is now known to be shy and usually gentle. And the chimpanzee is not merely an amiable muncher of bananas but is an enthusiastic hunter on occasion.

Primate research continues to be of three general types: investigators may study apes or monkeys in the hope of increasing our understanding of humans; they may observe primates simply to learn more about them; or frequently, they may attempt to achieve both goals. But whatever its purpose, observation of modern primates is enriched by an awareness not only of how apes and monkeys relate to humans, but also of how they relate to each other and to their ancestors. By understanding what caused primates to evolve as they have, we should be better able to see why they behave as they do.

**DEVELOPMENT OF MODERN PRIMATES**

The order Primates comprises more than one hundred and fifty living species. As we have seen, these fall within two suborders: Prosimii, which include tree shrews, lemurs, lorises, and tarsiers; and Anthropoidea, which include New World and Old World monkeys, apes, and humans. Though in many ways the primate species all are equally remarkable products of the evolutionary process, in this chapter we will consider primarily our own closer relatives, the Anthropoidea. These consist of the sixteen genera of Ceboidea, the New World monkeys; the fourteen genera of Cercopithecoidea, or Old World Monkeys; and the six genera of Hominoidea, the gibbons, siamangs, orangutans, gorillas, chimpanzees, and humans (Table 6–1 and Figure 6–3).

## TABLE 6–1 Living Genera of the Order Primates

| SUBORDER | SUPERFAMILY | FAMILY | GENUS | COMMON NAME | LOCATION |
|---|---|---|---|---|---|
| Prosimii | Lemuroidea | | 9 genera | Lemurs | Madagascar |
| | Daubentonioidea | | 1 genus | Aye-ayes | Madagascar |
| | Lorisioidea | | 5 genera | Lorises | Africa/Asia |
| | Tarsioidea | | 1 genus | Tarsiers | Southeast Asia |
| Anthropoidea | Ceboidea | | | New World monkeys | Central/South America |
| | | Callithricidae | *Callithrix* | Marmosets | South America |
| | | | *Cebuella* | Pygmy marmosets | South America |
| | | | *Saguinus* | Tamarins | Central/South America |
| | | | *Leontideus* | Golden lion tamarins | South America |
| | | | *Callimico* | Goeldi's marmosets | South America |
| | | Cebidae | *Pithecia* | Sakis | South America |
| | | | *Chiropotes* | Bearded sakis | South America |
| | | | *Cacajao* | Uakaris | Central/South America |
| | | | *Aotus* | Douroucoulis | Central/South America |
| | | | *Callicebus* | Titis | Central/South America |
| | | | *Saimiri* | Squirrel monkeys | Central/South America |
| | | | *Cebus* | Capuchins | Central/South America |
| | | | *Alouatta* | Howler monkeys | Central/South America |
| | | | *Ateles* | Spider monkeys | Central/South America |
| | | | *Lagothrix* | Woolly monkeys | South America |
| | | | *Brachyteles* | Woolly spider monkeys | South America |
| | Cercopithecoidea | | | Old World monkeys | Africa/Asia |
| | | Cercopithecidae | *Cercopithecus* | Guenons | Africa |
| | | | *Erythrocebus* | Patas monkeys | Africa |
| | | | *Cercocebus* | Magabeys | Africa |
| | | | *Mandrillus* | Mandrills | Africa |
| | | | *Papio* | Baboons | Africa |
| | | | *Theropithecus* | Geladas | Africa |
| | | | *Macaca* | Macaques | Asia/Africa |
| | | | *Cynopithecus* | Celebes black ape | Asia |
| | | Colobidae | *Colobus* | Guerezas | Africa |
| | | | *Presbytis* | Langurs | Asia |
| | | | *Pygathrix* | Douc langurs | Asia |
| | | | *Rhinopithecus* | Snub-nosed langurs | Asia |
| | | | *Nasalis* | Proboscis monkeys | Asia |
| | | | *Simias* | Pagai Island langurs | Asia |
| | Hominoidea | | | Apes and humans | Worldwide |
| | | Hylobatidae | *Hylobates* | Gibbons | Southeast Asia |
| | | | *Symphalangus* | Siamangs | Southeast Asia |
| | | Pongidae | *Pongo* | Orangutans | Southeast Asia |
| | | Panidae | *Pan* | Chimpanzees | Africa |
| | | | *Gorilla* | Gorilla | Africa |
| | | Hominidae | *Homo* | Humans | Worldwide |

*Note:* Authors differ in details of Primate classification. This table presents a classification that is widely accepted.

## Adapting to the Trees

As we saw in Chapter 5, all modern primates evolved from small ratlike insectivores that invaded the trees from the ground some 75 million years ago. In time, these creatures developed a number of adaptations that increased their suitability to an arboreal existence. The early insectivores, which got around as squirrels do today, gradually developed hands with *prehensile* fingers, capable of gripping. Claws began to turn into nails. Some groups developed a way of getting about that depended on a slow but sure four-handed movement, characterized by a grip whose strength was out of all proportion to the size of the animal. Pottos still move in this way, as do slow lorises (see Figure 6–4), and both have powerful hands and feet for grasping and clinging. Another means of locomotion was, as we have seen, leaping and clinging. Some early prosimians were great jumpers. They had long legs—in proportion, as long as those of kangaroos—and very short arms.

Most of the prosimians were extremely small. Some surviving species still are: the tarsier of the Philippines is no larger than a kitten. In time, because of natural selection, many of the prosimians became bigger. There are forces at work in all species that encourage the selection of larger individuals if there is no offsetting advantage in being smaller. For one thing, larger, more aggressive males have an advantage over smaller ones in competing for females, thus increasing the proportion of their offspring in the next generation. For another, an increase in size may protect an animal like a small prosimian from being eaten by

*FIGURE 6–3   There are three main geographical radiations of living Primates: the lemurs, confined to Madagascar; the New World monkeys, confined to Central and South America; and the Old World primates (prosimians, monkeys, apes, and humans), confined, apart from humans, to Africa and Southern Asia. These three geographical groups are believed to have been separate for about 50 million years.*

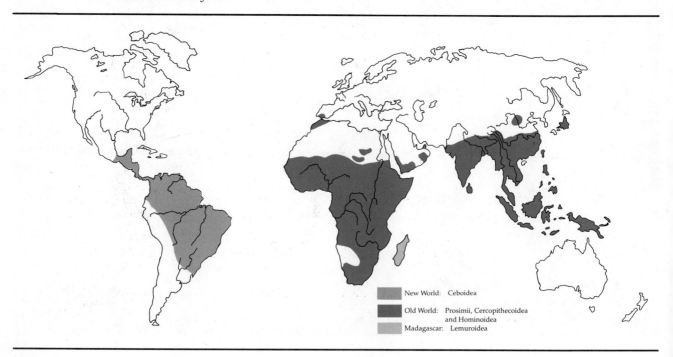

New World:      Ceboidea

Old World:      Prosimii, Cercopithecoidea
                and Hominoidea

Madagascar:    Lemuroidea

*FIGURE 6–4   The slow loris is so called because it moves extremely slowly and deliberately. It is very strong and can remain stationary for long periods suspended from a branch or supported by tree limbs, as it silently stalks an insect, bird, or lizard in the trees. The large eyes are an adaptation to nocturnal life. The slow loris lives in southeast Asia.*

snakes or hawks that are not powerful enough to take on bigger prey. In fact, a predator could encourage the evolution of larger animals in a population by killing a disproportionate number of the smaller ones, thus eliminating them as breeding stock. In reality it is more often the young animals that are caught.

Increased size brings problems with it, however. A large body is harder to hide than a small one. It also needs more food. If the animal feeds on fruit or tender leaves and shoots at the tips of branches, a balance will have to be maintained so that the survival advantage of being bigger is not outweighed by the disadvantage of being too heavy to get far enough out on the twig ends to reach the best food. In short, there is an optimum size for a particular way of living in a particular habitat. If the selection pressure for larger size is great enough, then the way of living may change. Thus a leaper may become a reacher, with longer arms that enable it to spread its weight among three or four branch ends, thereby reducing the weight on any one branch. Grasping hands with flat nails then become essential: claws will do for a very small climber but not for a bigger one, because they cannot carry the animal's weight.

Under these influences larger, heavier, long-armed, more dexterous primates began to appear, as we saw in Chapter 5, in the Oligocene epoch about 35 million years ago. Their food preferences began to be different. Accordingly, they sorted themselves out in different parts of the forest, in different kinds of trees, even in different parts of the same trees. Some of these longer-armed primates became quadrupeds, running easily along the branches on all fours. These were the monkeys. Others, whose arms became still longer, tended more in the direction of reaching, climbing, hanging, swinging. Some of them became the apes.

These early primates were well suited to life in trees owing to a number of adaptations that are still present in their descendants: the structure of their brains, their possession of fingernails and toenails and opposable thumbs, the way they use their senses of smell and sight and touch, and the way they bear and rear their young (Table 5–2). One quality in particular characterized all primates: the ability to climb by grasping.

## Monkeys, Apes, and Humans

The monkeys, possessed of all these advantages plus a size and structure that enabled them to move around easily in the trees, spread rapidly throughout the forests (Figure 6–5). One group spread across most of Central and South America, while another developed and spread across Africa, southern Europe, and southern Asia. Many monkey species later acquired new characteristics and specializations, but the monkeys' fundamental structure was set. And so, it might surprise the reader to learn, was the sensory system of all the higher primates, up to and including humans. The human brain is perhaps a dozen

*FIGURE 6–5   Monkeys have evolved a number of types of arboreal locomotion. The Old World monkey (left) leaps considerable distances between trees and uses its tail for balance and to control its position in flight. The New World monkey (right) uses its tail as an extra limb to grip the tree trunks and branches, freeing both its hands for feeding.*

times as large and vastly more complicated than that of any monkey, but most of this additional brain is devoted to memory, association, and speech; that is, to abstractions. So far as our method of perceiving the world around us is concerned, humans have advanced hardly at all beyond the stage reached by primates perhaps as much as 15 million years ago. We may not react like monkeys, but essentially we smell and taste, hear, touch, and see very much as monkeys do.

Anatomically, however, humans and monkeys are very different animals. Monkeys, being quadrupeds, retain many characteristics of primitive four-legged mammals. Their trunk is long, narrow, and deep, and their limbs are hung from it in a very special way that restricts them largely to using their arms and legs in a backward and forward plane, as in walking or running (see Figure 5–10). The general proportions of a monkey's trunk are much like those of a dog—and like a dog, a monkey tends to keep its arms and legs parallel. Even when stretching, it will reach out forward, as a dog does when it awakens from sleep, rises, yawns, and stretches out its legs. And in the trees, monkeys basically move as a four-legged animal moves, walking or running along the top of a branch. (See Figure 5–9 for a comparison of monkeys' and apes' skeletal features.) With apes, it is quite different—as it is with humans.

There are today five main genera of apes, divided into three families. One family includes the African gorilla and chimpanzee; the second includes their Asiatic relatives the orangutan; and the third includes the Asiatic gibbons. All are quite different anatomically from any monkey.

**Locomotion** The most obvious distinction between apes and monkeys is that apes are built for a different mode of travel, having short, wide, shallow trunks and long, free-swinging arms that rotate at the shoulders. These adaptations allowed early apes to reach out in all directions in the trees, climbing arm over arm.

From their probable beginning as efficient climbers, the different families of apes have adapted in different ways. The gibbons and siamangs (Hylobatidae), although they climb much of the time, especially when feeding, have evolved very long arms and hands and in this way are specialized for the horizontal arm-over-arm locomotion called *brachiation*. They can throw themselves from hand to hand, swinging under the branches through the treetops, often with their legs tucked up under their bodies. They can travel with considerable speed and extraordinary grace (Figures 5–11 and 6–6).

*FIGURE 6–6   Whereas the orangutan (upper left) and gibbon (upper right) are still fully arboreal, the gorilla (lower left) and chimpanzee (lower right) have developed knuckle walking as the form of locomotion most practical for their ground-based way of life.*

The orangutan (*Pongo*) moves steadily, climbing through the trees with all four limbs. So flexible are the shoulder and hip joints that its legs are like arms in use: the animal almost appears to be four-armed and four-handed (Figure 6–6). On the ground the orang moves quadrupedally with clenched fists and feet, though it occasionally walks on the palms of its hands. Both the gibbons and orang are fully adapted to arboreal life, however, and show no specific terrestrial adaptations.

The African apes (family Panidae), however, do show such adaptations, and the larger species—especially the mountain gorilla—have almost deserted the trees for the ground, though they still sleep in trees. Although the smaller chimpanzees are good climbers, all species of panids are adapted to terrestrial quadrupedalism and they walk on the soles of their feet and the knuckles of their hands. The terrestrial skeletal adaptations are seen in the bones of their wrists and hands, which are modified to support the weight of the animals on their knuckles—on the second phalanx counting from the tip of the finger (Figure 6–6). Here, normal hairy skin is replaced by hairless friction skin such as we find on the palms of our hands and the soles of our feet.

Thus the living apes, sharing a common ancestor which we believe was an arboreal climber and which underwent a reduction in the tail, have each in their own way modified this original locomotor adaptation together with their skeleton and musculature. Human ancestors have taken a fourth route—to terrestrial bipedalism. Although we are still quite able as climbers, our lower limbs have undergone profound changes in adaptation to walking on the ground.

**Changes in Anatomy**     Obviously, the adaptation that gave the apes the ability to climb with their arms and distribute their weight better provided them with an opportunity for growth. But having been granted this opportunity, what led them to exploit it? What advantage did the apes win by growing bigger?

There was, of course, a competitive advantage that any big animal has over a smaller one when it comes to eating or being eaten. But there is also an extended life span. Big animals tend to live longer and their rate of metabolism is slower than that of small animals: their internal organs simply do not have to work so hard, and therefore do not wear out so fast.

Any useful change often begets more change along the same line of development: it is a basic rule of evolutionary dynamics. Climbing prompted a series of further changes in the apes that altered the primate anatomy, providing on the one hand the potential for bipedal and tool-using humans and on the other the specialized adaptations of the modern anthropoid apes. In order to climb more effectively, the apes acquired a whole new complex of characteristics in their shoulders, their elbows, and their wrists that combined to make their arm move-

FIGURE 6–7   *Jane Goodall observed chimpanzees fishing with short twigs for termites in mounds. The chimpanzees prepared the twigs by stripping leaves and breaking them at a certain length: in fact, they made a tool.*

ments much more flexible. Apes can swing their arms out in a wide circle from their shoulders—forward, sideways, backward, and up. With their more flexible elbows they can straighten out their arms, and their wrists are much more mobile than a monkey's—more so, in fact, than a human's. An ape can hang from a branch by one hand and rotate its body completely around, thanks to the flexibility of its arm and wrist joints.

Nor did the changes that arose from climbing stop at the apes' arms and shoulders. Ultimately changes affected the whole of their upper bodies, giving them their characteristic short, relatively inflexible spine, the wide, shallow trunk with its resultant different arrangement of the internal organs, and a pelvis splayed out to provide additional room for the attachment of muscles. All these changes helped to produce animals that, from the waist up, physically resemble humans.

The results of the apes' shift from quadrupedalism to climbing and brachiation are profoundly important. If an animal evolves greater erectness and arm flexibility, it can reach farther and grasp, pluck, hold, examine, and carry with greater ease. The more often a hand performs these acts, the better it gets at doing them. A chimpanzee, as British primatologist Jane Goodall discovered, has the manual dexterity to strip the leaves from a twig (in other words, to make an implement) and deftly insert that twig into a small hole in a termite mound so that it can lick off the termites that cling to the twig when it is pulled out (Figure 6–7). This remarkable act of food-gathering requires not only precise manipulation but also intelligence. This is another way of saying that increased dependence on hands has an evolutionary effect on the brain. It is therefore significant that apes are, as a group, more intelligent than monkeys, whose hands are dexterous enough, but whose quadrupedal way of life limits their use, and thus limits the feedback that the use of hands has on the evolution of the brain.

## BASIS OF SOCIAL ORGANIZATION

Although monkeys and apes differ from each other in important ways, they share many characteristics. Of these, certainly the most interesting is that they are all social species (except perhaps the orangutan) and their societies are highly organized. We first need to ask ourselves several questions. What are the advantages of social life? Why are so many mammal and bird species social and why have the Hominoidea developed this characteristic to such lengths? Four kinds of advantage are usually proposed by zoologists:

1. Several pairs of eyes are better than one in the detection of predators and in their avoidance. Defense by a group is also far more effective. Three or four male baboons constitute an impressive display and can frighten any predator, even a lion. A single baboon is a dead baboon.

2. Food finding and food exploitation and handling, as well as defense (of a carcass, for example) are more efficient at times when food is in fairly ample supply. We shall see that in some monkeys social groups subdivide when food is sparse and widely scattered.

3. Reproductive advantages accrue from social groups because regular access to the opposite sex is ensured.

4. Social groups permit extensive socialization with peers and elders and the opportunity for learning from them. Among animals such as the higher primates, this is a factor of the greatest importance.

These factors are probably the most important in bringing about the selection of social life in animals such as primates. Although considerable variation may occur within a species, especially under different environmental conditions, only a few Old World primate species (including the gibbons and siamang, a large gibbon) normally live in groups consisting only of an adult male, female, and young. The remaining seventy-odd species of Old World primates all live in social groups that number as high as five hundred individuals but most commonly number between ten and fifty (Table 6–2).

But how are these societies organized? Far from being a structureless collection of rushing, squalling animals, primate societies are remarkably stable and usually serene and quiet. Order is maintained in primate societies through a complex interrelationship of several factors. One factor is the animals' prolonged period of dependence: infant apes and monkeys, like human infants, are far from self-sufficient, and maintain a close relationship with their mothers longer than most other animals.

**TABLE 6–2   Size and Distribution of Social Groups of Some Primate Species**

| PRIMATE | TROOP OR BAND SIZE | | DENSITY PER SQUARE MILE | HOME RANGE IN SQUARE MILES[a] |
|---|---|---|---|---|
| | Mean | Range | | |
| Langur | 18 | 3–50 | 12 | 0.01–5.0 |
| Savanna baboon | 40 | 8–500 | 10 | 2–15 |
| Gibbon | 4 | 2–6 | 11 | 0.1 |
| Chimpanzee | —[b] | 2–20 | 3–5 | 4–10 |
| Gorilla (mountain) | 12 | 3–27 | 3 | 10–15 |
| Humans | | | | |
| Bushmen | 34 | 16–61 | 0.08–0.65 | 50–150 |
| Australians | 35 | 25–40 | 0.3–2.0 | 100–750 |

[a] The home range is the approximate area covered by the troop or band in a year's foraging and hunting.
[b] Chimpanzee bands vary greatly in size and composition. It is now thought that bands belong to a larger group, called the community, which usually numbers about fifty, but is not normally together at one time.

During this time they learn some of the roles they will play as adults. Another factor is dominance—every adult has a social rank within the group. Also important are the other relationships among adults, which to some extent are determined by kinship, friendship, sexual contacts and competition for food, sleeping sites, and any other limited resources.

Thinking about these factors, one quickly sees that they are among the most important regulators of human society as well. Thus, for a very long time (we may assume) and for many species—for humans, for chimpanzees, and for baboons—the problem of life has been, and still is, largely the problem of getting along in a group.

**Learning in Childhood**    Sherwood Washburn and David Hamburg, looking at primate behavior from the point of view of an anthropologist and a psychiatrist, respectively, recognized the importance of group life when they wrote:

> The group is the locus of knowledge and experience far exceeding that of individual members. It is in the group that experience is pooled and the generations linked. The adaptive function of prolonged biological youth is that it gives the animal time to learn. During this period while the animal is learning from other members of the group, it is protected by them. Slow development in isolation would simply mean disaster for the individual and extinction for the species.

What is meant by "prolonged biological youth"? A kitten has become a cat by the time it is a year old. A male baboon, by contrast, takes seven to eight years to reach full social and biological maturity, a chimpanzee needs anywhere from ten to fifteen years, a human even longer. As a result, family ties among higher primates tend to be strong and lasting. This slow development is necessary for a higher primate to learn all the things it must to fit itself into the complex society into which it is born. In a society in which an individual must deal with many daily choices and varied personal interchange, a long period of youthful learning is an absolute necessity.

For a chimpanzee, childhood play is the equivalent of going to school. It watches its mother look for food, and looks for food itself. It watches her make nests, and makes little nests of its own—not to sleep in, just for the fun of it (Figure 6–8). Later, during a long adolescence, it picks up from its peers the physical skills it will need as an adult as well as the more intricate psychological skills required to get along with others: it learns not only how to interpret the moods of other chimpanzees but also how to respond to other individuals. Any chimpanzee that cannot learn to communicate fully with its fellows almost certainly will not live to grow up, for communication is the essential bonding of any society. All this time the learner is finding its own place among its peers, first in play, later in more competitive activity that will help determine its

FIGURE 6–8   *Each night, chimpanzees pre-*
*pare new nests for themselves by bending*
*tree branches over larger boughs to make a*
*bed.*

rank as an adult. In sum, two sources of learning, two sets of relationships, make up primate society. One of these is the family relationship
(mother-infant-sibling). The other is the larger relationship of the individual to all other members of its troop.

Primate behavior, like that of other highly evolved mammals, depends heavily on learning, in contrast to the less flexible behavior of
simpler animals. For this reason, the prolonged learning period is especially significant. The important role of learned behavior among primates also means, as Washburn and Hamburg have pointed out, that
the group as a whole has more knowledge and experience than its
individual members. This was demonstrated in a Nairobi game park
where a ranger had had to kill a baboon: for many years afterward, the
troop that had lost its member avoided the site of the killing, even
though all members of the troop had not witnessed the event.

Phyllis Jay's studies of langurs in India (Figure 6–9) yielded a wealth
of information on how the infants of one monkey species learn. All the
adult male langurs within a group are organized in a dominance hierarchy; so too are the females, though to a lesser degree. As soon as she
gives birth, however, a female moves out of the hierarchy, devoting her
full attention to her infant. The other females are both curious about
the infant and extremely protective of it; they may wait in line for a
chance to hold it. No matter what the mother's social status, however,
her first claim on her baby is respected.

FIGURE 6–9  A juvenile female langur (right) holds a complaining infant while adult females groom each other. As the infants get older, they become more adventurous (below).

After the infant reaches the age of about five months, its distinctive dark coat lightens to the color of an adult langur. Now the females no longer vie to hold it. It follows its mother about, copying her actions, learning to forage. It also spends much of its time in energetic activity, running, climbing, chasing, and wrestling—skills that will be invaluable as it reaches adulthood. As it plays with its fellows, it learns to get along as a member of the group.

Once young langurs are weaned, around the age of fifteen months, they become segregated by sex. The females stay near the center of the group, close to the adults, mixing more and more intimately with the adult females and their infants. Holding the infants and sometimes tending them while the mothers are away, they are gaining experience toward their own future role as mothers. The male juveniles, meanwhile, spend most of their free time playing. As they grow older, their play becomes ever more vigorous and wide-ranging, and, needing more room, they drift toward the periphery of the group, away from both the adults and the infants.

Through their play, the male juveniles establish the close social bonds that will later help to keep the group unified. As they compete for food or the best sleeping positions or the easiest passageways through the trees, they gradually establish the order of dominance they will carry with them into adult life. Gradually, too, they begin to have more contact with the older members of the group. One by one, each male subadult fights his way up the female hierarchy, dominating one female after another as he grows stronger and more confident. Eventually each will find a position among the adult males. When their period of adolescence finally ends, both females and males are equipped to take their places as fully adult members of the group. Without any formal course of instruction, simply by allowing their own tendencies to develop within the context of the group, they have learned all they need to know.

Other monkeys whose development has been studied are the baboons and macaques. The pattern they follow illustrates interesting social differences among the various genera in the male attitude toward the infants of a group. In a langur group, adult males are inclined to behave like the traditional Victorian father who kept himself apart from his young children. Langur males in captivity do show an interest in newborns, particularly male, but on the whole young langurs grow up in an almost exclusively matriarchal atmosphere. On the other hand, Japanese macaque males have been observed to cradle one- and two-year-old infants during the birth season. Paternal attention of this nature, which may persist for some time, is somewhat similar to that of hamadryas baboons. The subadult or young adult hamadryas male in fact acquires females for his eventual one-male (and many-female) family unit by first "mothering" infant females. For months—often a year or more—a young female enjoys a protective relationship with a male that is similar to the protection she received from her mother. The male readily carries the young female on his back, helps her over difficult terrain when she walks, and lets her huddle next to him at night. She will in due course become an adult member of his one-male group— his harem of females. In savanna baboon groups, adult males also show an intense interest in infants. They do not, however, assume responsibility for individual infants. Usually an adult male will approach a mother, smacking his lips to show he means no harm, in order to enjoy the pleasure of playing with the mother's infant. The savanna baboons live in multiple groups in which one male does not control a particular harem of females.

Why these differences? They are adaptations acquired in the interests of survival in different environments. Comfortable as some langur species are on the ground, no langur ever ventures more than a few yards from trees. The females do not require the male's protection and they usually do not get it. If a langur group is alarmed, it is every monkey for itself. Baboons are organized differently because they frequently move far from trees, and, if a predator approaches, females and infants alike depend on the adult males for protection. But an animal is hardly likely to risk its life to save a strange infant. In the course of their adaptation to life on the ground, baboon males have acquired a strong protective urge toward all infants that, in an emergency, gives males a motive to defend them.

**Dominance**  Part of growing up in most monkey and ape societies is establishing a place in the group's social hierarchy. In some species the social structure is loose; in others it is more rigid, with each animal having a precise rank in relation to the others. Often, as with langurs, the hierarchy is more significant among males than females; and females are submissive to males.

The phenomenon of male dominance is striking among macaques and chimpanzees and in many of the baboon troops that have been studied. Usually there is a dominant individual to whom the other males habitually defer; often two animals, sometimes as many as three or more, will team up as a coalition to hold a top position that none could hold alone. Below the top male (or males) the other adult males arrange themselves in descending order of authority. There is always a certain amount of jostling for position and occasionally some prolonged and bitter struggles for places at the top (Figure 6–10). Nevertheless, the overall dominance hierarchy tends to be remarkably stable. The high-ranking animals move confidently through their troop; the others defer to them as a matter of course in confrontations over food, females, selection of sleeping sites, grooming and being groomed, and so forth. The hierarchy may remain stable for long periods, although if a strange

FIGURE 6–10 *Confrontations among savanna baboons usually result in one individual either presenting its rump in defeat or scampering off. For these two wellmatched baboons, however, confrontation has resulted in fighting.*

animal enters the troop to stay, it may be involved in open conflicts until its place in the social structure is established. The dominant males take precedence when food is limited, making them most likely to survive in a famine; this is one way the characteristics that bring about dominance, such as strength and agility, are selected for in the troop.

Among baboons status is most important. A savanna baboon troop travels on the ground, where there is selective pressure to produce big, aggressive males to protect the troop against predators. As a result, there is marked *sexual dimorphism* in baboons; that is, the males are noticeably different from the females (Figure 6–11). They are much larger (often twice as heavy) and much stronger, have far bigger canine teeth and jaws, are a great deal more combative, and are less tolerant of lapses in behavior or threats to their status. These traits tend to create an authoritarian society in which a mere stare by a dominant male will remind a subordinate of the realities of its status.

Among baboons, as well as a number of other primate species, it is also the particular males, as we have seen (Chapter 4), who act as consorts to the females at the height of *estrus*, the period when a female is sexually receptive. Most of the characteristics that mark the dominant male baboon, such as his size, his large canine teeth, and his thick fur mantle, result from a high level of the hormone testosterone, the hormone that also governs his sexual activity. The baboon that dominates all others in the troop and heads the social hierarchy is termed the *alpha male*. Thus, the social dominance of a particular baboon is related to his personality, his strong sexual drive, and his physical appearance, all of which are heavily influenced by his testosterone level.

Following a very important long-term study by Shirley Strum of the baboon troops at Gilgil in Kenya, it has now become clear that adolescent males leave their home troops as a matter of course and move to neighboring troops. Here they will attempt to become assimilated by making friends with high-ranking females. The approach to the female will be made very slowly over a long period of time and in due course, if the male is accepted, he will begin to play with her infant for hours. Males generally make friends with infants as a means of winning female trust and neutralizing the aggression of other males. If such a male becomes accepted by the female, he courts her and becomes her "friend," and thereby becomes a full member of the troop. If he is sufficiently ingratiating and clever in developing his relationships, he may be able to copulate with his female or females at estrus. Recent evidence suggests that among the Gilgil baboons, sexual conquest can be achieved more effectively by building friendships than by achieving dominance in the male hierarchy.

Observation of baboons and better knowledge of blood relationships within the baboon troop have revealed that the long-term stability of the group depends not so much on the males but on certain high-ranking females that constitute an ongoing aristocracy of their own, based on mother-daughter and sister-sister ties. Once established, this aristocracy tends to perpetuate itself: the hierarchy of females is much more stable than that of males. The privileged—and usually related—females groom each other sociably, bringing up their infants in an atmosphere of comfort and security that is denied low-ranking females. The latter are

FIGURE 6–11   Hamadryas female with young, and male. The male is larger and heavier, and he carries a magnificent mane, which makes him look even larger.

forced to hang about at the edge of the group, alert to the possibility of a bite or a slap if they do not move aside for a higher-ranking animal. Unable to enter permanently into the established matriarchy at the center, they pass their timidity and generally low self-esteem on to their babies. Not surprisingly, the babies reared by the dominant mothers grow up with a far greater chance of achieving dominance themselves, having learned confidence and assurance from their mothers.

Among rhesus and Japanese macaques, an individual's rank within its age group is based on its mother's rank. Among baboons, this is also true within each sex, but males of any age consistently dominate females of similar age.

Stability is enhanced, then, by the fact that in most groups the hierarchy is based not only on male strength and aggressiveness but also on factors such as kinship and personality. But to understand more fully how dominance helps ensure a stable social structure, it is necessary to consider the part conflict plays in creating the hierarchy. Conflict can take three forms: play conflict, threat, and open conflict. The controlled and harmless conflict of young animals at play gives them the opportunity to develop precise motor control and coordination, but it also lays the foundation for their future social status. Once they reach adulthood, they seldom actually fight, normally relying on a threat to assert and maintain their relative positions. By averting open conflict, threat is obviously adaptive, for it avoids the risk of wounds and prevents constant strife within the troop. Every species has its own forms of threat signaling—an important form of communication in any social group (Figure 6–12). In addition to the part it plays in stabilizing the group itself, threat often will scare intruders away from the group's territory.

**Sexual Bonds**     As we saw earlier, Sir Solly Zuckerman's observations of baboons in the London Zoo during the 1930s led him to conclude that the members of primate groups are bound to each other by the urge to satisfy their sexual needs. In many mammals—deer are among the most familiar examples—males and females are together only during the breeding season, forming separate societies during the rest of the year. Because scientists generally believed that monkeys were sexually active the year around, they argued that sex was a logical explanation for the monkeys' staying together. This theory was bolstered by the effects of the crowded conditions under which primates often were studied in zoos or laboratories, for in such a situation animals use sexual behavior to establish dominance and submission, since many other means are not available. Studies of Japanese macaques at the Takasakiyama feeding station, for instance, revealed that a dominant male often will mount an inferior male—as he would when copulating with a female—to assert his right to a choice tidbit.

*FIGURE 6–12   Here a male savanna baboon is threatening the photographer. The main features of a baboon threat are the display of the immense canine teeth and the half-closed light-colored eyelids.*

Actually, as recent field studies have shown, many monkeys—for example, the rhesus and Japanese macaques—breed only in a specific season, and their closely knit societies continue even when there is no primary sexual activity. Thus, once again, the study of captive animals proved misleading. In the controlled environment of a laboratory, a monkey's endocrine system, which governs its sex hormones, is not subject to seasonal variations, and the monkey can copulate all the year around. In the wild, however, its hormones are influenced much more heavily by such external factors as day length, humidity, and diet, and the result is that most species copulate during only a few months of the year. The existence of a mating season is one means of ensuring that the young will be born at an auspicious time, when they are most likely to survive.

Consideration of the mating season brings us to an important physiological difference between the nonhuman primates and humankind. Although all primates have an *estrous cycle* (which in humans is somewhat different and is called the menstrual cycle) and although all cycles last approximately four weeks, humans alone lack the phase of "heat," or estrus, which is common to the majority of mammals. This, in higher primates, is a period of about three to five days when the female ovulates, shows (in the case of the chimpanzee and some monkeys) pronounced swelling of the genital region, and actively solicits male sexual attention.

Among savanna baboons, this is the period during which the chosen male will accompany the estrous female and keep all other males away. This *consort relationship* may last about three days and is believed to coincide with the period when fertilization is most probable. The male will copulate frequently with his mate during this period.

Female chimpanzees also present themselves for mating at this time only, during which they are both receptive and attractive to virtually all males in the band. In keeping with the generally relaxed, tolerant nature of chimpanzee society, mating in the wild is free of sexual jealousy; it is marked instead by a casual promiscuity. When a female is in estrus and eager to mate, any interested males in the troop must wait their turn—which should come soon, since copulation takes only a few seconds and is performed casually, sometimes while one of the protagonists offhandedly munches a banana and while curious youngsters look on or tug at the performing male. Dominant chimpanzee males, however, sometimes take females in estrus away alone "on safari," sometimes forcibly, for a few days or a week. During this period they form a temporary pair bond.

It has been observed that most higher primates do copulate throughout the estrous cycle, but that the female actively solicits copulation at estrus, and that at this time copulation reaches a peak frequency. Humans differ from nonhuman primates, for male humans are not aware of the period of estrus in females, which is no longer clearly apparent as in most other primates, but hidden.

The social structures of the apes are very varied. The gibbons and siamangs form family groups with one male and one female and young, and defend a small territory of forest with immense energy.

The orangutan, in contrast, is solitary. A female and its most recent young will travel together, but females without young and males lead solitary lives and come together only to mate.

The gorilla lives in family groups consisting of one senior silverback male, a number of mature females, and juveniles of both sexes. Maturing males will often leave the troop and forage alone until they are able to form their own harem.

Chimpanzees live in large mixed groups with many males (usually vying for dominance) and many females who form a relatively stable hierarchy. We shall return to the African apes toward the end of this chapter.

**Grooming**  Perhaps the most commonly observed form of social contact between higher primates is grooming. One monkey or ape grooms another by picking through its fur to clean out dirt, and also parasites and salt crystals, which it then eats. Physically, grooming is simply a cleaning mechanism, and it is highly effective, as one can see by comparing lions and baboons that inhabit the same area of the East African savanna. Although lions are clean animals, the backs of their necks, where they cannot reach to clean, are thick with ticks, whereas the baboons' hair is totally free of them.

But to primates, grooming is far more than a form of hygiene. It is the most important means of social interaction among members of a group, and it serves a variety of purposes. Though it usually occurs as part of the dominance ritual, grooming seems to be an effective instrument for reducing tension of all kinds, particularly among the more aggressive species, the baboons and macaques. At other times, it serves simply as an enjoyable pastime when the group is not in search of food. Much as humans gather in conversation groups, monkeys gather in grooming groups. The same function is served—the maintenance of friendly social relations. Being groomed is obviously enjoyable: the groomed animal sits or lies in an attitude of beatific contentment (Figure 6–13). Most grooming is done by females. Mothers regularly groom their young from birth. Equals groom each other in approximately equal amounts, while subordinates groom their social superiors much more frequently than they are groomed in turn. As one might expect, dominant males get the most grooming and give the least. There is, however, a semblance of reciprocity in a female's grooming of a male: after she has worked over him for perhaps ten minutes, she will turn and sit, inviting him to groom her. The male obliges by grooming her for about

FIGURE 6–13  *Grooming has two main functions: to remove parasites and keep the fur clean and to establish and maintain social relationships. Here a relaxed female encourages a dominant male to groom her, while a lower-ranking male watches from a proper distance.*

thirty seconds, then turns indolently and is groomed by the female for another ten minutes. The significant function of grooming in monkey society is that it cuts across hierarchical lines, establishing friendly relationships between individuals on various levels of the hierarchy who might not otherwise interact.

**Group Cohesiveness**   It seems clear that the degree of awareness exhibited by chimpanzees and baboons is such that they are not merely conscious of the activities and status of other troop members, but see deeper into personality. They show preferences; that is, they prefer to spend time with particular members of the troop, who may be their kin. In both species we see what looks very like friendship: certain pairs and trios (sometimes of different sex, but more often of the same) spend much time together and share experiences and food sources. When meat, a rare delicacy, is obtained, chimpanzees will share after the provider has had first pick; baboons will move aside to make room for a friend to get at the kill. It looks as if these primates are in some small way responding to each other's needs, even when they are adult and outside the mother-infant relationship. What we see is the innate altruism that rearing an infant implies being extended to reciprocal altruism between adults. Insofar as the members of a troop help one another, this behavior has an obvious adaptive value for the social group as a whole.

The degree of cohesiveness of a group, in fact, directly reflects the potential danger that threatens its members. Gorillas live in comparatively little day-to-day danger, and so individual male gorillas feel free to go off on their own, and many do—even for weeks at a time. The situation among Gombe chimpanzees, which are also in little danger, is somewhat similar. But they split into small units whose membership is constantly changing, and individuals often search for food alone, out of sight of the group's members. And chimpanzees seem little concerned with the safety of the group as a whole, because when alarmed, an individual chimpanzee will often make off without even giving a warning call.

It is quite common for male baboons and macaques to change groups, but most females probably pass their entire lives in the group into which they were born. Firm though group discipline may be, life need not be intolerable for a subordinate member. Living together from birth, the members of a group learn how to get along. Those who cannot stand each other keep at a distance. When tensions do arise, the monkeys involved usually stay apart until tempers have cooled. Only the attempts of one male to displace another in the hierarchy precipitate really vicious fighting. They crop up perhaps once every few months inside even a large group. But when every monkey knows its place, daily life is fairly peaceful.

For it is uncertainty that creates conflict. The hamadryas baboons in the London Zoo fought with savagery largely because they were strangers trapped and brought together from different troops, and they were too closely confined to avoid each other until differences could be settled more amicably.

In the wild, while the female hierarchy may be basically stable over long periods, it also shows some flexibility. This is because the behavior of a female is closely tied to the different phases of her reproductive cycle. As long as the female has a young infant she is so closely protected by the adult males that she is not subject to attacks from other females; during motherhood she is, in effect, almost outside the female hierarchy. A female in estrus is quite another matter. The word estrus is derived from the Greek *oistros*, a gadfly, and implies the frenzied behavior of an animal stung by such an insect. The estrous female is far more active than normal, both attacking other females and being attacked by them more frequently. Furthermore, when she is most attractive to adult males, at the height of estrus, she is often under the protection of an accompanying male and can use the status she derives from him to dominate a female normally superior to her. The result of this flexibility in the female hierarchy is a tendency to bickering, which is characteristic of female baboons and macaques. As we shall see, the situation among chimpanzees is different.

## ENVIRONMENT AND SOCIAL ORGANIZATION

The loss of estrus among humans was probably associated somehow with the development of increasingly permanent relationships between males and females. Thus it will be useful to consider here where that bond might have originated. The family unit we humans tend to take for granted—father, mother, and children—has no place among chimpanzees; though mother-infant and sibling-sibling ties are prolonged, there are no social fathers, nor can biological fathers often be identified. There is plenty of food in the forest (no need for a fatherly provider) and few predators (no need for a fatherly protector). Nor are there visible pair bonds among the East African savanna baboons, even though they are somewhat more subject to predators. Such bonds are present, however, in some other monkey societies, notably the gelada and hamadryas species, and among some langurs. The gelada and hamadryas baboons live in open country that is generally drier and has greater seasonal variations in climate, and hence in availability of food, than either the forest habitat of the chimpanzee or the woodland savanna home of East African baboons, where food is relatively abundant the year around (Figure 6–14).

FIGURE 6–14  The sleeping trees, to which a savanna baboon troop returns each night, are an essential feature in the home range of every troop in open savanna country. In this photograph, the troop has left its grove of acacia trees at dawn and is preparing to move out into the open grasslands to feed.

These environmental differences coincide with differences in social organization, a phenomenon first described by the British ethologist John H. Crook. Crook has studied the social organizations of many animals, including certain African weaver birds and antelopes as well as baboons. What struck him is the apparent uniformity with which all these otherwise entirely different creatures react to similar environmental change. So striking were his findings that he has used them as the basis for a hypothesis: *under similar environmental conditions, social animals will tend to develop similar social organizations.* Crook's conclusions about social organization are based on complex and subtle evidence that is beyond the scope of this volume. A look at three African monkey societies in the next few pages should make his point clear, however.

## Use of Territory by Baboons

The relationship between the social group and its environment is ultimately determined by the distribution and density of the natural resources essential to the group's survival, the density of competing animals, and by the pressure of predators. The social group becomes associated with a recognizable area of land or forest—called the *home range*—which contains sufficient space, food, water, and safe sleeping sites for all its members. Behavioral mechanisms bring about this spacing, which reduces the possibility of overexploitation of food resources and of conflict over those resources. The home range of savanna baboons may be partly shared with other groups of the same species; it is usually shared with other species. Within this range, it is usually possible to define a smaller area—called the *core area*—containing the resources absolutely essential for survival; in this case sleeping trees (Figure 6–15). The core areas becomes *defended territory* when it is actively defended against intruders from neighboring groups.

An overlapping home range pattern is characteristic of most monkeys and apes. Among gibbons and some monkeys, when the food supply is either very rich or sparse yet concentrated, and thus the area of required resources is small, the home range may be reduced to a defended territory, a smaller region that nongroup members will not be allowed to enter. In this case, which is the exception rather than the rule, threats are used to maintain control of the territory and its essential resources.

## Adapting to Different Environments

Baboons are extremely adaptable animals; they have not become as physically specialized as many other animals, and they are thus able to suit themselves to a wide variety of living conditions. With no material culture to rely on, however, baboons must change their social organization in order to adapt to different environmental conditions.

Of three species, the East African savanna baboon lives in the easiest surroundings: close to trees to which it can flee and in which it can

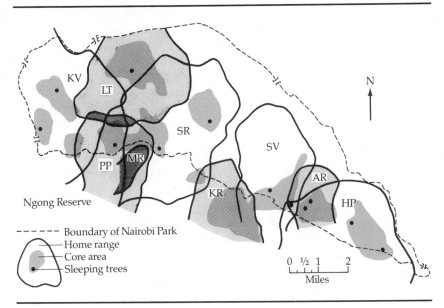

*FIGURE 6–15   This plan shows the home ranges and core areas of the baboon troops in the Nairobi Park. The home ranges overlap considerably, but the core areas, which contain the baboon's sleeping trees, essential to each troop, are quite distinct. (The letters refer to the different troops studied by Washburn and DeVore.)*

sleep, and in a climate where there is a year-round abundance of food. In this setting the troop is the all-important social unit; family relationships, except for mother-infant ties, are secondary. The nearest thing to a social father is a dominant male that, as a matter of course, exercises authority over some or all of the females in the troop. This male may be the biological father of many of the youngest infants, but that cannot be certain.

By contrast, geladas (a related genus but not a true baboon) are confined to mountain slopes in Ethiopia. There the climate is harsher, seasonal change is greater, trees are very rare, and food availability is more chancy. Male-female relationships, too, are very different from those which prevail on the savanna. The animals are found in large herds that, in areas or seasons of poor food supply, break down during the day into a number of wide-foraging separate units, each containing a single adult male with one or more females and assorted young (*polygynous* groups). The value of this arrangement is obvious: during times of food shortage, adequate food for females and young is far more important for the survival of the species as a whole than is food for extra males. Also, when food is short, more ground must be covered. So long as there is one strong male to protect the females, other males can be regarded as surplus, useful only for replacement or for forming new families of their own with young females. With this social structure the relationship between a particular male and females is far more durable than it is among savanna baboons. In that respect it resembles the human nuclear family unit more closely than does the organization of the savanna baboon troop. Significantly, when the wet season comes to the dry Ethiopian hills and food starts to be more abundant, the one-male groups coalesce into the larger multimale troops.

Hamadryas society is different again. This baboon lives in country even drier than the gelada's terrain, in rocky sections of Ethiopia and the near-desert of Somalia. In this environment one-male groups are the rule the year round, though for safety many groups come together at night on the sleeping cliffs. The male-female relationship is more close-knit than among geladas. Each hamadryas male is continuously jealous of its harem, requiring its females to stay very close to it at all times. When it moves, they move—or get bitten.

The implication of this short review of baboon adaptations is that the social and sexual patterns of behavior expressed by a primate species are to a great extent a response to a particular environment. There is some reason to believe that the one-male harem pattern may be the basic primitive pattern. If so, then the savanna baboon's and the chimpanzee's social adaptation of a large multimale troop could be considered no more than the product of the abundant food supply available to these species. It seems reasonable, therefore, to envisage the early evolution of the human family as an adaptive response to savanna conditions that either maintained or created one-male polygynous social groups.

**THE APES**     The environmental adaptations of the monkeys and their social organization make their study of particular interest to us; but it is, of course, not the monkeys but the apes that are our closest relatives among nonhuman primates.

**Asiatic Apes:**     The gibbon and orangutan are Asiatic species. By a great number of
**Gibbon and Orangutan**     external and internal measurements, including genetic ones, they are remarkably different from chimpanzees and gorillas. In fact they are in some ways less like a chimpanzee than humans are. This difference indicates a separation far back in time, before the separation of human, gorilla, and chimpanzee.

As we have seen, both the gibbon and orangutan are tree-dwelling animals today. Millions of years of climbing and total reliance on the fruits that grow in jungle trees have brought them to an extreme point of arboreal specialization. In the trees, they move superbly, each in its own way. The gibbon (Figure 6–16) is an airy flier that hangs from branches, swinging from one to another in a breathtaking arc, grabbing the next branch just long enough to launch itself in the direction of a

*FIGURE 6–16   A gibbon hangs by an arm and steadies itself with a foot while feeding. See also Figure 6–6.*

third. With this animal, arms and hands are everything. Its fingers are extremely long, specialized to serve as powerful hooks to catch branches. As a result of this finger specialization the gibbon has the poorest manual dexterity of any ape. And being the smallest ape, it has the smallest brain.

The orangutan is quite different (Figure 6–17). It is much larger: adult males weigh over 150 pounds, compared to the gibbons' 10 to 15 pounds. Obviously an animal of this size cannot go careening through the branches. Orangutans have developed four prehensile hands well-adapted for seizing or holding, and their limbs are so articulated that they can reach in any direction. There is almost nowhere in a tree that an orangutan cannot safely go, despite its great bulk, by careful gripping and climbing.

As we have seen, the gibbon and orangutan are most unusual socially among higher primates. When these specialized animals are compared with the general-purpose monkey-ape model that was probably ancestral to all higher primates, it is clear that the gibbon and orangutan have evolved in a direction entirely different from the one that might have led to humanity. Each is fully specialized for arboreal life. The gorillas and chimpanzees of Africa, on the other hand, have not traveled the exclusively arboreal route: they are both in different degrees adapted to ground dwelling.

## Gorillas: Research of Fossey

Most of what we know of the gorilla comes from the work of Dian Fossey, who began her extensive observations of mountain gorillas in 1967 and founded a research center in Rwanda that is still active. Fossey quickly discovered that, far from being the ferocious beasts of legend, gorillas are generally mild-mannered vegetarians who like to mind their own business (Figure 6–18).

While the orangutan and gibbon have evolved into specialized tree-dwellers, the gorilla's development has taken the direction of a great increase in size, along with a dietary switch from the fruit and leaves found in trees to a more general menu of fresh bark, larger leaves, roots, bamboo shoots, and other plants—herbal as much as arboreal vegetation. These two specializations of size and diet go together: we may suppose size and strength have been selected because other animals will not attack the gorilla while it is on the ground eating. And because the gorilla is so large, it needs a great deal of just the kind of coarse vegetation that it finds in large quantities in the places it inhabits. This great ape retains the equipment for climbing and reaching—the long arms, the deft hands, the good brain. Young gorillas are frisky and venturesome in the trees, but their elders are essentially ground animals. Having carved out a successful niche for themselves there, they have apparently been relatively stable members of the African rain forest community for millions of years.

FIGURE 6–17   The orangutan of Indonesian Sumatra and Kalimantan (Borneo) is the most seriously threatened of the great apes. It has immensely long arms and relatively short legs with short thumbs and big toes. It is mainly arboreal but does cover considerable distances on the ground in emergencies. This is a juvenile.

With no predators to fear except humans, and plenty of food available, the gorillas Fossey encountered lived in a state of mild and amiable serenity (Figure 6–19). Most of them live in groups of five to twenty, each group led by a powerful silverback male, so called for the saddle of grizzled silver hair that the males grow when they reach the age of ten. His dominance over the group is absolute, but normally genial. Occasionally a young gorilla will get too frolicsome and be silenced by a glare or a threatening slap on the ground from an adult. Sometimes a couple of females will begin to scream at each other until the leader glares at them, when they promptly calm down. Except for particularly irascible silverbacks, the leaders are usually quite approachable. Females nestle against them and infants crawl happily over their huge bodies. When a band of gorillas is at rest, the young play, the mothers tend their infants, and the other adults lie at peace and soak up the sun.

Like humans, gorillas yawn and stretch when they awake in the morning, and sit, dangling their legs over the sides of their nests. They pick their noses, scratch themselves when puzzled, and, if nervous or excited, they often begin to eat vigorously, much as a person might pull at a cigarette. Though there is great individual variation of temperament among gorillas, there is about them a curious reserve; they are normally rather quiet creatures and rarely use their immense strength.

Nonetheless, gorillas can exhibit strong feelings, especially when they feel threatened. They scream in alarm and as a warning to other members of the group. They toss leaves in the air. They also beat their chests. All gorillas, even very young ones, do this, rising up on two legs on the ground, or popping up amid the foliage of a tree to give a few brief slaps before fading out of sight. The full performance, however, which is given in response to more serious threat or high anxiety, is put on only by the silverback males, and it is as formal as the entrance of a fighter into the prize ring. It begins inconspicuously with a series of soft, clear hoots that gradually quicken. Already, the silverback expects to command attention because, if interrupted, he is liable to look around in annoyance. As he continues to hoot, he may stop, pluck a leaf from a plant nearby and place it between his lips. This curiously incongruous and delicate gesture is a prelude to coming violence, and when they see it, the other gorillas get out of the way. The violence is not immediate. First the gorilla rises to his full height and slaps his hands on his chest or his belly, on his thigh, or on another gorilla, producing a booming sound that can be heard a mile away. The chest beating over, the violence erupts. He runs sideways for a few steps, then he drops down on all fours and breaks into a full-speed dash, wrenching branches from trees and slapping at everything in his way, including any group members who do not have the wit to keep clear. Finally, there comes the last gesture: the silverback thumps the palm of his hand violently on the ground, and then sits back, looking as if he is now ready to hear the applause.

Though gorillas present a mild demeanor to the outside world, protected as they are by their immense strength, they can be aggressive in rivalry between males over females and in other aspects of reproductive behavior. Males reaching full maturity as young silverbacks can form their own family groups only by kidnapping females from other groups, by usurping the dominant silverback male (probably their father) in their own group, or by awaiting his death. Sometimes the females will support an up-and-coming male against an older one. The group leaders in turn have to defend their own females against kidnapping and maintain their authority over their groups. The kidnapping can usually be carried out by stealth as much as by overt aggression, but the takeover of a group from an aging male may be a very unpleasant affair. Sometimes two ambitious young silverbacks will fight each other; one or more of the older females may be killed, and quite often the youngest infant or infants are killed by the victorious male. (A similar bout of infanticide has been observed among some other primates, such as Indian langur monkeys. In this species it follows the takeover of a troop by a new dominant male, and has the effect of bringing the bereaved mothers quickly back into estrus. The new male will then copulate with the females who will now rear his progeny rather than the young of his predecessors.) In this way the newly promoted dominant male can begin mating and start his own family without further delay. This behavior has presumably been selected because it brings about the greatest multiplication of the group leader's genes.

Here we see sexual selection in action. The intermale rivalry described by Darwin is selecting sexual dimorphism: relatively large males, with powerful jaws and large canine teeth. Thus some features of gorilla dentition are associated not with diet but with patterns of behavior that have evolved as a result of the social structure of the species.

FIGURE 6–18   In Central Africa, Dian Fossey walks through the forest near her isolated field station with two young mountain gorillas. She has studied this endangered species in its native habitat since 1967. (Bob Campbell, © National Geographic Society)

## Goodall and the Gombe Chimpanzees

As with the gorilla, long and devoted field observations have helped us understand something of chimpanzee behavior. Louis Leakey knew of a troop of chimpanzees that lived in a hilly wooded tract near the Gombe Stream, a river running into Lake Tanganyika in western Tanzania. He was interested in anything that had to do with primates; furthermore, he believed that the present-day stream, with its woodland and grassland environment, closely resembled the environment of Olduvai 2 million years ago. He persuaded Jane Goodall to undertake a study of the Gombe troop.

When Goodall arrived in what is now the Gombe Stream Chimpanzee Reserve in 1960, she set up camp near the lake shore and began to spend her days roaming the hills and valleys, looking for chimpanzees

*FIGURE 6–19   Here mountain gorillas (the silverback is on the left) relax on a fallen tree after a morning's feeding. The Central African mountain environment in which these animals live has very high rainfall and the vegetation is lush. The group size averages eight animals.*

in an area of about fifteen square miles. Her plan was to watch the animals discreetly, not getting too close, just accustoming them to her presence, as a preliminary to closer acquaintance. Many months later she was still watching from a distance, still treated with suspicion by the shy chimpanzees. Ultimately, after a period of rejection that would

have discouraged a less dedicated person, she was accepted, not by all the chimpanzees but by many of them (Figure 6–20). She became very friendly with a few of them. Eventually she spent thousands of hours with them, sometimes in actual physical contact—handing out bananas, playing with a baby—more often just sitting quietly and watching a society of unimagined subtlety and complexity gradually unfold.

Two years after Goodall's arrival, a photographer, Hugo van Lawick, came to the reserve and underwent a similar process of scrutiny, familiarization, and slow acceptance, before the animals would act naturally in his presence. But in testimony to the chimpanzees' intelligence, they associated him with their human friend and accepted him in only a month. Goodall's studies and van Lawick's pictures of the Gombe troop (published in a book called *In the Shadow of Man*) reveal the chimpanzee to be an animal whose nature and social organization provoke all kinds of speculations about the emergence of humankind.

Ordinarily, when we look at the great apes in zoos, our vision is clouded by seeing them through the distorting glass of modern human eyes and in a setting that is so overwhelmingly humanized that the apes tend to look a great deal more simple-minded, a great deal more vulnerable, a great deal less competent than they actually are. But take humans back a few million years, divest them of all their accomplishments and social progress—all the things that now threaten the survival of the chimpanzee and gorilla—and the gulf between human and ape shrinks. Humans become less impressive, and apes more so, particularly when the work of scientists like Fossey and Goodall reveals how subtle and complex primate societies are.

Of all the great apes, the chimpanzee is, as mentioned, the least specialized. In size it is a neat compromise: small enough to get about in trees, and big enough to take care of itself on the ground against predators, particularly since it usually travels in bands, which are sections of a whole troop or community. As a result, it is at home in both worlds. Although still a fruit eater whose favorite staple is ripe figs, it will eat a wide variety of other fruit and vegetation, together with some meat: birds' eggs or fledglings, insects, lizards, or small snakes, and occasionally a young baboon, colobus monkey, or bush pig.

FIGURE 6–20 *Jane Goodall has been a pioneer in the study of wild animals. By undertaking a long behavioral study of wild chimpanzees since 1960, she has contributed greatly to our understanding both of chimpanzees and, by implication, of ourselves.*

**The Chimpanzee as Hunter**

Goodall reports that a hunting chimpanzee is unmistakable. Compared with other chimpanzee behaviors, there is something out of the ordinary about hunting behavior, observed only among males. There is, in it, something purposeful, tense, and inward that other chimpanzees recognize and respond to. Sometimes they just watch the hunter intently. Sometimes other males move to adjacent trees to cut off the escape of the quarry, a young baboon or small arboreal monkey. On several occasions observed by Goodall, the quarry was a young baboon whose

FIGURE 6–21   *The upper chimpanzee is holding the rib cage of a small monkey; the two lower chimpanzees are begging. When it has eaten enough, the hunter will share the remains of the kill.*

screams brought adult baboons rushing to its defense. In the ensuing hullabaloo the youngster more often than not escaped. But Goodall saw chimpanzees eating infant baboons often enough to realize that a small but fairly steady toll was taken of them.

Chimpanzees are excited by meat and clearly very fond of it. They chew it long and reflectively, usually with a mouthful of leaves added. Wads of this mixture are occasionally given to other begging chimps. Sometimes the carcass is shared by the successful hunter, who tears off pieces and hands them out (Figure 6–21). The curious thing about meat eating and meat sharing is that when these activities are going on, regular dominance patterns do not apply. A high-ranking chimpanzee that would not hesitate to assert itself over a lowly one for possession of fruit will respect its right to the possession of meat. Apparently something about having killed an animal gives an individual the right to keep it.

The revelation that chimpanzees hunt and eat meat—and share it as well, albeit often reluctantly—has enormous implications in explaining the development of hunting and sharing among hominids. We shall return to this important question in Chapter 9. It now becomes possible to speculate that these traits were brought to the savanna from the forest. We no longer have to puzzle over how a propensity for meat eating got started in a creature with a fruit-eating ancestry; it was probably there, as we now know it is in most primates. All it needed was encouragement in a new environment.

## The Chimpanzee as Tool User

Although chimpanzees are tool users and toolmakers in a limited way, they do not *need* tools. Nevertheless we know that the chimpanzee can develop a tradition of elementary tool use. We cannot know when the chimpanzees at Gombe first learned to fish for termites with straws (as we saw one do in Figure 6–7) or how long this took to become an established activity. Goodall has shown that each new generation learns it from the previous one. The youngsters have an opportunity to learn from their elders: they watch them intently, often copying what they do.

FIGURE 6–22 *Throwing stones and other objects is typical of chimpanzees trying to scare a threatening intruder or merely letting off steam.*

Another talent Goodall observed among the Gombe chimpanzees was for throwing things. Her accounts reveal that this activity was well established in the Gombe troop; a number of males tried it, and under a variety of circumstances. Even often woefully inaccurate throwing seems useful to a chimpanzee. In chimpanzee life there is a great deal of bluffing and aggressive display. During such activity an animal will jump up and down, wave its arms, hoot, shriek, and charge forward. This behavior looks especially disconcerting if it is accompanied by a shower of sticks or trash or stones (Figure 6–22). The fact that throwing is useful as an aggressive display explains why it is now established as part of the species' behavior.

At its present stage of throwing development, the chimpanzee is scarcely a star athlete, by human standards. Through lack of practice it cannot throw far or accurately—it cannot count on hitting anything more than four or five feet away. But the performance does not have to impress humans, only other chimpanzees, baboons, leopards, and the like. For that audience the display is extremely effective. Throwing clearly has selective value, and we can speculate that if chimpanzees are left to themselves long enough they might become better throwers than they now are.

Even now, potential for improvement exists among individual chimpanzees. There was one such at the Gombe Stream called Mr. Worzle (Goodall named all the chimpanzees as fast as she could recognize them, for ease of identification). Mr. Worzle accomplished the remarkable feat of becoming a superior stone thrower as a result of being exposed to an unusual challenge. In order to attract the troop to the camp area, where it could be more easily observed, Goodall made a practice of putting out bananas. This unnatural concentration of food also attracted baboons that lived in the vicinity, leading to abrasive confrontations. The baboons quickly learned which chimpanzees, mostly females and juveniles, they could intimidate by rushing at them. But they never could dislodge Mr. Worzle, who stood his ground, picking up whatever was handy and throwing it at them. Sometimes it was leaves. Once, to the delight of the baboons, it was a bunch of bananas. But slowly Mr. Worzle learned that rocks were best, and as time went on he depended more and more on rocks and started using bigger and bigger ones. Mr. Worzle's response indicates the ability to improvise that exists in an intelligent and physically adept animal when confronted by a new situation or given an opportunity to deal with an old one in a new way.

Recent work has revealed that encounters between primate troops or—in the case of chimpanzees—communities may in fact be sought and may become very aggressive. The best data come from Goodall's observations at Gombe. Here it was observed that parties of up to ten adult males, sometimes accompanied by females and young, may patrol peripheral areas near the boundary of the home range and actively search for signs of neighboring groups. Contact may result in displays until one or both groups give up or flee and return to the core area of their range. When single chimpanzees or very small parties are encountered, they may be chased and even attacked, often brutally, especially if they are females. Males have been observed setting out as a small group with the clear intention of stalking a neighbor. They silently move through the forest, avoiding the crackle of branches or leaves underfoot. Such behavior is known to have resulted in what can only be called brutal murder, clearly cold-blooded and calculated. Jane Goodall has recently described the last few years at Gombe as a four-year war, during which time an entire community was annihilated, so that the victorious males and their females were able to move into the unoccupied territory. This behavior looks all too familiar, and the whole question of intercommunity relations and aggression among chimpanzees is now a subject of active research. Its understanding is important to those studying the evolution and nature of human violence. At present, only humans and chimpanzees share this behavior of murderous intent and the calculated killing of members of their own species.

## Chimpanzee Politics

Studying chimpanzees and gorillas in the wild may seem the ultimate step in behavioral research, yet it has one serious disadvantage. It is extremely difficult to follow the behavior of groups of individuals for long periods in great detail; trees and undergrowth, the natural shyness of wild animals, and their tendency to move about, can interrupt observations at critical moments. On the other hand, observations of captive apes are unreliable insofar as their behavior is distorted in captivity by the unnatural conditions under which they live.

In 1971, an attempt was made to overcome this problem. A large two-acre moated enclosure was built at the Burger's Zoo, in Arnhem, Holland. Here a group of chimpanzees was settled—males, females and young—and they have developed into a most successful breeding colony that now numbers twenty-five individuals. Observation platforms were built, and observers were able to watch the behavior of inmates in extraordinary detail. In his *Chimpanzee Politics*, Frans de Waal describes the social life of these chimpanzees in a way that was never before possible. What he has found is truly remarkable—that the chimpanzees exhibit political behavior (defined as social manipulation designed to secure and maintain power status) of a kind previously believed to be found only among humans.

Throughout the past two decades, since Jane Goodall began her research at Gombe, we have been surprised (and delighted) again and again by the extent to which chimpanzees have been found to foreshadow humans in their social behavior. First the greeting and nursing behaviors, then the intermale competition, then their interest in using and making tools, then their enthusiasm for hunting, then their aggression, ambition, and apparent cold-blooded cruelty. Now, de Waal reveals to us that the whole social structure is based on political infighting; that whole passages of Machiavelli (who described the political manipulation of the Italian popes and the influential princely families such as the Medici and Borgias) seem to be directly applicable to chimpanzees; that the struggle for power and the resultant opportunism is so marked among chimpanzees that their social organization seems almost too human to be true. But it is true. The observations are sound, their interpretation unavoidable. Not all the political mechanisms seen at Arnhem are necessarily present in all wild communities, but they probably are present, and there is no doubt that the potential for this kind of political maneuvering is indeed part of chimpanzee nature.

The main difference between the wild and captive chimpanzees is quite superficial: the wild animals spend most of their waking hours in the quest for food. In contrast, the captive chimpanzees were fed daily, each evening, and therefore have far more leisure at their disposal to devote to politics and intrigue.

The work at Arnhem has given us important insights into many areas of chimpanzee behavior, which we can only briefly summarize here. In the first place, there is usually a clear-cut rank order, at least among the dominant individuals. The urge to power is a primary determinant of all male behavior. Second, female relationships are less hierarchic but much more stable than those of males. Senior females may be very influential and may even mediate between competing males. They may also confiscate a rock from the hand of an angry male!

Hidden beneath the power struggle and its resultant hierarchy is a network of positions of influence. Thus the most influential troop members at Arnhem were the oldest male and oldest female, no longer dominant in the obvious sense, but highly influential and able to pull strings behind the scenes. Newly dominant individuals were usually much less influential and dependent on coalition and alliance. Thus there is an overt and a covert aspect to chimpanzee politics. Altogether, power politics reigns supreme and is able to give chimpanzee society a logical coherence and even a democratic base. Every individual searches for social significance and continues to do so until a temporary balance is achieved, determining new hierarchic positions. Thus the hierarchy is a cohesive structure and brings stability that makes possible effective child care, play, cooperation, and undisturbed sexual activity. But the balance of power is tested daily, and if found to be weak is challenged: then the social structure is rebuilt.

At Arnhem, it appears that the rewards of power are more limited than in nature, for food is rationed and fairly distributed among the chimpanzees. Thus the rewards to males of high status were mainly sexual: access to estrous females. This limitation, however, did not prevent the apes from exhibiting almost every political subterfuge known to humans, including dominance networks and coalitions, power struggles, alliances, divide-and-rule strategies, arbitration, confiscation, collective leadership, privileges, bargaining, and frequent reconciliations (which usually take the form of kissing, open-mouthed). Almost all these behaviors have been at least briefly observed or suspected at Gombe, but they were never recorded with the frequency or in the detail made possible at Arnhem.

It is impossible in this book to describe the complexity and subtlety of chimpanzee politics. The reader should consult de Waal's short and very readable book. It is clear, however, that in terms of socialization, chimpanzee sensitivity, ambition, relationships, and social complexity differ very little from our own, and that the difference between us lies not so much in the level of social evolution, but in the appearance of human language. This event must have helped, surely, to define and stabilize relationships and social roles in the continuing power struggle that evidently characterized the evolution of human society.

Although it is clearly wrong to suppose that the behavior of the earliest hominids was exactly like that of gorillas or chimpanzees, or indeed any living primates, we can nevertheless draw certain conclusions and derive certain insights from our studies of primate behavior. We can be reasonably sure that the earliest hominids showed many of the social and individual characteristics that higher primates share with each other. It also seems probable that the earliest hominids were at least as intelligent and inventive as the African apes are today. These ideas will form a starting point for our explorations of early hominid behavior that follow in Chapter 9.

# Chapter 7

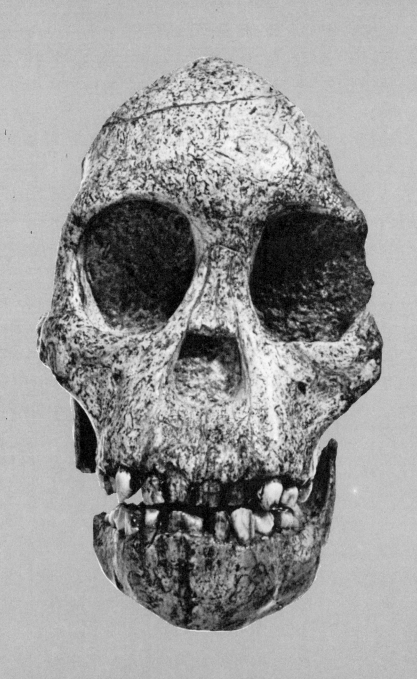

# The Transvaal Hominids

In each great region of the world the living mammals are closely related to the extinct species of the same region. It is, therefore, probable that Africa was formerly inhabited by extinct apes closely allied to the gorilla and chimpanzee; and as these two species are now man's nearest allies, it is somewhat more probable that our early progenitors lived on the African continent than elsewhere.

CHARLES DARWIN, 1809–1882.
*The Descent of Man.*

The importance of bipedalism—two-leggedness—cannot be overestimated. Bipedalism is much more than a mere rearing up and running about. Apes and monkeys have all sorts of structural handicaps that hamper them in this respect: they stand with knees bent, unable to extend their legs fully; they walk on the sides of their feet. They can move on two legs and sometimes do for short distances, but they are not made for it. Humans, however, cannot function properly in any other way. Somehow, somewhere, in the late Miocene or Pliocene, the adaptations of bipedalism made their appearance in at least one kind of primate.

## DART'S DISCOVERY OF THE TAUNG SKULL (1924)

The first tangible evidence that a two-legged primate existed in the distant past came from an unexpected place, the Transvaal region of South Africa. Raymond Dart (b. 1893), professor of anatomy at the University of the Witwatersrand in Johannesburg, South Africa, encouraged his students to send him rock fragments that contained fossils. In 1924, a student brought him an unusual fossil baboon skull that had come from a limestone quarry at a place named Taung, 200 miles from Johannesburg (see Figure 7–1). Hoping to obtain more fossils, particu-

161

FIGURE 7–1   *The earliest knowledge of* Australopithecus *came from the Transvaal in South Africa. At a number of sites in this area fossils were preserved in caves and hollows in the dolomite bedrock. Although their absolute age is not accurately known, they are broadly dated between 3 and 1 million years B.P.*

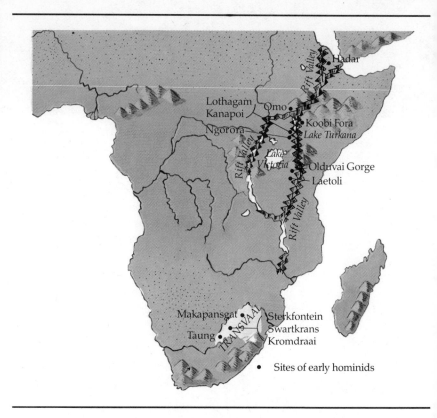

larly another baboon skull, Dart persuaded the quarry owner to save bone-bearing rocks, and in due course he was sent two boxes of broken rock containing fossils.

Dart found nothing of interest in the first box, but his eye hit on something very strange in the second. On the top of the heap lay, not a skull, but the next best thing to it: an oddly shaped rounded piece of rock that appeared to be the mold of the inside of a skull. Scarcely allowing himself to think what this might mean, Dart went through the rest of the box and found another piece of rock with a curved depression into which this mold fitted—the skull itself. In this second rock Dart could dimly perceive the outline of a broken piece of skull and the back of a lower jaw. He was looking from the rear at the inside of something's, or somebody's, head.

A fossilized cast of the skull of any species of primate would have been a notable discovery, but one look at this antique fragment sent Dart's mind racing. Here was no fossil baboon. The animal's brain capacity appeared to be three times larger than an ancient baboon's, and perhaps even larger than a modern adult chimpanzee's. The exciting thought struck Dart that he might be holding in his hands the "missing link" between ape and human.

Dart's first problem was to free the rest of the strange skull from the surrounding stone. Working with a hammer, chisels, and a sharpened knitting needle, he "pecked, scraped and levered" bits of stone from the front of the skull and the eye sockets. After days of painstaking dissection, an incredible face began to emerge. Rather than the long projecting jaw and large canine teeth that clearly identify both existing and fossil baboons, this face had the relatively smaller jaw and the more nearly vertical face of an ape; yet it was not overhung by the low brow of an ape, but surmounted by a forehead. From then on, Dart lay awake nights "in a fever of thoughts" about what kind of ape might have lived long ago on that grassy plateau.

Apes lived in tropical forests, but there have been no such forests in South Africa for more than a hundred million years. While ice advanced and retreated over much of the earth, and while mountains rose along the continental coasts, South Africa had always remained a dry, relatively undisturbed veld, much as it is today. Throughout prehistory, the nearest natural habitat of apes was more than 2,000 miles north of Taung. Could some different kind of ape have found a way to adapt itself to life in an arid, open land?

**The Evidence and Dart's Interpretation**

Dart continued his exacting labor with the baffling fossil until, on the seventy-third day of work, the stone parted and he saw before him the face and most of the skull of a child five or six years old (page 160 and Figure 7–2). It had a full set of milk teeth; the permanent molars were just beginning to erupt, and the canines, like those of humans, were quite small. After Dart studied his find more carefully, he realized that the set of the skull suggested that the child had walked upright. One thing that made him feel sure he was dealing with a true bipedal creature was the position of the *foramen magnum*, the large hole through which the spinal cord passes into the skull on its way to the brain. In apes and monkeys the foramen magnum is near the back of the skull, reflecting the sloping position of the spinal column in quadrupedal posture. But in the Taung skull it faced almost directly downward (Figure 7–3): the Taung child had carried its head over its spine like a rock balanced on the top of a pole. Whatever verdict the scientific establishment would eventually pass on the Taung child, Dart was certain that the creature had stood erect.

All previous discoveries of human predecessors had proved in the end to be authentic, if early, human beings, including Neandertal man and Java man. All are now classified as *Homo* despite certain primitive features. The child's face before Dart seemed the reverse: an ape with human features. It could not possibly be a human. It was too primitive, too small-brained. A prehuman, then, a link with the ape past? Taking

FIGURE 7–2    *In 1924 Raymond Dart startled the anthropological world by his discovery of a small fossil skull from a quarry at Taung in South Africa. (The height of the skull and jaw is about 5 inches.) The following year he named the Taung specimen* Australopithecus africanus *and boldly declared it to be a human ancestor. His claim was derided, but finds made many years later proved his fossil was indeed hominid.*

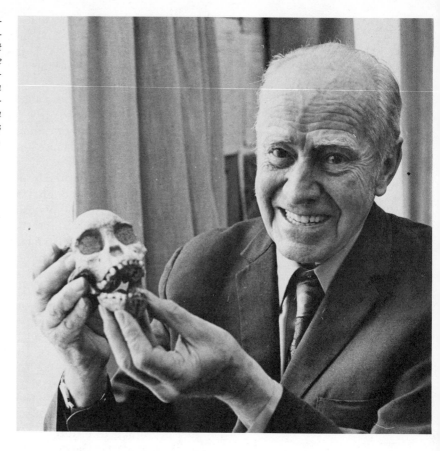

a deep breath, Dart announced to the world in 1925 that he had found a human ancestor that was not yet human. He gave it the formidable name of *Australopithecus africanus* (from *australis,* southern; and *pithekos,* ape)—African southern ape.

Because he was so confident of the significance of his find, Dart publicized his momentous news in record time. Less than four months after the skull had come into his hands, he wrote a full scientific report for the February 7, 1925, issue of the British magazine *Nature.* His report included the provocative statement, "The specimen is of importance because it exhibits an extinct race of apes intermediate between living anthropoids and man . . . a creature well advanced beyond modern anthropoids in just those characters, facial and cerebral, which are to be anticipated in an extinct link between man and his simian ancestor." That day, in South Africa and around the world, the headlines proclaimed that the missing link had been found. Actually, it was also the first link in a long chain of discoveries that would establish Africa as the probable place of origin of humankind.

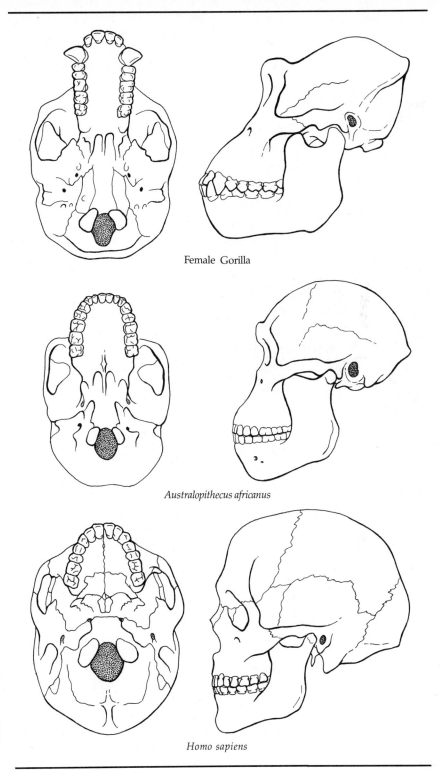

Female Gorilla

*Australopithecus africanus*

*Homo sapiens*

FIGURE 7–3  *Improvement in the balance of the head during human evolution has involved movement of the occipital condyles and associated foramen magnum (shown stippled) forward. (The occipital condyles are the bearing surfaces of the skull on the uppermost vertebra—the atlas; the foramen magnum is the hole in the base of the skull through which the spinal cord passes.) In this important character of the skull base,* Australopithecus *is intermediate between apes (here a gorilla (top) is illustrated) and modern humans (bottom). Scale approximately one-third actual size.*

## Dart's Claims Dismissed

FIGURE 7–4   *Dr. Robert Broom was a passionate fossil hunter and distinguished paleontologist. He kept working until his death at age 85.*

Dart's report was intensely interesting to a number of scientists in Europe, not so much for the human attributes he claimed for the Taung creature as for the inexplicable presence of an ape so far south. The general conclusion was that this was a young specimen of an ancient chimpanzeelike or gorillalike species; but how it had wandered where no ape had ever before been known to go was extremely puzzling. As a result, Dart's claims about the Taung child had to endure a long period of skepticism.

This suspicion may seem strange. After all, anthropologists spend their lives looking for increasingly primitive, ever more apelike fossils. Why are they so reluctant to recognize one when it turns up? There are numerous reasons. For one, there are many false alarms. If this book were to catalogue all the mistaken claims about hominid fossils made by layman and expert alike, it would have to be far longer than it is. At the time that Dart discovered the Taung skull, the fraudulent Piltdown skull (Chapter 10) represented the generally held concept of our early ancestors. It suggested that early humans already had large brains but still had apelike faces—a concept that satisfies modern human vanity, with its emphasis on the special quality of the human intellect. Dart's fossil was not so agreeable. It suggested the opposite: that face and teeth began to become recognizably human while the brain was still very small. And so anthropologists were cautious, even prejudiced, and attacks on Dart were not long in coming. Dart's child, several critics suggested, was only "the distorted skull of a chimpanzee." Taung became something of a byword; it was ridiculed in songs and on musichall stages.

Despite the criticism, Dart was encouraged by a warm congratulatory letter from Robert Broom (1866–1951), a Scottish physician who had hunted fossils, particularly fossils of mammallike reptiles, in many parts of South Africa (see Figure 7–4). Two weeks after the letter arrived, Broom himself appeared at Dart's laboratory. He spent a weekend studying the Taung child intensively and became convinced that as "a connecting link between the higher apes and one of the lowest human types" it was the most important fossil discovered up to that time. He said so firmly in an article in *Nature*. After the first flare-up of attention, however, Dart's child was either forgotten or dismissed by most scientists. Nonetheless, Dart and Broom continued to study the skull.

## Dentition of Taung

For his part, Dart worked away at the skull almost daily for more than four years. In 1929 he succeeded in separating the upper and lower jaws, which had been cemented together in the rock-hard mass of *breccia* (a mixture of sand, soil, and pebbles cemented by lime) that enclosed them. For the first time he could examine the entire pattern of the teeth and get a good look at their grinding surfaces.

What he found strengthened his case that the fossil was clearly not an ape or a baboon. In apes, as we have seen (page 111), the front teeth are large, because they are used for defense and for tearing up the tough vegetable matter that forms much of an ape's diet. Ape canines, in particular, are so large that there must be spaces between the teeth of the upper jaw to accommodate the lower canines when the jaw is closed (Figure 7–5). At the same time, apes' jaws are relatively longer than humans' jaws, and heavier, too, and the muscles needed to move them are more massive. The Taung child, although a young individual and therefore lacking typical adult characters, could be judged to be distinctly more humanlike than apelike in all these characteristics. Its nicely curved jaw was shorter than a young ape's and more lightly made. Its canines and incisors were relatively small and set closely together. In fact, though the molars were larger than is now normal, most of the teeth could have belonged to a child of today.

In the minds of Dart and Broom, any lingering doubts about the hominid nature of the creature vanished; but skeptics, they suspected,

*FIGURE 7–5 These drawings show the palate and a lateral view of the jaws of a gorilla, an adult* Australopithecus, *and a modern human. The striking difference in the size and form of the canine teeth is clear, and in the gorilla we can see the gap or diastema into which the lower canines fit on each side. The difference in the shape of the dental arcade in ape and hominid is also striking.*

*The lateral view also shows distinct tooth wear: the ape teeth are used to crush and tear; the hominid teeth are used to crush and grind, which causes the typical flat wear of the hominid dentition. Not drawn to scale.*

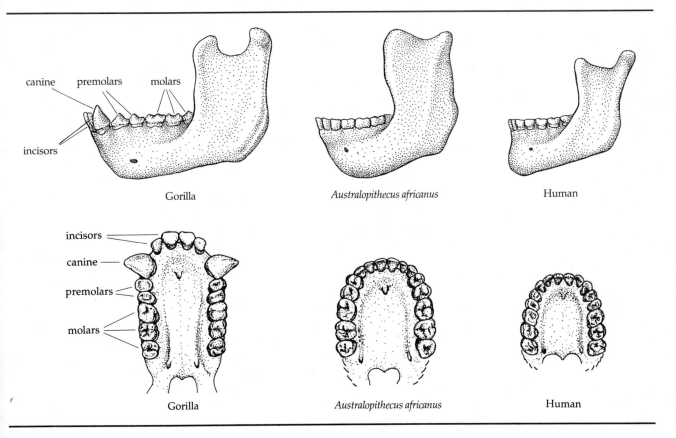

canine    premolars    molars

incisors

Gorilla

*Australopithecus africanus*

Human

incisors

canine

premolars

molars

Gorilla

*Australopithecus africanus*

Human

would take more convincing. What was needed was an adult skull, and also some legs or pelvic bones to support the claim of erect posture that the position of the foramen magnum suggested. Broom was determined to find this evidence, but it was not until the 1930s that he was free to begin a serious search.

**DISCOVERIES OF ROBERT BROOM**

The way was opened when Broom became curator of vertebrate paleontology at the Transvaal Museum in Pretoria. For the next year and a half, he was occupied with digging out, describing, and naming forty-four new fossil species of reptiles. He also unearthed a baboon jaw that at first appeared to be *Australopithecus*. It was not, but the publicity it engendered led two of Dart's students to tell Broom about some small skulls they had found in a quarry at Sterkfontein, a village not far from Pretoria (Figure 7–1).

**A Skull from Sterkfontein (1936)**

Ever since the first mining camps were opened during the South African gold rush of 1886, the people of the Sterkfontein area had been picking up fossilized remains of baboons, monkeys, and perhaps, unknowingly, hominids. By some extraordinary quirk of fate, the limeworks had even issued a little guidebook, ''Come to Sterkfontein and Find the Missing Link.'' When Broom first visited the quarry, the manager, who had worked at Taung and knew about the *Australopithecus* child's skull, promised Broom that he would keep a sharp lookout for anything resembling the skull of a hominid.

When Broom returned on August 7, 1936, the manager asked, ''Is this what you're after?'' and handed him two-thirds of a superb brain cast, which had been blasted out only that morning. Broom anxiously dug into the debris to find the skull that had served as the mold. Though he worked until dark, he found nothing. The next day, as he sorted the piles of stone, he recovered not only both sides of the upper jaw, but also fragments of the brain case. When the fragments were pieced together, Broom had parts of the skull of an adult *Australopithecus*.

***Australopithecus robustus* at Kromdraai**

For three years Broom, now in his seventies, continued to visit his fossil gold mine. One June day in 1938, the quarry manager met Broom and handed him a hominid upper jaw with one molar in place. He had obtained it from a schoolboy who lived on a farm at Kromdraai, less than a mile away. Broom found the boy, who responded to Broom's first questions by pulling out of his pocket ''four of the most wonderful teeth ever seen in the world's history.'' The boy also gave Broom a piece of a lower jaw. During the next two days, Broom and the boy sifted earth and found a number of scraps of bone and teeth. When the pieces were put together, Broom had most of another skull, though this one was different: the face was flatter than that of the Sterkfontein *Australo-*

*pithecus*, the jaw heavier, and, though the incisors and canines were still small, the molars were larger and less human.

When the newest findings were published, the situation seemed even more confused. The Kromdraai adult differed so markedly from both the Taung child and the Sterkfontein adult that it appeared increasingly likely to Broom that there were two species of early hominids in South Africa: the smaller, more slender "gracile" type with smaller molars that Dart had named *Australopithecus africanus*, and the heavy-jawed "robust" Kromdraai type with extremely large molars. Broom established a new genus and species for the Kromdraai type: *Paranthropus robustus*, robust near-man.

Years later, when numerous fossils of both types had been recovered, a clear scientific distinction would be made between them. One of the hominids—including the Kromdraai finds—would be called *Australopithecus robustus*, out of respect to its larger size and supposed weight of up to 150 pounds. The smaller, estimated to weigh from 80 to 100 pounds, would retain the name that it had originally been given, *Australopithecus africanus*. But when Broom set up a new genus for fossils from one small African site, his fellow scientists thought he was going too far. "Of course the critics did not know the whole of the facts," said Broom. "When one has jealous opponents one does not let them know everything." What he had not disclosed was that the fossils of animals found with the Kromdraai fossil were less archaic than the ones excavated with *Australopithecus africanus*, and thus represented a different period. Fossil horses abounded at Kromdraai; none apparently occurred at Sterkfontein, only one mile away. Many other fossil animal species were not shared by the two sites. Also, the breccia itself in which the Kromdraai creature lay seemed to be of a different age from that which held *Australopithecus africanus*. If the sites were occupied at various times—from several million to a half million years ago—then each might well have sustained a different species of hominid. Broom came to the conclusion that some of his *robustus* finds were as much as a million years younger than the Sterkfontein fossils—and this is still considered a correct interpretation.

Broom continued to search, and in due course he had more evidence to work with, having struck a rich find in a cave at Swartkrans (Figure 7–6) just across the valley from Sterkfontein. But the more new robust material he found, the more puzzled he became. Of the two types of *Australopithecus*, *A. robustus*, the larger, more recent hominid, seemed somehow the more primitive. Although a million years closer to us, it was not more humanlike; nor was it more apelike (Figure 7–7). Its jaws and molars were massive, less like those of modern humans than the jaws and molars of *A. africanus* were. These grinding teeth were huge in proportion to the size of its front teeth; for the canines were very small. Also, on its skull it had a bony ridge or crest called a *sagittal*

FIGURE 7–6 *The almost perfect jaw of* Australopithecus robustus *found at Swartkrans. Note the huge molars and premolars and diminutive front teeth that characterize* Australopithecus, *especially the robust forms. (This photograph is approximately three-fourths actual size.)*

*crest* to anchor large jaw muscles. These characteristics suggested that the creature was a vegetarian, that it chewed up large quantities of tough vegetable food, as a gorilla does today.

Could the younger, robust type be the human ancestor? That just did not make sense. How could a less human hominid occur so much later than a more human one? Assigning *A. robustus* a role in human ancestry raised awkward problems. For one thing, an animal does not get specialized jaw equipment—a heavy jaw, oversized grinding teeth, a bony ridge on its skull—overnight. It could be assumed that *A. robustus* had been following an evolutionary course toward a vegetarian life for a long time. Therefore the most reasonable expectation would be that the creature would continue to do so. Evolution does not work capriciously or fast. It would be much more logical to assume that, since humans were known to eat all sorts of things—to be omnivores—for at least three quarters of a million years, they probably had done so for a much longer time.

**Age of *Australopithecus africanus***

Broom set out to calculate the age of *Australopithecus africanus*, a task that was not easy. Accurate dating is impossible in South Africa, because of the way the fossils were obtained and, more important, because of the unique geological structure of the area. Most South African finds were made in lime-cemented breccia that had filled in ancient caves. This material had to be removed from quarries by blasting, which, of course, destroyed the stratigraphic pattern. In addition, because of the distinctive geology of South Africa, with no volcanic activity to deposit datable layers of ash, whatever stratigraphic clues could be discovered could not be matched with better-known and better-dated layers in other parts of the world. About the best that Broom could do was to carefully examine the animal fossils associated with the *Australopithecus* remains. To Broom's frustration, not only were all the large mammals extinct, but they also were not known in any other place; there was nothing he could compare them with. The very fact of their extinction suggested, however, that they must have been at least a million years old, possibly much older. Making a bold guess, Broom announced that *Australopithecus africanus* was probably 2 million years old, of Pliocene age.

His choice of 2 million years turned out to be more extraordinarily shrewd than it was shaky. For the moment, however, his announcement was greeted by the scientific community with hoots of derision. What bothered other scientists who examined the fossils or read about them was not the jaws but the rest of the head. They could not believe that a human ancestor with a brain scarcely bigger than a chimpanzee's had been running around on two legs in South Africa 2 million years ago.

Considering that this creature was estimated to be more than twice as old as any other known hominid, it did not seem remarkable to Dart or Broom that this peculiar mixture of ape and human characteristics

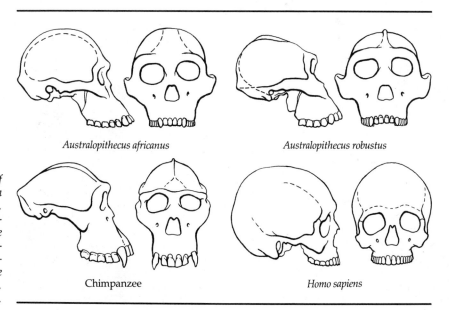

*Australopithecus africanus*

*Australopithecus robustus*

Chimpanzee

*Homo sapiens*

*FIGURE 7–7   The skulls of two species of* Australopithecus *are here compared with those of a chimpanzee and a modern human. Notice the absence of the crest on* A. africanus *and its narrower face. The large ape canine is not found in either species of* Australopithecus. *In the human specimen, notice the increase in the relative size of the braincase and the relatively smaller jaws. Not drawn to the same scale.*

should exist in a fossil. Two million years, they reasoned, might bring one pretty close to a common ancestor for humans and apes. That ancestor could well display a confusing and unexpected mingling of characteristics.

World War II came and went, and still *Australopithecus* was scarcely recognized in the scientific world. This was partly because Dart was an anatomist and all but unknown to the paleoanthropological establishment, all of whose brightest stars were in the United States, England, France, and Germany; it was also partly because the brains of these South African fossil creatures just were not big enough to satisfy other scientists prejudiced by the Piltdown skull. Perhaps *Australopithecus* was simply an aberrant chimpanzee.

**New Discoveries at Sterkfontein (1947)**

Meanwhile fossil evidence continued to accumulate. Soon after the end of the war, in 1947, Broom resumed working at Sterkfontein. One day a blast in some unpromising cave debris revealed the first of a series of important discoveries. When the smoke cleared away, the upper half of a perfect skull (Figure 7–8) sparkled brilliantly in the sunlight. Lime crystals encrusting its inner surface caught and reflected the light like diamonds. The lower half of the skull lay embedded in a block of stone that had broken away. The glittering skull was believed to be that of an adult female. Her jaw protruded, her forehead was low, but to the trained eye there was an unmistakable quality of humanness about her.

FIGURE 7–8   *The magnificent skull of* Australopithecus africanus *found at Sterkfontein by Robert Broom in 1947. Although the teeth and jawbone are missing, the skull is otherwise complete and undistorted—a rare find. (The photograph is approximately half actual size.)*

FIGURE 7–9 *These beautifully preserved jaws were found in 1949 at Sterkfontein by John Robinson, Broom's successor as curator at the Transvaal Museum. This specimen has unusually large canine teeth for* Austra-lopithecus africanus.

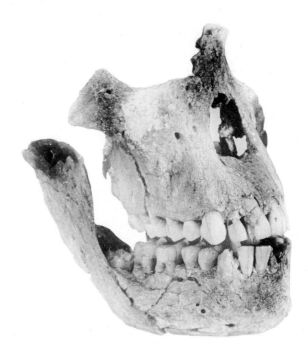

Her cranial capacity was 485 *cc* (see Table 8–1). Her discovery was followed by other important finds (Figures 7–9 and 7–10): first, a male jaw with an intact canine tooth worn level with the other teeth, as human canines are; and then, in August 1947, a nearly perfect female pelvis. This was, after the skull, the most important discovery. There was no doubt that it had belonged to a creature that had walked and run upright, as we do. Other fragments of pelvis and femur confirmed it many times over.

**Assessing *Australopithecus***

By 1949 the remains of more than thirty individuals had been recovered from the South African caves, and Wilfrid Le Gros Clark, professor of anatomy at Oxford University, undertook an impartial, definitive study. He studied the South African fossils and compared them in every detail of shape and structure with a series of ninety skulls of modern apes. His verdict was unqualified:

It is evident that in some respects they [the *Australopithecus* specimens] were definitely ape-like creatures, with small brains and large jaws. But in the details of the construction of the skull, in their dental morphology, and in their limb bones, the simian features are combined with a number of characters in which they differ from recent or fossil apes and at the same time approximate quite markedly to the *Hominidae*. All those who have had the opportunity of examining the original material are agreed on these hominid characters: the real issue to be decided is the question of their evolutionary and taxonomic significance.

*FIGURE 7–10   The skeletal remains of* Australopithecus africanus *found by Robert Broom in 1947 at Sterkfontein. These bones are believed to have belonged to a female no more than 4 ft. 3 in. tall. The pelvic bones were of exceptional importance in proving that* Australopithecus *was bipedal, as Dart had claimed in 1925. (The photograph is approximately one-fourth actual size.)*

By the mid-1950s a total of five sites had yielded several dozens of individuals of both *Australopithecus africanus* and *Australopithecus robustus.* The growing fossil record confirmed Broom and his assistant, J. T. Robinson, in their certainty that they were dealing with two quite different creatures. Furthermore, another South African, C. K. Brain, had made detailed studies of the sediments in the various sites, and his findings had begun to produce more evidence of the relative age of the two types. The smallest *A. africanus* specimens were invariably more ancient, and at the site of Makapansgat, which Dart had excavated in 1947, they seemed to evolve toward somewhat larger forms. By contrast, the robust type was always of more recent date. It seemed that throughout its known existence it evolved little, or not at all.

## FOSSILS AND ARTIFACTS

*FIGURE 7–11   Raymond Dart firmly believed that* Australopithecus africanus *used animal bones as a wide variety of tools. Here he demonstrates a pick (top) and a scraper (bottom).*

Which, if either, of the two South African fossil types led to humans still remained an unanswered question. If stone tools could be found associated with either type, some light might be shed on the matter.

At first, Dart and Broom were preoccupied with the fossils. *Australopithecus* was such an ancient and controversial character that for a number of years after its discovery the argument was less over whether it was or was not a tool user than over whether it was or was not an ape. In 1947, after eighteen years of concentrating on his work in anatomy at the University of Witwatersrand, Dart returned to the search for "dawn man." He analyzed thousands of fossilized animal bones associated with further remains of gracile *Australopithecus* that had been found in cave deposits 200 miles to the north of Sterkfontein, at Makapansgat (Figure 7–1). Dart concluded that *A. africanus* had employed tusks and teeth for cutting tools, jaws for saws and scrapers, and leg bones for bludgeons (Figure 7–11). His arguments, though ingenious, were not widely accepted. Today it seems clear that these extensive deposits were not of tools but of bones collected and gnawed by carnivores, mainly porcupines. The study of the origin and formation of assemblages of fossils is termed *taphonomy*.

Broom sought other clues, other cultural objects essential to hominid status. For years, he and his colleagues hunted for stone tools that might be associated with either the robust or the smaller, gracile hominids. For years they found none. Then, in 1953, some simple pebble tools were discovered on a terrace in the Vaal valley, which had been formed during what was thought to be the same dry period in which the hominids had lived: they were fist-sized pieces of stone from which a few chips had been removed. At the time it seemed impossible to most archaeologists that they could have been made by *Australopithecus*, whose brain was no larger than that of a modern ape and so the question of tools continued to haunt Broom and many other paleoanthropologists.

### Pebble Tools at Sterkfontein

But in 1957, once again new evidence was discovered. Working close by the cave at Sterkfontein that was yielding up a gratifying supply of *A. africanus* remains, Broom's successor, J. T. Robinson, and an archaeologist, Revil Mason, dug into a layer of red-brown breccia and found several hominid teeth and nearly 300 pebble tools. To the untrained eye these objects would have looked like naturally fractured stone, but close examination showed that chips had been flaked off two sides; the head of the stone was left round (Figure 7–12). A hammer-stone held in the hand and guided by understanding had shaped these pebbles to cut, scrape, and possibly kill. Not only their shape and the fact that they had been worked indicated that these were tools, but their location also did. The Sterkfontein cave is near the top of a hill where stones of

FIGURE 7–12  *These primitive hand-axes and choppers from Sterkfontein were the first to be discovered in association with hominid remains in South Africa. Recent research has shown that they were associated not with* Australopithecus africanus, *but with* Homo habilis, *and are from a higher level of the cave deposits. This type of simple stone tool is discussed in Chapter 9. (These drawings are approximately 40 percent of natural size.)*

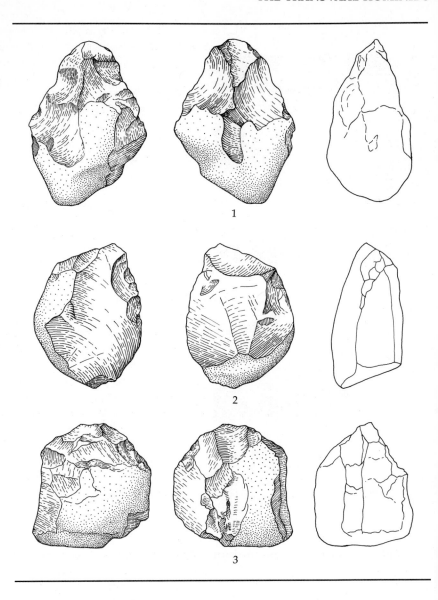

that kind do not occur naturally, but such stones are common in the valley about half a mile away. Because stones do not climb hills unaided, they must have been carried to the site of the cave.

For fifteen years, the situation was not entirely clear. The breccia that yielded the teeth and stone tools was believed to be somewhat more recent than that which yielded the skulls and teeth of *Australopithecus africanus,* but there were not enough teeth from the breccia containing tools to permit exact identification of the teeth with *Australopithecus* or with later hominids. Since 1966, a very thorough and painstaking excavation has been carried out by Phillip Tobias, Dart's successor as professor of anatomy at the University of Witwatersrand, and his assistant Alun Hughes. This work has made it clear that the teeth and stone tools excavated by Robinson and Mason come from a more recent period than the *Australopithecus africanus* fossils. Indeed, Tobias and Hughes found, along with stone tools, a fragmentary skull which is much more advanced than that of either *Australopithecus* and which clearly belongs to the genus *Homo*. It now seems quite certain that toolmaking humans lived in the Sterkfontein cave after *Australopithecus africanus*. Recent faunal and stratigraphic research suggests that the *Australopithecus*-bearing strata at Sterkfontein date from between 3.0 and 2.5 million years B.P., while the *Homo* and tool-bearing strata date from between 2.0 and 1.5 million years B.P. There was a considerable gap of time between the age of these two fossil beds.

Since 1965, C. K. Brain, assisted by Elizabeth Vrba, has been working at Swartkrans. In a meticulous excavation they have resolved many of the problems associated with this site. In the first place they estimate that the fossil-bearing strata there date from about 1.5 million years ago (contemporary with the more recent Sterkfontein bed). Second, they have established that the *Australopithecus robustus* fossils that characterize the deposits are accompanied by fossils of *Homo* and a few stone tools, similar to those from the more recent Sterkfontein bed. Thus we now have good evidence of the contemporaneity and age of early *Homo* and *A. robustus* in Southern Africa. (More recent deposits in the Swartkrans cave yielded a jaw of *Homo erectus*—see Chapter 10.)

Since 1977 Vrba has been reexamining Broom's famous breccia-filled cave at Kromdraai. She has already found further specimens of *A. robustus* and on the basis of extensive faunal analysis, has suggested a date of about 1.8 million years B.P. for these deposits.

The situation in the Transvaal is now becoming clear. Although the dates do not have the precision of those established by potassium-argon, the faunal and stratigraphic researches of Tobias, Hughes, Brain, and Vrba combine to give us a coherent picture of two periods. During the earlier period, about 2.5 million years ago, the gracile *A. africanus* occupied the Transvaal alone and left no known associated cultural remains. During the later period, about 1.5 million years ago, the region was occupied by two kinds of hominid: *Australopithecus robustus*, probably adapted to a tough, fibrous vegetable diet and probably without industry; and the more humanlike form we call *Homo*, associated with a clearly recognizable stone-tool industry. It is generally believed that *Homo* (though not necessarily these specimens) evolved into modern humans, and *A. robustus* became extinct. No later remains of *A. robustus* are known from South Africa.

**Holocene**

10,000

**CENOZOIC**

*Dryopithecus*

*Apidium, Parapithecus,*
*Aegyptopithecus,* and
*Propliopithecus*

*Amphipithecus*

Early prosimians

65 million

**MESOZOIC**

First mammals

Age of Reptiles

225 million

**PALEOZOIC**

---

YEARS A.D. — DISCOVERIES

| YEARS A.D. | DISCOVERIES |
|---|---|
| 1977 | Vrba starts work at Kromdraai |
| 1966 | Tobias starts work at Sterkfontein |
| 1965 | Brain starts work at Swartkrans |
| 1957 | Robinson and Mason find tools at Sterkfontein |
| 1950 | Definitive assessments by Le Gros Clark published |
| 1948 | *Paranthropus* found at Swartkrans |
| 1947 | *Australopithecus africanus* skull and pelvis found at Sterkfontein; Dart discovers *Australopithecus* at Makapansgat |
| 1938 | *Paranthropus robustus* discovered by Broom at Kromdraai |
| 1936 | Broom's first adult *Australopithecus* found at Sterkfontein |
| 1925 | Dart's publication on *Australopithecus africanus* |
| 1924 | Dart discovers *Australopithecus africanus* from Taung |

---

| YEARS B.P. | FOSSIL RECORD | |
|---|---|---|
| | | *HOMO SAPIENS* |
| Pleistocene | | *HOMO ERECTUS* |
| 2 million | *Australopithecus robustus* at Kromdraai and Swartkrans | *AUSTRALOPITHECUS AFRICANUS AND AFARENSIS* |
| | *Australopithecus africanus* at Sterkfontein and Makapansgat | |
| Pliocene | | |
| 5 million | | |
| Miocene | | |
| | *Sivapithecus* in Europe and in Asia | |
| 10 million | | |
| | *Dryopithecus* in Asia | |
| | *Dryopithecus* in Europe | |
| 15 million | | *PROCONSUL* |
| | *Proconsul* in Africa | |

THE TRANSVAAL HOMINIDS
The history of discoveries in South Africa is a fascinating story still unfolding (top right). The age of the fossils (bottom right) is still a matter of some uncertainty because potassium-argon dating is not applicable in the area, owing to the absence of volcanic activity there during the Cenozoic (see also Figure 8–20).

# Chapter 8

# The Great Savanna

Ex Africa semper aliquid novi.
("Africa always has something new.")

**PLINY THE ELDER, 23–79.**
*Natural History,* Book VIII.

Fifty million years ago, the grasses evolved and began to spread throughout the world. They were adapted to particular climatic conditions—intermittent wet and dry seasons that provided insufficient rain to support forest. As rainfall patterns changed, particularly during the Miocene, the grasses spread over great areas of North America, East Asia, and Africa; in Africa they extended over the eastern side of the continent, from Ethiopia to the Cape. The grasslands usually contained scattered trees, but essentially they constituted an open habitat distinct from forest and woodland, a habitat to which a whole new range of herbivorous animals were destined to become adapted. These vast African plains, known as savannas, were to play an important part in hominid evolution.

The questions that archaeologists were trying to answer in the Transvaal—whether the early hominids made tools and where the first stone tool industries occurred—brought the attention of anthropologists to another part of the African savanna. During the 1950s, Louis and Mary Leakey, both distinguished archaeologists, were finding the remains of an extensive pebble-tool industry 2,000 miles north of the Transvaal grasslands of South Africa in a dry river canyon in northern Tanzania (Figure 8–1).

## DISCOVERIES AT OLDUVAI

Olduvai Gorge is an abrupt rent in the earth, some 25 miles long and 300 feet deep. Like a miniature Grand Canyon, its sides display different strata laid bare by the cutting of an ancient river (Figure 8–2). A German entomologist named Wilhelm Kattwinkel found the gorge in 1911 when he almost fell into its depths as he broke through some bush on the edge. A hasty exploration showed the place to be a rich source of animal fossils. Some of the fossils that Kattwinkel took back to Berlin were so unusual that an expedition headed by Hans Reck was sent out in 1913 to explore further. Its investigations were ended by World War I, and after the war Reck was unable to raise funds to resume operations. Eventually he wrote to Louis Leakey (1903–1972), the young curator of the Coryndon Memorial Museum at Nairobi, Kenya, urging him to take over, but Leakey had to wait until 1931 before he could raise the money for an expedition to Olduvai.

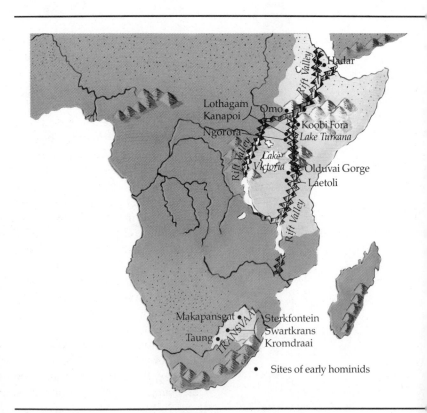

FIGURE 8–1   *Southern and Eastern Africa, with sites in which fossils of* Australopithecus *have been discovered. All lie to the eastern side of the continent where parkland and savanna have proliferated during the last 10 million years.*

FIGURE 8–2   Olduvai Gorge is a remarkable landform as well as a fossil gold mine. In this photograph Louis Leakey points out to visitors some features of interest.

One season spent exploring the gorge was enough to convince Leakey that Olduvai was a site "such as no other in the world." He found pebble tools in his first year there, long before they were discovered in South Africa, and no doubt he wondered if they could have been made by a creature similar to *Australopithecus.* For years Leakey searched the clearly stacked strata of the gorge in vain, unable to find the maker of the tools. As money and transport permitted, Leakey returned to the gorge, along with his wife Mary (b. 1913) and their sons. From each of the four principal beds that overlie one another from the river bottom to the surface of the plain some 300 feet above, the Leakeys eventually recovered an enormous number of animal fossils. They identified and classified more than a hundred species, most of them extinct and some unknown to science until the Leakeys discovered them.

**Discovery of**
***Australopithecus boisei***
**(1959)**

For twenty-eight years the Leakeys (Figures 8–3 and 8–4) were engaged in one of the most persistent and unrewarding efforts in the history of anthropology. Olduvai was far from the museum at Nairobi where Louis Leakey worked, and they could seldom spend more than a few weeks a year at the gorge. The trip was expensive, and in the early years it took several days to get to Olduvai on the very rough road from Nairobi.

The gorge was stiflingly hot, and water had to be hauled from a spring thirty-five miles away. It was not until the 1950s that the Leakeys were able to begin extensive excavation at Olduvai, and until July 17, 1959, all they knew was that they were the possessors of a small collection of what they believed to be the oldest implements ever seen, collectively called the *Oldowan* industry.

On that morning Louis Leakey awakened with a fever and headache. His wife insisted that he remain in camp. But the work season was drawing to an end and the day could not be lost, and so Mary Leakey drove to the point where the party was working. As she walked slowly along the hillside of Bed I, the lowest layer of the gorge, a piece of bone exposed by recent erosion caught her eye. She recognized it as a piece of skull. Searching higher along the slope, she suddenly saw two big teeth, brown-black and almost iridescent, just appearing from the eroding hill. She marked the spot with a small piece of stone and sped back to camp.

Louis heard the car racing up the road and sprang up in alarm, thinking that his wife had been bitten by a snake. But as the car stopped he heard Mary shout, "I've got him!" The "him," she felt sure, was a hominid fossil—the early human they had been seeking for so many years. Louis's fever and headache forgotten, he jumped in the car and the couple drove back as fast as they could.

The Leakeys went to work with camel's-hair brushes and dental picks. The palate to which the teeth were affixed came into view, and then fragments of a skull emerged. In order not to lose a single precious scrap, the couple removed and sieved tons of scree, fine rock debris, from the slope below the find. At the end of nineteen days they had about four hundred fragments.

While undertaking the delicate task of assembling the bits and pieces, the Leakeys continued to excavate the site. Not only had they discovered the oldest hominid skull found to that time in eastern and central Africa, but they had also unearthed what appeared to be a campsite of this ancient creature. Scattered on what had been the margins of an ancient lake were many tools made of flaked stone and pebbles, along with waste chips. Lying about too were the fossil bones of animals that the residents of the campsite had killed and eaten—complete remains of rats, mice, frogs, lizards, birds, snakes, tortoises, and some young pigs, and parts of small antelopes. But there were no remains of large animals. Nearly all these bones were broken; but the near-human skull and tibia and fibula (the two bones of the lower part of the hind leg) that appeared at the same site were not. It seemed clear that the hominid had killed the other animals.

The skull that took shape from the fragments uncovered at the campsite was that of a nearly mature male (Figure 8–5). That the wisdom

*FIGURE 8–3   A distinguished archaeologist, Mary Leakey worked with her husband Louis at Olduvai from 1935, and today she still carries on her painstaking research in Tanzania.*

FIGURE 8–4  *Louis Leakey was somewhat eccentric, yet he was a passionate, brilliant man. Here he is shown examining some of his important and numerous discoveries.*

teeth were unworn and that the suture joining the two halves of the skull, the *sagittal suture*, had not yet closed indicated that it was a young adult. In brain size and in general appearance the young male broadly resembled *Australopithecus robustus* of the south. The molars were extraordinarily large and heavy, but detailed study confirmed that they were, in their structure, undoubtedly hominid teeth. The skull had the characteristic massive face and teeth and rugged low cranium of *A. robustus* but was even larger and more specialized. These differences led Louis Leakey to set up a new genus for what he believed was the earliest tool-user, and he named it *Zinjanthropus boisei*. (*Zinj* means "eastern Africa" in Arabic; *Boisei* honored Charles Boise, who had helped to finance the Leakeys' search for early humans.) Later, it was decided that the skull was more properly referred to as a new species of the genus *Australopithecus*; the creature is now called *Australopithecus boisei*. The skull is so much more heavily built than that of *A. robustus* that it is often described as super-robust.

**Age of *A. boisei***

Fortunately, the approximate age of the Leakeys' fossil could be determined, because it was found sandwiched between layers of volcanic ash. Scientists extracted minerals containing potassium from the volcanic ash covering *A. boisei* and also from an older volcanic bed that underlay the site. When they analyzed these layers by the then-new method of potassium-argon dating, they were able to fix the startling age of about 1.75 million years, an age repeatedly confirmed by later potassium-argon tests. This dating of the fossil was extraordinary in itself, but it also had a valuable side effect: suddenly Broom's original claim of an age of 2 million years for the early South African *Australopithecus africanus* changed from being a wild guess to being an inspired deduction.

The question of which of the early hominids (Figure 8–6) was the first to use tools, and when, continued to haunt paleoanthropologists. The evidence from Olduvai seemed to suggest to the Leakeys that *Zinjanthropus* might be the toolmaker. But only a year after they had found the first skull, they found another.

**Discovery of *Homo habilis* (1960–1964)**

Early in 1960 the Leakeys' son Jonathan uncovered some teeth and bone fragments of the second hominid. Though found at broadly the same stratigraphic level as *A. boisei* and not far away, these bones, Louis Leakey realized, represented a creature far closer to humankind than the heavily built *A. boisei*. Two years passed before further specimens were found to confirm this interpretation, but by 1964 the Leakeys and their collaborators were ready to announce their new discovery.

Though as old as *A. boisei*, the new fossils represented a distinct

FIGURE 8–5   Zinjanthropus, *the immense skull found by Mary Leakey at Olduvai in 1959. It is now classified as* Australopithecus boisei. *(This photograph is approximately 65 percent actual size.)*

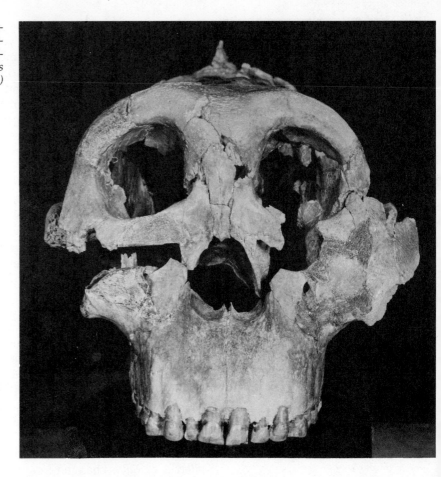

species. It was clearly of the gracile type and even more humanlike than the gracile South African *A. africanus.* In fact, it seemed sufficiently human to be separated from the known *Australopithecus* species altogether. Louis Leakey and his co-workers described the fossil species as a true human that deserved to be classified in the genus *Homo.* He christened his find *Homo habilis,* "handy" man, believing that now he really had discovered the toolmaker.

That *Homo habilis,* and not the super-robust *A. boisei,* was indeed the toolmaker has now been widely accepted. The Leakeys subsequently collected from Olduvai a whole series of *Homo habilis* fragments, indicating that this type lived there for more than half a million years, using much the same primitive tool culture the entire time. (Later, *Homo erectus* fossils also were discovered at Olduvai, together with a more advanced stone culture.)

**Classifying *Homo habilis***

*Homo habilis* earned neither name nor credentials easily. It was primitive and still relatively small-brained. A few anthropologists preferred to identify it as an advanced type of the gracile *A. africanus* not deserving *Homo* status at all. Some still identify it in this way. Its qualifications as a distinct species have been in question from the day it was named.

Was it human or not? Should it be called *Homo habilis* or *Australopithecus habilis*? Compared to the certified human beings that came after, it seems scarcely human; compared to the more primitive types that preceded, its human credentials suddenly improve. This disconcerting shift of perspective always occurs when the eye runs down a series of fossils that are related to one another through direct descent. The differences between them are differences in degree—not in kind—and obviously become more pronounced as one takes one's example from more widely separated time zones. Some of the more obvious characteristics of *Homo* are comparative: an "increasingly large" brain, a "higher" forehead, a "more delicate" jaw, and "longer" legs. But in a continuous series, where does one draw the line?

That question continues to arise, but it is conceivably the wrong question. Since all creatures are bundles of characteristics, many of which may be evolving at different rates, drawing a line that is based on these characteristics will always cause trouble. Early in this century, the British anatomist Sir Arthur Keith chose to draw the line marking the appearance of humanity where the brain capacity touched 750 cubic centimeters (cc). Anything below that, according to Keith, was not human; anything above it was (*Homo sapiens* is usually within the 1,200–1,600 cc range; see Table 8–1). More recently, Sir Wilfrid Le Gros Clark put the minimum at 700 cc. Clark's choice, unlike Keith's, was not arbitrary; it reflected the state of the fossil record at the time it was made—no accepted "human" skulls were known to exist with cranial capacities of less than 700 cc. Implicit in this situation, of course, was the possibility that an apparently human specimen with a slightly smaller brain might be discovered any day.

*Homo habilis* laid this problem right on the scientists' doorstep. The great difficulty in deciding whether or not it was human lay in the fact that the so-called type specimen, the first one to be found and named *Homo habilis* by the Leakeys, had a brain capacity estimated to be about 657 cc—just under Clark's limit. Since then three other *habilis* skulls from Olduvai have been measured by two experts, Phillip Tobias and Ralph Holloway. They came up with surprisingly uniform figures for these skulls. They range in capacity from 600 to 684 cc and average about 642 cc. Too small-brained for a human? Perhaps, but probably too large-brained for a typical gracile *Australopithecus*, whose mean cranial capacity is only about 450 cc.

What is the meaning of brain size? How significant is the steady

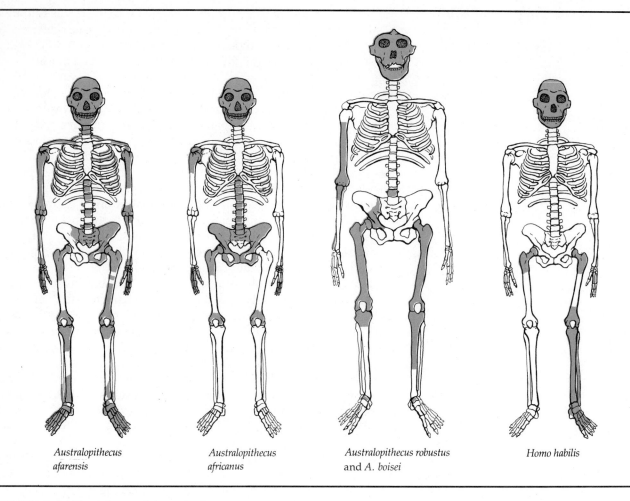

| Australopithecus afarensis | Australopithecus africanus | Australopithecus robustus and A. boisei | Homo habilis |

*FIGURE 8–6    The skeletons of* Australopithecus afarensis *from Ethiopia*, A. africanus *and* A. robustus *from South Africa, and* A. boisei *and* Homo habilis *from East Africa are reconstructed from fragments of many individuals. In the case of* A. boisei *and* A. robustus, *the drawing is highly imaginative and the skeletal material is combined, for we have very limited remains (shown in color). (*A. africanus *was approximately four feet tall, and the others are drawn to scale.)*

increase in cranial capacity that we find in human evolution? Large brains are found in large animals generally, and the brains of elephants and whales are very much larger than those of humans. As a general rule, among mammals brain size can best be interpreted when it is related to body size, and a doubling of body size during the evolution of a lineage will usually result in a considerable increase in brain size (see Chapter 13). When we look at the figures in Table 8–1, therefore, we should consider the size of the animal itself. For example, the stature of *A. afarensis* varied from 3.5 to 5 feet tall, while that of modern humans varies from 4.5 to 6 feet approximately. The difference in *relative brain size* is therefore not quite as great as the table might suggest. It should not be forgotten, however, that many human populations, of pygmies

TABLE 8–1  Comparison of Cranial Capacity

| | RANGE OF CRANIAL CAPACITY (cc) | AVERAGE CRANIAL CAPACITY (cc) |
|---|---|---|
| Lemur | 10–70 | – |
| Chimpanzee | 282–500 | 383 |
| Gorilla | 340–752 | 505 |
| *Australopithecus afarensis* | 380–500 | 440 |
| *A. africanus* | 435–530 | 450 |
| *A. robustus* | – | 500 |
| *A. boisei* | 506–530 | 515 |
| *Homo habilis* | 600–752 | 666 |
| *H. erectus* | 775–1,225 | 950 |
| Modern adult human | 1,000–2,000 | 1,330 |

*Note:* Measurements of cranial capacity are given in cubic centimeters (cc—a cubic centimeter is about the size of a sugar cube); the size of the brain itself is usually somewhat smaller because the cranial cavity also contains other structures. The above figures are approximate: for lemurs, the figures refer to several species of different size; for the two African apes, they are based on rather small samples; and in the case of the fossil groups, the samples are extremely small and may prove to be misleading (only a single complete specimen of *A. robustus* is known and measured). Specimens included under *A. africanus* and *H. habilis* are from the sites listed in Table 8–3. In the case of modern humans, rare extremes exceeding even the approximate range given above have been found; the average figure is based on a limited number of samples. Slight variations of these figures will be found in other authors' work.

As a general rule, and within an order, species of animals with larger brains are more intelligent than those with smaller brains, but this does not hold among species of different body size. The significance of brain size is considered in Chapter 13 (page 341). Within a species, variations in brain size are not believed to be related to intelligence among normal individuals.

for example, fall into the range of stature for *A. afarensis* and yet have brains in the region of 1,200–1,350 cc.—three times as large. A consideration of stature is therefore not going to alter very seriously the significance of the figures for Hominidae listed in Table 8–1.

It is clear that brain size and tooth shape and length of leg all evolved at different rates and this common evolutionary phenomenon is called *mosaic evolution.* As a result, it is difficult to define sequential species on the basis of these characteristics. Nevertheless, classification and naming are necessary. The best way to deal with this problem may be to assign a time, rather than a set of physical characteristics, to mark the emergence of new species. Of course, if paleoanthropologists choose to classify in this way, they must recognize that they will always be plagued by some blurring of characteristics.

A recent proposal of this kind placed the dividing line between the ancestral *Australopithecus* and the descendant *Homo* at about 2.3 million years B.P. (Figure 8–7). If this boundary line is accepted, then it follows that we should put the 1.75-million-year-old *habilis* into the genus *Homo* and call the species *H. habilis.*

FIGURE 8-7 *This diagram of the hominid lineage symbolizes the complexity of the evolutionary process and indicates the amount of variability (shown by the horizontal dimension) present at any one time. The successive species are separated by time lines (shown in color). These are arbitrary divisions, but they represent the only effective way of subdividing such a lineage. A. robustus is here shown to have evolved locally from the South African A. africanus. We have no fossil evidence of the origin of A. boisei, but it is reasonable to assume that it shares common ancestry with A. robustus in view of their numerous similarities.*

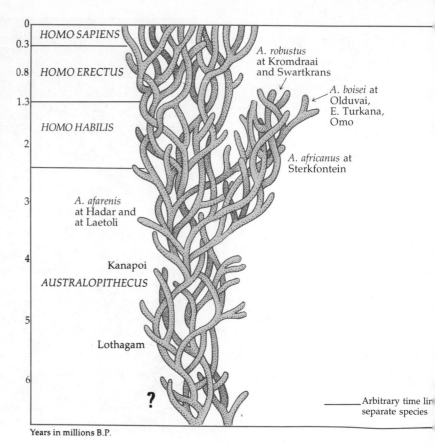

HOMO SAPIENS

HOMO ERECTUS

HOMO HABILIS

*A. afarensis* at Hadar and at Laetoli

Kanapoi

AUSTRALOPITHECUS

Lothagam

?

*A. robustus* at Kromdraai and Swartkrans

*A. boisei* at Olduvai, E. Turkana, Omo

*A. africanus* at Sterkfontein

———— Arbitrary time line separate species

Years in millions B.P.

Does the evidence suggest that two hominids existed simultaneously? South Africa does not give us a good answer, because the sites are of different ages. But if we look at the two types from Olduvai, it is clear that *Australopithecus boisei* is so very robust that it and *Homo habilis*, which is extremely gracile, are different. They certainly coexisted—they were even found at one site on the same ancient living or *occupation* floor. At a later date (about 1.2 million years ago), evidence suggests that *A. boisei* coexisted with *H. erectus* at Koobi Fora (see Chapter 10).

In the 1960s, looking back over *Homo habilis*'s shoulder deeper into time was impossible. There simply was nothing known that was definitely older than *H. habilis*. Although many scholars suspected that the gracile South African fossils might be older, they could not, at that time, prove it. Broom's guess that *Australopithecus africanus* was about 2 million years old held, however, and the faunal evidence tended to support this age (Figures 8-8 and 8-20).

**OMO AND TURKANA**  The only way to clear up the mystery was by finding more fossils, by dating more precisely the ones that had been unearthed, and by digging deeper into time. In the hope of doing so, an ambitious international expedition was organized in 1967 to look for hominid remains in Ethiopia. The expedition was under the direction of Yves Coppens and Camille Arambourg from France and the American anthropologist F. Clark Howell. Its destination was a remote spot in the southern part of the valley of the Omo River, just north of Lake Turkana (Figures 8–1 and 8–9). Though one of the most desolate places anywhere south of the Sahara and one of the hottest, the area had several attractions. For one thing, it had been visited thirty-five years before by Arambourg, who had found it rich in animal fossils. For another, it bore a striking resemblance to Olduvai. It, too, is part of the Rift Valley geological complex, a giant crack in the earth that, running north-south through Africa, once was marked by chains of lakes and rivers and edged by towering escarpments. Much of the Rift Valley is dry now, its lakes shrunken, some of its cliffs worn away, its stones baked in the sun. There is no river at all today in Olduvai Gorge, except during flash floods, although the gorge was made by a river. At Omo, as at Olduvai, deep-cut riverbeds speak of ancient days and long-vanished landscapes. The Omo River still runs down from the Ethiopian highlands and empties into Lake Turkana, just over the border in northern Kenya. Lake Turkana itself has grown and shrunk twice in the last 4 million years. It is still a sizable lake 185 miles long, but it has shrunk considerably from its original size, and is still shrinking. The brutal, arid lands around it are largely unexplored.

The Rift Valley is an unstable area on the earth's surface where the earth's crust is still moving. It has long been a center of volcanic activity and is pockmarked by cones and craters. Due to neighboring volcanic activity, Olduvai has invaluable layers of datable volcanic ash; so does Omo. Both places supported more life in the past than they do now. Laced with rivers, much greener, carrying a far larger animal population than they do today, each provided the lush water-edge environment, the forest-becoming-savanna, that the early hominids are believed to have preferred.

But Omo is also different from Olduvai, and the differences are what made it particularly appealing to the 1967 expedition. At Olduvai, the most accurate and useful pages of the volcanic timetable are crowded into an 800,000-year period that is not quite 2 million years old and are contained in layers not totalling much more than 100 feet thick. At Omo the strata being investigated are more than 2,000 feet thick and span a far longer period of time. Moreover, they contain a great many layers of volcanic ash at varying intervals, some of them only 100,000 years apart, some more widely spaced, each datable by the potassium-argon

FIGURE 8–8  *Some early hypotheses of human evolution are here shown in the form of very simplified evolutionary "trees" representing the hominid lineage. The earliest, prepared by Le Gros Clark (A), is not very different from the scheme presented in Figure 8–7. By 1967 views were diverging greatly: Loring Brace proposed a very simple scheme, though recently he has come to recognize a branch for A. robustus (B). Tobias's was more complex (C). By 1971 new finds caused Louis Leakey to add even more branches to the hominid tree. His scheme (D) has three main side branches; Donald Johanson's latest (E) has just one.*

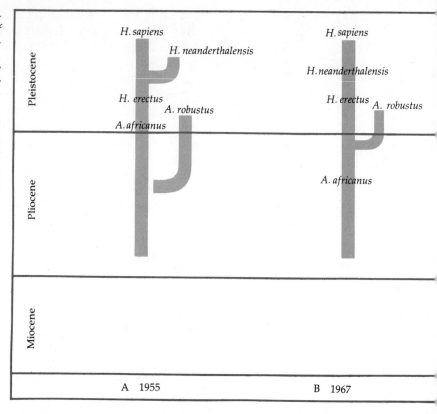

method. Together, these layers of ash can be used by scientists to step backward into time and into the earth, determining an approximate date at each step.

One does not have to dig at Omo to go deeper into time. The strata have been heaved up in the past and now lie at an angle to the earth's surface. One need only walk along to find successively older layers revealing themselves.

The Omo story begins a little over 4 million years ago and continues to about 1.5 million years B.P. This date conveniently overlaps with the deposits at Olduvai, which begin at 1.8 million years B.P., so that the two sites between them give us an almost unbroken story for the last 4 million years.

## Omo Hominids (1967–1974)

In this area of great promise, Arambourg, with Coppens, picked the spot he had worked before and knew to be productive. A second group, under Clark Howell's direction, went a short distance up the Omo River to tap a previously unexplored area. A third group, headed by the Leakeys' son Richard, picked another untapped spot, farther north and

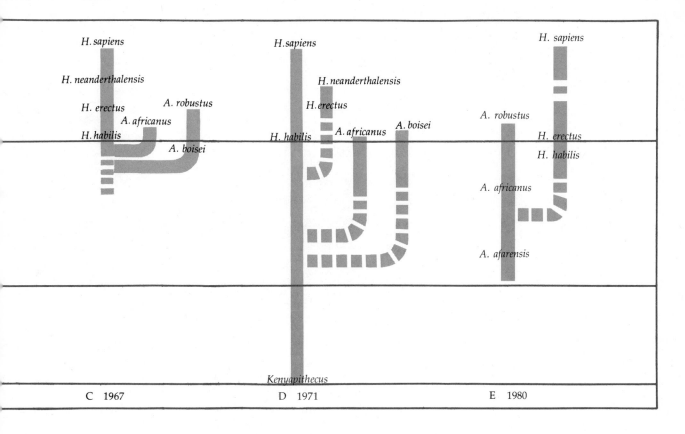

H. sapiens

H. neanderthalensis

H. erectus     A. robustus

A. africanus

H. habilis

A. boisei

H. sapiens

H. neanderthalensis

H. erectus

H. habilis     A. africanus     A. boisei

Kenyapithecus

H. sapiens

A. robustus

H. erectus

H. habilis

A. africanus

A. afarensis

C   1967      D   1971      E   1980

across the river from Howell. As it turned out, Richard Leakey's choice was the only one that proved somewhat unfruitful. He found plenty of material there, but the strata were not old enough to be of interest to the expedition. He decided to disassociate himself from the project and returned home to Kenya to do some prospecting.

The other members of the expedition persevered where they were. Immediately they began recovering extinct animal fossils of extraordinary richness and variety. The great number of dated layers at Omo made it possible to trace the evolutionary changes that had taken place in some eighty species of mammals. Six genera and eight species of extinct pigs laid their secrets bare in the strata. Twenty-two kinds of antelope were discovered, and several extinct saber-toothed cats. Altogether, more than 150 species of fossil animals have been found at Omo. These discoveries were so varied and told such a clear story that matching fossils from other places with those from Omo became a distinct possibility.

In addition to all the useful animal fossils found at Omo, traces of hominids began to appear. The French group first found a jaw. Both

*FIGURE 8–9   This aerial view of the Omo Valley in southern Ethiopia shows uplifted fossil-bearing deposits of the Shungura formation. The harder layers of rock are the datable volcanic tuffs.*

parties found teeth, eventually more than 200 of them; then came other jaw fragments, parts of two skulls, and several arm and leg bones. It has been a spectacular haul and an enormously significant one, for several reasons. First is the age of the oldest specimens, more than twenty teeth: 2.5 million years. These teeth are almost certainly those of a small gracile hominid resembling the South African *A. africanus.* Also of significance was the fact that remains of this hominid were found along with super-robust fossils some half a million years older than the *A. boisei* found at Olduvai. Furthermore, similar specimens continued to turn up in various layers, dating right up to 1.5 million years ago. *A. boisei* apparently lived at Omo for at least a million years.

**Robust Hominids at Koobi Fora (1969–1976)**

Meanwhile, Richard Leakey flew south in a helicopter, across the border into Kenya and along the eastern shore of Lake Turkana, previously called Lake Rudolf (Figures 8–1 and 8–10). Here, Leakey spotted some likely sites from the air and set his helicopter down almost on top of what has turned out to be one of the richest mines of hominid fossils ever found.

The results of work near Lake Turkana carried out by a large group of scientists directed by Richard Leakey and Glynn Isaac of the University of California at Berkeley were sensational: at the sites east of the lake, named Ileret and Koobi Fora, they discovered three superb skulls, more than two dozen *mandibles* (lower jaws) or parts of mandibles, some arm- and leg-bone fragments, and some isolated teeth, amounting

FIGURE 8–10 *Richard Leakey's team has had astounding success in finding fossil hominids in the desert regions east of Lake Turkana in Kenya. With more than 150 fossil hominids found, his success was unprecedented.*

to more than one hundred specimens in all. Much of this material is of the super-robust *A. boisei* type and dates from nearly 2 million years ago to about one million years ago (Figure 8–11). When these East Turkana fossils are combined with the Omo finds, there is enough material in the way of young and old individuals, both males and females, and enough variation in dentition, for the outlines of a variable population of the super-robust *Australopithecus boisei* to begin to reveal itself.

Having a population to study instead of an individual fossil is extremely important. No two people today are exactly alike; no two *Australopithecus* creatures were, either. For that reason, drawing conclusions from a single fossil is risky. Measurements can be taken of a single fossil, and theories built up as a result of those measurements; but this information may be misleading because the fossil may not be typical. Only when a large number of specimens are available can variations be taken into account. If visitors from outer space were to describe and name *Homo sapiens* by examining one skeleton—that of a short, heavy-boned Eskimo—they certainly might be excused if they thought they had another species when they discovered a second skeleton—that of a six-and-a-half-foot, slender-boned Watusi tribesman from central Africa.

That is why the *A. boisei* population that is emerging is so valuable. It begins to indicate some of the limits of variability beyond which no members of the species go. Any creature that does exceed those limits in any way can be presumed to be something else. And those limits are now well enough defined to make it quite clear that the gracile *Australopithecus* specimens *are* something else; doubt about the distinctiveness of the two forms has now evaporated.

*A. boisei*, on the other hand, is not significantly different from the robust types of South Africa, which also exist in sufficient numbers to constitute a variable population with limits of its own. Like *A. robustus* (Figure 7–7), *A. boisei* had a bony crest along the top of its skull, but its crest is more pronounced for the anchoring of even bigger muscles to work a more massive jaw containing larger molars. This complex of features indicates a life adapted to eating large amounts of coarse, tough vegetable matter. It is the same adaptation as *A. robustus* but more highly evolved.

Because on further analysis the known differences between *A. robustus* and *A. boisei* have proved to be almost entirely differences in size, some workers today consider both groups to be geographical subspecies of the single species *A. robustus*. Whether the remains in fact represent one or two distinct contemporary biological species is something that can be finally determined only when a great deal more fossil evidence is available. For our discussion it is convenient to continue to distinguish them as separate species.

The question of the number of species represented by varied samples of fossils has always been a difficult one. Paleoanthropologists concerned with these matters are sometimes divided into *splitters* and *lumpers*. Splitters divide their samples into groups with small variability, so that many species and genera are recognized. Lumpers accept wide ranges of variability within groups and so recognize only a few species and genera. In the early days of paleoanthropology, almost every find that varied even the smallest amount from another was given a separate specific or generic name. The result was a splitter's taxonomy with thirty-seven genera and one hundred and eleven species of Hominidae! Following our present understanding of the variability of modern species, no one today would recognize such a number; nevertheless, there is some divergence of view. Here are two extreme classifications of the family Hominidae (Table 8–2). The classification used in this book lies between these two extremes.

### Gracile Hominids at Koobi Fora (1969–1976)

The picture that *A. boisei* gives us is that of a creature that became stable and well adapted to its own niche—until challenged by another hominid. Unfortunately for *A. boisei,* there was another hominid, and the challenge came.

The East Turkana finds also include late gracile fossils. The finest specimen is that known simply as ER 1470, an almost complete cranium and face, but with the skull base and jaw missing (Figure 8–12). It retains the large face of *Australopithecus* with its strongly built zygomatic arches (which carry the jaw muscles) and evidence of large molar teeth (which are missing). But these features are combined with a much larger cranium with a capacity of about 775 cc.—far larger than that found in earlier forms, and the whole skull is more lightly built. For a million years this type was contemporaneous with *A. boisei;* coexistence of the two creatures has been confirmed without question. At first their paths—their ways of making a living—almost certainly did not cross. As time went on this situation must have changed. Though *A. boisei* did not evolve rapidly, the gracile hominid did. Its brain became larger, and this development may have spelled disaster for all the robust *Australopithecus* populations, both north and south. *A. boisei* disappeared in East Africa about a million years ago; *A. robustus,* we believe, had disappeared in South Africa by the same time. There are, in fact, no reliably dated robust specimens anywhere that are less than a million years old. The number of different kinds of environments that the emerging gracile hominid could occupy was probably increasing along with its brain size and its capabilities as a hunter, and with this growing adaptability it may have forced its larger cousins into extinction.

What is the gracile type that appears at Koobi Fora? Richard Leakey suggests that some specimens are similar to *Homo habilis* from Olduvai;

*FIGURE 8–11    This skull (KNM-ER 406) of* Australopithecus boisei *found by Richard Leakey at Koobi Fora is similar in many ways to that found by his mother at Olduvai (Figure 8–5). (This photograph is approximately 30 percent actual size.)*

TABLE 8–2   Alternative Classifications for the Hominidae

| LUMPER'S CLASSIFICATION | | SPLITTER'S CLASSIFICATION | |
|---|---|---|---|
| 2 Genera | 4 Species | 7 Genera | 11 Species |
| *Australopithecus* | *africanus* | *Australopithecus* | *afarensis* |
| | *boisei* | | *africanus* |
| *Homo* | *erectus* | *Paranthropus* | *robustus* |
| | *sapiens* | *Zinjanthropus* | *boisei* |
| | | *Pithecanthropus* | *erectus* |
| | | *Sinanthropus* | *pekinensis* |
| | | *Atlanthropus* | *mauritanicus* |
| | | *Homo* | *habilis* |
| | | | *heidelbergensis* |
| | | | *neanderthalensis* |
| | | | *sapiens* |

this opinion has been seconded by others. Leakey will not give species names to his finds; he simply calls all robust types *Australopithecus* and all gracile types *Homo*, regardless of age, preferring to leave the precise naming of species to others.

**Discoveries at Hadar (1973–1976)**   Five hundred miles to the northeast, near the Awash River in northern Ethiopia, at a barren and arid place called Hadar (Figures 8–1 and 8–13), extraordinary new discoveries are giving gracile hominids an even earlier date. An international expedition led by Maurice Taieb and Yves Coppens from France and Donald C. Johanson from the United States has made the most remarkable finds of fossil hominids in the history of paleoanthropology. The story began in 1973, when, during the first season at Hadar, Johanson found a hominid knee joint washed out of a slope. This discovery in itself would not have been so remarkable if the geologists and paleontologists had not assigned it a date of more than 3 million years B.P. Furthermore, an examination of its anatomy proved conclusively that the creature to whom the knee belonged walked erect (Figure 8–14). Here was evidence of fully evolved bipedalism far older than anything known before. Hadar suddenly became the most intriguing prehistoric site on earth.

Johanson and his group returned to Hadar in the fall of 1974, and on November 30 he wrote in his diary: "To locality 162 with Gray A.M. Feel good." He later wrote: "When I got up this morning I felt it was one of those days when something terrific might happen." On the way home from locality 162, at about noon, Johanson and his student Tom Gray made a short detour to look in a particular gully that had intrigued Johanson. In it the two men discovered the most remarkable find in all paleoanthropology: the incomplete skeleton of a hominid—more than 3 million years of age. Given the name Lucy, the skeleton (from locality 288), which was 40 percent complete, represented a very small gracile *Australopithecus* (Figure 8–13). Although the knee joint and the pelvis again carry the marks of fully evolved bipedalism, the skull is primitive, as are other features of the skeleton, and is somewhat more apelike than that of *A. africanus* from South Africa.

The 1975 season brought further remarkable discoveries. From a single site (locality 333) one of Johanson's team, Mike Bush, found further hominid fossils: this time a mixed collection of some 200 teeth and bone fragments, representing at least thirteen individuals including males, females, and at least four children. The strange thing about this precious haul was that the hominid bones were all associated and from a single level, not mixed with animal bones as such fossils usually are. Because of their close association, it has been supposed that they might represent part of a single social group and are therefore possibly genetically related. They have been called "the first family."

*FIGURE 8–12   Most important of Richard Leakey's finds from Koobi Fora is this skull, discovered in 1972 and known as ER 1470, which is about 1.8 million years old. It has an unusually large cranial capacity of 775 cc. and is now considered to belong to the species* Homo habilis. *(The photograph is approximately 60 percent actual size.)*

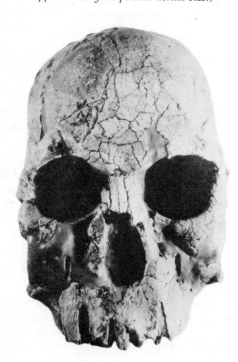
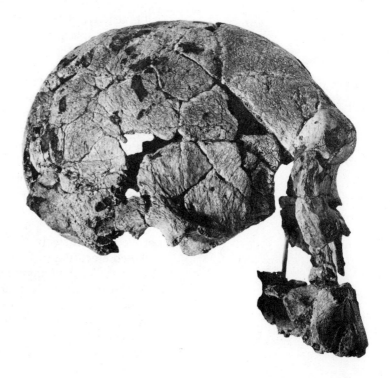

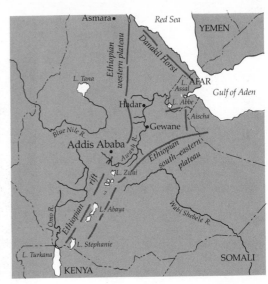

FIGURE 8–13 *Important hominid remains have been recovered from the extensive stratified deposits at Hadar (right) in the Afar region. Near where the people are sitting in the top photograph, Donald C. Johanson (at the bottom center) and his team discovered the bones of a skeleton, in 1974. After three and a half weeks of mapping, collecting, and sieving, the bones were gathered into the most nearly complete early hominid yet found (bottom row, right photograph). "Lucy," as the skeleton is called, lived by a lake about 3.5 million years ago; she was only 3.5 to 4 feet tall and died when she was in her early twenties. Johanson and his colleagues believe she is best classified as a new species,* Australopithecus afarensis. *Also found in this region was a complete palate, dated at around 3.3 million years. In the bottom left photograph it is compared with a cast of a* Homo erectus *palate (left) that is perhaps a million years old. Their similarities suggest that the Afar palate is ancestral to* Homo.

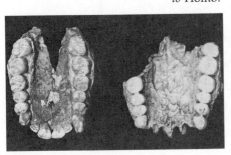

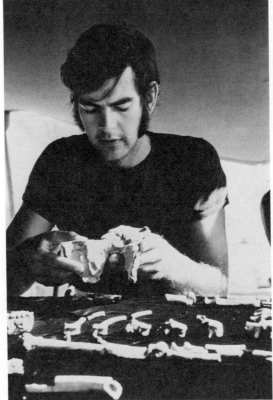

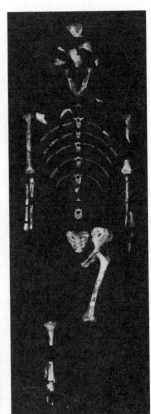

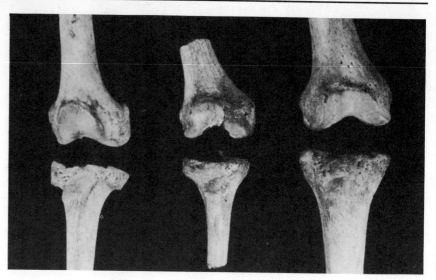

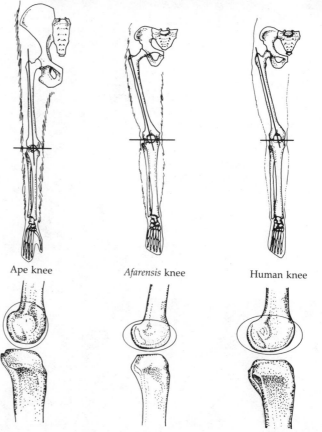

Ape knee                    *Afarensis* knee                    Human knee

FIGURE 8–14   *The interpretation of the*
Australopithecus afarensis *knee bones
(top) can be understood from this figure. The
critical character is the plane of the condyles
of the knee joint in relation to the shaft of
the femur. In the ape (left) the alignment is
such that the leg is straight when the knee is
extended. In humans (right) and in A. afarensis (middle) the angle is such that the leg
is angled at the knee. This is a product of the
broadening of the pelvis (middle). The lower
drawing shows that the bearing surfaces of
the knee condyles are broadened in bipedal
species as an adaptation to the greater
weight transmitted through the knee.*

The final field season of 1976 was concerned mainly with stratigraphy and dating. We now believe that this group of fossils probably falls into the time range 2.8–3.3 million years ago (Figure 8–15). The potassium-argon dates in this section agree with fission-track dates and have been cross-checked by the chemical signatures of the tuffs (page 27), while the fauna (in particular the pig fossils) from the section also supports the dates. Figure 8–15 also shows how the paleomagnetism of the section conforms roughly to the paleomagnetic record. In summary, the

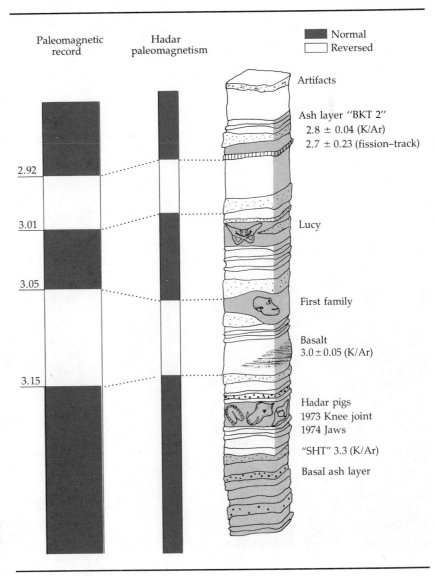

*FIGURE 8–15   Stratigraphic column at Hadar showing chronometric dates in million years B.P. and best fit paleomagnetic match. Compare Figure 1–13.*

site is quite well dated, although further dates from below the fossil-bearing strata would help sandwich the lower collection of fossils.

The fossils from Hadar have been described by Johanson and his associates. The characteristics of the group have caused Johanson, Coppens, and Tim White to recognize a new, earlier, and more primitive species of *Australopithecus*—*A. afarensis*. The characters of this species are described below.

Their size varies considerably both within a sex and between sexes (sexual dimorphism), so that small females, like Lucy, may be only 3 feet 6 inches tall, while large males might be as much as 5 feet tall. Weight probably varied from 25 to 50 kilograms. The individuals, though small, were powerfully built: the bones were thick for their size and carried markings suggesting that they had been well muscled. As we have seen, they were fully bipedal (a claim to be confirmed by some other discoveries, which will be described below). Their arms were slightly longer and their legs slightly shorter, relative to their trunks, than those of modern humans (an apelike character). Their hands had curved apelike fingers and wrist bones, but the fingers were not long—like those of an ape—but shorter like our own, with a fully opposable thumb. Their skulls (Figure 8–16) were small, almost chimpanzeelike, with a cranial capacity of approximately 380–500 cc. (Table 8–1)—hardly different from that of chimpanzees.

Finally, the dentition is of great importance: it is claimed to be significantly more apelike than that of any other species of *Australopithecus*. In particular, the canine is somewhat pointed with a large root and is reminiscent of that of an ape; it also shows noticeable sexual dimorphism (Figure 8–17). It is associated with a small diastema in the upper

*FIGURE 8–16 Composite reconstruction based on* A. afarensis *fossil skull fragments found at Hadar. Reconstruction by Tim White and William Kimbel. The photographs are approximately 30 percent of actual size.*

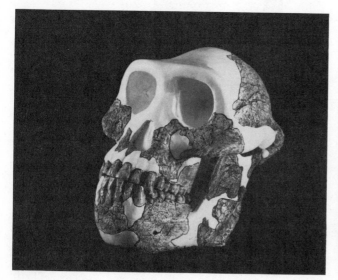
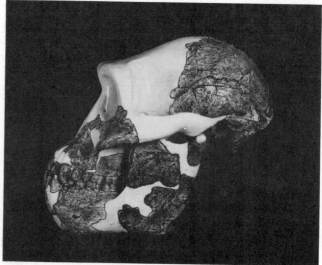

FIGURE 8–17 *Comparison of Hadar with chimpanzee and human dentitions. At the top, a comparison of the male and female canines of each species. Notice the pointed ape canines and the blunt human teeth, together with the considerable sexual dimorphism in the ape and Hadar teeth. Below this the three mandibles are illustrated: notice the intermediate shape of the Hadar mandible. The lines show the alignment of the first lower premolar in relation to the molar series as a whole. Below, the first lower premolar is illustrated. The ape premolar is one-cusped, the human premolar is two-cusped. The Hadar premolar illustrated has a small lingual cusp (arrow) and is intermediate in form.*

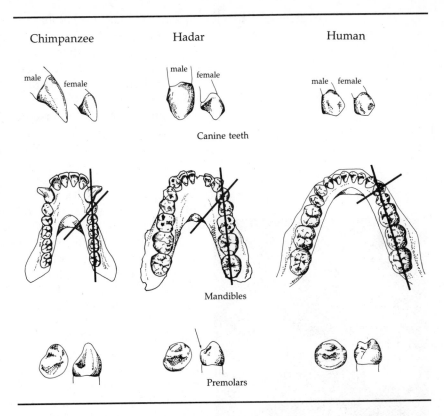

jaw. At the same time, the first lower premolar is also remarkable as lacking or having only a small internal (lingual) secondary cusp; yet the tooth is not truly apelike, for the apes have no second cusp, but only one single large one. It is, as Johanson says, a tooth in transition. This feature and the form of the canine serve to separate the group from the gracile South African *A. africanus.*

The molar teeth show the sort of wear we associate with humans, and the form of the jaw is perhaps more human than apelike, but in the shape of the palate and in the profile of the face, the skull is more apelike (Figures 8–16 and 8–17).

Altogether the *A. afarensis* fossils show a remarkable group of traits that place them squarely in the Hominidae, yet closer to apes than any other species. Eight years' work has made *A. afarensis* one of the best known of all fossil hominid species.

The species *A. afarensis* includes not only the Hadar fossils; we can add to it some skull fragments from the lower member at Koobi Fora and some teeth from the lower levels at Omo, all dated to almost 3 million B.P. The species also includes fossils from another site, Laetoli, which lies in northern Tanzania.

## Discoveries at Laetoli (1974–1977)

Since 1974 Mary Leakey has returned to Laetoli, a site south of Olduvai (Figure 8–1). The site was first visited by the Leakeys in 1935 and later by the German prehistorian L. Kohl-Larsen. Louis Leakey collected some fossils of Pliocene monkeys, which included some loose teeth, among them a canine tooth. This tooth has recently been reexamined and has turned out to belong to the species *Australopithecus afarensis*; it is of great interest, because its discovery actually predates all the discoveries of Robert Broom in South Africa (Chapter 7). It was in fact the first evidence of an adult *Australopithecus* that was ever recovered. In 1939 Kohl-Larsen collected a hominid upper jaw fragment with two teeth, which was called *Meganthropus africanus*. We now know that these finds also belong with the Hadar fossils to the species *A. afarensis*. In 1974 Mary Leakey returned to the site, and from eroding Pliocene strata in this area, she has collected more than twenty fragmentary hominid jaws (Figure 8–18), including those of eight adults and three children, and they are conveniently sandwiched between two volcanic ash strata dated 3.6 and 3.75 million years B.P. They have striking affinity with the contemporary fossils of Hadar and it is claimed that they belong to the same species; they also have much in common with the later *Homo habilis* fossils from Olduvai. Indeed, there is little remaining doubt that the ancestors of the genus *Homo* were populations that, if they were not those actually discovered at Hadar or Laetoli, would nevertheless be classified with them among the early members of the widely dispersed and successful genus *Australopithecus*.

Paul Abell, a geochemist working at Laetoli, made another discovery that was, if anything, more remarkable than the fossil finds. Sandwiched in layers of volcanic ash were found the preserved footprints of a whole range of animals, including elephants, rhinoceroses, many types of antelope, three kinds of giraffe, a saber-toothed cat, and many other species, all now extinct. One of these other species was a hominid: clearly impressed in the ash layer, hominid tracks cover a distance of more than 150 feet. Portions of the tracks are slightly eroded, but several intact prints are preserved (Figure 8–19). The pattern and form of the footprints are like those made in soft sand by modern humans and suggest (like the other evidence) an evolved bipedalism. The smaller and larger footprints (on the basis of modern people's foot size) suggest a stature ranging from about 4 to 5 feet. This discovery is a most remarkable one, and it is unique in paleontology for the number of mammalian species represented: a large proportion of the Laetoli Pliocene fauna has left its imprint. Above all, it is quite clear that *Australopithecus afarensis* was walking very like a human being nearly 4 million years ago.

Up to now we do not have any fossil evidence of the origin and evolution of bipedalism. By about 3.3 million years ago, when the first

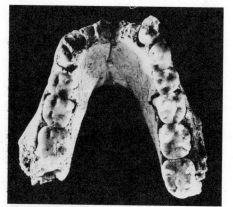

*FIGURE 8–18   This hominid jaw from Laetoli was discovered in 1974 and is dated about 3.7 million years B.P. It has been selected as the type specimen of Australopithecus afarensis. The upper photograph shows the relatively large but damaged canine tooth in the top right-hand corner. The lower photograph shows the jaw from the right-hand side.*

evidence of it appears in the fossil record, we already find footprints and a knee joint that appear fully modern. Further discoveries at Hadar, however, of hand and foot bones and of shoulder and pelvic girdles, make it clear that early *Australopithecus* was not in fact fully modern in its anatomical adaptations to bipedalism insofar as the genus still bore many features that allied it with a climbing mode of locomotion. These features suggest either that these creatures still climbed trees with some regularity, or that their ancestors did so. There is no doubt, however, that their locomotor adaptations had so far evolved that they had reached an efficient and effective bipedalism and that this was their primary mode of locomotion.

## Origins of Gracile and Robust Hominids

But we are still faced with the question of where the gracile and robust *Australopithecus* species evolved. Is one perhaps African and one Asian? We must not forget that the present lack of evidence of *Australopithecus* in Asia does not necessarily mean it was absent from that continent. Some evidence relating to this question comes from two more discoveries, from another part of the Rift Valley. Predating the fossils from Laetoli and Ethiopia, we have an arm bone found in 1965 by a Harvard University expedition at Kanapoi at the south end of Lake Turkana. It is some 4 million years old, is probably hominid, and may have belonged to a gracile type. Then there is a half mandible, which clearly belongs to a gracile hominid, which was found in 1967 at Lothagam, west of Lake Turkana (Figure 8–1). Its age: 5.5 million years. It seems plausible from this slender evidence that East Africa is the home of the gracile lineage that leads to humans, while the robust *A. boisei* might have been an immigrant from elsewhere. Because of its close relationship to *A. robustus*, it may have come from South Africa. It seems most probable that the robust lineage was originally a product of an early gracile form in South or East Africa.

## Early Stone-Tool Evidence

One of the surprises at Koobi Fora is the presence of stone tools, few and far between, but possibly as old as those at Olduvai Gorge. Somewhat older tools have been found by the French-American excavations beside the Omo River. Here, remains of stone-tool industries have been found in sites that are dated at more than 2.0 million years B.P. Scattered flakes are believed to originate from earlier deposits. Only in beds from 2.1 to 2.0 million years old, however, do we find a recognizable collection of artifacts made to a regular pattern in undisturbed datable deposits. But these artifacts are not associated with any hominid fossils. Recent work at Hadar has taken the archaeological record back still further. In the last (1976) field season, archaeologists Helene Roche and Jack Harris (from France and New Zealand) discovered an old land surface with basalt Oldowan tools, together with elephant molar and

*FIGURE 8–19   At Laetoli have been found a unique record of the footprints of animals dated from about 3.7 million years B.P. The footprints of a large proportion of the fossil species are present, including those of Australopithecus afarensis shown in this photograph.*

bone fragments. The site overlies a tuff (BKT 2) dated by potassium-argon and fission-track at 2.7–2.8 million B.P.; Harris dates the tools conservatively at about 2.5 million B.P. (Figure 8–20).

This discovery takes the age of the first known archaeological evidence back another half million years. If the date can be bracketed by further chronometric estimations from overlying tuffs, we shall feel secure in attributing stone-tool manufacture of a regular pattern to this early time. Unfortunately, it has been impossible for anyone to return to Hadar since early in 1977. Clearly the potential for further work is immense, and Johanson and his team will no doubt be back again to consolidate and extend their work as soon as politics allows.

Because *A. boisei* was contemporary with sites bearing stone tools, this raises again the question of whether *A. boisei* was a toolmaker. It may turn out to have been at least a tool-user, if not a toolmaker, but one whose dependence on them was never great because of its vegetarian diet. We do not know, and we may never know.

Such a limitation in technology could explain why *A. boisei* did not survive. Increasing tool use is correlated with better manual dexterity and with the evolution of a more complex brain. If *A. boisei* had ever been interested in expanding its diet to include meat, its preoccupation with tools would probably have been greater. But these were already activities of the gracile *Australopithecus*. By 2 million years ago *A. boisei* and *A. robustus* were perhaps already doomed to disappear, for the competition was to become too much. The gracile *Australopithecus* may even have hunted the much slower robust species. And for some thousands of years, the robust species might have observed their smaller, livelier, more intelligent, and increasingly dangerous cousins, oblivious of the fact that their successor was evolving before their eyes.

For the present, this scenario settles the problem of where the small and large species of *Australopithecus* went—the small became the genus *Homo*, the large became extinct.

## *AUSTRALOPITHECUS* AND *HOMO HABILIS* REVEALED

Let us review what the fossil evidence has told us about the gracile *Australopithecus* and its successor, *Homo habilis*, bearing in mind that the following description is tentative.

**Daily Life**

*Australopithecus* was not an ape. It lived either on the edge of the forest or out on the open plain, but always within a day's walk of water. It was there a long time, certainly for 3 million years, maybe more. It probably spent its days in small troops of males and females with their attendant children, plus some infants carried by their mothers. It walked on two legs as we do. It could run well, and did, to catch lizards, hares, rats, and other small prey. Its world was thronged with animals, as East Africa is today: enormous herds of antelope, zebra, and other

*FIGURE 8–20  The approximate time spans of some of the deposits mentioned in the text. The South African dates are generally less reliable than those for East Africa and Ethiopia. The South African deposits usually represent a short time span that falls somewhere in the range of time indicated. The East African and Ethiopian deposits are deep, and the range indicated is that actually represented by the deposits: fossils are found at many levels.*

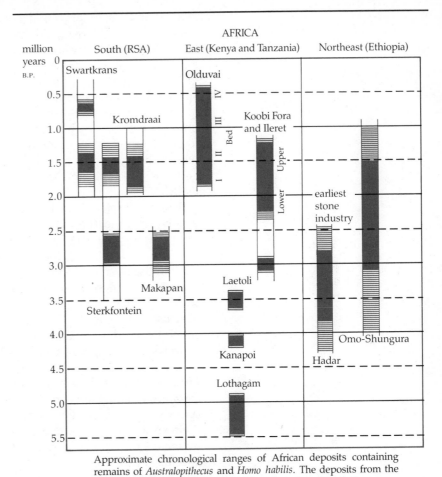

Approximate chronological ranges of African deposits containing remains of *Australopithecus* and *Homo habilis*. The deposits from the northeast and east are better dated than those from the south.

herbivores. It moved among them, watching the smaller gazelles for a sick or crippled individual that it might kill, alert to the possibility of picking off a newborn calf. *Deinotherium* (a type of elephant now extinct), the rhinoceros, and the powerful black buffalo it sensibly avoided.

Its world also contained the lion, leopard, hyena, and a large, now-extinct, saber-toothed cat. All preyed on it from time to time. But it moved in compact bands, and possibly carried sticks, bone clubs, and crudely chipped rocks, and it exhibited a strong sense of group defense in the presence of any threat. All these things enabled it to go about its daily business—searching for roots, berries, insects, and whatever game it could manage to catch—without serious threat from the big cats, which generally preferred to prey on antelope, as they still do. *Australo-*

*pithecus* and *Homo habilis* may even have been able to drive single leopards or lions away from kills they had made; it could have done this to hyenas, provided the hyenas were not too numerous. When it had killed or scavenged game, it may have cut the game up by using sharp-edged chopping tools freshly prepared from pebbles and then have smashed the bones with hammer-stones to extract the marrow.

*Australopithecus* was agile, keen-sighted, alert. It was more intelligent than the baboons with which it shared the savanna, and it had nothing to fear from them—although a single male would probably have been no match for a single male baboon, because *Australopithecus* was lighter and less powerful and lacked the baboon's powerful jaw and canine teeth.

The gracile male was between four and a half and five feet tall and weighed perhaps between sixty and eighty pounds; females were considerably smaller. The color of their skin is unknown but we can guess that it was probably dark and lightly covered with fine hair. Its face was similar in some ways to that of an ape. Its jaw stuck out more than a modern human's, and it had no chin. Its nose was wide and flat, scarcely projecting; its forehead was low and sloping, the bony ridges over its eyes quite prominent. The top and back of its head were very small by modern standards—markedly so, compared to that large forward-thrusting face (Figure 8–21).

Judging by the smallness of its brain and by the brain's presumed proportions, these early hominids probably could not talk. But they certainly must have been capable of a number of expressive nonverbal sounds, such as those we find among most primates, which others of their kind understood. No doubt they also communicated as apes do by means of a subtle and varied range of gestures, body movements, and facial expressions.

Where *Australopithecus* and *Homo habilis* passed the night is not known. Living in savanna areas with forest edges or scattered trees, they may have taken to the trees to avoid predators, for at night the latter would be most active and the sleeping hominid most vulnerable.

How do we reconstruct this sketchy description of the life of *Australopithecus* and *Homo habilis?* What makes it likely to be true? As we have seen, evidence about the Pliocene environment and way of life is accumulating—evidence of the vegetation, climate, and fauna, and of the food remains and stone tools used by *Homo habilis,* as well as the bones themselves, which tell us so much. But there are more behavioral clues than these, as we shall see in Chapter 9.

In the discussions that follow in Chapters 9 and 10, we shall be using the generic term *Australopithecus* to refer to the ancestor of *Homo habilis.* The story of human evolution is concerned with the nature and fate of the gracile form. Its heavily built cousins *A. boisei* and *A. robustus* have no further part in this history and will not be referred to again.

**Origin of the Hominidae**     There, for the present, the story of the early hominid fossils ends. The similarities between the remains of *A. afarensis* and the African great apes are clear, but we have no fossil evidence of the common ancestor, or of its transformation into either a hominid or a chimpanzee. In particular, as we have seen, we have no fossil evidence of the evolution of bipedalism, for by the time of *A. afarensis,* the evolution of bipedalism is almost complete.

*FIGURE 8–21   This reconstruction of Australopithecus africanus required a good deal of imagination on the part of the artist, Jay H. Matternes, because we have no direct evidence of the soft parts of the body. The assumptions made, however, are reasonable, and the result is probably not very misleading.*

## TABLE 8–3   Fossil Record of *Australopithecus* and *Homo habilis*

| TYPE | SOUTH AFRICAN FINDS | AGE (MILLION YEARS)[a] | EAST AFRICAN FINDS | AGE (MILLION YEARS)[b] |
|---|---|---|---|---|
| **Gracile** | | | | |
| *afarensis* | | | Hadar (Coppens, Taieb, Johanson, 1973–1976) | 3.5–2.8 |
| | | | Laetoli (M. Leakey, 1974–1977) | 3.75–3.6 |
| | | | Kanapoi (Patterson, 1965) | c. 4.0 |
| | | | Lothagam (Patterson, 1967) | c. 5.5 |
| | | | Omo (Howell, 1967–1974) | 3.0–2.3 |
| *africanus* | Taung (Dart, 1924) | c. 2.0 | | |
| | Sterkfontein (Broom, 1936, 1947) | 3.0–2.5 | | |
| | Makapansgat (Dart, 1947) | 3.0–2.5 | | |
| *habilis* | Sterkfontein (Robinson, 1957–1958; Hughes, 1973–1976) | 2.0–1.5 | Olduvai (M. and L. Leakey, 1960–1969) | 1.8–1.6 |
| | | | Omo (Howell, 1967–1974) | 2.3–1.5 |
| | Swartkrans (Broom and Robinson, 1949–1952) | 2.0–1.5 | Koobi Fora (R. Leakey, 1969–1976) | 2.2–1.5 |
| **Robust** | | | | |
| *boisei* | | | Olduvai (M. and L. Leakey, 1959) | 1.75 |
| | | | Omo (Howell, 1967–1974) | 2.5–1.5 |
| | | | Koobi Fora (R. Leakey and Isaac, 1969–1974) | 2.2–1.2 |
| | | | Peninj (R. Leakey and Isaac, 1964) | 1.5 |
| *robustus* | Kromdraai (Broom, 1938) | 2.0–1.5 | | |
| | Swartkrans (Broom, 1949) | 2.0–1.5 | | |

[a] Dates attributed to South African sites are based not on potassium-argon analysis but on comparative analysis of fauna, and are not as accurate as potassium-argon dates. Nevertheless, these dates probably do bracket the times during which lived the populations that the fossils represent.
[b] Most of the dates attributed to the East and Northeast African sites are based on at least a few potassium-argon determinations and, although there may be some errors, they are more reliable than those for South African sites.
*Note:* The exact status of some of these fossils is quite uncertain because details about them have not been published in full. Descriptive and analytic studies of some of the more recently discovered fossils are still awaited.

The period of 6 to 4 million years B.P. is the span of time that still eludes us in the hominid story, and it is a time that may tell us of this critical transition that determined the hominid adaptation and ultimately the nature of humankind (Table 8–3). Biochemists have suggested a time of 5 ± 1.5 million years B.P. for the ape-hominid split, and there seems little reason to postulate an earlier date on the basis of the present evidence. One or two million years would probably have been sufficient time for the locomotor evolution that we believe occurred.

What was the common ancestor of humans and African apes like? We can make a number of statements on this subject with some assurance:

1. It was not a biped. Neither chimpanzees nor gorillas show any evidence of ancestral bipedalism either in their present anatomy or in that of their distant *Proconsul* ancestors.

2. It was not a knuckle-walker. Neither modern humans nor any fossil hominids (including *A. afarensis*) show any evidence of knuckle-walking adaptations in their ancestry. Studies of hand and wrist bones in both groups make this clear.

3. Both hominids and great apes are good tree climbers. Hominids suffer from not possessing a prehensile foot, but this loss of prehensibility is clearly a product of bipedalism. The arm, on the other hand, has all the anatomical features of the arm of a climbing primate and is structurally quite comparable to the arms of the great apes (even including the orangutan).

4. In a decade of research, American anatomists and anthropologists, especially J. T. Stern and J. C. Fleagle, have established by detailed study of anatomy and muscle action that climbing brings about adaptations in the hindlimb that are preadaptive for bipedalism. That is to say, the muscles and muscle-action required in climbing can be used with minimal modification for bipedalism. They have also shown that climbing adaptations of the forelimb are preadaptive for hand-over-hand brachiation such as we sometimes see in ape locomotion. Climbing adaptations also require minimal modification for apelike quadrupedalism, and only the hand and wrist are modified for knuckle-walking.

Thus it seems a reasonable hypothesis, with the present evidence and our present knowledge, that the common ancestor of human and African ape was an ape that was an arboreal climber with no specializations for quadrupedalism, bipedalism, or brachiation.

As we saw in Chapter 1, fossils are found only under conditions suitable for their preservation. It is unfortunate that the forest floor is not such a place. The humic acids produced by rotting vegetation will quickly dissolve the calcium phosphate of bone, and unless an arboreal primate happens to die in a flash flood and be buried in a sandbank or washed to a lake shore, its bones are not likely to be preserved. Thus not only do we have a very poor fossil record of forest-living apes, but we are not likely to find much evidence of our common ancestor. Fossils from the period of savanna adaptation will continue to be discovered, but from an earlier period, when our ancestors lived more exclusively in the forest, they will most probably be rare or absent altogether.

If we accept the argument presented here, plus the other evidence offered in this chapter, we may conclude that:

1. Hominids have been separate from apes for probably 5 million years.

2. They had evolved into at least two different kinds by about 2.5 million years ago.

3. One kind continued to evolve, producing the bigger brain and

primitive culture of *Homo;* the other kind became extinct by about 1 million years ago.

Other theories are built on the evidence we have presented. Some authors believe at least three, if not four, separate lineages were evolving alongside each other in Africa alone. New discoveries may prove these authors right, but for the present the simple statement of two evolving lineages represents a reasonable hypothesis. But the hypothesis can take two forms. In one, *Australopithecus africanus* and the older *A. afarensis* both lie on the line leading to *Homo.* In the second, *A. africanus* is placed on a side branch leading to the robust species (Figure 8–22). The first scheme is perhaps the most generally accepted. The second scheme, however, is becoming increasingly attractive as we learn more about the early *A. afarensis* fossils from Hadar and Laetoli. When these fossils have been fully compared with other specimens from East and South Africa, we may have to conclude that *A. africanus* was not an ancestor of humankind but the first stage in the evolution of the robust lineage (Figure 8–7), which may turn out to have originated in South Africa.

And so it is in science. The deductions we make at any time can be based only on the data we have in hand; later evidence may corroborate a hypothesis, question part of it, or disprove it altogether. We must therefore always be open to new ideas and new facts, ready to change our minds and modify our beliefs. The evolution of hypotheses is characteristic of the scientific search for truth.

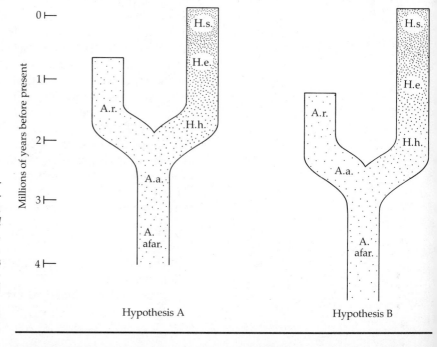

*FIGURE 8–22   In hypothesis A, Australopithecus afarensis* gives rise to A. africanus, *which then divides into two lineages, one leading to* A. robustus *and the second leading to* Homo sapiens. *In hypothesis B,* A. afarensis *splits into two lineages and* A. africanus *is ancestral only to* A. robustus *and* A. boisei. *A. afar. = Australopithecus afarensis; A.r. = A. robustus and A. boisei; H.h. = Homo habilis; H.e. = Homo erectus, and H.s. = Homo sapiens.*

# Chapter 8 Overview

| | YEARS A.D. | DISCOVERIES |
|---|---|---|
| **HOLOCENE** | | |
| 10,000 | 1974 | Hominids found at Laetoli |
| **PLEISTOCENE** | 1973 | Hominids first found at Hadar |
| | 1969 | Oldest stone tools found at Omo |
| 1.5 million | 1967 | First Koobi Fora expedition |
| | | First Omo expedition |
| **PLIOCENE** | | |
| 5 million | 1960 | Discovery of first *Homo habilis* bones at Olduvai |
| | 1959 | Discovery of *Zinjanthropus boisei* at Olduvai |
| | 1954 | Discovery of two hominid milk teeth at Olduvai |
| **MIOCENE** | | |
| *Ramapithecus* | 1939 | First hominids found at Laetoli |
| | 1931 | First Leakey expedition to Olduvai |

*Dryopithecus*

| | YEARS B.P. | FOSSIL RECORD | HOMINID LINEAGE |
|---|---|---|---|

*Homo sapiens*

25 million

**OLIGOCENE**

1 million — Most recent gracile and *A. boisei* at East Rudolf

*Homo erectus*

A. robustus in South Africa

*A. boisei* and *habilis* at Olduvai

2 million — Most recent *A. boisei* and gracile at Omo

*Homo habilis*

Earliest *A. africanus* in South Africa

A. robustus in South Africa

Gracile *A. afarensis* at Hadar

3 million

*A. africanus*

A. boisei in East Africa

*Apidium, Parapithecus, Aegyptopithecus,* and *Propliopithecus*

35 million

Oldest gracile and *A. boisei* fossils at Omo

Gracile at Laetoli

4 million — Age of Kanapoi

*A. afarensis*

*Amphipithecus*

5 million

**EOCENE**

Lothagam jaw

6 million

**CENOZOIC**

7 million

8 million

58 million

9 million

**PALEOCENE**

Early prosimians

65 million

## THE GREAT SAVANNA

The story of discoveries in Northeast and East Africa is as exciting as that of South Africa and new discoveries are reported every year. Dating of fossil deposits is far more secure in these areas than in South Africa because there has been much volcanic activity since the early Miocene and potassium-argon dating is therefore possible. Many of the deposits, moreover, are very thick and span a considerable time range (Figure 8–20).

# Chapter 9

# The Evolution of Hominid Behavior

As unto the bow the cord is,
So unto the man is woman;
Though she bends him, she obeys him,
Though she draws him, yet she follows;
Useless each without the other!

HENRY WADSWORTH LONGFELLOW, 1807–1882.
*The Song of Hiawatha*, x.

As we have seen, human evolution probably began with an unspecialized, arboreal, climbing primate that we would classify as an ape. It was probably somewhat smaller and somewhat shorter-armed, possibly somewhat more general in its food tastes than the chimpanzee of today, hence more willing to explore a variety of food sources. The world, in short, was wide open to it. It could go in any of several directions.

**HOMINID LOCOMOTION**

**From the Trees
to the Ground**

If in one part of this ape's range there are large forests and an abundance of fig trees, there will be little reason for the animal not to stay in the trees and become increasingly specialized as a fruit eater. In another part of the range, or at another time, however, the environment might be somewhat different: fewer fig trees, but an abundance of seeds, berries, tubers, insects, and other food on the ground. Such a situation may have existed about 4 to 6 million years ago. At that time tropical forest extended through a good part of Central Africa as it does today. Of course, there also existed a comparably large amount of forest edge, and open woodland with opportunities for tree dwellers to descend to the ground and eat the berries, roots, insects, and other food that

215

abounded in the open. Such a place where two ecological zones meet is called an *ecotone*. It presents new opportunities for survival, for if an animal adapts to the ecotone, it can exploit the food found in both zones. Advanced apelike creatures thronged the forests, probably as a number of species, some of which must have lived on the forest edge. Like a good many monkeys and apes today, some of these creatures (among them our ancestors) undoubtedly came to the ground when opportunities for feeding presented themselves.

If it is understood that these "decisions" to come to the ground were repeated billions of times by millions of apes in thousands of different places, then one begins to get a better idea of the process of evolution: it was a gradual one, so gradual as to be imperceptible except over a great span of time. Opportunity and aptitude went together. No one decision by one ape or group of apes had any evolutionary meaning whatsoever. But in places that, century after century, provided a better living on the ground for apes able to exploit it, the animals best adapted to living and feeding on the ground were the ones that spent most time there and whose descendants became still better adapted to this environment and life-style.

The apes were not forced out of the trees. It is true that during the Pliocene the forests dried up and retreated, subtracting several million square miles of living space from the possible ranges of tree-dwelling apes. But the process was so gradual that at no time could it have affected the evolving habits of individual animals and the extent of the forest-edge ecotone was not greatly altered. Variations of climate from one year to the next were all that concerned them. If a river goes dry and the trees along it die, the animals that formerly thrived there simply move away, taking their various ways of living with them. They do not abandon living in trees because some trees disappear; they simply find other trees.

## Tool Use and Bipedalism

In his *Descent of Man*, Charles Darwin wrote: "The free use of arms and hands, partly the cause and partly the result of man's erect position, appears to have led in an indirect manner to other modifications of structure . . . . As they gradually acquired the habit of using stones, clubs or other weapons, they would use their jaws and teeth less and less. In this case the jaws, together with the teeth, would become reduced in size." Thus Darwin believed that bipedalism led to weapon use and then to smaller jaws and teeth.

In contrast, the American anthropologist Sherwood Washburn suggested that tool using might have preceded walking on two legs; more than that, it probably helped to develop walking. He pointed out that apes, unlike monkeys, were characteristically upright even before they left the trees. Whereas monkeys ran along branches on all fours or jumped about in them, apes climbed hand over hand. They swung from branches, sat upright in them, and sometimes even stood on them. Their arms were well articulated for reaching in all directions, and the important, interrelated development of stereoscopic eyesight, larger brain, and improved manual dexterity had already evolved. Apes, in short, had the physical equipment and the dawning brain potential to use their hands in new and useful ways. That certain of them did so is suggested by the knowledge that chimpanzees, man's nearest relatives, are simple tool users today. As we have seen, they throw stones and sticks as weapons. They use sticks, rocks, and handfuls of leaves for digging, cracking nuts, wiping themselves, and sopping up water.

Like Darwin, most authors have believed that humans were bipedal from the time they first stepped away from the trees, and that it was this characteristic that gave them the opportunity to become tool users and toolmakers, by freeing their hands to carry things. If hominids found it advantageous to walk on two legs from the beginning, the argument goes on, then, to make it easier for them to get about in that way, natural selection would inevitably improve their pelvis, leg bones, foot bones, and muscles.

If we accept that at some time in the late Miocene certain apelike creatures found themselves becoming increasingly adapted to life on the ground, we must also accept that, being apes, they had the potential for walking erect and for using their hands. This brings up two important matters. First, the things these creatures spent their days doing—poking up roots with sticks, turning over stones for grubs and beetles, snatching at or swatting small lizards and frogs, cracking nuts with rocks—all tended to improve and develop the manual dexterity that they already possessed. Second, because they found themselves in greater danger from predators on the ground than in the trees, they were probably very slow to abandon trees entirely, doing so only as their ability to run about developed. That ability depended on leg structure. By standing up, a ground dweller could see potential enemies much better over the tops of bushes and tall grass, as baboons do to this day. Over an extended period the individuals that had the longest legs and stood up most often would be the ones that could see predators best and run for safety first. They would be the best adapted and ultimately might abandon the trees.

The critical matter here seems to be a combination of environmental pressure and timing. Populations of higher primates that left the trees as quadrupeds remained quadrupedal, like the baboon. Those which became climbers had the potential for erect posture and hand use. Some of them became specialized as brachiators; the long-armed, brachiating gibbons are now firmly established in the trees. Others were able to develop their potential for erectness and live on the ground. The timing must be just right: the populations not wedged too tightly into any particular niche were best able to adapt to a new opportunity on the ground. That way, they developed a competitive advantage over any later creatures who tried to follow suit. And, gradually, some of them became hominids. The others remained in the forest and went in slightly different directions, becoming modern chimpanzees and gorillas.

## Physical Adaptations

To achieve good bipedalism, the hominid predecessor had to go through evolutionary changes in the shape and proportions of the foot, leg, and pelvic bones, and in the muscles of the leg and buttock. A chimpanzee can walk quite comfortably on its hind legs, but not for any length of time. It can also run surprisingly fast. But the chimpanzee simply is not built properly for what humans know as efficient running and walking (Figure 9–1). Its legs are too short, its feet are not the right shape, its big toes stick out to the side like thumbs, instead of forward to give spring to the stride, and its propulsive buttock muscles are rather small and poorly placed. What muscles it can use for bipedal walking are attached to its bones in such a way that insufficient leverage is provided to achieve a vigorous stride. The chimpanzee proceeds in a kind of waddle or rolling gait, because it must shift its body weight at each step to position it over the leg that is on the ground.

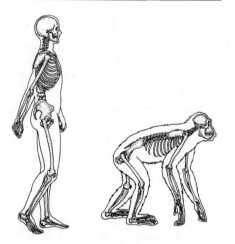

FIGURE 9–1  *The posture of human and chimpanzee compared. The forms of the skull, vertebral column, pelvis, limbs; hands, and feet reflect the means of locomotion.*

A more efficient way of walking erect is to have the legs longer and the knees closer together, as they are in humans (see p. 200). This is made possible by a marked change in the shape and proportions of the ancestral leg and foot bones and particularly in the ancestral pelvis (Figure 9–2). There has been a twisting and flattening of the two large pelvic flanges, which not only sets the trunk more vertically on the legs, but also provides better anchorage and far better leverage for the three sets of buttock muscles that are used in walking. We know that these changes were almost complete in *Australopithecus afarensis* by 3.75 million years ago.

## Knuckle Walking

Sherwood Washburn also maintained that erect walking was the final stage in a process that first had to proceed through an intermediate stage: the style of four-legged locomotion known as *knuckle walking*. As we have seen, two of the great apes are knuckle walkers today: the chimpanzee and gorilla (Figure 9–3). (As Washburn says, this is exactly the position a football lineman takes before the snap of the ball.) According to Washburn, knuckle walking could be regarded as a kind of half-way step between quadrupedalism and bipedalism.

The anatomist Charles Oxnard, among others, has pointed out, however, that the human shoulder blade most resembles that of the orangutan, which is not a knuckle walker. This similarity suggests that the ancestral hominid was an accomplished climber while in the trees and, accustomed to an erect posture, might have walked bipedally immediately on descending to the ground (as the gibbon does now), without ever going through a knuckle walking stage.

And if a human being is specialized for walking upright, with all the muscular and skeletal adaptations that make it possible, so too is an ape specialized for its kind of locomotion: a modern knuckle walking chimpanzee has a very complex arrangement of muscles, ligaments, and bones, particularly in the wrist and the bases of the fingers, which enable it to proceed comfortably on all fours. Knuckle walking should not be regarded as an inferior or intermediate way of getting around, but simply as a different way. It is a way developed by a kind of ape that never entirely left the forest and consequently could get along with a different form of locomotion, appropriate to the animal's own needs. For a different ape, one that lived in more open country and often used tools, knuckle walking was not so good. Fossil wrist and hand bones of *Australopithecus afarensis* at Hadar, or from Olduvai and other *Homo habilis* sites in Africa provide no evidence for ancestral apelike knuckle walking adaptations. Most scholars now believe that protohominids never did pass through a knuckle walking stage; they became bipedal hominids without any intermediate locomotor adaptations, though the transition was gradual.

## Manipulation, Bipedalism, and Brain Development

From squatting in a tree to strolling upright in a meadow is an enormous evolutionary leap. Any explanation of the change can only be specula-

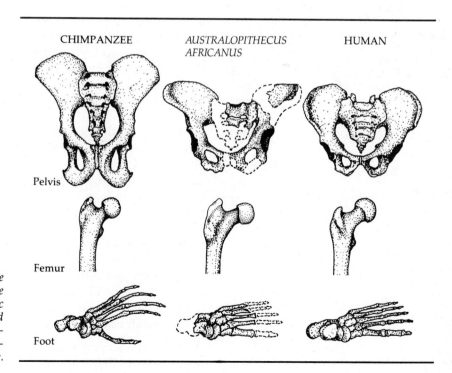

CHIMPANZEE     *AUSTRALOPITHECUS AFRICANUS*     HUMAN

Pelvis

Femur

Foot

FIGURE 9–2   *These comparisons emphasize the humanness of* Australopithecus: *note the shortening and broadening of the pelvic structure, the lengthening of the "neck" and the larger head of the upper end of the femur, and the large, robust, and nonopposable big toe.*

FIGURE 9–3   Knuckle walking is a means of quadrupedal locomotion peculiar to chimpanzees and gorillas. These animals put their weight on the soles of their feet and on the outer surface of their fingers, which carry specialized, ridged, hairless friction skin, such as is found on the palms of our hands.

tive. But some speculations have an uncanny way of hanging together. For a confirmed weapon and tool user, the most useful way of getting about is on two feet, because the hands are left free to carry things. Chance success with throwing stones and sticks may have led to dawning realization that rocks and clubs were invaluable as weapons in defense, and even for bringing down small game. In due course, these talents could have made the creatures that possessed them rather formidable, allowing the animals to venture farther and farther from the safety of the trees. Eventually they could have become completely ground-oriented by day, with natural selection evolving creatures that were more and more adept at running on two legs.

As a bit of fossil evidence to back up claims of early weapon and tool use, Washburn calls attention to the extreme smallness of the male *Australopithecus* canine tooth. In all other large ground-dwelling primates—in chimpanzees, gorillas, and, particularly, baboons—the male's canine is an enormous tooth, a true fang. Among its uses are self-defense and intimidation against the large and dangerous predators ground dwellers are exposed to. For a male hominid to be able to get along on the ground without such a tooth, we must supply some other means of self-defense. Although no early archaeological evidence for weapons has yet been recognized, this logic would suggest that weapons have been vital for 4 or 5 million years—long before *Homo* evolved.

To an animal increasingly involved with manipulation, brain development becomes much more important, and changes in skull size and shape can be considered as possible results of selective pressure to provide increased brain space. By this time the tangled triple influence of bipedalism, brain development, and manipulation of objects cannot be separated. As one attribute develops, faster development in another takes place, which in turn encourages further development in the first.

## Problem of Causation

There may be disagreement as to whether weapon or tool use first stimulated walking or walking first stimulated weapon and tool use, but there is absolutely no disagreement on the way in which both related to brain development or on the importance of positive feedback among weapons, tool use, and walking. *Positive feedback*—a process in which positive change in one variable component of a system brings about positive changes in other components of that system, which feed back to reinforce change in the first component—is a widely known phenomenon. Its effects are obvious in the buildup of unusually large waves in the ocean under the right conditions, when the waves themselves help create bigger waves. A problem is revealed, however, when the elements that make up the evolutionary feedback model (Figure 9–4) are broken down:

1. Out in the open, early hominids needed weapons to defend themselves because they had small canines.

FIGURE 9–4  *Numerous feedback systems occur in nature and are often interlocking. Negative feedback maintains stability, but positive feedback brings about major adaptive changes that constitute evolution. Shown here in simplified form is a positive feedback system that has been important in human evolution.*

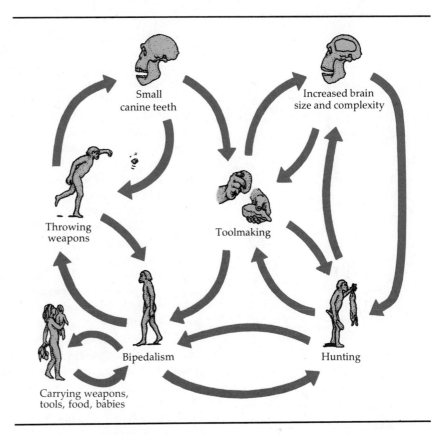

2. They had small canines because they no longer needed big ones.

3. Because they were becoming erect they had greater opportunities to use weapons. With weapons they were better able to defend themselves.

4. Big canines for defense were no longer necessary; their canines became smaller.

This is a classic feedback model. Once it is set up, it is not hard to see how each element affects the other, including that all-important by-product, development of the brain. The only trouble is that the argument goes in a circle: canines don't get small because you need weapons and a bipedal stance to protect yourself against having small canines!

**Seed-Eating Hypothesis**    This circularity in reasoning was pointed out by the British anthropologist Clifford Jolly, who writes that the more nearly perfect a feedback model is, the more nearly impossible it is to get the model started. If everything depends so neatly on everything else, he observes, nothing will happen. In thinking about this dilemma Jolly tried to find an element that did not depend on the others, something that got its initial

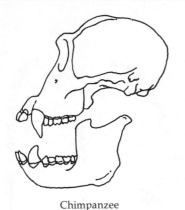

Chimpanzee

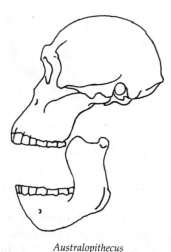

Australopithecus

FIGURE 9–5   *The braincase of* Australopi-
*thecus is larger, and its skull better bal-
anced than that of the chimpanzee. But the
most striking difference between the chimpanzee skull and that of* Australopithecus
*lies in the dentition. The* Australopithecus
*teeth are of even height and wear relatively
flat; the jaw is powerfully built to grind as
well as crush.*

thrust from some outside influence. Like many other anthropologists, he was struck by the remarkable differences between the teeth of the earliest hominids and those of the other apes (Figure 9–5). Those small canines and incisors, together with the abnormally large molars, had to be explained in some way.

Because teeth and jaw structure obviously are related to eating habits, Jolly tried to account for the dental peculiarities of the ancestral hominid by seeking a shift in feeding—a movement away from reliance on fruit to reliance on something else. Noticing that modern humans still depend on cereal grains, the seeds of domesticated grasses, for their diet, Jolly speculated that at some time in the past ancestral hominids might have begun to include seeds as at least a part of their diet.

Jolly's argument for this hypothesis is complicated, and some of the dental evidence is beyond the scope of this book, but the main points fall together in enough ways to make up an intriguing case for his idea. To begin with, there is the ecological niche itself: the more open country at the ecotone and seasonal variability in the weather (alternating rainy and dry seasons are necessary if a grassland is to maintain itself). Open country, with its grains, contains a large untapped source of food for an ape that has enough manual dexterity to scoop, pick, or strip something as small as seeds. The gelada baboons can do so today; so too can some chimpanzees that have adapted to seasonal open-country life, going out during dry periods when the yield of food in the forest is low. There is no reason why a hominid ancestor could not also have done it.

What is needed to become an efficient seed eater? Very large molars, for one thing, to grind up large numbers of small, hard objects, together with plenty of enamel on the faces of the teeth to withstand the grinding. This combination is exactly what we find in *Australopithecus*. Also, proper hinging of the jaw and powerful muscles are essential to develop power for easy crushing, together with enough flexibility to permit the side-to-side motion that is necessary for grinding. But all the flexibility in the world at the back of the mouth will do no good if rotary movement is limited by large canine teeth interlocking in front. Help yourself to a small mouthful of peanuts or sunflower seeds and chew them up, and you will notice two things. First, as you swivel your jaw to grind up the seeds, your front teeth will move as much as or more than your back ones. If you try to check this front-tooth movement, as oversize canines would check it, you will find the side-to-side movement of your back teeth limited. Second, you will find that the highly arched roof of your mouth, together with a thick and flexible tongue, acts as an efficient mechanism for constantly pushing the mouthful back under the molars for further grinding, until the food is in a condition to be swallowed. The combination that has just served you well—large molars, small canines, rather small incisors, and an arched palate—is characteristic of *Australopithecus,* but not of apes. (In other primates, females may have small canines, but males still have large ones. Only in humans are male canines small.)

Here, Jolly suggests, lies the clue to the peculiar dental evolution of the earliest hominids, and also the initial thrust that started the feedback process. If there is a wealth of seeds to be eaten in a new environment, and a selective advantage in the evolution of smaller male canines in order to exploit this diet more efficiently, smaller canines will result.

"But," an alert skeptic will say, "what about baboons? Don't baboons have very large canine teeth for protection on the ground? If they became seed eaters, why didn't they lose those teeth too?" The answer to this question goes back to the fundamental difference between hominids and monkeys. One has the erect inheritance and potential for tool use that the other lacks. If hominids can develop a talent for using weapons to protect themselves or at least intimidate potential attackers, they do not need big canines at all. Savanna baboons do need them—and they still have them. Gelada baboons, who live on mountain slopes and not the savanna, show some modifications that support Jolly's hypothesis. They are to some extent seed eaters, and their molars are larger and their canines smaller than those of other baboons that eat more succulent food, such as the lower stems of grasses.

Jolly's comparisons, while not conclusive in themselves, make an arguable theory for the appearance of the "third ape" (the first two being the chimpanzee and the gorilla) on the ground and out in the open at an early date. That creature probably had a talent for using tools and weapons that not only made possible the modification of molars and canine teeth to adapt to a diet emphasizing seeds, but also encouraged further tool use, manual dexterity, and bipedalism, all of which combined to stimulate further development of the brain.

Anthropologist Richard Kay, however, points out that fruit-eating primates (frugivores) have thicker molar enamel than leaf-eating species (folivores). Also, the ability to crush seeds in fruit, as well as nuts, was almost certainly an important adaptation among some forest-living forms, and many of these do not show significant canine reduction. The implication is that seed eating may not be the cause of canine reduction.

Sherwood Washburn, like some others, thinks diet cannot explain how *Australopithecus* evolved its peculiar dentition of large molars and small canines. In Washburn's view these features must be traced to other activities—to the gradual increase of tool and weapon use and the development of hunting. Jolly may agree with Washburn on the importance of tool use, but mainly to explain how human teeth evolved from *Australopithecus* teeth. Jolly is looking further back; he is interested in finding how *Australopithecus* teeth evolved from ape teeth.

From these arguments we can conclude that a change in diet to seeds and tough vegetation was probably more important at an early stage of hominid evolution, and the development of hunting and tool use was more important later on. There is no doubt that at some time tool use and toolmaking became the critical factors in the increasingly swift shaping of humankind and also in the increasingly important role that hunting would play in hominid life.

Finally, we can now be sure from the fossil record not only that bipedalism was a very early development but that brain enlargement was relatively late. The fully bipedal *A. afarensis* had a brain no bigger than that of a chimpanzee, and although the creature was smaller in body size, it was probably no smaller than the pygmy chimpanzee (*Pan paniscus*). Brain expansion, on the other hand (Table 7–1), did not really get under way until the time of *Homo habilis,* and from that period we find stone tools made to a regular pattern. We have to conclude that the chart in Figure 9–4 is probably valid but that some components of the system were possibly operating before others. All, however, began slowly and in so doing left no record: we shall perhaps never have certain knowledge of the actual sequence (if it was a sequence) of events. Our knowledge of living primates and the archaeological and fossil records give us this sequence as a working hypothesis:

| | |
|---|---|
| Throwing objects ⎫<br>Tool use ⎭ | Seen in living primates and therefore probably ancient |
| Bipedalism ⎫<br>Reduced canines ⎭ | Evident by 3.75 million years B.P. |
| Toolmaking | Evident by about 2.5 million years B.P. |
| Hunting and scavenging ⎫<br>Increasing brain size ⎭ | Evident by 1.75 million years B.P. |

## EARLY TECHNOLOGY

The origin of tools in human evolution must have occurred through trial and error. The nearest we can come to reconstructing that process is to remind ourselves that there was a time when our ancestors could do with fewer tools than chimpanzees can do now. They must have worked their way up from a similar (but not necessarily identical) limited capacity to shape something for a purpose—a grass stem for poking into a termite mound, a chewed-up mouthful of leaves to serve as a sponge, a stick or branch as something to be brandished in an effort to intimidate, a rock to throw.

A group of not-too-large apes will seem more formidable standing erect because they will appear larger; in fact, the erect posture is sometimes used by nonhuman primates as a gesture of threat. The brandishing of sticks or branches will enhance that effect, and may have been enough, on occasion, to swing the balance to the hominids in a set-to with hyenas over possession of a kill. The earliest use of implements by our ancestors, ground-dwelling scavenger-hunters, may have received its strongest impetus from its value in threat displays against competing species. For an immensely long time, the found implement was the only type of implement, picked up and then thrown away when its immediate use was over. But there must have come a stage at which *Australopithecus* (or its ancestor) began to recognize more and more clearly the usefulness of certain objects and, as a result, tended to hang on to them longer, until it may have begun carrying them around much of the time. The great abundance of wood, and the fact that it is softer and easier to work than stone, suggests that the earliest hominids may have used wood a great deal. They also probably used the long bones of some of the larger animals. But the great triumph of our ancestors as creators of culture came much later and is seen most clearly in the legacy they have left us of worked stone. All the oldest surviving artifacts are implements for cutting and chopping, not weapons. We can therefore recognize a clear succession: tool use, tool modification, toolmaking.

## Earliest Stone Industry: The Oldowan

The magnet that drew Louis and Mary Leakey back to Olduvai Gorge year after year was the large numbers of extremely primitive stone implements. Mary Leakey made the study of these objects her special province. Her first monograph on the stone culture at Olduvai covers material taken from the gorge's lowest strata, known as Beds I and II, and a time period that extends from 1.8 million years ago to 1.2 million years ago (Table 9–1).

Certain details of the lives of the creatures who lived at Olduvai so long ago have been reconstructed from the hundreds of thousands of bits of material that they left behind—some stone, some bone; some large, some extremely small. No one of these things, alone, would mean much, but when all are analyzed and fitted together like a gigantic three-dimensional jigsaw puzzle, patterns begin to emerge that speak across the gulf of time.

Mary Leakey found that there are two stoneworking traditions in Olduvai. One, the Acheulian, appears only in Bed II and will be discussed in Chapter 11. The other, the Oldowan, is the older and more primitive and occurs throughout Bed I, as well as at other sites in somewhat earlier deposits we have already mentioned (see page 205). It consists mainly of what anthropologists for a long time called pebble tools but what Mary Leakey prefers to call *choppers*. The word *pebble* suggests something quite small, and her term is an improvement, for many of the chopping tools at Olduvai are of hen's-egg size or larger, some of them three or four inches across.

An Oldowan chopper (Figure 9–6) is about the most basic "human"-made, "human"-used implement that one can possibly imagine and the earliest artifact from the Stone Age recognized by archaeologists. It is, typically, made from a cobble, a stone that has been worn smooth by sand and water action. The stone selected is often that of a close-

| TABLE 9–1 | Stratified Beds and Fossils at Olduvai Gorge | |
|---|---|---|
| APPROXIMATE AGE (YEARS) | BED | FOSSILS AND INDUSTRY |
| 100,000–400,000 | Upper beds | *Homo sapiens* |
| 400,000–700,000 | Bed IV | Fossils of *Homo erectus* Late Acheulian hand-axes and cleavers |
| 700,000–1.2 million | Bed III | No fossils Few artifacts |
| 1.2–1.65 million | Bed II | *Homo erectus and Homo habilis* Early Acheulian and Oldowan tools |
| 1.65–1.8 million | Bed I | *Australopithecus boisei* and *Homo habilis* Oldowan choppers |
| 1.9 million | Volcanic lava | |

*Note:* The ages of the Upper beds are still rather uncertain. Bed I carries the most reliable dates.

FIGURE 9–6  *An Oldowan chopper is usually made by striking some flakes from a rounded cobble to give a cutting edge. It is the simplest stone implement.*

grained, hard, smooth-textured material like quartz, flint, or chert. Many cobbles at Olduvai are of hardened lava that flowed out of the volcanoes in the region.

Oval or pear-shaped, and small enough to fit comfortably in the hand, such a water-rounded stone could be gripped firmly without hurting the palm. What an early toolmaker had to do to turn it into a tool was simply to smash one end down hard on a nearby boulder, or balance it on the boulder and give it a good whack with another rock. A large chip would fly off. Another whack would knock off a second chip next to the first, leaving a jagged edge or perhaps a point on one end of the stone. With luck this edge would be sharp enough for the hominids to cut up meat, to saw or mash through joints and gristle, to scrape hides, to sharpen the end of a stick. There are large choppers and small ones. The tool presumably was held as one would hold a rock while banging downward with a direct hammering or chopping motion. The small chips knocked off during the manufacture of choppers are known as *flakes*. Sharper than choppers, they probably were used for slicing and cutting. They undoubtedly became dull very quickly, for although stone is hard, its edges break easily.

The names of many of the ancient tools imply a way of using them. It should be understood clearly that a name like "chopper" describes a use that can only be guessed at by the archaeologist. The guess may appear overwhelmingly logical, but it is still a guess.

An implement like a chopper is recognized readily by an expert, although to you it might be indistinguishable from a stone that has been pointed or edged by nature. The ancient tool kit contains implements that are still more primitive than choppers, and with luck they can be found and with skill recognized. An unworked stone that bears the marks of a great deal of banging and battering may have been used as a hammer or as an anvil. Also, the presence of stones of a kind that do not normally occur at a site indicate tool use, even though the stones themselves have not been chipped. These unchipped stones are called *manuports,* meaning they have been moved by human intervention. As for actual manufacture, the presence of large numbers of chips or flakes in one spot is an indication that toolmaking took place there. Choppers are by no means the most common tool found in the earliest sites. Much more numerous are the smaller chips and naturally shaped stones. The latter, of course, were the principal source of tools for millions of years before it occurred to anyone to try to sharpen a stone. They are identifiable today only by the context in which they are found. Other early implements that may have been used cannot be recognized.

The culture that Mary Leakey's work at Olduvai reveals was left by a 1.8-million-year-old hominid that most anthropologists believe was too small-brained even to talk. Just as the intricacies and subtleties of chimpanzee or baboon society turn out to be much more complex than anyone realized a generation ago, so too does the culture of the early bipedal hominids. The Leakeys concluded that the creature responsible for turning out this varied tool kit was of the genus *Homo,* and therefore called it *Homo habilis,* because of the elaborateness of the culture Mary Leakey unearthed, not because of the size of the brain. If it could make tools rather than merely use them, and make them to a regular pattern, the Leakeys argued, then it was a human.

## Occupation Floors

Perhaps the most impressive of all the things Mary Leakey has turned up at Olduvai are *occupation floors.* These are ancient land surfaces where hominids lived for periods of time, dependent on the local vegetation and the local game. They are, in effect, nearly 2-million-year-old campsites and are identifiable by heavy concentrations of fossil material, stone tools, and debris, which are confined to a depth of only a few inches. The earth those hominids squatted on is still there, with the remains of what they made and ate scattered about.

Gradually, and without much disturbance, blown dust, encroaching vegetation, rising water, and mud covered each of these occupation floors. Thus, the objects that 2 million years later the Leakeys were to uncover laboriously and catalogue thoroughly remained exactly where they had been dropped (Figure 9–7). Elsewhere in Olduvai the artifacts

FIGURE 9–7 *This plan of an ancient land surface shows the distribution of bones and stones discovered at a site in Bed I of Olduvai Gorge by Louis and Mary Leakey. The circle of rocks suggests the alignment of the base of a windbreak or hut—the earliest known.*

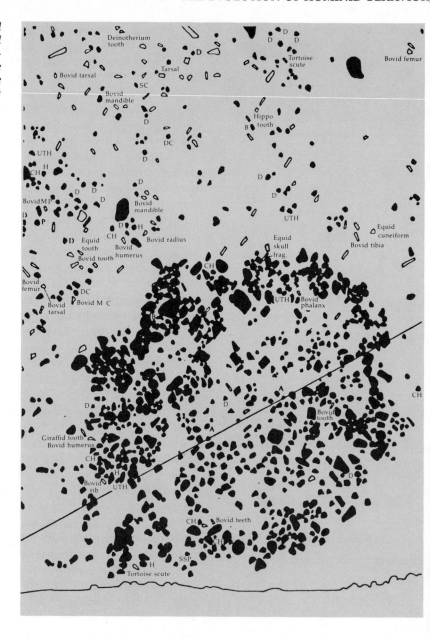

and bones are spread through layers of sand and clay that may be several feet deep. In these places it is clear that river action has moved the objects about, swirled them together, and dumped them from time to time, making their position relative to one another not very meaningful. But as one lays bare an occupation floor, one can learn something about the life that its owner lived.

What did *Homo habilis* leave there? One site contained a lot of fish heads and crocodile bones, together with fossilized papyrus plants, indicating at least that the site was next to water that probably provided some food. Other sites contain the bones of flamingos. This evidence says that the nearby water was a lake, shallow and slightly alkaline as many East African lakes are today, for only such conditions produce the tiny shrimps flamingos eat.

Ten occupation sites have been identified at Olduvai, out of about seventy fossil- or tool-bearing sites scattered along a twelve-mile stretch of the gorge. On one floor the cultural debris is arranged in a most peculiar manner. A dense concentration of chips and flakes from tool manufacture is mixed in with a great number of small, smashed animal-bone fragments, all crowded into a roughly rectangular area some fifteen feet wide and thirty feet long. Surrounding this rectangle is a space three or four feet wide with hardly any of this cultural junk; the ground is nearly bare. But outside that place, the material becomes relatively abundant again. How can we account for this extraordinary arrangement? The most obvious explanation is that the densely littered central section was a living site surrounded by a protective thorn hedge, inside which hominids relaxed safely while they made their tools and ate their food, tossing out over the hedge whatever they did not simply drop on the floor.

**The First Shelters**  At another site is a roughly circular formation of stones, about fourteen feet in diameter (Figure 9–7). The other stones on that occupation floor are widely and haphazardly scattered. By contrast, the circle is a dense concentration of several hundred stones carefully arranged in a ring by somebody—somebody who also took the trouble to make higher piles of stones every two or three feet around the circle. That this configuration survives after nearly 2 million years is staggering. This ancient arrangement of stones brings to mind the kind of shelter being made today by the Okombambi tribe of southwest Africa (Figure 9–8). They, too, make low rings of stones, with higher piles at intervals to support upright poles or branches, over which skins or grasses are spread to keep out the wind.

Although the predictable debris is found inside the stone circle, indicating that some activity took place there, the evidence shows that a wider variety of activities took place outside, which makes sense. The interior dimensions of this somewhat irregular circle are only about eight feet by twelve feet, which would have made the enclosure rather crowded were all kinds of activities carried out in it. Furthermore, the group that used the shelter included some extremely good hunters or scavengers. The surrounding area contains the fossilized remains of giraffes, hippos, and many antelopes, and the tooth of the ancient kind of elephant, *Deinotherium*. This group was eating big game and may

FIGURE 9–8   *This shelter of branches and grass, built by the Okombambi people of Namibia, is probably little different from those that have been built for the last two million years. The evidence from Olduvai Gorge, Bed I, suggests a structure of this type (see Figure 9–7).*

have found it more convenient to eat out in the open rather than in the confines of the shelter.

The chronicle of Olduvai does not say whether these hominids actually killed any of those large animals, whether they chased any of them into swamps and helped them die, whether they brought home meat from found carcasses, whether they more commonly preempted the kills of other carnivores. But it makes clear that some scavenging did take place. Under microscopic investigation, some bones show the marks of the teeth of carnivores, and superimposed upon them, the score marks of stone-flake incisions. There is no doubt that when an extremely large carcass became available it was butchered and eaten. Two sites at Olduvai Gorge are known to have been *butchering sites* (Figure 9–9). One contains the skeleton of an elephant, the other that of a deinotherium. Since those animals weighed several tons each, it was obviously impossible to move them; the thing to do was to settle down where the carcass was and chop and chew away at it until its meat was gone. Judging from the evidence at these butchering sites, that is exactly what happened. At each there is an almost complete skeleton of a huge animal, its bones disarranged as if they had been tugged and hacked apart. Lying among the bones are the discarded choppers and other stone tools that did the hacking.

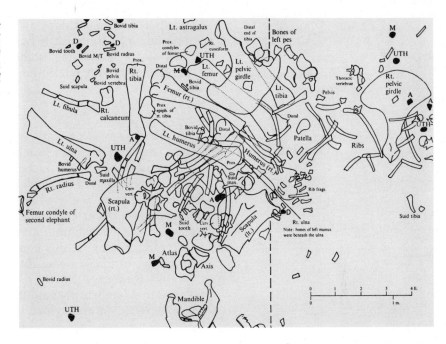

FIGURE 9–9  *This plan shows part of the ancient living floor of a butchery site in Bed I of Olduvai Gorge. Stone tools (solid black) are mixed in with almost the entire skeleton of an elephant, together with other food remains.*

Certain Olduvai sites are rich in antelope bones: some skulls are cracked open at the precise point on the front where the bone was thinnest. Other sites are crammed with the shells of large tortoises. One is littered with snail shells. Another contains a giraffe head, but nothing else belonging to that animal; clearly, it was brought home to be eaten.

The clues are many, and enthralling. What do we make of little concentrations here and there of very small bones, most of them broken into tiny pieces? Would any hominid have collected handfuls of skeletal fragments of mice, shrews, small birds, and lizards and then carefully placed them in piles? It seems wildly unlikely, and Mary Leakey concluded that these strange little heaps are probably what is left of hominid feces. Our ancestors were eating those small animals whole, bones and all, much as a modern human eats a sardine. The bones were ground up into very small fragments by chewing, then passed through the intestines and deposited where the Leakeys found them.

This wealth of information from Olduvai indicates without question that by about 2 million years ago hominids were living at a cultural level that no one a few decades ago would have believed possible. Because progress in the early Stone Age was slow, the beginnings of the Oldowan tool industry are probably far older than would be indicated even by the Hadar site, which dates tools at about 2.5 million years B.P. (Chapter 8). But how much older no one yet has the slightest idea. We know that toolmaking and hominid evolution go hand in hand, but the earliest steps are unknown. It will surely be hard if not impossible to distinguish between a worked tool from such a remote period and a found one, something our ancestors might have been experimenting with while they began to discover the advantages of walking erect.

## EVOLUTION OF THE FAMILY

As we have seen, there is a great deal of dispute and uncertainty about when, why, and even how our ancestors became bipedal ground-dwelling creatures. But vital characteristics of hominids must surely be traced to the introduction of a forest ape to the savanna. One such characteristic is the *nuclear family* of father, mother, and children. Particularly interesting are the extended intimacy between male and female and the existence of a father figure, a male head of the family.

We cannot know at this late date what early hominid groups were like, but we can make some shrewd guesses about them. Because early hominids were most closely related to ancestors of chimpanzees, and because they probably shared the savanna environment with ancestors of baboons, it is useful to look for clues in the social organization of the living descendants of those animals.

### Sex and Estrus

As we learned, human females are alone among primates in lacking a well-defined period of estrus associated with ovulation. During this time nonhuman primate females exhibit various physiological signals such as an attractive scent and a swollen peritoneal region, in some species. They are also more than usually sexually receptive to males, solicit their attention, and are capable of conceiving. In contrast, human females can and do initiate sexual activity at any time of their cycle, and males are unable to determine, by observing any such signs as the female chimpanzee shows, the stage of a female's cycle. This is a very striking and important development in human evolution. What determines who copulates with whom is no longer a physiological mechanism, but either personal choice, social sanction, or both because a female can solicit a male's attention at any time she chooses. She can therefore attract the male of her choice. Similarly, a man can approach a woman of his choice at any time. The possibility of choice of a sexual partner means that partners can be friends, and it also means that society may determine sexual alliances.

### One-Male Groups

We saw clues in Chapter 8 as to where and why that extended intimacy between human male and human female might have originated. Recall John Crook's hypothesis—under similar environmental conditions, social animals will tend to develop similar social organizations—and the application of that hypothesis to baboons. If social organization is shaped by environment (Crook would have it understood that the shaping does not take place directly, but over a long time, initiated by and reinforced by selection), an ape, in moving out of the forest to live in seasonally dry country, would have a social organization to conform to the requirements of that environment. Further, it would have adapted in the way that other primates have. These modifications obviously would have varied from place to place. Just as different baboon species have differing life-styles, surely hominids did, too, depending on where they lived and on how severe the seasonal food- and water-getting problems were. Where such problems were at their worst, extra male hominids may have been considered just as expendable as surplus male hamadryas baboons, and one-male family units may have been the usual social adaptation.

This speculation supplies a father figure for our small-toothed, open-country, erect ape—a figure that is missing in the easygoing chimpanzee society reported from Gombe. It was not the peculiarly human characteristic of month-long sexual attractiveness and receptivity that introduced the father to the family (although, later in evolution, such receptivity may have become one of the forces that encouraged him to keep coming back to it). On the contrary, at the stage of which we are speaking, as we try to identify the beginnings of a human family structure in a creature that is not yet human, the determining factor may well have been environmental. If so, the long-term association of a male with certain females was an economic one. Under the conditions we have outlined, one-male groups were the most efficient arrangement for survival.

Crook's hypothesis seems to suggest that the male-female bond is a very old one, for it is based on adapting to the environment and therefore could logically be expected to manifest itself soon after hominids first encountered seasonal food shortages in woodland savanna. Other primatologists believe that the one-male group may be the original primitive primate social pattern and that the promiscuous multi-male troop is a derived adaptation to more richly and evenly distributed food resources. That could take the one-male group back well beyond the earliest *Australopithecus*.

Those who disagree say that to explain family formation it is not necessary to look as far afield as baboons. They keep their eye on the chimpanzee, and attribute the beginnings of family formation to meat eating and food sharing—traits chimpanzees display, though in a feeble form. These activities, says Sherwood Washburn, a strong advocate of this view, were the influence that led to the development of more lasting male-female bonds. Because a developing taste for meat leads to an improvement in hunting techniques, and because the practice of hunting involves more effective tools and weapons and more efficient bipedalism, the Washburn model implies a somewhat later date for family formation. This hypothesis—which implies that the family evolved as a response to unequal access to highly desirable food resources (because only male chimpanzees hunt) and therefore food would be shared between the sexes—is an important one. Probably both seasonal food shortages and the evolution of hunting played some part in the development of male-female ties. We shall return to this topic later in this chapter.

## EVOLUTION OF MALE AND FEMALE ROLES

Everyone agrees that the changing role of the male in hominid evolution, however it emerged, was important. It has affected the evolution of different male and female roles in daily living; the division of labor; the development of teaching elaborate and appropriate new skills to the young; the development of the concept of a home base; and matters of hunting, food gathering, child care, and food sharing. All are interconnected. Together they make for a complex feedback system.

### Physical Differences

Differing roles suggest evolutionary shaping to fit those roles. For example, males are usually bigger and stronger than females now, with a more heavily built skeleton and more powerful musculature, and they may have been so throughout hominid evolution. These attributes are predictable for protectors and hunters; the relationship between role and physique is simple and direct. But males can also run faster than females, and here the reason is neither simple nor direct. If speed on foot were merely a matter of size and strength, then the largest and strongest male would be the fastest runner. Because he demonstrably is not, there must be another reason why a lithe female should not be so swift as a bulkier male: she cannot be if she is going to be the mother of larger-brained children. The best-designed pelvis for bearing such children is not the best-designed one for running, or even for the most efficient walking.

As we saw earlier, hominids became capable of mechanically efficient bipedalism because of marked changes in the shape and proportion of leg and foot bones and, especially, of the pelvis. But these early changes in the human pelvis did not make the open space in its center, the birth canal, big enough for the large-brained babies that would evolve. In order to achieve that, the whole pelvic structure would have to get bigger, and that change would defeat the evolutionary process of developing a compact, narrow pelvis, efficient for bipedal walking. The pelvis of the modern human female cannot be as compact as the human male's (Figure 9–10) without being too small to permit passage of the head of a baby. The female pelvis is therefore a compromise—not compact enough for the *most* efficient walking but large enough for the birth of a large-brained infant. As hominids became more human and larger-brained, the birth canal might have become even larger than it is. That it did not is due to the demands of bipedalism, and is one cause of the difficulties in childbirth some modern women experience.

FIGURE 9–10  *Among humans the greatest skeletal difference between the sexes is found in the pelvis. The most important differentiating feature is the female's large birth canal, which causes numerous minor differences in the shape of the bones that constitute the pelvis. Especially noteworthy is the breadth and form of the blade of the ilium and the angle below the pubic bones.*

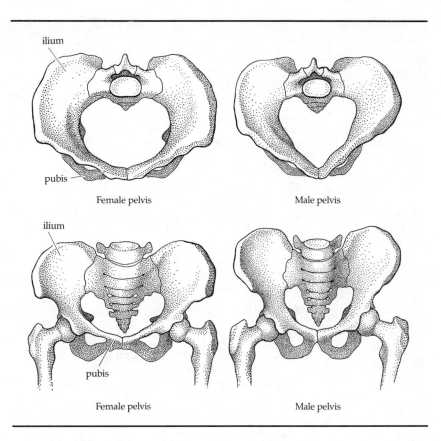

Female pelvis                    Male pelvis

Female pelvis                    Male pelvis

### Prolonged Youth and the Female's Role

When hominids entered the savanna, we can be sure that they began to evolve differences in the roles played by males and females. Hominid females were closely tied to infant care. Not only did hominid infants mature more slowly, but they were becoming more helpless at birth. This was because one solution to the small-pelvis, large-brain problem is for the female to give birth to the infant at an earlier stage in its development, before its head gets too big, and go through a correspondingly longer period of caring for the infant. Clearly, human infants enter the world much earlier in their development than other primates, at a stage in which their brains and bodies are too unformed to let them walk and forage for themselves. (See Table 9–2 for a comparison of chimpanzee and human development.) At birth the human brain is one-fourth its eventual size; the baboon brain is three-quarters grown.

Ape and monkey infants can hang on to their mothers' fur with feet as well as hands. Within a day or two, for example, a baboon baby can cling unaided to its mother's hair while she moves around in search of food and water, and it later rides on her back; within twelve months the little baboon is more or less on its own. The human baby, by

## TABLE 9–2    Development of Humans and Chimpanzees

| AGE | CHARACTERISTIC BEHAVIOR | PERCENTAGE OF ADULT BRAIN SIZE |
|---|---|---|
| **Human child** | | |
| At birth | Depends completely on mother for food, transportation, and protection<br>Exhibits grasping reflex: automatically grabs an object that touches its palm<br>Stretches arms outward, then together over its chest, in a grasping gesture, when its head falls backward<br>Vocalizes by crying | 25 percent |
| 3 months | Raises its head when lying down, supporting its weight on its forearms<br>Turns body from back to side<br>Vocalizes through cooing | 35 percent |
| 6 months | Sits up unsupported<br>Exhibits coordination: reaches purposefully for an object and grasps it<br>Vocalizes through babbling one-syllable sounds | 45 percent |
| 9 months | Stands upright when supported; takes a few steps holding on to an adult<br>Crawls on all fours | 50 percent |
| 1 year | Stands upright and walks unsupported<br>Responds more to play objects than to playmates<br>Responds to verbal commands and says first words | 60 percent |
| 2 years | Runs upright<br>Moves quickly from sitting to standing position<br>Uses a cup as a drinking tool<br>Plays as much with playmates as with play objects<br>Exhibits great interest in objects<br>Speaks with a vocabulary of more than fifty words and uses two-word sentences | 70 percent |
| 4 years | Actively practices motor skills: running, jumping, hopping<br>Plays extensively with other children<br>Has the ability to understand and use language with precision | 80 percent |
| 8 to 9 years | Learns to cooperate with others and masters control over impulses and aggression with a group<br>Thinks in abstract terms and exhibits great interest in solving problems | 95 percent |
| 12 to 14 years (puberty) | Exhibits increasing interest in the opposite sex | 100 percent |

contrast, is utterly dependent on its mother. It has to be carried and supplied with almost all its needs for at least two years; it may take six years for it to be able to care for itself as well as a baboon can at twelve months. The carrying of babies as well as food and tools must have been an important factor in the evolution of bipedalism.

**TABLE 9–2 (Continued)**

| AGE | CHARACTERISTIC BEHAVIOR | PERCENTAGE OF ADULT BRAIN SIZE |
|---|---|---|
| **Chimpanzee** | | |
| At birth | Depends completely on mother for food, transportation, and protection<br>Exhibits grasping reflex: clings to its mother's chest with hands and feet<br>Stretches arms outward, then together over its chest in a grasping gesture | 45 percent |
| 3 months | Sits up unsupported<br>Exhibits coordination: reaches purposefully for an object and grasps it | 50 percent |
| 6 months | Stands upright when supported; takes a few steps holding on to an adult<br>Moves about on all fours | 60 percent |
| 9 months | Stands upright and walks unsupported<br>Actively swings through trees, leaping from branch to branch<br>Plays with other young chimpanzees | 65 percent |
| 1 year | Runs upright and on all fours | 70 percent |
| 2 years | Engages in social activities with chimps of all ages except infants | 75 percent |
| 4 years | Completely independent of mother for food and transportation<br>Plays much of day with other chimps and its mother<br>May make and use tools to obtain food and drink<br>Begins to vocalize, using noises to express fear, excitement, anticipation of food, and pleasure during grooming | 85 percent |
| 8 to 9 years (puberty) | Spends increasing amount of time in social grooming and in feeding itself as it devotes less time to play<br>Begins sexual interest and activity | 100 percent |

With influences like these at work, it is logical to assume an intensification of the differences in the roles played by hominid males and females, particularly as females became more and more necessary to their infants for longer and longer periods and perhaps became more dependent for food on males with whom they were beginning to associate longer. Longer association encourages mutual support. New behavioral twists become possible, one of them being the slow beginning of reciprocal food sharing.

**Food Gathering**   Baboons rarely share food; chimpanzees sometimes do. The food shared in either instance is meat. Hominids also may have had traces of the meat-sharing trait when they left the forest. As they became increasingly good walkers and extended the range of their activities accordingly, the chances of their finding small animals to kill, and later beginning deliberately to hunt them down, obviously grew. The incentive to share food must have grown accordingly. A hominid cannot eat an entire baby antelope on the spot. What he might well do is share it with other hunters then and there, and carry what is left back to the infant-encumbered females with whom the male associates. Because hunting involves chasing prey, sometimes for considerable distances, some group members must be left behind, most probably females with infants. "Behind" should be at best a place where those less mobile members of the group are reasonably safe, and at worst a place that the hunters can find again—in short, this marks the beginnings of a home base.

Hunters are not always successful. More often than not they return empty-handed. As a result, in nearly all hunter-gatherer societies hunters supply only part (usually less than half) of the group's food. It is the gatherer's responsibility to ensure a dependable supply of fruit, seeds, nuts, and other vegetable materials together with the smaller items of animal food such as eggs, snails, and small game. Food gathering is a behavior very different from what we find in monkeys and apes. These creatures pick and eat food as they need it. Food gathering implies that more food than is immediately required is picked and then placed in containers: consumption is postponed. In addition to the vital function of evening out the ups and downs in the food supply created by the unreliability of hunting, such things as nuts and grain, unlike quickly rotting meat, keep a long time and may be rationed out in small quantities as needed.

Gathering supplies of small food items requires considerable foresight and an entirely new approach to the extraction of resources. It is one of the most important developments in human evolution, and one of our entirely original behaviors—it is found in no other primate. The novel use of leaves, bark, or skin as containers and of digging sticks to reach roots and bulbs—developments particularly associated with females today—is not a less important technological advance than the use of stone flakes as cutting tools.

In a recent book, anthropologist Nancy Tanner suggests that women were responsible for developing gathering and its associated tools because of the nutritional requirements of pregnancy and nursing and the overt demands of hungry children. She believes that for this reason women, rather than men, had the motivation for technological inventiveness, for creativity in dealing with their environment, for learning about plants, and for developing tools to increase the extraction of resources.

If food is gathered and brought home to base it is to be shared, and there seems no doubt that gatherers, of whichever sex, must have been in the habit of regularly sharing what was collected. This development is without question immensely important in the history of early hominid behavior.

The whole question of gathering and its technology has been neglected by paleoanthropologists because perishable tools leave no evidence in the archaeological record and their presence can only be assumed. But so ignoring them leaves us with only half a picture. Their importance in widening the resource base of the early hominids cannot be exaggerated. The early advances in hominid behavior and technology were probably shared by both sexes, each playing its own part in developing hominid survival strategies.

How far this division of labor had progressed by the time of *Australopithecus* is debatable; certainly its progress was uneven. There is no evidence that *Australopithecus* used containers to gather food, but the lack of evidence does not mean they were not used, for all such materials are perishable.

Could *Australopithecus* have invented such objects? Could *Homo habilis*? All that can be said is that at some time prior to 1 million years ago female hominids had probably already begun collecting and keeping more food than they could eat at the moment themselves. The existence of rather sophisticated toolmaking techniques recently described by Mary Leakey from such an early period should make paleoanthropologists extremely cautious about making firm pronouncements on what early hominids could or could not do. The more we learn about our ancestors, the more capable they seem to have been.

## HUNTING AND SCAVENGING

One area of their lives in which our ancestors were marvelously successful was hunting; many of our physical characteristics and some of our most deeply ingrained emotional traits stem from our long career as hunters. Although the development of agriculture and the dramatic rise of civilizations in the last five thousand to ten thousand years tend to obscure the fact, our ancestors almost certainly lived by hunting and gathering for more than a million years, perhaps for 2 or 3 million years. Thus, out of the last 2 million years of their evolution as bipedal hominids, our ancestors probably spent 99 percent of their time as hunters and gatherers.

How did the first hominids practice hunting as a way of life? How may it have developed? To answer these questions, we should recall the hunting behavior of the chimpanzee while we examine the behavior of animals more fully adapted to a carnivorous life-style.

## Cooperation and Food Sharing among Social Carnivores

The African savanna was inhabited by meat eaters that still roam and hunt there: lions, leopards, cheetahs, spotted hyenas, and wild dogs. By observing the hunting practices of these carnivores, we may, as George Schaller proposes, gain some insight into how *Homo habilis* developed hunting techniques to satisfy its inherent desire for meat. Schaller has written: "Since social systems are strongly influenced by ecological conditions, it seemed [to me] that it might be more productive to compare hominids with animals which are ecologically but not necessarily phylogenetically [evolutionarily] similar, such as social carnivores." Lions, hyenas, and wild dogs all are social animals that have developed two vital traits: they hunt in groups, and they share their food.

Cooperative hunting has many advantages; Schaller lists no fewer than five that give a group of hunters a big edge over an individual working alone. First, the group is consistently more successful in killing. Two or more spotted hyenas, working together, kill an animal after a hunt more than three times as often as a lone hyena does. Second, a group can kill larger animals than one hunter can. The most dramatic example is probably the wild dog, which, working as a member of a pack, can bring down zebras that weigh up to 500 pounds, though the dogs themselves weigh only about 40 pounds each. Third, all the food caught by a group will probably be eaten on the spot, so that none is wasted. This is often not possible for one hunter, which eats as much as it can and then must wait until it is hungry again. By that time scavengers may have found the carcass and finished it. That is why the leopard, a solitary hunter, is put to the trouble of hauling its kills into trees where hyenas, jackals, and dogs cannot reach them. The fourth advantage is what Schaller calls division of labor. He cites the example of wild dogs—one dog remains behind to guard pups in the den while others hunt for food, which they bring back in their bellies and regurgitate for the pups and the adult guard. The final advantage of cooperative hunting takes into account the power ranking on the savanna based on size, with the lion at the top, the leopard next, followed by the hyena and the wild dog. Numbers can overbalance size. Frequently, a lioness is unable to defend the carcass of a giraffe against a dozen hungry hyenas.

Another advantage that we might cite is the greater variety of hunting methods that is open to a group than to a lone animal. Among these is a kind of relay-race effect achieved by wild dogs. One or two adults start a chase by running right after the prey, keeping constant pressure on it. As it flees, it is apt to run in a wide circle, which enables trailing dogs to watch the action and then save steps by cutting across the arc of pursuit and close in for the kill. Another example: lions drive prey toward hunting partners lying in ambush. They also surrounded it, so that whichever way it bolts there may be a lion in a position to attempt a kill. A group hunting together can sometimes maneuver the quarry into a cul-de-sac: out onto a promontory, into a swamp or a river, into a gully from which it cannot escape. Hominid hunters probably used all these techniques.

Another very important aspect of social carnivores' behavior is food sharing. Lions fight and snarl—and, though rarely, kill each other—over their food. The trait suggests incomplete social evolution: that is, they may have learned to cooperate in the field but not yet at the table. Hyenas and wild dogs are much better adapted in this respect. Dogs are extraordinarily scrupulous; the pups in the pack, being slower runners, are likely to be the last to arrive at a kill. The adults usually content themselves with a few bites, then move aside to let the youngsters have their fill before settling down for their own meal. Sometimes they go hungry and must hunt again, but good care of pups has great survival value for a species in which mortality among adults seems to run high.

## Development of Hominid Hunting

Cooperation and sharing, then, confer strong benefits on social carnivores. For savanna-living hominids these same benefits could have accrued. The more widely they ventured, the greater would have been their chance of coming upon small prey such as hares, fledgling birds, and the newborn young of larger herbivores. Not only would they be increasingly stimulated to chase and kill these creatures but, even more important, they would be encouraged to be on the lookout for them and to think more and more about how and where to find them. Hominids' ambitions perhaps grew as they realized that crippled or old individuals of larger species were within their capabilities as social hunters. But the bigger the game, even with weakened animals, the greater the need for cooperation. And with proportionally larger amounts of meat on hand as a result of successful cooperation, the greater the opportunity and the incentive to share it.

Here again, positive feedback could have operated. The more successful a kind of behavior is in an animal intelligent enough to remember its actions, the more likely that animal will be to continue trying what has worked before. Each animal caught strengthens the urge to look harder for more prey. This phenomenon was observed by Jane Goodall among the Gombe chimpanzees. A chance catch of a young baboon would stimulate a good deal of hopeful hunting energy. But because of their poor success as hunters, their misguided enthusiasm, and the large number of alternative food sources, the chimpanzees would be discouraged quickly by failures. Hunting would cease to arouse interest—until the next lucky kill rekindled the urge. Stimulated by more frequent success in the open and perhaps also by a greater need to hunt and scavenge because of a less stable food supply there, hominids could have made hunting, which was unimportant to the survival of chimpanzees, into a pattern of behavior that was increasingly vital to their survival.

Sharing, just as much as cooperative hunting, would have improved the survival chances of a hominid. It is painful to watch a sick or injured baboon trying to keep up with the troop. Other baboons do not feed or look out for it in any way; being largely seed, grass, fruit, and root eaters, they need large quantities of their food to maintain their energy, which means they have to spend most of the day feeding themselves. Therefore the sick individual must manage on its own, and even though the other animals may move slowly throughout the day, the disabled one still may not be able to forage because it is devoting all its strength merely to keeping up. In such a situation it will get weaker, find it harder to keep up, and eventually be picked off by a hunting carnivore. Bringing back food to a place from which a disabled individual does not have to stir for a critical few days might mean the difference between life and death. Hominids and social carnivores will do so, but a baboon with a broken leg or a case of dysentery is almost certainly a dead baboon. A similarly stricken hominid might have survived.

Combine the peculiar attributes of a hominid with the cooperative hunting and food sharing of a social carnivore, and the result, in earlier stages, could be something like *Australopithecus*, a hunter that goes about its business in a new way—on two legs and with weapons—its wits constantly being sharpened thereby until it eventually becomes a very efficient hunter indeed.

Because apes and monkeys are diurnal (active during the day), Schaller, like virtually everybody else, assumes that the early hominids were, too, and that they did all their hunting and scavenging in daylight. This speculation is overwhelmingly logical. For one thing, the night is dangerous; a small hominid out scavenging after dark would have been all too likely to run into saber-toothed cats, lions, leopards, or hyenas, which hunt at night. For another, bipedal hominids were tall enough to see considerable distances, and mobile enough to cover a good deal of ground. This ability suggests that they observed sharply what was going on around them and that much of their activity was directed toward scavenging. Too slow to run down healthy large animals by themselves, they probably relied on lions and wild dogs to do that for them, and then ran up in a noisy group and drove the predators away. They would also have found less competition from other predators during the day. Finally, some characters of *Homo* do seem to suggest adaptation to intense exercise in heat (see page 310).

By *Homo habilis* times, about 2 million years ago, it is almost certain that hominids were sufficiently skillful hunters to make all but the largest herbivores afraid of them. It is likely that they competed with wild dogs and the great cats, fighting with them over their kills and over the found carcasses of large dead animals. In those fights, numbers, aggressiveness, and weaponry undoubtedly decided the issue.

Still, hunting started on a very modest scale, limited to the chance finding of small animals. Equally important, probably both in the earliest stages and thereafter, was scavenging, finding game already dead, either from natural causes or killed by other animals capable of being intimidated and driven away. This might be called the opportunistic side of meat eating, and here, once again, hominids probably resembled social carnivores. Although a lion will drive hyenas off a fresh kill, the hyenas are capable of gathering reinforcements to drive away the lion. Two or three lions will turn the tables again.

## Communication and Hunting

If animals are to cooperate during hunting, aggression between individuals must be discharged harmlessly or suppressed. It has been suggested that aggressive behavior among male hominids became reduced as a result of the emergence of one-male groups—for there is certainly more male–male aggression within multi-male troops. At the same time, the beginning of language—a mode of communication that could convey something more than mere feelings—would have led to greater trust, greater understanding, and greater cooperation between individuals of both sexes.

Others disagree. Although they would admit that language may be a useful moderator of aggressive behavior (you curse somebody or complain instead of hitting him with a club), they do not believe that it was necessary in stimulating cooperation and altruism. That, they maintain, resulted from family formation, long mother-infant relationships, and food sharing, long before language came along. Submissive behavior was already highly evolved. In fact, they insist, *Australopithecus* was too small-brained to have been able to talk. They contend that speech was beyond the capacity of hominids before the emergence of *Homo erectus* a little over a million years ago.

Furthermore, early hominids may not have needed to talk. The real value of language, in addition to the enormous stimulation it gives to brain development, is that it permits the conveying of symbols referring to objects in the environment and ideas that are beyond the power of grunts and gestures to communicate. Nonverbal communication (which we will examine in Chapter 13) can be surprisingly subtle and as we have seen it permits a remarkably high degree of communication among such animals as chimpanzees; but though we may assume that hominids knew more than chimpanzees and thus needed to communicate more, how much more is hard to say. Like everything else, language origins were gradual and slow in coming. We simply do not know, and probably never will, how or when language began. Schaller sensibly observes that speech is not necessary during hunting and would scare game. Carnivores do not communicate while so engaged; indeed, some hunt at night, using stalking techniques that require silence and make visual communication difficult.

If hominids were organized into one-male groups—a hypothesis that now seems increasingly probable—then it would have been necessary for some social structure above the group level for the formation of a band of hunters. The model of the gelada monkey seems a suitable one to throw light on the society of early hominids. On this premise we can suppose that under certain conditions the one-male groups would have come together to form a larger unit from which the hunting band would have emerged. Such a two-level structure seems to be the necessary basis for the evolution of human society.

**Schaller and Lowther's Experiment**

Having made the many keen observations about the lives of social carnivores that have provided a base for our discussion here, Schaller prudently backed off from claiming too direct a connection between hominid life and that of modern carnivores. He remarked that there are many styles of hunting among them and that at present we have no way of telling which, if any, were adopted by hominids, or even if different hominids did different things at different times. Nevertheless, the analogies are there, and they are extremely provocative—so much so that Schaller decided to turn himself into an early hominid for a few days to find out more about what these early hominids may or may not have been able to do.

Selecting the Serengeti Plain in East Africa as an environment whose climate and large herds of grazing animals are still very close to the presumed conditions of a couple of million years ago, Schaller and a fellow scientist, Gordon Lowther, conducted two experiments as hunting-scavenging hominids. The first experiment was conducted on the open savanna (Figure 9–11), where the two men walked, a hundred yards apart, for a total distance of about a hundred miles over several days. Their main target was baby gazelles, which, in the first week of life, do not run but crouch in the grass. They found eight and could easily have caught them all. An excellent food supply for an early hominid, but there was a catch to it: five of the young were spotted within a few minutes of one another at a place where pregnant females had gathered to deliver their fawns. Since birth among most of the plains herbivores is concentrated into very short seasons, Schaller concluded that catching gazelles was a poor long-term proposition: marvelous for a few days, poor the rest of the time.

He and Lowther stumbled over other things on that same walk, however—a hare they could have caught, a couple of adult gazelle carcasses partly eaten, a cheetah making a kill that they could have preempted. Conscientiously adding up all the bits of pieces of meat

*FIGURE 9–11* Australopithecus *lived in a savanna environment with animals that were not very different from those we see today. In this reconstruction,* Australopithecus *has been placed in a modern setting.*

they could have eaten, including some scraps of brain from one kill gnawed almost clean, they came up with seventy-five pounds of meat.

Their second experiment, conducted in a woodland strip edging the Serengeti's Mbalageti River, lasted a week. There they had better luck. Choosing as their territory the riverbank where the herds came to drink, they ran into competition from sixty or seventy lions that were also hanging around. They found four lion kills, but these had all been picked so clean that nothing was left but some brains and the marrow in the larger bones. As tool-using hominids, they could have recovered the marrow by smashing the bones open with rocks. They found a

*FIGURE 9–12   As part of their experiments on hunting-scavenging hominids, Schaller and Lowther themselves smashed animal bones to recover the marrow and stalked a young blind giraffe.*

partly eaten buffalo that had died of disease, and they could have recovered about 500 pounds of meat from it. In addition they found an eighty-pound zebra foal, abandoned and sick, and an oddly acting young giraffe that they discovered was blind when they succeeded in catching it by the tail. It weighted about 300 pounds (Figure 9–12).

Schaller's experiment is fascinating, but it has limited value because of the short time span it involved. The game supply for early hominids was unpredictable, rising and falling seasonally, according to drought, disease, and migration. To cope with this, hominids must have been under some selective pressure to become increasingly artful hunters, to learn how to stalk, ambush, and kill healthy animals when there were no old and sick ones to be had. It is unlikely that they used any one hunting technique, but rather they probably developed a varied repertoire of methods of obtaining meat, whether by hunting or by scavenging. But the uncertainty of hunting highlights the importance of the women—gathering seeds, nuts, roots, and fruit for them to fall back on—just as hunter-gatherers do today.

Some anthropologists make a direct comparison between the hominid hunting-and-gathering life and that of certain modern hunter-gatherers like the Kalahari San Bushmen, but that comparison is misleading, according to Schaller. The Bushmen have been pushed into a semidesert area with sparse game; the bulk of their food has to be vegetable. But early hominids, small and relatively unintelligent though they must have been, may have gotten more meat than modern Bushmen. Whether they did or not, however, is not the important point. What counted in the long run was the activity of hunting itself. The challenges of hunting stimulated the brain. One of the strongest influences in the intellectual evolution of humans, as Sherwood Washburn keeps emphasizing, was undoubtedly their activities as hunters. But Washburn maintains that to account for a hunting tradition in early hominid behavior one need look no further than a chimpanzee, with its natural inclination to hunt. Hunting changed our ancestors by enlarging their horizons and their mental capacity. Gradually they learned to hunt better, to think and plan better, and to use and make better tools and weapons.

## LOVEJOY'S HYPOTHESIS

The American anatomist Owen Lovejoy has synthesized some of the points made in this chapter with a hypothesis that contrasts with Jolly's seed-eating hypothesis. Lovejoy suggests that the initial thrust of the feedback model in Figure 9–4 came not so much from a change in diet as from a change in reproductive strategy (Figure 9–13). He points out the need for mobility of each individual chimpanzee, including mothers, for feeding is a significant cause of mortality among their infants. He surmises that if a hominid infant is to survive, in spite of the fact that

*FIGURE 9–13  Pliocene adaptations of early hominids according to Lovejoy, drawn as a feedback system. Compare Figure 9–4, which applies to a later period when tools were in use.*

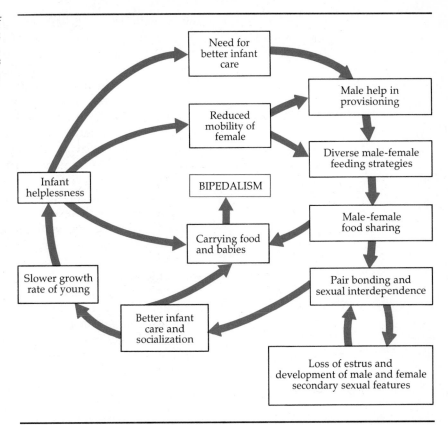

during hominid evolution it is becoming increasingly helpless, female mobility would have had to be reduced while the baby was more or less continuously carried. This need to carry helpless infants would have been a most important reason for evolution of bipedalism, which frees the arms and hands. Lovejoy, however, also suggests other ways of improving parenting, the most important of which would be for the males to help in provisioning the mothers and young. He believes that an effective strategy would have been for males to obtain food away from base, so that the females would have more available locally. This system would reduce their need to travel widely, as well as removing male competition for the food supplies around the base. Thus it would lower accident rates for infants, maximize the females' familiarity with the core area of their home range, reduce exposure of females and young to predators, and generally allow intensification of child care.

But Lovejoy goes further. He believes this division of labor would have brought about the development of pair bonding between a female and male, presumably on a fairly long-term basis, so that the male would eventually be provisioning only his particular female and his own genetic offspring. They would be safer and better fed, which would increase the inclusive fitness of both parents. This hypothesis seems eminently reasonable, especially because we have examples of this strategy from a number of living species such as gibbons, siamangs, and some New World monkeys. Pair bonding, he claims, also implies extension of the period of receptivity in the female hominid with no recognizable estrus at ovulation so that copulation would become more frequent and strengthen male-female bonds. These bonds would also be strengthened by evolution of the striking secondary sexual characters that are unique to humans. Such characters include the permanently rounded breasts of the female, the rounded buttocks—both due to permanent deposits of fat—the male's large penis, and the hair forms and patterns of both sexes.

Thus Lovejoy proposes the surprisingly early development of a pair bond between male and female. Because polygamy is very common in modern human societies (being permitted in about 85 percent of them), we would have to suppose that this is a late development that logically follows when particular males are able to provision more than one female and her young. But perhaps the most important and least controversial element in Lovejoy's scheme is the early appearance of bipedalism. Basically he accounts for it as a product of the need to carry helpless infants and their provisions, easily and efficiently. For this purpose bipedalism is clearly better than any other form of locomotion.

We shall probably never know the exact order of events in human evolution. Behavior, which leaves few clues for us, precedes the anatomical changes it evokes, and we still have much to learn about the timing of anatomical evolution in the Hominidae. We now do know something, though, of the timetable of events (page 224), and the new scheme proposed by Owen Lovejoy goes a long way toward making sense of the fossil evidence. Stone toolmaking and brain expansion were late and were not involved in early Pliocene developments. If bipedalism evolved because it freed the hands, it was for carrying babies and food at least as much as, if not more than, for toolmaking. The evidence for the origin of the human family is, however, more speculative: we have discussed it already (page 232) and we shall return to the problem again in a later chapter (page 321).

**A Reconstruction**  From observing the behavior of other animals and examining the evidence of tool use and living floors given in this chapter, we are now able to make some behavioral speculations about *Australopithecus* and *Homo habilis*. We have an image of a social hominid with a structure of one-male groups which constitute the beginnings of a family. Its wider society was intricately and hierarchically organized on the basis of dominance among males and hereditary status among females. This hominid had moved from the forest into more open country; there it exploited a growing variety of foods, including the seeds of herbs and grasses. It had brought with it to the savanna the ape's potential for bipedalism, for tool use, and for meat eating. On the savanna there were very real advantages in developing these traits, and the hominid exploited them all. From the fossil evidence we know that it was an erect walker 3.75 million years ago and would have been bipedal long before that. Distinct male and female roles—of protector-hunter and homemaker-gatherer, respectively—were perhaps beginning to assert themselves. Here we find ourselves once again in the circle of positive feedback, for these roles not only were necessary for protection and sharing in order to take care of larger-brained, slower-developing infants and their mothers, but also were made possible by the larger brains that this new way of life, with its reliance on sharing, bipedalism, and tool use, encouraged.

The size of the area through which hominid groups might move to exploit all kinds of food resources began to grow as their physical ability to roam these ranges increased. Opportunities for new sights and experiences grew correspondingly. So too did the selective pressure to evolve larger brains capable of storing more and more information about the larger world. With increased movement came the stimulus to carry things—tools, weapons, containers—for greater distances, itself a further stimulus to bipedal walking—and to further exploration.

We have absolutely no way at present of calculating the range of a hominid band, which surely varied from place to place and from good year to bad. It was almost certainly measured in the scores of square miles, and may well have been in the hundreds (see Table 6–2). With that expanded range went all the advantages that could accrue to a mobile group living in it: the ability to escape local disasters of drought or flood, to take advantage of local bounty as it developed seasonally, and, most important, to remember where, when, and how to exploit that large domain. Simply by increasing the options available, a large-brained hominid that could walk considerable distances increased its chances for survival.

Estimates of the number of individuals in a hominid band range from a dozen or so up to fifty. These estimates are based on the known sizes of chimpanzee, gorilla, and baboon troops, and on the practical size limits that would be put on (and are still put on) hunter-gatherer bands by the day-to-day problem of finding enough food and water for all their members.

As to how long *Australopithecus* or *Homo habilis* lived, that too is a subject for speculation. A chimpanzee has a life expectancy of about twenty-five years in the wild, although it may have the physiological potential to live as long as sixty years. *Australopithecus*, of similar size, could be expected to have the same potential. But as with chimpanzees, this potential apparently was severely reduced under actual living conditions. The paleoanthropologist Alan Mann has been examining the rate of tooth development among immature specimens of some South African gracile *Australopithecus* fossils and the rate of tooth wear among adults of that same population. His studies indicate that none of the individuals whose teeth he examined got past forty and that only about one in seven lived as long as thirty years. Their mean life span, he estimates, was about twenty years, which says a good deal about the hazards of life for *Australopithecus*. In the absence of modern medicine and technology, the mean life span of modern humans is probably about thirty to thirty-five years, while in the West it is now about seventy years.

Movement to the savanna may have led to the evolution of human beings, but it would be millions of years before this revolutionary development would have any payoff in easier living or greater longevity. Meanwhile, the evolution of the bipedal hominid *Australopithecus* continued, slowly, over millions of years. The large species of *Australopithecus* eventually became extinct, while the smaller *Australopithecus* species was to become the world's cleverest hunter and continue to change and evolve more complex social institutions, more sophisticated technology, and a more effective means of communication. The first recognizable stone-tool industries appear about 2.5 million years ago. With them appears the earliest human, *Homo habilis*, with a brain significantly larger than that of *Australopithecus*. The hominid that had evolved by one million years ago carried a brain that had more than twice the volume of the brain of the earliest members of the genus *Australopithecus*. This far more humanlike hominid we call *Homo erectus*. We shall now turn to the evidence for the further evolution of this lineage, which led eventually to us.

# PART III

# THE EVOLUTION OF HUMANKIND

# Chapter 10

# Discovering
# *Homo erectus*

Then felt I like some watcher of the skies
When a new planet swims into his ken;
Or like stout Cortez, when with eagle eyes
He stared at the Pacific—and all his men
Looked at each other with a wild surmise—
Silent, upon a peak in Darien.

**JOHN KEATS, 1795–1821.**
*"On First Looking into Chapman's Homer."*

Because most of what we know about early humans is based on fossil evidence, it is worth mentioning that fossil finds, as far as their influence on knowledge goes, fall into two rough categories. First are the discoveries of previously unknown fossil types, finds that provide brand-new insights into the evolutionary picture; second are those which confirm or enlarge information about a type of fossil already discovered. The first kind—the heart-stopper, the producer of wild surmises—makes newspaper headlines. But the second kind should not be underrated, because, to the scientist, it is perhaps at least as important. To get a good idea of the characteristics or dimensions of a species, one must have a series of fragments or skeletons from a number of individuals. Without such a series, a single fossil may be simply a curiosity, a provocative and exciting one, no doubt, but still something that cannot be fitted with any sense of certainty into the overall order of things until a number of like fossils are found and examined. It is the patient, more obscure, and always time-consuming comparative study of later finds, often made years after the original one, that eventually turns the wild surmises into scientific conclusions or destroys their credibility.

In this chapter we describe the discovery of the fossils that follow *Homo habilis*, fossils that today are seen collectively as representing the species *Homo erectus.* Currently, *Australopithecus afarensis* (possibly *A. africanus*) followed by *H. habilis* and *H. erectus* are believed to have existed successively in geological time and to form a lineage leading to us. Of course, all populations of a species probably did not evolve into its successor species, for some isolated groups may have survived for a while without substantial change only to become extinct later. Nevertheless, the fossil evidence clearly suggests that the succession of species from *A. afarensis* to *H. habilis* to *H. erectus*—and the further evolution of *H. erectus* into *H. sapiens*—broadly represents the course of human evolution (see Figure 7–7).

To describe the discovery of the fossils of *Homo erectus,* which existed in the Old World between about 1.5 and 0.7 million years ago, we will return to the nineteenth century, to a discovery made thirty-five years earlier than that of *Australopithecus africanus.*

## WORK OF EUGENE DUBOIS

### Nineteenth-Century Background

In the mid-1800s the Western world's interest was focused on the present and the future. It was an age of human progress and accomplishment, of prosperity, and of inventions that made life easier and more civilized: running water and lighted streets, iceboxes, sewing machines, elevated railways, lawnmowers, typewriters, and telephones. It is understandable, then, that the new theory about humankind's descent from prehistoric apes provoked doubt and opposition. In this atmosphere of progress and self-approval, the claim that humankind was merely an offshoot of the ape was rejected by much of the public and by many eminent scientists as well. No one had yet found any fossils proving a link between apes and humans. Most of those who doubted our primate origins did so not merely through acceptance of the Biblical account of creation, but also because for a long time there was no convincing fossil evidence to support Darwin.

Some scientists took the lack of any fossils of intermediate humanlike apes as proof that no such creatures had ever existed. At the other extreme, some of Darwin's early supporters rushed forward with fanciful pedigrees for humankind, making up in enthusiasm for what they lacked in evidence. Even believers in human evolution were confused by the outpouring of rival experts' family trees for humankind, full of imaginary apish ancestors with scientific-sounding Greek and Latin names.

Eugene Dubois (Figure 10–1) was born in Holland in 1858, into this atmosphere of often bitter debate over human origins. Although the Dubois family was conventional and religious, the home atmosphere was not one of narrow-minded provincial piety, and the boy's interest in science was encouraged. Dubois went to medical school and then, choosing academic life over medical practice, became an instructor in anatomy at the Royal Normal School in Amsterdam. He was fascinated

FIGURE 10–1   *An 1883 photograph shows Eugene Dubois (1858–1940) as a teacher in Amsterdam.*

FIGURE 10–2   *Ernst Haeckel's work on the ancestry of humankind was one of the first attempts to deal with the specifics of evolution. Although his genealogical chart, which starts with a blob of protoplasm and ends with a Papuan, contains misconceptions and fictitious creatures, it is in some ways surprisingly accurate, considering the dearth of knowledge in his day. The animals illustrated were chosen as representatives of the taxonomic groups to which successive human ancestral species were believed to have belonged.*

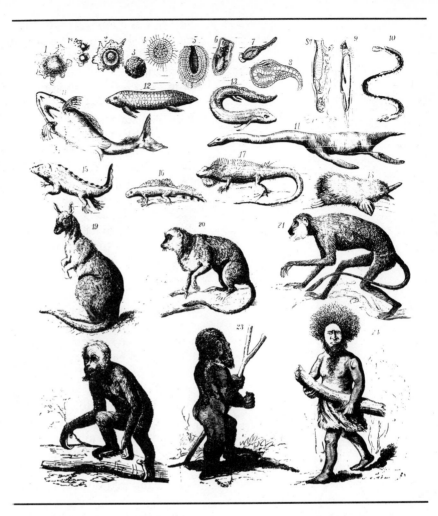

by the many different family trees that were being published in both learned and popular journals and was much influenced by the work of Ernst Heinrich Haeckel, a German zoologist who had predicted in some detail what *should* be discovered about the course of human evolution (see Figure 10–2). For six years Dubois delivered his lectures and gave no hint of the wild idea that was taking hold of him: to establish the human place in evolution and set the record straight once and for all, by finding a fossil of a primitive creature that was the clear forerunner of humans.

**Dubois' Search for the Missing Link**

Dubois began to take up his vocation by going over all the clues he could find. One important clue was the first Neandertal fossil, which had been discovered in 1856, two years before Dubois was born (see Chapter 14). For many years the Neandertal remains were the only trace of a primitive skeleton in the human closet. Dubois, a firm believer in evolution, considered the Neandertal fossils to be definitely human, and very ancient. To him they suggested that the search for even more primitive creatures should be carried out in some region of limestone deposits and caves similar to the European habitat of Neandertal; but they also suggested to him that Europe was not the place to look for a missing link. The creature that provided the evolutionary link between ape and human, Dubois reasoned, must have lived long before Neandertal, at a time when Europe was far too cold to permit their survival. The forebear he wanted to find must have lived in a tropical part of the world that had been untouched by the glaciers of the ice age.

Other clues as well pointed to the tropics. Darwin had suggested that our tree-dwelling progenitors lived in "some warm, forest-clad land"; Alfred Russel Wallace had also recommended that our forebears be sought in a tropical zone. Wallace had lived in Malaysia for eight years, and he had noticed that the islands of Sumatra and Borneo (Figure 10–3) are the home of both the gibbon, the oldest living ape, and the orangutan, one of the most advanced species of ape. He wrote, "With what interest must every naturalist look forward to the time when the caves of the tropics be thoroughly examined, and the past history and earliest appearance of the great man-like apes be at length made known." Wallace's curiosity about these islands and their caves proved contagious, and Dubois began to think seriously of going to the Dutch East Indies to explore the caves himself. The more he read about the geology and natural history of the region, the more convinced he became that the missing link would be discovered there. The islands once had been part of continental Asia; before the seas had inundated the lower land, turning the mountaintops into islands, animals could have wandered down freely from the north.

At age twenty-nine Eugene Dubois set out to solve the mystery of human origins, to find the fossil of a creature with both apelike and humanlike traits that would prove the relationship between humans and apes. Dubois' planning focused on Sumatra, then under Dutch rule and therefore a practical place for a Dutch citizen to launch a paleontological expedition. In 1886 he told some of his colleagues at the University of Amsterdam that he had reason to believe he would solve the mystery of human origins. They tried to dissuade him, and one even politely suggested that Dubois was slightly mad. His requests for financial backing were turned down flatly by both philanthropists and government bureaucrats. But Dubois was determined to get to Sumatra, and finally he was sent there by the Dutch East Indian Army, in which he enlisted as a doctor.

For the first two years in Sumatra, his investigations of a great many limestone caves and deposits yielded only teeth that were too recent to interest him; they belonged mainly to orangutans. When word came in

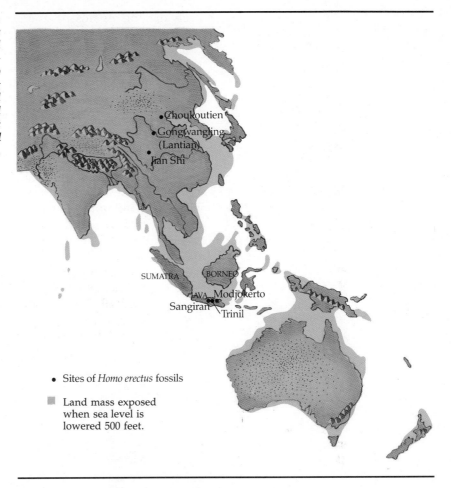

FIGURE 10–3 *During glacial periods, when far more water was locked up in the polar ice caps than today, the world sea level fell. During the coldest periods, the maximum lowering of the sea level appears to have been about 500 feet. This receding would have considerably enlarged land masses available for occupation by plant and animal life, shown here colored. Throughout the Pleistocene, the sea level fluctuated extensively.*

• Sites of *Homo erectus* fossils

▮ Land mass exposed when sea level is lowered 500 feet.

1890 of the discovery of a very ancient skull at Wadjak, Java, Dubois persuaded the government to send him to that neighboring island (Figure 10–3). The colonial government, showing new interest in his work, supplied him with a native crew of convict laborers and two Dutch officers to oversee them. With such backing, excavations began on a grand scale.

Dubois managed to buy the Wadjak skull that had brought him to the island, and then he promptly found another. Both were modern in appearance and too recent to have belonged to a missing link. But the region was extraordinarily rich in fossils of many kinds, and Dubois set up several digging parties at different locations. By 1894 he had shipped to the Netherlands 400 cases of fossil bones, including specimens of many extinct and previously unknown animals.

At one site to the north, Dubois' foreman reported an unexpected problem. He had found that for many years natives of the area had been digging up fossils and selling them to Chinese merchants as "dragon bones" to be ground into powder for an ancient and popular Chinese medicine. The local fossil hunters, unwilling to give up a profitable business with the Chinese, would not sell any of their finds to Dubois' party. To make matters worse, the foreman soon discovered that his own workmen were stealing the fossils they unearthed and carrying them off to sell to the local traders. When called upon for help, the colonial government issued an order outlawing the sale of any fossils to Chinese merchants in Java.

**Discovery of**
***Pithecanthropus* (1891)**

To Dubois, the most promising site on the island seemed to be an exposed and stratified embankment along the Solo River, near the small village of Trinil in the center of Java (Figure 10–4). Here, in the months when the river was low, Dubois could survey a forty-five-foot-high bank of ancient river deposits, clearly defined layers of fine volcanic debris, and sandstone.

In a stratum about four feet thick just above the stream level, Dubois came upon a rich store of animal fossils: a stegodon, an extinct hippopotamus, a small deer, an antelope. Before he could pursue these interesting finds, the rains set in and he had to abandon his excavations at the river until the following autumn. In August 1891 he and his crew

*FIGURE 10–4  At this bend in the Solo River at Trinil, Java, Dubois excavated the terraced bank where the Java fossils were found, at a depth of forty-eight feet.*

FIGURE 10–5 *The brown skullcap of* Pithecanthropus erectus *was Dubois' greatest find. It was to be nearly forty years before another skull of this kind was found. (This photograph is approximately 60 percent of actual size.)*

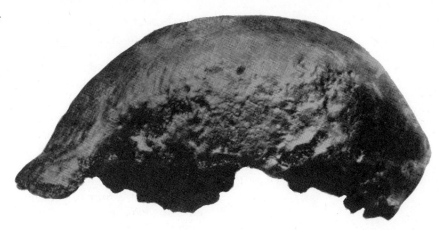

FIGURE 10–6 *The first femur that Dubois found appeared very modern and indicated an upright posture. The growth of bone on its inner surface near the top is an unusual pathological condition that is also found in modern humans but has no evolutionary significance. (This photograph is approximately 20 percent of actual size.)*

set to work once more, digging down through the strata with hoes, hammers, and chisels—crude implements by later standards, but Dubois was one of the first scientists ever to attempt a systematic search for fossils. In September he found his first recognizable fossil of a primitive primate: a single, apelike tooth.

On first inspection, this fossil seemed to Dubois to be the wisdom tooth of an extinct giant chimpanzee. Later, comparing it with molars of other apes, he noticed a strange wrinkling of the crown, suggesting that it was, instead, the tooth of an orangutan. As Dubois mulled over the molar, the digging went on for another month. Then, only three feet to the side of where the tooth had been unearthed, and in the same layer, a workman discovered a heavy, brown rock that looked like a turtle's shell. After the earth was brushed away from the new find, it looked more like part of a skull. "The amazing thing had happened," wrote the English anatomist G. Elliot Smith years later; "Dubois had actually found the fossil his scientific imagination had visualized." Though he did not know it at the time, it was the evidence Dubois had crossed half the world to find.

The skull (Figure 10–5) was unlike any ever seen before. Clearly, it was too low and flat to be the cranium of a modern human. After detailed study of both the skullcap and the tooth, Dubois reported: "that both specimens came from a great manlike ape was at once clear." Despite his expert knowledge of anatomy he found the skull peculiarly hard to place more precisely than that.

Shortly after these finds were made, the rains came, the river rose, and digging again had to be suspended until the following year. When digging resumed in 1892, Dubois cut a new excavation in the same deposit about thirty-three feet from where the strange cranium had been buried. There, ten months after the apelike skull was found, he discovered another, even more surprising, primate fossil. This one (shown in Figure 10–6) was unmistakable. It was the left femur, or thighbone, of a primate that had walked erect! It resembled a human thighbone in almost every respect, except that it was heavier. In October, another tooth quite like the first turned up. Could the curious teeth, the problematic skull, and the unexpected thighbone all have belonged to the same individual? The implications were staggering.

Dubois measured and studied the apelike skull and the humanlike femur from Trinil and in 1892 announced that the skull and femur had belonged to the same creature that he believed to have been an upright species of chimpanzee that he called *Anthropopithecus erectus*. It soon occurred to him, however, that the creature whose anatomy was indicated by these bones and teeth was of exactly the sort that Haeckel had suggested as a human precursor. Haeckel had named this hypothetical ancestor *Pithecanthropus* (from the Greek *pithekos*, "ape" and *anthropos*, "man"). In 1894, Dubois claimed that he had found the real *Pithecanthropus*, and he renamed his extraordinary find, *Pithecanthropus erectus*. By appropriating this name for his Java find, Dubois boldly filed his claim to have found, as he cabled his friends in Europe, the "Missing Link of Darwin." He attributed it to a late Pliocene age.

The bones of *Pithecanthropus erectus* were one of the greatest fossil finds ever made, and even though he had only these few incomplete specimens Dubois fully realized their importance. We now believe that *Pithecanthropus erectus* was actually an early human, a vital link in the chain of human evolution, not the half-ape Dubois had supposed it to be. We now believe this skull to date from the early Pleistocene—between 800,000 and 900,000 B.P. (Figure 5–1).

**Java Controversy**     Even before Dubois could show his discoveries to colleagues in Europe, his precious fossils became the focus of a raging scientific controversy that embroiled him throughout the rest of his life. His first cabled reports were met with skepticism. Some critics insisted that the fossil bones did not belong together at all, and suggested that Dubois simply had made the mistake of mixing the skull and teeth of an ape with the thighbone of a human who had died nearby. One member of the Netherlands Zoological Society, writing in a Dutch newspaper in 1893, ridiculed Dubois' jigsaw-puzzle methods, asking whether more finds at the site in Java might not eventually lead to announcements of an even stranger creature: if another, more human, skull was discovered within fifty feet of the other bones, this unfriendly commentator queried, would this mean that *Pithecanthropus* had two skulls, one apelike and one humanlike?

To those unwilling to acknowledge any link with any form of anthropoid ancestor, *Pithecanthropus* was pure insult. Clergymen hastened to assure their congregations that Adam, and not the crude half-ape half-human brute unearthed in Java, was the true human ancestor. Dubois was denounced from pulpit and from platform, for scientists were almost as angry and skeptical. The combination of apelike head and upright posture ran directly contrary to the belief that the development of a larger, better brain had come first in the separation of the human stock from earlier anthropoids. Scientists expected a being with a human head and an apelike body, not the reverse.

The arrival of the fossils themselves for close inspection did not settle the arguments. Only six weeks after Dubois reached Holland in 1895, he presented *Pithecanthropus* to the Third International Congress of Zoology at Leiden. Almost at once, a great quarrel broke out over where to place this Java "ape-human" in the scheme of evolution. Opinion seemed to harden along national lines: most German scientists believed that *Pithecanthropus* was an ape that had humanlike characteristics; most English ones thought it was a human that had apelike attributes; and American experts tended to consider it a transitional form more along the lines Dubois had suggested.

Dubois gave his colleagues as much detailed knowledge of *Pithecanthropus* as he could. He exhibited the bones at scientific meetings throughout Europe, showed them to any scientist who wanted to examine them, and published detailed descriptions. He had to acquire the skills of a dentist, photographer, and sculptor. In order to make accurate brain casts, he spent weeks learning to use a fine dental drill, with which he could clean away minute stone particles inside the skullcap. He invented a special "stereorthoscope" camera, designed to photograph the fossils in various planes without distortion. For the public he sculpted a life-size reconstruction of *Pithecanthropus* (see Figure 10–7), ordering his son to pose for him during a school vacation. He patiently defended his claim for *Pithecanthropus*, carting the bones around in a battered suitcase, and seemed to develop an almost personal attachment to the fossil ancestor whose bones were a constant companion.

In spite of all Dubois' efforts, the attacks on *Pithecanthropus* continued. Dubois took them personally. Deeply hurt by the refusal of other scientists to accept his interpretation of the bones, he withdrew the remains of *Pithecanthropus* from the public realm, hid them under the floor of his dining room, and became almost a recluse.

In 1920 the discovery of an ancient skull in Australia led scientists to urge that *Pithecanthropus* be let out of solitary confinement, but Dubois was obstinate. He added to the problem by announcing for the first time that he had the two Wadjak skulls and would allow no one to see them, either. At this time Henry Fairfield Osborn, head of the American Museum of Natural History, appealed to the president of the Dutch Academy of Sciences in the hope that this material, essential to science, would be made available. Soon afterward, in 1923, Dubois opened his strongboxes for Aleš Hrdlička of the Smithsonian Institution, and thereafter again exhibited *Pithecanthropus* at scientific meetings. He also released a cast of the *Pithecanthropus* skull that indicated a brain of about

*FIGURE 10–7   Dubois' model of* Pithecanthropus *holds an antler.*

850 cc, well above the range of 275 to 750 cc of the apes and below th 1,000–2,000 cc range of modern humans (see Table 8–1).

Today there still remain some unanswered questions about Dubois discovery. Do the bones really belong to the same creature? To suppose that two different primates—an unknown species of ape and an un known species of human—had lived in Java at exactly the same time and had died within thirty-five feet of each other at Trinil, seemed to Dubois far more improbable than to suppose that the various bone belonged to one creature with both apelike and human characteristics The skull is unquestionably that of an early human of the species w now call *Homo erectus*, but one tooth at least may have belonged to a prehistoric orangutan and experts now suspect that the thighbone migh have come from a higher stratum and belonged to a more modern form of human.

Because of the great controversy over whether *Pithecanthropus* was a human, an ape, or a true "missing link," Dubois' brilliant detective work in locating the fossils seemed only to add to the mystery of human origins instead of solving it. While anthropologists argued over the Java bones and Dubois withdrew into his home in Holland, the controversy was being settled elsewhere.

## TWENTIETH-CENTURY DISCOVERIES

### The Mauer Jaw (1907)

On October 21, 1907, a new clue to the human past turned up in Germany. On that day, two workmen were digging in a huge commercial sand pit near Mauer (see Figure 10–8). Several fossils previously had been unearthed there, and geologists from Heidelberg University had asked the owner of the pit to save any bones that were found, particularly anything that looked human. This day, digging nearly eighty feet below the ground level, one of the workmen struck a large jawbone with his shovel and split it in half. The jaw (see Figure 10–9 looked human but seemed much too large. Professor Otto Schoetensack of the university was notified and took possession of the jaw, which he cleaned, repaired, and studied with growing excitement. The fossil was so wide and thick that, without its teeth, it might have been mistaken for the jaw of a large ape. But the teeth were remarkably like those of modern humans. They had bigger roots and were slightly larger than our teeth, but showed all the characteristics that distinguish modern human teeth from those of the ape, including small canines and molars worn flat by chewing. In a monograph describing the find, Schoetensack created a new human species on the basis of this lower jaw—*Homo heidelbergensis*, or Heidelberg man. Today the fossil is considered by many experts to be a European example of the once widespread species *Homo erectus*.

From the jaw alone, it was impossible to tell much about what "Heidelberg man" looked like. Much more revealing was the place where the fossil was discovered. The jaw had lain in strata of rock

FIGURE 10–8   Since the earliest discoveries in East Asia, a number of sites in Europe and Africa have yielded remains of Homo erectus. In this map, the coastline is shown as it might have been during the Mindel glaciation when the sea level fell. The site of the Piltdown "discovery" has been added, together with important archaeological sites mentioned in the text.

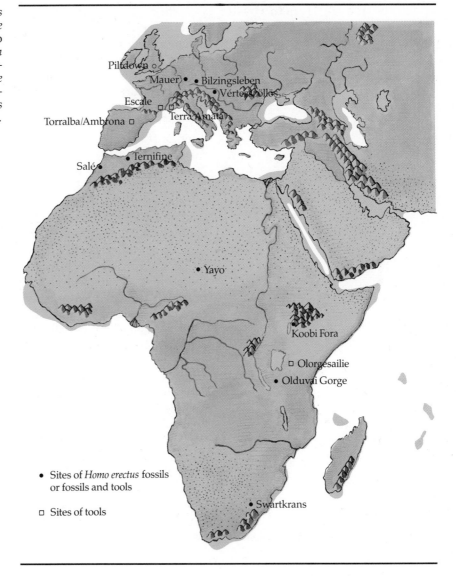

Piltdown

"Mauer" • Bilzingsleben
Vértesszöllös
Escale
Terra Amata
Torralba/Ambrona □

• Ternifine
Salé •

• Yayo

Koobi Fora

□ Olorgesailie
• Olduvai Gorge

• Sites of Homo erectus fossils or fossils and tools

□ Sites of tools

• Swartkrans

where other extinct animal fossils also were found. Because the era when these animals had lived was known, the Mauer jaw could be roughly dated: it belonged to someone who lived during the middle phases of the Pleistocene, in a warm phase of the ice age. This discovery was the first hint that humans existed so far north, into the wintry climates of Europe, at so early a date. Today we attribute to the Heidelberg jaw a date of 500,000–700,000 years B.P., which places it in the middle Pleistocene.

## Search for Human Fossils in China

Despite the importance of the Mauer jaw, it was too small a piece of evidence to throw much light on its owner's place in human evolution. It was nearly two decades before another fossil somewhat like it was found, this time in China.

The discovery of "Peking man" in 1927 involved a piece of scientific detective work almost as remarkable as Dubois' exploit in Java. This ancestor was added to the human family tree simply because a small band of scientists had gone to China determined to hunt it down. Even after Dubois' success in Java, the prospect of searching for a primitive human in China could appeal only to people prepared to spend their lives hunting for a needle in one haystack after another. But a Canadian physician, Davidson Black (1884–1934), was sure that he would unearth a human ancestor in China if only he looked long and hard enough. And so in 1919, when he was offered an appointment as professor of anatomy at Peking Union Medical College, which was being set up with funds from the Rockefeller Foundation, he eagerly accepted.

Black's conviction was based both on geologic evidence showing that the ancient climate and geography of China were quite suitable for a primitive human to exist there, and on the theory that patterns of evolution are closely related to climatic conditions. Also supporting his feeling was a single tantalizing piece of fossil evidence that some early primate had once inhabited China. In 1899 a European paleontologist, Dr. Haberer, had chanced upon an unusual fossil tooth among some "dragon's bones" about to be ground up for medicine in a druggist's shop in Peking. The tooth was among the more than a hundred bones the doctor picked up in various Chinese drugstores and sent to paleontologist Max Schlosser. Schlosser identified the tooth as a "left upper third molar, either of a man or a hitherto unknown anthropoid ape" and predicted hopefully that further search might turn up the skeleton of an early human.

Black's hopes of finding time for fossil hunting when he reached China were dissolved by an adviser from the Rockefeller Foundation, who warned him to concentrate on anatomy, not anthropology. It was not until 1921 that the search for early humans in China actually began.

*FIGURE 10–9   The Heidelberg jaw (center) is here compared with the jaw of a chimpanzee (left) and that of a modern human (right).*

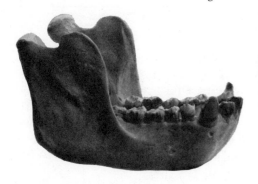 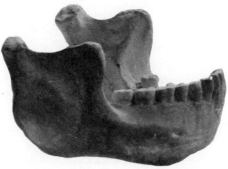 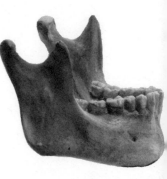

That year a group led by John Gunnar Andersson, a Swedish geologist, began to dig at a site twenty-five miles southwest of Peking, near the village of Choukoutien (see Figure 10–3). Excavations were proceeding at a rise called Chicken Bone Hill near an old limestone quarry, when Andersson was told by his workmen that much better fossils could be found on the other side of the village, at Dragon Bone Hill, beside another abandoned quarry.

The Chinese had been digging "dragon bones" out of this spot and others like it for hundreds of years, and no one will ever know how many powdered fossils have passed harmlessly through the alimentary canals of dyspeptic Chinese. Whatever the losses may have been to paleoanthropology, some of the limestone caverns in the hillside were still richly packed with interesting material. There were bits of broken quartz among the limestone deposits around an ancient cliffside cave. The quartz would not naturally be associated with limestone, Andersson knew; it must have been brought there—perhaps by some tool-making peoples of the past.

A great many fossils were dug out of the rock and shipped back to Sweden for study. Twenty different mammals were identified, many of them extinct species. But Andersson's toolmaker was not easily found. A likely tooth turned up, but it was then identified as the molar of an ape. Finally, in 1926, when one of Andersson's associates had given up and returned to Sweden and the digging had stopped, a closer study of this molar and another tooth found later suggested that they might indeed be human. The teeth were sent back to Andersson, who turned them over to Davidson Black for his expert appraisal. Preoccupied though Black was with medicine, he had never lost interest in the Choukoutien digs. He was certain that the tooth came from a human of great antiquity, and he persuaded the Rockefeller Foundation to support a large-scale excavation of the site.

*Sinanthropus* **Discovered (1927)**

Work started up again at Dragon Bone Hill in 1927. At some remote time in the past, water had honeycombed the limestone of the hill with caves and fissures. The caves in turn had filled with the deposits of running water and with the debris of collapsing roofs. By the twentieth century, when modern quarrying cut away one face of the hill, the former caves appeared only as fossil-bearing rock distinct from the limestone. Digging in this hard, compacted fill material proved difficult; blasting was often necessary. Just as much of a problem was the troubled political condition of China. Antiforeign riots were flaring, and bandits controlled the countryside around Peking. For weeks at a time they isolated the dig from the city. Nevertheless, work at the dig continued. On October 16, 1927, three days before the first season's work was to end, Birgir Böhlin, field supervisor, found another early human tooth. As he hurried to Peking to take it to Black, soldiers stopped him

*FIGURE 10–10   The excavation of the cave filling at Choukoutien was a gigantic undertaking. Work continued at the site from 1927 until 1937.*

several times, without suspecting that he carried a scientific treasure in his pocket.

Black studied the tooth exhaustively. Struck by its size and its cusp pattern, he became convinced that it was a very ancient human molar. Without waiting for any further proof, Black announced the discovery of a new genus and species of prehistoric human: *Sinanthropus pekinensis,* "Chinese man of Peking." Scientists were startled, and although Black traveled around the world to let them examine for themselves the evidence (which he carried on a watch chain in his waistcoat pocket), many refused to recognize *Sinanthropus* as a legitimate ancestor on the evidence of only one tooth.

When Black returned to Peking in 1928, his belief in the humanness of *Sinanthropus* was vindicated. His associates were waiting with fragments of a primitive human jaw they had dug out of the cave. And as tons of earth were excavated from the hillside and sifted for signs of fossil fragments, further teeth and several small fragments of human bone came to light.

Then, in 1929, W. C. Pei, a Chinese paleontologist working with Black, turned up the first skull of *Sinanthropus.* Work was about to be closed for the year when Pei opened up two caves at the extreme end of a fissure. On the floor of one was a large accumulation of debris. Pei brushed some of it away, and suddenly, partly surrounded by loose sand and partly embedded in travertine (a water-formed rock), there lay revealed the object of all the searching—a nearly complete skullcap. Even at first glance, Pei felt certain that it was a skullcap of *Sinanthropus.* After removing the skull and part of its stone bed from the cave, Pei carefully wrapped it up, set it in the basket of his bicycle, and pedaled the twenty-five miles to Black's laboratory in Peking. Black showed Pei's discovery to Roy Chapman Andrews, an American scientist. "There it was, the skull of an individual who had lived half a million years ago," Andrews wrote. "It was one of the most important discoveries in the whole history of human evolution. He could not have been very impressive when he was alive, but dead and fossilized, he was awe-inspiring."

Black spent the next four months freeing the skullcap from the surrounding stone. When it was entirely clean he separated all the bones, made a cast of each one, and then reassembled the pieces. Black was now able to make a reliable estimate of the brain capacity of *Sinanthropus.* It came to about 1,000 cubic centimeters, marking its owner as definitely humanlike in this respect.

## Intensive Work at Choukoutien

The news made headlines around the world. Excavations at Choukoutien were reorganized on a broader basis and went on for almost ten more years, finally taking on the proportions of a grand engineering project.

As work advanced, a whole hillside was sliced off, revealing deposits

*FIGURE 10–11  Franz Weidenreich (left) succeeded Davidson Black (right) at Peking Union Medical College in 1934 and pursued the excavations at Choukoutien with equal fervor.*

160 feet deep (Figure 10–10). They can be compared with an apartment building about sixteen stories tall, each story packed solid with blown-in debris combined with the abandoned rubbish of long-departed tenants. Layer on layer, the Choukoutien caves were filled through the ages with strata of clay, with soil carried in by the wind, with limestone drippings, with rock fallen from the ceiling—all sandwiching layers of human and animal debris. It is clear that large carnivores occupied the caves for long periods of time. Bones of extinct creatures like the cave bear and a giant hyena, together with the remains of animals on which they preyed, occur at certain levels. At others, it is equally clear that human beings drove the carnivores out and took over the caves for themselves. At first the animal and human layers alternate fairly regularly, but toward the top, humans take over permanently.

A total of 1,873 workdays were devoted to dynamiting and removing some 20,000 cubic meters of rock and earth and sorting through the debris for fossils. The findings constituted an encyclopedia of prehistory that has given us a great part of our knowledge of these people. By 1937, parts of more than forty men, women, and children had been unearthed; these fossils included 5 complete skulls, 9 fragmentary skulls, 6 facial fragments, 14 lower jaws, and 152 teeth.

Black organized the work, kept detailed records of all the finds, classified them, and made casts, drawings, and photographs of the heavy volume of material pouring into Peking. Tragically, he did not live to savor the full bounty of Choukoutien. He died of a heart attack in 1934, but he had seen enough to realize its extraordinary significance.

The Rockefeller Foundation sought carefully for a successor and chose Franz Weidenreich (1873–1948), then a visiting professor of anatomy at the University of Chicago (Figure 10–11). Before the Nazis drove him from his native Germany, Weidenreich had completed important studies of the evolutionary changes in the pelvis and foot that made possible our upright posture. His studies supported the contention of Darwin and Huxley that humankind is a descendant of some ancient anthropoid stock but not of any recent genus.

## Assessment of *Sinanthropus*

After Weidenreich's arrival at Choukoutien in 1935, only two more seasons of undisturbed digging could be carried out. Fighting between Chinese and Japanese guerillas broke out nearby, and the archaeologists had to take refuge. With the approach of World War II, Weidenreich concentrated on making accurate drawings and casts of the Peking skulls and published detailed photographs and descriptions of every important fossil. He began a classic series of studies of the Peking fossils—*The Mandibles of Sinanthropus, The Dentition of Sinanthropus, The Extremity Bones of Sinanthropus, The Skull of Sinanthropus*. All four supported Black's conclusion: *Sinanthropus* was not a link between apes and humans but an actual human, though a very primitive one. Weidenreich placed *Sinanthropus* solidly in the human lineage because mem-

*FIGURE 10–12   Skulls of a female gorilla,* Sinanthropus, *and a modern Chinese (all equally reduced). Notice the size and form of the braincase in relation to the jaws.*

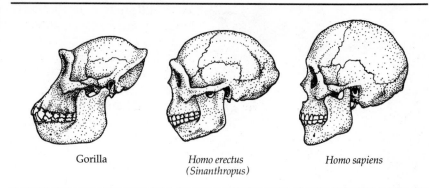

Gorilla                    *Homo erectus*                *Homo sapiens*
                           *(Sinanthropus)*

bers of the species undoubtedly could walk upright on two legs. "Apes, like man, have two hands and two feet, but man alone has acquired an upright position and the faculty of using his feet exclusively as locomotor instruments," said Weidenreich. "Unless all signs are deceiving, the claim may even be ventured that the change in locomotion and the corresponding alteration of the organization of the body are the essential specialization in the transformation of the prehuman form into the human form."

The teeth and dental arch of *Sinanthropus* testified further to human status. The canines were not the projecting fangs of the ape, and the dental arch was curved, not oblong. Still more evidence lay in the skull. Weidenreich arranged the skulls of a gorilla, *Sinanthropus,* and a modern human in a row, so that even a glance revealed their striking differences: the extremely low skull of the gorilla, the somewhat higher skull of *Sinanthropus,* the rounded skull of a modern human (Figure 10–12). The low vault of the gorilla skull houses a brain averaging about 500 cc; the higher dome of *Sinanthropus* held one of about 1,000 cc; the high cranium of the modern human encloses a brain averaging about 1,330 cc. Because *Sinanthropus'* brain was so small, some scientists questioned the creature's human status. Weidenreich cautioned that brain size alone is no absolute determinant. One species of whale, he pointed out, has a brain approaching 10,000 cc, but this amounts to one gram of brain for each 10,000 grams of body weight, compared to our ratio of one gram for every 45 grams of weight (Table 8–2). "Neither the absolute nor the relative size of the brain can be used to measure the degree of mental ability in animals or man," he added. "Cultural objects are the only guide as far as spiritual life is concerned. They may be fallacious guides too, but we are completely lost if these objects are missing."

### Culture at Choukoutien

At Choukoutien cultural objects were not missing. The continuing excavations produced thousands of stone tools. They were simple choppers with only a few chips removed, but they were made to a pattern.

In the largest cave that was explored, 100,000 stone tools and fragments, most of quartz, were found. Some of them lay with charred bits of wood and bone. The charring, it was evident, had not resulted from some accidental fire, for the hard-baked red and yellow clay of ancient hearths often underlay the carbon. *Sinanthropus* had mastered the use of fire. The charcoal in some of the hearths was as much as twenty-two feet deep—dramatic evidence that the first humans did not permit the fires to die out. There were also some tools fashioned from animal bones and antlers, as shown in Figure 10–13.

The bones of thousands of animals were strewn about in the caves. Nearly three quarters of them belonged to deer, which must have been the favorite meat of *Sinanthropus*. There also were bones of giant sheep, zebra, pigs, buffalo, and rhinoceros, and traces of monkeys, bison, elephant, and even such river dwellers as the otter. All the mammalian bones came from species long since gone from the earth. About twenty feet below the lowest outer threshold of the big cave, the expedition found *Sinanthropus'* garbage dump, a stony amalgam of thousands of scraps of bone, stone chips, and hackberry seeds. All in all, by their fires and their handiwork as well as by their bodily structure, the specimens found in China indubitably established their right to a place in the human genus. Recent Chinese research places the human occupation of the cave between 450,000 and 500,000 B.P.

**Relationship of**
***Pithecanthropus* and**
***Sinanthropus***

Weidenreich's assessment corroborated Black's earlier conclusion that *Sinanthropus* was humanlike. In 1929 Black had compared his Peking skull with Dubois' detailed description of *Pithecanthropus*. He concluded that the skulls were two specimens of the same type of creature. In each, the bones of the skull were thick, the forehead was low and sloping, and massive brow ridges jutted out over the eye sockets.

In 1931, on an upper terrace of the same Solo River whose banks had harbored the bones of Dubois' *Pithecanthropus*, fragments of eleven somewhat more recent skulls were excavated by Dutch geologists. This

*FIGURE 10–13 Two antler tools. Bone and antler tools were found in abundance at Choukoutien. (The photograph is approximately one-sixth actual size.)*

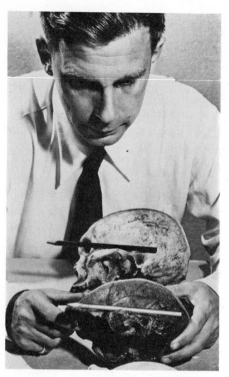

*FIGURE 10–14   G. H. R von Koenigswald worked in Java in the 1930s and managed to find more specimens of* Pithecanthropus. *He helped establish that* Sinanthropus *and* Pithecanthropus *were of the same genus.*

discovery encouraged G. H. R. von Koenigswald (b. 1902), a German paleontologist (Figure 10–14), to keep searching for more specimens of *Pithecanthropus*. Eventually, in 1937, in a region to the west called Sangiran, he found pieces of three more skulls, definitely human and definitely very old—and presumably remains of the same *Pithecanthropus* that Dubois had found forty years before. When the most complete skull was assembled, it scarcely could have been more like Dubois' fossil. "It was a little eerie," said von Koenigswald, "to come upon two skulls . . . which resembled each other as much as two eggs." In 1936, von Koenigswald had excavated a child's skull at Modjokerto, Java, which later proved to be that of a six-year-old *Pithecanthropus*.

In 1939 a historic meeting of *Sinanthropus* and *Pithecanthropus* took place in Weidenreich's laboratory, when von Koenigswald paid a visit and brought his Java fossils along to compare them with the Choukoutien finds. The two scientists concluded that *Pithecanthropus* and *Sinanthropus* were indeed close relations. "In its general form and size [the Peking skull] agrees with the Java skull to such an extent that it identifies *Pithecanthropus* too, as true man, and a creature far above the stage of an ape," said Weidenreich, upsetting the judgment of Dubois that *Pithecanthropus* came long before the first humans.

The assessment of von Koenigswald and Weidenreich was later corroborated by Sir Wilfrid Le Gros Clark. *Pithecanthropus*, Le Gros Clark said, appeared slightly more primitive, with a brain of about 900 cubic centimeters and a slightly heavier jaw. In addition, the animals killed and eaten by *Pithecanthropus* were a little older than those found at Peking, and no tools were found with *Pithecanthropus*. Despite these differences the two ancient beings were strikingly alike.

Von Koenigswald and Weidenreich had agreed that *Pithecanthropus* and *Sinanthropus* differed little more than "two different races of present mankind," and Le Gros Clark came to the same conclusion. He proposed dropping the *Sinanthropus* classification, which implied a separate genus, for it was doubtful that the two formed even separate species. He suggested that both should be identified as *Pithecanthropus*, and distinguished only by their specific names, *Pithecanthropus erectus* for the Java finds and *Pithecanthropus pekinensis* for the Peking ones.

The aging Eugene Dubois bitterly opposed Le Gros Clark's conclusion, continuing to insist that his own find was quite distinct from all others. But von Koenigswald and Weidenreich were little disturbed by his protests. More upsetting was the rumble of war.

## Fate of the Java and Peking Fossils

In Java, von Koenigswald knew that it was only a matter of time until the island would be seized. He quietly gave some of his most valuable fossils for safekeeping to a Swiss geologist and a Swedish journalist, neutrals in the conflict between Allies and Axis. (The journalist put the teeth in milk bottles and buried them one night in his garden.) When the Japanese occupied Java in 1942, they demanded that von Koenigswald give up his fossils. He surrendered a few, but he substituted plaster casts for some of the originals.

At the end of the war, von Koenigswald tracked down and reassembled all the fossils. "My happiness was complete," he said, "when I learned that my precious specimens had been saved. Large parts of my collections, many of my books, and all of my clothes had been stolen, but Early Man had survived the disaster." Von Koenigswald later exhibited *Pithecanthropus* in New York and then took the bones to the Netherlands and then on to Frankfurt, Germany, where they now remain.

The Peking fossils were not so fortunate as the Java fossils. By the autumn of 1941, the scientists working at Choukoutien were more immediately threatened than they had been before by the war. After some debate about what to do with the fossils, the Chinese scientists appealed to the president of the Peking Union Medical College to have the irreplaceable Peking remains taken to safety. It was arranged to send the collection to the United States. The boxes of fossils were entrusted to a detachment of Marines who were evacuating Peking. At 5 A.M. on December 5, 1941, nine Marines, with their baggage and the fossils, went by special train to the port of Chinwangtao, where the steamship *President Harrison* was waiting for them.

But the rendezvous was never kept, for on December 7 Japanese bombs were dropped on Pearl Harbor and total war came violently to the Pacific. Somewhere between the Peking depot and the *President Harrison,* the boxes with all that existed of *Pithecanthropus pekinensis*—fossil pieces representing about forty individuals—disappeared. They never have been found. It seems that the Peking people, after lying buried at Choukoutien for nearly half a million years, reappeared for only twelve short years before disappearing again, perhaps forever. Fortunately, a superb series of casts had been prepared in Peking and these were saved. We also have Weidenreich's outstanding descriptions and photographs.

The fate of the Peking fossils remains one of the great international mysteries, but their standing as humans is secure. However fleeting their reappearance, their bones and the Java fossils offered incontrovertible proof of humankind's lengthy existence. These ancestors emerging from the past were not what their descendants expected them to be, for they seemed crude, primitive, and low of brow. But not only did they live successfully in their environment several hundred thousand years ago; they also walked like modern humans and bore human intelligence. In short, they were humans, not transitional forms between animals and humankind.

It is only in the last decade or so that the growing number of finds and increasing familiarity with the fossils themselves have generally

*FIGURE 10–15   This reconstruction of the skull and jaw of* Homo erectus *is based on numerous fossil finds. The general form of the face can also be reconstructed with reasonable accuracy, but we have no evidence of such important features as nostrils, lips, and hair. He was most unlikely to have been clean-shaven!*

convinced scientists that, for all their geographic dispersion, all these remains represent a single species of human that varies considerably in different locations. The Java and Peking fossils were given a single scientific name, *Homo erectus* (Figure 10–15), which places them in a different species but in the same genus as *Homo sapiens,* the name given to modern humans.

## MEANING OF THE FOSSILS

By the time anthropologists were able to resume the search for early humans after World War II, human ancestry had been traced, as we have seen, to forebears more primitive and apelike than *Homo erectus.* Yet there was still no clear conception of the human lineage, nor of the relationships between the various fossils found in different parts of the world. Had the human body evolved toward its modern form more rapidly than the human brain, or had the brain outstripped the body in early human evolution? Were many species of early humans evolving at different rates and in different ways in various parts of the world? Or was there one consistent pattern governing human evolution worldwide? In part, these crucial questions could not be answered at the time because the answer was obscured by the most peculiar human fossils of all—the skull and jawbone of a creature known as Piltdown man.

## The Great Piltdown Hoax

When they turned up in a gravel pit on an old farm in Sussex, England, in 1911, the Piltdown fossils were seen as an important new clue to the human past. Their discoverer was an amateur archaeologist named Charles Dawson. Dawson reported that while taking a walk near a place called Piltdown Common, he spotted unusual brown flints being used to mend the road. He asked where they had come from and was led to a nearby farm where workmen were digging gravel. The gravel pit looked to him like a possible source of fossils, and he asked the men to save any old-looking bones they might unearth. On his later visits to the farm he retrieved several parts of a seemingly ancient human skull. Dawson told his story and showed the fossils to A. Smith Woodward of the British Museum, and together the two made an exhaustive search of the gravel pit. They found many fragments of the skull, apparently smashed and scattered by the digging, as well as half of a slightly damaged jaw. On December 18, 1912, the two men introduced Piltdown man to the members of the Geological Society of London. Smith Woodward named this creature *Eoanthropus dawsoni*, or "Dawson's dawn man."

At first sight, the Piltdown man was a complete surprise (Figure 10–16). The skull seemed to be that of a modern human, with an imposingly large braincase and a vertical forehead with slightly ridged brows. But it also had the more primitive-looking jaw of an ape. The jaw was almost exactly like a chimpanzee's, except that the molars were ground down the way a human's teeth are worn by chewing and the canine was missing. Unfortunately, the small section of the jaw that could have proved whether it fit the skull, a structure called the condyle, had been broken off.

The small braincase and humanlike thighbone found in Java had suggested that the human body had evolved more rapidly than the brain. Because it was originally considered to be of Pliocene (and later, middle Pleistocene) age, that is, as old as *Pithecanthropus*, the Piltdown skull suggested the opposite: that the brain evolved first. Just as some scientists had doubted that the different Java fossils belonged together, some skeptics now felt that the Piltdown skull did not go with the jaw. But many of the world's leading experts welcomed Piltdown into the family of human ancestors.

Over the years, troubling discrepancies began to be noticed in the Piltdown fragments. The maturity of different parts seemed to vary, and one expert complained that Piltdown was not only human-brained and ape-jawed, but appeared to have a middle-aged skull, a young jaw, and an elderly set of teeth! But the downfall of Piltdown did not come until the 1950s, when so many genuine fossils of early humans and their ancestors had been found that Dawson's discovery was seen to stand out like a transistor radio in a collection of stone hand-axes. All the other fossils confirmed that the human brain had evolved toward its modern form somewhat more slowly than the remaining physical equipment. Piltdown must be, then, an evolutionary freak—or could it be a fraud?

The first scientist to test the latter idea was J. S. Weiner, then a lecturer in Oxford University's anatomy department, which was headed

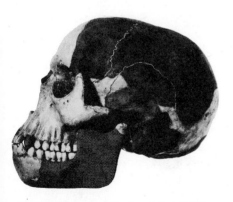

FIGURE 10–16 *The fraudulent Piltdown skull, here reconstructed, led scientists astray for forty years in their understanding of human evolution. The black shaded area of the skull and jaw are the original fragments. The remainder is reconstruction.*

by Sir Wilfrid Le Gros Clark. Weiner tried out his suspicions of Piltdown man on Le Gros Clark, who doubted at first that the fossils could be fraudulent. Then Weiner took a chimpanzee jaw from the anatomy department collection, filed down the teeth to resemble those of Piltdown, and stained his handiwork to make it look like a fossil. Placing the jaw on Le Gros Clark's desk, he said he had found it in the anatomy collection and asked what it could be. The resemblance to the Piltdown jaw was remarkable. Convinced that Weiner must be right, Le Gros Clark joined him in initiating a reexamination of Dawson's discovery.

This was the beginning of the end for Piltdown. Tests that should determine the relative age of fossil bones by measuring the amount of fluorine absorbed from the ground water showed the Piltdown jaw and skull to be of different ages, and when a magnifying glass was used on the teeth, file marks showed up clearly. In 1953 Weiner, Le Gros Clark, K. P. Oakley, and others announced that the jaw was a hoax.

Further tests proved the rest of Piltdown fraudulent as well. Fragments of several modern skulls, along with what turned out to be an orangutan's jaw (and a few genuinely ancient animal bones to suggest the age of the deposit), had been planted in the gravel bed. Who put them there, and why, has never been determined. The circumstances suggest that Dawson could have been the perpetrator, but a number of young paleontologists also had the knowledge and the skill needed to have carried out such a hoax. Dawson died in 1916, thirty-seven years before the forgery was finally detected.

Whoever did contrive the Piltdown hoax had gone to great pains to carry it out. All the fragments were made to appear antique with potassium dichromate, a chemical that gave them the dark brown color of fossils. The forger, besides filing down the teeth and knocking off the telltale condyle joint of the jaw, had also removed the canine tooth, which is long and pointed in an orangutan. (Soon after Dawson announced his discovery of the Piltdown skull, Smith Woodward, the anatomist to whom Dawson had first taken the bones, made a model of what he thought Piltdown's canine ought to look like. When Dawson revisited the gravel bed, a worn canine tooth almost identical to the model "turned up.")

**Pattern of Human Evolution**

Once the Piltdown puzzle was disposed of, scientists began to perceive more clearly the basic pattern of our evolution from the prehistoric apes; *Australopithecus, Homo erectus,* and many more recent finds from other parts of the world fell into place. A great many new fossils and living sites of *Homo erectus* have been discovered in recent decades, making the evolutionary picture even more complete.

In 1955 jaws and part of a skull were discovered in a sand pit in Ternifine, Algeria (Figure 10–8), showing that *Homo erectus* once had inhabited North Africa. In 1960 a *Homo erectus* skull turned up in East Africa in the rich deposits of Bed II at Olduvai Gorge, where Louis and

Mary Leakey had already found the bones and tools of that species' ancestor. Three years later, a fossil skull somewhat older and more primitive than those of *Sinanthropus* was discovered in China, at Gongwangling, near the town of Lantian, 600 miles southwest of Peking (Figure 10–3). The Chinese also discovered some teeth at Jian Shi and obtained more fossils from Choukoutien, including a fine skull. (The cave site has now been made a museum.) In 1960 an extraordinarily well preserved skull was found in a cave at Petralona in northern Greece, with some rather modern features. In 1965 a quarry in Vértesszöllös, Hungary, thirty miles from Budapest (Figure 10–8), yielded the occipital bone of a skull that seemed to indicate a larger brain than any discovered up to then.

Further discoveries followed: from Salé, in Morocco, North Africa, in 1971 came a frontal bone that appears to belong to a very late and modern-looking specimen of *Homo erectus*, with striking similarities to the Peking fossils. At the same time in East Africa, at Koobi Fora, Richard Leakey found a considerable number of skull and bone fragments approximately 1.2 million years old that include a superb skull (Figure 10–17). On the west shore of Lake Turkana, his team has discovered the most complete skeleton ever found of *Homo erectus*, be-

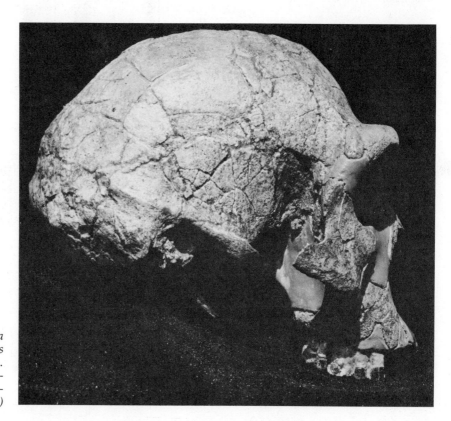

*FIGURE 10–17   This skull from Koobi Fora in Kenya is one of the best-preserved skulls that belong to the species* Homo erectus. *The present evidence suggests it is 1.5 million years old. (This photograph is approximately one-third actual size.)*

longing to a twelve-year-old boy, 5 feet 4 inches tall and probably weighing over 140 pounds, which is dated by potassium/argon to 1.6 million B.P. Again, the similarities to the Peking finds are quite clear. Down in the Transvaal, Brain's work at Swartkrans had meanwhile solved a number of questions relating to the strange jaw found there in 1949 and called *Telanthropus capensis* (because it was so much more modern in appearance then *Australopithecus*). This specimen has now turned out to be most probably a South African specimen of *Homo erectus*.

The age of these skulls is not accurately know, except for the East African specimens, because it has been impossible to use potassium-argon dating. Age estimates have been made for each, though. Figure 10–18 shows the time spans during which it is believed the deposits were laid down and which therefore bracket the supposed age of the fossils.

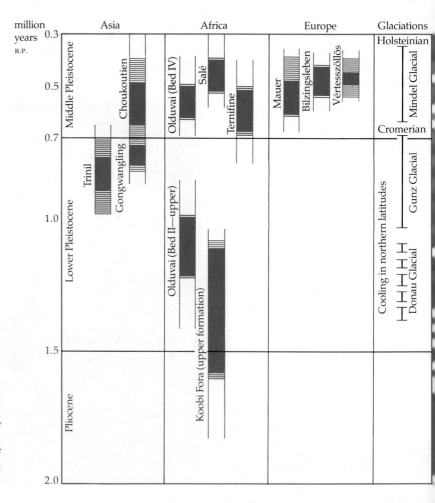

FIGURE 10–18 *This chart shows the approximate ranges of time of the deposits which contain fossils of* Homo erectus *mentioned in this chapter. The exact age of the fossils themselves has not yet been determined with any accuracy. The time spans of the Pleistocene ice ages are indicated on the right.*

FIGURE 10–19 *A representative selection of fossils of* Homo erectus. *The thighbone is exceptionally robust, as is the pelvis, but in most other respects the skeleton is modern in form. The skull and jaw, however, are still very different from those of* Homo sapiens: *the skull is low and long, the jaws and teeth powerful, and the lower jaw robust but chinless.*

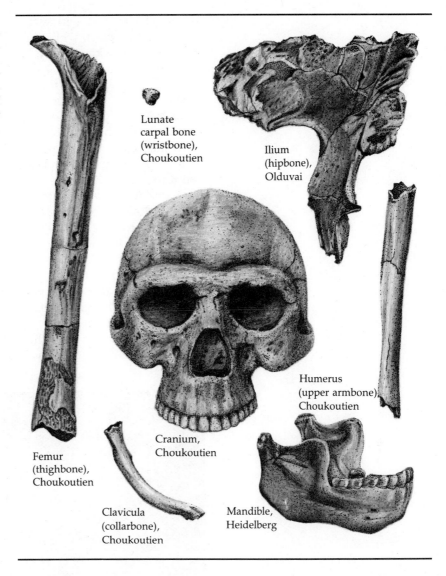

Lunate carpal bone (wristbone), Choukoutien

Ilium (hipbone), Olduvai

Humerus (upper armbone), Choukoutien

Femur (thighbone), Choukoutien

Cranium, Choukoutien

Clavicula (collarbone), Choukoutien

Mandible, Heidelberg

As all these fossils were compared and studied, it became apparent that there were some broad similarities among them (Figure 10–19). Taxonomists were now able to clear up the confusion caused by the initial naming of the fossils, in which each was given its own separate genus and species. Names like *Pithecanthropus* and *Sinanthropus* were discarded: *Homo erectus* encompassed them all. The great wave of discoveries in recent years has demonstrated the wide range of living sites and physical characteristics of *H. erectus* and has shown that over the million years of their existence they slowly evolved from the earlier *H. habilis* toward a form almost indistinguishable from early *H. sapiens*.

The skull found at Vértesszöllös, for example, has a cranial capacity typical of *H. sapiens,* while the Gongwangling skull is almost too primitive to be put with the rest.

In the search for the first humans, much of the initial excitement over the discoveries of the fossil hunters centered on human skulls. Along the way, however, scientists have accumulated a vast store of other evidence: tools and artifacts these people made and used, such as those unearthed in Choukoutien, and the bones of the animals that were their contemporaries. At some sites, as we shall see in Chapters 11 and 12, no human bones were found, but the artifacts told much about the people who used them. No fossil bones of *Homo erectus* have been discovered yet in India or the Middle East, but tools like those they used elsewhere have been found in both areas, and so *H. erectus* is assumed to have lived there as well. In some places, the combination of human bones and artifacts has presented a puzzle. The fossil occipital bone at Vértesszöllös, for example, suggests that its owner was an advanced *H. erectus,* and yet, mysteriously, these people used more primitive stone tools than their smaller-brained contemporaries in other parts of the world. The explanation is almost certainly related to the nature of the rock available in the region. We have learned that the quality of available material is one of the most important determinants of the type and quality of stone tools made at a site.

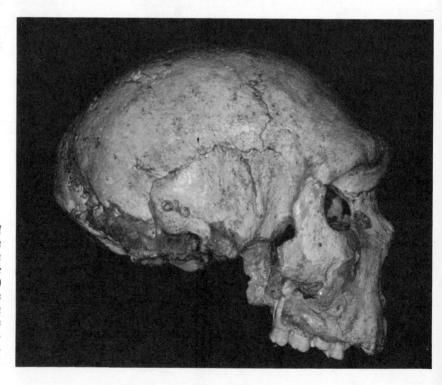

FIGURE 10–20   *This almost perfect skull (but without a mandible) was discovered in a sealed cave near Petralona in northern Greece. It is the heavily built skull of a male and may date from as long ago as 700,000* B.P., *though it may be younger. It bears some characters of* H. erectus *together with other more modern Neandertal-like features as well, and can be considered to be transitional between late* H. erectus *and the earliest* H. sapiens.

One small group of discoveries links *Homo erectus* to their predecessor *Homo habilis*. In 1936 and 1937, when von Koenigswald was excavating in Java, he discovered some fragments of jaw in deposits that may be considerably older than the Trinil deposits and seem to represent an earlier population than Dubois' *Pithecanthropus*. These specimens he named *Pithecanthropus dubius*, and today they are believed to be possibly about 1.5 million years old. Further dates are required to establish without doubt the age of these fossils. The fragments have much in common with the *Homo habilis* remains from Olduvai and Koobi Fora (see pages 185–197). They may prove to form the evolutionary link between *Homo habilis* (which seems to have been confined to Africa) and the later *Homo erectus* fossils now known to have ranged from Africa to Asia to Europe (Figure 10–18).

A second group of discoveries links *Homo erectus* with its descendent species *H. sapiens*. The European fossils from Heidelberg, Vértesszöllös, and Petralona are all late (probably 700,000–500,000 B.P.) and carry a number of characters associated with early *H. sapiens* (see page 367) and even the later Neandertal people. The classification of these specimens is presently controversial precisely because they do fall on the boundary between the two species. The age of the Petralona cranium is uncertain. Claims for its age range from 100,000 to 1,000,000 years B.P. The fauna,

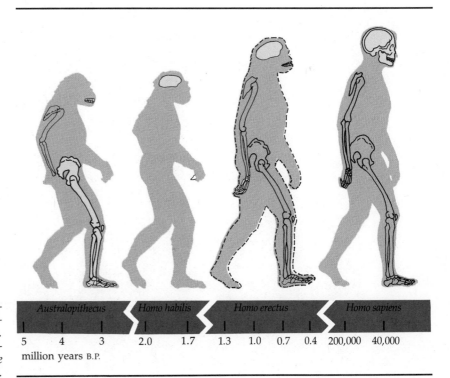

FIGURE 10–21 *Evolution of the entire human body did not occur at one period. Different organs evolved at different times. These diagrams show the succession of evolutionary developments that produced the present-day form of* Homo sapiens.

however, seems to suggest contemporaneity with the Heidelberg jaw and the Vértesszöllös occipital. Petralona is the only complete skull from this period in Europe. It appears to be what we might expect from such a period and does indeed seem to bridge the transition between *H. erectus* and *H. sapiens* (Figure 10–20).

Thus the fossil sequence from the earliest *Homo habilis* in Africa to the last *Homo erectus* in Europe is slowly falling into place. Problems and gaps remain, but if discoveries continue at the present rate, we will see clearly the overall pattern of this phase of human evolution. We already know that human evolution is definitely *mosaic* in kind; that is, the different parts of the body did not evolve toward *Homo sapiens* together and at the same rate (Figure 10–21). The evidence from *Australopithecus, Homo habilis,* and *Homo erectus* together makes it clear that the locomotor apparatus—the human pelvis, legs, and feet—evolved long before the brain and jaws. Small-brained *Australopithecus* was bipedal and very like humans from the waist down; *Homo habilis* shows us the beginning of the evolution of the brain and culture; flat-crowned *Homo erectus* was almost indistinguishable from modern humans in the anatomical structures that equipped them for bipedalism, but they were heavy-jawed and their brain was still evolving. It was only during the later evolution of *Homo* that the head took on its present shape.

# Chapter 10 Overview

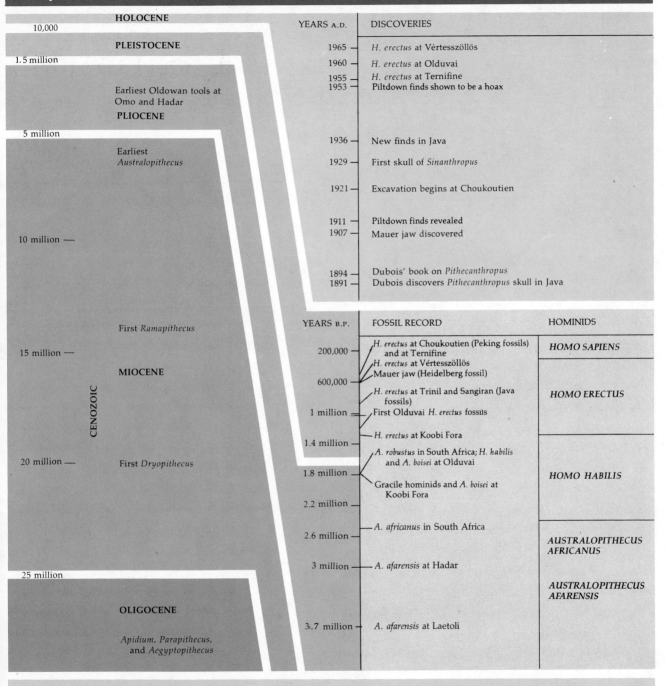

| | | YEARS A.D. | DISCOVERIES |
|---|---|---|---|
| HOLOCENE | 10,000 | | |
| PLEISTOCENE | 1.5 million | 1965 — | *H. erectus* at Vértesszöllös |
| | | 1960 — | *H. erectus* at Olduvai |
| | | 1955 — | *H. erectus* at Ternifine |
| | | 1953 — | Piltdown finds shown to be a hoax |
| Earliest Oldowan tools at Omo and Hadar | | | |
| PLIOCENE | 5 million | 1936 — | New finds in Java |
| Earliest *Australopithecus* | | 1929 — | First skull of *Sinanthropus* |
| | | 1921 — | Excavation begins at Choukoutien |
| | 10 million — | 1911 — | Piltdown finds revealed |
| | | 1907 — | Mauer jaw discovered |
| First *Ramapithecus* | | 1894 — | Dubois' book on *Pithecanthropus* |
| | | 1891 — | Dubois discovers *Pithecanthropus* skull in Java |

| | | YEARS B.P. | FOSSIL RECORD | HOMINIDS |
|---|---|---|---|---|
| 15 million — | | 200,000 — | *H. erectus* at Choukoutien (Peking fossils) and at Ternifine | HOMO SAPIENS |
| MIOCENE | | | *H. erectus* at Vértesszöllös | |
| | | 600,000 — | Mauer jaw (Heidelberg fossil) | HOMO ERECTUS |
| | | | *H. erectus* at Trinil and Sangiran (Java fossils) | |
| | | 1 million — | First Olduvai *H. erectus* fossils | |
| | | 1.4 million — | *H. erectus* at Koobi Fora | |
| 20 million — First *Dryopithecus* | | 1.8 million — | *A. robustus* in South Africa; *H. habilis* and *A. boisei* at Olduvai | HOMO HABILIS |
| | | | Gracile hominids and *A. boisei* at Koobi Fora | |
| | | 2.2 million — | | |
| | | 2.6 million — | *A. africanus* in South Africa | AUSTRALOPITHECUS AFRICANUS |
| | | 3 million — | *A. afarensis* at Hadar | |
| 25 million | | | | AUSTRALOPITHECUS AFARENSIS |
| OLIGOCENE | | 3.7 million — | *A. afarensis* at Laetoli | |
| *Apidium, Parapithecus,* and *Aegyptopithecus* | | | | |

CENOZOIC

## DISCOVERING *HOMO ERECTUS*

Discoveries of *Homo erectus* have been made throughout the Old World since the first Java finds in 1891. *Homo erectus'* predecessors, *Homo habilis*, were intermediates between the ancestral *Australopithecus* and themselves. The evolutionary process was a continuous one; the subdivisions of this lineage and the names given to those subdivisions are arbitrary. It is not the naming of these ancestors but their nature that is the subject of the science of paleoanthropology.

# Chapter 11

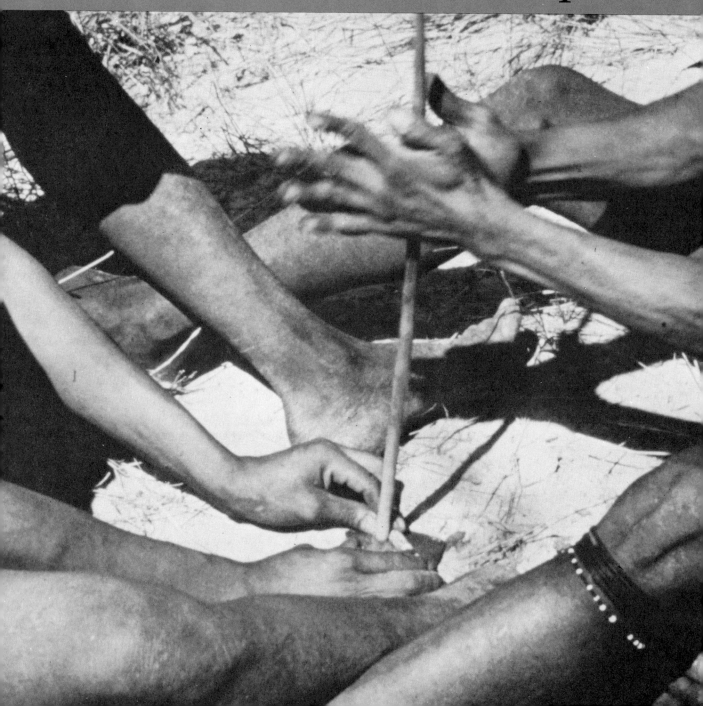

# Environment and Technology

**Man is a tool-making animal.**

BENJAMIN FRANKLIN, 1706–1790.

The fossil discoveries recorded in the last chapter, together with the archaeological sites dating from the same period, tell us much about *Homo erectus*. In this and the following chapter, we will review this evidence as a whole, looking both at the bones and at the material culture of these rapidly evolving people. To begin, we will consider an extraordinary piece of detection carried out a few years ago in the south of France.

**TERRA AMATA**  On a late spring day about 400,000 years ago, a band of perhaps fifteen men, women, and children stopped at a sandy cove on the Mediterranean coast. They were looking for somewhere to camp, and they chose a site on a sand dune protected by a limestone cliff, at the mouth of a valley. Today, the city of Nice, France, rises around their ancient campsite, but archaeologists have unearthed the place, called Terra Amata (see Figure 10–8), where these fifteen primitive visitors once made a brief stopover. From the assortment of fossil bones, stone tools, and imprints left behind and from the consistency of the sand in which this record was deposited, archaeologists have been able to estimate that the group stayed only about three days. Further, they can describe, in extraordinary detail, just what the visitors and their numerous successors did before moving on. It is possible to tell what kind of shelter they built, what sort of meals they ate, how they made their tools, and even, from imprints on the floor of the hut, where they slept and what they slept on.

## Site and Excavation

The story of the discovery begins in October 1965, when a construction site near the cliff road to Monte Carlo attracted the official prehistorian of Marseilles, thirty-year-old Henry de Lumley. De Lumley's interest in the site had been whetted eight years before when laborers preparing the ground for new apartments had uncovered a stone tool and a few flint flakes. But at that time the contractors went broke, and no further work was done until 1965. That year, bulldozers moved in again, and de Lumley stood by, watching the site carefully. As a bulldozer sheared off about three feet of ground, some objects glinted in the sunlight. De Lumley spotted what he quickly recognized as beach pebbles that had been shaped by human hands.

In France, where prehistoric artifacts may crop up anywhere, archaeology takes precedence over new construction—for a time, at least. Before long more than three hundred archaeologists, students, and interested amateurs were involved, and between January and July of 1966, they quickly dug down through hundreds of thousands of years of geologic history, until they uncovered an ancient beach that bore traces of human habitation. In the end, they had sliced vertically through more than seventy feet of the Terra Amata hill.

While inching down through the eight feet of Paleolithic deposits, each worker excavated a small area. The site had been divided into sections a meter (thirty-nine inches) square, marked off by strings tied to stakes around the edges of the excavation. Thus the dig was carried out horizontally, layer by layer. The diggers drew to scale on graph paper the plans of their particular squares and marked the exact location of each discovery. In this way the location of every relic found could be precisely identified, because relative position, as we have seen, reveals much about the identity and origin of a fossil or tool. The subsequent juxtaposition of all the charts, coupled with photographs and casts of the finds, enabled de Lumley to reconstruct the various levels of the ancient habitation.

In five months, de Lumley's team exposed 35,000 objects, which were recorded by 1,200 charts, 9,000 photographs, and 108 square yards of casts. In all, the Terra Amata site afforded one of the most unexpected and valuable archaeological treasures ever found in one small area. "It is as if we are reading a book," de Lumley said while the rewarding excavation was still in progress. "Each layer is like a page that we read, and as we read, we know the story of early man."

## Huts and Living Floors

The first page to be read was the twenty-by-forty-foot floor of a hut. Several holes, about a foot in diameter, within this floor space suggested that the roof of the hut had been held up from the inside by two or

*FIGURE 11–1    Footprints of early humans are extremely rare. This one from Terra Amata is about 400,000 years old. It is a rather broad right foot (heel to the bottom).*

more posts, perhaps the trunks of dead trees washed up on shore. In the center of the dwelling was a hearth, a fairly compact area of baked and discolored sand partially surrounded by pebbles someone had placed there to protect the fire from the northwest wind, still the prevailing wind in Nice today. The fact that the hut was such a drafty affair as to require a windbreak of this sort led de Lumley to surmise that it may have been made of saplings or branches. A circular area around the fireplace was free of litter, suggesting that the inhabitants slept there. Only a few steps away from the hearth, de Lumley uncovered a toolmaker's workshop, in the middle of which was a flat stone. Here, he guessed, the toolmaker had sat; tools and chips lay scattered about the seat. The most dramatic of all the discoveries was a nine-and-a-half-inch footprint (Figure 11–1) made by an adult whose heel had slipped slightly when stepping in the mud.

If there had been no other discovery, this occupation floor alone would have been enough to excite anthropologists everywhere. But the richness of the site exceeded de Lumley's dreams. His interpretations of the evidence are extraordinarily detailed and give us a vivid account of *Homo erectus;* a colorful fragment from the past.

Huts had stood in three locations at one time or another: some had been built on a sandbar, some on the beach itself, and others on a dune. They had been built over perhaps a century, although those on the dune, not so old as the others and built one on top of the next, had apparently resulted from consecutive annual visits to the cove by the same band.

The dune where the later camps had been set up was evidently an ideal spot, protected by a limestone cliff and close to drinking water from a spring nearby. The huts there (Figure 11–2) are believed to have been oval in shape, but they varied in size, measuring from twenty-six to forty-nine feet long and thirteen to almost twenty feet wide. Their shape could be determined from the bracing stones still lying in a ring around many of the living floors and from the imprints of stakes or saplings stuck into the sand very close together around the edge to form the walls, which corroborated de Lumley's original belief that the structures were drafty, sapling-walled constructions. At the center of the huts lay the hearths—shallow pits, either unlined or with pebbled surfaces—each shielded by its little stone windscreen (Figure 11–3).

The size of the huts suggested to de Lumley that the groups of inhabitants had been relatively small, some consisting of perhaps no more than fifteen individuals. On this basis he conjectured that the groups were made up of men out on a short hunting foray. This opinion, however, is not shared by most authorities, who point out that it would not have been feasible for the men to transport, in their arms or on their backs, an appreciable quantity of meat over any great distance to the women and children of the band who had been left behind.

FIGURE 11–2   *This drawing reconstructs the kind of huts that Henry de Lumley excavated at Terra Amata. The hut has been cut away to show the method of construction. The exact form of the roof is uncertain, but this type of construction is common today in Africa, as can be seen in the photograph of a !Kung Bushman hut. The drawing shows some worked stones in the center. The oval of rocks and the central postholes were the main clues to the size and form of construction.*

No human bones were found to provide proof for either opinion, but something of the life of the more recent dwellers could be visualized through the details extracted from the living floors (Figure 11–4). In a corner of one of the later huts, not far from a hearth, lay a large, smooth stone scarred with tiny scratches. To de Lumley's eye those scratches indicated that meat had been cut on the stone with a smaller piece of sharp stone; bones of many animals were found nearby.

*FIGURE 11–3  On one of the Terra Amata hut floors, a windscreen of stones still shields a shallow hearth (left).*

Close to this "kitchen" area de Lumley came upon another unusual find: specimens of fossilized human excrement. It seems these were not the most hygienic of humans, though a kind of toilet zone does seem to have been set up in the hut. Analysis of fossil pollen found in the feces indicated the time of year the hut had been built and occupied—late spring or early summer, when certain flowers, among them yellow broom, were in blossom and shed their pollen over everything that the prehistoric campers ate.

It was also a time when many game animals would have been abundant on the flood plain of the Paillon River, not far from the campsite. Surely the presence of game was no coincidence. These humans were above all hunters, and the Terra Amata bands must have chosen the site in the late spring because hunting was good there at that time.

The animal remains found throughout the site corroborate that speculation. There were bones from birds, turtles, and at least eight kinds of mammals. The hunters did not spurn rabbits and rodents, but they preferred larger, meatier prey. Many bones were those of the young of big game. Red deer were represented in greatest numbers, followed in descending order of abundance by an extinct species of elephant; wild boar; ibex or wild mountain goat; Merk's two-horned rhinoceros, now extinct; and the extinct wild ox. Only the wild boar still lives in the environs of Nice, and it is smaller than its forebears.

The visitors obviously concentrated on hunting while at Terra Amata, but they also had a taste for seafood. Shells of oysters, limpets, and mussels, creatures that are fairly readily gathered, are found at the site. The presence of some fishbones and fish vertebrae indicated that the dune campers caught fish occasionally as well.

### Dune Campsites

According to de Lumley, the occupants of the earlier huts, on the beach and sandbar, differed in several ways from the people who camped on the dune. For whatever reason, they built bigger fires. They seem also to have been less competent toolmakers. They left behind several examples of their rather crude skill, including such pebble tools as a pick, flaked on one face only, rough *bifaces* (oval cobbles chipped on two sides of one end), scrapers, cleavers, choppers, and projectile points.

The dune dwellers made many of the same tools as their predecessors but employed a more advanced technique of manufacture—flaking chips off a core and then shaping the chips, rather than the core, into tools. They apparently traveled to find proper materials: a projectile point fashioned from a kind of volcanic rock found only in the Esterel region, some thirty miles to the west, was unearthed at a dune site.

The dune dwellers used tools manufactured from bone as well as stone. The leg bone of an elephant had been ground to a point. Another bone too had been hardened in fire, and the fragment of a third was blunt with use. A fourth tool had a long, sharp end and may have been

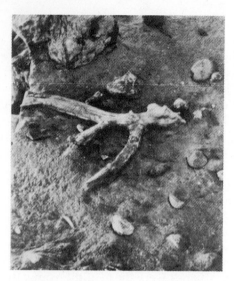

*FIGURE 11–4   An antler, together with pebbles and tool chips, lies on the hut floor at Terra Amata. The antler may have been used as a pick for digging or for freeing shellfish from rocks.*

employed as an awl to pierce hides, perhaps to make clothing. Around one hearth impressions in the sand, unmistakably those of animal skins, suggested that *Homo erectus* either sat or slept on hides.

The discovery of several pieces of red ocher, worn to a nub, seemed to imply that these people may also have decorated their bodies, perhaps even for ceremonial purposes. The ocher may, however, have had a more practical application: some people living in sunny areas today still mix it with fat and use it as a sunburn preventive. (As we shall see in the next chapter, experts think that *Homo erectus* were relatively hairless, and so this preventive may have been needed.)

One of the most intriguing finds was a spherical imprint in the sand. Was it left by a bowl? De Lumley thinks so, and believes that the bowl, presumably of wood, was used to store water. He theorized that the hut dwellers might also have cooked in such a container, filling it first with water and then adding hot stones ("potboilers") to raise the water temperature, a method of boiling food followed by many American Indian tribes. The possibility that the *Homo erectus* tool kit included vessels provides rich ground for further speculation. Such containers may well have been used by women and children to gather nuts, berries, and seeds, thus facilitating the division of labor that is the hallmark of developing human society.

This entire reconstruction, based as it is on de Lumley's interpretations, is necessarily speculative and has been questioned in certain details by archaeologist Paola Villa and others. Nevertheless it is probably correct in its broad outline and reflects part of the lifestyle of those times.

**Other Clues**     The dig at Terra Amata was a tour de force of modern archaeology. Not only did it reveal the life of *Homo erectus*, but it disclosed much about the climate, geography, flora, and fauna of the times. The results of studies by paleontologists and geologists, for instance, made it possible to reconstruct the countryside of Nice at the time of the hunters' visits. Terra Amata was colder and more humid then. The Mediterranean was about eighty-five feet higher than it is today, and the sea covered most of the plain of Nice and partly filled what is now the Paillon River valley. That is why Terra Amata, once on the shore of the sea, now overlooks it from a hillside.

Where the hunters of Terra Amata went after their short visits, and why, after visiting the cove for many years, they never came back to that site, are mysteries still. But what happened to their ancient settlement is no mystery at all. When the last bit of archaeological evidence had been carefully lifted from the ground in July 1966, the bulldozers inexorably closed in. Today, luxury apartments stand where *Homo erectus'* huts stood more than 400,000 years ago; Terra Amata continues to be one of the oldest occupied spots in human history.

## CHARACTERISTICS AND ACHIEVEMENTS

What sort of people visited this cove on the coast of Europe 400,000 years ago? The finds at Terra Amata, although extraordinarily useful, include no hints—other than the single human footprint in the soft sand—about the anatomical makeup of these European members of the genus *Homo*. Other sites, however, give us a good idea of what these people probably looked like.

### Anatomical Development

As we have seen, fossils of *Homo erectus* are now known from many areas of the Old World, from Peking in the east to Heidelberg in the west, and south to the Transvaal and Java. These fossils clearly indicate that anatomically comparable human populations existed more than a million years ago on both the east and west sides of the Indian Ocean. Toward the top of Bed II at Olduvai lies a fine braincase of *Homo erectus* more than a million years old that falls close to the range of variation of finds from Choukoutien in China. As we discussed in Chapter 8, in the lower levels of the gorge, which date back nearly 2 million years, are fossils indicating the presence of the earlier species of *Homo*, *H. habilis*, whose skull and teeth seem to be intermediate between *Australopithecus* and the later *H. erectus*.

Physically, *Homo erectus* represented a considerable step away from *H. habilis*, which had evolved a larger brain relative to their size than modern apes have but were still comparatively small—pygmy-sized creatures (Figure 11–5). *Homo erectus*, from our limited evidence, were larger. The best evidence suggests that females stood just under, and males well over, five feet tall. They stood straight-backed, and their legs were long and straight. In fact, the thigh bones of *H. erectus* that have been unearthed are not easy to distinguish from those of modern humans. Even if we exclude the doubtful femora from Java, the remainder show only a few minor characteristics that together distinguish them from modern humans. The rest of their skeleton was also much like modern humans'. No complete set of *H. erectus* hand bones has been found, but their skill at making tools suggests that they had hands not unlike ours, capable of both power and precision grips.

Although *Homo erectus* were not built quite like their forebears, neither did they resemble us exactly (Figure 11–6). Their bones were heavier and thicker than a modern human's, implying that they had evolved a very powerful musculature. These skeletal differences, however, are not extreme and fall within the range of modern human populations. Below the neck, differences between *Homo erectus* and modern humans could be detected only by an experienced anatomist. Nevertheless, they do appear to have been a powerful, muscular, heavily built people adapted to a life-style that by our standards would probably seem very tough indeed.

From the neck up, however, *Homo erectus* looked markedly different from *Homo sapiens*. From the fossils we possess we can deduce that

FIGURE 11–5 *Although imaginative, these reconstructions probably give a reasonable approximation to the posture and form of* Homo habilis *and* Homo erectus. *The main differences between them probably lie in the size and robustness of the body and the size of the brain, but as we saw in Chapter 7, we have little direct evidence of the stature of* Homo habilis.

Homo habilis

Homo erectus

*Homo erectus* had a low, rather narrow, sloping forehead; thick, jutting brows; and a massive jaw with no chin. The lower canine teeth, still a little larger than ours, showed a slight tendency to interlock with the teeth of the upper jaw. The head was very robust, the skull bones thick. The cusp pattern and shape of their molars set them about midway between *Homo habilis* and *Homo sapiens*. Also, the basic proportions of *H. erectus'* head had begun to change: it became higher-domed than that of *Homo habilis*, and their forehead receded less. Their brain was expanding. Taken together, these changes tended to humanize their looks; nevertheless, their face was probably the least modern thing about *Homo erectus*.

**The Brain**  Far more than their increased height, their strength, erect stature, human gait, or improved grip, the remarkable change in *Homo erectus'* brain and behavior clearly marked them as human. The sharpest difference between *Homo erectus* and all the primates who preceded them was the large size of their brain and the complexity of behavior this larger brain made possible. Though the size of the braincase cannot always be relied on as an accurate measure of brain power, it is generally true that among animals of similar size, species with large brains are more intelligent than those with small brains. The capacity of a modern ape's skull—even the gorilla's—averages only about 500 cc. The cranial capacity of *Australopithecus* was similar, though larger in relation to body size, while the cranial capacity of *Homo habilis* varied from 600 to 750 cc. *Homo erectus*, however, had a braincase of between about 775 and at least 1,225 cc, putting the brainier members of the species well within the range of modern humans, whose cranial capacity varies between the extremes of 1,000 and 2,000 cc (see Table 8–1).

**Territorial Expansion**

As the early populations of *Homo erectus* multiplied, some stayed on in the tropics, developing the skills, language, and social organization that enabled them to flourish as hunters of big game on the savannas. But as numbers increased, the range of *Homo erectus* expanded. They did

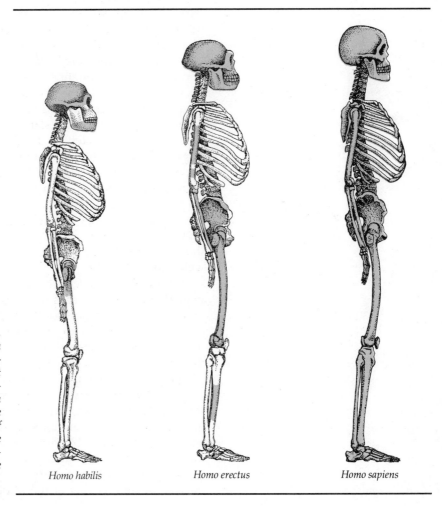

*FIGURE 11–6    Though stockily built,* Homo erectus *was becoming very modern in most features and distinct from* H. habilis; *the differences in the skull are the most striking. In addition,* Homo erectus *probably had longer legs and shorter arms than their ancestors. Stature is a very variable characteristic, and some living races of* Homo sapiens *are smaller than the average* Homo erectus *and no bigger than the skeleton of* Homo habilis *shown here. The bones known from the right side are colored. Compare Figure 7–6.*

Homo habilis        Homo erectus        Homo sapiens

not migrate in the sense of pulling up stakes and immediately moving hundreds of miles to a new location. Instead, the expansion into new habitats was accomplished by a process anthropologists call *budding*. A few individuals would split away from a prospering group and found their own autonomous band in nearby territory, where the food resources were perhaps somewhat less plentiful. If they could make a go of it, by finding sufficient resources or by developing appropriate technology to increase the extraction of resources, their population would grow, and later generations might split off into other marginal areas.

*Homo erectus'* dispersion across several continents occurred during a time of great change of the world's geography and climates (see Figure 15–2). In a series of cold waves that represented what we now call the Ice Age, snow-fed glaciers spread over the northern continents. Rainfall may have increased greatly in the tropics at this time, producing great stretches of grassland and lakes in the now uninviting North African desert. Even in the tropics, temperatures fell. Between these cold spells, the glaciers melted away and temperatures were often warmer in Europe and Asia than they are today, while the tropics may have experienced long periods of drought.

With so much of the world's water locked up in ice and snow, sea levels dropped greatly at times, and land bridges between continents appeared. Java, now an island in the Indonesian archipelago, was for a long time connected to the Asian mainland. Similarly, Africa might for a time have been linked to Europe across Sicily, and to Asia through Egypt and Ethiopia (Figure 11–7). It is not yet known exactly when and where these land bridges appeared, nor which ones *Homo erectus* used. In part, the problem is that for tracing those migrations we depend on knowledge of the age of skulls, skeletons, and archaeological sites found in various regions of the world that we do not yet possess. It is possible, however, to sketch a reasonable picture of events based on the best evidence available.

When *Homo* evolved from *Australopithecus,* a vast tropical corridor of woodland and savanna surrounded the Indian Ocean, running up the east coast of Africa, across the Indian subcontinent, and down into the Indonesian archipelago. Because of the wide dispersal of early *Homo,* we can safely assume that their ancestors had been living in many parts of this corridor, either dispersing through it from some ancestral home or evolving in several of its parts.

Like their forebears, *Homo erectus* probably drifted back and forth throughout the tropics, with new bands branching off from more settled populations as their numbers increased. Some of these new bands also spread north, probably along several routes at different times. Some dispersed north from Java into China; others spread north from Africa across land bridges to Europe, or entered Europe after skirting the Mediterranean by way of the Middle East, Turkey, and the Danube.

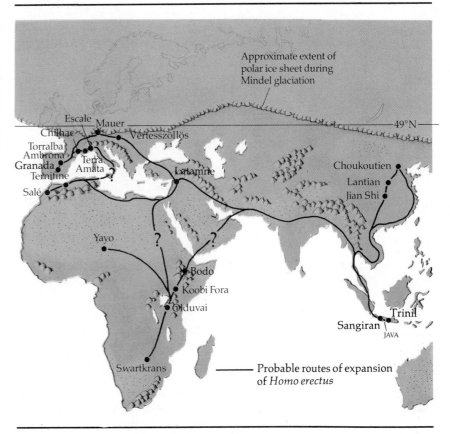

FIGURE 11–7   Homo erectus *were much more widely dispersed than* Australopithecus *and (apart from the Japanese monkey) were the first primates to survive the winters of the north temperate region. During interglacial periods they reached at least latitude 49° north. This map shows the sites of some major finds and gives an idea of probable routes of expansion and gene interchange.* Homo erectus *may have occupied many other areas as well. We do not know if they originated in one particular area.*

Evidence of the early expansion of *Homo* from southern Asia into Europe and China is rare. The earliest inhabitants were presumably few and left little behind them. A recently discovered site in southern France, at Chilhac, however, carries a potassium-argon date of 1.8 million years B.P. and contains tools similar to those from Bed I at Olduvai Gorge of the same age. From China (at a site called Jian Shi) we have some molar teeth which are probably 750,000 years old and which certainly belong to *Homo*. These two small clues are all we have, but they are highly suggestive.

From a little later, perhaps 700,000 years B.P., we have more evidence. Remains of hearths have been recognized by some archaeologists in a cave at Escale, near Nice, in France, and fire was used extensively at Choukoutien as well as at Vértesszöllös about 500,000 years ago. By this time the climate had changed and long periods of cold developed in these northern regions (see Figure 15–2). What led humans to brave the winters in these places can only be guessed. It may have been the pressures of multiplying human populations; it may have been the search for new or more fertile hunting grounds. In any case, changes in the world's geography and climate sometimes facilitated the northward expansion of *Homo erectus'* range and sometimes reversed it.

Once humans became so widely dispersed, they began to adapt to a new diversity of changing climates and environments. *Homo erectus* was probably forced to retreat from their northern outposts many times during the cold of this changeable age. The fossil record clearly shows that numerous animal species less adaptable than humans perished during the times of advancing ice.

The slowly pulsating climatic changes we associate with the Pleistocene and the corresponding expansion and contraction of the territory available for human occupation have been characteristic of the last million years of the earth's history. The selective pressures put upon humankind by their changing environment have been a factor of primary importance in the evolution of modern *Homo sapiens*.

**Use of Fire**    Confronted with such trying conditions, these middle Pleistocene people were forced to meet the challenge of winter with their wits. How they first learned to tame fire and use it to their advantage will never be known. Two explanations are possible. One is that they learned to capture and carry fire when nature offered it, as when a volcano erupted, when lightning struck in the dry grass of the plains, or when some outcrop of coal or shale oil burst into flames by spontaneous combustion. Early humans must have observed such wildfire. Fire has a fascination even to sophisticated modern people, and perhaps this fascination has always existed in the human race. Perhaps an early human approached a natural fire fearfully but curiously. He or she could easily have managed to hold a burning twig and, touching that twig to a shrub or tuft of grass, could have multiplied the flame. One can imagine the sense of power and wonder that this person would have then experienced. The warmth of fire is felt quickly, and even the inexperienced *Homo erectus* must have imagined its usefulness in a cold cave and attempted to bring the fire indoors. Another possible theory for the discovery of fire connects humans even more closely with its actual production: they may once have accidentally made fire while chipping flint tools with iron pyrites. Sparks struck in this way may well have landed in piles of leaves used as bedding, or in the hair of animal skins, and begun to smolder.

However fire was discovered, having captured it, humans learned to keep it going in their hearths. Undoubtedly these early fires must have gone out many thousands of times before people became wise enough to keep supplies of fuel on hand, and skillful enough to invent methods for preserving hot embers, perhaps banking them with sod (as is still done in remote corners of the world where the matchstick has not made its appearance). When a fire went out, the loss must have been keen and the wait a long one before a natural blaze could be captured again.

Only by continuous friction between certain woods, or by sparking from certain rocks such as flint and iron pyrite used in combination, can fire be made. So far no pyrite firestones have been found among the relics *Homo erectus* left behind. The earliest known firestone, a round lump of iron pyrite grooved by repeated strikings, dates back only 15,000 years, hundreds of thousands of years after the last of these early humans. Even in modern times, some primitive tropical hunter-gatherers have not known how to make fire.

Nevertheless, once people learned to use and control fire, the idea surely would have caught on rapidly and *Homo erectus* would have begun to live by fire, at least throughout the northern world. Here they could not have survived without it. On the winterless plains of Africa, where humans could thrive in the open without needing fire, relics of its undoubted use date back to only about 60,000 years ago, though it may, of course, be considerably older. Recent evidence suggests that fire may have been used intermittently in Africa as long ago as 1.5 million years B.P.

## Evidence from Choukoutien

Excavations at the great cave of Choukoutien have given a remarkable view of the importance of fire to the first humans. When groups of *Homo erectus* first arrived there about half a million years ago, they may have spent their first few winters along the crevices and ledges of the cliff, wrapping themselves in hides while building some sort of make-shift shelters against the bitter winds. Choukoutien was the kind of site these first northerners picked out wherever they settled; it was not far from water, and it gave them protection and a commanding view of a grassy plain where herds of grazing animals could be spotted.

The great cave in the cliff offered a good place to come in from the cold, but the humans had to fight the animals around them for possession of it. As we have seen, the oldest and deepest layers of fossils in the cave show that *Homo erectus* made their home there, and were driven out again, many times over many generations. At a certain point, however, humans took full and permanent possession of the cave; this is the point at which the evidence of fire becomes continuous. Fire was the key to humans' control of the cave. Their flaming brands and the light of their all-night fires kept at bay even the giant cave bears.

Besides the protection it afforded, fire was a key to survival in other ways. The origin of cooking was undoubtedly the result of an accident: food that fell into the fire turned out to be tasty and tender when retrieved and allowed to cool. Once *Homo erectus* discovered the art of cooking, they seem to have cooked much of what they caught. The Choukoutien cave floor was littered with charred bones of sheep, large horses, pig, buffalo, and especially deer. Roast meat not only was more appetizing and tender, it gave *Homo erectus* a benefit they did not know about—it killed parasites and offered increased food value, for heat breaks down some of the chemical compounds of tough meat and releases nutritious juices. Cooking also tenderizes food and may have brought about the reduction in molar size that was to characterize the evolution of *Homo sapiens.*

*Homo erectus* discovered other practical uses for fire. It broadened their choice of tools and weapons. The observation that bone or antler grows hard in the heat of a campfire, or that green wood does not always burn completely and instead hardens, must have led humans to employ fire in toolmaking. Among the bones fossilized at Choukoutien were pieces of fire-hardened tips of antlers, which probably served as hammers for chipping away the rough edges of split-stone tools and fashioning cutting edges on them; the points of wooden spears found at other sites had likewise been hardened in fire to increase their piercing power. Similarly, sticks could have been tempered with flame before they were sharpened for use as digging implements.

Although we cannot know for certain how *Homo erectus* used fire, the evidence left behind in places like the Choukoutien caves allows us to make logical assumptions about that use. With an increasingly well-developed brain, and with growing prospects of foresight and reflection, *Homo erectus* almost certainly had within reach the simple mental processes required to capture fire, keep it alive, and roast and hunt with it. After learning to make stone tools, humankind's most dramatic and important cultural advance was the taming of fire.

## STONE TOOLS

From what we have seen so far in this chapter, *Homo erectus* might be labeled as "migratory workers," people who returned to certain sites with some regularity. They probably made their rounds according to the seasons, living on game, fruit, and vegetation as they became abundant. Most of our specific knowledge about their habits is based on their occupation sites, and these are especially rich in stone tools.

In the drawers of museum and university collections around the world are hundreds of thousands, possibly millions of prehistoric stone tools. These date from the entire period during which early humans used stone tools—the Stone Age. This abundance may seem amazing when we consider the extreme scarcity of fossils of the humans who made them, and yet it is entirely logical. Stone is one of the most enduring substances on earth, and tools were almost invariably made of the hardest kinds of stone. Once made, they were virtually indestructible, whether they happened to fall into the mud of a swamp or were slowly covered by rubbish in the floor of a cave. Because stone implements are so indestructible, we can assume that practically all that have ever been made are still lying around somewhere. It is no surprise that a good many of them have been found, any more than it would be surprising for some archaeologist of the future to stumble over a quantity of Coca-Cola bottles entombed quietly where they had been dropped, one by one, beneath the pier of a waterside amusement park.

Another reason for the abundance of stone tools compared to fossil bones is that whereas individuals had only one skull to leave behind, they had any number of stone implements. They made the tools quickly and easily. As fast as they broke them or lost them or blunted them, they made new ones, starting when they were children and continuing throughout their lives. Even among beginners in the tool business, one toolmaker might have produced anywhere from dozens to hundreds of tools before dying. Of course, we do not know what the rate of tool production at that early date was, or how many members of a band made tools. It may be that only a few of the most able ones did, although the likelihood is that, once toolmaking had become characteristic of hominids, it was common to all members of each group.

At any rate, certainly by the time of *Homo erectus*, toolmaking was universal. Not only had humans become much more dependent on tools by then, but they were also making better ones. This improvement, in turn, changed their way of life and increased their dependence on their technology.

Much attention has been paid to the question of tool use, and sophisticated experiments have been conducted by several paleoanthropologists. J. Desmond Clark, Louis Leakey, S. A. Semenov, and most recently Larry Keeley, for example, tried to work out a scientific basis for determining how tools were used. The method was to make several duplicates of a specific tool, use each one in a different way—chopping wood, cutting flesh, skinning animals, scraping hides, digging roots— and then examine their edges under a microscope to see if the different uses had produced different kinds of wear. As a by-product of this study, a great deal of practical knowledge was gained about what kinds of tools are best for what kinds of jobs.

**Oldowan Industry**   In addition to being named according to their presumed use, stone tools are classified according to their workmanship, or their presumed method of manufacture. As seen in Chapter 9, chopping tools, first found by the Leakeys in East Africa, constitute the so-called Oldowan industry. Similarly worked tools bear that name no matter where they are found—whether in China, Hungary, or South Africa.

The Oldowan industry lasted for at least a million and a half years, perhaps much longer. How it got out of Africa, if that is really where it first arose, is unknown. The most probable route for exportation of the industry was through the Middle East; from there it could have branched out into both Europe and Asia.

It was not until 1963 that a relatively clean and undamaged Oldowan site was opened up in Europe: Vértesszöllös, in Hungary (Figure 11–7). Four different occupational levels were detected. They are thin, suggesting that small groups lived there briefly. Although some layers are merely scatterings of debris, the debris is significant. It includes not only a number of burned objects, indicating the use of fire, but also tools in considerable abundance, and the smashed bones of some fifteen species of small animals. Among the tools are many flakes and choppers, simply chipped on one or two edges and primitive enough to qualify as Oldowan. Even more significant was the eventual discovery of ancient human footprints and parts of a human skull, suggesting a form no longer typical of *Homo erectus* but not yet fully *Homo sapiens*.

The types of tools found at Vértesszöllös are much the same as those found at Choukoutien as well as those at Olduvai, but the site is probably older than Choukoutien and was inhabited some 500,000 years ago at least. Most other sites associated with *Homo erectus* or their descendants are characterized by a different kind of tool industry—the *Acheulian* industry. To understand what gave the new style its novelty, it is necessary to learn something about the various ways in which stone can be shaped.

## Materials and Techniques

Rocks of a coarse, granular composition, like granite, are almost useless for making chipped tools; they do not fracture along smooth, clean edges but tend to crumble. Certain other rocks, like common feldspar, tend to break only along certain fracture lines and hence cannot be controlled by the toolmaker.

The ideal stone from the point of view of the toolmaker is one like flint or chert: hard, tough, and of a smooth, fine-grained consistency. Stone of this type behaves somewhat like glass; it fractures rather than crumbles, and cone-shaped flakes can be knocked off it that are razor-sharp. Flint was the most common of the desirable tool stones in western Europe, and the typical Acheulian implement was a flint hand-axe. In many places where flint was unobtainable, quartz, quartzite, and other rocks were used and the simpler Oldowan tools often persisted, as at Choukoutien and Vértesszöllös.

In a very real sense the presence of good stone helped determine the distribution of peoples during much of the Paleolithic era. This is one reason why so many of *Homo erectus'* artifacts are found in or near rivers, which are an almost endless source of pebbles and pieces of rock. (Of course, *Homo erectus* would also have stayed near rivers for the fresh water supply.)

Combining various kinds of stone with various ways of working them produces a surprising variety of results. The finer-grained the stone, the flatter and more leaflike the flakes that can be chipped loose from it. The size and shape of these flakes can be further controlled by the ways in which they are separated from the original stone. They may be knocked loose by a hammer or pried loose by a pointed stick or bone. The angle at which the hammer blow is struck can be changed to produce either a small, thick flake or a large, thin one. Also, different kinds of hammers produce different kinds of flakes. Relatively soft hammers of wood or bone produce one kind, hard stone ones another, and a wooden point pressed against the edge of the stone will produce still a different kind. Even the way a tool is held while it is being made will affect the kind of flake that can be struck from it: when it is held in the hand, the results are not the same as when it is balanced on a rock.

Every toolmaker must have had a good deal of skill, based on necessity, on years of practice, and on an intimate knowledge of the natures of different stones. For each stone has its own qualities, which vary further depending on whether the stone is hot or cold, wet or dry. But the basic principles of toolmaking are fairly simple. If you decide to try it, you may be surprised at how hard a blow it takes to crack or flake a stone, but if you do it right, the stone will behave in a predictable way.

## Core and Flake Tools

Despite all these variations in techniques and materials there are still only two basic categories of tools: *core tools* and *flake tools*. To make a core tool, take a lump of stone and knock chips from it until it has the desired size and shape; the core of stone that remains is the tool (Figures 11–8 and 11–9). A flake tool, as its name implies, is a chip struck from a core. It may be large or small and its shape may vary, depending on the shape of the core from which it was struck. It may be used as it is, or may itself be further flaked or chipped, somewhat in the manner of a core tool. In any event, the flake itself, and not the core from which it was struck, is the tool.

In the earliest days of toolmaking, flake tools were very simple. Whatever happened to fly off a core would be put to use if it had a sharp edge. In general, flakes were used as cutters, because their edges were sharper than the edges that could be produced on core choppers, which were more useful for heavy hacking. As time went on, more and more skills were developed in the manufacture of flakes, and eventually it became a much more sophisticated method of toolmaking than the core technique.

## Acheulian Industry

The Acheulian toolmaking industry characterized by a prepared core made its earliest appearance about 1.4 million years ago. Its earliest forms bear several names like "Chellean" and "Abbevillian," but "Acheulian" is the principal style and the principal name that covers it through most of the world and for several hundred thousand years. (The name comes from the small town of Saint Acheul in the Somme Valley in France.) The Acheulian was a clear step forward. It spread rapidly, probably from Africa into Europe and eastward, at least as far as India.

The characteristic implement of the Acheulian industry is the biface, a tool whose cutting edge has been flaked more carefully on both sides to make it straighter and sharper than the primitive Oldowan chopper. This may seem like an awfully small improvement, but it was a fundamental one and made possible much more efficient tools. The purpose of the two-sided, or bifacial, technique was to change the shape

*FIGURE 11–8   Toolmaking is not simple but requires skill and much practice. Most people, however, can learn how to make simple tools. These photographs show François Bordes making a chopping tool (bottom right).*

Bordes begins with a rounded quartzite lump and a smaller hammer-stone (top left). With two or three blows he can produce a rough but serviceable cutting edge (bottom right). Such tools as this were a basic weapon and hunting implement for over a million years. They have been discovered in Africa, the Middle East, Asia, and Europe.

FIGURE 11–9 *It is not difficult to see how
a simple chopper (left) developed into a very
primitive biface or hand-axe (right). Both
these tools are from Olduvai.*

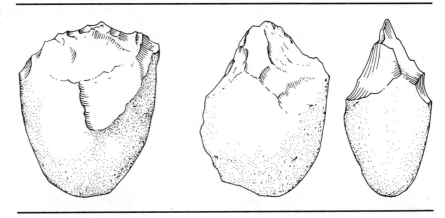

of the core from essentially round to flattish, for only with a flat stone
can one get a decent cutting edge. The result was the *hand-axe*, the
typical and first-to-be-recognized implement of the early Stone Age.
The first step in making an Acheulian hand-axe was to rough out the
core until it had somewhat the shape of a turtle shell, thickest in the
middle and thinning to a coarse edge all around. This edge could then
be trimmed with more delicate little scallops of flaking (Figure 11–10).
The cutting surfaces thus produced were longer, straighter, and considerably keener than any Oldowan chopper could offer.

One technological improvement that permitted the more controlled
working required to shape an Acheulian hand-axe was the gradual
implementation, during the Acheulian period, of different kinds of
hammers. In earlier times, it appears, the toolmaker knocked flakes
from his stone core with another piece of stone. The hard shock of rock
on rock tended to leave deep, irregular scars and wavy cutting edges.
But a wood or bone hammer, being softer, gave its user much greater
control over flaking. Such implements left shallower, cleaner scars on
the core and produced sharper and straighter cutting edges. In time,
the use of stone on stone was pretty much restricted to the preliminary
rough shaping of a hand-axe, and all the fine work around the edges
was done with wood and bone (Figure 11–11).

Acheulian hand-axes were usually pear-shaped or pointed and ran
somewhat larger than chopping tools. Some have been recovered that
were more than two feet long and weighed upward of twenty-five
pounds. Obviously these were far too heavy and cumbersome to have
been used for the kind of cutting and scraping that the smaller ones
were designed for. One suggestion is that they may have been fitted to
broomlike handles and poised over traps, set to fall and split the skulls
of animals that triggered them.

Another type of implement that appears for the first time in the

Acheulian industry is the *cleaver*. A cleaver had a straight cutting edge at one end and actually looked much more like a modern axehead than the pointed hand-axes did. It was probably used for heavy chopping or for hacking through the joints of large animals.

Present-day knowledge about the early development of the Acheulian industry is somewhat general, somewhat sparse, and somewhat disorganized. An extremely useful source of the information we do have is Olduvai Gorge. The Olduvai living floors may tell us a great

*FIGURE 11–10   Making a hand-axe is more difficult than making a chopping tool, as these photographs of Bordes illustrate.*

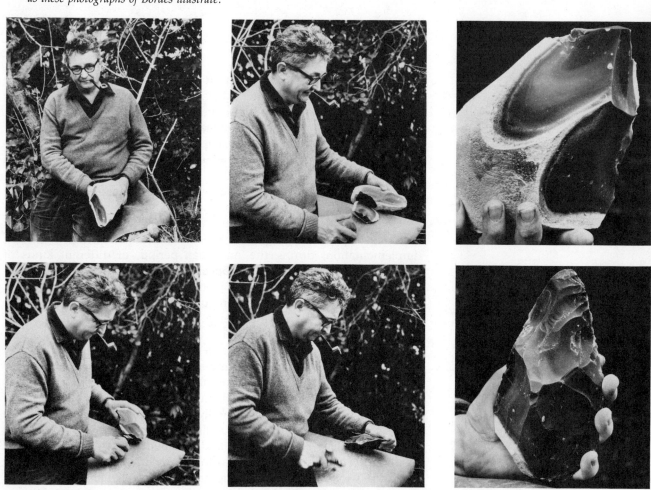

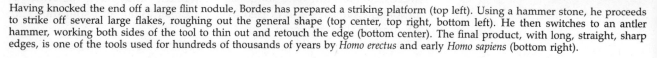

Having knocked the end off a large flint nodule, Bordes has prepared a striking platform (top left). Using a hammer stone, he proceeds to strike off several large flakes, roughing out the general shape (top center, top right, bottom left). He then switches to an antler hammer, working both sides of the tool to thin out and retouch the edge (bottom center). The final product, with long, straight, sharp edges, is one of the tools used for hundreds of thousands of years by *Homo erectus* and early *Homo sapiens* (bottom right).

*FIGURE 11–11 Many of the developed Acheulian hand-axes were carefully and well made. Tapering to a slender tip, this 200,000-year-old hand-axe was shaped with a stone hammer. Then its edges were refined with a hammer of hard wood or bone, whose more resilient blows yielded small chips.*

deal about the evolution of *Homo habilis* and *Homo erectus* but they tell us a great deal more about the development of the stone industries. As we ascend the strata in the gorge, we pass from a simple Oldowan industry, with little more than a variety of choppers, to a much more varied tool kit. In Bed II we come across the first bifaces (Figure 11–9), witnesses to the beginnings of the Acheulian culture. Here we find some eighteen kinds of implements including—in addition to the choppers and simple bifaces—scrapers, burins (chisels), awls, anvils, hammer-stones, and round stone balls. The marked increase of scrapers in Bed II suggests the beginning of an industry in hides and leather, which needed preparation with this kind of tool. There is also a huge amount of so-called débitage, or waste: the small flakes and chips that would naturally accumulate in a spot where implements were being made over a long period (see Table 9–1).

Further matching up of tools with fossil evidence from this confused early period will undoubtedly take place and lead to further clarification. Cultural evidence from the middle Pleistocene onward is varied and rich. It reveals the development of a large number of subcultures during the long span of the Acheulian. These have many names, each usually identifying a local way of toolmaking. Humankind obviously was moving in many cultural directions by this time, and as these different threads met, crossed, tangled, disappeared, and emerged again, the fabric of human society became increasingly complex and increasingly widespread. Acheulian tools of one type or another are found in all major river valleys of western Europe and Africa.

## Cultural Adaptation

One thing to bear in mind is that the more highly developed a culture is, the faster and more complex will be its response to local conditions. By the middle of the Acheulian period, the sophisticated toolmakers were capable of living on the seashore, in the temperate forest, on temperate grasslands, or on the subtropical savanna. Whatever specialized tool kits they needed for successful life in these places, they made.

When we realize the immense period of time over which these changes took place, however—at least a million years—we get a strong sense of cultural stagnation. Life then was conservative; it crept on from millennium to millennium without apparent change. In some places there appears to have been no cultural development: *Homo erectus* were still using the same Oldowan tools in China that their ancestors had used a million years earlier. Yet the people had evolved physically. It therefore seems very probable that this period saw very important developments in aspects of material culture other than stone tools—in containers, shelters, clothing, traps—and, of course, in social organization and language.

| | YEARS B.P. | EVIDENCE OF BEHAVIOR | ARCHAEOLOGICAL ERAS |
|---|---|---|---|
| **HOLOCENE** | | | **UPPER PALEOLITHIC** |
| | | Fire used in Africa | **MIDDLE PALEOLITHIC** |
| Peking man | | | |
| | 250,000 — | | |
| Günz glaciation | | | |
| Java fossils (Trinil and Sangiran) | | | |
| 1 million — **PLEISTOCENE** | 500,000 — | Fire used extensively at Choukoutien / Terra Amata inhabited | |
| *A. robustus* and *boisei* extinct | 600,000 — | Hearths at Vértesszöllös | |
| | 700,000 — | Possible evidence of fire at Escale | |
| | 750,000 — | | |
| | | *Homo erectus* expansion into China | |
| *Homo Habilis* at Olduvai | 1 million — | | **LOWER PALEOLITHIC:** oldest period of Old Stone Age |
| 2 million — | 1.25 million — | | |
| | 1.5 million — | Earliest appearance of Acheulian tool industry at Olduvai | |
| | 1.75 million — | | |
| | | Oldowan tool industry at Olduvai and at Chilhac, France | |
| | 2 million — | | |
| | | Stone tools at Omo | |
| **PLIOCENE** | 2.25 million — | | |
| | 2.5 million — | Earliest known stone tools at Hadar | |
| | 2.75 million — | | |
| | 3 million — | | |

THE ADVANCEMENT OF *HOMO ERECTUS*

Assigning absolute dates to geological and archaeological events between 50,000 and 1.5 million years ago is particularly difficult. The dates given here are based on a wide range of geological and paleontological evidence.

# Chapter 12

# Hunting, Gathering, and the Evolution of Society

**It is far from easy to determine whether Nature has proved a kind parent to man or a merciless stepmother.**

**PLINY THE ELDER, 23–79.**
*Natural History,* Book VII, 1.

## THE ARCHAEOLOGY OF THE HUNTERS

The interpretation of archaeological sites is not always as straightforward as it may appear. There is no doubt that the sites in Olduvai Gorge excavated by the Leakeys have been correctly interpreted; they are indeed ancient land surfaces preserved more or less as they were left by early hominids. It often happens, however, that some movement occurs in such deposits, and in more extreme cases the archaeological remains may be washed out by heavy rains or river action and redeposited in another place. Such deposits are called secondary sites. In many instances the stones and bones may be sorted by the moving waters of a river and deposited in very dense accumulations which have the superficial appearance of being the result of human activity.

The distinction between primary and secondary sites in archaeology is an important one. In the past, investigators have sometimes been misled into believing that bones or stone tools scattered on an ancient river bank represented an original living floor. In many cases microscopic analysis of the material is required which will reveal if the bone or stone has been battered or "rolled" in the flowing river, or still remains in an uneroded condition.

Such a site is Olorgesailie in southwestern Kenya, where for many years it was thought by some archaeologists that there was definite evidence of hunting and butchery. Here, at one site, in an area only twelve by fifteen meters, Glynn Isaac unearthed bones and teeth of at least 14 adult and 76 juvenile monkeys of the now extinct species

*Theropithecus oswaldi.* Mixed with them was more than a ton of hand-axes and cobbles (altogether 4751 artifacts). The date is estimated at about 450,000 years B.P. It seemed to some that a massive organized slaughter had been conducted on the site, followed by a tremendous amount of butchery. A band of hominids appeared to have ambushed and killed a big troop of these formidable animals (the males almost the size of the hunters). The density of bones and stone tools was most unusual.

Glynn Isaac, however, believes it most likely that the stone tools and bones were washed down the river, sorted, concentrated and deposited in distinct areas on its banks. Taphonomic studies have shown that such a hypothesis is a possible explanation for these dense accumulations of material. The site contains a huge hoard of heavy stone tools, and the evidence suggests that *Homo erectus* was systematically butchering these giant gelada monkeys and perhaps even hunting them, upstream from the actual site, and that this probably continued over a considerable period of time.

We must bear the difficulties of archaeological interpretation in mind as we turn to look at the evidence for the hunting prowess of *Homo erectus.*

## Hunter's Diet

As we saw in Chapter 9, the fossil evidence shows that *Homo habilis* groups consumed a wide variety of animals, some of which they presumably caught and some of which they scavenged. But they evidently lacked the ability to be thoroughly consistent hunters. The picture changes dramatically with *Homo erectus. Although they undoubtedly continued to rely heavily on plants for nourishment*—as do practically all modern humans—they possessed both the cunning and the equipment necessary to assure themselves of meat with fair regularity. If hunting had been merely an occasional exercise for their predecessors, it became for *Homo erectus* a major occupation.

Like all evolutionary change, this crucial development was a slow matter of advantage and capacity reinforcing each other. Humans did not become hunters because some individuals decided they liked meat. Instead, a creature able to catch, eat, and digest meat was favored, at a particular time and place, in the competition for survival. Hunting makes available far more food per square mile of the African savanna than plant life can provide. As vegetarians, humans can make use of only a limited number of the things that grow on the ground—mainly roots, nuts, fruits, berries, and some tender shoots. The most abundant plants—the grasses of the savanna and the leaves of the forest trees—contain a high proportion of cellulose, which cannot be digested by the human stomach. But the animals that live on the things that humans cannot digest may themselves be both edible and nourishing. Through hunting, previously inedible vegetation, converted to edible meat, became available as a food source for humans.

Hunting not only increased the amount of food available, but, as mentioned in Chapter 11, it also provided better food. Meat, particularly when cooked by fire, is a much more concentrated form of nourishment, a more efficient source of energy, than wild vegetables, fruits, and berries. Venison, for instance, yields 572 calories (calories measure the energy available in food) per 100 grams of weight, whereas the same weight of most fruits and vegetables yields well under 100 calories. One medium-sized animal would have provided, in a compact, easily carried form, the same amount of energy as the results of a whole day's foraging for vegetables. (Nuts yield more calories than most meats and were undoubtedly a vital part of early humans' diet when and where they could find them, but nuts grow only in certain localities, and most of them are seasonal, whereas game is widely available throughout the year.)

Another very important factor in the development of hunting and the evolution of *Homo erectus* is the seasonality of vegetable food in the temperate regions. In tropical savanna regions with their biennial wet and dry seasons, the supply of vegetable foods is more or less continuous, as the success of the vegetarian savanna monkeys demonstrates. In north temperate zones, however, there is a real dearth of vegetable foods after the nuts and berries have been consumed in the fall. In the winter and early spring, meat would have been a major part of the diet of *Homo erectus* groups that had expanded into the temperate zones. Hunting was an essential adaptation for any groups who were to succeed in the bitter winters of northern Eurasia.

## Skin Adaptation

Because meat eating brought clear-cut advantages for survival, natural selection favored individuals who had in some small degree the physical or mental traits that made them better hunters. Most of the physical traits required for hunting probably had been acquired by *Homo habilis*. *H. habilis* walked erect and were probably good runners, although *H. erectus* were probably taller and thus could run faster and see farther. Furthermore the hands and arms of *H. habilis* may have been adapted for fairly accurate throwing, a fundamental hunting skill.

Another major physical change that possibly had occurred by the time of *Homo erectus* was adaptation of the skin. When hominids started diverging from the African apes, they probably were just as hairy as those animals are now. In time, their hair must have grown less dense and the sweat glands in their skin more numerous. By the time of *Homo erectus* the skin probably had become relatively hairless and had developed a greater number of sweat glands (Figure 12–1). This change sharply differentiates humans from other primates. Today, though we still have as many hair roots as apes, our hair is generally much shorter and finer, and over large areas of our bodies it is almost invisible. Conversely, we have from 2 to 5 million sweat glands, more than are found in any other primate, and these are far more productive of sweat.

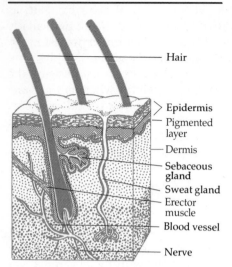

- Hair
- Epidermis
- Pigmented layer
- Dermis
- Sebaceous gland
- Sweat gland
- Erector muscle
- Blood vessel
- Nerve

*FIGURE 12–1   The skin is an organ of astonishing complexity. It is the barrier between the relatively closed system of a human body and its external environment; it is strong, elastic, waterproof, protective, and self-repairing. Beyond this, it serves as a sense organ, an excretory organ, a heat control mechanism (involving hair and sweat glands), and as the organ of individual identification. It responds to environmental stress, both directly (sun-tanning and healing) and indirectly (sweating).*

Scientists are not sure why this change in body hair took place, but it seems connected with an increasing ability to sustain strenuous physical exertion. As we have seen, most meat-eating animals hunt at night. As hominids ancestral to humans moved from the protective forests onto the open savanna and became *daytime* hunters, they faced a new problem. They generated a great deal of body heat *(metabolic heat)* in the hunt, just at the time of day when the temperature of the air was high and so the cooling effect of the air low. To maintain a constant body temperature, essential to any primate, a very efficient cooling mechanism was required. A logical evolutionary adaptation to this biological need was the increased number of sweat glands producing far more sweat per gland and the reduction of hair cover. During heavy exertion or in hot weather, the sweat glands bathe the body in moisture. Evaporation of this moisture cools the surface of the skin and the blood just below it. Dense hair would inhibit evaporation and would get matted and clogged with dried sweat. Hence, the theory goes, the marked decrease in hair density.

There are, of course, other savanna animals that sweat heavily during strenuous exertion and yet retain a full coat of hair; zebras are an example. But their metabolic rate is noticeably lower than that of humans, and their dependence on grazing allows them to lead a much less active life. Strenuous exertion is rare and occurs mostly during the cooler night, when predators are active.

Sweating is not an unmitigated blessing for humans. As biologist William Montagna points out, sweating represents a major biological blunder in some ways, for it drains the body of enormous amounts of moisture, requiring fairly constant replenishment, and depletes the system of sodium and other essential elements. But higher primates all require regular supplies of drinking water, and so this requirement was nothing new. Sweating humans were certainly better equipped to exert themselves for long periods in the tropical sunlight than their ape and monkey relatives were, and it can be assumed that the dramatic changes in skin, however they occurred, made it possible for humans to engage successfully in their new way of life.

## Hunting and Intelligence

If all the important physical adaptations that equipped humans for hunting had already been achieved by *Homo erectus'* predecessors, what made *Homo erectus* much better hunters than their predecessors had been? The answer almost certainly lies in the enormous increase in the size and adaptive capabilities of the brain. Hunting was more than a physical activity; it helped to create a new way of life, involving language, culture, and social organization. Hunting became as much a matter of the mind as of the body.

We have seen that one indication of *Homo erectus'* increasing mental ability is the refinement and improvement of their technology. Their stone tools and weapons were improvements over those of their predecessors, and they also had wooden spears, which made hunting safer and more effective. Even if they only jabbed with the spear rather than throwing it, they still could attack an animal without getting within immediate reach of its claws and teeth. And a spear embedded almost anywhere in an animal's body is likely to disable the animal; a stone, to be equally effective, must be thrown accurately to hit a vulnerable spot.

Perhaps as important as any improvement in weapons technology was a change in tactics. We can suppose that with a bigger brain *Homo erectus* had a greater attention and memory span. By being able to remember information from their own and their fellows' past hunting experiences, they could amass knowledge of animal behavior, plan ahead, work out strategies, and roam farther afield than their forebears without getting lost. Furthermore, they could cooperate more subtly with fellow hunters, increasing their chances of making a kill. With better cooperative tactics, organized groups of *Homo erectus* could take on much larger animals than *Homo habilis* had dared to. There was a definite advantage in trying for big game; more meat could be obtained for less time and labor.

## HUNTING METHODS

*Homo erectus'* success as hunters must have depended to a large extent on their guile and their understanding of their quarry's behavior. If so, just how did they hunt? Some methods are documented in the remains found in excavated sites; others can be inferred by examining hunting techniques employed in modern times by hunter-gatherers—by ethnographic analogy. As we have shown in Chapter 9, many of these methods have close parallels in the animal world, and the similarities suggest that early humans, faced with the same hunting challenges that confront most social carnivores, responded in the same way. If *Homo erectus* adopted tactics that paralleled those of other predators, they almost certainly did so unconsciously. But their evolving brain enabled them to make conscious improvements in hunting methods as well.

They were clever enough to have looked carefully for the weaknesses of the animals they hunted, big or small. The large number of fossil remains of immature mammals found at *Homo erectus* sites indicates that these people had learned well the advantages of picking younger, weaker animals as their prey. African hares are quick but vulnerable, and they, too, must have figured as part of *Homo erectus'* diet. How easily they can be caught by an intelligent (and agile) human was demonstrated by Louis Leakey, who ran them down and captured them with his bare hands. The technique is simple. The hunter, on spotting a hare, need only watch its long ears. When the hare is about to dodge, it lays its ears all the way back. Seeing this telltale sign, the hunter veers immediately either to the left or to the right, which gives a fifty-fifty chance of picking the way the hare is going to go. If the hunter has guessed correctly and is quick, the animal will be caught. If the hunter misses, the hare usually will run for cover and freeze there. The hunter, with the advantage of the primates' highly developed color vision, will see through the animal's camouflage, and simply go over and pick up the prey.

**Persistence Hunting**

Because *Homo erectus* could not have run down much of their larger quarry, they probably used a technique that anthropologist Grover S. Krantz has called *persistence hunting*. Development of this method, too, required insight into the behavior of animals, such as the tendency of antelopes and gazelles to move in an arc when trying to escape from a pursuer, giving the intelligent hunter the opportunity to cut them off. But the key to persistence hunting is persistence: never allowing the animal to rest, but keeping it constantly in motion until it grows so tired it can go no farther; when it slumps from exhaustion, it can be killed easily. *Homo erectus* may have had to keep up the chase for hours on end. The Tarahumara Indians of Mexico have been known to pursue a deer for as long as two days. Although the hunters may at times lose sight of their quarry, they never lose track of its spoor—hoofprints, droppings, and other signs of its passage—and relentlessly continue the pursuit until the deer collapses.

Stalking can bring down far larger animals than deer. Though their predecessors did eat large animals, either scavenging dead animals or bringing down weak ones, *Homo erectus* were a more skilled people. They deliberately hunted and killed such formidable creatures as ancient elephants, which were considerably bigger than their modern counterparts (Figure 12–2). It seems incredible that an animal as huge and tough as an elephant could be killed with nothing but bone and stone weapons and wooden spears. Yet Pygmies still use poisoned wooden

*FIGURE 12–2   The close of an elephant hunt. Except that they use iron-headed rather than flint-pointed spears, these Mandari hunters of the Eastern Sudan, Africa, could be reenacting a Paleolithic elephant hunt.*

spears to hunt elephants. Normally, Pygmy hunters go out in groups; when they come across an elephant, one hunter will attack it with a spear. As the animal charges the attacker, the other hunters dash toward it from different angles and plunge in their spears. They keep this up until the tormented animal dies. Some Pygmies even hunt elephants alone. They wear no clothing, but smear their bodies with animal dung to mask the human smell. Once they have located an elephant herd that has paused to rest in the midday heat, they sneak up on it, and with a favorable wind, stalk one of the beasts. When they are within three or four yards, they rush forward and spear the animal in the neck, then beat a quick retreat to escape the thrashings of the wounded elephant while the poison takes effect. An even more audacious method involves waiting in the bush for a herd to file past. When the last one goes by, the hunter darts between its legs and plunges a lance with a barbed head into its belly. The elephant is unlikely to be killed at once but probably will wander through the jungle, dazed with pain and becoming increasingly weary; the hunter must follow it until it weakens enough to be killed. The use of poisons makes these techniques possible. Without poisons *Homo erectus* would have found the task far harder to accomplish.

**Ambush**

If persistence hunting was indeed used by *Homo erectus*, it undoubtedly took a serious toll on the hunters' energy, and it had the distinct disadvantage of leaving the hunters stranded so far from camp that they could take back only a small part of the meat. A more productive method would have been a surprise attack by several hunters, who might have waited in ambush for their prey.

One ambush method that *Homo erectus* appears to have developed and refined was the use of bogs as traps for catching individual animals, or even entire herds. At Olduvai Gorge Louis Leakey unearthed fossil evidence of herds of extinct forms of cattle and gazelles that had been driven into a swamp by hunters and killed as they attempted to free themselves from the mud. The leg bones of one still stood in the clay; the hunters apparently had butchered the rest of the carcass and carried it off.

**History of Torralba and Ambrona**

Excavations carried out in Spain have been claimed to indicate further evidence of hunting by *Homo erectus*. The relics at Torralba and Ambrona, like those at Terra Amata in France, were first hit upon accidentally by a commercial enterprise. In 1888 workers for a Belgian company were digging trenches in preparation for laying a water main for a railroad when they came upon a few huge bones (Figure 12–3). The bones turned out to be the remains of an extinct species of elephant (*Elephas antiquus*), which had straight, rather than curved, tusks almost ten feet long. The bones remained only curiosities until 1907, when a

FIGURE 12–3   Ancient elephant bones excavated at Ambrona are jacketed in plaster and reinforced with rods to protect them during removal to the laboratory for study.

Spanish aristocrat and amateur archaeologist, the Marqués de Cerralbo, began to excavate at Torralba. Off and on for four years the Marqués dug and collected fossils, including the remains of at least twenty-five elephants. He also found several kinds of stone and bone tools, sharpened tusks, and fragments of wood, apparently worked by humans. It was the first collection of *Homo erectus* artifacts ever assembled.

Cerralbo's work was justly celebrated, and many of his conclusions were sound; his conjecture that Torralba represented the most ancient site of a human settlement in Europe held firm as late as 1958, when earlier sites were discovered at Vallonet, in France. Unfortunately Cerralbo died before he was able to publish his extensive and well-illustrated study of his work at the site. His digging was not as thorough as this literary work might have been, however; by today's standards it was hardly systematic. A great deal of work still remained to be done at Torralba, but it was more than half a century before anyone undertook it. Then in 1960 anthropologist F. Clark Howell visited the fallow trenches and soil heaps. A quick examination told him that this was still rich ground, and the following year he came back to begin new excavations.

During one summer's work Howell and his assistants unearthed the remains of six additional elephants at Torralba and another dozen at the larger site of Ambrona nearby (Figure 12–4). By the end of the third season, the diggers, under the direction of Howell's associate, anthropologist L. G. Freeman, Jr., had found more than fifty beasts. Torralba was completely excavated. Ambrona had been only about a third uncovered when Howell turned his attention to the Omo River area in southern Ethiopia. After nearly twenty years, Howell and Freeman returned in 1980 and began work again. Neither the Marqués de Cerralbo nor Howell discovered any human fossils or evidence of human-made shelters at either Torralba or Ambrona.

## Elephant Butchery

The study of fossilized pollen at the sites has revealed that it was very cold in Spain during this period between 300,000 and 400,000 years ago, so cold that the ground bore traces of frost patterning and resembled land in northern Alaska today. The summers were warm enough only to have thawed out the surface; the subsoil remained frozen the year around. Digging into this once-frozen soil, Howell found evidence suggesting that the hunters used fire to stampede the elephants: bits of charcoal and carbon were widely scattered across the ancient valley (Figure 12–4). The assumption that the hunters had spears as well as stone weapons is based on the discovery of small pieces of wood; some fragments, in rotting away, left hollows in the ground that could be filled with plaster to reveal the pointed shape of the original wood.

When this site was first excavated, it seemed to anthropologists that the evidence suggested a major hunting and butchery site. After killing

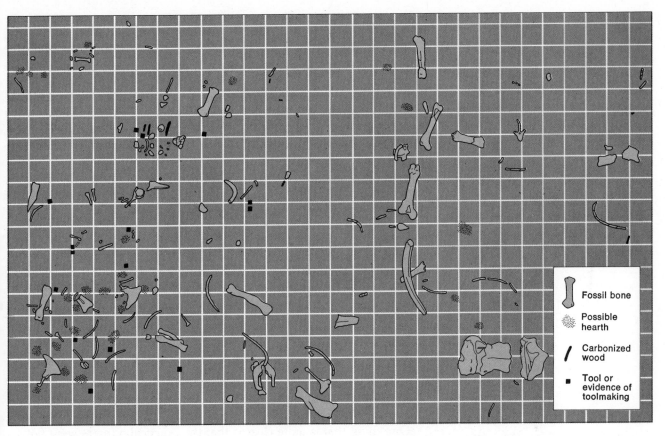

Fossil bone

Possible hearth

Carbonized wood

Tool or evidence of toolmaking

*FIGURE 12–4   Plotted on one-meter squares, the bones, tools, and charcoal at Ambrona were all recorded for each level excavated. The bones and tusk which can be seen in Figure 12–5 appear to the right of center in this plan.*

the elephants in the bog, the carcasses, it seemed, would have been stripped and the hunters would have taken the meat nearby for further processing. Here, as the debris they left behind seems to indicate, they reduced it to smaller pieces and cracked some of the bones for marrow. What they did with the skull is a mystery; the only one found at Ambrona had the entire crown smashed away, presumably so that the brain could be extracted and eaten.

Once the hunters had cut up the meat, they seem to have feasted on it nearby, at spots marked by clusters of crushed and burned bones. But when the four-ton size of an individual elephant is taken into account, it hardly seems possible that the hunters, no matter how numerous, could have eaten anything but a very small portion of the meat. They must have carried most of it off to their base camps, perhaps in some preserved form. The smoke-curing process seems too advanced for *Homo erectus*, but they probably had learned to dry their meat in the sun, as many people do today. In addition to preserving the meat, drying would have much reduced the weight of the meat, rendering it more easily transportable. (Plains Indians used to dry buffalo they killed; the flesh of an entire cow, cut up and dehydrated, weighed only forty-five pounds.)

How did the hunters go about sharing the meat? The ashes, bones, and tools of Torralba and Ambrona cannot answer this question directly, but one small, indirect clue emerged from the excavations. Analysis of the clusters of splintered and burned bones showed that each pile contained examples of most of the animal species known to have been killed and butchered at the site. Thus the hunters would seem to have distributed the spoils of the hunt equally among themselves; such egalitarianism is in fact a mark of hunter-gatherers today.

From one animal at Torralba, the skeletal remains of the left side only were found, lying skin side up. The cranium and pelvis had been removed from their natural position within the skeleton and the other bones do not appear to have been cracked for the marrow. Could this elephant have been singled out for special treatment and its bones assembled in a symbolic way, perhaps as part of a ritual? A more probable explanation may be that in trying to free itself from the mud of the bog, the animal toppled onto its left side, completely worn out. It may have sunk so deeply into the muck that only its right side could be butchered. But then why was the remaining part eventually flipped over, as the position of the skeleton would seem to indicate?

Across the valley at Ambrona a tusk and five long bones were discovered lying in a straight line near other parts of the animal's skeleton (Figures 12–4 and 12–5). At first it was thought that these huge bones may have served as a bridge across a boggy area, but then scientists determined that this spot was not a swamp at the time.

One thing that is quite clear is that the practical hunters were not so reverent that they avoided turning parts of their prey into tools. Among the many artifacts found at Torralba were some that had been made from animals' long bones and ribs, which had been fractured lengthwise down the middle. The pieces were then flaked by stones to produce tools that may have functioned as picks, cleavers, or hand-axes.

It has not been possible to give these sites a reliable date; the charcoal is too old for radiocarbon dating and the river deposits contain no volcanic rock or ash. The botanical and geological evidence, however, indicates an age of at least 300,000 and probably nearer 400,000 years B.P.

**QUESTIONS AND CONCLUSIONS**

The conclusions we have reviewed here have been questioned recently following new analyses by taphomonist Pat Shipman. She has reexamined some of the bones from these two sites using a Scanning Electron Microscope (SEM), which has enabled her to determine the types of damage to which the bones have been exposed. Surprisingly, she was only able to confirm the existence of cut-marks made by humans on 1% of the bones in her sample. What she did find was much evidence

FIGURE 12–5 *This view of the excavation at Ambrona shows the remarkable linear arrangement of elephant tusks and leg bones, which suggested that humans were responsible for their disposition.*

of abrasion from the surrounding sediments which might have obliterated the cut marks on other bones had they been present in the first place. The implications of her research are twofold:

1. There is clear evidence that hominids did indeed butcher at least some of the animals preserved at these sites, if not all. Both the stone tools and the cutmarks confirm this.

2. The material as a whole may prove to constitute a secondary deposit because the bones show considerable rolling and abrasion. At the least this implies that the bones have moved within the gravel beds as a result of the slumping of the sediments or the cycles of freezing and thawing to which the land was subjected. At the most it implies that the deposit is entirely a product of water action and does not represent an ancient land surface.

Thus it now seems possible that the interpretation of these sites which we have discussed is somewhat too detailed: the conclusion that we are looking at major butchering areas now requires further corroboration. From this development we can see how new techniques of analysis (such as use of the SEM) bring more refined and more reliable interpretations of archaeological data.

The travel imposed on *Homo erectus* by their wandering and migratory prey must have enormously affected their life. It forced them to cover new ground and exposed them to varied new experiences and sensations. All primates are curious, and doubtless *Homo erectus* explored the diverse features of their enlarging world with interest. They must have had to solve new problems, such as how to transport food and water and fire as they moved from one hunting ground to the next. No direct evidence has been discovered so far to show that they had receptacles of any sort, but it is inconceivable that they could have managed without at least crude skin bags made of animal hides or perhaps containers made of wood, leaves, or even clay. It is unlikely that these hunters carried many stone tools with them; the elephant bones sharpened for use as tools at Torralba and the chips around the toolmaker's "bench" at Terra Amata suggest that they manufactured most of their implements on the spot.

The hunters' wanderings may have played a part in *Homo erectus'* remarkable expansion out of the tropics, if only in preparing them for the adjustments that the new environment would force on them. When they did begin to expand their range northward, the cooler climates made taming of fire, and probably also construction of clothing of some sort, a necessity. Both these behaviors can be related to hunting. The cold, harsh winters of the north deprived *Homo erectus* of a year-round supply of vegetable food and put an even higher premium on their skill as hunters. How successfully they met these challenges is widely evident. Of hearthside fires, where they cooked the meat that hunting had supplied them with, we have ample evidence in the continuous layers of ash in the cave at Choukoutien. Clothing could have been made from the pelts of animals they had killed; impressions in the ground at Terra Amata and elsewhere show that *Homo erectus* used hides for something.

**NEW SOCIAL DEVELOPMENTS**

The records of achievement left by *Homo erectus* at Choukoutien, Torralba-Ambrona, Terra Amata, Olduvai Gorge, and other sites may not seem like much for their million-year tenure. And yet in successfully adopting hunting-and-gathering as a way of life, humans had taken a major step toward setting themselves apart from their animal ancestors and establishing the genus *Homo* as supreme among the creatures of the earth. The dependence on hunting and expansion into temperate regions of the Old World must have profoundly influenced human social organization.

The expansion into temperate zones (shown in Figure 11–8) was perhaps the high adventure of those million years during which *Homo erectus* established themselves as nature's dominant species. Before the great expansion, their immediate ancestors had been evolving by the dictates of natural selection in much the same way as other animals had: adapting imperceptibly to their environment, living in loose social groups, depending on a generally benign environment for food and warmth, having very little awareness of the past or thought for the future. But when *Homo erectus* spread into the world's previously unpeopled regions, their relationship to natural selection began to alter. *Homo erectus* prevailed over the obstacles of new environments not because they developed new bodily equipment but because they had a better brain. By meeting the challenges of changing conditions with solutions of their own making, rather than waiting until evolution created solutions for them, humans passed a crucial milestone: for the first time, a creature, however unconsciously, took an active part in its own adaptation and its own evolution. The invention of a "cultural environment" was the most significant contribution *Homo erectus* made to human evolution.

## Hunting, Gathering, and Family Interdependence

Cultural development requires a particular social environment: it depends on the existence of a home base and interdependence among people so that their relations are frequent and stable. We saw in Chapter 9 that *Homo habilis* society must have begun to operate according to certain patterns of social interdependence. As *Homo erectus* evolved, the links of dependence among individuals strengthened and became more numerous—babies depended upon mothers, youngsters upon adults, hunters upon other hunters, hunters and gatherers upon each other, and men and women upon each other; eventually, groups depended upon groups.

*Homo erectus* probably had to cover a large territory to find their food. It has been estimated that it took as much as ten square miles to support one hunter; a band of thirty people might have ranged over an area of 300 square miles in supplying itself with meat. Even if *Homo erectus* groups were as successful in their hunting as primitive hunting tribes are today, through most of the year the kills probably provided no more than a fourth of the food a band needed to live on. The rest had to be supplied by vegetable foods, probably gathered by the women. (In the northern temperate zone, the proportion of the diet that was meat would have been higher, especially in the winter and early spring.) As meat became more and more important in the human diet, women would have become more and more dependent on the men to supply it for them; similarly the hunters' dependence on the women gatherers to supply the vegetable mainstay would have grown.

By the time of *Homo erectus*, when hunters were tackling larger and more dangerous prey than *Homo habilis* had, more hunters working together were needed, and specialization of work had become more necessary. The division of labor between men and women, which today is accepted—or challenged—as a traditional social arrangement, had by then become essential to survival (Figure 12–6). Men and women living separately, every individual for himself, would almost certainly have starved; working together in distinct roles as hunters and gatherers, they formed a successful economic team (Figure 12–7).

*FIGURE 12–6* Homo erectus *probably evolved a pattern of division of labor similar to that of these present-day !Kung San. While the men search for meat, the women gather and dig vegetable foods.*

FIGURE 12–7 *Two !Kung brothers and their wives go out in the morning to find food. The men carry springhare poles, bows, and quivers of arrows for hunting; the women, one carrying two children, will gather plant foods.*

While this increasingly essential life-style was forging a stronger male-female relationship, and while larger brain size and slow infant development were reinforcing the infant-mother relationship, still another relationship was further developing: that of male to female to young. This three-way interdependence was perhaps the most important of the new kinds of social bonds. However ancient its beginnings may have been, it was evolving, and it was to become the basic unit of human society: the family.

As we saw in Chapter 9, Owen Lovejoy suggested that one-to-one male-female interdependence ("monogamy") may have appeared among groups of *Australopithecus* with the evolution of bipedalism (pages 246-248). On the other hand, research on primate social behavior and ecology (page 146) points to the more probable development of one-male harem groups ("polygyny"). Biological considerations such as the degree of sexual dimorphism in *Homo sapiens* and earlier hominids support the latter suggestions, because permanently monogamous species like the gibbon show no difference in size between the sexes.

Although it never can be known for sure what pattern of sexual relationships existed among early hominids, we can be fairly certain that male-female interdependence was important. It also seems possible that such interdependence was strengthened through females exchanging sexual favors only with supportive males. From here on, increasing interdependence and some division of labor probably developed among *Homo habilis*, as we have seen in Chapter 9, fostering relationships among men and women within the band. By *Homo erectus'* day, these bonds undoubtedly were more clearly established. If a *Homo erectus* band encompassed twenty to fifty individuals, as most experts believe, it included perhaps three to a dozen family units.

All sorts of human families exist today, and the European or American nuclear type is not the only form. The earliest families may have evolved under the leadership of the father, the mother, or the uncle (all these systems are to be found today) and may have included several females for a male or, very rarely, several males for a female. Common to all types of families is three-way interdependence. One male usually assumes some special responsibility for one or a few females and their children, while the females assume special responsibility to the males and their own children, and the children feel a special commitment to their parents.

This interdependence is a matter of degree. Children in particular may have been viewed in those early times as the charge of the entire band rather than of their parents alone. Yet the ties that distinguish families within a society must have been growing markedly stronger. Because family ties seem to be associated with sexual taboos and mate-selection rules, these behaviors, too, may have developed at this time.

As we discussed in Chapter 9, the estrous cycle of hominid females gradually became modified into the menstrual cycle, so that human females were not only capable of year-round sexual receptivity but were always attractive to males. Men and women must have come to exert more control over their sexual behavior and could decide when, and with whom, they mated. This physical change increased the all-important element of choice, and led to what has been called the individualization of sex. Mating would be less casual, and mates would become friends and partners.

This "partnering" probably was not permanent or monogamous. Furthermore, because hunting was communal, sharing meat probably was also, so that a man would not have been expected to provide all the meat a woman needed. Sharing hunted and gathered food, a two-way process, was surely important as a bonding mechanism, as it is today. Nevertheless, it seems inescapable that certain men and women would have attracted each other, become friends, and formed some sort of relationship that they and the group recognized. They would have bedded down together, kept one another company when the band was on the move, shared their resources, and paid particular attention to each other's needs. In addition, a man would have taken an interest in the children of the woman he favored, even if he did not specifically recognize them as his own. He would have taken her male children on hunting forays as soon as they were strong enough to keep up, and would have formed close ties with these protégés as he initiated them into his particular skills.

Kinship ties in the group almost certainly would have been extended by the presence of a few grandparents—men and women who were past their hunting and childbearing days but who were honored for their skills at toolmaking or teaching, or valued simply as baby-sitters. They may also have held a position of authority and influence in the band as elders. With the development of recognized kinship ties, continuity of genetic lines would have taken on firmer definition.

**Incest Taboo**

As these family patterns were more deeply etched into the emerging society, undoubtedly avoidance of *incest*, sexual relations between closely related individuals, was more marked. Incest inhibitions are evident in some apes and monkeys. Among Japanese and rhesus macaques, for instance, there is apparently some sort of restraint against sex between mother and son; in chimpanzees this inhibition usually is extended to include brother and sister, although in other ways the sex lives of chimpanzees are promiscuous. In modern humans a taboo against incest is found in all societies (though a few societies have carefully defined exceptions). At some time during human evolution, then, the partial inhibition became a hard-and-fast taboo. It seems fair to suggest that as *Homo erectus* grew more aware of kinship structures within the community, a sanction against sex within the family became more pronounced. Perhaps familiarity inhibited sexual interest. This change may have functioned to retain the stability in the family and the broader social structure. It is clear that bonds within the family will always be threatened by incest; and development of bonding between descent groups (discussed below) depended upon extending the incest taboo to a widening group of kin. That extensive inbreeding can be genetically undesirable (as we saw in Chapter 4) was surely not known to these people, yet in this respect also the taboo was an advantageous behavior pattern.

**Exogamy**

*Homo erectus'* tendency to look around widely for mates probably grew, and eventually they reached beyond their own band to select partners from neighboring groups. This practice, which anthropologists call *exogamy*, certainly had advantages. Speech would have enabled *Homo erectus* to name and symbolize relationships between families and descent groups, and development of blood ties between such groups through exchange of mates would have encouraged intergroup harmony. If competition for game among neighboring bands was a potential problem at the time, this development could have been of great social importance. When bands with adjoining hunting ranges are related, sharing develops; when game and other foods become scarce, the bands can hunt freely over one another's ranges. By bringing in mates strange to the group, exogamy made family ties and band identity even more important. Rules of exogamy—which today cause individuals to marry outside their social group and may even specify the outside group into which they must marry—are characteristic of all existing human societies and are undoubtedly an ancient custom, and certainly one of extraordinary importance.

**Home Base**  With strong family ties and individualization came another cultural development vital for society's growth: the idea of a home base. In a society more complex than that of most primates, subgroups of hunters or foragers are likely to be isolated from the main group for a time. As we have seen, there is some evidence that *Homo habilis* invented the base camp, to which individuals or subgroups would return after dispersing to perform specific social functions. Certainly, constant association as a group would not have been possible for *Homo erectus*, whose hunters ranged far and whose young were becoming increasingly dependent. The solution was a place, however temporary, where the children could be looked after and the fires kept burning, where the women could stockpile the fruits of their gathering, and where the men could bring their supplies of meat after a day or two on the hunt.

By the time of *Homo erectus* we have evidence of at least two kinds of homes: one temporary, one permanent. If the hunters were following migrating animals, the bases were used only as long as the animals were in the area. Terra Amata was a temporary home of this sort. Even there, the visitors saw fit to build huts for shelter each time they came. The huts we believe were built in consecutive years on the same sand dune at Terra Amata suggest a group with a well-ordered annual schedule and perhaps even a feeling of attachment for a favored spot. Choukoutien was not a temporary home. There, where in one cave the layers of hearth ashes were twenty-two feet thick, the base must have been more or less permanent (although during some periods it may have been a seasonal home): no doubt it was in a favored location where water and game were within close range most of the year.

In developing the idea of a home base, *Homo erectus* and their predecessors were unique among primates. Many animals mark off territories they regard as peculiarly their own, and some monkeys and apes show a preference for certain clumps of trees to sleep in within their ranges. The most highly evolved social carnivores, the African wild dogs, have a den—a permanent home base—to which they always return. But no other primate group has anything like a permanent base.

With a home base, humankind had a new social blueprint. For one thing, the existence of a home meant that the sick or infirm no longer faced abandonment along the way; now they had a place where they could rest and mend in comparative safety. "For a wild primate," Sherwood Washburn and Irven DeVore write, "a fatal sickness is one that separates it from the troop, but for man it is one from which he cannot recover even while protected and fed at the home base. . . . It is the home base that changes sprained ankles and fevers from fatal diseases to minor ailments."

Thus development of the home must have affected the normal life span. Still, only a few *Homo erectus* individuals are believed to have attained the age of forty, and anyone who survived until fifty would have reached a ripe old age indeed. Most died much earlier, as shown by the evidence from the cave at Choukoutien: 50 percent of the human bones found there belonged to children under fourteen.

For the long-range development of human society, the real importance of the home base was that it provided a medium for cultural growth. Within the safe circle of its carefully tended fire could grow a fellowship, a self-awareness and trust, a sense of community that was new on earth. There people could begin to learn more than simply how to survive; they could improve their tools and weapons, fashion a language, and look not only to the past but to the future.

## INTRASPECIES AGGRESSION

### Theories of Aggression

The home, for all it contributed to human growth, also could be involved in another, and much less desirable, hallmark of human society (according to some writers)—one that some observers think they can trace to *Homo erectus* and before. That is the modern human's unhappy tendency to do violence to other humans.

Author Robert Ardrey hypothesized that people instinctively guard whatever territory they consider their own, such as that of a home base, and will defend it, violently if necessary, against all intruders. He suggested that an inborn drive for aggression carried over from animal forebears explains all humans' violent behavior, from wars to riots to throwing dishes in a domestic quarrel. Konrad Lorenz, Austrian authority on animal behavior, argued that this innate drive will express itself in one way or another; if it is not channeled productively, in society's terms, it will burst out destructively—sooner or later, but inevitably.

Most anthropologists and ethnologists today disagree with Lorenz's and Ardrey's hypothesis. They believe that humans have no specific innate drive for aggression but merely the potential for this kind of behavior, and that this potential is shaped by society. When people are threatened or think they are threatened by another, their response might just as well be to flee the threat as to fight the provoker. All vertebrate animals are provided with a dual innate response to danger of *fight* or *flight*. Thus all species have the possibility of peaceful coexistence. Among humans, culture and experience determine which response they make.

Anthropologist David Pilbeam does not believe that aggressive behavior is innate either in humans or in monkeys and apes. "The degree to which such behavior is developed," he states, "depends very considerably indeed upon cultural values and learning. Territoriality, likewise, is not a 'natural' feature of human group living; nor is it among most other primates."

Pilbeam's analysis is borne out by observation of several hunter-gatherer peoples living today, such as the !Kung San of the Kalahari Desert in southern Africa. The !Kung are not particularly territory-minded, and among themselves they are not usually aggressive, regarding hospitality and generosity as normal. Even milder are the Tasaday people, discovered living in Stone Age primitiveness in the Philippine jungle. These quiet, gentle people appear to live in harmony with their surroundings and each other, and apparently exhibit no driving aggression in any aspect of their society.

### Aggression among *Homo erectus*

*Homo erectus*, too, probably were peaceable. They lived by the club and spear, it is true, but only to feed themselves and their kin. Sharing food was basic to their existence, and because their possessions were limited by the kind of life they led, covetousness and greed could hardly have driven *Homo erectus* to violence.

Yet the possibility of conflict within or between bands cannot be entirely eliminated. Much that we know portrays *Homo erectus* as solid and industrious social humans, sharing the burdens of a primitive existence. Yet, among the fossils unearthed on the cave floor at Choukoutien are reminders that they were savages, living in a savage world. Charred human bones were found, and human skulls smashed in at the base. This evidence can be explained in many ways; some archaeologists conclude that the first humans practiced cannibalism and ate the brains of the dead. Savage as this act is now considered, it does not necessarily make *Homo erectus* less human. In fact, it could be taken as evidence of a forward step in human development.

Among the tribal peoples that have been known to practice cannibalism in recent times, the act is nearly always carried out not for the sake of food but as a ritual (Figure 12–8). The distinction between dietary and ritual cannibalism is important; it is extremely rare for people to eat other people merely for food. Writing of some present-day head hunters, G. H. R. von Koenigswald explained, "The head hunter is not content merely to possess the skull, but opens it and takes out the brain, which he eats in order by this means to acquire the wisdom and skill of his foe." The very evidence suggesting that the first humans ate each other and each other's brains, then, might suggest that they had some spiritual notion that cannibalism could increase their powers.

Conflicts between bands, if they occurred, must have been rare in an uncrowded world that offered few natural examples of creatures systematically setting upon their own kind. It appears likely that cruelty and war were later developments. They probably came after humans

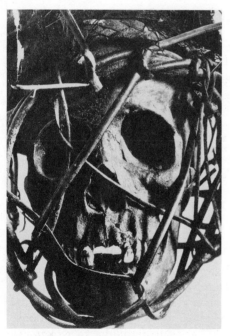

FIGURE 12–8   Bornean headhunters usually keep the skull of the man they have killed as a trophy. The base of the skull is always damaged; the foramen magnum has been enlarged and the brain removed. It is normally eaten, an example of ritual cannibalism. (See also Figure 15–18).

settled down on the land, became a more numerous species, and forged cultures that encouraged individual and group pride in possessions, territories, and beliefs, even as they fostered art, science, and literature.

These are today's problems, of course, and there is little reason to think they afflicted *Homo erectus*. They were confronting their own challenges and, with perseverance and imagination, solved them remarkably well. To their success we owe our flaws and triumphs.

**HOLOCENE**

10,000

---

*HOMO ERECTUS* (c. 1.0–0.5 million B.P.)

| | | |
|---|---|---|
| Peking fossils | | |
| Torralba/Ambrona and Terra Amata | Physical characteristics | Males over and females just under 5 feet tall. |
| Olorgesailie | | Cranial capacity from 775 to 1,225 cc.; heavily built skull |
| Hearths at Escale | | More sweat glands and less hair than previous hominids |
| | | Heavier and thicker bones than most modern human's |
| Günz glaciation | | |
| Java fossils | Subsistence | Scavenged, foraged, and gathered food |
| **PLEISTOCENE** | | Hunted larger animals, such as ancient elephants, than did previous hominids |
| *A. robustus* and *boisei* extinct | | At least in northern areas, probably hunted as a major means of getting food, especially in winter |
| Earliest Acheulian tools | | Used spears and possibly spheroids as weapons, and the techniques of ambush and persistence hunting |

1 million —

*H. habilis* at Olduvai

2 million —

| | | |
|---|---|---|
| | Social organization | Division of labor between the sexes and interdependence more firmly established than among previous hominids |
| | | Extended kinship ties, incest taboos, and exogamy probably appeared |
| | | Established temporary and permanent homes |
| | | Probably lived in bands of 20 to 50 individuals |

Earliest Oldowan tools at Hader

3 million —

**PLIOCENE**

*AUSTRALOPITHECUS* (c. 3 million B.P.)

4 million —

| | | |
|---|---|---|
| | Physical characteristics | Males about 4.0–4.5 feet tall; females somewhat smaller |
| | | Cranial capacity ranging from about 435 to 530 cc. |
| | Subsistence | Scavenged and foraged and hunted small animals in tropical regions |
| | | Primarily dependent on vegetable foods, which possibly were collected |
| | Social organization | Lived in social groups |
| | | Division of labor between the sexes and prolonged bonds between males and females possibly began to appear |

5 million —  Early *Australopithecus*

---

HUNTING AND THE EVOLUTION OF SOCIETY

The evolutioin of human society resulted to a great extent from development of gathering and hunting to increase food resources, the division of labor, and the expansion into the north temperate zones.

# Chapter 13

# The Evolution of Language and the Brain

He gave man speech, and speech created thought,
Which is the measure of the universe.

> PERCY BYSSHE SHELLEY, 1792–1822.
> *Prometheus Unbound,* II, iv, 72–73.

Speech was given to man to disguise his thoughts.

> *Attributed to CHARLES MAURICE de TALLEYRAND,* 1754–1838.

## WAYS OF COMMUNICATING

As the social life of humans grew more complex, the ability to communicate must also have developed. Language, we can now see, was humankind's passport to a totally new level of social relationship, organization, and thought; it was the tool that allowed humans to vary expressions to meet changing conditions instead of being limited by less flexible patterns of communication, as the other primates are.

## Early Theories on the Origins of Speech

When did humans learn to speak? How did they start? What did their first words sound like? Investigators have been seeking answers to these questions for thousands of years. In ancient Egypt the pharaoh Psammetichus ordered two infants reared where they could hear no human voice. He hoped that when at last they spoke, uninfluenced by the sound of the Egyptian tongue, they would resort to their earliest ancestors' language, which he confidently assumed lurked within them. One child finally uttered something that sounded like *bekos,* or "bread" in the language of Phrygia, an ancient nation of central Asia Minor. Phrygian, said Psammetichus triumphantly, was obviously humankind's original tongue.

Many centuries later King James IV of Scotland tried a similar experiment with two babies. The result, he let it be known, was that his experimental subjects spoke passable Hebrew. This report must have pleased Biblical scholars of the day, for they had contended all along that Adam and Eve had conversed in Hebrew. A Swede of the late seventeenth century believed otherwise: he announced that in the Garden of Eden God had used Swedish, Adam Danish, and the serpent French.

As time went on, all sorts of theories sprang up about the origins of speech. The eighteenth-century French philosopher Jean Jacques Rousseau envisioned a group of tongue-tied human beings getting together and stammering out more or less overnight a language they could use. Why they felt the need for one, and how they communicated with each other before they had invented the words to communicate with, Rousseau failed to mention. His contemporary, the German Romantic historian Johann Gottfried Herder, also espoused the notion that language was human-made, not God-instilled, as most people believed. Anything so illogical, so imperfect as language could hardly be attributed to a divinity, Herder argued. But he would have none of Rousseau's ideas, either. Instead, he saw language springing from the innermost nature of humans, in response to an impulse to speak. Just how language took shape Herder could not say, but he imagined that it started when humans began imitating sounds of the creatures around them, using eventually the imitative sounds as the words for the animals themselves. This theory, known today among those who disagree with it as the "bow-wow thesis," was followed by a number of others, similarly named and ridiculed, ranging from the whistle-and-grunt thesis to the ouch-ouch, which claimed that language rose from exclamations of pain, pleasure, fear, surprise, and so on.

Darwin's concept of human evolution provided a new way of approaching the problem of the origin of language. Scientists are now beginning to develop some theories about how we came to speak. Furthermore, they have some reason to believe that *Homo erectus* was the first creature to begin to depend on language for communication. Studies of animals, particularly monkeys and apes, both in the laboratory and in the wild, have given us an understanding of the foundation on which language is based; they have shown that there is considerably more of the ape in talkative humans than most people think. Examination of that foundation is necessary, because understanding what communication was like before there were words helps make clear why and how language evolved and emphasizes the tremendous biological and cultural changes that it made possible.

**Communication among Animals**

The lower animals and insects have some intriguing ways of communicating. Honeybees perform a kind of dance on the honeycomb; the dance accurately transmits information about the direction, distance, and nature of a food source. Dogs and wolves·use scents to communicate in addition to barks, howls, and growls; they also use a system of visual signals that includes not only facial expression and body movement but also the position of the tail.

Communications get more complex as the social organizations of animals do, and next to ourselves the nonhuman primates have the most intricate systems of all. Far from depending only on vocalizations, nonhuman primates seem to rely heavily on combinations of gestures, facial expressions, and postures as well as scents and sounds (Figure 13–1). They apparently are able to lend many shades of meaning to this body-language vocabulary. Often, they use sounds as a means of calling

*FIGURE 13–1   Facial expression is one of the most important modes of nonverbal communication in both chimpanzees and people. The functions of such expressions in the two species are quite closely related.*

FIGURE 13–2 *A dominant male chimpanzee reassures a young male who is presenting his rump in appeasement. As a result, the younger male now feels able to turn and face his superior.*

attention to their other signals. On some important occasions, however, only sounds will do. On discovering something good to eat, a monkey or ape will let out a cry of pleasure that brings the rest of the troop running; sensing danger, it will give a shriek that causes its companions frantically to seek shelter.

This wordless communication system serves the nonhuman primates extremely well. As social animals living in troops, they use it to keep in touch with one another at all times. More important, it enables individuals to display their feelings and to recognize at a glance the intentions and moods of others, enabling them to avert conflict. Many of the signals express the established hierarchy of dominance and submission within the troop (see Figure 13–2). A subordinate male chimpanzee, seeing signs of aggression directed at him by a male of superior rank, backs up to the other and presents his rump in a gesture of appeasement—unless he intends to challenge the other male. Different signals, vocal and visual, keep the troop from becoming scattered when it is on the move or roaming over a territory foraging for food. Still other signals promote mating behavior or foster good mother-infant relations. A mother chimpanzee has been observed to calm her disturbed youngster simply by touching its fingers lightly with hers (Figure 13–3). So complex and so delicate is this language of gesture in the chimpanzee that it cannot be said to be less evolved than our own. It serves to maintain an extremely complex social system (p. 156).

Yet for all its complexity, and however well suited it may be to the chimpanzees' needs, such a communication system falls far short of human language. As far as is known, nonhuman primates in the wild cannot name specific things; they have no way of referring to their environment and cannot communicate thought via the complex phonetic codes called words that are used by humans. Nor do they seem able to refer to the past or future with the aid of their signals. For them, what is out of sight is out of mind. The signal system narrowly circumscribes what can be communicated, and vocalizations and facial expressions are not under voluntary control.

This is not to say that the nonhuman primates' vocal signals are entirely unspecific. Some apes indicate the desirability of the food they are eating by the intensity of their food calls. During normal feeding, chimpanzees emit food grunts; but for a favorite food they give the more excited food bark. They still cannot say "banana," of course, but they communicate something more than simply "food." Even more specialized is the danger-call system of the African vervet monkeys, which have three alarm calls for three kinds of attackers. The vervets use a chitter for snakes, a chirp for ground-dwelling carnivores, and a *r-raup* sound to warn of birds of prey. It has been shown by playing back to them tape recordings of their alarm calls that a chirp is enough to send the vervets scrambling to the tips of branches, well out of reach of ground animals, whereas a r-raup launches them from the trees into the thickets below, where birds cannot get at them. As the young mature, they are able to make finer distinctions between the different alarm calls. A cry of "Watch out—eagle!" is beyond their capabilities, but it is also beyond their needs. They do not have to know whether it is an eagle or a hawk diving on them; what matters is that they get the message that the danger is from above, and flee in the right direction.

**Limbic and Nonlimbic Communication**

In their function, as well as in their causation, the vocal and visual signals used by nonhuman primates can be divided into two kinds. The majority of these signals, probably all the vocal signals, express inner emotional and physiological states and involuntarily accompany such states. They allow all members of the troop to monitor the emotional

*FIGURE 13–3 Among chimpanzees, as among humans, physical contact is a most important means of communication between individuals. Even a touch is reassuring. This photograph is of wild chimpanzees in Tanzania.*

status of all other members. All signals of this sort are generated by a group of structures in the brain known collectively as the *limbic system* (or the "emotional brain"). These signals come from below the level of conscious awareness, just as the human scream is generated. (We will take a closer look at the limbic system later in this chapter.)

In contrast to these signals, some gestures appear to communicate conscious will or intent. A chimpanzee holds out its hand as a gesture of submissive greeting, or raises it in threat. A young baboon anxiously presents to a superior male, backing rump first toward him. A mother chimpanzee uses her hand to beckon to her infant or repel its approach. These conscious gestures, which are normal, voluntary movements, have taken on a role in communication. Because of the intentions and wishes they symbolize, they fall into a category very different from the expressions of emotion we have considered above. They are generated not by the limbic system but by the higher centers of the brain, just as human language is. It is for this reason that chimpanzees are excellent gestural mimics and, as we shall see, they can learn sign language.

Both kinds of communication are seen in our own behavior. We, too, have a repertory of wordless signals that universally express emotions. A person has only to smile to demonstrate friendly intentions; clenched fists and jaws, scowls, and frowns are unmistakable signs of anger or disappointment; the laugh, the cry, the scream are direct expressions of inner psychological and physiological states. Humans even have acquired an involuntary signal other primates do not have: the blush, over which most people have little or no control, but which sends a clear message about what is going on inside the brain. And when humans are most excited, they often show it by speechlessness. Such basic signals are in a different category from the many other body motions humans use, such as shaking and nodding the head, shrugging the shoulders, and clapping the hands; these are really abbreviated substitutes for spoken language and vary in meaning from one place to another. Nonverbal communication is still an essential component in modern human relationships (see Figure 13–1).

But signals are less important to humans than they are to other animals, for they make up a smaller part of humans' communication system. Much of the information necessary for social interaction among humans is conveyed vocally; a blind human can communicate satisfactorily. But deafness from birth is tragic: because babies born deaf cannot hear and imitate spoken words, they can learn to speak only with great difficulty. Fortunately, they can use sign language; a real language, even if it is nonvocal.

## Nature of Language

Language provides a magnificently efficient and versatile means of communication. It is a complex system of vocal signals to which meanings have been assigned by cultural convention and the number of

meanings that can be so assigned is, in practice, infinite
of sounds conveys conscious thought at least ten time:
other method of signaling can—faster than hand signs, r
or even other kinds of vocalizations. Through langua;
step outside themselves and give things and people name
others and themselves, and refer to the past and the future. Most
important of all, language gives people the capacity to share their
thoughts. As Sherwood Washburn and Shirley Strum write: "It is the
communication of thought, rather than thought itself, that is unique to
man, makes human cultures possible, and that is the primary factor in
separating man and beast." Discussion, bargaining, and democratic
processes became a possibility for the first time.

This insight provides one of the reasons specialists are so sure *Homo
erectus* must have had some form of language: so many of their activities
required sharing thought. To carry out hunts such as those documented
by the varied archaeological evidence, they must have been able to lay
plans in advance; name animals and tools; identify places; and refer to
both the past and future. Moreover, the division of labor that must
have marked *Homo erectus'* society would have been all but impossible
if men and women had been unable to communicate about their separate responsibilities or could not agree to meet at a particular spot once
food-gathering was completed. As their society grew more complex,
they would have used words to sort out family relationships and to
establish ties with neighboring bands.

Furthermore, language was the new and extraordinarily efficient
means by which humans acquired and passed on from one generation
to the next that flexible network of learned, rather than inherited,
behavior patterns and the knowledge that allowed them to alter their
environment and adapt to new ones. A simple culture now had a
symbolic form that changed its whole nature. From this point in human
evolution, culture and its medium—language—would be necessary for
survival.

## ABILITY TO SPEAK

Though it has long been clear that this watershed in evolution occurred
largely because of the ability to use words to communicate symbolic
meaning, it was not at all clear until recently why humans alone, and
not their intelligent close relatives among the apes, learned to speak.
After all, apes have much of the vocal apparatus—lips, a tongue, and
a larynx or voice box with vocal cords—that humans have.

### Talking Apes?

An eighteenth-century French physician and philosopher, Julien Offroy
de la Mettrie, imagined that apes were on about the same intellectual
level as retarded humans and that all they needed to turn them into
"perfect little gentlemen" was speech training. Not until early in the

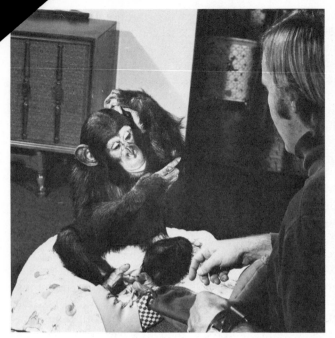 

*FIGURE 13–4   Two Ameslan hand signals. In the "tree" sign, one hand holds the opposite forearm upright by the elbow, and the free hand is fluttered back and forth. The sign meaning "hat" is made by first placing the hand on top of the head and then making a repeated patting motion.*

twentieth century, however, were any scientific attempts made to teach apes to talk. One couple worked with a chimpanzee called Viki, and only after six years of the most painstaking effort on their part and a great deal of frustration on hers did she manage to say, on cue, what sounded like "Mama," "Papa," "up," and "cup." It was clear that although accomplished gestural mimics, chimpanzees cannot mimic vocally, as humans can.

A more recent experiment made by Beatrice and Robert Gardner produced a more startling result. A chimpanzee named Washoe learned by age five to understand more than 350 hand signals of the standard American Sign Language of the deaf (Ameslan), and to use at least 150 of them correctly (see Figure 13–4). With these, she learned to name things and express her wants and needs in those names. Another chimpanzee, Sarah, learned to communicate with her keepers by selecting from a number of plastic signs which carried particular meanings, which she placed upon a magnetic board. A third chimpanzee, Lana, learned to communicate by pressing buttons on a keyboard. A gorilla, Koko, recently trained by Penny Patterson of Stanford in Ameslan, has learned a vocabulary of over 350 hand signals and understands many more. Others are teaching the orangutan. Constant training by humans enables these apes to associate visual symbols not only with concrete objects, but also with such abstracts as adjectives, verbs, and even prepositions. With these symbols it is claimed that they can construct simple sentences, which they use to express their desires. It is said that they can also lie, abuse their trainers, and invent new expressions. Examples of the latter include "water bird" for swan (Washoe), "white tiger" for zebra, and "eye hat" for mask (Koko). Koko has also combined signs to make entirely new words. Evidently, with human help, apes can by imitation learn symbols and use a symbolic means of communication, but in all cases they do so by gesture or manipulation rather than by means of their vocal apparatus. Whether the ape's use of symbols amounts to the use of language depends on the definition of *language* employed. Such a definition is very complex and numerous definitions have been proposed. The apes can certainly use a symbolic mode of communication, even if it does not amount to anything approaching human language.

### The Pharynx

Viki's frustration and Washoe's success have led to clearer understanding of what is involved in human speech. Spoken language requires equipment, both physical and mental, that apes and monkeys simply do not have (see Figure 13–5). The adult human tongue, for example, is thicker than that of monkeys and apes, and unlike theirs, it bends in a sharp angle into the throat. In addition, the human larynx, with its vocal cords, lies farther down the throat than the ape larynx. The part of the throat above the larynx, the pharynx, is proportionately much longer in humans than in any other primates.

FIGURE 13–5 *Scientists have assessed the speaking ability of* Homo erectus *by comparing the vocal apparatus of a modern adult and a baby with that of a chimpanzee. To form words, sounds must be modulated by the areas above the larynx.* Homo erectus, *however, are believed to have had a vocal tract similar to the one shown below. The larynx sits higher up in the throat than in modern adults, limiting the size of the pharynx. The vocal tract of a modern newborn baby probably resembles* Homo erectus' *more than does a modern adult's. The implication is that if* Homo erectus *talked, they did so with a more restricted range of vowel sounds.*

The pharynx serves as a combined opening for the windpipe, which goes to the lungs, and the gullet, which leads to the stomach. The anchor for the base of the tongue, it also plays a fundamental part in producing speech, and this is where the longer human pharynx becomes important. It is the pharynx that modifies the sounds made by the vocal cords and gives them the tones that a listener recognizes as language. To provide this control, the muscles of the pharynx walls and

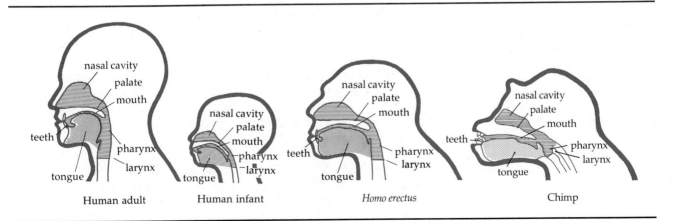

Human adult    Human infant    *Homo erectus*    Chimp

the base of the tongue move continuously during speech, constantly and precisely varying the dimensions of the pharynx—the greatest width of the pharynx is at least ten times its narrowest. These dimensional changes produce much the same effect on sounds that an organ achieves with its dozens of pipes of different lengths and diameters, each making a particular tone. The pharynx is extremely important to speech; it is quite possible to speak intelligibly without the larynx or tip of the tongue as long as the pharynx and base of the tongue are intact.

Monkeys and apes, lacking the human vocal equipment, vary the shape of only their mouths when they vocalize; there is practically no movement of the pharynx, the musculature of which is rudimentary. They can produce only a limited number of distinct sounds—ten to fifteen in most cases—and because of limitations of the brain's cortex they cannot combine them at will to form words.

The same limitation restricts the vocalization of human babies, who at birth are unable to make the vowel sounds typical of human speech. For at least six weeks a baby's tongue remains immobile during its cries. It rests almost entirely within the mouth, as in nonhuman primates, and the larynx sits high in the throat. This arrangement permits babies to swallow and breathe at the same time without danger of choking. By the time they reach the babbling stage, at around three months, the base of the tongue and the larynx have already begun to descend into the throat, enlarging the pharyngeal region. Not until then are infants physically equipped to make the speech sounds that distinguish them from their simian relatives.

## Centers of Vocal Communication: The Cerebral Cortex

Other equally important reasons why humans can talk and the nonhuman primates cannot, have to do with the brain. When people use their voices to communicate, they are doing more than making noise. They are codifying thought and transmitting it to others in a string of connected sounds. The coding begins in the *cerebral cortex*, the convoluted outer layer of the brain. The cortex (or *neocortex*) has three areas of importance in speech production (Figure 13–6). All occur on one cerebral hemisphere only, usually described as the dominant hemisphere, because speech is so important in human life. The dominant hemisphere is the left hemisphere in almost all right-handed people, while in many left-handed people it is found on the right side. (The nondominant hemisphere is associated with concepts of proportion and relationship in space and sound that are expressed in art and music.)

One region important in the generation of speech is called *Broca's area*. Located toward the front of the brain's dominant hemisphere, it sends the code for the succession of *phonemes* (speech sounds) to an adjacent part of the brain (the motor cortex) controlling muscles of the face, jaw, tongue, palate, and larynx; thus it helps set the speech apparatus in operation. Injury to Broca's area produces the form of *aphasia*

FIGURE 13–6   *Areas of the brain cortex involved with speech production are shown in the left drawing. The drawing at right shows the arcuate fasciculus, which links Wernicke's to Broca's areas. Wernicke's area and the angular gyrus are also involved in decoding of speech.*

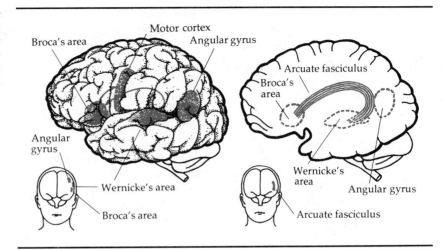

(loss or impairment of speech) in which articulation is slow and labored.

The second region is *Wernicke's area*, located farther back on the dominant hemisphere, in the temporal lobe; it is vital to the process of comprehension. Damage to Wernicke's area usually produces another form of aphasia: speech that is fluent but meaningless. A bundle of nerve fibers transmits signals from Wernicke's area to Broca's, making possible the vocal repetition of a heard and memorized word.

The third region, adjacent to Wernicke's area, is the *angular gyrus*. It occupies a key position at the juncture of the portions of the cerebral cortex connected with vision, hearing, and touch—the parts of the brain that receive detailed information from the world outside the body. Linked to these sensory receivers by bundles of nerve fibers, the angular gyrus operates as a kind of connecting station, permitting one type of incoming signal to be associated with others. For example, the angular gyrus makes it possible for the brain to link a visual stimulus produced by the sight of a cup with the auditory stimulus produced by a voice saying "cup" and with the tactile stimulus produced when the hand picks up the cup. The importance of these associations is clear when we think of the way children learn the words for things: when children ask "what's that?" and are told by their parents, they match the image of the seen object with the sound of the spoken word and thus absorb the name for it, automatically filing the sound for that association in their memory bank. This process of association and memorization is the first and most basic step in the acquisition of language.

**Limbic System**   The brains of monkeys and apes are broadly similar to humans' brains but are significantly less developed in some important areas. An ape's angular gyrus is small and there is limited association between infor-

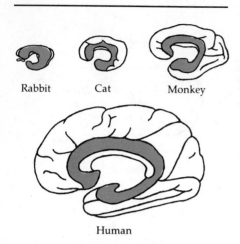

Rabbit     Cat     Monkey

Human

*FIGURE 13–7   These drawings of the brain in partial section show the relative size of the limbic regions in different species (approximately to scale). The limbic system is the "emotional brain" in all mammals, including humans. It is connected with the expression and decoding of much of the nonverbal communication that plays such a big part in the social life of mammals. Though still large and important in humans, it is no longer the largest component of the brain, as it is in other mammals. The limbic system lies beneath the neocortex which is distinctive of mammals and reaches its greatest development among primates.*

mation signals coming from different senses. Apparently, incoming signals are routed mainly to another part of the brain altogether: the limbic system (see Figure 13–7). All mammals, including humans, have this evolutionarily ancient region lying near the core of the brain, a kind of netherworld of neurological activity. Among other things, it activates the physical responses that go with hunger, fear, rage, and sexual activity, and it triggers the feelings that accompany these responses (Figure 13–8). If a monkey sees a predator, the visual signal feeds into the limbic system and produces a physical reaction—the sounding of the danger call, perhaps—and also makes the animal feel fear. Similarly, sexual signals sent out by a female chimpanzee go to the limbic system of a male, causing him to feel sexually stimulated and prompting a sexual response.

In other words, information channeled to the limbic system from the outside produces an instantaneous, unthinking, adaptive response. As anthropologist Jane Lancaster writes, the limbic system "makes the animal want to do what it has to do to survive and reproduce."

As we have seen, among the responses that are directed by the limbic system are vocal signals—cries of fear or pleasure, for example—that are quite distinct from language. That communication through signals like these is controlled by this part of the brain can be demonstrated by laboratory experiment. When electrodes are planted in the limbic system and related structures of a monkey and its brain is stimulated electrically, the animal responds with its repertory of cries, even though the situations that normally stimulate those sounds (aggressive behavior by a dominant male, food, enemies) are not present. Furthermore, other monkeys of the same species in the laboratory react to these sounds (by cringing, searching for food, taking an alert stance) just as though they were bona fide signals. Similar experiments have been performed on human subjects during brain surgery, and they react in a similar way. When certain parts of the human limbic system are stimulated, the patient responds with sounds.

The sounds produced through the limbic system in both ape and human are not the sounds of speech. For that distinctive emblem of humanness it was necessary for other parts of the brain, specifically the angular gyrus and Wernicke's and Broca's areas of the cortex, to develop fully. It was through this development and the evolution of the speech apparatus that emerging humans began to speak and left the inarticulate apes far behind.

In the cortex evolved the means of producing complex vocal sounds that could be used to communicate intent, will, and desire, as could the gestures discussed earlier used by nonhuman primates. Language is a learned vocal and symbolic communicatory system that is cortical in origin. It can be used to refer to all kinds of objects, processes, and concepts, and indeed it is practically unlimited in its value to human society. It was probably the most important development in human evolution, because it made possible our extraordinary cultural adaptations.

## EVOLUTION OF SPEECH

It is obviously impossible to pinpoint when *Homo* began to use language: the development of speech and other human characteristics was infinitely gradual. The process may have begun when they started making and using tools. If *Australopithecus* had at first depended upon gestures to communicate, such hand signals would no doubt have eventually become inadequate; the hominids literally would have had their hands full, carrying tools or food. Thus the ability to use sounds voluntarily to attract attention and to make meaning clear would have proved a great advantage.

FIGURE 13–8 *Chimpanzees have a complex repertoire of facial expressions, as varied as our own. Most facial expressions are components of the multimodal communication system generated by the limbic system.*

But, for the process of naming things to start, the vocal apparatus had to be modified, the brain had to evolve. This development must have taken hundreds of thousands of years. Some small mutations may have enabled *Australopithecus* to make a few voluntary sounds, providing an edge in the competition for survival. The ability to signal one another through a more extensive repertoire of phonemes would have been a definite advantage when *Homo habilis* were gathering food or hunting. And then, as the number of phonemes grew, brain development could have permitted more precise differentiation between them and new combinations of them, so that primitive words may have taken shape. All the while the brain and vocal apparatus would have been involved in a feedback relationship with each other, changes in one fostering development of the other: the success of the cortex in forming a rudimentary sound code would have affected the vocal apparatus, and this, in turn, would have helped enlarge the speech centers of the brain, and so on until, by the time of *Homo erectus,* the rudiments of language might have appeared. Then the first humans were ready to begin combining a few separate sounds, or words, representing specific elements of terrain, the hunt, the family, and seasonal changes, into simple combinations that conveyed a great deal of information.

### Lieberman and Crelin: The Vocal Apparatus

What this first human speech sounded like depends on how far the dual development of vocal apparatus and cortical brain equipment had progressed. Recent investigations have given a clue to the state of that development. Linguist Philip Lieberman's analysis of the character of modern speech emphasizes the importance of the human vocal equipment. He points out that the pharynx is essential for producing the vowel sounds *a* ("ah"), *i* ("ee"), and *u* ("oo"), which are crucial to all modern languages, from English to Kirghiz. Virtually all meaningful segments of human speech contain one or more of these sounds. Combining these vowel sounds with a wide assortment of consonants, the human vocal apparatus not only can produce an infinite number of variations but also, and more important, can connect them with great rapidity in the coded series of sounds that is language.

The key to this process is the putting together of separate phonetic segments into a sound that can be understood as one word. A person saying "bat," for instance, does not articulate the fragments of sound represented by the letters *b*, *a*, and *t*, but combines these elements into one syllable. This ability to combine sounds gives the voice the ability to put together and transmit upward of thirty phonetic segments a second.

Had the pharynx developed enough in *Homo erectus* to produce the complex sounds characteristic of modern speech? Lieberman thinks not. He places *Homo erectus'* speech at a much cruder level, basing this opinion on a fascinating piece of detective work attempted with the aid of anatomist Edmund S. Crelin. He tried to estimate the position of the larynx in the throats of fossil humans: he believes that it was placed much higher than it is in modern humans. He then proceeded to reconstruct the pharyngeal, nasal, and oral cavities of early humans. Then Lieberman measured the reconstructed vocal tracts. He related these measurements to the dimensions of the vocal tract of modern humans and to the tract's sound-making capabilities; then he fed the figures into a computer programmed to calculate the resonances that corresponded to the range of shapes each vocal tract could have produced.

Lieberman and Crelin concluded that early humans would have had to communicate verbally much more slowly than modern people—perhaps even as slowly as one-tenth the speed we can maintain. Although their results have not been widely accepted, their technique is remarkable for its ingenuity. More recent research on the base of the skull by Jeffrey Laitman and E. S. Crelin indicates that the important developments in the vocal tract did not begin to evolve before the time of *Homo erectus* and were not fully completed in the Neandertal people.

**Krantz: The Brain of *Homo erectus***

Anthropologist Grover Krantz confronted a problem that has puzzled anthropologists for a long time: why did the quality of *Homo erectus'* stone tools remain static for so long? Over many thousands of years, no matter where found, they show little sign of improvement. Why did they not become sophisticated more quickly? Krantz poses an ingenious explanation that may shed light on the acquisition of language by the first humans. He suggests that *Homo erectus'* brain was not well enough developed to allow them to begin to speak as early in their lives as a child does today. Because *Homo erectus* were short-lived, they therefore had a shorter period in which to use language in order to acquire and augment the skills necessary for toolmaking.

Although this argument may have value, it is important to realize that brain size alone does not make speech possible. The complexity of brain structure and, above all, its internal organization are the primary factors in the evolution of language. At the same time, a great deal of learning can occur, including toolmaking, without language skills.

**Speech among the First Humans**

Even with the speech limitations that we might predict, *Homo erectus* still would have been able to communicate a great deal about themselves and the world around them. It is necessary only to listen to very young children to see how effective language can be, even in its simplest form. Between the ages of eighteen and twenty-four months, only half a year or so after children first speak, they begin to use two-word sentences. The sentences are neither copies of grown-up speech nor reductions of it, but the children's own inventions, conforming to what would seem to be native, universal rules of grammar. They are made up of so-called *open words*, words that can be said by themselves and still mean something, such as the nouns "blanket," "milk," and "baby"; and *pivot words*, often prepositions, adjectives, or verbs such as "on" and "hot." At this age, children put words together to describe the world or to get people to act ("pajama on"), but they are not used to express emotion.

Only when the children are three or four do they begin to put feelings into words. Before then they rely, as nonhuman primates must, on the workings of the limbic system to call attention to their needs. Rather than say "I'm angry," or "I'm afraid," they demonstrate physically how angry or afraid they are. They find temper tantrums, whimpering, or crying a much easier way to communicate; that is, they find emotions easier to act out than to explain. As any parent knows, children have little difficulty in making themselves understood. There is no reason to think that *Homo erectus*, speaking even the simplest of sentences reinforced by gestures and hand signals, could not have communicated just as well with their early version of human speech.

Whatever it sounded like, and at whatever age they began to use it, *Homo erectus'* language was a tool used in its own right—a tool to drive like a wedge into the environment, hurrying the split from nature that marked their development and foreshadowed ours. For the first time in human history, cultural evolution, because of speech, began to outpace biological evolution, as instinct and emotion were counterbalanced by symbol and custom.

**The Brain**

Possibly the most striking evidence for the evolution of language is the increase in size of the large hominid brain. Evidence for this increase is the expanding cranial capacity that we see in successive hominid fossil skulls. As we saw in Chapter 11, the cranial capacity trebled during the last 3 million years; certainly a very rapid rate of evolution. But to see this figure in perspective, we need to relate it to body size, for a simple increase in body size itself (accompanied by an appropriate increase in brain size) can occur rapidly in evolution and is not an unusual occurrence. To relate brain size to body size, we need to calculate how large a brain a typical ape would have if it were to have a body with the same size as ours. The answer reveals that the present human brain is 3.1 times larger than we would expect for a primate of our build. It appears then that the brain's trebling in size occurred in spite of the slight increase in our body size. This is perhaps the most significant anatomical fact about the species *Homo sapiens*.

This characteristic is perhaps even more striking when we remember that the monkeys and apes have the biggest brains in relation to body weight of any land animal. California psychiatrist Harry Jerison has introduced the *Encephalization Quotient* (EQ) to compare relative brain sizes. The EQ is calculated by relating the brain size of each species to the size expected for an average mammal of the same body weight. By definition, an average mammal has an EQ of 1.0. If the relative brain size is smaller than average, then the EQ will have a value of less than 1.0; if the relative brain size is larger than average, then the EQ will range above 1.0. Figure 13–9 summarizes very briefly his results. Insectivores and rodents are in one group, with EQs generally below 1.0. Ungulates (hoofed mammals), carnivores, and prosimians make a second group, with EQs slightly over 1.0. Monkeys and apes are quite distinct from these other groups, with EQs ranging between 1.0 and 5.0. Humans have an EQ of nearly 8.0. Here again we see that humans are absolutely distinctive in the size of their brains.

If we relate brain weight to body weight and generate a simple ratio, we get further remarkable results (Table 13–1). Here, surprisingly, humans do not come at the top of the list; the highest positions are occupied by two small New World monkeys. It was in fact these monkeys which occupied the top section of the monkey and ape histogram in Figure 13–9. This anomalous state of affairs can be understood as a product of a higher primate with relatively small body size, for another fact of brain development is that small animals in any particular order have relatively larger brains than large species. For the same reason, large animals (within any particular order) have relatively smaller brains. Thus, as Table 13–1 shows, the elephant and whale, which have the largest brains of any animals (of about 4,000 cc and 6,000 cc respectively), have relatively small brains within their respective orders. The most anomalous figure in Table 13–1 is that for the porpoise. Although good data on the brain and body sizes of porpoises are very limited, it does appear that this group of marine animals have exceptionally large brains, and this ratio is particularly striking in the smaller species. The dolphin brain is famed not only for its size but for the extent of its convolutions, which imply a relatively immense neocortex. The expla-

FIGURE 13–9  *Encephalization Quotient (EQ) is shown here for seven groups of mammals. In each group the mean is shown by the dot and the range by the vertical line. The upper range for higher primates is generated by certain small and distinctive New World monkeys.*

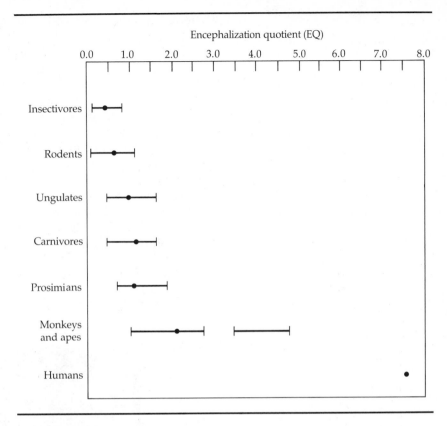

TABLE 13–1  **Ratio of Weight of Brain to Weight of Body in Certain Mammals**

| MAMMALS | BRAIN-BODY RATIO |
|---|---|
| New World, squirrel monkey | 1:12 |
| New World, tamarin, a marmoset | 1:19 |
| Porpoise (dolphin) | 1:38 |
| Higher primates | |
|    Humankind | 1:45 |
|    *Australopithecus afarensis* (estimated) | 1:100 |
|    Old World monkey (*Macaca*) | 1:170 |
|    Gorilla | 1:200 |
| Elephant | 1:600 |
| Sperm whale | 1:10,000 |

nation for this remarkable-looking brain is still one of the great mysteries of modern biology.

If primate brains are relatively large, we may then ask if the proportions of the different parts separate them from other orders of mammals. We have seen (Figure 13–7) that the development of the neocortex is distinctive of mammals and especially of primates, a characteristic that becomes clear in dissection and measurement. The jackal, a large-brained carnivore, has a brain of about 64 grams, the same size as that of the macaque monkey. In the jackal the cerebral hemispheres form 60 percent of the brain, but in the monkey they constitute 78 percent of the brain.

With the order Primates, however, the story is different. It has been claimed that the human brain is preeminent in the development of the neocortex and especially the prefrontal and association areas. According to British psychologist Richard Passingham, however, the evidence for these claims is still flimsy and they cannot be substantiated at present. He demonstrates convincingly, though, that in the relative proportions

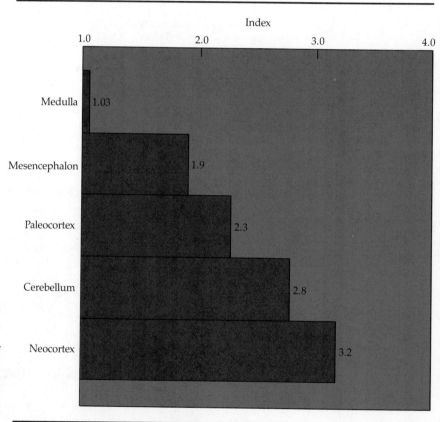

FIGURE 13–10  *Indices comparing the size of parts of the human brain with values predicted for a primate of the same body weight. The index is the actual value of the weight of the part in humans divided by the predicted value. Notice that not only the neocortex but other parts, particularly the cerebellum, show considerable development. The parts are labelled in Figure 13–12.*

of the main subdivisions of the brain, including the neocortex, the human brain does indeed differ from those which might be expected in monkeys and apes of similar body weight (Figure 13–10). He points out, however, that this difference is in fact predictable from higher primate data, and that if the brain proportions are related to brain size and not body size, they can be predicted in a brain of human size (Figure 13–11). We have known for some time that the functional areas of the brains of apes and humans were comparable (Figure 13–12); now we can conclude from evidence presently available that the human brain is indeed a standard higher primate brain that has simply been increased in size by a factor of 3.1. No new structures appear to have been introduced at this gross level of measurement.

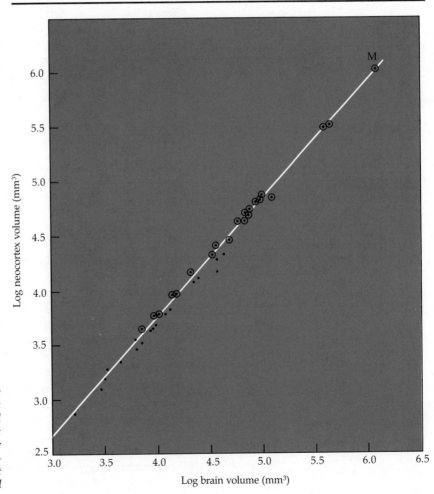

FIGURE 13–11 *When we plot the volume of the neocortex (in cubic millimeters) as a function of the volume of the brain, we find that the relationship is the same throughout the primates. The slope of the line is steeper than 45 degrees because the neocortex is relatively larger in larger brains by a constant proportion: · prosimians; ⊙ monkeys and apes; M humans.*

*FIGURE 13–12   Comparison of ape and human brains shows that the human brain is not only bigger but more deeply folded. The form of the brain of* Homo erectus *can be guessed at only by the shape and size of the endocranial cast; it was clearly human.*

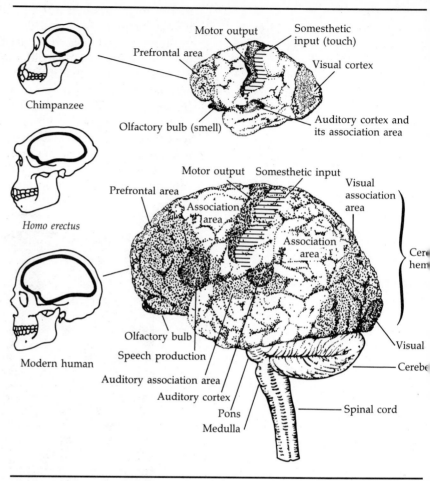

When we come to consider the more detailed structure of the neo-cortex, of the neurons, and of their interconnecting pathways, we may be forgiven for expecting something distinctively human. Ralph Holloway of Columbia University summarizes the evidence that human brains have larger and more complex neurons (the individual brain cells) and many more interconnections among them than other primate brains. He shows too that the brain cells are less densely packed than in other primates. It appears, however, that one rule governs the density of brain cells in all mammals, varying in size from elephant to mouse. The human brain, surprisingly, obeys that rule. In fact, the human brain has the same number of neurons in a radial section of the cortex as any other mammal, for although the cells are less dense, the cortex is thicker. Thus, in both its microscopic and macroscopic structure, the human brain is a standard, though large, primate brain.

We can therefore conclude that the unique human potential has been made possible by our large brain. Expansion of a standard primate brain has provided us with behavioral possibilities undreamed of in other, even closely related, species. This brain, absolutely as well as relatively large, with its absolutely large number of neurons (about $10^9$) and its unbelievably large number of dendritic interconnections (about $10^{12}$) gives us the human potential for making tools, talking, planning, dreaming of the future, and creating an entirely new environment for ourselves. The primate laws of relative brain growth have been followed in all respects, both macroscopically and microscopically, except in one factor: the brain–body ratio. That factor of 3.1 has lifted humans far above their animal cousins into a new order of organic life.

The size of the brain, therefore, crudely measured in cubic centimeters, tells us something very profound about human nature. Our brain is not so much different from other brains, it is bigger. We are not a whole new experiment in the evolutionary process, but a superprimate. A quantitative change in the evolving human brain, however, has produced a qualitative change of extraordinary significance.

**HOLOCENE**

10,000

| | AGE | MODERN HUMAN |
|---|---|---|
| Terra Amata | Birth to 6 weeks | Tongue immobile during cries and larynx high in throat |
| Peking fossils | 6 weeks to 3 months | Base of tongue and larynx have begun to descend in the throat |
| | | Babbling |
| Hearths at Escale | 1 to 1½ years | Cranial capacity of about 750 cc |
| Günz glaciation | | Begins speaking |
| Java fossils | | |
| **PLEISTOCENE** | 1½ to 2 years | Uses two-word sentences |
| *A. robustus* and | 3 to 4 years | Begins to express feelings in words |
| boisei extinct | Adult | Cranial capacity of 1,000 to 2,000 cc |
| Earliest Acheulian tools | | Larynx low in the throat, enlarging the pharyngeal region |
| | | Through speech, normally able to convey thought at least ten times faster than would be possible by any other form of signaling |

1 million —

*H. habilis* at Olduvai

2 million —

| | AGE | *HOMO ERECTUS* (c. 1.0–0.5 million B.P.) |
|---|---|---|
| | 6 years | Cranial capacity reaches about 750 cc |
| Earliest Oldowan tools | Adult | Cranial capacity ranging from about 775 to 1,225 cc |
| | | Larynx probably higher in the throat than it is in modern humans and pharyngeal region therefore smaller |
| | | Probably communicated more slowly than modern humans do |

3 million —

| | AGE | *AUSTRALOPITHECUS* (c. 4 million B.P.) |
|---|---|---|
| **PLIOCENE** | 6 years | Cranial capacity about 350 cc |
| | | Probably almost entirely dependent on nonverbal communication |
| | Adult | Cranial capacity ranging from 380 to 530 cc. |
| | | Limbic communication paramount but first voluntary sounds of cortical origin probably appearing in certain populations |

4 million —

5 million — Early *Australopithecus*

EVOLUTION OF LANGUAGE

Statements about the evolution of language are necessarily merely informed guesses, but they are based on a wide range of evidence.

# PART IV

# MODERN HUMANITY

# Chapter 14

# Discovery of Neandertals and Their Contemporaries

The savage . . . breathes only peace and liberty; he desires only to live and be free from labour.

> JEAN JACQUES ROUSSEAU, 1712–1778.
> *A Discourse on the Origin of Inequality.*

And the life of man, solitary, poore, nasty, brutish, and short.

> THOMAS HOBBES, 1588–1679.
> *Leviathan*, Pt. 1., Ch. 13.

**FIRST VIEWS OF NEANDERTAL**

Of all the kinds of prehistoric peoples, certainly those who project the clearest image are the Neandertals. For many they are *the* Stone Age humans, shambling, beetle-browed louts who prowled the earth during the time of the glaciers. The Neandertals got such a poor reputation among the general public because they were grievously misjudged by the experts. Until recently, many paleoanthropologists regarded Neandertals as a brutish breed that at best represented an insignificant side branch of the human family tree. Only now is this misjudgment being remedied: much new evidence demonstrates that some, if not all, Neandertals may have been our immediate ancestors. From 100,000 years ago to about 40,000 years ago they and their contemporaries greatly expanded the regions occupied by humans, devised ingenious stone tools to exploit nature, developed a complicated society, and opened the door to the world of the supernatural. Clearly, they were people of great accomplishments.

Why did the experts misjudge the Neandertals? Many reasons could be given—the scarcity of fossils, errors in reconstructing bone fragments, and other technical difficulties. But perhaps more important, these problems were compounded by an accident of timing. To tell the story of the Neandertals, we have to return again to the previous cen-

355

tury—to a time even before publication of Darwin's *On the Origin o Species*, when almost no one believed that humankind had ever had primitive ancestor.

The first fossil skull ever to be positively identified as belonging to an ancient human was that of a Neandertal. No one was prepared fo the sight of a primitive-looking skeleton in the human closet, and wher such a skeleton was found in 1856, it brought on a crippling case o ancestor-blindness. Having nothing with which to compare the firs Neandertal skull except the skull of a modern human, scientists of the time were struck more by the differences between the two than by thei similarities. Today the reverse is true. Compared to their predecessors *Homo erectus*, Neandertals showed considerable evolutionary advance ment. They might have been a little shorter than the average moder Westerner, and considerably heavier-featured, squatter, and more mus cular than most, but they were well on their way toward modernity.

**First Discovery (1856)**     The first Neandertal to be recognized as a primitive human wa discovered in 1856, not far from the city of Düsseldorf, Germany, wher a tributary stream of the Rhine flows through a steep-sided gorg known as the Neander Valley, "Neanderthal" in Old German (see Fig ure 14–6). In 1856 the flanks of the gorge were being quarried fo limestone. During the summer, workmen blasted open a small cav about sixty feet above the stream. As they dug their pickaxes into th floor of the cave, they uncovered a number of ancient bones. But th quarriers were intent on limestone; they did not pay much attention t the bones, and most of what was probably a complete skeleton of Neandertal was lost. Only the skullcap, ribs, part of the pelvis, an some limb bones were saved.

The owner of the quarry thought these fragments belonged to a bea and he presented them to the local science teacher, J. K. Fuhlrott, wh was known to be interested in such things. Fuhlrott had enough knowl edge of anatomy to realize that the skeletal remains came not from bear but from a most extraordinary human with thick limb bones an a heavy, slanted brow. The bones seemed very ancient to him. T account for the apparent antiquity and odd location of the relics, h concluded that they belonged to some poor mortal who had bee washed into the cave by Noah's flood.

Knowing that this judgment was bound to be disputed, Fuhlro called in an expert, Hermann Schaffhausen, professor of anatomy a the University of Bonn. Schaffhausen agreed that the bones repre sented one of the "most ancient races of man." He had in mind an ag of no more than a few thousand years; the fossil fragments could hav come, he suggested, from some barbarian who had lived in norther Europe before the Celtic and Germanic tribes arrived.

**Missing Links in
the Chain of Being**

Schaffhausen can hardly be criticized for missing the truth about the bones from the Neander Valley: the scientific community of 1856 did not realize that humankind had been on earth for a substantial length of time. And no respectable scientist believed that humans had ever existed in any form other than that of the modern human. Such a notion would have been directly contrary to the belief in *Genesis* and in what was known as the Chain of Being, a grandly conceived hierarchy of all living things. In it, every creature had a rank: starting with the lowliest worm, the hierarchy progressed steadily upward through ever more advanced species and finally reached the pinnacle of nature, humans themselves. Creatures positioned close to each other on this chain naturally showed some similarities; even at this time, people admitted that they resembled apes in their outward form. But similarity between types of creatures did not mean that there was any genealogical connection. The separate links of the Chain of Being were thought to have been fixed forever at the Creation; species never changed and certainly never evolved from the lowlier forms.

As we have seen (Chapter 1) this orderly scheme still held in 1856, but it was being shaken both by changing ideas about the age of the earth and primarily by the appearance of animal bones unlike those of any living creature, suggesting to some dissenting thinkers that the Chain of Being did not tell the full story of life. Extinct animals were not the only threat to the established scheme. Records exist of a few primitive-looking human fossils that were found as early as the year 1700, and many finds probably went unrecorded before (and after) that. Remains that are now also known to be Neandertal had been uncovered in Belgium in 1829 and on the north face of Gibraltar in 1848. Unlike the bones from the Neander Valley, however, these finds received no publicity, and science was not forced to grapple with their significance. But when Darwin's *On the Origin of Species* was published in 1859, the tidy scheme of the Chain of Being began to collapse, and the way was open for recognition of fossilized human ancestors of not completely human form.

*Homo neanderthalensis?*

Experts familiar with human skeletons and skull structure could see some very peculiar things about this Neandertal skull (see Figure 14–1). It was clearly humanlike, yet it had strongly developed eyebrow ridges and a retreating forehead, and was much flatter on top and more bulging in the back than the skull of any modern human. At the time, it was easier to regard the skull as a deformed specimen of a modern human skull than to accept the possibility that human ancestors actually looked like that. That opinion of the skull—that its owner has been a not very ancient pathological idiot—prevailed for many years.

Darwin heard about these remarkable bones but never investigated

FIGURE 14–1   *The skullcap from the Neandertal is the most famous fossil discovery ever made. Following its discovery in 1856, it was thought by many to be the skull of some pathological idiot. Today we know that it belonged to an early, but by no means primitive, member of our own species,* Homo sapiens. *(This photograph is approximately one-half actual size.)*

them. But his friend and supporter Thomas H. Huxley undertook a thorough study of the unprecedented skull. In the condition in which it was discovered, the cranium could hold sixty-three cubic inches (1030 cc) of water; complete, it would have contained seventy-five cubic inches (1230 cc), which is not far from the average cranial volume of many modern people. Therefore the brain must have been of modern size, too; and the limb bones, though on the bulky side, Huxley found to be "quite those of an European of middle stature."

"Under whatever aspect we view this cranium," wrote Huxley in 1863, "we meet with ape-like characteristics, stamping it as the most pithecoid [apelike] of human crania yet discovered." In view of the large cranial capacity, however, Huxley did not see Neandertal as an ancestral form. He wrote: "In no sense can the Neandertal bones be regarded as the remains of a human being intermediate between men and apes." Although they were more nearly allied to the higher apes than the latter are to the monkeys, he concluded that they were nonetheless human. "In still older strata," Huxley wondered, "do the fossilized bones of an Ape more anthropoid, or a Man more pithecoid, than any yet known await the researches of some unborn palaeontologist?"

Meanwhile, a second skull had been brought to England from the Natural History Society collections in Gibraltar, where it had been discovered in a cave in 1848. When it was exhibited at the meetings of the British Association for the Advancement of Science in 1864, it was seen quite clearly to be a second example of a human with the hitherto unique but recognizable shape of the Neandertal skull.

Only William King, professor of anatomy at Queen's College in

Galway, Ireland, accepted the German fossil as an extinct form of humanity. In 1864 King suggested that the specimen be placed in a separate species, *Homo neanderthalensis*. In giving the fossil the genus name *Homo*, King was acknowledging a general similarity to humankind; but he felt that he could not add the species name for modern humans, *sapiens*, because, as he wrote, "The Neanderthal skull is so eminently simian . . . I am constrained to believe that the thoughts and desires which once dwelt within it never soared beyond those of the brute."

King's assessment was closer to being correct than anyone else's, but he changed his thinking when he heard what the German anatomist Rudolf Virchow had to say. In a closely reasoned paper, Virchow stated that the man from the Neander Valley was not ancient at all, but a modern man who suffered from rickets in childhood and arthritis in old age; and, at some time during his life, he had received several stupendous blows on the head. This pronouncement, coming from a highly respected source, effectively silenced all further speculation.

How could authorities such as Rudolf Virchow conclude that the Neandertal bones were modern? The incompleteness of the fossil was one factor: because the skull lacked a face and a jaw, it was hard to tell what the original owner had looked like. Also, no one could say for certain that the Neandertal bones were really old, for no stone tools or bones of extinct animals had accompanied the fossil, and no reliable methods of dating existed. Without proof of great age, it was thought best to err on the side of caution and presume a date not too remote from the present. It would not be fair to indict the cautious scientists of the day for inclining toward the safest position. Those who accepted the theories of Darwin were open-minded by any standard. It took a large measure of intellectual courage to surrender the accepted wisdom of centuries for Darwin's brave new world of evolution.

The Darwinians, to their great credit, were actively interested in discovering a primitive human ancestor from the moment *On the Origin of Species* appeared. But they had no way of knowing where to look. Huxley, a bold and brilliant man, believed that there was little hope of finding fossils that would reveal human evolutionary history. Some of the evolutionists did not even think that it was necessary to peer into the past. They believed that the present offered examples of humans who were intermediate between the evolutionists themselves and some primitive ancestral form. One presumed authority pointed to mental institutions: "I do not hesitate to uphold . . . that microcephali and born idiots present as perfect a series from man to ape as may be wished for." Although such surmises received only slight approval, they do suggest one reason for failure to understand the evolutionary significance of Neandertal. Scientists evidently did not expect evolutionary intermediates to turn up in a cave, and so they never really gave the evidence a fair chance.

As soon as Virchow had announced that the odd appearance of the bones from the Neander Valley was the result of disease rather than antiquity, the fossil ceased to disturb anatomists. They simply forgot about it. Prehistorians, however, were still very interested in finding an ancient fossil ancestor of *Homo sapiens*—as long as the fossil looked like a modern human; anything that resembled an animal ancestor, an ape or monkey, was rejected automatically.

## Discoveries at Spy (1886)

*FIGURE 14–2 The skull of Spy I, though incomplete, shows clearly the long head and brow ridges typical of Neandertals. (This photograph is approximately one-fourth actual size.)*

In 1886, additional primitive-looking fossils appeared. A cave near a town called Spy in Belgium (see Figure 14–6) yielded two skeletons. One skull, probably from a female, was reminiscent of the original fossil from the Neander Valley, although the cranium was higher and the forehead somewhat less slanted. The other skull was virtually identical to the German find (see Figure 14–2). Coincidence? Yes, said Rudolf Virchow, dismissing the Spy skeletons as further diseased specimens of modern humans. But this explanation began to sound hollow. Not only was such a coincidence of pathological deformity most unlikely, but these fossils were definitely very old—along with them were found primitive stone tools and remains of extinct animals. Most scientists were obliged to admit that an archaic people, distinct from modern humans, had indeed lived in Europe during some bygone era.

The fossil skeletons found at Spy lacked some parts, but they were complete enough to serve as models for a rough sketch of the Neandertal race. These people were short and thickset. Their heads were long and low, with large brow ridges. Their faces were massive and protruding, with a heavy jaw but a receding chin. Could these have been our ancestors? Nearly all scientists said no. They were willing to give Neandertal a place on the human family tree but not on any branch shared by modern humanity. Some authorities felt that the Neandertals might represent an offshoot from the main evolutionary line; if they were related to humans at all, they were poor and distant relatives.

By this time the initial shocked reaction to Darwin's theory of evolution was over, and the disturbing idea that humans had been around for tens or hundreds of thousands of years was becoming accepted. The fossils from Spy indicated that the Neandertals were ancient peoples, not modern ones deformed by disease. And Dubois' discovery of small-brained *Pithecanthropus* (Chapter 10) helped put the Neandertals in perspective. Although most experts were not yet willing to trace our lineage through a Neandertal stage of evolution, their belief that humankind could never have looked so primitive as Neandertal was now recognized as perhaps a subjective feeling, and thus open to debate. At this time, when the riddle of human ancestry was already confusing, new evidence appeared that complicated the problem further.

## La Chapelle-aux-Saints (1908) and Other Finds

In the first decade of the twentieth century, archaeologists were at work in the Dordogne region of southwestern France (see Figure 14–6). From the 1860s on, countless stone tools had been found in southwestern France, proof that the Dordogne had been a population center in ancient times. Beginning in 1908 a magnificent series of Neandertal fossils was also discovered. One of the first to turn up was the skeleton of an old man in a cave near the village of La Chapelle-aux-Saints (Figure 14–3). A nearby cave at Le Moustier, from which quantities of stone implements had been excavated earlier, yielded the skeleton of a Neandertal youth. A rock shelter at La Ferrassie produced adult male and female Neandertals and later the remains of several children (see Figure 14–4). Another rock shelter at La Quina held parts of several Neandertal skeletons.

The great value of this material was its completeness. The bones from Spy had given a rough portrait of the Neandertal people, but as long as the fossil record remained essentially fragmentary, venturesome scholars could leap to extremes and see them as either *Homo sapiens* or gorilloid. The wealth of skeletal material from southwestern France now seemed to promise enough data to set the vividest anthropological imagination to rest. Now scientists would be able to reconstruct what a Neandertal looked like and study the physical resemblances—or lack of them—between Neandertals and modern humans.

*FIGURE 14–3   The skull of the old man of La Chapelle-aux-Saints shows he lost many teeth during life. He was less than five feet tall, bent by arthritis, but he had a large cranial capacity of about 1,600 cc (the average modern human capacity is 1,330 cc). (This photograph is approximately one-third actual size.)*

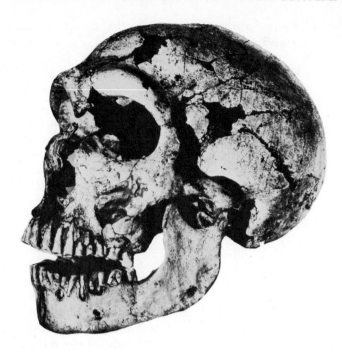

*FIGURE 14–4  The male skeleton from La Ferrassie, buried with five others, had an even larger cranial capacity than La Chapelle—1,640 cc. His front teeth show a rare type of extreme wear that is found today among some Eskimo tribes and other hunting people. It may have been caused by chewing animal skins to soften them for clothing. (This photograph is approximately one-third actual size.)*

## Boule's Reconstruction (1911–1913)

The man from La Chapelle-aux-Saints was selected for a detailed reconstruction of what was thought to be a typical Neandertal. The task of rebuilding the skeleton fell to a French paleontologist named Marcellin Boule, of the French National Museum of Natural History. On this project, Boule had an unusually fine set of bones to work with. The materials were well preserved, and although some of the bones were broken, almost everything of importance was available except some teeth and vertebrae. Despite the completeness and good condition of the bones, Boule proceeded to commit an astonishing series of errors— and they were not corrected for decades. Boule misconstructed the bones to make the skeleton appear almost apelike from head to toe (see Figure 14–5). He mistakenly arranged the foot bones so that the big toe diverged from the other toes like an opposable thumb, which implied that Neandertals walked on the outer part of their feet, like apes. Boule's interpretation of the knee joint was equally incorrect: he declared that Neandertals could not fully extend their legs, which resulted in the bent-knee gait that observers could readily see the skeleton would adopt if it could walk. In every respect, the posture of Boule's reconstruction seemed nonhuman. Unfortunately, photographs of Boule's reconstruction appeared in many textbooks during the first half of this century.

The most devastating conclusion of Boule's study was on the intelligence of the man from La Chapelle-aux-Saints. Boule ignored the fossil's large cranial capacity. He looked only at the long, low skull— and perceived severe mental retardation. He cited the interior of the skull as support for this judgment; measuring the space behind the retreating forehead, the paleontologist determined to his satisfaction that there was not much room for the frontal portion of the brain, which was then thought (incorrectly) to be the center of higher intelligence. And so Boule ranked the fossil man's brainpower somewhere between that of apes and modern humans, but closer to the apes.

Boule wrote disparagingly of the "brutish appearance of this muscular and clumsy body, and of the heavy-jawed skull that declares the predominance of a purely vegetative or bestial kind over the functions of the mind. . . . What a contrast with the men of the next period, the men who had a more elegant body, a finer head, an upright and spacious brow, and who were the first to merit the glorious title of *Homo sapiens!*" Boule was willing to grant the Neandertals the honor of the genus *Homo*, but he relegated them to a separate, aberrant species that had died out long ago.

Marcellin Boule was a man of excellent reputation and formidable diligence, virtues that made his errors all the more serious. Between 1911 and 1913, he published his conclusions in three exhaustive volumes. Packed with detail and ringing with confidence, these monographs had tremendous influence on scientists and the public alike. Although a few prehistorians stuck to their view that Neandertals were respectable ancestors of modern humans, practically everyone now felt that such a lineage had been proved impossible.

The sheer force of Boule's work was not the only reason for its acceptance. Some circumstantial evidence pointed toward an evolutionary gap between the Neandertals and the later Cro-Magnons, those elegant "men of the next period" to whom Boule refers, who by this time were acknowledged to be the immediate ancestors of present-day humans. (The Cro-Magnons are discussed in Chapters 16 and 17.) Even if the Neandertals were not quite as debased as Boule supposed, they definitely looked different from the Cro-Magnons, and no one had come across a fossil that indicated an evolutionary transition between the two. Without an intermediate fossil, it was only prudent to assume that the Cro-Magnons derived from stock that had been occupying Europe or some other part of the world during or possibly before the era of the Neandertals, thus granting the Neandertals no significance in human evolution.

Archaeologists believed that there was no cultural connection between Neandertal and Cro-Magnon peoples. The stone tools of the Cro-Magnons seemed markedly more sophisticated than Neandertal implements. And when archaeologists dug down through successive layers in caves, they sometimes found sterile layers between the Neandertal deposits and the deposits left by Cro-Magnons, indicating that no one had occupied the cave for a time. These layers containing no sign of human occupation were interpreted as proof that the Neandertals had become extinct without having given rise to the Cro-Magnons.

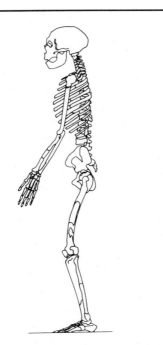

FIGURE 14–5 *Marcellin Boule overlooked the effects of arthritis when he reconstructed the skeleton from La Chapelle-aux-Saints and so implied that all Neandertal people walked with stooping gait and bent knees. The reconstructed skeleton was five feet and one inch tall.*

During the following decades very little was said in support of the European Neandertals as human ancestors. Boule's analysis not only won almost universal acceptance but also inspired some views even less flattering than his own. The noted anatomist Elliot Smith wrote in the 1920s of the "uncouth and repellent Neandertal man" whose "nose is not sharply separated from the face, the two being merged in what in another animal would be called a snout." Smith further commented that Neandertals were not only marred by a "coarse face" and a "peculiarly ungraceful form" but probably had "a shaggy covering of hair over most of the body." Despite the clearly human formation of the Neandertal hand, Smith claimed that it "lacked the delicacy and nicely balanced cooperation of thumb and fingers which is regarded as one of the most distinctive human characteristics."

## DISCOVERY OF ARCHAIC *HOMO SAPIENS* BEYOND EUROPE

Boule had depicted Neandertals as creatures that might have had a hard time surviving, much less thriving, in the world. But if territorial range is any measure of success, these "uncouth and repellent" people seem to have done quite well. As the years passed, Neandertal fossils were found all over Europe, from Rumania and the Crimea in the east to the western lands of Spain and the Channel island of Jersey (see Figure 14–6). Still, as long as there was no evidence of them outside Europe, they could be written off as a localized evolutionary aberration. Prehistorians could safely claim that the main line of human evolution belonged elsewhere, in a still-unlocated Eden. (This problem-dodging tactic has been called the "over-there" school of prehistory.)

### Broken Hill Fossils

In 1921 some laborers mining lead and zinc ore in Zambia (previously Northern Rhodesia), thousands of miles from Europe, uncovered a skull and other human bones that somewhat resembled Neandertals. The fossil fragments came from a cave in a knoll called Broken Hill (see Figure 14–7), which rose above plateau country just north of the Zambesi River, at a place called Kabwe. The presence of stone tools and extinct animal bones indicated considerable age.

This fossil human from Broken Hill had a heavy skull and receding forehead like the European Neandertals. The heavy bar of bone over the eyes was even more pronounced than any yet seen. But there was also a progressive trait: the limb bones were straighter and slenderer than those of the European Neandertals.

The newly discovered fossil (Figure 14–8) was called "Rhodesian Man." Where did it fit into human evolution? Some scholars, echoing Virchow, proclaimed that the Rhodesian was a modern-day mortal deformed by disease. A British expert entrusted with the job of describing the bones for his fellow scientists went to the opposite extreme. Following Boule's example, he declared that the formation of the pelvis "leaves no doubt that the gait of Rhodesian Man was simian, and that he walked

FIGURE 14–6  *The earliest Neandertal discoveries were made in Western Europe, especially in southwestern France. During the Würm ice age, when Neandertals flourished, sea level was lower than today (see shading), and vast areas of fertile grassland and woodland were added to the present lands that border the Atlantic Ocean. This map also shows the sites of early H. sapiens fossils discussed in this chapter. Only the sites of some fossils mentioned in the text are indicated.*

with a stoop." He considered the creature "nearer to the Chimpanzee and Gorilla than was Neandertal Man."

**Asian Fossils**  Many scientists, however, believed that Rhodesian Man was an African version of the Neandertal type. They began to wonder if some members of the breed had lived in Asia. A positive answer was soon forthcoming. During 1931 and 1932, fragments of eleven individuals were dug from the banks of the Solo River at Ngandong (see Figure 14–7) in Java. The fossils, collectively named "Solo man," consisted of several skulls that were almost perfect but lacked their bases and faces, and other bones that were badly shattered. There were enough fragments to suggest a kinship with the Neandertals, although the thickness and low dome of the skulls suggested an even earlier evolutionary level and a close genetic link with *Homo erectus*.

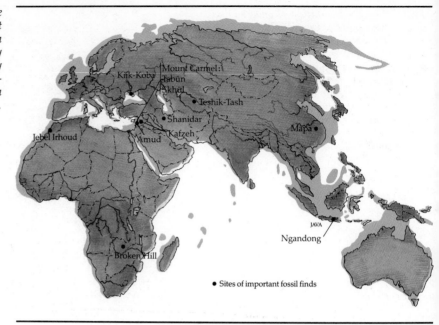

*FIGURE 14–7   During the first half of the twentieth century, people related to the west European Neandertals were discovered in many sites outside Europe. Although they show some variation in skull shape, they bear many characteristics that unite them genetically. As in Figure 14–6, the lowered sea level is indicated by shading.*

The gap between Java and Europe was filled in 1938 by a find in the desolate Bajsun-Tau Mountains of south-central Russia, about seventy-eight miles south of Samarkand (see Figure 14–7). A cave in a cliff called Teshik-Tash (the Pitted Rock) yielded the fossilized remains of a boy with clear similarities to the Neandertals of Europe.

## Discoveries from Israel

During the early 1930s a joint Anglo-American expedition was looking for fossils in what is now Israel, then called Palestine. The expedition had extraordinary good luck in two caves on the slopes of Mount Carmel, overlooking the Mediterranean near Haifa (see Figure 14–7). The first find, at Mugharet et-Tabūn (Cave of the Oven), was a female skeleton, definitely Neandertal-like but possessing a skull slightly higher-domed than usual and with a more vertical forehead (see Figure 14–9). A second Mount Carmel site, Mugharet es-Skhūl (Cave of the Kids), yielded remains of ten individuals. Some resembled Neandertals in a few features: others looked more advanced, and one approached the appearance of modern humans. This last individual displayed only a trace of the Neandertal brow ridge, but the forehead was steeper, the jaw more delicate, the chin more pronounced, and the shape of the cranium distinctly modern. Today we have further important discoveries from Israel: a rather Neandertal-looking skeleton from Amud (north of the Sea of Galilee) and another thirteen of the more modern-looking skeletons from Kafzeh (south of Nazareth). The variation exhibited is striking. The sites from this region appear to span a period from about 70,000 B.P. to 40,000 B.P.

*FIGURE 14–8   People somewhat similar to the European Neandertal tribes flourished during the same period in Africa. This skull from Broken Hill, in Zambia, is exceptionally powerfully built. The hole in the temporal bone (arrow) was probably caused during life by a small tumor. (This photograph is approximately one-fourth actual size.)*

The total impression left by these people is that they occupied an evolutionary middle ground between the Neandertals and modern humans. But the assumption that all Neandertals belonged to a dead-end species was, by the 1930s, so deeply entrenched that most experts could not believe that the Mount Carmel specimens might be direct ancestors of people living today. Some paleoanthropologists concluded that the fossil people from Palestine were hybrids—products of interbreeding between true Neandertals and true modern-type people who lived somewhere in the same area. The children of such a union could be expected to show a blend of primitive and modern traits. Those who favored this view were quick to maintain that such interbreeding may have been rare and need not have affected the main course of human evolution; Louis Leakey even suggested that any mating between Neandertals and people of modern type might well have produced sterile offspring, like a mule born of a horse and a donkey.

The most recent analysis of these cave sites suggests that the more Neandertal-like fossils such as the Tabūn woman and the Amud man are early while the Skhūl and Kafzeh people are late. Rather than a hybridization of two types, we may be seeing the evolution of a more primitive into a more modern form.

## SEARCH FOR THE ORIGIN OF MODERN HUMANS

All those who relegated Neandertals to a side branch of human evolution believed (and some still believe) that modern humans existed somewhere on earth during the Neandertal era. A few scientists suggested that *Homo sapiens* existed millions of years ago. Most authorities, however, dated the origin of humans like ourselves to 200,000 or 300,000 years ago. They believed that early "true humans" waited in the wings all through the heyday of the Neandertals, biding their time in an unknown land. Then, between 30,000 and 40,000 years ago, these true humans supposedly leaped into the evolutionary spotlight, either killing off the Neandertals or allowing them to succumb to their own ineptitude.

*FIGURE 14–9   On the left is the skull of the woman from the cave of et-Tabūn on the slopes of Mount Carmel, who shares many of the features of the Western European Neandertals. On the right is skull No. 5 from the neighboring cave of es-Skhūl. This male skull shows more modern features than the earlier one at et-Tabūn: the chin is more pronounced, the forehead steeper, and the brow ridges lighter. (Both photographs are approximately one-fourth actual size.)*

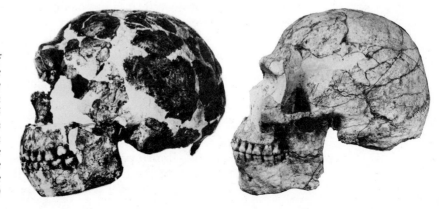

If modern humans existed so long ago, where were they hiding? Generations of scholars devoted their careers to a search for a very ancient but modern-looking ancestor. Marcellin Boule, for one, presented two fossils as proof of the great antiquity of modern humans. One, found in Italy, was called "Grimaldi man"; the other was Piltdown man, from England. But Boule's choices were poor. A recent analysis of the Grimaldi site has shown that the fossil is actually of rather recent vintage, postdating the Neandertals. The disproof of Piltdown was simpler—and, as we saw in Chapter 10, considerably more embarrassing to those who had believed that fossil was our ancestor.

## Swanscombe and Steinheim Skulls (1933–1936)

The fossil that came closest to proving the early origin of modern humans was a skull discovered in the mid-1930s in some gravel deposits in the Thames Valley, near the village of Swanscombe, England (see Figure 14–6). Detailed geological knowledge about that part of England and the animal fossils found above and below the skull in a number of ancient terraces along the river enabled scientists to assign the Swanscombe fossil an approximate date of 200,000 to 300,000 years B.P. The skull consists of only three bones: both parietals and the occipital. When first studied, these bones appeared to fall within the range of variation of modern *Homo sapiens*: their size, their proportions, and particularly their curves seemed much the same as a modern human's (Figure 14–10), and they definitely were not those of *Homo erectus* or Neandertal.

Inasmuch as science for many years regarded Neandertals as much more primitive than ourselves, the modern-looking yet ancient Swanscombe fragments were obviously a gift for those who saw all the Neandertal fossils as representing a separate branch of hominid evolution. A fascinating alternative solution begins to suggest itself if we now turn to another skull, which had been discovered at Steinheim, in Germany, in 1933. This, too, has been dated with great care, and its age appears to be approximately the same as the Swanscombe fossil's. The shape of the back of its head is also more or less similar. What the Steinheim fossil adds to the picture is a face, for the front of the skull has been preserved. It is not modern. It has quite heavy brow ridges and a low forehead that are neither quite primitive enough to fall within the range of variation of *Homo erectus* nor advanced enough to fall within the range of variation of modern *Homo sapiens*. Clearly it is an intermediate type. If the skulls were related, as they seemed to be, the Swanscombe fossil could be considered not a modern human but in fact a very early Neandertal.

## Evaluation of Swanscombe (1964)

The debate about Swanscombe wavered back and forth until 1964, when two British paleoanthropologists, the editor of this book and J. S. Weiner, for the first time enlisted the help of a computer to ascertain the status of a fossil skull. They took seventeen different measurements of

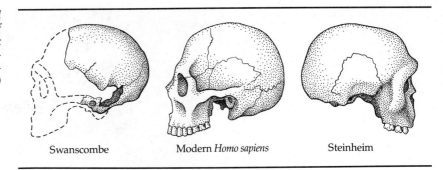

FIGURE 14–10 The Swanscombe and Steinheim skulls compared with the skull of a modern human being. The form of the back of the skull is quite comparable; the differences lie in the face. (This drawing is approximately one-fifth actual size.)

Swanscombe     Modern *Homo sapiens*     Steinheim

the Swanscombe and Steinheim skulls; then, for comparison, they measured various Neandertal skulls and a large population of modern skulls, to give some indication of the variability that can be expected in a natural population. The computer was programmed to work out "distance functions"—numerical statements of morphological resemblance. Its opinion was added to the debate: the Swanscombe fossil was no more modern than the Steinheim skull. Instead of being precociously sapient, both skulls were in many respects equally primitive and distinct from the large-brained Neandertals that followed them. Thus, what seemed to be evidence for the presence of a modern human far back in time was discounted again.

The examination by computer of the Swanscombe fossil is one of many helpful new approaches to prehistory. During the nineteenth century and much of the twentieth, scientists had the inevitable task of making sense out of a mere handful of fossils. Dates were uncertain or sometimes impossible even to guess at. A lack of information about human variability often caused experts to make too much of one trait or another from a single find. It is easy to go wrong about fossils—for example, exaggerating the significance of a curve at the back of a skull or incorrectly reconstructing features when parts are missing. Today these errors and inadequacies are being corrected. Statistical mathematics has reduced subjectivity in analyses of fossils and artifacts, just as the invention of various sorts of radiometric techniques has enabled archaeologists to establish ancient dates far more accurately than used to be possible. Anthropologists and archaeologists no doubt still make mistakes, but let us hope they are fewer than ever before, because more objective methods of analysis are available.

## Arago Discovery (1971)

In 1971 a new discovery was made of fossil humans from approximately the period of the Swanscombe and Steinheim fossils. Henry and Marie-Antoinette de Lumley excavated a cave at Arago near Tautavel in the Pyrenees (see Figure 14–6). Along with stone implements, the de Lumleys found the partial skull of a man about twenty years old (see Figure

FIGURE 14–11    *The skull from Arago is much more robust than those from Swanscombe and Steinheim. (This photograph is approximately two-thirds actual size.)*

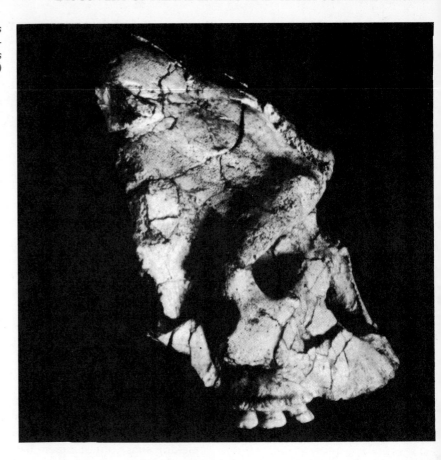

14–11) and two partial jaws of other individuals. The man had a forward-jutting face, heavy brow ridges, a slanting forehead, and a braincase somewhat smaller than the modern average. The two jaws were massive and somewhat resembled the Mauer jaw of much greater antiquity (p. 262); they seemed well suited to chewing coarse food. Altogether the fragments appear to be more archaic in form—that is, closer to *Homo erectus*—than Swanscombe and Steinheim.

A jaw fragment from another cave in the Pyrenees near the village of Montmaurin is of the same age (about 250,000 B.P.); it also fits this general type. A further fragmentary skull somewhat like the Arago specimens has been discovered at Bilzingsleben in East Germany, though it is possibly somewhat older. It is anatomically very close to *H. erectus*. Together these specimens give us an idea of hominids intermediate between *Homo erectus* and the later European Neandertals; some are morphologically close to *Homo erectus*, some closer to Neandertals.

## REASSESSMENT OF NEANDERTAL

Improvements in dating and evaluating techniques have proved particularly fruitful for the study of the later Neandertals of Europe. New fossils have now been identified in many parts of the world—China, southern and northern Africa, Iraq, Czechoslovakia, Hungary, Greece, and elsewhere—bringing the number of individuals of archaic *Homo sapiens* to more than three hundred. With the discovery of new and better evidence has come a drastic change in the appraisal of the European Neandertals and their contemporaries throughout the world.

The old prejudices began to evaporate in 1955, when several scientists suggested that Boule may have been in error in describing the posture of the Neandertal from La Chapelle-aux-Saints as slumped. Even children learning to walk, it was pointed out, or apes standing on their hind legs, have a fully upright trunk. The major turnabout came in 1957, when two anatomists, William Strauss and A. J. E. Cave, took a second, closer look at the fossil from La Chapelle-aux-Saints. The fossil was supposed to be typical. Strauss and Cave, however, detected a deformation of its bone joints indicating that this Neandertal had suffered from a severe case of arthritis, which affected the formation of the vertebrae and the jaw. Strauss and Cave spotted many other mistakes in Boule's reconstructions. The big toe was not opposable; the foot was definitely not a "prehensile organ," as Boule had said. The neck vertebrae did not resemble those of a chimpanzee, nor was the pelvis apelike in structure. All in all, Strauss and Cave found Neandertal to be quite modern in shape. They wrote: "If he could be reincarnated and placed in a New York subway—provided that he were bathed, shaved and dressed in modern clothing—it is doubtful whether he would attract any more attention than some of its other denizens." (see Figure 14–12).

By removing the taint of apishness that had been associated with Neandertals for so long, the Strauss-Cave study effectively revived Neandertals' candidacy as possible ancestors of modern humans. It is

*FIGURE 14–12  Homo erectus, early Homo sapiens, and Neandertal form a series of variable populations that succeeded each other in many parts of the Old World. Here they are represented by typical skulls. (This drawing is approximately one-fourth actual size.)*

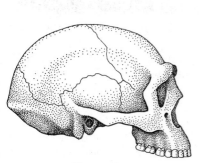

Homo erectus

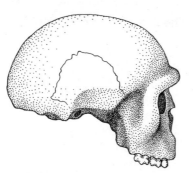

Early *Homo sapiens* (Steinheim)

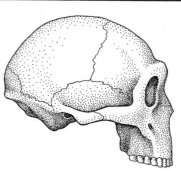

Late Neandertal

still true, of course, that the fossil from La Chapelle-aux-Saints does not look much like Cro-Magnon or most humans of today, and many paleoanthropologists continue to deny an ancestral relationship for the western European specimens. Some of the skeletons uncovered at Mount Carmel, however, definitely cannot be dismissed from the human lineage on the basis of looks. Some of these Middle Eastern fossils therefore establish a possible evolutionary link between the early *Homo sapiens* of Steinheim and modern human beings.

## Species and Speciation

Study has shown that the ranges of variation archaic *Homo sapiens* and modern humans overlap. Indeed, the more we learn about fossils of this period the greater the overlap appears to be. This similarity eventually forces a critical question: are they, and is Neandertal in particular really so different from modern *Homo sapiens* as to merit being considered another species? Fifty years ago anybody rash enough to raise such a question would have been laughed out of the room. Today, with the overthrow of prejudices of the sort Boule displayed and with the clarified status of the Swanscombe fossil, most paleoanthropologists agree that the Neandertals and their contemporaries were sufficiently human in mind and body to have been members of our species, *Homo sapiens*. On the end of this title is tacked the subspecies name *neanderthalensis* (or *rhodesiensis* or *soloensis*), denoting some difference from fully modern people. But *sapiens* places them all squarely in the human fold.

This placement does not mean that there are not differences between the subspecies; there are plenty. To understand and evaluate both the differences and similarities, though, it will be necessary to reconsider for a moment how speciation takes place and what makes a species.

The classic definition of a species is, as we have seen, one or more groups of individual organisms, the members of which interbreed with one another in nature or are enough alike in structure and behavior that, if they had access to one another, they could interbreed and produce fertile offspring. They are genetically isolated from other species. This concept recognizes that all breeding populations within species are not always in contact with one another. If geographic separation goes on for a long time, the different populations may become so changed through evolution that if they should come together again they might no longer interbreed. In this case it would be correct to say the original single species had split into two species.

This is an extremely simplified statement of a very complex and subtle process. For one thing, separation is often behavioral: if one animal acts in a way that makes it impossible for it to breed with another, the separation between the two is as real as if they were kept apart by a mountain range. Consider the races of song sparrows that inhabit North America (see Figure 14–13). Some song sparrows habitually migrate north to Alaska every year; others remain in Mexico during

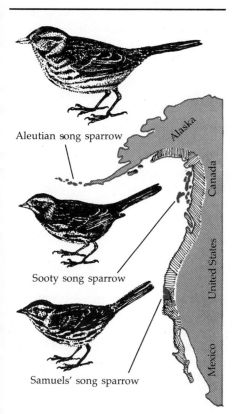

*FIGURE 14–13 At present there are thirty-four subspecies of the song sparrow (Passerella melodia) in North America; three are shown here. Their approximate breeding ranges (dark color) and those of fourteen other subspecies along the West Coast (hatched) are also indicated (from the West Coast to the Midwest of the United States are the breeding ranges of five other subspecies). The subspecies vary greatly in color and size, but if we look at representatives of all thirty-four, we find a continuous, gradual series.*

the breeding season. Theoretically both populations could interbreed, but their habits as migrants do not give them a chance to. What tends to hold them together as a species is the existence of a large number of sparrows that breed between the extreme northern and extreme southern breeding areas. Through these intermediary birds, the individuals on the northern and southern fringes keep in genetic touch through gene-flow, discussed in Chapter 4. Their genes are distributed inward from the edges of an enormous pool of genes that represents all the traits of the species; at the same time, they keep receiving genes that are passed out toward them from the center of the pool. This mingling reduces any tendency toward extreme differentiation along the edges. In other words, genetic contact with the main body of birds tends to ensure that the outlying members of the species continue to look and act pretty much like all the others. As long as the contact is maintained, the species remains intact. Two opposing influences determine the course of speciation in any group of organisms: one is environmental and selective, tending to create differences; the other is genetic and connective, tending to distribute the same traits through a population.

If we were collecting sparrow fossils and had only a couple of Alaskan specimens and half a dozen from Mexico, how would we relate them, particularly if we had no knowledge of any sparrows living anywhere else? Would we recognize the obvious differences between them and assign them to different species, or would we still consider them the same kind of bird? It is that problem which continually confronts paleoanthropologists. Their sample of human specimens is often so small that it is next to impossible for them to learn enough about the distribution of the people they are studying to tell whether their samples are from opposite fringes of one, rather varied population or whether they are truly separate and different species.

Current species theory emphasizes whole populations, not individuals. It deals with the entire gene pool of the species. It recognizes that differences exist among individuals or groups of individuals and that such differences continue to have a chance, through interbreeding, to be reabsorbed into the whole gene pool and in this way continue to be expressed as part of the species' genetic makeup. Older theory tended to look at an evolving species as a solid tree trunk with distinct limbs branching off it from time to time as new species were created. The newer theory, by contrast, visualizes a species as a tangle of interlocking strands that separate and join again in no orderly pattern. How they join is not so important as that they do join. These constant joinings represent the individual mating decisions of countless members of the species and the fate of numerous small populations. If a population drifts away from the main body to such an extent that these rejoinings no longer take place, then it will become a separate gene pool and eventually, perhaps, a separate species.

**Characteristics of Western Neandertals**

This flexible model of a species fits rather neatly what we know about *Homo erectus*. It emphasizes the broad similarities that exist among the various known specimens and it acknowledges their differences by assuming that a good deal of variety will inevitably manifest itself in any widely distributed species. Their successors present us with a similar situation, but compared with *Homo erectus* fossils, their remains are numerous. The difficulty is not so much with rarity as it is with how to interpret a rather embarrassing and perplexing abundance.

The first finds came from western Europe and were all named after the Neandertal discovery. Most of the fieldwork of the last century and the early part of this one was done by Europeans, and much of it was concentrated in their own countries. As discovery followed discovery, it became increasingly clear that these Neandertal peoples were already well established in Europe about 75,000 years ago.

Though variable, this western European Neandertal, now called the "classic" type, is not hard to recognize. Although the cranium is large and could accommodate a brain just as big as a modern human's, it is differently shaped. It has a lower, flatter crown, and its interior space is equal in size because the skull is longer and bulges more at the back and sides. There is a very characteristic swelling at the back to which the neck muscles are attached—the Neandertal "bun." The face has four distinctions: a chin still very receding (as in earlier forms) under large projecting jaws, large nasal region, the whole constituting a large prognathous face; large teeth and palate—the incisors especially large, usually shovel-shaped and showing marked wear; round orbits for the eyes; and extremely prominent brow ridges curving over each eye and connected across the bridge of the nose. It is this continuous ridge of bone that gives classic Neandertals their famous beetle-browed look.

The rest of the skeleton suggests a rather short but powerfully built body. Neandertals stood just over five feet and had broad, rounded chests. Only minor features of the pubic bone and scapula clearly separate the Neandertal from a modern skeleton. The long bones of their limbs were robust and slightly curved, which may have given them a somewhat bandy-legged appearance. Their hands were large but their fingers were short and stubby. That their feet, too, had stocky proportions is borne out not only by the bones themselves but by the astonishing preservation of actual Neandertal footprints (Figure 14–14). The Neandertal was heavily muscled and appears to have been very strong.

Neandertals existed in western Europe right up to about 35,000 years ago, and then they disappeared. If we had only the evidence of western Europe to go by, Neandertals would seem to follow the classic pattern of speciation. They were noticeably different from modern humans, and in addition to disappearing rather abruptly, the classic Neandertal in western Europe was replaced by people like ourselves. There is no clear blending, little evidence of gradual shading from one type to the

*FIGURE 14–14   The short and strong tibia (shin bone) on the right is from Spy. It is noticeably different from the less robust, non-European tibia on the left, which is from es-Skhūl. (The photograph is approximately one-fifth actual size.) The plaster cast of a Neandertal footprint from an Italian cave suggests a broad, short foot. (The photograph is approximately one-fourth actual size.)*

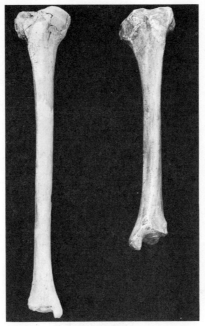

other. This separation suggests two competitive species, one replacing the other, with the more advanced one perhaps exterminating the more primitive one.

## Eastern Contemporaries

But of course, the classic western European Neandertal is not the only population to consider. As we have seen, other populations with different characteristics have been found (see Figure 14–15). Significantly, some of the traits exhibited by the fossils from the latter places are not nearly so extreme as those of the western European classic Neandertal. These eastern European and non-European peoples tend to be less massive, taller, and more finely made. Their forearms and legs are not as robust and not as curved (see Figure 14–14). Their skulls are a bit more lofty and their faces a trifle smaller, with bony features more like our own.

Perhaps a typical representative of these eastern peoples is a complete skeleton of a hunter, precisely dated by radiocarbon at 46,000 years B.P., which was dug out of a cave at Shanidar in the mountains of northern Iraq in 1957 (see Figure 14–7). This man had been a victim of a hazard peculiar to cave dwellers in areas that were earthquake-prone: he had been crushed by a massive fall of rock from his own ceiling. At the time of his death he was about forty years old and had bad teeth. He was five feet three inches tall and, like his western cousins, somewhat barrel-chested; but, like the es-Skhūl people, his

FIGURE 14–15  *The wide distribution and variability of* Archaic Homo sapiens *is suggested by these four examples. (The skulls face different directions so that their most nearly complete side will show.)*

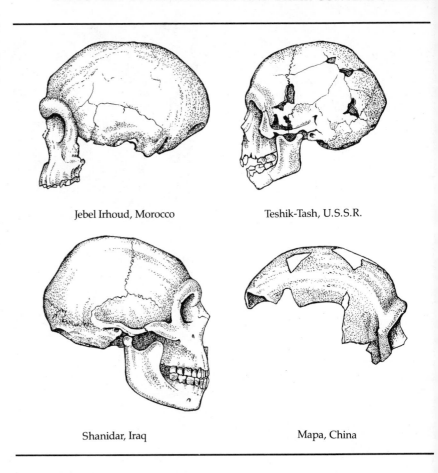

Jebel Irhoud, Morocco                    Teshik-Tash, U.S.S.R.

Shanidar, Iraq                    Mapa, China

eyebrow ridge was less thick and heavy, giving the whole upper part of his face a more modern look. Further research in the Shanidar cave yielded five more adults; together with a baby previously found, they totaled seven almost complete skeletons, all showing this curious hint of modernity in the upper face, some of them with traces of other characteristics that separated them from the classic Neandertal model.

**Neandertal and the Species Model**

This provocative evidence from the Near and Middle East tells a story entirely different from that told in western Europe. It suggests an extremely varied gene pool capable of producing all kinds of individuals but moving, between 70,000 and 40,000 years B.P., in the general direction of modern humans.

We cannot simply ignore those squat people from the icy caves of western Europe, however. Somehow we must fit them into our species model. Perhaps the best way to do so is to regard them as fringe dwellers like the sparrows that breed in Alaska, representatives of a population living under different environmental conditions and subject to different selection pressures than the main group of their kind, and probably even separated from the main group toward the end. The history of the Australian aboriginal people can be considered a parallel instance. Cut off for at least 30,000 years on a remote island, they have evolved their own distinct racial charcteristics (pp. 483–484).

Isolated perhaps for a good many thousands of years at a time, one or many local populations could have evolved in what now appears to have been a primitive direction. But calling them primitive is misleading. Is the form of European Neandertals really primitive or is it simply adaptive? Their large brain shows they were advanced in this respect; their "primitive" bodies may merely reflect that in a very cold climate the stockiest people with the shortest limbs will be the most efficient conservers of body heat. (This is an example of Bergmann's "rule" described on page 474). In such an environment, they, and not the slender more "advanced" people, would have the survival advantage. In view of the arctic environment in which they lived, this seems a reasonable explanation for at least part of their morphology.

## Neandertal and Human Evolution

Let us conclude, then, that the archaic *Homo sapiens* were a widespread and widely varied group; not all of them exhibited the extreme characteristics of the classic Neandertal type. Their gene pool evolved over a long period out of that bequeathed to them by *Homo erectus*; some in turn bequeathed their gene pool to modern humankind. The disappearance of the Neandertal people from western Europe may or may not have been the result of actual extermination. If they were killed, they were killed by members of their own species, by their distant cousins perhaps—not by a different kind of creature altogether. They may also have simply become extinct because they finally failed to adapt successfully to the environment, like so many animals and hominids before them. Or they may have been genetically swamped by hordes of immigrants (see Chapter 16).

We now begin to get a picture of a world that may never have held more than one species of *Homo* at any one time. The vine stems may have been extremely tangled, and a few creepers may have strayed, like the classic Neandertal, far enough from the central cluster to have withered and died. If we wish to begin thinking about species, we would do well to examine the cluster vertically, not just horizontally; we must take into account the element of time. When we do, the image of a vine becomes more compelling, with *Homo erectus* occupying one section of it and archaic *Homo sapiens* another, higher up and later in time, as Figure 14–16 shows. To find out where one human line stops and the other starts, we have to select a time and slice through the vine there to see what we get. Because evolution does not proceed in all places at the same rate or even in the same way, wherever we slice we will find inconsistencies. If the slice is wide enough to include places like South Africa and Java, where other people lived contemporaneously with Neandertals and shared some but not all of their traits, the inconsistencies become very plain. Nevertheless, the general indications of species relationships persist. They become more meaningful as one thinks more about the evolving gene pool as a whole, and not about individuals.

Neandertals were the last of the archaic humans, not the first. Behind them stretched 5 million years of slow evolution, during which *Australopithecus* evolved into *Homo*, which eventually gave rise to *Homo sapiens*. The earliest *Homo sapiens* evolved into many varieties, such as the Swanscombe/Steinheim/Arago group and the different kinds of archaic humans, and eventually into modern humans.

FIGURE 14–16 *The evolving gene pool of the hominid lineage contained many semi-isolated populations, some of which fused with each other, while some became extinct. This diagram symbolizes the complexity of this process, though we have no idea of the actual number of differing populations, varieties, and races involved. The more recent species of our lineage occupied a shorter time span than the earlier ones because the positive feedback loops portrayed in Figures 9–4, 18–2, 18–5, and 18–25 have accelerated the evolutionary process in this cultural animal.*

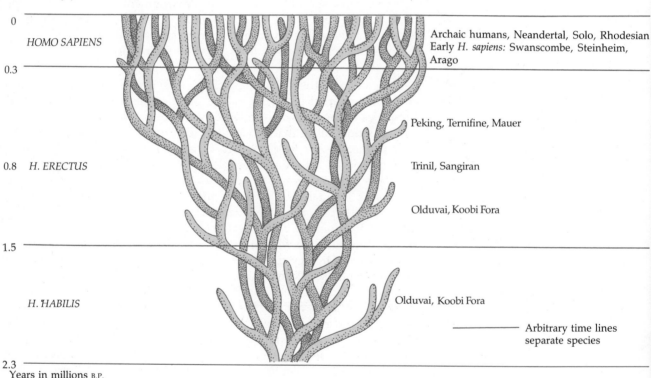

| | |
|---|---|
| 0 | |
| HOMO SAPIENS | Archaic humans, Neandertal, Solo, Rhodesian Early *H. sapiens*: Swanscombe, Steinheim, Arago |
| 0.3 | |
| | Peking, Ternifine, Mauer |
| 0.8 H. ERECTUS | Trinil, Sangiran |
| | Olduvai, Koobi Fora |
| 1.5 | |
| H. HABILIS | Olduvai, Koobi Fora |
| | Arbitrary time lines separate species |
| 2.3 | |

Years in millions B.P.

| Time | Event | YEARS A.D. | NEANDERTAL DISCOVERIES | | PUBLICATIONS |
|---|---|---|---|---|---|
| | **HOLOCENE** | | | | |
| 10,000 | | | | | |
| 100,000 — | Neandertal fossils | 1971 — | At Arago | | |
| | Swanscombe, Steinheim, Arago fossils | 1965 — | At Hortus | 1964 — | Swanscombe report |
| | | 1961 — | At Amud | | |
| | | 1957 — | At Shanidar | 1957 — | La Chapelle reconsidered by Strauss and Cave |
| 500,000 — | Peking finds | | | | |
| | **PLEISTOCENE** | | | | |
| | Hearths at Escale | | | | |
| | | 1939 — | At Monte Circeo | 1939 — | Full publication of finds at Tabūn and Skhūl |
| | | 1938 — | At Teshik-Tash | | |
| | | 1935 — | First Swanscombe discoveries | | |
| | Java finds (Trinil, Sangiran) | 1933 — | First Kafzeh discoveries; at Steinheim | | |
| | | 1931 — | At Solo, Skhūl, and Tabūn | | |
| 1 million — | H. erectus expansion into China and perhaps Europe | 1926 — | Gibraltar child | 1928 — | Monograph on Rhodesian finds |
| | | 1924 — | At Kiik-Koba | | |
| | A. robustus and boisei extinct | 1921 — | At Broken Hill | | |
| | Earliest Acheulian tools | 1914 — | At Ehringsdorf | 1913 — | Boule's monograph on La Chapelle finds |
| 1.5 million — | | 1909 — | At La Ferrassie | | |
| | | 1908 — | At La Chapelle, Le Moustier, and La Quina | | |
| | H. habilis at Olduvai | | | | |
| | | 1886 — | At Spy | | |
| 2 million | | | | | |
| | | | | 1864 — | King creates species Homo neanderthalensis |
| | | | | 1863 — | Huxley's report on the Neandertal skullcap |
| 2.5 million | **PLIOCENE** | | | 1859 — | Darwin's On the Origin of Species |
| | Earliest Oldowan tools | 1856 — | In Neander Valley | | |
| | | 1848 — | In Gibraltar | | |

## DISCOVERY OF NEANDERTAL AND CONTEMPORARIES

The greatest period of discoveries was between 1900 and 1940, and most finds came from Europe and the Near East. Finds from Africa and China are very rare. Today more research effort is being put into the earlier periods that preceded Neandertals and their contemporaries.

# Chapter 15

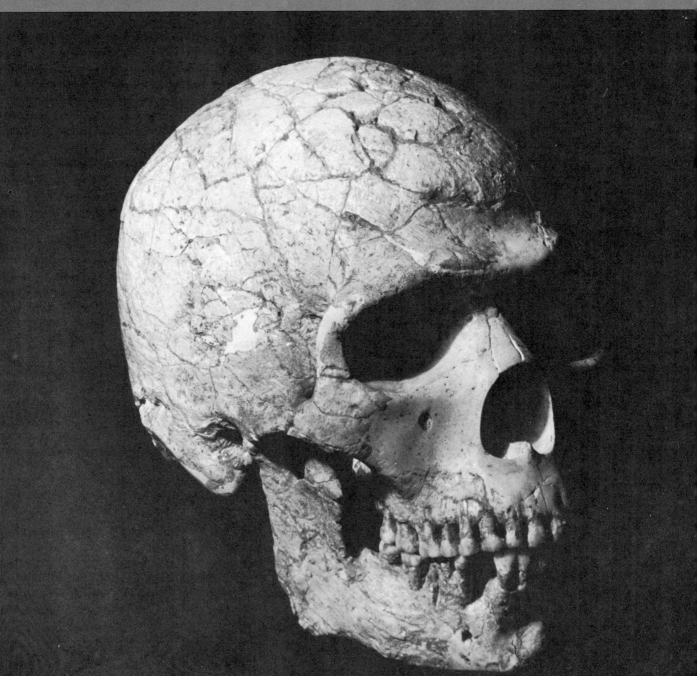

# Archaic *Homo sapiens:* Culture and Environments

Man is no more than a reed, the weakest in nature. But he is a thinking reed.

BLAISE PASCAL, 1623–1662.
*Pensees,* **VI,** 347.

## RANGE AND ADAPTATIONS OF EARLY *HOMO SAPIENS*

Two hundred and fifty thousand years ago the human population was probably less than 3 million. But this unimpressive total is deceptive, for even then humankind occupied far more of the earth's surface than any other mammal species. Most of Europe was then woodland, frequently interrupted by lush meadows, with temperatures so warm that water buffalo thrived in central Germany and monkeys chattered in dense woodlands along the northern Mediterranean coast. Most of Asia was less hospitable, and human bands avoided the heartland of that continent because of the harsh winters and dry, blistering summers. But human groups scattered around the entire southern perimeter of Asia, from the Middle East to Java and northward into central China. In all probability the most densely populated continent was Africa. This sprawling land mass may have contained more people than the rest of the world put together.

The sorts of lands settled by these various people reveal much about their ability to deal with nature. They almost invariably lived in grassy or partially wooded country. There was a very good reason for this preference: these regions supported the herds of grazing animals that provided much of the meat in the human diet. Wherever animals were lacking, humans stayed away. The unoccupied areas included the deserts, the rain forests, and the dense evergreen woods of the north—a very substantial portion of the earth's surface. A few herbivorous animal species did exist in the forests of north and south, but they tended to wander alone or in small groups, for the scantiness of forage and the difficulty of moving through the thick growth of a forest made herd life impractical. To find and kill solitary browsers and grazers was so difficult at this stage of human development that it seems probable human groups could not prosper in these regions.

Another environment that resisted human invasion for a long time was the tundra of the far north. Here, obtaining meat was not the problem. Enormous herds of reindeer, bison, and other large, vulnerable animals found ready forage in the mosses, lichens, grasses, and shrubs of the nearly treeless tundra country. People, however, could not yet cope with the extreme cold of the region. Early *Homo sapiens* consequently stuck to the same lands that had supported their *Homo erectus* ancestors: the savannas and open thorn woodlands of the tropics, and the grasslands and open deciduous woodlands found in the temperate latitudes.

## Evidence of Adaptations

It is remarkable that paleoanthropologists have been able to learn as much as they have about the world of these early people, considering the distance in time and the scant evidence left behind. Many materials essential to early humans are highly perishable. Foods, hides, sinews, wood, plant fibers, and even bone last no time at all except under the rarest conditions. The few scraps of organic materials such as these that have survived often seem more tantalizing than informative. Take a sharpened piece of yew wood, thought to be about 300,000 years old, found at Clacton-on-Sea in England (the wood was preserved because the site was waterlogged). This wooden point may have come from a spear—having been dried over flames, it was hard enough to penetrate the hides of animals. It may have served some entirely different purpose, however, such as digging up edible roots.

Yet such seemingly ambiguous clues can be interpreted. In a case like that of the yew fragment, common sense helps. Humans certainly were using both spears and digging sticks well before this artifact was made, but a person would probably be more likely to take the trouble to harden a spear point than a digging implement. Similarly, we have every reason to believe that people who lived in cool climates wore some sort of clothing many hundreds of thousands of years ago, even though their garments, undoubtedly made of animal skins, have not endured. It also seems certain that shelters were regularly constructed; as we have seen, the impressions of postholes and sapling tips at Terra Amata prove that people knew how to make simple huts of branches (and probably animal hides) even back in *Homo erectus* times.

A posthole here, a piece of wood there, a bit of sharpened bone, an occasional hearth: these are whispered hints of human achievement in remote times. Some clues to the past speak more firmly. Geological deposits laid down during a period can reveal a good deal about climate, including the temperature and the amount of precipitation. Pollen found in deposits can be identified under a microscope, indicating exactly what kinds of trees, grass, or other vegetation prevailed. But most important for the study of prehistory are, of course, stone tools.

**Stone Industries**     Wherever archaeologists find tools, they know that humans once lived there. A comparison of tools from one site with contemporaneous tools from another site may suggest cultural contacts between ancient populations; comparison of tools in successive layers can help trace the cultural progress and the skill of the early peoples who left them.

Stone tools reveal that although the humans living 250,000 years ago were modern enough to deserve the title *Homo sapiens,* as toolmakers they still had a great deal in common with their less advanced *Homo erectus* forebears. They made their tools according to a style that had originally appeared hundreds of thousands of years earlier: the Acheulian tradition (Chapter 11), with its characteristic implement, the hand-axe. As we have seen, the Acheulian hand-axe would have been suitable for many purposes. It might have been wedged into a thick wooden club to form a compound implement like a modern hatchet or axe. More probably, it was always hand-held; perhaps a piece of animal hide was wrapped around the butt to protect the user's hand.

The double-edged hand-axe was supplemented by stone flakes, which were sometimes notched or given a saw-toothed edge for finer work on carcass or wood. Evidence shows that some people preferred flakes to the larger of the hand-axes; others rounded out their tool kits with heavy cleavers. In general, though, at the time of early *Homo sapiens,* the basic outlines of the Acheulian tradition were still followed by people in all parts of the world, except the Far East, where somewhat cruder single-edged implements were still being used.

**Prepared Tortoise Core:**     The lack of inventiveness indicated by the worldwide uniformity of
**Levallois Technique**     stonecrafting gave way very slowly. Gradually, the hand-axe was improved, if only in small ways: the cutting edges became sharper and more regular. Other stone tools in the deposits left by early *Homo sapiens* people point to greater willingness to experiment. Some particularly ingenious craftsmen initiated a major new technique for making flake tools. Instead of simply banging away at a large piece of flint to produce flakes, they developed a sophisticated and much less wasteful manufacturing process (see Figure 15–1). First, a flint nodule was chipped around the side and on the top. Then this prepared core was rapped at a point on its side. The blow resulted in a flake of predetermined size and shape, with long, sharp cutting edges. This *Levallois technique,* as it is called, represents a remarkable insight into the potential of stone, for no tool is visible until the very end of the process. In the making of a hand-axe, the tool gradually and reassuringly takes shape; but a

*FIGURE 15–1 The Levallois flake has a distinctive predetermined shape. The tool-maker first prepares a nodule by trimming its sides (top right). Then he further refines this core by flaking small chips from the front and back surfaces. This is known as a tortoise core because of its appearance. A final brisk blow at one end removes the finished flake (bottom right), already sharp and in need of no further retouching. (These drawings are approximately one-third actual size.)*

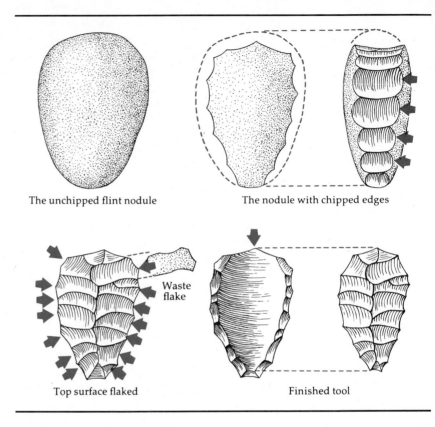

The unchipped flint nodule    The nodule with chipped edges

Waste flake

Top surface flaked    Finished tool

Levallois flake springs full-blown out of a core of flint that in no way resembles a tool. The Levallois method seems to have originated about 200,000 years ago in Africa, and to have spread outward from there, although it may have been discovered independently in several places.

When all the kinds of evidence of early *Homo sapiens* are put together—tools, a few fossils, a bit of organic material, along with pollen and various geological clues to climate—the people of that remote time start to come alive. These sturdy folk were master hunters and gatherers who could cope with all but the harshest environments. Culturally, they clung to the traditions of the past, but they were slowly inventing their way toward a tighter, more secure hold over nature.

Theirs was a fairly hospitable world. But it was destined to change—abruptly by geological measures—and the regions we now call temperate were to become as inhospitable an environment as the human race has ever known.

**THE RISS GLACIATION AND RISS-WÜRM INTERGLACIAL PERIOD**

About 250,000 years ago, the weather in the northern hemisphere began to grow colder. Glades and meadows in the deciduous woodlands of Europe broadened at an imperceptible rate; the tangled lush woodlands along the Mediterranean gradually withered; and the expanses of spruce and fir in eastern Europe slowly yielded to the expanding steppe, or grassy plain. Similar changes occurred in China. The increasing cold did not necessarily mean that the basic patterns of human life were about to change. Because *Homo sapiens'* way of life was nomadic to begin with, they had simply to follow wherever the herd animals led. But certainly the pressure to develop a different material culture was felt by groups that formerly had no pressing need for fire, clothing, or artificial shelter. These groups now had to take a lesson in cold-weather survival techniques from more northern people, who had been practicing such arts ever since the days of *Homo erectus.*

Snow was falling in the mountain ranges of the world, more snow than could melt during the summer. Year by year it piled up, filling deep valleys and compacting itself into ice. The stupendous weight of the ice caused its lower layers to behave like very thick putty, sliding outward from the valleys as the ever-accumulating snow pressed down from above. Inching through the mountain ranges, the great fingers of ice plucked boulders from cliffsides and used them like a giant's scouring powder to grind the once-green land down to bedrock. In the summer, torrents of meltwater carried the debris of sand and rock dust out in front of the advancing ice, where it was later picked up by winds and blown across the continents in great yellowish-brown clouds. And still the snow continued to fall, until in some places the ice sheets grew more than a mile thick, burying the mountains and causing the very crust of the earth to sag under the load. At their fullest extent, the great sheets of ice called glaciers covered more than 30 percent of the world's land surface, compared to a mere 10 percent today. Europe was almost entirely icebound. The surrounding ocean and seas offered a limitless source of moisture for snow, which fed separate glaciers spreading outward from the Alps and the Scandinavian ranges to cover vast stretches of the continent.

This glacial age, known as the Riss, was one of the worst climatic traumata in the 5-billion-year history of the earth. Although as many as 10 similar glaciations are believed to have occurred during the last 1 million years of the Pleistocenes (see Figures 11–7 and 15–2), humans had never before lived so far north and been so profoundly affected by such extreme changes in the earth's climate. The Riss glaciation was the first ice age to try the endurance of *Homo sapiens.* They were to survive perhaps 100,000 years of bitter cold, interspersed with mild spells, before the northern part of the earth warmed up again—for a time.

**Changes Around the World**

The effect of the climatic changes was enormous. During these cold periods, the wind patterns of the world were disrupted. Rainfall increased in some places and diminished in others. Patterns of vegetation were greatly altered. Many animal species died out or evolved new, cold-adapted forms, such as the cave bear and woolly rhinoceros.

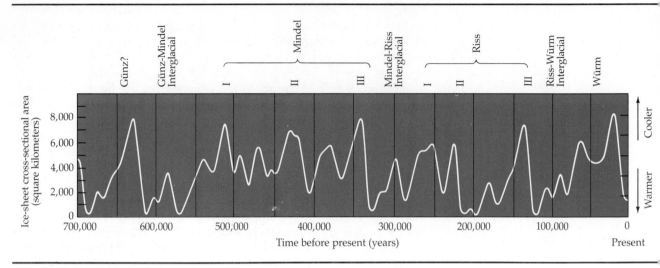

*FIGURE 15–2   The Pleistocene ice ages were most probably caused by periodic variations in the geometry of the earth's orbit, and such variations as are believed to have occurred concur with evidence from other sources (oxygen isotope analysis of deep-sea cores). From these data it has proved possible to calculate the cross-sectional area of ice sheets at any time during the last 700,000 years. As we see in this chart, the main peaks of cold weather occur approximately every 100,000 years, but many other cold oscillations come between these peaks. Although correlation with the named northern European ice ages is not secure, those indicated may be correct.*

During some particularly severe phases of the Riss glaciation, what is now England and other parts of northern Europe, which had been so pleasant when the earliest *Homo sapiens* lived there, became so bitterly cold that midsummer temperatures were often below freezing. The temperate woodlands of central and western Europe were transformed into tundra or steppe. As far south as the shores of the Mediterranean, trees gradually died and were eventually replaced by grassland. No hominid fossils are known from Europe during the coldest phases of this glaciation, and it seems likely the climate was too cold for humans.

What happened in Africa is less clear. In some places, reduced temperatures apparently were accompanied by greater rainfall, allowing trees or grass to grow on formerly barren parts of the Sahara and Kalahari deserts. At the same time, changing wind patterns had a drying effect on the dense Congo rain forest, causing it to give way in parts to open woodland or grassland. Thus, while Europe was becoming less habitable, Africa was probably becoming more so, favoring an expansion of people through much of that continent.

The land resources available to human groups during the Riss ice age also were increased by a worldwide lowering of sea levels. So much water became locked up in the huge ice sheets that the level of the oceans dropped by as much as 500 feet, exposing to the elements large areas of the continental shelves, those shallow submarine plains that reach outward from the continental margins, in some places for hundreds of miles, before dropping off steeply to the ocean floor far below. The baring of formerly submerged land gave humans access to millions of square miles of new territory, and there is no doubt that they took advantage of this dividend of the ice age. Each year, bands and their game must have wandered farther into newly drained land.

## Stimulus to Intelligence and Ingenuity

During the 100,000 years of the Riss glaciation, surviving inhabitants of northern latitudes suffered hardships that were unknown during the balmy period of the earliest *Homo sapiens* peoples. These hardships may have had a stimulating influence on human intelligence. As we saw in Chapter 12, it seems likely that the great increase in cranial capacity that had already occurred during the era of *Homo erectus* was due at least in part to expansion out of the tropics and into cool regions, where ingenuity and flexibility of behavior were more necessary for survival. *Homo erectus* pioneers had to learn to use fire, develop clothes and shelter, and adjust to complex seasonal schedules for the availability of animals and, primarily, vegetable food. The Riss, with its widespread ecological disruptions, would have tested—and perhaps selected—intelligence in the same way.

Recently, at Lazaret in southern France, the de Lumleys made a spectacular find—remnants of shelters that had been constructed *inside* a cave. These simple shelters, dating to just before the end of the Riss, about 125,000 years ago, were tents, probably consisting of animal hides anchored by stones around the perimeter. Perhaps the hunters who occupied the cave from time to time set up the tents to give families some privacy or to keep off water that dripped from the ceiling. But the weather must have been a consideration, too. The entrances of the tents faced away from the cave mouth, suggesting that winds blew cold and hard even at this spot close to the Mediterranean.

## Riss-Würm Interglacial Period

Around 125,000 years ago, the long climatic agony of the Riss began to taper off and another period of warmth began. It was to last about 50,000 years. Glaciers shrank back into their mountain fastnesses; the seas rose; and northern latitudes all across the world once again became an inviting place for humans. A few intriguing fossils dated to this period testify to continuing modernization of *Homo sapiens*. From La Chaise, Biache St. Vaast, Fontéchevade, and other sites in France come skull fragments, perhaps 100,000 years old, that seem more advanced than the more ancient humans from the Pyrenees.

## Cranial Capacity of Neandertal

From the time the warm period following the Riss glaciation reached its midpoint, about 100,000 years ago, the occupants of Europe were the classic Neandertals, and the transitional period from the early *Homo sapiens* people was ended. These European Neandertals had evolved gradually, we assume, from people like those from Arago and the later, more modern Fontéchevade people. The human jaw was still massive and chinless; the face was still out-thrust; and the skull was still low, with a sloping brow. But the volume of the braincase was now at the present-day size.

In fact, from the limited sample available from this period, it seems that the mean size of the Neandertal brain (some 1,600 cc) was significantly larger than that of modern Europeans. This size has long presented paleoanthropologists with a puzzle, for the meaning of this figure is hard to determine. We know that brain size is related broadly to body size (Chapter 13) and it seems that the most likely explanation is that the large brain was a product of the large and robust bodies of these people, whose physical adaptations can to some extent be compared with those of today's Eskimo. Whatever the reason, there is no justification in supposing that the Neandertal people lacked intelligence compared with ourselves, though that is not to say that their brains were necessarily similar to our own.

Why did the expansion of the brain cease about 100,000 years ago? Because intelligence is of such obvious value to humanity, why would the brain stop growing larger and presumably better? Physical anthropologists C. Loring Brace has one interesting explanation. In his view, human culture in Neandertal times reached a point at which almost all members of a band had a fairly adequate chance of survival so long as they could master the traditions of their band. If language were sufficiently developed and if intelligence were sufficiently high that the least brainy members of a band could be taught the necessary survival techniques, then increased brain size would confer no further evolutionary advantage. Some individuals were especially innovative, of course, but their ideas would be communicated to everyone, and the whole band would benefit from any advance. Thus, according to Brace, the raw intelligence of humanity as a whole became stabilized, although people continued to increase their knowledge about the world.

**Evidence of Intelligence**      This idea is certainly speculation, and most anthropologists prefer a more down-to-earth approach. They feel that the only fair way to assess the powers of the Neandertal brain is to find out how Neandertal peoples dealt with the world. These anthropologists turn to stone technologies and detect evidence of quickening intelligence everywhere. As we have seen, the old Acheulian tradition of hand-axes persisted, but it was becoming ever more varied. The double-edged hand-axes now came in many sizes and shapes, often so symmetrical and painstakingly trimmed that esthetic impulses seem to have guided their makers. When people made small hand-axes for roughing out spears or notched flakes to strip the bark off spear shafts, they made them just right, taking care to shape the implements for maximum efficiency at their intended work (Figure 15–3).

In toolmaking, Europe seems to have been a center of innovation. Because it is bounded by seas on three sides, the early *Homo sapiens* bands living there had had no easy avenue of escape to warmer regions during the Riss glaciation, and even the Neandertals were isolated occasionally, when cold spells occurred during the warm era following the Riss. Disruptive environmental changes in Europe would have been a sharper spur to experimentation than the more equable climates of Africa or southern Asia.

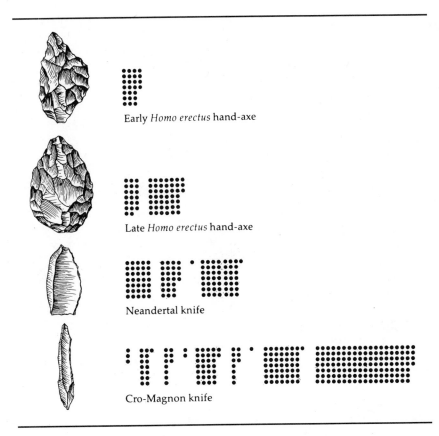

FIGURE 15–3 *Steady progress in the manu-*
*facture of tools is traced in this diagram,*
*which shows how increasing numbers of*
*blows (dots) and of different steps (clusters*
*of dots) in toolmaking led to finer tools and*
*more efficient utilization of the raw material.*
*The most primitive tool required 25 blows*
*and one step; the latest and most sophisti-*
*cated took 251 blows and nine complex*
*steps. The first and second tools shown rep-*
*resent the Acheulian toolmaking techniques*
*of* Homo erectus; *they were rough-hewn*
*from single pieces of flint. The third was*
*made in Neandertal times by the Mousterian*
*technique, which involved chipping a flake*
*from a core and then modifying the flake.*
*The bottom tool—a knife so sharp one edge*
*had to be dulled to permit grasping—was*
*shaped by the more intricate Aurignacian*
*technique of Cro-Magnon (see Chapter 16).*

Early *Homo erectus* hand-axe

Late *Homo erectus* hand-axe

Neandertal knife

Cro-Magnon knife

## WÜRM GLACIAL PERIOD

About 75,000 years ago, that spur was applied to Neandertal people with renewed force as, once again, glaciers began to grow (see Figures 15–2 and 15–4). This most recent glacial age, known as the Würm, was not severe at first. The Würm initially brought snowy winters and cool, rainy summers. Nevertheless, open grassland spread, and formerly wooded portions of Germany and northern France were transformed into tundra or a forest-tundra mixture where open areas of moss and lichens alternated with groups of trees.

During preceding ice ages, the early *Homo sapiens* bands had pulled back from such uncongenial lands. Now, in the summer at least, the Neandertals and their northern neighbors stayed, subsisting off the herds of reindeer, woolly rhinoceros, and mammoth (see Figure 15–5). They had to be first-rate hunters, for tundra country offered little vegetable food to tide them over on lean days. Recent evidence from Russia shows that settlements extended right up to the Arctic Ocean northwest of the Ural mountains. Here there are indications of huts built with mammoth tusks and skins, warmed by small fires, together with remains of polar bears, which evidently were hunted. No doubt the death

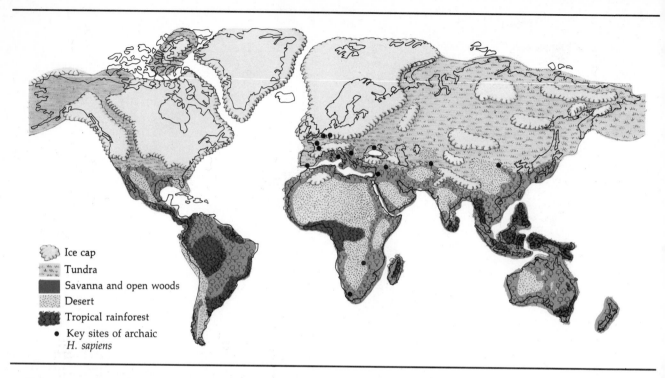

Ice cap
Tundra
Savanna and open woods
Desert
Tropical rainforest
● Key sites of archaic
  H. sapiens

*FIGURE 15–4   This map gives an idea of
the climate and vegetation of the world at
the first peak of the Würm glaciation, about
70,000 years ago.*

toll was high on the northernmost frontier, and bands remained small
and scattered. Away from the frigid border of the ice sheets, populations
were denser.

To understand the extent these populations depended on cultural
adaptations, we must remember that hominids are biologically adapted
to a tropical climate. Hominids had evolved an efficient system of per-
spiration to prevent overheating in the tropics but had not previously
needed to develop a counterbalancing system equally effective against
overcooling. Such changes require a long time to evolve. These people
did not have to wait for such evolutionary changes to cope with the
cold: they were intelligent enough to deal with the problem without
depending on evolution. They generated extra heat with well-controlled
fires, put on carefully made hide clothes, and either took shelter in
caves, or, where there were no caves, carefully constructed their own
shelters.

### Sunlight and Skin Color

One physical change that was associated with *Homo sapiens*' expansion
into northern lands was associated less directly with cold than with the
scarcity of sunlight during winter in the higher latitudes. Their skin
probably got lighter. There is no certain evidence, but it seems likely
that *Australopithecus* and early, tropical *Homo* as well, had been quite

FIGURE 15–5 *The eight-ton, twelve-foot-tall woolly mammoth was ideally suited to the rigors of ice-age Europe. Shaggy hair and a layer of fat insulated it from the cold, and its ears were small to reduce heat loss. The woolly mammoth disappeared about 10,000 years ago, possibly unable to adapt to the increasingly temperate climate of its last home, the grazing grounds in Siberia and North America. Complete animals, with muscles and skin intact, have been found in frozen ground in Siberia.*

dark-skinned. In equatorial regions, brown skin has an advantage. Overexposure to ultraviolet rays of the tropical sun is harmful to skin, and many experts feel that as the hominid skin became less hairy and more exposed, the *melanocytes* (the cells that produce the skin-darkening pigment melanin) compensated by producing extra pigment, which blocked the ultraviolet rays.

But the presence of a screen of pigment inhibits photosynthesis of vitamin D in the skin. This decrease of vitamin production is not a serious problem in the tropics, where there is so much sunlight that enough of the essential vitamin is made anyway. When people settled permanently in regions with less sunlight, however, they did not get enough vitamin D; pigment was no longer a protection but a drawback. This problem was exacerbated by onset of cold. The well-fitted hides worn against the cold decreased the amount of sunlight that could fall upon the skin. If the human of the north was to get enough vitamin D, any skin exposed would have to be able to absorb light and synthesize vitamin D extremely rapidly. In these conditions, a level of pigmentation that could further the contribution of vitamin D to the body's chemistry was better for survival, and so lighter skin evolved. In this way we can account for the evolution of the light-skinned northerner.

The significance of vitamin D in the lives of the early *Homo sapiens* populations was considerable. Today we know that humans can obtain the vitamin only from milk and fish oils, and so eating fish can substitute for exposure to sunlight. Further, we have learned that deficiency in the vitamin causes the bone-bending disease rickets. It is no surprise, therefore, that we find many skeletons of northern peoples, especially children, showing direct evidence of a deficiency in the vitamin. And

FIGURE 15–6   *The disk (above left) is all that remains of what started as a much larger core. Refinements in the initial shaping of the core, and in the way it was struck, permitted the toolmaker to flake the core until it was almost all used up. Such technical mastery could then turn the flakes into tools like the double-edged scraper (middle) and the thin-bladed point (right), both shown in full view and profile. (The photographs are approximately half actual size.)*

### Disk-Core Technique: The Mousterian Industry

it is equally unsurprising that among the Cro-Magnon people who followed them in these icy regions, and whom we know to have had fishing tackle, the incidence of the disease is greatly reduced. The importance of sunlight to survival of early *Homo sapiens* in northern lands, and the limitations that it placed on their further expansion, cannot be exaggerated.

The tenacity of the archaic humans of the north and the thriving state of those in milder areas must have been due, at least in part, to further cultural advances. During the early Würm, the Neandertals invented a new stoneworking method that brought about the permanent ascendancy of the versatile tools made from flakes over those made by shaping a heavy core. Fine flake tools had now been made for a long time by the Levallois technique, but the new method was far more productive. Stone tool remains indicate that many Neandertals now trimmed a nodule of stone around the edges to make a disk-shaped core; then, aiming hammer blows toward the center of the disk, they repeatedly rapped at its edges, knocking off flake after flake until the core was almost entirely used up. Finally, the unfinished flakes were further trimmed to give them edges for work on wood, carcasses, or hides (Figure 15–6).

The great virtue of this new *disk-core* method was twofold. It permitted production of large numbers of usable flakes with little effort. And because flakes can be retouched easily to give them a shape or edge, the new technique ushered in an era of specialization in tools. Neandertal tool kits were far more versatile than those of earlier peoples. François Bordes, a French archaeologist who is the world's foremost expert on Neandertal stonecrafting, lists more than sixty distinct types of cutting, scraping, piercing, and gouging tools. No one band of Neandertals used all these implements, but the kit of a given band nonetheless contained a great many special-purpose tools, such as saw-toothed implements and stone knives with one blunt edge that enabled the user to apply pressure more firmly. Different tool kits were probably prepared for different needs. And new weapons may have been made at this time. Spears may have been created, when some pointed flakes were attached to long pieces of wood by being wedged into the wood or tied with thongs. With such an arsenal of tools, human beings could exploit nature as never before.

Everywhere north of the Sahara and eastward as far as China, these retouched flakes became the preeminent tools (see Figure 15–7). The tools made within this broad area are collectively called *Mousterian* (see Figure 15–8), after the French site of Le Moustier, where flake tools were first found in the 1860s.

*FIGURE 15–7   Archaic* Homo sapiens *were widely dispersed throughout the Old World, but were unable to expand their territories into northeastern Asia or Australia. They nevertheless adapted to a wide variety of ecological zones.*

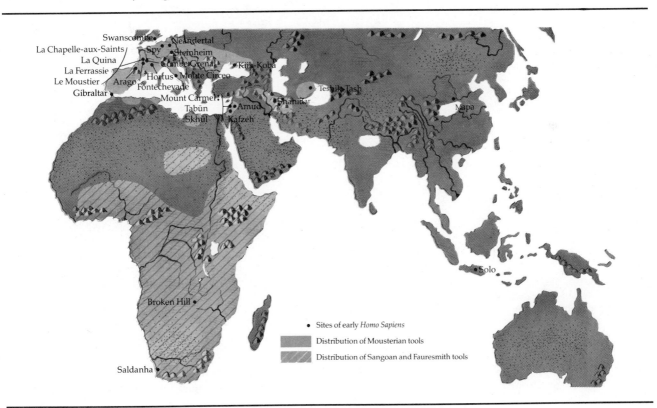

- Sites of early *Homo Sapiens*
- Distribution of Mousterian tools
- Distribution of Sangoan and Fauresmith tools

FIGURE 15–8 *Flint tools of the typical Mousterian. Points are carefully worked and retouching is carefully done, usually on two sides. These tools are of finer workmanship than the Denticulate Mousterian in Figure 15–10. (Drawings are approximately one-half actual size.)*

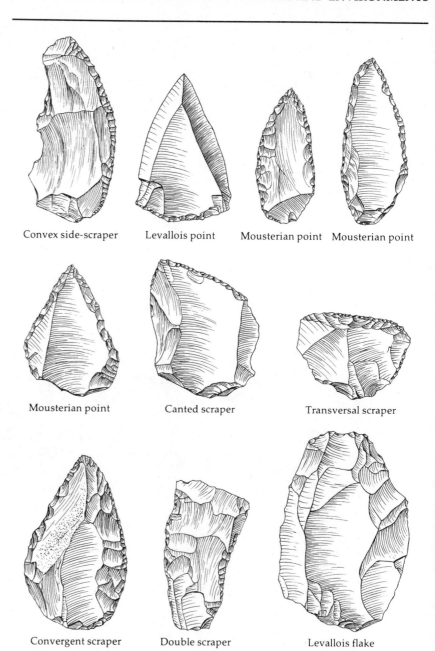

Convex side-scraper    Levallois point    Mousterian point    Mousterian point

Mousterian point    Canted scraper    Transversal scraper

Convergent scraper    Double scraper    Levallois flake

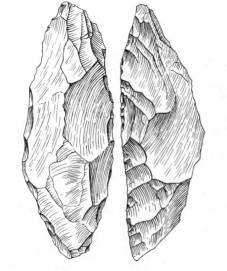

FIGURE 15–9 *A Sangoan pick. (The drawings are approximately one-third of the actual size.)*

## Fauresmith and Sangoan Industries

South of the Sahara, two distinct new styles appeared. One, called the *Fauresmith* tradition, was a highly evolved version of the Acheulian, including small hand-axes, a variety of scraping tools, and narrow flake knives. The Fauresmith kit was used by people living in the same type of grassy landscape favored by earlier Acheulian hunters. The other new style, called *Sangoan,* was characterized by a long, narrow, heavy tool (see Figure 15–9), which may have served as a combination machete and stabbing weapon, as well as some hand-axes and small scrapers. This style, like the Mousterian, represented a major departure from the Acheulian tradition. Although the tools look crude, they were well suited to cutting and shaping wood.

## Expansion and Adaptations

From 75,000 to about 35,000 years ago, these people conquered a whole series of habitats that had repulsed their ancestors. The European Neandertals accepted the challenge of tundra country and won. Some of their African contemporaries, equipped with Sangoan tools, penetrated the fringes of the Congo forests and hacked paths through the dense vegetation that had replaced much of the grassland during rainy times. Others were spreading across the vast plains of the western U.S.S.R., and still others ventured into the rugged mountain chains of southern Asia and out the other side, opening up the Asian heartland to human existence. But this expansion was slow and was performed by the population as a whole, not just a few individuals. No band was suicidal enough to pack up its scanty possessions and walk a hundred miles into an area that its members knew nothing about. These conquests were achieved not by dramatic migrations, but by gradual budding.

Specialization was the order of the day. The northern Mousterians must have been the supreme clothesmakers of the world, as indicated by their numerous scraping tools, which could be used in preparing hides. The Sangoans may have been the most skilled woodcrafters.

Perhaps they learned to construct traps to catch forest creatures that, wandering singly through the woods, were much more elusive than herds grazing on a savanna. People also were beginning to focus on hunting certain kinds of animals, a remarkable shift from the catch-as-catch-can approach that had characterized hunting in the earliest times. Proof of the specialization among hunters can be seen in one European tool kit, known as *Denticulate Mousterian* because it emphasizes flakes with toothed or notched edges (Latin *dens,* tooth), such as those shown in Figure 15–10. Denticulate Mousterian tools are almost always found in association with the bones of wild horses. Apparently, the people who made these tools had so thoroughly mastered the knack of killing horses that they ignored all the other grazing animals around them and spent their days in quest of the kind of meat they liked best.

Where key resources were lacking, these people undoubtedly tried to overcome the difficulty. On the treeless plains of central Europe, they began to experiment with bone tools that could take the place of wood. Water was another resource in short supply over large parts of the earth's surface, and humans always had been forced to stay within walking distance of streams, rivers, lakes, or springs. But some very dry lands were invaded by utilizing water vessels. Recently, in the sun-

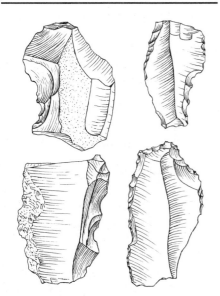

*FIGURE 15–10    Four examples of typical Denticulate Mousterian tools, characterized by notched flakes and usually associated with the butchery of horses. (Drawings are approximately one-half of the actual size.)*

baked Negev region of Israel, shells of ostrich eggs were unearthed along with Mousterian tools. These large eggshells would have held enough water to enable a band to survive a journey across the parched hills from one water hole to another.

The sheer abundance of Mousterian tools is in itself enough to affirm that their makers outstripped their predecessors in their ability to gather a living from nature. There is no doubt that these people considerably enlarged the dominion of humankind. The conquests of new territories that occurred during this period were the greatest expansion of humankind since *Homo erectus* had wandered out of the tropics and into cool latitudes hundreds of thousands of years earlier.

## RITUALS AND ART

Discovery after discovery has shown that these archaic humans very probably started some of the activities and beliefs that are considered most characteristic of humankind. They conceived of a life after death. They attempted to control their own destiny through magical rites. They may even have taken the first hesitant steps into the realm of art. And they cared for aged and handicapped individuals. In fact, it seems they were the first humans to display the complete spectrum of behavior that can be considered to constitute modern human nature.

### Hunting Rites and Magic

It seems very probable that Neandertal people and their contemporaries, like modern hunter-gatherers, had rites related to that most vital activity, hunting. The outcome of the hunt affected every individual. It was a matter of great importance that the supply of animals remain plentiful and that the hunters of the band enjoy good luck and safety in the hunt. But nothing in their world was guaranteed. Hunters could be injured. A long spell of bad weather could cut down on the catch. Animal herds might be destroyed by disease, changes in the predator population, or a host of other ecological factors. Mysterious forces operating beyond the horizon could interfere with or prevent animal migrations, causing herds to disappear.

Prior to this era, these various liabilities probably were regarded as largely beyond human control. But the Neandertals apparently attempted to manipulate the hidden forces of their universe that controlled success and failure in the hunt: they seem to have practiced hunting magic. One clue to their efforts comes from the Grotto della Basua, the "Cave of Witches," west of Genoa, Italy. In the depths of the cave, almost 1,500 feet from the entrance, Neandertal hunters threw pellets of clay at a stalagmite that to this day has a vaguely animal shape. The inconvenient location of the stalagmite rules out the possibility that this was merely a game or a kind of target practice. The fact that the Neandertal hunters went so far back into the farthest reaches of the cave to throw the pellets suggests that this activity had magical meaning of some kind.

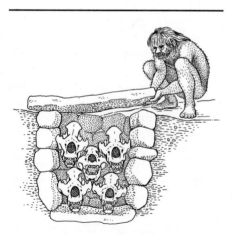

FIGURE 15–11   *Discovery of bear skulls stacked in a pit supports the idea that the cave bear was the center of a Neandertal cult. Such skulls may have been the first hunting trophies.*

In 1970, Ralph Solecki discovered evidence of a deer ceremony at a cave in Lebanon. Here, about 50,000 years ago, a fallow deer was dismembered, the meat placed on a bed of stones and sprinkled with red ocher. The natural pigment was almost certainly intended as a symbol of blood—the blood of the earth, in a sense. The rite seems to represent a ritualistic or magical attempt to control life and death in the deer kingdom.

### Bear Cult

The most famous example of Neandertal hunting magic is the bear cult. It came to light when a German archaeologist, Emil Bächler, excavated the cave of Drachenloch between 1917 and 1923. Located 8,000 feet up in the Swiss Alps, this "lair of the dragons" tunnels deep into a mountainside. The front part of the cave, Bächler's work made clear, served as an occasional dwelling place for Neandertals. Farther back, Bächler found a cubical chest made of stones and measuring approximately three and a quarter feet on a side. The top of the chest was covered by a massive slab of stone. Inside were seven bear skulls, all arranged with their muzzles facing the cave entrance. Still deeper in the cave were six bear skulls, set in niches along the walls. The Drachenloch find is not unique. At Regourdou in southern France, a rectangular pit, covered by a flat stone weighing nearly a ton, held the bones of more than twenty bears (Figure 15–11).

The object of these rites was the cave bear, *Ursus spelaeus*, now extinct. This barrel-chested brute outweighted the grizzly and measured nine feet from nose to tail (Figure 15–12). Swift, powerful, and less predictable than any herd animal, it occupied a difficult environment, wintering in caves and ranging throughout the rugged, densely wooded sections of the European mountains during the milder seasons of the year.

The Neandertals' stone chests of bear bones were not simply trophies, like stuffed animal heads hanging in the dens of modern game hunters. If contemporary examples of hunting magic are any guide, the Neandertals were up to something much more serious. Rites involving bears are still performed—or at least were performed until quite recently—by a number of northerly hunting peoples, living in the wild lands that stretch from Lapland across Siberia and into the arctic regions of the New World. Certain Siberian tribes worship the bear as the mythical first human, and they make profound apologies to the animal before killing it. In other cases, the bears are considered to be intermediaries between humans and the reigning spirits of the land. The Ainu of northern Japan used to capture a cub and treat it as an honored guest through most of the year (sometimes the women even nursed the cub); then, in the winter, the bear was sacrificed at the conclusion of a long ceremony, and the Ainu men drank its blood while the presiding shaman prayed to the Creator. These people believed that the spirit of the sacrificed bear would return to the forest and report the hospitality

FIGURE 15–12 *The cave bear was probably easy to kill during hibernation. Neandertals had to remove the bears from caves needed for living quarters. No doubt the danger of bears was the principal reason their skulls were treated as sacred objects.*

it received. Supposedly, a favorable report would persuade the forest gods to arrange for good hunting the following year.

**Beginnings of Art**

That the beginnings of art may also have occurred during these times is a logical deduction, for the Cro-Magnon people who lived about 25,000 B.P. were already accomplished artists who created engravings, statuary, and magnificent cave paintings. The only prehistoric arts for which there can be any surviving evidence are the visual kind. If music was played during Neandertal times, it is lost forever. The Neandertals may have been excellent singers and perhaps even imaginative dancers; dancing is an important form of expression among all known hunting peoples. But what little is known about the visual art of the Neandertals indicates a generally low level of artistic accomplishment.

The Neandertals occasionally made use of such natural pigments as red or yellow ocher and black manganese. These occur at Neandertal sites in powder form and sometimes in pencil-shaped pieces that show signs of being rubbed on a soft surface, such as human skin or animal hides.

There is no sign of a representational engraving or statue from the era of the Neandertals. Nor have deposits yielded a single perforated tooth that might have been used in a necklace, a very common personal ornament among hunters, including later Cro-Magnons. There are a few tantalizing indications, however, that the Neandertals were beginning to sense the visual possibilities of the materials around them. A cave at Tata in Hungary has yielded both a small engraved stone (Figure 15–13) and a piece of ivory that had been trimmed into an oval shape, polished, and then coated with ocher. At the cave of Pech de l'Azé in southern France, a Neandertal bored a hole in an animal bone; the bone may have been an amulet of sorts. From another French cave at Arcy-sur-Cure come a pair of oddities—two fossils of marine animals. These are very humble objects indeed, perhaps mere curiosities, but art objects they probably are—they have no obvious utilitarian function.

FIGURE 15–13   *This small stone from a Mousterian site at Tata in Hungary, dated 50,000 years B.P., carries an engraved cross. We do not know its significance, but the stone is the earliest known example of artistic or symbolic decoration. (This photograph is approximately three-fourths of the actual size.)*

**DEATH AND BURIAL**

Of all the various indications of the humanlike behavior of the Neandertals, their practice of burying the dead is the best documented and easiest to interpret. Death is life's bitterest fact, the inescapable defeat at the end of the long struggle to survive and prosper, and humans are not the only creatures saddened by it. Many animals seem momentarily distraught when death claims one of their number; elephants, for instance, have been observed trying to revive a dying member of the herd, even attempting to get it back on its feet by lifting it with their tusks. But only people anticipate the event far in advance, acknowledging that inevitably it will occur, dreading it, refusing to accept it as conclusive, and taking some solace in a belief in an afterlife. One mark of this belief is ritual burial of the dead—not known from any earlier stage of human culture.

**Evidence of Burial Customs**

The Neandertals were not credited with deliberately meaningful burial of their dead until more than a half-century after their discovery. The original Neandertal bones taken from the cave in the Neander Valley of Germany may have belonged to someone who was buried by members of the group, although no one suspected so when the bones were found in 1856. The two fossils discovered at Spy in Belgium in 1885 had indeed been buried; apparently fires had been lighted over the bodies, perhaps in an effort to counteract the chill of death. But no one had guessed in 1885 that Spy had been the scene of an ancient burial. Then, in 1908, the cave of La Chapelle-aux-Saints in France almost shouted its evidence of a Neandertal funeral rite. The excavators found an ancient hunter who had been laid out carefully in a shallow trench. A bison leg was placed on his chest, and the trench was filled with broken animal bones and flint tools. These various articles might have been seen as provisions for the world beyond the grave, for it was well known that many primitive peoples bury their dead with food, weapons, and other goods. Yet even then most experts failed to make the connection that now seems obvious.

**La Ferrassie (1912–1934)**

The evidence continued to turn up. In 1912, two more Neandertal graves were found at the site of La Ferrassie, not far from the cave at La Chapelle. The diggers who carried out the excavation wrote:

We have been able to recognize, at the base of the Mousterian layer, the existence of two small trenches measuring 70 centimeters wide by 30 centimeters in depth, very precisely cut in half-sphere form in the underlying red-yellowish loamy gravel, filled with a mixture of nearly equal parts of the black earth of the Mousterian fireplace above and of the underlying gravel. The existence of artificially dug graves was absolutely obvious. . . . This is, then, in the clearest way, proof of a funeral rite.

The excavation of the Ferrassie site took many years, and the complete results were not published until 1934. This rock shelter appears to have served as a family cemetery. Six Neandertal skeletons were eventually exhumed: a man, a woman, two children about five years old, and two infants (see Figure 15–14). The most perplexing grave was located in the rear of the shelter. Here, in a gently sloping trench, the lower skeleton and the skull of a child were interred, separated by a distance of about three feet. The skull was covered by a triangular limestone slab whose underside displayed a number of cup-shaped impressions, possibly symbolic markings of some sort. Why were the head and the rest of the body separated? One authority, the Abbé Bouyssonnie, a French prehistorian, has suggested that the child was killed and beheaded by a wild animal, and that the head was intentionally buried upslope from the body so that, in the afterlife, it might somehow find its way down the slope and rejoin the trunk. This is a pure guess, but there must be some reason for the odd arrangement.

### Traditions of the Mousterian Industry

As more and more Neandertal graves were found over the years, a larger puzzle emerged. It relates not to the meaning of specific funeral rites but to the identity of the people who performed them. Almost every Neandertal burial site in western Europe is associated with the toolmaking tradition known as *Quina-Ferrassie* (see Figure 15–15). Yet this tradition is only one of four main styles that François Bordes believes were used in western Europe. In addition to the Quina-Ferrassie style (containing a high proportion of flake tools used for scraping), there are the *Denticulate Mousterian,* the *Typical Mousterian* (highly developed pointed tools), and the *Mousterian of Acheulian Tradition,* or MAT in archaeological shorthand (a diverse kit that includes numerous handaxes. Figure 16–7.) In Bordes's opinion, these four basic tool kits represent distinct cultures—different peoples occupying the same general area but having little contact with one another. No human bones have been found associated with Denticulate tools, or with tools of the Mousterian of Acheulian Tradition. Did only the Quina-Ferrassie people, then, believe in a life after death? Not necessarily. In the first place, burial is not the only ritual way of entering the afterworld; Bordes speculates that the people of the other tool styles may have exposed corpses to the elements on platforms outside their caves or placed them in trees, as some modern hunter-gatherers still do. Or they could have practiced cremation, a practical solution to the problem of frozen ground. But there is an alternative explanation: Lewis Binford believes the different tool styles may prove to be different tool kits developed for different purposes by the same people. The different kits may have

*FIGURE 15–14　The care that Neandertals lavished on their dead is made clear at La Ferrassie, France. Here archaeologists have discovered what may be a 50,000-year-old family cemetery, containing the skeletons of two adults and four children. (The drawing here shows a site about eighty-five feet long.) The presumed parents were buried head to head (at sites 1 and 2 in the drawing); two skeletons (3 and 4), possibly of their children, each about five years old, were neatly interred near their father's feet. The significance of the nine small mounds is not clear, but one contained the bones of a newborn infant and three beautiful flint tools (5). The triangular stone (6) covered the grave of a six-year-old child.*

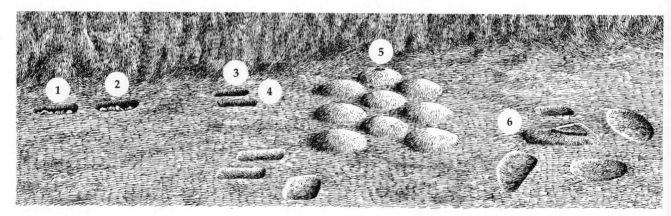

a functional rather than a cultural significance. A good case can be made for this hypothesis.

## Non-European Burials

This European puzzle remains unanswered. But from other parts of the world we have evidence that many contemporary people also buried their dead. Far to the east, on the Crimean peninsula that juts into the Black Sea, the graves of two individuals were found at a cave at Kiik-Koba in 1924. One trench held the remains of a one-year-old child resting on his side with his legs bent. This skeleton was in poor condition because later inhabitants of the cave had dug a pit for their fire directly over the grave and inadvertently disturbed the bones. Three feet away from the child was the grave of a man, also lying on his side with his legs tucked up. The body was oriented east-west—as were the Spy fossils and five out of six of the Ferrassie fossils. Possibly the orientation had something to do with the rising or setting sun.

The early 1930s saw the discovery of the magnificent set of human burials at Mount Carmel in Israel (see pages 366–367). On the terrace at the mouth of the es-Skhūl cave, five men, two women, and three children had been placed in shallow graves. The legs of all of the bodies were pulled up so tightly that the feet touched the buttocks. There is little other suggestion of ritual—with a single startling exception. One forty-five-year-old man held in his arms the jawbones of a huge boar. Did the boar cause his death? Or do the jaws represent a hunting trophy, proclaiming the man's prowess to whatever spirits might meet him in the afterlife?

The most amazing burial of all was that in the Shanidar cave in Iraq (see page 375 and Figure 15–16). There Ralph Solecki dug down through compressed deposits to uncover a total of nine burials. At the back of the cave, in a layer estimated to be 60,000 years old, he found the grave of a hunter with a badly crushed skull. As a routine procedure, Solecki collected samples of the soil in and around the grave (shown in Figure 15–17) and sent them to a laboratory at the Musée de l'Homme in France. There his colleague Arlette Leroi-Gourhan checked the pollen

*FIGURE 15–16 Kurdish shepherds, helping with the excavations at Shanidar, still use the cave to shelter themselves and their animals during the cold winters, much as their predecessors did thousands of years ago.*

count, hoping it would provide useful information on the climate and vegetation prevailing during Neandertal times.

What she found was completely unexpected. Pollen was present in the grave in unprecedented abundance. Even more astonishing, some of it appeared in clusters, and a few clusters had been preserved along with the parts of the flowers that had supported them. No birds or animals or wind could possibly have deposited the material in such a way in the recess of the cave. Clearly, masses of flowers had been placed in the grave by the companions of the dead man. Leroi-Gourhan believes that the Neandertal hunter was laid to rest on a woven bedding of pine boughs and flowers; more blossoms may very well have been strewn over his body.

Microscopic examination of the pollen indicated that it came from numerous species of bright-colored flowers, related to the grape hyacinth, bachelor's button, hollyhock, and groundsel. Some of these plants are used in poultices and herbal remedies by contemporary peoples in Iraq. Perhaps the mourners, too, felt that the blossoms possessed medicinal properties and added them to the grave in an effort to restore health to the fallen hunter in the afterlife. On the other hand, the flowers may have been put there in the same spirit that moves people today to place flowers on graves and gravestones.

FIGURE 15–17 *The skeleton known as Shanidar 4, which pollen tests show was buried with bunches of wild flowers related to hyacinths, daisies, and hollyhocks. The age is circa 60,000* B.P.

These people must have sensed the precious quality of life more keenly than other creatures before them, because burial rites, at the most fundamental level, represent a commitment to human conservation. Burial rites declare that some essential quality of human life, call it spirit or soul, cannot be destroyed but continues to exist after death, somewhere else, in some other form.

## The Old and the Handicapped

This growing sense of the value of life is reflected not only in death rites but also in the Neandertals' treatment of old or handicapped individuals. The man of La Chapelle-aux-Saints, for instance, was long past his prime when he died. His skeleton reveals that he had been bent over by arthritis and could not possibly have taken part in a hunt. Even the act of eating must have been difficult for him, because he had lost all but two teeth. Had he lived at some earlier time, he might well have been abandoned to starve after his economic usefulness to the group was over. But the Neandertals evidently were not ruled by such stern logic. This man's companions unselfishly provided food, and they probably even softened it for him by partially chewing it.

Concern for the handicapped is suggested also by remains at Shanidar. Some of the bones found there belonged to a forty-year-old man

who probably was killed by a rockfall. Study of his skeleton revealed
that before his accidental death he had had the use of only one arm;
his right arm and shoulder were poorly developed, probably from a
birth defect. Despite the major disability, he lived to a ripe age. His
front teeth are unusually worn, suggesting that he spent much of his
time chewing animal hides to soften them for use as clothes or perhaps
that he used his teeth in lieu of his arm to hold objects.

**Evidence of Violence**

The fact that these people could find a place in their society for aged
or handicapped individuals does not necessarily mean that they were
always full of love for their fellow humans. It is impossible to know the
reason for increased evidence of violence. Perhaps it was due to an
increase in population, dependent upon inadequate technology to obtain resources. At many sites there is plentiful evidence for the darker
side of human nature. A fossil of a man found at es-Skhūl bears the
traces of a fatal spear wound. The point of a wooden spear, long since
decayed, had passed through the top of the man's thighbone and the
socket of the hipbone, ending up inside the pelvic cavity.

Another ancient act of violence is recorded in the Shanidar deposits.
One of the ribs of the fossil of a hunter from the Iraq cave was deeply
grooved by the point of a weapon, probably a wooden spear. The top
had penetrated the man's chest and perhaps punctured a lung, but this
hunter somehow had survived the wound, for the bone shows signs of
healing. The original Neandertal man from Germany also had survived
a grievous injury, although his recovery was incomplete: his left elbow
bones were so misshapen that he could not have raised his hand to his
mouth. Whether the damage was done by human or beast will never
be known. There may be a hint, however; T. Dale Stewart points out
that in the three specimens from es-Skhūl, Shanidar, and the Neander
Valley the injuries involved the left side of the body. This side would
tend to be most easily injured in combat between right-handed opponents.

**Cannibalism and Ritual**

That Neandertals and their contemporaries sometimes killed one another should surprise no one—especially in view of the evidence from
Choukoutien. Perhaps more surprising is the ample evidence that they
also ate one another. In 1899 the mutilated remains of about twenty
individuals—men, women, and children—were found at the site of
Krapina in Yugoslavia. Skulls had been smashed into fragments; limb
bones had been split lengthwise, presumably for their marrow, and
there were traces of charring, hinting that the human meat had been
cooked. In 1965 another collection of charred and shattered human
bones, again involving at least twenty individuals, was found at the
cave of Hortus in France. The remains were mixed with other animal
bones and food refuse, as if some ancient inhabitants of the cave had

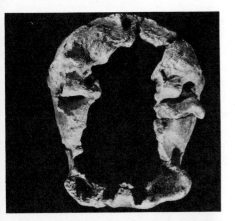

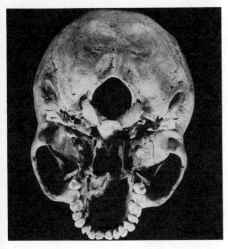

*FIGURE 15–18   The cast of a skull from Ngandong, in Java (top), shows the face and base of the skull broken away. Below it for comparison is a basal view of an unmutilated Indian skull from North America. Note the central foramen magnum through which the spinal nerve cord passes.*

### A Cult of Skulls?

drawn no distinction between human meat and that of a bison or reindeer.

Some paleoanthropologists feel that the cannibalism at Krapina and Hortus was dietary cannibalism—motivated by nothing more than hunger. They suggest that a band of Neandertals, having run short of other game, decided that in such an emergency their neighbors would make a life-saving meal. This idea does not get much support from a study by physical anthropologists Stanley M. Garn and Walter D. Block, who looked at the problem of cannibalism from the viewpoint of practical dietetics. According to the arithmetic of the two anthropologists, the edible muscle mass of a 110-pound man skillfully butchered would yield about 10 pounds of useful protein—not much food compared to the meat of a mammoth or a bison. Furthermore, as we have seen, contemporary peoples who practice cannibalism are not driven simply by hunger or blind ferocity. Members of some societies cannibalize as part of a ritual, believing that they acquire strength and courage by eating the flesh of an enemy. There are also rare documented cases of murderers eating the flesh of their victims in order to prevent the ghost of the dead from haunting them; or the relatives of a murdered person may eat the victim's flesh, in the belief that it will aid them in their quest for revenge. The slaughters at Krapina and Hortus, however, seem more savage and less selective than any cannibalistic rite of today.

Ritualistic motives appear more likely at another ancient feast on human flesh. The evidence is in the group of skulls excavated on the banks of the Solo River in Java. Though eleven skulls were dug up, no other skeletal parts were found, except for two shin bones. The facial bones had been smashed off every skull, and not a single jaw or tooth was left (Figure 15–18). The bodiless isolation of the skulls is enough to hint at some ritual intent. Even more suggestive is the treatment of the opening at the base of the skull. The foramen magnum is normally about an inch and a quarter in diameter. In all but two of the Solo skulls, it had been widened considerably by hacking with stone or wooden tools. Similar mutilation of skulls was carried out at Choukoutien, as we have seen, and has been observed among cannibals of the present day, who widen the opening so they can reach into the skulls to scoop out the brains.

Not all authorities accept a direct connection between cannibalism and the widening of the foramen magnum. Certain contemporary peoples keep skulls as trophies or as cherished momentos of departed relatives. They clean the skulls by opening the base and removing the brain. It is doubtful, however, that any of the skulls from Java were cherished, because, in every case, the face had been knocked off, and at least one person had been killed by a crushing blow to the back of the head.

Bodiless skulls of Neandertals have been found in Europe as well as

Asia, prompting speculation about a worldwide skull cult. One skull, belonging to a five- or six-year-old child, turned up in a cave on the Rock of Gibraltar. The discoverer, struck by the absence of any other human bones, suggested that the solitary skull had been placed there as a trophy or sacred relic. A similar find occurred at Ehringsdorf, Germany. Here, the jaw of an adult, the remains of a ten-year-old child, and the cranium of a woman were unearthed. The woman had been clubbed repeatedly on the forehead; her head was severed from her body; and, as at Solo, the foramen magnum had been enlarged. Although some experts believe these skulls could have been brought to their strange state by natural causes—hyenas, the pressure of falling rock, and so on—another skull, from Monte Circeo in Italy, about fifty-five miles south of Rome, would seem to resolve such doubts.

In 1939 the owner of a seaside inn at Monte Circeo decided to expand his premises to accommodate his steadily increasing trade. When workmen dug into the limestone to make room for a bigger terrace, they bared the entrance of a cave, about fifteen feet above sea level. Apparently the cave had been sealed off by a landslide long ago, transforming it into a pristine time vault such as archaeologists dream of. The proprietor of the inn and several of his friends crept on their hands and knees along a narrow corridor leading into the hillside. The corridor opened onto a chamber where no human had set foot for perhaps 60,000 years. By lantern light the explorers could see that in this eerie sanctuary a shallow trench had been scooped out of the ground near the farthest wall. A single skull rested there, surrounded by an oval ring of stones (Figure 15–19).

Subsequent examination of the skull showed that it had belonged to a Neandertal man who had been killed by a blow to the temple. Once again, the foramen magnum had been enlarged. This mutilation, plus the presence of the ring of stones, provided plain evidence that a ceremony had been staged in the cave.

The stone-encircled skull at Monte Circeo could signify almost anything. Consider a rite of some contemporary head-hunting tribes in New Guinea. When a child is born into a tribe, the tribesmen kill a man from another tribe; the father or a near relative of the infant beheads the victim and opens the foramen magnum to extract the brain, which is baked with sago (a starch made from the pith of a palm) and eaten. All this is done in the belief that the newborn child cannot be assigned a name without the ritual treatment of the brain of a man whose name is known; an anonymous corpse would not do. This violent rite is so alien to Western culture that its explanation seems incredible, despite the testimony of eyewitnesses. The practice could not possibly be guessed at if there were only a mutilated skull and some sago to go by. Although it does no harm to speculate about the rite at Monte Circeo, our chances of being correct are not much better than those of a New

*FIGURE 15–19   Monte Circeo man was a classic Neandertal found in an Italian cave sealed for some 60,000 years. He was about forty years old and had been murdered. His right temple was smashed, and a hole was cut in the base of his skull, probably for picking out the brain. He seems to have been a victim of ritual cannibalism: his skull had been carefully centered in a ring of stones. (This photograph is approximately one-half actual size.)*

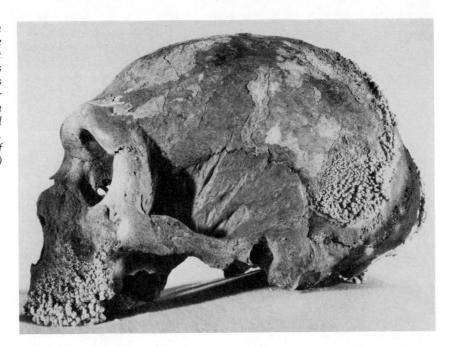

Guinean hunter trying to guess why Western people traditionally launch a ship by breaking a bottle of champagne across the bow.

These ancient rites of burial and cannibalism may be only the visible tip of an iceberg of hidden ceremonies. Practically all known primitive peoples have special beliefs and practices pertaining to key steps in the human life cycle, and it is at least reasonable to assume that the Neandertals and their contemporaries did too. Birth, for instance, may have been treated as more than a purely biological event. Perhaps they had ritualistic ways of ensuring the safety of the mother, welcoming the child into the world, giving it a name, and aiding its chances of good fortune later in life. Other likely occasions for ceremonies were attainment of puberty, initiation of hunters, marriage, and choice of a leader. Serious illness, too, might have called for a special attempt to enlist help from extrahuman sources or to drive malevolent spirits from the body of the afflicted person. But death, no doubt, stirred the ritual impulse most deeply of all.

| | YEARS B.P. | FOSSILS AND ARTIFACTS | GLACIAL STAGES |
|---|---|---|---|
| **HOLOCENE** 10,000 | | | |
| **UPPER PALEOLITHIC** 35,000 | | | |
| **MIDDLE PALEOLITHIC** 100,000 | | | Würm |
| | 50,000 | Skhūl fossils, bear burial, Kafzeh fossils | |
| | | Tabūn, Amud, Shanidar fossils | |
| | | Charred skulls at Hortus | |
| | | Shanidar flower burial | |
| | | La Quina, La Chapelle burial, La Ferrassie, Spy fossils | |
| | | Teshik-Tash goat horn burial | |
| **Homo erectus at Choukoutien** | | Disk-core technique of toolmaking originated | Riss-Würm interglacial |
| **LOWER PALEOLITHIC** | | Broken Hill fossils | |
| Mindel glaciation | | Kiik-Koba burials | |
| 500,000 — | | Earliest burials | |
| | | Classic Neandertals in Europe | |
| | | Solo fossils with smashed bases | |
| | 100,000 | Fontéchevade skull | |
| | | Ehringsdorf skull with smashed base | |
| | | Tent shelters in caves at Lazaret | |
| Hearths at Escale; *H. erectus* expansion into Europe | | | |
| | 150,000 | | Riss |
| Java finds (Trinil; Sangiran) | | Arago fossils | |
| Günz glaciation | 200,000 | Levallois technique originated | |
| 1 million — *H. erectus* expansion into China | | | |
| | 250,000 | Swanscombe fossil | Mindel-Riss interglacial "The Great Interglacial" |
| | | Steinheim fossil | |
| *A. robustus* and **A. boisei** extinct | | | |
| | 300,000 | | |
| | | | Late Mindel |
| Acheulian industry originated | 350,000 | | |

*Mousterian industry* / *Acheulian industry* (vertical axis labels)

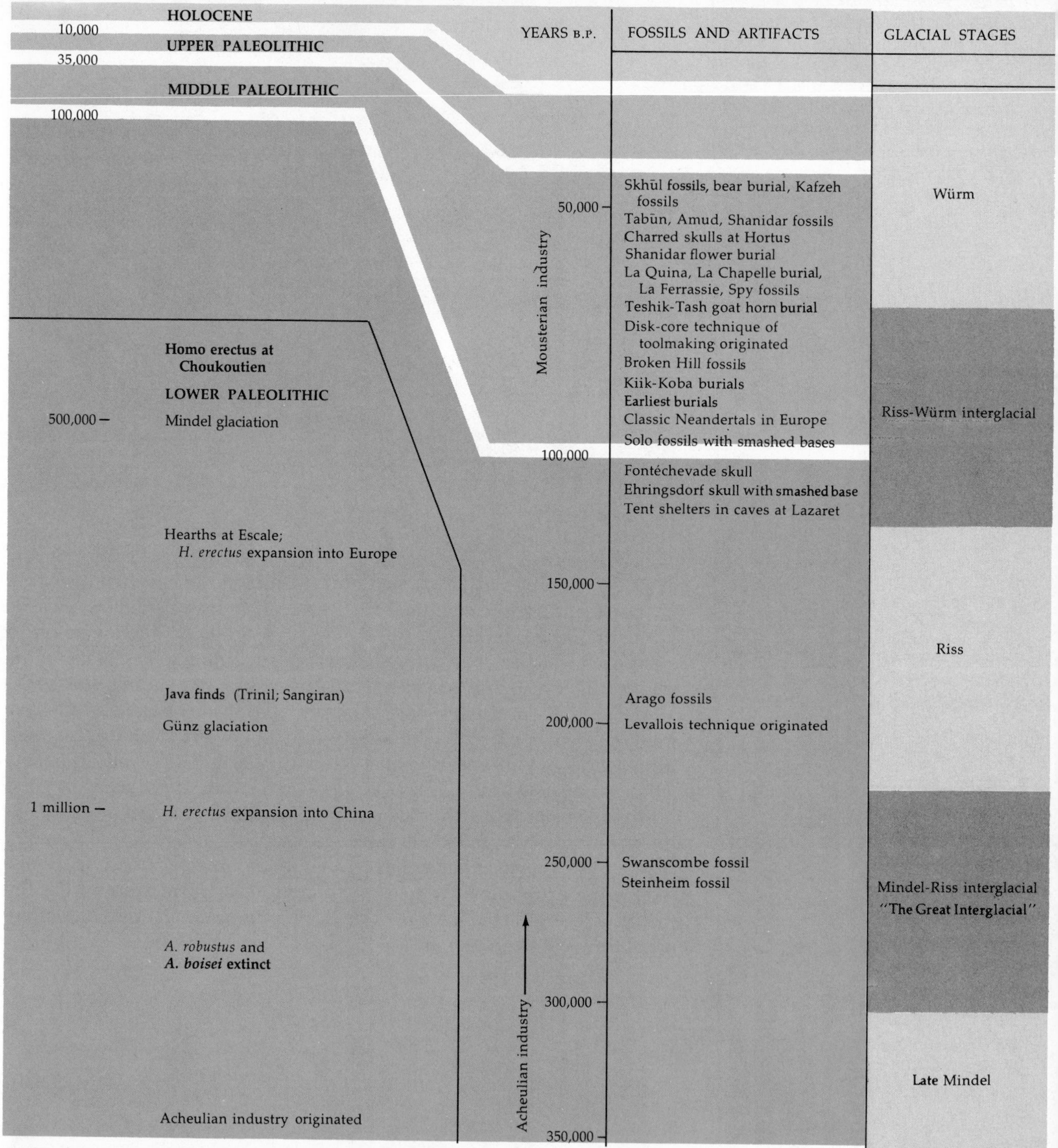

NEANDERTAL ENVIRONMENTS AND CULTURE

The age of many of these specimens is still in doubt but the order of antiquity shown here is probably correct. The dates of the glacial and interglacial phases are still extremely uncertain.

# Chapter 16

# Enter Cro-Magnon

The troubles of our proud and angry dust
Are from eternity, and shall not fail.
Bear them, we can, and if we can we must.

A. E. HOUSMAN, 1859–1936.
*Last Poems*, ix.

**FIRST MODERN PEOPLE**

In recent years prehistorians have begun to seek the origins of modern humankind in diverse parts of the globe—in Africa, the Orient, Australia, and the Americas. But the story of the discovery of the first modern people begins in the Dordogne region of France (Figures 16–1 and 16–2), where four generations of archaeologists from many countries have excavated and analyzed and argued since 1868, when the first Cro-Magnon site was laid bare. This important discovery takes us back again to the nineteenth century, twelve years after the first Neandertal find, but still long before anyone really understood its implications or the full meaning of human evolution.

**Discovery in the Dordogne (1868)**

The discovery was made prosaically enough by a gang of railway workers cutting into a hillside just outside the village of Les Eyzies. They dug out the earth from an overhanging rock shelter in one of the many limestone cliffs that loom over the village, and with the dirt came bones and what looked like stone tools. Scientists summoned to the site soon uncovered the remains of at least four human skeletons: a middle-aged man, one or two younger men, a young woman, and a child two or three weeks old. The skeletons were similar to those of modern humans and were buried with flint tools and weapons, seashells pierced with

411

Combe Grenal
Cro-Magnon
Lascaux

Dolni Vestonice
Mladec
Dordogne
Solutre

Předmost
Šipka
Pavlov
Sungir
Kostenki

SIBERIA

Choukoutien

Skhūl
Tabūn
Kafzah
Amud

Singa

Niah

Java Trench

Timor Straits

Florisbad

Lake Mungo

▰ Land Masses—18,000 B.P.

▱ Ice sheets—18,000 B.P.

▲ Sites of Cro-Magnon fossils

• Sites of Upper Paleolithic tools

FIGURE 16–2 Most of the sites where humans are known to have lived about 30,000 years ago are in Europe, particularly in the Dordogne in southern France. The caves in which these people sheltered themselves from the ice-age glaciers also protected and preserved their artifacts and bones for hundreds of centuries.

holes, and animal teeth similarly perforated, probably to make ornaments.

The name of the rock shelter was Cro-Magnon, in garbled recognition of a local hermit called Magnon who had lived there. And so the name *Cro-Magnon* was affixed to these newfound humans. In the strict archaeological application, which we shall follow here, the name applies only to the people who lived in southwestern France from about 35,000 to 10,000 years ago, a period in Europe technically known as the Upper Paleolithic. Bit in a broader sense, the name Cro-Magnon has been used to refer to the first modern peoples everywhere. They appeared at different places on the earth at different times—the earliest secure date ascribed to their emergence is about 40,000 B.P.

The limestone cliffs in the Dordogne region seem peculiarly adapted for human habitation (see Figure 16–3). These masses of rocks were formed more than a hundred million years ago by the accumulation of tiny lime-containing animals on the floor of the shallow ocean that once covered most of Europe. The skeletons of these minute animals formed, in time, a building material that was to be immensely useful to humankind. Strong but water-soluble, the exposed lime of the Dordogne cliffs is honeycombed by rivers and waterfalls, which hollowed out ledges, shelters, and caves.

The entrance to one cave, Font-de-Gaume, halfway up a cliff that juts out into a little valley, effectively commanded the approach of animals, friends, or enemies. Surely, over tens of thousands of years these cliffs positively affected the formation of human character in this region. In a sense, they provided a stage setting that enabled humans to see themselves as dominant creatures in their local environment. During the times when they lived there more or less permanently, the cliff dwellings must have enhanced their sense of identity and contributed to early stirrings of community pride. Here were their burial pits and the secret shrines where rituals of the hunt were performed. Here were the scenes of their mating and the birthplace of their children. The special beauty of the area around Les Eyzies must have aroused strong attachments to home and earth, and hunters returning after long trips in pursuit of game could hardly have failed to welcome the sight of these lush valleys and protective cliffs with pride and satisfaction.

A more concrete advantage of the Dordogne region was the extraordinary natural riches it offered its prehistoric inhabitants. The Massif Central, a mountainous plateau that covers most of central France, begins about fifty miles east of Les Eyzies. Its high plains would have been a fruitful summer hunting ground that provided reindeer, horses, and bison in abundance. West of Les Eyzies, the coastal plain stretching toward the Atlantic was also good grazing ground. The Vézère River ran then in much the same course as it does now, providing water and, to the successors of Cro-Magnons who learned to take advantage of it,

FIGURE 16–3   *Excavation of a rock shelter in the Dordogne called Abri Pataud. A steel grid has been constructed to enable the excavator to plot the depth and position of every fragment of archaeological evidence. The overhanging limestone cliffs extend upward and outward.*

a ready supply of fish. Many of the caves and shelters face south, offering warmth and protection from the cold winds of winter. Although many peoples around the world 30,000 to 20,000 years ago were probably nomadic, following game through seasonal migrations, it seems likely that the hunters who lived in this fortunate region were able to stay there for the greater part of the year.

## Characteristics of Cro-Magnon

In the years since the discovery of the fossils in France, the ancient skeletal remains of people of modern appearance have been turning up all over the world: in Hungary, in the USSR, in the Middle East, North Africa, and South Africa, in China and Southeast Asia, and even in Australia and North and South America (see Figure 16–1 and 16–

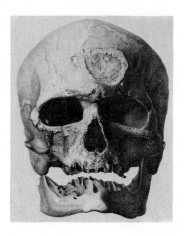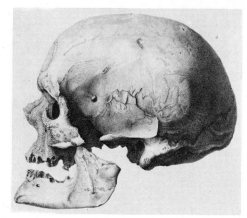

*FIGURE 16–4    Nineteenth-century drawing of the fossilized skull from Cro-Magnon, France, the first of the very early specimens of modern* Homo sapiens *to be found. Notice the well-developed chin and high forehead. (The drawings are approximately one-quarter actual size.)*

11). Not all the fossils are complete, of course, and some are no more than fragments, but everywhere they are anatomically modern.

The bones of these fossils are frequently less massive than those of their predecessors. Further, their skulls are generally like the skulls of people living today: with a definite chin; a high forehead; small, even teeth; and a cranial capacity equal to that of modern humans (see Figure 16–4). We also believe that these people had, for the first time, the necessary physical equipment for constructing complex and elaborate patterns of speech such as we ourselves use. The existing human languages are closely related and probably originated about the time of the first Cro-Magnons. Possibly, the range of vocalizations available to them was also just as great as what we hear today. We have no evidence, beyond that which was discussed in Chapter 13, of any kind of language that may have preceded this period.

## FATE OF NEANDERTAL

But what became of the Neandertal men and women and those who lived outside western Europe and struggled so hard against the world around them to sustain their developing humanity? As we have seen (Chapter 14), some paleoanthropologists believe that many, though not all, evolved into modern *Homo sapiens*. Others make no exceptions and feel that all, including the European Neandertals, evolved into modern humans. Still others, a minority nowadays, insist that all the heavily built populations became extinct and were replaced by modern people who had evolved from an unknown genetic stock in an as yet unlocated Eden.

### Sequence of Tools

Only a few years ago, textbooks cited the sequence of tool-bearing layers in caves and rock shelters in western Europe as absolute proof that all Neandertals became extinct. It was thought that the tools made by Neandertals declined in number and quality as the end of their period neared; then no tools were made at all, resulting in sterile layers with no sign of human habitation; then brand-new styles of tools abruptly began. This was interpreted as a clear sign of one people becoming extinct and another arriving on the scene.

Although an off-and-on sequence of tool-bearing strata—Neandertal layers fading into sterile layers followed by Cro-Magnon layers—is indeed found at some Neandertal sites, archaeologists have now discovered many exceptions. At some sites, successive layers show that tool-making proficiency rose, rather than declined. Also, sterile layers do not always appear between layers containing Neandertal and Cro-Magnon tools; more often, there is no break, indicating that occupation of the site was virtually continuous. Finally, the differences between Neandertal and Cro-Magnon tools do not necessarily indicate that one culture disappeared to be replaced by an unrelated one. This last fact may hold the key to the Neandertal mystery. Closer study of the differences between tools could suggest how Neandertals, far from being replaced by Cro-Magnon, actually evolved into them.

**Flakes and Blades**

With few exceptions, the tools associated with Neandertal peoples and their contemporaries all over the world are categorized as *Middle Paleolithic*, a word derived from the Greek *palai* (long ago) and *lithos* (stone); the term is a broad one that covers Mousterian tools and related types like the Sangoan and Fauresmith in eastern Asia, Africa, and elsewhere. (The *Lower Paleolithic* includes earlier stone industries such as the Oldowan and Acheulian.) The comparable term for tools associated with the next (Cro-Magnon) phase of evolution is *Upper Paleolithic* (*upper* because these tools appear in layers lying on top of the earlier tools). [One important exception to this statement is at the site of St. Césaire, discovered in France in 1979, where a Neandertal skeleton has been found with an Upper Paleolithic tool assemblage (see page 417).] Most Middle Paleolithic tools consist of flat flakes of fine-grained rock shaped and retouched to provide the desired working edge. Upper Paleolithic toolmakers produced flakes, too, but they specialized in a kind known as *blades*, which are essentially parallel-sided and at least twice as long as they are wide. This shift in the fundamental unit of the tool kit is marked enough that many collections of Middle and Upper Paleolithic tools can be distinguished at a glance.

Blades are more economical to make than flakes, because they yield more than five times as much cutting edge per pound of stone. Progress is also apparent in craftsmanship. Tools of the Upper Paleolithic are more finely made, requiring extremely precise chipping to produce the desired point, notch, or cutting edge. And there are many more kinds of special-purpose tools. Upper Paleolithic kits often include a high percentage of *burins*—chisel-like tools useful, as we shall see, for cutting bone, antler, and ivory.

Without a doubt, then, Upper Paleolithic tools are superior to those made by the Neandertals. Clearly the changeover in tool styles occurred quickly. Earlier generations of paleoanthropologists, working under the assumption that the Neandertals belonged to a separate species of humankind unrelated to Cro-Magnon, naturally saw the changes in stone tools as proof that the Cro-Magnons moved in and took over. But now that the Neandertals are seen as genetically closer to the Cro-Magnons, scientists are beginning to wonder if the shift in tools can be explained by a rapid evolution of tools rather than by the arrival of a new culture. If Upper Paleolithic implements developed out of Middle Paleolithic styles of stoneworking, the transition should be indicated by some tools that display characteristics of both types. Now, after years of speculation, evidence of a transition has appeared.

**Perigordian Industry**     First found in southwest France, the two earliest Upper Paleolithic tool types are *Perigordian* and *Aurignacian*. The Aurignacian (Figure 16–5) is so completely unlike any typical Middle Paleolithic style that it almost certainly was imported to western Europe. Tools resembling the Aurignacian have been unearthed from an earlier level in eastern Europe, suggesting that immigrants brought their new tool style from there.

The Perigordian style (Figure 16–6) of Upper Paleolithic tools is another story. Despite some claims that it is an import from the East, more and more evidence supports a European origin. The Perigordian now can be seen to have grown directly out of the Mousterian of Acheulian Tradition, that most complex and ingenious of all Middle Paleolithic Mousterian types (see Figure 16–7). At a number of sites in Europe, successive Mousterian layers dated near the end of the Neandertals' time show a steady increase in the ratio of blades to flakes. The frequency of certain favorite Upper Paleolithic tools, such as burins, also rises. The shift is gradual, and no discontinuity indicates one culture of people came to an end and were abruptly replaced. At St. Césaire, as

*FIGURE 16–5   Typical Aurignacian tools of the Upper Paleolithic. Although some similarities with the Quina-Ferrassie tradition can be recognized, the Aurignacian appears to have developed in the East: probably in western Asia. The most typical Aurignacian tool is the blade, much longer and narrower than any scraper. The Aurignacian retouching is very fine. The tools are made from a specially prepared core. (These drawings are approximately one-half actual size.)*

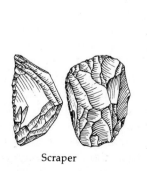

Scraper

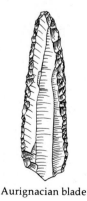

Aurignacian blade

Scraper

*FIGURE 16–6  Typical Perigordian tools of
the Upper Paleolithic. This tradition began
with strongly marked Mousterian features
and included Mousterian points, flakes, and
denticulate tools (compare Figures 15–8 and
15–10). Later, Perigordian tool kits contained a high proportion of burins and
points. (These drawings are approximately
one-half actual size.)*

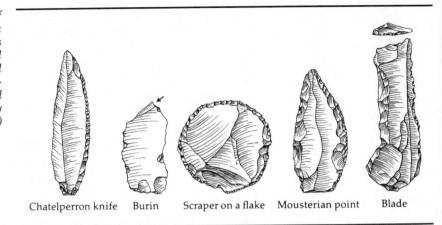

Chatelperron knife    Burin    Scraper on a flake    Mousterian point    Blade

we have seen, part of a Neandertal skeleton has been found with an
early Perigordian (or Châtelperronian) tool assemblage dated about
32,000 B.P. This could imply a transition, with evidence that the Neandertals were developing Upper Paleolithic tools. In contrast, however,
the French anthropologist Bernard Vandermeersch believes quite the
opposite—that the evidence shows that Neandertals and modern humans were contemporaries in Europe, which implies that the modern
people must have come from elsewhere, most probably the East.

Evidence for indigenous evolution of the Upper Paleolithic out of the
Middle Paleolithic has also been found at some sites in eastern Europe,
Asia, and Africa, but most archaeologists are steering clear of generalizations until the evidence has been analyzed more thoroughly. The
truth is that no one really knows how toolmaking traditions change.
Are innovations spread by migrations, barter, conquests, or word of
mouth, or by exchange of individuals between neighboring bands? Are
changes spurred by rising intelligence, increasing linguistic capability,
or some other factor not even guessed at? It seems most likely that all
these factors played a part.

### Fossil Record

Fossils would give us a more direct line of inquiry than tools into the
fate of the Neandertals, provided enough could be found. With a complete series of fossils from all over the world dated from about 50,000
to 30,000 years ago, any amateur could study the remains and tell what
happened to the Neandertals. Regrettably, the trail of humanity through
this period is not yet well enough marked by bones.

No Neandertal fossil has been given a reliable date more recent than
40,000 years B.P. (though Mousterian cultures survived in southern
France after 35,000 B.P.). A date of about 34,000 B.P. has been published
for a frontal bone of modern form found at Velika Pečina in Yugoslavia.
After that, the oldest securely dated modern peoples from Europe are
from near the town of Pavlov in Czechoslovakia; they lived about 26,000

years ago. The earliest Upper Paleolithic cultures in western Europe date from 34,000 B.P., but in Poland and Hungary they appear to have been present since 40,000 B.P. From elsewhere, we have few well-dated sites: a skull from Niah in Sarawak (on the island of Borneo) carries an astonishingly early (but questionable) date of 40,000 B.P., and another from Florisbad in South Africa is dated 35,000 B.P. Whereas the Florisbad skull carries a mixture of archaic and modern features, the earlier Niah skull is completely modern in form. There are also remains of two skeletons from Australia dated about 25,000 B.P. (page 431). These remote finds only make the transition from archaic to modern more mysterious. If further finds prove the early date of Niah to be reliable (neither carbon-14 nor potassium-argon dates can be relied on without question, especially if determined only once), then we will have evidence of a Southeast Asian population of modern appearance that predates the European populations. The same may prove true in South Africa, when new dates of other modern skulls have been checked and confirmed. There is indeed some indication that western Europe was backward at this time in the evolution of modern humankind, and this condition may well be attributable to the barriers of ice of the Würm glaciation (Chapter 15).

The world was certainly fully populated throughout the period between 40,000 and 30,000 B.P. But populated by whom? On one side of the gap in the fossil evidence were the robust, archaic humans. On the other side are the Cro-Magnons and their contemporaries: modern from head to toe, talented as artists, and eventually to be initiators of the idea of writing. Are the striking differences between them simply a

FIGURE 16–7 *Typical tools of the Mousterian of Acheulian tradition, which appeared during the Middle Paleolithic. The presence of up to 40 percent hand-axes characterizes this variety of Mousterian industry.*

Point, with thinned butt

Double scraper on blade

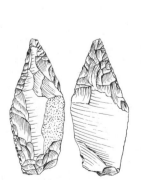
Bifacial point

Cordiform hand-axe

## Anatomical Comparison: Archaic and Modern People

result of their separation in time? If so, how did human evolution cross the gap so fast, and where, and when, and why?

The first step in attempting to trace human evolution through this fascinating 20,000-year period is to assess the physical difference between archaic and modern humans, a procedure that is not as easy as it sounds. When two extreme fossil types—for example, the old man from La Chapelle-aux-Saints and the middle-aged man from the original Cro-Magnon site—are viewed side by side, the difference seems tremendous (Figure 16–8). The classic Neandertal has a long, low cranium, bulging at the sides, with a protruding bun at the rear, a slanting forehead, and a heavy brow ridge. The Cro-Magnon has a high cranuim, rounded at the rear and vertical at the sides, with a vertical forehead and no brow ridge to speak of. The faces are quite dissimilar, too. The Neandertal has an out-thrust face, a broad nose, and a large, chinless jaw. By contrast, the face of the Cro-Magnon, with its regular features, was entirely modern.

But these are the extremes. Some other Neandertals have definite chins, smaller jaws, rather high-vaulted craniums, little sign of a bun at the back of the skull, fairly steep foreheads, and only a moderate brow ridge. And some Cro-Magnons have a rather pronounced brow ridge, sloping foreheads, and large jaws.

Visual comparison of fossils is such a fallible approach that paleoanthropologists have been resorting more and more to statistical comparisons of tooth size, cranial height, brow formation, and so on. These efforts have gone a long way toward dispelling old impressions. Many scientists once believed that Neandertals had strayed far from the mainstream of human evolution. But as we have seen in Chapter 14, they had not—the range of variability of most Neandertal features overlaps

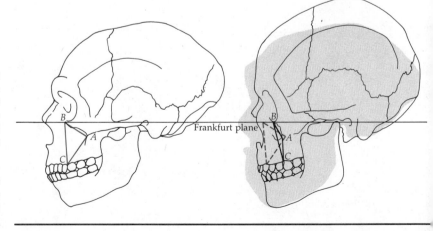

FIGURE 16–8  The Neandertal skull of La Chapelle, left, is here compared with an anatomically modern skull. The horizontal line called the Frankfurt plane, which passes through the lower margin of the orbit and the auditory meatus or ear-hole, enables the skulls to be drawn in the correct orientation. The differing triangles ABC indicate the altered position of the jaws in relation to the braincase and face. Other striking differences include size of the brow ridge, development of the chin, and shape of the braincase.

with the modern range of variability. Occasionally you might see Neandertal features just by strolling through the nearest crowd, although no individual will have a complete array of Neandertal characteristics. Similarly, most early authorities believed that the western European Neandertals were remarkably homogeneous. Their alleged lack of variety was interpreted to mean that they had somehow lost evolutionary flexibility, become specialized, and come to a dead end. Now, however, statistical analyses have indicated that the range of variability within Neandertal populations was as great as the variability among *Homo sapiens* today.

**Regional Survey**   It helps to know that archaic humans came in many shapes and sizes, and that these are sometimes matched by the various conformations of the first modern humans. There is no doubt that somewhere the evolutionary gap was crossed by a steady progression of changes, each so small as to be imperceptible, yet all adding up to the differences between Neandertals and Cro-Magnons. What follows is a brief, region-by-region summary of the skeletal material supporting the belief that through long series of small changes the features of most archaic populations in the world become those of modern peoples.

In the Middle East, an ancestral relationship between the archaic and modern people seems probable (see Figure 16–9). This is the only locality where a series of candidates for an intermediate type of human has appeared. The fossils from es-Skhūl and Kafzeh in Israel seem to belong between the two camps. The skulls display a fairly even blend of archaic and modern traits.

In eastern Europe, an ancestral relationship seems entirely possible, for the most recent of the archaic specimens appear rather advanced and the oldest of the modern forms appear rather robust. In particular, the skulls from Mladec, Pavlov, and Předmost and a jaw from Sipka in Czechoslovakia, which are among the oldest Upper Paleolithic skulls (some probably more than 30,000 B.P.), have many archaic features.

In Southeast Asia, an ancestral relationship also seems possible, because fossils from Australia (dated only about 10,000 B.P.) hint at an anatomical link between the skulls from the Solo River in Java and the most ancient fossils of Australian Aborigines, which date back to 25,000 B.P. and were full-fledged modern *Homo sapiens*.

In Africa, apart from the Florisbad skull, which has some archaic characteristics, transitional specimens are lacking. A number of modern but rugged-looking skulls have turned up, however, in eastern and southern Africa. These fossils could be more than 40,000 years old, although their dates—and those for such robust skulls as the one found in Zambia—are still imprecise. An ancestral relationship between the two types is considered possible, and some paleoanthropologists feel that the African *Homo sapiens* were the first to have crossed the threshold to modernity.

FIGURE 16–9  *This sequence of skulls from Israel shows some of the changes that occurred in the evolution from archaic to modern human beings. From left to right, they are from et-Tabūn, Amud, and below, from es-Skhūl, and an Upper Paleolithic Natufian site in Israel. (These photographs are approximately one-quarter actual size.)*

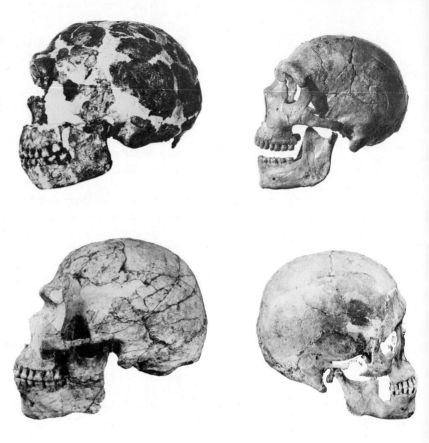

## Problem of Western Europe

One area has been left off this list of places where evolution of archaic into modern humans is generally regarded as possible or probable. Western Europe is one of the richest fossil fields in all the world, and it has been scoured carefully for more than a century. Yet no fossil truly intermediate between the European Neandertals and the Cro-Magnons has ever been found, though a new discovery of a Neandertal frontal bone from Hahnöfersand in northern Germany has been claimed to show many modern features and carries a date of about 36,000 B.P. Because this is the only fossil found to date that comes close to fitting into the middle ground, many scientists are still inclined to exclude the western European Neandertals from the direct line leading to modern humans.

Agreement on this point is far from universal. C. Loring Brace, among others, believes there is no justification for treating western European Neandertals differently. Brace feels they showed ˜definite signs of evolving in a Cro-Magnon direction. He further suggests they may be older than is believed. In his opinion, their progressive tendencies are muted by this hitherto unsupposed antiquity. It is true that no well-preserved fossil from the region can be reliably dated, for most were dug up earlier in this century, when excavation and dating techniques were crude. Some recent studies suggest that the fossils from La Ferrassie, La Chapelle-aux-Saints, Monte Circeo, Spy, Neandertal, and elsewhere are approaching 60,000 years old—an age that would lend support to Brace's point that European Neandertals had time in which to evolve a modern appearance.

A good case can be made for the opposite viewpoint, however, that western European Neandertals missed the turn toward modernity and later died out. Geological factors may have influenced their fate. During severe cold phases of the Würm glaciation, the Scandinavian and Alpine ice sheets pushed toward each other and even came within 300 miles of meeting in Germany. Neandertals trapped behind the glaciers might have been more or less isolated from the evolutionary advances occurring elsewhere in the world. Although the isolation would have been neither total nor permanent, such geographic features could have operated as a fine-mesh genetic screen, severely limiting east-west contacts. In this way, the people of western Europe might have periodically pursued an independent evolutionary course.

If these people were indeed an evolutionary dead end, what accounts for their demise? The usual answer is that invading hordes from the east exterminated the western Neandertals. Some paleoanthropologists speculate that the classic Neandertals were in no condition to resist when and if the invaders arrived. These scientists point to the fossil evidence indicating that some western European Neandertals suffered from rickets, caused by lack of vitamin D. But vitamin deficiency alone could not account for the death of hundreds of thousands of people. Possibly the invaders carried a disease against which the Neandertals had no immunity. In contrast, some writers have conjured up the specter of ecological catastrophe, suggesting that the European Neandertals were so inflexibly adapted to cold that they could not adjust to the warm spell that began around 39,000 years ago and lasted for 2,000 years. This notion makes little sense, however; Neandertals had thrived during earlier warm spells, and it is hard to imagine a warm spell being stressful, let alone fatal.

A more persuasive explanation for the disappearance of the western European Neandertals at the hands of invading Cro-Magnons involves cultural ability. In modern times the overwhelming of one group by another, as the American Indians and the aborginal Australians were overwhelmed by the invading Europeans, has always turned on cultural and especially technological advantage, and ultimately on the relative abilities of each competing population to extract resources from the environment. This was surely also the cause in the transition from Neandertal to Cro-Magnon: aspects of culture and technology quite probably not represented in the fossil record were almost certainly a critical factor in that competitive situation (if such it was), as they always are today. Language ability was probably one important factor in the development of a broadly superior culture.

The debate is bound to continue for years, for the evidence of stone tools suggests at least some indigenous cultural linkage between Neandertals and Cro-Magnons in western Europe. And even if the western Europeans were overwhelmed by invaders, some racial crossing must have taken place. No evidence is known to date, however, of the contemporaneity of the two racial types in Europe. Nevertheless, it is unlikely that the genes of the western European Neandertals disappeared entirely from humankind.

This supposition is based on our understanding of what has been called *genetic swamping*, a common occurrence when a large population overruns and absorbs a smaller one. The genes of the smaller population are preserved but make little contribution to the physical characteristics of the successor population. In the succession of Cro-Magnon, we can also postulate a similar *cultural swamping*. As we have said we see this phenomenon within historical times, in instances where whole cultures, languages, and religions have died out and been replaced to a great extent by the culture of more numerous invaders, even though the people who carried the ancient culture have survived as a genetic minority.

## FROM NEANDERTAL TO CRO-MAGNON

A fundamental question remains. If most of the archaic humans evolved into anatomically modern populations, as seems likely, why did such a change take place? What evolutionary forces could explain remodeling of the human skull from the form that had characterized humans since *Homo erectus* times, a quarter of a million years or so before? Until that question is firmly answered, the transformation of archaic into modern people will remain enigmatic.

### Brace's Hypothesis

One hypothesis directed to this problem focuses on the Neandertal face. Anyone seeing a Neandertal skull for the first time is struck by the appearance of the face. What conceivable purpose could that long and decidedly out-thrust facial structure serve? Many authors believe that Neandertal teeth suggest an answer to this question. They view the large face with projecting jaws as a supporting structure for the very large teeth. According to Loring Brace, the size of the front teeth in particular was a sort of "technological" adaptation. Brace thinks that Neandertals regularly used their front teeth as a built-in tool, serving as pliers to hold one end of some material such as wood or hide so that one hand would be free to cut, scrape, or pierce the material with a stone implement. This application is also inferred from examination of the wear on the incisor teeth and their form, which is called *shovel-shaped*. This term implies that the incisors are strengthened on their inner borders in a way that gives them a curved and shovel-like shape. Patterns of wear on the incisors of some fossils suggest that the Neandertals softened animal hides by chewing them; people may also have twisted plant fibers or straightened wooden shafts with the aid of their teeth.

To provide room for the big, strong front teeth that work of this sort would favor, the face had to extend well forward. Furthermore, the jaw had to be large and thick to withstand the stresses generated when the teeth were used as gripping, tearing, or hide-softening tools. Other skull features may have been affected, too. Probably the heavy brow ridge of the Neandertals functioned as a structural support to take up chewing stresses. Probably the shape of the back of the skull was dictated by the massive tooth-bearing structures up front. The bunlike extension of the rear of many Neandertal skulls may have acted to balance the out-thrust face, distributing the weight of the head evenly above its supporting point at the top of the spine. More important, the neck muscles, which balance the head upon the vertebral column, would be more effective in supporting the heavy face and jaws given the longer lever arm provided by the extended bun. Another possible explanation for the elongated skull brings in rotary motion. The head is swiveled from side to side partly by means of the neck muscles. Extension of the back of the head again gives the muscles a longer lever arm to work with, lightening the task of moving the heavy, forward-jutting face.

Why would the skull evolve into its modern form? Brace feels that improvements in stone implements caused the Neandertals to rely less and less on their front teeth as a built-in tool. This decreased reliance led to gradual reduction in tooth and jaw size, which in turn permitted reduction in the face and other features of the skull, giving rise to people with heads like ours.

**Pilbeam's Hypothesis**    Many scientists feel that Brace's hypothesis cannot account adequately for the transformation of the archaic Neandertals and their contemporaries into people of modern appearance, and they offer alternatives. David Pilbeam proposed another sort of evolutionary mechanism that might have contributed to the changes in the human skull. He suggested that with the possible exception of western European Neandertals, the archaic head gradually became more modern in form because of the evolution of the upper part of the throat into a pharynx capable of producing the full range of modern vocalizations. As we saw in Chapter 13, when, in modern human development, this essential part of the vocal tract starts to take on its final shape (at the age of three months), the larynx moves down in the throat, and the base of the skull, which is rather flat at birth, takes on a concave arch. The pharyngeal space is thus formed in front of the topmost vertebrae, and the arch in the base of the skull serves as a roof.

Pilbeam believes that the evolution of the pharynx's arched roof may have affected the overall structure of the human skull. As the arch formed, the base of the skull shortened (just as the ends of a piece of cloth that is lifted slightly in the middle pull together). If the starting point for this process were a long, low skull, the shortening of the skull base might have caused the facial region to pull inward from its formerly out-thrust position. With the face thus pulled in, the whole braincase would have had to become higher to contain the same amount of brain tissue. And as this shaping happened, the brow and the sides of the skull would have become more vertical. Thus, the Neandertal skull could have been transformed into a modern *Homo sapiens* skull. Neandertal and modern skulls are, in effect, just different ways of packing the same quantity of brain tissue. The overall shape of the package is dictated by only one of its dimensions—the length of the base of the skull—which is in turn related to the presence of a modern pharynx.

Pilbeam's logical chain of events explains the evolutionary changes that turned archaic into modern humans. The development of a modern pharynx could have occurred very rapidly, for speech was now becoming an extremely valuable adaptation. Natural selection might have worked at maximum speed to weed out the slow talkers and foster better speaking ability. It is almost impossible today, tens of thousands of years later, to sense the powerful evolutionary pressures that might have been launched when this new element was introduced into the vocal tract. The development of a modern pharynx, with its huge potential for communication, could very well explain a leap in physical and cultural evolution. Changes in teeth or noses probably would not have gone forward at the same rapid pace.

## Transition Completed

The most probable answer to our question of why the modern head form evolved is that all the factors that have been mentioned were at work: the pharynx almost certainly increased in length, and the jaws, teeth, and associated bony structures were indeed reduced in size. The changes at the back of the skull were most probably no more than a product of the important new developments taking place at the front.

Much has been learned of the period of transition between Neandertal and Cro-Magnon times, and much remains to be learned. Hardly any relevant fossil evidence is available from some crucial areas of the world: Arabia, at the crossroads of two continents; the endless reaches of central Asia; and the subcontinent of India, rich in game and characterized by the sort of warm climate that early humans favored for millions of years. Nor can paleoanthropologists say when the transformation started. Perhaps some modern-looking individuals began to appear in archaic populations 60,000 or even 100,000 years ago.

Whenever and wherever it began, the evolutionary transition probably affected most of humankind. From the savannas of Africa to the hills of Czechoslovakia and eastward to China, humans were joined in an enormous gene pool—a great mixing vat in which traits of appearance or behavior could be exchanged by interbreeding among neighboring bands of hunter-gatherers. Because exogamy (see page 323) was probably well established by this time, an evolutionary surge in one place eventually made itself felt everywhere else in the gene pool; humankind climbed toward modernity as a unit. By about 30,000 years ago the changes were largely complete, and the world was populated with people who looked like ourselves. People were living in larger bands than they ever had before. Cultures were branching and rebranching along countless idiosyncratic paths, like a plant that has lived long in the shade and is suddenly offered the full strength of the sun. Successful initiatives in technology or art or symbolmaking brought on more initiatives, and cultural change steadily accelerated.

## A NEW BREED

### Variability

Like people living today, these first modern people developed characteristic physical types from region to region, and even from site to site within a region (Figure 16–10). Their environment, its climate and its

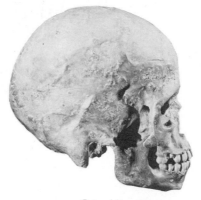

Grimaldi

Chancelade

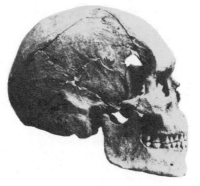

Combe Capelle

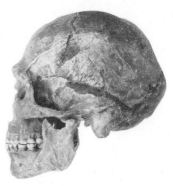

Předmost

*FIGURE 16–10 Four European Cro-Magnon skulls show some of the variation we would expect to find in a population the size of that which occupied Europe. These are from Grimaldi in Italy, near the border with France on the Mediterranean coast; from Chancelade and Combe Capelle in France; and from Předmost in Czechoslovakia. All are dated at about 20,000 to 25,000 B.P. (These photographs are approximately one-fourth actual size.)*

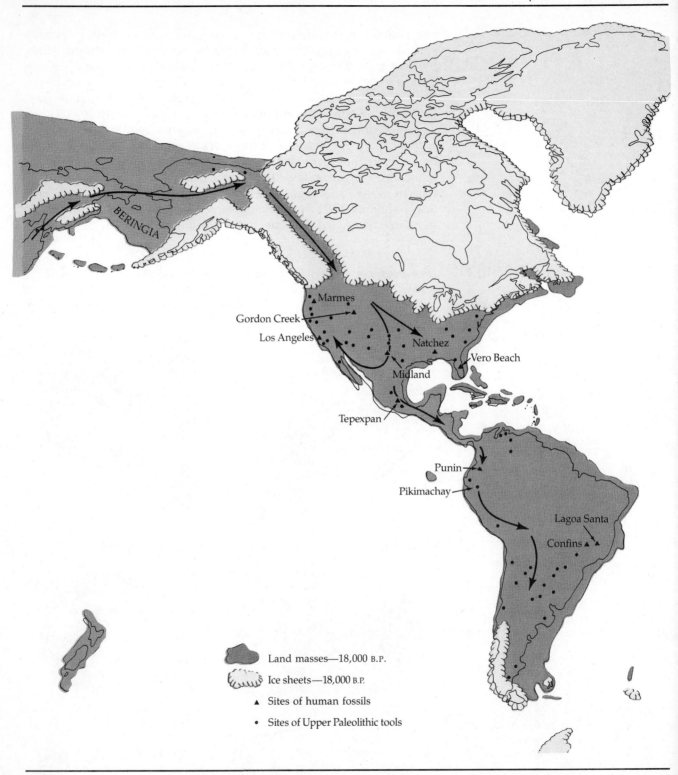

Land masses—18,000 B.P.

Ice sheets—18,000 B.P.

▲ Sites of human fossils

• Sites of Upper Paleolithic tools

BERINGIA

Marmes

Gordon Creek

Los Angeles

Natchez

Vero Beach

Midland

Tepexpan

Punin

Pikimachay

Lagoa Santa

Confins

FIGURE 16–11   *Much is still to be learned about the arrival of humankind in the New World. This map gives an idea of the most probable migratory route of the invaders, and of the extent of the land mass during the last glaciation. Carbon-14 and racemization dates from many sites suggest that humankind entered North America before 20,000 B.P. and possibly as early as 50,000 B.P.*

food supply account for some of these variations. Such physical characteristics as tallness and shortness, dark skin and light skin, straight hair and curly hair, had formed and would continue to evolve during the millennia when the human body had to accommodate itself to both heat and cold and to the variations of sunlight in different latitudes. The relatively short, thick body of the Eskimo, for instance, conserves heat better than the tall, thin bodies of some African Negroes, which present a much greater area of skin to be cooled by the air. Similarly, thick, straight hair, in the opinion of some scholars, might help to maintain the temperature of the brain in cold climates, whereas tightly curled hair seems an adaptation guarding against hot tropical sunshine; it is a noticeable characteristic of genetically unrelated people in Africa and the islands of Southeast Asia and the South Pacific.

## Advantages of the Large Gene Pool

By 20,000 B.P. many of the physical changes wrought by the environment had largely reached their present state. That peoples varied in physical type from one location to another may be related as much to demography as to geography, for there was a great increase in numbers of people and a continued division of human populations into many fairly isolated groups. The gene pool grew with the expanding total population, but it remained divided into small breeding populations that still partially inhibited gene flow.

When the population of a species is relatively small, the genetic material available to it is relatively limited in scope, and the variant physical types may be few. But as the population increases it also begins to vary more, simply because greater numbers provide more opportunities for variations to appear. When gene flow within a large population is limited, as it was at this period, the variations may become specialized, adapting to local environments according to the dictates of natural selection and perhaps the chance consequences of the founder effect (Chapter 4).

## NEW LANDS

These first anatomically modern people lived during the second half of the last ice age, known as the Würm glaciation in Europe and the Wisconsin in North America. Warm and cold periods followed one another in close succession—close at least by geologic time—and with each cold interlude the glaciers advanced and withdrew. Islands rose and fell, and natural causeways and corridors appeared, making new traffic routes for the comings and goings of humans. Along one of these ancient routes these people may have moved northward from what is now China into the chilly reaches of Siberia. Along another one they apparently migrated from Siberia, across the wide land bridge of Beringia, now covered by the Bering Sea, into the continent of North America (Figure 16–11).

FIGURE 16–12 *"Unearned" resources refers to migratory herds that live for part of the year outside the home range of the hunting bands. Herds that feed in the mountains during the summer may come down to the valleys during the winter, where they are hunted. Thus the valley hunters are drawing on food resources of the entire region, without actually traveling through it. The figure shows the relationship of the zones of food production to the home base.*

### The Americas

Exactly when early humans first entered the Americas is still quite uncertain. It had been believed for many years that the oldest evidence for the first Americans did not predate 10,000 B.P., and there was no sure evidence of tool traditions of very much greater antiquity. Recently determined radiocarbon dates based on bone collagen, however, have indicated ages of 17,000 and 23,000 years for a skeleton and skull found in 1933 and 1936 by workmen at Laguna Beach and Los Angeles in southern California. There is some doubt, however, about the exact provenance of these remains; they had no cultural context, and because it was possible to carry out only one carbon-14 date in each instance archaeologists are somewhat doubtful of their age. Radiocarbon dates from North American archaeological sites are now accumulating, however, and some twenty-eight dates take the evidence of human activity well beyond the 10,000 B.P. mark. An extremely well-dated site in Peru (Pikimachay) has yielded good evidence of human occupation by 19,000 B.P., but no skeletal remains. More recently, dates obtained by the racemization technique (page 30 have suggested a much earlier appearance of humans in California: about 45,000 B.P. Although these dates are as yet inadequately calibrated, it does seem possible (on the basis of the early date from Peru) that humans may indeed have entered North America, probably by the ice-free corridor shown in Figure 16–11, much earlier than has been supposed. Further evidence is still needed. It is clear, though, that all the known skeletal material is anatomically modern; there is no evidence of archaic humans or of their Mousterian tool industry.

Winter grazing and hunting grounds

Summer feeding grounds

**Australia**  Although the vast ice caps of the Würm glaciation locked up enough of the world's water to drop sea levels as much as 400 feet, adding great expanses of dry land to the continents, such extensions never joined Australia to the mainland of Southeast Asia. The subsidence of waters from the comparatively shallow Sunda Shelf united Borneo, Java, and Sumatra to the mainland of Southeast Asia and probably exposed enough small islands to make island hopping feasible. But between Australia and the shelf at the edge of the Asian mainland still remained the 26,000-foot-deep waters of the Java Trench—sixty miles of open sea. How did humankind manage to get across it?

It was long assumed that humans did not reach this major island continent until the ancestors of the modern Aborigines migrated there by boat, probably from Southeast Asia, some 8,000 to 10,000 years ago. Then in the 1930s, finds indicated an earlier human arrival, and in 1968 archaeologists digging near Lake Mungo in New South Wales discovered a 25,000-year-old skeleton of a woman, unmistakably modern in her anatomy, and artifacts dating back as far as 32,000 years B.P.

The millennia around the year 30,000 B.P. represent a period of time long before any archaeological evidence for the existence of boats. Yet the evidence from southern Australia clearly indicates that people living more than 30,000 years ago somewhere in Southeast Asia already must have invented some sort of watercraft. Was it simply a raft of bundled bamboo and reeds, meant for offshore fishing? Or was it perhaps a primitive version of the dugout canoe used today by modern Melanesians? Even more intriguing is the question of how the voyagers happened to journey to Australia. Were they carried there inadvertently by a wayward current or, according to one far-out speculation, by a massive tidal wave like the one that rolled out from the island of Krakatoa during a volcanic eruption there in the nineteenth century? Did they go to Australia purposefully and if so, what drew them? We do not know.

**Diet and Hunting**

Like the migrations of all the hunter-gatherer peoples who had gone before them, the movements of these people were concentrated on getting food. In the means they used to achieve this end—in their implements, their techniques, their social organization, their choice of habitation—they went far beyond what anyone had done before. Their diet included almost every sort of food the earth provided, and they became enormously adept at acquiring those foods. Indeed, in living off the land, and living well, they must have been far more successful than anyone before their time or since.

When the first hominid groups developed their skills as hunters, they tapped a source of food energy unavailable to their mainly vegetarian predecessors. When they began to hunt migratory grazing animals and an occasional predatory animal whose territory extended beyond their own, their intake of food energy began to draw upon a still wider range of resources. Thus, when territorial expansion took humans into the temperate zone, where grazing herd animals sometimes migrate between winter and summer feeding grounds, their food intake tapped nutritional energy from distant sources that sometimes were extremely different from the resources supplied by their own immediate environment. Cro-Magnons, harvesting the reindeer of the Dordogne region, were benefiting from the nutrients of the northern pastures and coastal plains where the reindeer herds did some of their grazing but where people seldom, if ever, ventured. Anthropologists call this kind of long-distance food collection living on *unearned resources* (see Figure 16–12). Of all the ways in which organisms had adapted to and drawn sustenance from their environment (short of actually controlling it) this was the most sophisticated. Not until agriculture was developed did humans' exploitation of nature become more effective.

Modern archaeological techniques give us a glimpse of the variety and complexity of the ecological adaptations accomplished by the Cro-Magnons. In the next chapter we will look at the technology of these people in more detail and at their arts and their beliefs about the world in which they lived.

# Chapter 16 Overview

| | | YEARS B.P. | EMERGENCE OF MODERN HUMANS | TYPES OF *HOMO SAPIENS* |
|---|---|---|---|---|

10,000 — **NEOLITHIC AND MESOLITHIC**

35,000 — **UPPER PALEOLITHIC**

**MIDDLE PALEOLITHIC**
Neandertal in Europe, Asia, Africa

100,000 —

Iron Age
Bronze Age: pottery
Copper Age

New Stone Age (Neolithic)

**PRESENT-DAY HUMANS**

Arago, Swanscombe, and Steinheim; Levallois technique

10,000 — Mesolithic
First agriculture: domestication of plants and animals

Peking finds

20,000 — Cro-Magnon, Dordogne: date of first discovered modern fossil skull

– Lake Mungo, Australia: skeletons
– Předmost: robust modern skulls

**FIRST MODERN HUMANS**

500,000 —

30,000 — Lake Mungo, Australia: artifacts
Velika Pecina
– Florisbad: modern and archaic features; most recent Mousterian tools

Hearths at Escale;
*H. erectus* expansion into Europe

40,000 — La Quina, La Chapelle, La Ferrassie, and Spy: Neandertal fossils; oldest Upper Paleolithic tools found; Niah: modern skull

Günz glaciation

Skhūl and Kafzeh: blend of archaic and modern features

1 million —
*H. erectus* expansion into China

50,000 — Sipka jaw fragment: blend of archaic and modern features

*A. robustus* and *A. boisei* extinct

Tabūn, Amud, Shanidar: archaic skulls; very few modern features

**TRANSITIONAL: ARCHAIC AND MODERN**

**LOWER PALEOLITHIC**

60,000 — Monte Circeo: classic Neandertal

Acheulian industry

70,000 —

1.5 million —

Mousterian industry appears; disk-core technique used

**ARCHAIC**

80,000 —

*Homo habilis* at Olduvai

Broken Hill: very robust skull, large palate, modern limbs

90,000 — Earliest evidence of classic Neandertal in Europe

2 million — Oldowan industry

ENTER CRO-MAGNON

This chart shows the approximate chronology of the Middle to Upper Paleolithic sequence. No dates are entirely reliable, and many are not based on carbon-14 dating but on more indirect dating methods.

# Chapter 17

# Technology, Magic, and Art

Human life is everywhere a state in which much is to
be endured and little to be enjoyed.

SAMUEL JOHNSON, 1709–1784.
*Rasselas*, Ch. 7.

## AN END TO WANDERING

In the fertile valleys of Egypt, on the frigid plains of Siberia, and along
the seacoast of Africa, humans were demonstrating that they not only
could stay alive but could actually prosper under conditions of extraordinary diversity. Cold was no barrier to their existence; when meat was
scarce their food became fish; and at least in one area we have evidence
that with foresight and planning they harvested natural grains. After
centuries of nomadism, of moving from place to place in pursuit of
game or of fresh supplies of plant food, humans were finally able to
stay in one place and systematically exploit the seasonal resources of
one locality. They were, in short, becoming the masters of the world
they inhabited.

### A New Life-Style

This change in subsistence inevitably produced profound changes in
their physical well-being and mode of living. For one thing, these first
modern humans were probably healthier than their predecessors. With
sufficient food and a more rounded diet, they must have been stronger
and more alert, better able to outrun and outmaneuver many of the
animals they hunted. The skeletal evidence suggests they also lived a
bit longer, and the extra time on earth allowed them not only to accumulate more knowledge but to pass on more of their knowledge to
their children and grandchildren.

FIGURE 17–1  *The oldest known firestone, this iron pyrite is from a Belgian cave. The Cro-Magnons were apparently the first to discover that flint and iron pyrite used in combination yielded sparks hot enough to ignite tinder. (The stone is here enlarged one and a half times.)*

Along with better health, their efficiency as food producers gave them other advantages. Because they were often able to lead a more sedentary life, they could acquire more material goods, objects which would have been impractical to own as long as they were on the move but which made providing for food and shelter easier. The inhabitants of several late Cro-Magnon sites in central Europe, for instance, were shaping objects from clay and, as we shall see, even firing them in dome-shaped kilns. Even more important than material wealth was the evolution of social behavior—a base for the full development of language, art, and religion and for the complex forms of social and political organization that are the hallmark of all developed human cultures.

During the 20,000 or so years of their tenure, these people made more technological progress, and in so doing gained more control over their environment, than had been made or gained in all the million years of human experience that preceded them. They were the master stoneworkers of all time, improving old techniques to produce stone tools of greater effectiveness and variety. The Cro-Magnons also exploited other materials—bone, antler, and ivory—that had been little used earlier, selecting and working each to best advantage in fashioning not only new weapons and new tools but domestic inventions and decorative objects as well. They learned to build better fires more easily and to use them for new purposes. Some Cro-Magnon shelters were but a step away from real houses; they were more durable than earlier shelters and afforded more protection against the elements. And when the climate changed, they invented ways to deal with it. Technological innovation and cultural adaptation almost replaced physical evolution, and humans' links to their animal past were now beginning to lie more and more behind them. These people still depended on nature, but nature no longer ruled them.

**Mastery of Fire**  The Cro-Magnons added new dimensions to the humans' use of fire. For one thing, they were the first to leave proof of their ability to strike a fire quickly whenever they needed one. A cave site in Belgium yielded a beautifully rounded piece of iron pyrite (Figure 17–1). This substance is one of the few natural materials from which flint will strike sparks that will set dry tinder on fire; sparks struck from two flints or two ordinary rocks are not hot enough to do so. What is more, the Belgian pyrite has a groove showing where it had been struck again and again with pieces of flint. Because iron pyrite is not easy to find lying about on the ground, each such firestone was undoubtedly a cherished item that would have been carried where a band roamed.

A more dramatic example of the growing mastery of fire, evidence of which has turned up in sites in the Soviet Union and France, seems prosaic at first glance: shallow grooves dug into the bottom of a hearth, and a channel curving away from the hearth like a tail. So simple an innovation may well have been overlooked many times in earlier archaeological excavations, but in fact it was the first small step toward the blast furnaces of modern steel mills. The grooves and channels in those prehistoric fireplaces allowed more air to reach the fuel, and fires in them could thus burn hotter.

The people who built these special hearths needed them because of the type of fuel they used. In an area where wood was scarce, they had to turn for fuel to a material that normally does not burn well: bone. Although bone is hard to ignite and burns inefficiently, being only about 25 percent combustible material, it gives off adequate heat. That these people did burn it is proved by the lack of charred wood and the considerable quantities of bone ash found in their specially vented hearths.

The hearth was home, and Cro-Magnons, who changed so much else, also changed the concept of home. Though some lived in the same caves and rock shelters that had protected their predecessors, they seem, in some places at least, to have kept cleaner house than those earlier tenants; litter was thrown outside instead of being allowed to pile up inside.

It was in regions that offered no ready-made habitations that the home improvements were most noticeable. Particularly in central and eastern Europe and Siberia, remnants of many sturdily built shelters have been found in open country (see Figure 17–2).

**Solutrean Laurel Leaves**

Improvement in stone tools was crucial to the Cro-Magnons' new technical mastery. It is ironic that despite all efforts at deciphering them no one really knows what purpose was served by the most beautiful examples of this new skill. Anyone who has ever held and examined a tool such as the magnificent eleven-inch-long "laurel-leaf" blade (Figure 17–3) must eventually wonder how this implement could have been used. Too delicate for a knife, too big and fragile for a spearhead, so

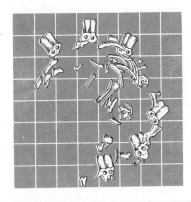

FIGURE 17–2  *Careful mapping of an upper Paleolithic site in the Ukraine shows mammoth bones lying in a semicircle, suggesting that they were part of a round structure. The original dwelling was probably dome-shaped, covered with hides, and weighted down with other bones, as depicted in the reconstruction.*

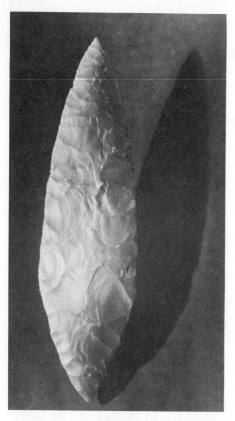

*FIGURE 17–3   A laurel-leaf blade is so delicate it could have served no practical purpose. The blade—eleven inches long but only four-tenths of an inch thick—may have been a ceremonial object or even the proud emblem of a master toolmaker. These finely chipped blades are part of the Solutrean tool industry.*

beautifully crafted a piece of flint seems to be a showpiece. Clearly, to produce an object of such daring proportions required craftsmanship bordering on art, and many archaeologists think this masterpiece and others like it may have been just that—works of art which served an esthetic or ritual function rather than a utilitarian one and which may even have been passed from one person or group to another as highly prized items.

If the large laurel-leaf blades were made for no useful purpose, they were clearly, then, an instance of technology transcending itself. The smaller, everyday implements on which such showpieces were modeled had strictly practical functions. They are known in the thousands and come in various styles from sites all over the world. Stone points in various sizes have been found in western and central European excavations in cultural levels called *Solutrean*—a style typified by finds from Solutré in France. There is no doubt that many of these points could have served most effectively as spear points or knives with razor-sharp edges. They were significant items in the armory of a people who depended for their existence less and less on the simple strength of their biceps and more and more on their brain power and the efficacy of their weapons.

The small stone blades of Cro-Magnons were unquestionably sharp and efficient. Modern experiments have shown that well-made flint projectile points are sharper than iron points of a similar type and penetrate more deeply into an animal's body. Flint knives are equal, if not superior, to steel knives in their cutting power. The only drawback of flint is that, because of its brittleness, it breaks more easily than metal and has to be replaced more often.

The importance of such blades in the lives of Cro-Magnon hunters lends authority to the theory that the large, nonutilitarian examples, of which at least several dozen have been found, might have been ritualistic objects representing the quintessential spear point. They might, too, have been used as a primitive currency for trade. On the other hand, it has also been suggested that a magnificent laural leaf might have been simply a *tour de force* tossed off by a virtuoso toolmaker to demonstrate his talent. If so, any admiration or praise his work received was well deserved. The laural leaf is without doubt a splendid creation, and fewer than a handful of people in the world today are skilled enough in the ancient craft to produce one.

## Tool Specialization

However different the various tool industries of this period may have been in style, in character they had much in common. Human groups everywhere produced tools more specialized than any used before. Archaeologists identify sixty to seventy types of tools in the kits of some Neandertals—scrapers meant to be held horizontally, knives with blunted backs, others with double edges, and so on. But they count

FIGURE 17–4 *This Upper Paleolithic burin is the first chisel—a new and important technological development. Its main use was perhaps to make other tools of wood or bone. (This photograph is approximately one-half actual size.)*

more than a hundred types in the tool kits of the Cro-Magnons—knives for cutting meat, knives for whittling wood, scrapers for bone, scrapers for skin, perforators, stone saws, chisels, pounding slabs, and countless others. Among the innovations of Cro-Magnons are two-part *composite* tools. They are believed to have begun putting bone and antler handles on many of their stone tools, such as axes and knives. By providing them with a firmer grasp and enabling them to use much more of the muscle power in their arms and shoulders, the handles increased the power the user could put into a blow with a tool through leverage by as much as two to three times.

One of the most important tools the Cro-Magnons developed was the cutter called a burin (see Figure 17–4). It is tempting to say they invented the burin, but it had existed in a few Neandertal tool kits and even in those of *Homo erectus*. In the hands of these modern people, however, the burin was gradually improved and became more important and much more prevalent. A burin was a kind of chisel. Today the name is given to a fine steel cutting tool used by engravers in preparing copper plates. In the Stone Age it was a tool with a strong, sharply beveled edge or point used to cut, incise, and shape other materials, such as bone, antler, wood, and sometimes stone. It differed from most other stone tools of prehistory in that it was not used by itself to kill animals, cut meat, clean hides, or chop down saplings for tent poles. Rather, like the machine tools of the modern age, its chief function was the manufacture of other tools and implements. With a tool that made other tools, the Cro-Magnon technology could expand many times faster than ever before.

The burin probably helped produce many wooden implements, but only fragments of these have survived. The best record of the object's effectiveness, then, is found in the surviving tools it shaped. These superb tools, like the burin itself, stand out as a mark of Cro-Magnon sophistication. Besides wood, three organic raw materials—bone, antler, and ivory—helped supply the needs of the Cro-Magnons' ever-expanding economy, and the burin made possible their widespread exploitation. *Homo erectus* and earlier *Homo sapiens* had used bone to some extent for scraping or piercing or digging, but not nearly so much as the Cro-Magnons did. In a typical Neandertal site perhaps twenty-five out of a thousand tools turn out to be made of bone; the rest are stone. In some Cro-Magnon encampments the mix may be as much as half-and-half, or even greater.

Bone and antler and ivory were the wonder materials of these times, much like plastics today. Less brittle and therefore more workable than flint, much stronger and more durable than wood, they could be cut, grooved, chiseled, scraped, sharpened, shaped. They could be finely worked into tiny implements like needles, or used for heavy work. A deer antler makes an excellent pick, a mammoth's leg bone cracked lengthwise needs only minor modifications and a handle to become an efficient shovel. Ivory could be steamed and bent, adding yet another dimension to toolmaking.

Best of all, the very animals hunted and depended on for food provided these materials in abundance. All animals have bone, of course, and many large animals—red deer, reindeer, mammoth—had antlers or tusks as well. Antlers seemed almost to be nature's gift to humans, because they did not even have to kill an animal to obtain them: every year deer shed their old ones, which lay on the ground for the picking up. Because reindeer and red deer were at one time or another perhaps the most abundant game animals in western Europe, antler was used there more than bone or ivory. In parts of eastern Europe and Siberia, where wood was relatively scarce, skeletons from giant mammoths that had died a natural death or had been trapped by hunters were a source of tools. A mammoth tusk might measure more than nine feet and weigh more than a hundred pounds; a lot of implements could be made from that much ivory.

With its strong chisel point, the burin could easily scratch or dig into ivory or bone without breaking. To cut up a bone, the toolmaker could incise a deep groove around the bone and then, with a sharp blow, break it cleanly at the cut, just as a glazier today cuts a groove in a glass pane before breaking it. To get slivers for needles, points, and awls, it was necessary only to draw a burin repeatedly lengthwise down a bone to score two parallel grooves deep enough to hit the soft center. Then the piece of hard material between the grooves was pried out and ground to shape (Figure 17–5). Other pieces of bone could be turned into spatulas, scrapers, beads, bracelets, digging tools, and more.

In addition to domestic utensils, bone and antler provided spear points, lances, and barbed harpoon tips, with which the hunters took advantage of bountiful supplies of game. Probably at no time since have there been so many grazing animals roaming the earth: Europe and Asia had mammoth, horses, red deer, pigs, reindeer, and bison; Africa had all the animals known there today, as well as a great many others that are now extinct—enormous relatives of buffalo, hartebeest, and zebra.

The scene was set for hunting-and-gathering humans to reach the peak of successful adaptation. Full exploitation of these rich resources gave an extraordinary amount of control over their environment, and formed the stable basis for still further cultural developments.

## CRO-MAGNON: HUNTER PAR EXCELLENCE

Two dazzling examples of Cro-Magnon hunting success have been unearthed by archaeologists in Europe. Near the town of Pavlov, in Czechoslovakia, excavations have revealed the remains of more than 100 mammoths in one giant bone heap; near Solutré, in France, an even more staggering bone pile contains the fossils of an estimated 10,000 wild horses lying in a tangled heap at the bottom of a high cliff. The mammoth bones are apparently the remains of the giant beasts trapped in pitfalls; the horses had perhaps been stampeded off the cliff over many years, even generations, by intelligent hunters who were familiar down to the last detail with the terrain of the region and the behavior of their victims.

It is likely that the people of this period—including the ancestors of the tribes who would in time be ranging the plains of North America— understood as much about hunting large herd animals as any human group in history. They undoubtedly knew just what plants the animals preferred to eat; when seasonal migrations began and how fast the animals traveled; what panicked them and what soothed them. They knew how to drive them into pit traps; how to snare them with baited thong nooses, and how to guide them into natural or human-made corrals, either by stampeding them or herding them quietly from a

*FIGURE 17–5   The slow process of making a needle out of an antler can be broken down in six steps.*

1. Preparing to make a needle, the toolmaker holds an antler in his hands. On his lap are a burin and a piece of grooved sandstone, which was cut with a burin.

2. Having scratched the outline of a triangle on the antler with a burin, the toolmaker finishes carving the triangle. He must cut deeply to completely separate it from the antler.

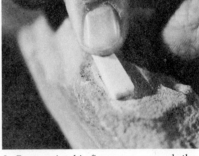

3. By pressing his finger on one end, the toolmaker has lifted the triangle from the antler and now rubs its wide end against sandstone to thin the triangle so that it can be pierced.

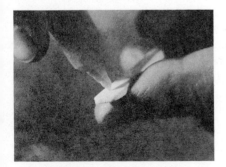

4. To make the needle's eye, the toolmaker holds the triangle and gently begins to bore a hole in it. He will turn the triangle over and work on the other side to refine the eye.

5. The eye—only one-sixteenth of an inch in diameter—is finished, and the toolmaker uses a burin to shape the triangle into a rounded needle.

6. To finish the needle, the toolmaker sharpens the point by rubbing it back and forth in a groove in a piece of sandstone. The finished needle is pointed enough to penetrate leather or skins easily.

discreet distance. Once trapped, the animals could be dispatched with spears or knives and butchered on the spot. The meat was then taken back to camp, perhaps in processed form, possibly cut up in strips and smoked or sun-dried.

There can also be little doubt that these hunters knew a great deal about the anatomy of their victims and the virtue of eating certain of their organs. Today the inland Alaskan Eskimos save the adrenal glands of slaughtered caribou to give to young children and pregnant women. Chemical analysis of the gland reveals an astonishingly high content of vitamin C, an essential element but one hard to come by in the standard diet of the Eskimo. Without overestimating the earlier hunters' knowledge in these matters, it can be assumed that they, too, knew exactly which parts of the animals they hunted were good, and also which parts were good for them.

## Spear Throwers and Points

These people's profound understanding of their prey, combined with significant technical advances in their hunting equipment, paid off in increased food supplies. Hunters had long had wooden spears with fire-hardened tips or sharp stone heads to thrust or throw at their prey, but the effectiveness of a thrown spear against even a young deer, to say nothing of a thick-skinned giant aurochs (a kind of extinct wild ox), must have been limited, especially if the animal was in full retreat. These hunters made the spear an effective weapon for killing their prey at a greater distance by inventing the *spear thrower*.

The oldest tangible evidence of this rodlike device dates from about 14,000 years B.P. It comes from the cave of La Placard in France. Here several fragments of spear throwers were discovered, including a length of bone with a hooked end that looks like nothing so much as an oversized crochet needle. All told, more than seventy reindeer-antler spear throwers have turned up in southwestern France and near Lake Constance along the northeastern border of Switzerland. There is a curious dearth of them elsewhere in the Old World, perhaps because they may have been made of perishable wood and rotted away. By about 10,000 years ago, the wooden spear thrower was being used by the Indians of North and South America; the Aztecs called it the *atlatl*. The Eskimos employed it until recently, and Australian Aborigines still use it today, calling it a *womera* (Figure 17–6).

The spear thrower is, in the simplest explanation, an extension of the arm. It is one to two feet long, with a handle at one end and a point or hook at the other that engages the butt end of the spear. Hunters hold the thrower behind their shoulder, hook up, and lay the spear along it so that the spear points forward and slightly upward. During the throw they keep hold of the thrower, which may have a thong tied to its end to go around their wrist. When throwing, they swing their arm forward and snap their wrist, launching the spear with

*FIGURE 17–6   The method of throwing a spear has not changed since spear throwers were introduced in Magdalenian times, about 15,000 years ago. Here an Australian is shown poised to throw his stone-tipped spear. The womera can be clearly seen.*

FIGURE 17–7 *This Magdalenian harpoon is beautifully made and is part of a highly evolved collection of fishing tackle. (This photograph is approximately actual size.)*

great velocity from the end of the thrower at the top of its arc, in this way taking advantage of the centrifugal force generated. The spear travels faster than if hand-thrown because the extension of the throwing arm provides more leverage; the spear thrower's end moves faster than the hand holding it.

Modern experiments have demonstrated the great advantage a spear thrower gives. A seven-foot spear can be thrown no more than sixty or seventy yards when launched directly from a hunter's hand, but it can be projected up to 150 yards with a spear thrower, and it can kill a deer at thirty yards. This increase in range gave hunters a tremendous advantage. No longer having to get within a short distance of their prey, they could more often get a throw at the animals before the game ran away. Now they could, when the occasion arose, hunt alone instead of in a group, because it was no longer necessary to surround an animal in order to spear it. And, of course, the spear thrower made hunting safer, for hunters did not have to get so close to dangerous teeth, antlers, and hooves. The benefits are obvious: hunters who killed more often and got hurt less lived better and longer lives.

The first spear throwers were undoubtedly of wood, as the Australian womeras are today, but soon they were also being made from antler. A group of late Cro-Magnon people known as the *Magdalenians* embellished many of their throwers with carved figures and designs and may even have painted them. One ancient Magdalenian thrower bears traces of red ocher in its hollows, and some have black painted into the eyes. Other throwers display exquisite renderings of animals, including horses, deer, ibex, bison, birds, and fish. At least three show an ibex defecating, held still by the art of the engraver in a vulnerable moment, when a kill may be made. These carvings on weaponry represent a combination of esthetics and utility that is echoed in many aspects of the Cro-Magnons' life.

Other functional advances were in the spear itself. By this time, hunters had realized that a barbed point does more damage than a smooth one. Harpoon-style points, fashioned from bone or antler, often had several barbs on one or both sides (Figure 17–7). Another development stemmed from the difficulty of killing an animal outright by one spear wound alone; hunters would have to follow their wounded prey for a while until loss of blood made it weak enough for them to kill. To speed this process, some hunters developed bone spearheads with grooves along each side—runnels apparently designed to increase the flow of blood from the wound.

**Bow and Arrow?**     An interesting puzzle is the use of the bow and arrow. There is no clear-cut archaeological evidence that people used such a weapon until the very end of the period of the Cro-Magnons. But because bows are normally made of wood and sinew or gut, it would be a lucky accident indeed if any had survived the last ice age, and so the lack of evidence cannot be taken as conclusive. A couple of bows have been uncovered in Denmark that date back approximately 8,000 years, and a larger number of stone-tipped wooden arrow shafts, perhaps 10,000 years old, have been found in campsites of ancient reindeer hunters in northern Germany. In a cave in La Colombière, in France, there have been found small stones, possibly more than 20,000 years old, with pictures scratched on them that may represent feathered projectiles; whether these were arrows or dartlike spears, however, is uncertain.

It is clear, though, that these people had the wit and ingenuity to invent the bow. They must have known that saplings bend under tension and spring back when released; they had leather thongs and almost certainly knew that dried animal gut and sinew make a strong and flexible cord. Believing this, many archaeologists today are convinced that some hunters indeed used the bow before 10,000 B.P., despite the lack of physical proof.

Certainly the bow would have given hunters an enormous advantage. The spear thrower, no matter how valuable an aid, required them to break cover and stand out in the open where they could be spotted by their prey; an unsuccessful launch would scare off the target. But with the bow, hunters could remain hidden. If they missed with the first arrow, they might have time to shoot again. Moreover, the arrow was swifter than the spear and its striking power was greater over a longer distance. It could be shot at a variety of animals—big and small, standing, running, or on the wing—with a better chance of hitting them.

### Fishing Gear

*FIGURE 17–8   The leister is a three-pronged fishing spear. The middle prong (not visible here) is shorter than the other two. Here an Australian employs the implement, which has been in use for at least 10,000 years.*

Perhaps even more significant than the invention of the spear thrower or bow in helping these Upper Palaeolithic people expand their food supply and make a living in varied environments was their development of fishing gear. Human groups had earlier availed themselves of the bounty offered by streams, rivers, and the sea; but for some fishing now became almost a way of life.

One ingenious development from this period (about 12,000 B.P.) was a device called the *leister* (Figure 17–8): a tridentlike spear with a point and two curving prongs of bone that held the fish securely after it had been lanced. Another was the *fish gorge,* a small sliver of bone or wood, perhaps two inches long, with a leather or sinew line tied around its middle. A fisherman dropped his baited line into the water; the gorge, once swallowed by a fish, cocked sideways in its throat in such a way as not to come out easily; and the fisherman hauled in his catch.

From a slightly later date, we have evidence suggesting that in South Africa and perhaps in Europe, people began catching fish in much greater numbers than ever before. Small, grooved, cylindrical stones found in South Africa may have been weights on nets made of thongs or plant fibers. With a net, two or three fishermen could catch a whole school of fish in one sweep.

The *weir,* a stone corral for trapping fish still employed by primitive peoples, was probably also used at this time. This technique would have been especially effective on rivers such as the Dordogne and Vézère in France, where spawning salmon swarm upstream in great numbers. It seems likely that at the spawning season, parties went to the fishing grounds to lay in a supply of salmon for the whole band, which may have had its home base miles away. The fish may have been cleaned and perhaps sun-dried or smoked where they were caught, and then carried to camp. At Solvieux, in France, a large rectangular area carefully paved with small stones has been excavated. Its placement and design strongly hint that it was a fish-drying platform.

## Sedentary Life and Sewn Clothing

As human groups learned to tap the potential of rivers and seas, climatic changes complemented their improving technologies. The rising sea level that was associated with the retreat of the ice submerged the Atlantic continental shelf and so increased the area of warm, shallow sea in which many species of fish could breed. The systematic exploitation of the waters' abundant protein resources—which included great quantities of shellfish as well as fish—was highly significant, not only because it broadened the base of the human diet but because it helped lead humans toward the next great step in cultural evolution: settled living. With fish and shellfish as a dependable supplement to their regular meat and plant foods, people did not have to move around so much in quest of sustenance. With nets they could gather more food with less effort than they could as nomadic hunter-gatherers, and thus one place could support a greater number of people. The beginning of a sedentary way of life was a crucial development, closely related to what became a rapidly expanding population.

As the last ice-age peoples learned to help themselves more efficiently to nature's bounty, they also found ways to protect themselves more effectively from nature's rigors. The fabrication of carefully sewn, fitted clothing was part of the equipment that enabled them to conquer the far north and eventually to penetrate North America.

The hide clothing of these people was probably much like that of the Eskimos. A tunic or pullover with tightly sewn seams to keep heat from escaping, pants easily tucked into boots, and some sort of sock, perhaps of fur, would have been warm enough in all but the coldest weather. For frigid days, outer clothing consisting of a hooded parka, mittens, and high boots would have kept a person from freezing. What is our evidence for clothing of this sort? Female figurines from Stone Age Russia look as if they are clothed in fur. Furthermore, even in more moderate climates, good sewn clothing seems to have been an advantage; the earliest eyed needles that have yet been discovered were fashioned by the same expert Solutrean workers of Europe who produced the laurel-leaf blades.

## ART AND RITUAL OF CRO-MAGNON

### Cave Art

Until now, our discussion of Cro-Magnons has centered on their improvements in working stone and particularly bone, and on the cultural developments furthered by these technological improvements. Notable as these changes are, it is their intellectual and spiritual achievements that make Cro-Magnons so impressive to us today. Particularly striking is their astounding artistic ability, a talent that seems to have sprung full-blown out of nowhere. There are dozens of examples of Cro-Magnon cave art in France alone. These date from approximately 28,000 to 10,000 B.P. Cro-Magnons were close observers of the animals they hunted as well as magnificent artists. More than that, the record they left behind shows that they had a sufficiently sophisticated way of life to be able to appreciate and encourage their own talents and to work them into their rituals.

From all evidence, the prodigious output of paintings and carvings of Cro-Magnons is closely associated with their spiritual life. One strong indication is seen in the places they chose to put wall paintings. The caves in the Dordogne are basically of two kinds. The rock overhangs, more or less open and facing out over the valleys, can be made livable by adding barriers of brushwood or animal skins to keep out the wind and snow. These are the rock shelters that Cro-Magnons lived in (Figure 17–9). They are full of the signs of many generations of occupancy;

*FIGURE 17–9  Seen from a cliffside ledge north of Les Eyzies, the Vézère Valley presents a peaceful panorama little changed since Cro-Magnons surveyed the scene. At left, the ledge leads past a shallow rock shelter, one of hundreds of prehistoric dwellings that are still unexcavated.*

tools lie in all strata in their floors together with buried skeletons. Hearths abound, tending to become bigger as they become more recent.

Some fragments of wall decoration have been found in these open shelters; perhaps originally there were more that have since been destroyed by exposure to the elements. But the most spectacular Cro-Magnon wall art is confined to true caves: deep underground fissures with long galleries and passages. These caves have their own subterranean pools and rivers, their festoons of stalactites and stalagmites. They are dark, mysterious, and very cold; they could be entered only by people holding stone lamps or torches. Certainly these caverns were inappropriate as dwelling places, and they contain little or no evidence of having been lived in. By nature removed from day-to-day life, these caves quite probably were used by Cro-Magnons as shrines.

**Painting and Hunting Magic**

Some attention has been given by archaeologists to the theory that Cro-Magnons used these underground passages for certain rites. The fears inspired by low, damp corridors and total darkness might have been similar to those provoked in other ways by some modern puberty initiation rites. Cro-Magnons were socially developed enough to have elaborate rites of this sort, and the evidence from the cave called Le Tuc d'Audoubert suggests such a practice (Figure 17–10). Another interesting point about cave art has been brought out by the late Abbé Henri Breuil, the French priest who devoted his life to the study of prehistory, and by Johannes Maringer, who has also studied this art intensively. The paintings or engravings were often made in the least convenient places for viewing: in narrow niches, behind protrusions of rock, sometimes in areas that must have been not only difficult but actually dangerous for the artist to work in. "It is simply impossible," says Maringer, "that this art should have been invented, in these locations, to give pleasure to the eye of the beholder; the intention must always have been to veil it in mysterious secrecy."

What was its purpose, then? According to Maringer and numerous other experts, cave art was a vehicle for magic—more specifically, a vehicle for a form known as *sympathetic hunting magic*. Cro-Magnons were strong and intelligent, and they were well equipped with all kinds of weapons from spears and knives to slings. They knew how to make traps for small animals and pitfalls for large ones. They could ambush animals and stampede them. And, as we have seen, they have left impressive records of their prowess behind them. Nevertheless, despite their formidable powers, they walked always in the shadow of unpredictable and incomprehensible events, which they may have seen as malign forces. Doubtless they felt it necessary to try to forestall misfortune and injury—and perhaps death, for some of the animals they came up against were extremely dangerous. Doubtless, too, they believed, like so many people living today, that magic could help them not only dodge misfortune but also gain control over the animals they wished

*FIGURE 17–10   Two twenty-four-inch-long clay bison lean against a limestone block in a remote chamber of Le Tuc d'Audoubert Cave near Ariège, France.*

to kill. By painting the animals' pictures they became in effect the animals' masters and strengthened their chances of dealing them a mortal wound during the hunt. Even today many isolated peoples believe that creating the likeness of a person or thing gives the person who created it some supernatural power over the subject.

This interpretation of the paintings as hunting magic has a variety of evidence to support it. First, and most direct, is the large number of animals painted with spears lodged in them or marked with the blows of clubs, as though the artists intended to illustrate what they hoped would be the outcome of a chase (Figure 17–11). Less obvious are the drawings of rectangular enclosures with animals seemingly trapped in them. The most frequently seen example of these is in a cave at Font-de-Gaume near Les Eyzies, where a magnificent painted mammoth seems to be caught in a pitfall even though its enormous tusks thrust beyond the snare.

There is also a hint of hunting magic in the practice of superimposing one picture over another. This phenomenon has been observed over and over again in the caves. In one spot at Lascaux in France, the paintings are four layers deep, even though there is plenty of empty wall space nearby. If the painters had meant simply to express themselves or give pleasure to others, they would probably have started with a clean wall surface for each animal depicted. The concentration of paintings in one spot, one atop another, suggests that placement of the painting was somehow important and that the overpainting was done for a purpose. Certain areas of the cave were favored for some reason, and it would be logical to suppose that paintings that had previously brought hunters good luck might in themselves come to be regarded as good hunting magic. Because all ritual depends on duplicating as closely as possible a procedure that has proved successful in the past, certain spots in the cave would come to be regarded as lucky.

In some instances entire caves seem imbued with an aura of good fortune. In Les Combarelles in southwestern France nearly three hundred animals crowd onto the cave walls. Perhaps it is this crowding that produced still another phenomenon of Cro-Magnon wall art: the tendency to overpaint one animal's head on another's body. Where space was at a premium, it would have been more provident to use the magic already available than start afresh. Or perhaps artists simply looked for a less arduous way of working magic, for many of the cave paintings obviously took time and effort to execute. It is not difficult to imagine wishful hunters contemplating a beautifully painted bison and deciding to take a magical shortcut by substituting a deer's head for the bison's.

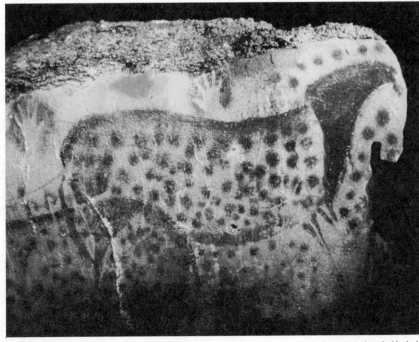

FIGURE 17–11 *Pelted with dots, a painting of two horses in the Pech-Merle Cave (Dordogne) combines two kinds of symbols for what could be simple decoration or signs of hunting magic. The dots, in black and red ocher, could represent projectiles; the handprints surrounding the horses, a person's power over his prey. Taken together, the dots and hands would then be an invocation to the supernatural, intended to assure the hunters of a successful kill.*

Hunting magic could also explain the occasional human-beast figures found in caves, strange-looking creatures with human bodies and animal or bird heads, often appearing to be engaged in some kind of dance. These shaman or sorcerer figures may be straightforward pictures of hunters disguised as animals, intended to guarantee successful stalking. On the other hand, they may be more symbolic. Perhaps they were projections of the hunters' feeling that a painting showing a ritual dance by a magician or shaman would work more potent magic on the game. The human-beast figures may even have been attempts to represent a superhuman being, such as a spirit of the hunt or the deity of the animals.

**Art and Fertility**

Although hunting magic logically explains a great deal of Cro-Magnon cave art, that art is open to other interpretations. For some authorities these animals and cryptic geometrical signs are sexual in nature, and the paintings are fertility magic. Pairs of animals were often shown together, sometimes in the act of mating. Horses, does, and cows were painted with swollen bellies (as in Figure 17–12), which have been interpreted as a sign of advanced pregnancy. In other paintings, udders were enlarged, as if to emphasize the rich supply of milk that the mother would be capable of giving to any offspring that might be born.

Fertility of the game hunted was a natural concern for the hunters. Scarcity of food must have been a periodic problem in many regions.

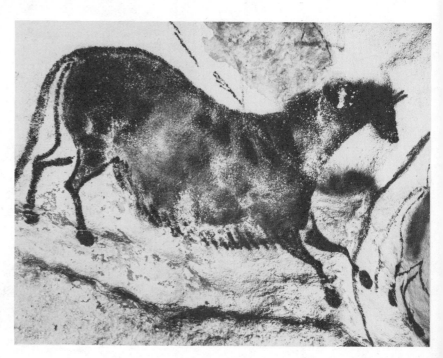

FIGURE 17–12   A pregnant horse gallops across the limestone ceiling of Lascaux. The slash marks above its shoulders may indicate spears.

During the colder episodes of the last glacial period Cro-Magnon hunters killed mammoths, woolly rhinoceroses, ibex, steppe horses, and particularly reindeer, which flourished in large numbers in the tundra environment. When the climate warmed from time to time, they undoubtedly hunted the deer, bison, and wild cattle that replaced the cold-adapted species. But the need to feed increasing numbers may well have led Cro-Magnons to encourage the natural productiveness of their game with fertility magic.

Other authorities think that Cro-Magnon cave art, though sexual in content, is far less utilitarian in its purpose. Instead of fertility magic, they see it as an attempt to express in visual symbols the dual forces in human nature—male and female. The most notable spokesman for this post-Freudian point of view is French anthropologist André Leroi-Gourhan, who has made an extensive study of Cro-Magnon cave art. Leroi-Gourhan has charted the frequency of occurrence of the various kinds of animals and signs, along with their locations in the caves and their positions in relation to each other. He thinks that most of the paintings and drawings have specific sexual connotations—that deer and bear are masculine, as are such signs as spears and clubs, whereas cattle and bison, as well as the enclosed figures that other authorities identify as traps in support of the theory of hunting magic, are feminine.

During the last fifteen years Alexander Marshack has been examining the smaller portable items of upper Palaeolithic art under a low-powered microscope. He has made many surprising observations, and drawn some startling if controversial conclusions. A beautiful 2½-inch-long horse carved in mammoth ivory from the site of Vogelherd in Germany is the earliest known example of animal sculpture, dating from about 30,000 B.C. The carefully carved ear, nose, mouth, and mane have been worn down by persistent handling. At some time during this use a fresh angle or dart has been engraved in its flank, apparently symbolizing an act of actual or ritualized killing. The object was touched and used, often, and seems to have served some important purpose.

A second example described by Marshak is the image of a horse engraved on a horse's pelvis from the site of Paglicci, in Italy. Microscopic examination of the image indicated that the horse had been symbolically killed twenty-seven times. Twenty-seven feathered darts or spears were engraved on and around the horse, each made by a different engraving point and in a different style, evidently over a considerable period of time. This horse was clearly a symbol that could be used in an appropriate way when required.

The large painted horse from the cave of Pech-Merle (Figure 17–11) proves to have somewhat similar characteristics: the black and red dots on its body are made of many pigments and ochers; they were applied over a period and so it seems that the horse was used continually as an important symbol.

But Marshak has noticed other details. On some portable items he has found small marks, often in series, made at different times by different tools, which seem to indicate some sort of notation or numerical record. One particularly interesting antler fragment, from La Marche in the Dordogne, shows both a pregnant horse (which has been "used" a number of times) and a lengthy notation consisting of small notches in rows made from the tip downward, in lines of eleven (Figure 17–13).

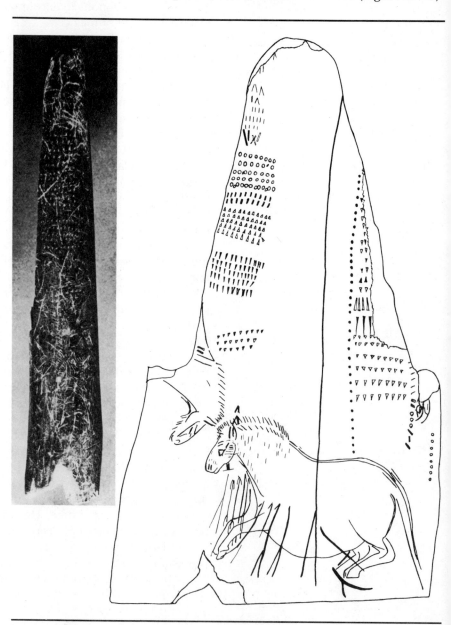

FIGURE 17–13  *Fragment of antler tool, La Marche, France. This is the earliest known artifact containing two types of notations; cumulative markings and naturalistic sketches. The markings may be related to the gestation period of a horse.*

Marshack points out that eleven is the number of months in the gestation of a horse. Other notations on other fragments suggest the phases of the moon were being logged.

Marshack's work has opened our eyes to the fact that the Cro-Magnon people were very much more sophisticated than anyone had supposed, and were not only great artists but were also possibly on the brink of developing arithmetic, and even perhaps the beginning of very primitive writing. We do not yet understand the meaning of all the material that they have left us, but we do know that they are ancestors for whom we should have the greatest respect.

Whatever the pictures' meaning, the skill of the artists and the beauty of their work is astonishing. Every animal is an individual portrait, drawn from life, by painters in complete control of their medium. Their outlines were sure and bold. They painted in various tones of black, red, yellow, and brown obtained from natural clays and mineral oxides. Sometimes they mixed their colors with charcoal and animal fat to make a thick pigment, which they used like a crayon or daubed on with moss, frayed twigs, or even a primitive paintbrush made of hair. At other times, they seem to have blown dry colors directly onto the wall in powder form, possibly through a hollow bird bone. Once applied to a wall, these colors were slowly absorbed by the limestone. This begins to explain their phenomenal durability. Thanks to the constant humidity and temperature of the caves, much of Cro-Magnon art in western Europe has retained its original brilliance for 10,000 to 20,000 years, some of it for even longer.

## Sculpture and Ceramics

In addition to painting, Cro-Magnons showed considerable proficiency as sculptors and engravers. In early examples of their skill, they incised the outlines of animals on cave walls. Later artists went on to develop the more advanced technique of carving subjects in high relief, often utilizing the contours of the walls. Le Cap Blanc, near Les Eyzies, has a marvelous set of horses done in this way. The entire frieze is about forty feet long; the largest horse is seven feet long. As the bulging sides of the horses' bodies reveal, the artists incorporated the natural curves of the rock into their work with great skill. Apparently, more than one artist was guided by the formation and the structure of the rock in carving this frieze, for the animal figures appear to have been worked on at various times.

Cro-Magnon artists also made complete statues in the round. In doing so, they left us a means of gaining further insights into Stone Age life and thought. The statues are normally of stone, bone, or ivory, although some were carved out of a mixture of clay and ground bone that had been fired to make it hard. The first evidence of firing comes from the site of Dolni Vestonice in Czechoslovakia. At a settlement dated about 27,000 B.P. is a kiln where the bone and clay mixture was fired into a new, rock-hard material. This is the first example in technological history of a process that was to become ubiquitous and would eventually be used in producing glass, bronze, steel, nylon, and most of the other materials of everyday life—that is, the combination and treatment of two or more dissimilar substances to make a useful product unlike either starting substance. It would be another 15,000 years or so before other people, living in Japan, learned to turn clay into pots; yet, as the evidence from Dolni Vestonice attests, ceramics had already been invented.

When the kiln hut was first investigated in 1951, its sooty floor was littered with fragments of ceramic figurines. There were animal heads—bears, foxes, lions. In one particularly beautiful lion head was a hole simulating a wound, perhaps intended to help some hunter inflict a similar wound on a real lion. The floor was also cluttered with hundreds of clay pellets bearing the fingerprints of the prehistoric artisan; he probably pinched them off his lump of unbaked clay when he first began to knead and shape it to his desire. And there were limbs broken from little animal and human figures. They may have cracked off in the baking, or when the ancient ceramist tossed aside a work that failed to please him.

## Female Figurines

*FIGURE 17–14   This Czech clay figure from Dolni Vestonice shows the Venuses' typical traits: huge breasts and belly and shapeless arms. This figure's legs are now broken, but they probably had no feet. (This photograph is approximately one-half actual size.)*

More intriguing than any waste fragments or even clay animal figures on the hut floor are the human statuettes found there, particularly the female figures. Unlike the animals, these are not naturalistic but almost surreal. They have a very wide distribution in Upper Palaeolithic sites over much of Europe and eastward as far as western Siberia and the Ukraine. Although they vary a good deal in appearance, they have some significant things in common. The most obvious of these is that the sculptors' interest was focused on the torso. Arms and legs are extremely small in proportion to the trunk, and in some cases they are merely suggested (see Figures 17–14 and 17–15). Heads are also small and typically show little attempt to portray features, although the famous Venus of Willendorf, a four-inch figurine made of limestone, does have a wavy hairdo executed with considerable care (see Figure 18–16). All the emphasis is on the bodies, with their female characteristics—breasts, belly, and buttocks—greatly exaggerated in size. They look like tiny earth goddesses or fertility figures, and a good deal of informed speculation suggests that this is what they were. Many of them show the polish of long use and some the remains of red ocher, which indicates that they were symbolically painted.

Some evidence for the idea that they were fertility figures is based on where these statuettes are found and when they are believed to have been made. The majority of them come from the period of the Upper Perigordian, a late Paleolithic culture of western Europe that existed between 20,000 and 25,000 years ago. During this period, the weather ranged from cool to very cold. In the cold periods it was bitter

FIGURE 17–15 *The Venus of Abri Pataud, the armless body of a woman incised in a small piece of rock, is one of the few art objects found at the excavation. It was made some 20,000 years ago.*

in the extreme, especially on the eastern European plains; nevertheless, many peoples continued to live there. Some made their homes in shallow pits they dug in the ground and then roofed over with hides or other material. The vague outlines of the walls of many of these sunken huts may still be seen. The interesting thing is that these sites contain abundant examples of these female figurines, where they are often found lying right next to the walls or buried near hearths. The figurines themselves often taper to a point at the bottom, as if they had been designed to be stuck into the earth or into a base of some sort.

On this evidence it is fairly clear that the figurines were closely associated with the daily life of the peoples who made them and have a significance utterly unlike that of the wall art that was created in secret, deep in underground caves. Speculating on their purpose, various authorities have proposed various theories. To Johannes Maringer the figurines seem to point to a change in the status of women. Maringer thinks that a combination of harsh climatic conditions and a relatively sedentary way of life account for that change. When people settle down in one place for considerable periods, the home becomes important; and homemaking is usually regarded as the woman's prerogative. In the cold of the windswept eastern steppe, it was perhaps the women who had the job of planning, rationing, utilizing, and storing supplies so that the group could get through the winter. Storage pits were found in many sites, some with animal remains. Probably, women would also have been responsible for making the fur clothing that the people are thought to have dressed in. They perfected the eyed needle, and by sewing carefully they could make warm clothing that fitted the body well, particularly around the arms and legs.

But the role of women would also have been important because of their procreative function. The mysteries of fertility and birth made women the guardians not only of hearth and home but of life itself. In the minds of some experts the female figurines are cult objects. They

*FIGURE 17–16   The skeleton of a man lies just as the body was buried 23,000 years ago in an ocher-sprinkled grave at Sungir, northeast of Moscow. The man was ceremoniously laid to rest, laden with beads, a headband of carved mammoth ivory, and the teeth of arctic foxes, in what appears to have been a burial ground—suggesting the hunter-gatherers of Sungir lived part of the year in a settled community where they developed complex customs.*

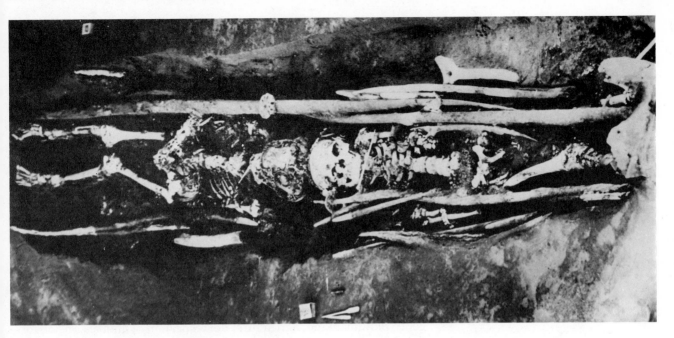

FIGURE 17–17   *The skeletons of two boys who died 23,000 years ago lie head to head in a grave at Sungir in Russia. The elaborateness of their grave suggests that the boys were laid to rest amid solemn ritual, perhaps with a view to an afterlife.*

represent the tribal ancestresses from whom the group is descended, assuring them of continuity as a group and increasing their population and the population of the animals they hunted. Whether the little figures were worshipped as goddesses or simply venerated as good-luck charms is not known.

## Burial Customs and Rites

Death as well as life concerned the Cro-Magnons, and their treatment of the dead was careful and thoughtful. The bodies were often placed in graves dug in the ashes of previously occupied living sites, and in many places it was a common practice to sprinkle the deceased with red ocher, perhaps in an effort to bring back the flush of life to pallid skin (Figure 17–16). The practice of including grave offerings, begun in Neandertal times, was expanded by their successors in Eurasia to extraordinary heights of funerary luxury. An example is the grave of two boys (shown in Figure 17–17) that was excavated during the 1960s in a Paleolithic settlement about 130 miles northeast of Moscow, at Sungir. The grave suggests either that the boys were very important or that the settlers who lived at Sungir 23,000 years ago had some fairly elaborate ideas about an afterlife. The boys—one seven to nine years old, the other twelve or thirteen—were laid out in a line, skull to skull. Both had been dressed from head to toe in clothing decorated with ivory beads carved from mammoth tusks, and they wore bracelets and rings of the same material. On the older boy's chest lay a disk of mammoth tusk carved into the shape of a horse, and both boys were equipped with an assortment of ivory weapons such as lances, spears, and daggers. The lances had been formed from a split mammoth bone that had been warmed over a fire in order to be straightened, a technique that requires considerable sophistication.

**Conclusions**    The more we learn about these earliest of modern people from the evidence of their living sites, the narrower the gap becomes between them and ourselves. But it will never be entirely closed. The intimate details of social life, the games children played, the gestures and courtesies that give a society flavor—all these have necessarily vanished. We have no knowledge of how one addressed another, or what words they used. And we will never know.

Some details have enlightened us, however, and some generalizations can be made. As these first modern people stretched their powers, they came to dominate nature in ways their ancestors could not have dreamed of. Their ability to exploit a variety of environments led to a great growth in their numbers, and populations increased as much as ten times in some parts of the world. By the end of this period, some 12,000 years ago, they had set the stage for the last steps in the emergence of humankind: agriculture, domestication of animals, metalworking, complex forms of social and political life, writing, and perhaps even war.

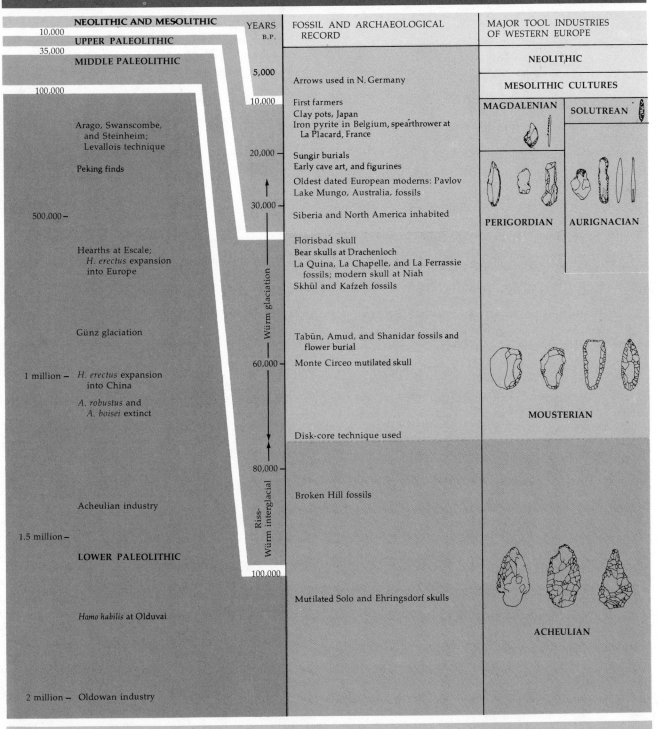

| | YEARS B.P. | FOSSIL AND ARCHAEOLOGICAL RECORD | MAJOR TOOL INDUSTRIES OF WESTERN EUROPE | | |
|---|---|---|---|---|---|

NEOLITHIC AND MESOLITHIC — 10,000

UPPER PALEOLITHIC — 35,000

MIDDLE PALEOLITHIC — 100,000

Arago, Swanscombe, and Steinheim; Levallois technique

Peking finds

500,000 —

Hearths at Escale; H. erectus expansion into Europe

Günz glaciation

1 million — H. erectus expansion into China

A. robustus and A. boisei extinct

Acheulian industry

1.5 million —

LOWER PALEOLITHIC

Homo habilis at Olduvai

2 million — Oldowan industry

YEARS B.P.:
5,000
10,000
20,000
30,000
60,000
80,000
100,000

Würm glaciation

Riss-Würm interglacial

FOSSIL AND ARCHAEOLOGICAL RECORD:

Arrows used in N. Germany

First farmers
Clay pots, Japan
Iron pyrite in Belgium, spearthrower at La Placard, France

Sungir burials
Early cave art, and figurines

Oldest dated European moderns: Pavlov
Lake Mungo, Australia, fossils

Siberia and North America inhabited

Florisbad skull
Bear skulls at Drachenloch
La Quina, La Chapelle, and La Ferrassie fossils; modern skull at Niah
Skhūl and Kafzeh fossils

Tabūn, Amud, and Shanidar fossils and flower burial
Monte Circeo mutilated skull

Disk-core technique used

Broken Hill fossils

Mutilated Solo and Ehringsdorf skulls

MAJOR TOOL INDUSTRIES OF WESTERN EUROPE:

NEOLITHIC

MESOLITHIC CULTURES

MAGDALENIAN     SOLUTREAN

PERIGORDIAN     AURIGNACIAN

MOUSTERIAN

ACHEULIAN

TECHNOLOGY, MAGIC, AND ART

Many of the dates given to finds are based on indirect evidence and are estimates; the dates given to cultural phases are approximations.

# Chapter 18

# The Human Condition

But man, proud man,
Drest in a little brief authority,
Most ignorant of what he's most assured,
His glassy essence, like an angry ape,
Plays such fantastic tricks before high heaven
As make the angels weep.

**WILLIAM SHAKESPEARE, 1564–1616.**
*Measure for Measure,* II, ii.

**THE STORY OF HUMANKIND**

It is hard to realize that the story we have recounted in these chapters took more than 30 million years in its enactment. The development of technology alone has taken well over 2 million years. During this incredibly long period of emergence, the animal that became *Homo sapiens* has been shaped by environment and social experience—both body and culture changing in adaptation.

Evolutionary biology, of which paleoanthropology is a division, makes this much clear to us: each species is a product of its genes and its environment. That is, each characteristic of every species is a product of mutation and natural selection and in a very immediate way *fits* its environment. Fishes have fins, horses have hooves, primates have hands. Each characteristic of the human body is also a direct product of the interaction between genes and environment. This is not to say that natural selection is directed or moves toward any goal; nor does it mean that the characteristics that *have* been selected by the environment are the only ones that could have been. Nature shows us that there is more than one solution to any problem. If in the long run we do not understand the genesis of every human characteristic, we know at least that we can never understand either the genesis or function of a characteristic without considering the environment in which it evolved.

**Environmental History and Adaptation**

The story of the human environment is relatively clear and forms the first strand of the story of human evolution. The tropical rain forest was the womb from which human ancestors emerged into the world. As our ancestors evolved, they moved out from the shelter of the forest to occupy more open woodland and the tropical savannas throughout the Old World. As they expanded north into temperate zones, they came to occupy an increasing number of different *biomes*, or ecological zones. To temperate grassland and woodland alike they adapted, and eventually to the cool taiga (subarctic coniferous forests) and icy tundra. They moved in and out of the northern taiga and followed game to alpine pastures. They evolved the flexibility to live in all these different biomes—and were the first organism to do so.

This flexibility humankind owed, of course, to the second strand of our story: to the evolution of a remarkable and extraordinarily adaptable body and of an astounding brain. We have seen how *Australopithecus* has come to be recognized as the first hominid and that this creature was certainly a biped with very human teeth. *Australopithecus* was adapted well to the new life-style of the savanna dweller—flexible in behavior, omnivorous, and highly social. The genus seems to have been a constant part of the savanna fauna for at least 4 million years. From it sprang bigger-brained forms: these were the first true humans, *Homo habilis*. Next in line were *Homo erectus*, who invaded the temperate zones. Expansion continued northward until the Neandertals and their contemporaries entered the arctic regions, equipped with highly developed technology. These people were already biologically modern, members of our own species, *Homo sapiens*. Following them, we find modern people who were indistinguishable physically from ourselves settling throughout the Old World and entering the New World and Australia. This expansion marked the beginning of modern times.

The human organism, miraculous though it may seem in its complexity, was still a product of natural selection: the human brain was no more than what was needed for survival in all these different environments. From an average of perhaps 400 cubic centimeters some 5 million years ago, human cranial capacity has risen to vary between 1,000 and 2,000 cubic centimeters. This increase in size has been exceedingly rapid by evolutionary measures, and has produced a brain of unprecedented complexity.

**Altruism and Bioaltruism**

*Altruism*—the act of helping others at some cost to oneself—has been claimed to be a unique characteristic of humans, and for many years biologists were unable to see how it could be that such a characteristic could possibly emerge as a result of natural selection. The question was discussed by J. B. S. Haldane as long ago as 1932, and he suggested that altruism of a kind would be selected if it prompted the survival of dependents or near relations. This obviously applies to the situation when a mother risks her life for her offspring. Since the essence of natural selection was competition, however, it was not clear how behavior that went against that overriding fact could be selected.

One hypothesis put forward originally by Charles Darwin and later developed by the British biologist V. C. Wynne-Edwards was based on the concept of *group selection*. If natural selection operated on social groups rather than individuals, then any behavior which benefited the social group, even at the expense of the individual, would presumably be selected. This point of view was discussed at length during the 1960s. It was not, however, generally accepted, and it was soon pointed out that other explanations were available which did not depend on the idea of a totally integrated group. Indeed we know that however well integrated the social group may be, a certain amount of competition continues within it.

Recent work by sociobiologists has, however, thrown light on this difficult question, and their ideas are of immense interest to anthropologists. When Hamilton introduced the concept of inclusive fitness in 1964 he gave us the key to understanding altruism in many social species (see page 87). The examples of altruism seen among insects and, for example, among birds which give warning calls (which we have discussed), is not of course what we think of as altruism among humans. This animal type of altruism has been conveniently called *bioaltruism*. Human altruism is expected to be voluntarily performed and disinterested.

When we come to examine social primates, we can identify a new kind of altruism. When baboons or chimpanzees form alliances, they will often take risks on behalf of one another which look very like human altruism. While in some cases they may be related, this is not always so. The American biologist Robert Trivers has examined situations of this kind and has introduced the term *reciprocal altruism*. Evidently there is an unspoken understanding between such individuals that "one good turn deserves another." It is in many ways a very human behavior pattern when members of a group of individuals agree to help each other when at risk. All that is required is that the aid should be reciprocated and that the advantages of such behavior should outweigh the disadvantages. It is also necessary that individuals do not cheat. Reciprocity is an important basis for much of human social life, and there are strong sanctions against cheating.

Do humans show any kinds of altruism which are not based in some biological advantage and not seen in other species? Edward O. Wilson, who has discussed this question at some length in his book *Human Nature*, has concluded that since we too (with our brains) are a product of natural selection, it it not likely that we should have developed behavior which operates against natural selection. If biological fitness demands altruism, then it will appear in human societies; but if altruism operates to lower individual and inclusive fitness, then it surely would never become established as a common behavior pattern. He writes:

> Genes hold culture on a leash. The leash is very long, but inevitably values will be constrained in accordance with their effect on the human gene pool . . . Human behavior—like the deepest capacities for emotional response which drive and guide it—is the circuitous technique by which human genetic material has been and will be kept intact. Morality has no other demonstrable ultimate function.

A review of instances of human altruism produces few examples in which there is not a well recognized reward for the risks taken, even if the reward is promised in the next life. Human society has developed reciprocal altruism to the point when it is all-pervasive, and society has developed sanctions against failure to act altruistically—against selfishness. Experienced swimmers are expected to save a drowning person even if they are completely unknown to them, and frequently do so. So strong is the pressure to act in this way that a policeman was recently drowned in England trying to rescue a dog from the waves.

Much human behavior is nonadaptive or maladaptive. We can choose not to bear children, we can commit suicide as individuals or as a nation. But we may question whether altruism lies in this category. As Wilson says, the genetic leash is long. Whether we can become free of that leash is another question. What we do know, however, is that reason has given us freedom from the lower brain centers, the limbic system, which makes animals do what they have to do. Because we are many and have reason as our guide, we can afford, biologically speaking, to take risks; we can risk our genes in living out our dreams. The ultimate human mystery lies perhaps in locating the origin of those dreams and

*FIGURE 18–1  From bipedal* Australopithecus *on the savanna to Cro-Magnons in the Dordogne, from Oldowan choppers to Solutrean eyed needles, human development has been the result of the interaction of environment, body, and culture.*

*Homo habilis*

*Homo erectus*

the new goals they have set us; goals that arise far from our biological heritage and yet give meaning to the lives of so many people. Human adaptability gives us freedom to follow those goals, at whatever cost.

**Cultural History** This immense adaptability led to the third strand of our story—the uniquely human characteristic that was also a response to the environment: culture (see Figure 18–1). Culture consists in the first place of those behaviors and ideas which are the property of the society and which are maintained by mutual learning and teaching among its members. In human evolution, language became a new means for transmitting and recording cultural data. Language was a unique and revolutionary organic adaptation; probably the most important development in human evolution. It opened up new possibilities of existence and paved the way for a second aspect of human culture: technology.

The first developments of technology came at an unimaginably slow rate. Any idea of progress would have been entirely foreign to early people; only the very simplest ideas were entering their heads. But progress did occur, however slowly. From using stone flakes they found on the ground as knives, people learned to prepare their own sharp flakes and their own simple choppers. Slowly, over millions of years, they improved the cutting edge and varied the form of tools for different purposes. The large hand-axe and the knifelike blade appeared; manual skill became essential to the development of technology. In the cave dwellings of the northern hemisphere the priceless and virtually irreplaceable fire began to be kept alive in the hearth. The rate of change quickened and cultural developments came more rapidly (Figure 18–2). In the cold winters a relatively complex technology was particularly

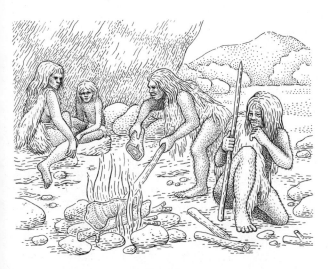

Neandertal

Cro-Magnon

crucial for human survival. Although we have little direct evidence, we can safely assume that not only containers but also clothing, wood and bone tools, and shelters of different kinds became an essential part of our ancestors' survival kit. People learned from each other, and from time to time an invention was made, but what today we see as a progressive journey was for these early people simply the way things were; their life-style was the only one they could imagine.

## Domestication of Plants and Animals

Eventually, humans learned to change their environment in a more fundamental way. They began to follow wild game and protect it from other predators so as to reserve it for themselves. They learned to select and breed animals: they domesticated sheep and cattle. They planted seeds and harvested cereals, becoming farmers.

Identification of the first evidence of the domestication of animals presents problems: the process of turning wild animals into tame ones will generate no identifiable archaeological remains, though after a considerable period of selective breeding, new breeds can be recognized by changes in skeletal structure. Dogs, sheep, goats and cattle were probably the first animals to be bred selectively, at an approximate date of about 10,000 B.P. in the Near East (Figure 18–3). There is some uncertain evidence from cave art in western Europe that horses may have been carrying bridals at a somewhat earlier time. But the hard evidence comes from a much later period. One of the most significant sites is that of Lukenya Hill, near Nairobi, Kenya, where cattle bones dated 4,000 B.P. are present on human occupation floors. Since cattle are not indigenous to Africa south of the Sahara, these animals must have been driven in from the north, which proves that they had reached a certain level of domestication by this time. Indeed, from that date on, domesticated cattle, sheep, goats and horses are found widely throughout the Old World.

The beginning of agriculture is still a mystery, and its details may always remain so. The first evidence of agriculture—of sowing, harvesting, and selecting wild barleys and wheats—dates from about 10,000 B.P. and comes from the Near East (Figure 18–3). It also appeared about this time, or soon after, in at least three other parts of the world: North China, Mexico, and Peru. The independent development of agriculture in these different regions is one of the most remarkable events in human evolution. The plants and animals domesticated in each area were different (Table 18–1), but the techniques were the same: the farmers collected and sowed seeds and then selected the high-yielding varieties for continued planting.

Hunting persisted in many areas and in some where humans herded animals agriculture did not follow until much later, even though the land and climate were suitable. Clearly, development of agriculture must have been slow, involving a number of steps. It probably followed an increase in population, which would create the need for a greater

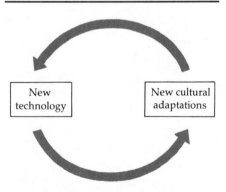

FIGURE 18–2 *Positive feedback loops can be constructive and creative, or destructive: in either case they tend to accelerate change in their components. This loop brings about very rapid cultural and technological changes.*

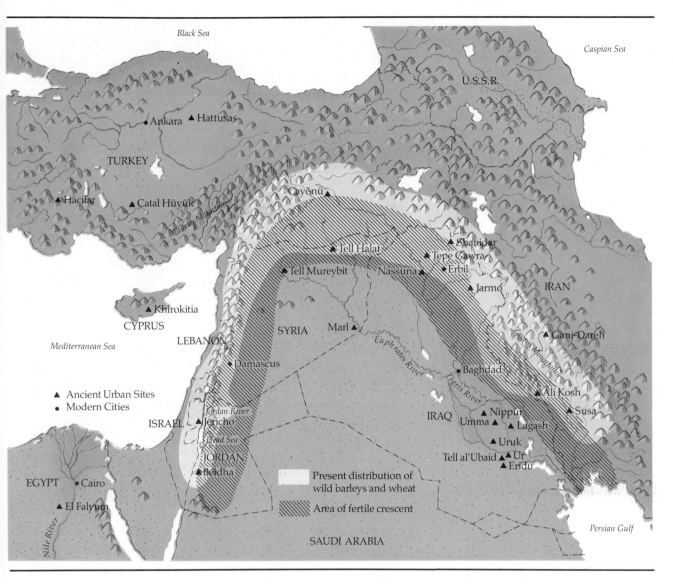

*FIGURE 18–3 This map of the Near East shows the fertile crescent where agriculture began about 10,000 years ago. During the last 5,000 years the rainfall of this region has become much less. Now much of the area is no longer suitable for agriculture. The reduction of rainfall was followed by the development of the earliest known system of irrigation in the valleys of the Tigris and Euphrates rivers. The earliest villages and towns also developed in this region of agricultural wealth.*

and more reliable food supply. And it occurred only where the appropriate plants and animals existed and the climate was right. Such an environment was the "fertile crescent" in the Near East. Robert Braidwood of the University of Chicago, who worked during the 1960s in northeastern Iraq, describes how some 10,000 years ago the climate and plant and animal life were ideal for innovation of agriculture. Within the zone, he wrote, "occur in nature a remarkable constellation of the very plants and animals which became the basis for the food producing pattern of the Western cultural tradition. Nowhere else in the world

**TABLE 18–1   Some Wild Vegetables and Animals Domesticated in the Three Primary Zones of Agricultural Development.**

| ZONE | PLANTS | ANIMALS |
| --- | --- | --- |
| Near East | Almonds<br>Apricots<br>Barley<br>Dates<br>Figs<br>Grapes<br>Lentils<br>Olives<br>Peas<br>Rye<br>Wheat | Cattle<br>Goats<br>Horses<br>Pigs<br>Sheep<br>Dogs |
| China | Bananas<br>Coconuts<br>Millet<br>Rice<br>Soybeans<br>Sugar cane | Banteng<br>Cattle<br>Pigs<br>Yak |
| South and Central America | Avocados<br>Beans<br>Chili<br>Cocoa<br>Corn<br>Gourds<br>Potatoes<br>Squashes | Alpaca<br>Guinea pig<br>Llama |

were the wild wheats and barley, the wild sheep, goats, pigs, cattle and horses to be found together in a single environment." The rainfall was right for agriculture without irrigation, but not sufficient to encourage the dense growth of forest, which would have been a stumbling block to primitive farmers.

**Civilization**   Although the agricultural revolution has not to this day reached all the earth's peoples, just about all the land suitable for agriculture is being farmed. Agriculture has made possible a vast increase in the world's population (see Figure 18–22) and it set the stage for a further cultural development of equal significance—development of cities and metal technology: the coming of civilization.

The most ancient city known to us is Jericho, which lies in present-day Israeli-occupied Jordan, on the west bank of the Jordan River (Figures 18–3 and 18–4). This city was first built about 10,000 B.P. and was no doubt a smaller settlement before then. The surplus food that agriculture made available in the region evidently enabled people to live in dense communities where they depended on farmers to supply them with their food—as we do today. This entirely novel situation allowed the city dwellers to specialize in arts and crafts of an ever-widening variety, and this specialization was to form the basis of modern civilization. Trade flourished: at Jericho, hematite, greenstone, obsidian, sea shells, and salt all passed through the city, together with much else of which we have no trace. The north-south trade route on which the city lay was an important stimulus to its development. But civilization probably would not have grown from these early roots without improvements in agriculture. The greatest cities grew in areas of rich agricultural land, where productivity was greatest; they reflected the foundation on which they necessarily were based.

FIGURE 18–4   An aerial view of Jericho encompasses the modern city and the fifty-foot-high dirt mound under which lie buried the many cities and walls of ancient Jericho. One of the most recent excavations can be seen: the trench cutting from left at the bottom of the photograph.

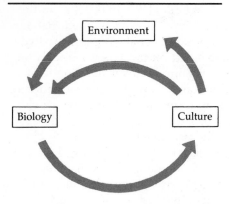

FIGURE 18–5   *This feedback loop shows the increasing influence of culture on our biology—our heredity. The biological rate of change always lags behind the cultural rate of change, a lag that implies failure in adaptation.*

The earliest achievements of civilization—including writing, organized religion and government, weaving, and metal technology—are too numerous to list, let alone discuss, but they bring us by an accelerating process of development from prehistory into history. Above all, it was developing technology that brought about the astonishing growth and complexity of human culture.

Environment, human biology, culture: these three are the threads of the human story we have told. During humankind's emergence each acted on the others in mutual feedback (see Figure 18–5); any change in one necessitated adjustment in the others. This relationship was something new in evolution, for learning to change the environment was something no animal had ever done before, beyond building a nest or preparing a small arena for courtship. Humans were to change their environment drastically—and as we can now see, to their ultimate disadvantage. But this was humankind's unique achievement, and it constitutes the story of human prehistory. Human work and human nature are indeed one. All are directly and systematically related to each other.

## HUMAN VARIABILITY

Within this dynamic system unique to humankind, in which the human body and its environment are related through culture, all three components show considerable variability. In this condition, humankind is not alone in the animal or plant worlds. Variability in behavior and appearance is characteristic of all living organisms as their environment varies, and it is probably no greater in humans than in many other species. Every individual (except identical twins) carries different genetic material; differences due to age and sex also exist. Beyond, we find variability that has evolved in response to local (and equally variable) environmental conditions. This type is especially noticeable as we pass from one continent to another or as we cross seas and mountain ranges, and observe populations that have adapted to very different environments. These are the human *geographic races:* the major units into which *Homo sapiens* can conveniently be subdivided.

The study of racial differences is important for a number of reasons. First, it provides us with many striking and fascinating characteristics of human groups. Second, the study can also indicate, to some degree, ancient, prehistoric relationships among different peoples. And third, the racial differences themselves are mostly examples of rather precise environmental adaptations, and so the racial differences illuminate our understanding of evolution, especially human evolution. The differences are also a most important key to better knowledge of human genetics. And, finally, the racial traits associated with certain diseases represent an important medical problem that requires continuing study.

**Geographic Races**     Because geographic races are extremely variable and merge with one another, they can in no sense be described as "pure." Indeed, their definition has been a source of controversy among anthropologists since their existence was first recognized, and it has even been said that races do not exist. This attitude, however, seems to contradict the evidence of our own eyes. American anthropologist Stanley Garn defines geographic races as collections of populations sharing a number of recognizable traits that are produced by a period of historical confinement within a certain geographic area. As Garn points out, resemblances within geographic races are far greater than those between them and this is the basis for their recognition. Nevertheless, differences within races are great, especially if traits are considered separately. In each geographic region there are tall populations and short populations, heavy-set people and slim people. On the other hand, some differences, such as those in skin color or hair form, which are extremely striking, transcend races and are a product of adaptations to a climate shared by different races. Thus people with dark skin can be found in almost all geographic races.

Because the distinctions among the races are not clear-cut and because gene flow always occurs between them where they are in contact, there are many ways of classifying the races. Classifications by different authors have listed from two to two hundred races. Such classifications are essentially subjective. The classification that follows is based on the main geographic races as they are most commonly recognized. Genetic differences *between* races, however, are believed to be fewer than those recorded *within* the major races. The distinctions between the races are, though, recognizable and useful. Also, in this discussion, we are using the term *race* purely in its biological sense to describe the biological nature of recognizably different human populations. The term carries no political implications or value judgments.

In our brief review of racial characteristics, we will refer to traits of three main kinds: (1) anatomical features, often superficial and visible, such as hair and lip form; (2) internal physiological traits, such as metabolic rate and hormone activity, growth rate, color blindness, and genetic diseases; and (3) characteristics of the blood (actually a subdivision of the physiological traits).

**Anatomical Features**     Anatomical features such as hair and lip form are well recognized as differing among races. The actual appearance of the hair is produced by differences in the structure and cross-section of the hair (Figure 18–6). Other external differences are caused by pigmentation (which affects skin, hair, and eye color), eyelid form (the presence or absence of the *epicanthic fold;* see Figure 18–7), breast and nipple form, patterns of hair on the head and the body, frequency of balding, fingerprint pattern (see Figure 18–8), and body build. There are also differences in the

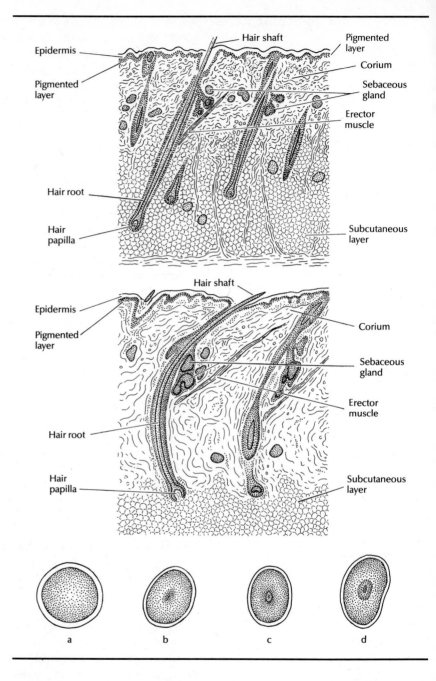

FIGURE 18–6  *Racial differences in hair form are as striking as those in hair color. Straight-haired races have a straight hair shaft (above), and those with tightly curled hair have hair shafts curving through the dermis (middle). The cross-section of the hair is even more important in determining hair form (bottom):* a *is from an American Indian,* b *is Caucasian,* c *is Australian, and* d *is African.*

teeth, in deposition of fat beneath the skin, and in minor details of the skeleton.

In 1833, the German C. L. Gloger showed that subspecies of mammals and birds that inhabit damp shady places are more darkly colored than those which live in drier, sunnier regions. Human skin colors follow "Gloger's rule": the darkest-skinned populations seem to have been associated originally with wet, tropical, forested regions. As humans spread north into cooler regions, their skin must have lightened because they no longer needed the protective melanin pigment (which produces darker skin color), but did need the vitamin D the skin produces in the presence of ultraviolet light (which production darker skin color impedes—see page 391). Today the lightest-skinned people are found in the cool northern temperate zones, where the clothing that must usually be worn keeps sunlight from the body. We do not yet understand in detail the full significance or genetic basis of the complex skin-color variations, but without doubt they represent an important environmental adaptation, possibly to more than one climatic factor.

Other rules like Gloger's reflect differences in body build. In 1847 Carl Bergmann, a German physiologist interested in the relationship

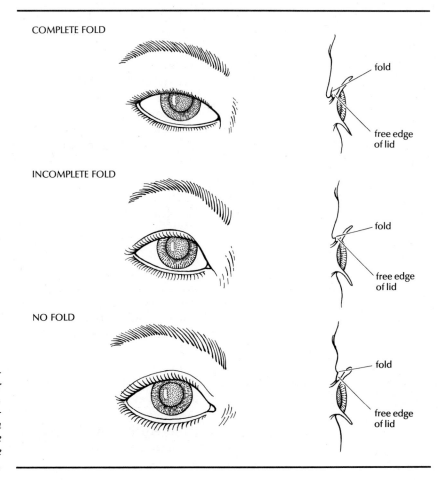

COMPLETE FOLD

INCOMPLETE FOLD

NO FOLD

fold

free edge of lid

FIGURE 18–7 Asiatic peoples are distinguished by an extra fold of skin in the upper eyelid which covers all or part of its edge. This fold is also found among some American Indians and among some of the Khoisan peoples of South Africa. By increasing the thickness of the eyelid, the fold may give the eye extra protection against harsh climates.

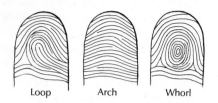

FIGURE 18–8  *Different races vary in the frequency of the three basic fingerprint patterns. Arches are relatively rare throughout the world and occur in no more than 16 percent of individuals. A majority of loops characterizes Caucasians and Africans. Asiatics and American Indians have a majority of whorls. Australians have the highest frequency of whorls (73 percent) and the lowest of arches (1 percent.)*

between body mass, surface area, and heat production in warm-blooded animals, observed that populations occupying the coldest parts of a species' range tended to be bulkier, that is, more compact, than those living in the warmer parts ("Bergmann's rule"). In 1877, the American J. A. Allen added that animals with the largest bodies are found not in the coldest part of the range but somewhere in the center (Figure 18–9). He further stated that the protruding parts of the body, such as limbs, fingers, ears, and tails, tend to be relatively shorter in the cooler parts of the range than in its warmer regions ("Allen's rule"). In cool regions, these adaptations in body build decrease surface area in relation to weight, reducing heat loss. In warm regions, they increase surface area in relation to weight, thus increasing heat loss (Figure 18–10). Human populations follow these rules derived from animal studies, and it is clear that populations known only from their fossilized remains did the same (see page 377).

Not all anatomical traits can be as easily understood as adaptations to the environment. We do not yet properly understand the function of hair form, lip form, epicanthic fold, and many other traits. From our knowledge of the adaptations of other animals, however, it seems most probable that these features are not the product of neutral mutations but are each valuable adaptations to present or past environments.

One of the neatest demonstrations of environmental adaptation is that relating nose shape (expressed as the nasal breadth ÷ nasal height) to humidity of the air (expressed as vapor pressure). Moistening the air is a prime function of the nasal epithelium; the moisture content of the air must be brought up to 95 percent relative humidity at body temperature before the air enters the lungs, otherwise they will be damaged. It seems clear that people adapted to areas of dry air (e.g., Asiatics) tend to have narrow noses while those adapted to moist air (e.g., Central Africans) have broad noses. The correlation can be demonstrated statistically and the explanation appears valid.

The important thing to remember is that differences are slight. Anatomical traits vary continuously: noses vary from narrow to broad, hair varies by infinitesimal gradations from straight to tightly curled and skin color from so-called white (a pale cream) to so-called black (a very dark brown). The German anthropologist Von Luschan recognized thirty-six gradations in this color spectrum. These features are determined by numerous genes and are not discretely segregated into just a few phenotypes.

## Physiological Traits

Physiological traits that vary among races are probably less well known than the more obvious anatomical differences; but they are also significant and reflect adaptation. The basal metabolic rate, which is related to the level of body heat production, varies, as might be predicted, according to mean annual temperature. Bone growth rate and maturation age also seem to vary, though both are also greatly influenced by nutrition. The age at which teeth appear and their order of eruption vary significantly. Third molars (wisdom teeth), which appear in Europeans between seventeen and twenty years of age, appear in East Africans at age thirteen. Protein structure, keenness of taste, drug sensitivity, balance of urinary substances, color blindness, and sex hormone activity also show measurable differences. And the better we become able to measure these sometimes trivial differences, the more of them we are likely to find.

Probably the most important physiological differences in race are those subtle genetic variations that give rise to disease. Because they are based on only one or two genes, these traits are discrete; that is, they are either present or absent. We discussed one of them—sickle-cell anemia—in Chapter 4. Some genetic diseases are just as dangerous but are limited to small populations rather than affecting whole races. In the Mediterranean region, there is *favism,* which is a genetically determined allergy to the broad bean and results in severe anemia; the same area also has *familial Mediterranean fever,* an obscure condition causing acute fever and much pain. Other hereditary disorders are much more widespread and occur more commonly in one race than another. One such disorder is *phenylketonuria* (PKU), inability to develop an essential enzyme, which usually results in brain damage and mental retardation. It is most prevalent among some groups of Caucasians.

*FIGURE 18–9   J. A. Allen studied the dimensions of animals in relation to their overall range. He showed that the larger animals were usually found in the middle of the animal's range. This is also true of humans, as can be seen in this map. The black lines join populations of greatest stature in each continent.*

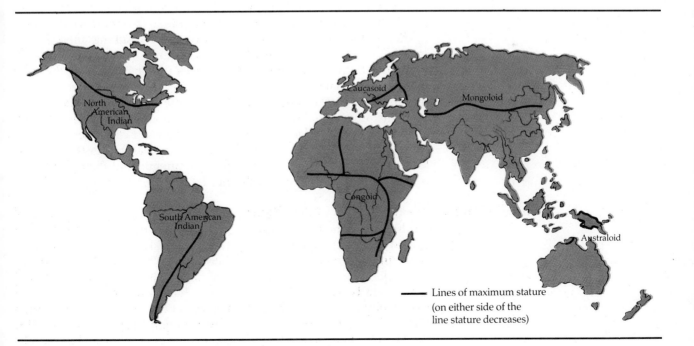

A disease like sickle-cell anemia, but appearing mostly in the Mediterranean region and in parts of Asia rather than in Africa, is *thalassemia*.
In the homozygous state (two Th$_2$ alleles), the resulting anemia is so
serious that afflicted individuals rarely reach reproductive age. But homozygous individuals who completely lack the Th$_2$ allele may die early
from serious malaria. It is in the heterozygote state that the trait is
present but not serious, and provides some protection from malaria.
Thus the advantages and disadvantages of the gene in the population
have remained in balance so long as malaria itself continues to thrive.
Although most genetic diseases may simply be part of humans' genetic
load, it is likely that some, like sickle-cell anemia and thalassemia, are
part of such an adaptive equilibrium, termed *balanced polymorphism*.

**Blood Groups**     The third group of racial traits, the blood groups, have great medical
significance. When the possibility of blood transfusions was first investigated during the nineteenth century, it quickly became clear that introducing one individual's blood into another's bloodstream could be
fatal. Blood consists of a liquid component, the *serum* or *plasma*, and
three main types of cells: the *red cells*, which contain the red pigment
hemoglobin, carry oxygen to all the parts of the body; the much larger
*white cells*, or *leucocytes*, defend against infection; and the smallest cells,
the *platelets*, maintain the circulatory system as a whole. The red cells
have a protein coat called an *antigen;* when introduced into another

individual, the antigen triggers production of an *antibody,* a protein that helps protect the body against foreign substances. Microscopic examination of the blood of two people mixed together has shown that difficulties with transfusions come from the reactions between antigens and antibodies.

Safe transfusions now rest on biologist Karl Landsteiner's discovery in 1901 of the existence of different *blood groups.* Transfusions of the wrong kind of blood can cause the recipient's red blood cells to *agglutinate,* or clamp together, and sometimes burst. The agglutination can result in clots that block the blood's flow. Landsteiner discovered that the blood (actually the antigen) of one individual could trigger production and agglutination of another individual's antibodies, causing clots. Landsteiner labeled with the letter O the blood of individuals which was never agglutinated by the serum of other persons but which would in turn agglutinate the blood cells of others. Blood of individuals that was agglutinated he labeled A. The blood that agglutinated A blood (and was not group O) and could itself be agglutinated by A blood, he labeled type B. Thus he had three types: A, B, and O. Blood group A carries antigen A and develops anti-B antibodies. Blood group B contains antigen B and develops anti-A antibodies. Group O contains no antigens, but develops both antibodies. Group AB (discovered later) carries antigens A and B but produces neither antibody. Thus type AB people can receive A, B, or O blood, but types A and B can receive only their own groups and type O; and type O people can receive only type O blood. Type O people, then, are universal donors, while type AB people are universal recipients. (The distribution of types A and O throughout the world is shown in Figure 18–11.)

Discovery of the ABO blood groups was followed by the discovery of many others (some of which are listed in Figure 18–12), most important of these is the *rhesus* (Rh) system (1940). The rhesus system is responsible for an important disease that can kill newborn babies by destroying their blood cells. The cause of the disease is incompatibility between mother and child for the rhesus antigen D. If the mother is Rh-negative (lacks the D antigen) and the child is Rh-positive (possesses the D antigen), then the mother may form anti-D antibodies at the time of the child's birth, when some of the child's blood may enter the mother's bloodstream. In a second pregnancy, this antibody can pass through the placental barrier, coating and destroying the red blood cells of the child if it has Rh-positive blood. This second child will have acute anemia at birth (there is no problem if the second child has Rh-negative blood). The anemia can be treated only by extensive blood transfusions, but the disease can now be prevented by giving the mother an injection of powerful anti-D antibody after the birth of the first Rh-positive child. The injection destroys any Rh-positive red cells from the infant remaining in the mother's bloodstream, and so inhibits anti-D antibody production.

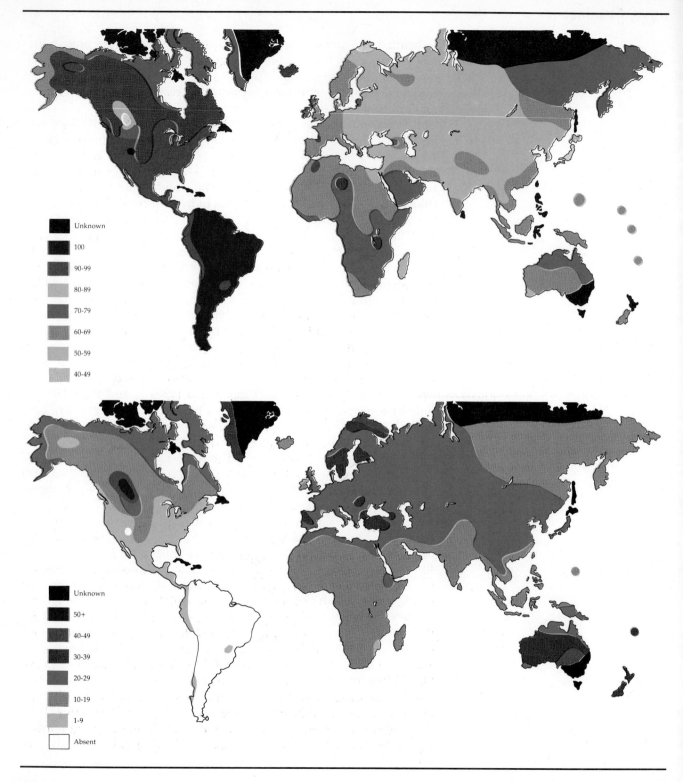

| | |
|---|---|
| Unknown | |
| 100 | |
| 90-99 | |
| 80-89 | |
| 70-79 | |
| 60-69 | |
| 50-59 | |
| 40-49 | |

| | |
|---|---|
| Unknown | |
| 50+ | |
| 40-49 | |
| 30-39 | |
| 20-29 | |
| 10-19 | |
| 1-9 | |
| Absent | |

Although individuals vary widely in their blood types, populations vary in the frequency or proportions of different alleles (the gene states that determine blood types) and their resultant antigens. These frequencies have been recorded for many human populations and make useful genetic markers for the major geographic races. (Some of those which separate the races most strikingly are shown in Figure 18–12.)

The study of blood groups, an important medical advance, led to understanding of their role as adaptations to disease antigens. The carrier of blood group B has some protection against infant diarrhea, groups $A_1$ and B protect against plague, and group O against bronchial pneumonia. ($A_1$ and $A_2$ are subdivisions of group A.) Those with rhesus gene D and MNS gene N (see Figure 18–12) are particularly susceptible to smallpox. Group A individuals also seem most liable to stomach cancer and pernicious anemia, while gastric and duodenal ulcers tend to affect persons of group O. Thus the frequency of genetic diseases and blood group genes in different races may result from selection by the infectious diseases to which populations have been exposed. We have quite good evidence that the American Indians of the northern plains evolved a high incidence of gene $A_1$ as a result of recent exposure to smallpox (see Figure 18–12).

Research into the relationship of disease and human genetics is still at an early stage, but is progressing rapidly. A particular medical and genetic problem is presented by people who carry a genetic condition like sickle-cell anemia in places where malaria is no longer present. Without the malaria to maintain the balance of the polymorphism, the sickle-cell gene will eventually be lost, as a result of natural selection against both homozygotes and heterozygotes. But that will be slow; meanwhile doctors cannot help those who carry the gene and suffer anemia.

It is still not clear what the adaptive significance of many of these traits is, whether they are anatomical or physiological. But all contribute to better understanding of the nature of race, and further research will undoubtedly clarify their meaning. In the following discussion of the geographic races, we will see some of the anatomical and genetic markers associated with each group. But do not emphasize these markers too much. As we have seen, geographic races are most readily recognized by a configuration of traits; considered singly the traits will cross and blur racial boundaries.

When we study the distribution and environments of human races, we usually consider the situation before 1492—the year Columbus arrived in the New World—and before sea voyages had a major influence on population movements. Of course, humans have always been on the move, and they were before 1492. But since then human populations have in many cases spread widely beyond the places where they evolved and have hybridized extensively. Figure 18–13 shows the approximate pre-1492 distribution of the geographic races.

FIGURE 18–11   These maps give some idea of the distribution and frequency of the two commonest ABO blood group alleles, O and A. This is an example of the kind of genetic data now available for human populations. The upper map charts the distribution of the predominant group O allele, which is common in the New World and especially South America. The lower map plots the group A allele, which is reasonably common in the Old World, but rare in many parts of the New World and virtually absent from South America. Remarkable concentrations are found among Scandinavian Lapps and Blackfoot Indians of Western Canada. The latter is possibly the result of a local smallpox epidemic, introduced perhaps by Europeans, in which the allele was selected.

FIGURE 18–12   *The frequencies of some blood group alleles present in different major races show the extent of racial differentiation in these genetic characters. Those of greatest significance are highlighted. Three different alleles for the rhesus positive condition are listed (cDe, CDe, cDE). Alleles of blood serum components gamma globulin and haptoglobin are also listed.*

| Blood Group System | Allele | World range | Caucasians | Africans Congoid | Africans Khoisan | Asiatics | American Indians | Australians and Oceanics |
|---|---|---|---|---|---|---|---|---|
| ABO | A₁ | 0–45 | 5–40 | 8–30 | 0–15 | 0–45 | 0–20 | 8–38 |
|  | A₂ | 0–37 | 1–37 | 1–8 | 0–5 | 0–5 | 0 | 0 |
|  | B | 0–33 | 4–18 | 10–20 | 2 | 16–25 | 0–4 | 0–13 |
|  | O | 39–100 | 46–75 | 52–70 | 75–78 | 39–68 | 68–100 | 51–79 |
| Rhesus | cde– | 0–46 | 25–46 | 4–29 | 0 | 0–5 | 0 | 0 |
|  | cDe+ | 0–95 | 1–5 | 34–82 | 84–89 | 0–4 | 0–7 | 1–9 |
|  | CDe+ | 0–95 | 39–55 | 0–21 | 9–14 | 60–76 | 32–68 | 68–95 |
|  | cDE+ | 0–61 | 6–17 | 0–19 | 2 | 19–31 | 23–61 | 2–20 |
| MNS | N | 8–78 | 33–51 | 39–53 | 41 | 37–45 | 9–35 | 73–97 |
|  | NS | 5–74 | 25–65 | 22–59 | 41 | 38 | 5–22 | 69–74 |
| P | P | 4–84 | 41–64 | 50–84 | ? | 17 | 15–79 | 12–67 |
| Lewis | Lewis | 0–67 | 34–50 | 41 | ? | 39 | 0–34 | 0–67 |
| Duffy | Duffy | 0–100 | 37–82 | 0–6 | 8 | 90–100 | 22–99 | 100 |
| Diego | Diego | 0–34 | 0 | 0 | 0 | 0–5 | 0–34 | 0 |
| Gamma globulin | Gm | 23–100 | 23–37 | 100 | 100 | 100 | 100 | 100 |
| Haptoglobin | Hp¹ | 9–87 | 9–44 | 40–87 | 29 | 23–28 | 32–73 | 46–63 |

▨ Most significant allele frequencies

**Africans**   The African peoples include all those whose homeland is south of the Sahara Desert. Through Sudan, Ethiopia, and Egypt, they blend with the lighter-skinned Caucasians of the north, and many Caucasian features are found among essentially African peoples as far south as Tanzania. In the southern part of Africa, we find remnants of the Khoisan peoples—mainly the short, yellow-skinned people we call the San Bushmen. These people are believed to have once occupied a far greater area of southern Africa, possibly as far north as Tanzania, but they have been squeezed into the Kalahari Desert between the waves of black Africans coming south and white Caucasians who spread north from the Cape of Good Hope. The "Cape Colored" people of the Western Cape are a cross mainly between the Khoisan peoples and colonizing Europeans.

Like the other major geographic races, the Africans vary enormously at a local level, and many local races have been described and named. All these people, however, have a number of features in common, including increased melanin pigmentation of skin, hair, iris, and gums; spiraling hair whose curl is sometimes extremely tight; lips that are turned outward; broad noses; and relatively hairless bodies—all characteristics that seem to be broadly related to high mean temperatures

FIGURE 18–13 There are no hard lines at racial boundaries and intermediates of all kinds exist. This map gives an idea of the distribution of the major geographical races before 1492.

*FIGURE 18–14   This African shows the typical tightly curled hair and facial features of the black Congoid people of Central Africa.*

and high levels of sunlight (insolation) in the African environment. African blood characteristics (listed in Figure 18–12) are highly variable. The Congoid group (Figure 18–14) includes all Africans but the Khoisans and probably was originally adapted to the humid forested regions of Central Africa. The Congoids are quite closely related to the Caucasians, having a high incidence of the Caucasian blood group gene $A_2$ and the rhesus negative gene, which the San Bushmen do not have at all. All the Africans are high in rhesus positive, though the San people exceed the Congoids in the frequency of it as well as of group O. Two other genetic characteristics include a relative absence of red-green color blindness and a high frequency of the abnormal hemoglobin that gives rise to the sickle cell and partially protects them against malaria.

Although the Khoisan people (Figure 18–15) are close to the Congoids physiologically and in blood characteristics, they are distinct enough in body form for some to call them a separate geographic race. They have yellow skin, epicanthic folds, small stature, small teeth, and high breasts. Early in life they lose subcutaneous fat (fat under the skin) over most of their bodies and thus have deeply wrinkled skin. The females, however, retain deep fat deposits on their buttocks, a trait called *steatopygia*. According to Garn, steatopygia may be an adaptation to the feast-and-famine cycles of the hunting-and-gathering way of life. Stored fat could be essential for someone to survive famine and is particularly adaptive in women, for whom pregnancy is a biologically important period of stress. Indeed, this characteristic may well have been much more widespread in the past (Figure 18–16).

Africans are now spread through most of the world, having migrated (or been taken forcibly) to Arabia; North, Central, and South America; and Europe. Africa itself has received Caucasians, Indians, and Malays among others, so that new genes are continually entering the African gene pool.

**American Indians**

We know that the aboriginal peoples of the Americas arrived during the colder phases of the last glaciation from eastern Asia, and they certainly share many physical characteristics with the Asiatic peoples that occupy that region. The American Indians (sometimes called Amerindians) typically have coarse straight black hair, brown eyes with occasional epicanthic folds, and scanty body hair and beards, though some grow full beards (Figure 18–17). Their skin varies from almost Caucasian white in northwestern Canada, to reddish brown in Central America and the Andes, to a pale yellow in the equatorial rain forests. In Patagonia they are again almost white. They also vary in stature, from the tall people of the Great Plains of North America to the small people of the tropical forests of South America. They generally have relatively long trunks with little spinal curvature, and their feet and hands are relatively small. Like Asiatics, their skulls tend to be short and rounded.

*FIGURE 18–15   The Khoisan or San people
of southern African have more tightly curled
hair than their northern neighbors and much
lighter skin. They are also rather small in
stature and have epicanthic eye folds, though
these are not as well developed as among
Asiatic peoples. (See also Figure 18–12.)*

Many American Indians also have shovel-shaped incisor teeth, as do the Asiatics.

The blood groups of American Indians vary, but in Central and South America almost all are group O. The incidence of group A ranges from 1 percent in southern North America to 35 percent in the north. In

*FIGURE 18–16   Small figurines like the
eleven-centimeter-high Venus of Willendorf
in Austria were widespread in Europe after
about 20,000 B.P. Their anatomy seems to
suggest that deep subcutaneous fat deposits
were an especially desirable adaptation
among these hunting-and-gathering people.
The fat deposits are still found today in Hot-
tentot women (a remnant group of the
Khoisan people). Here the condition is illustrated by a woman of the !gwi tribe.*

FIGURE 18–17    *These Apache Indian girls show the typical features of the American Indians. Their straight black hair is very striking.*

contrast to the Asiatics, blood group B is absent. The gene for blood type M (in the MNS system) reaches a high of 95 percent in Central America (with very low incidence of N), and the rare Diego positive blood type shared with Asiatics reaches a worldwide peak of 34 percent in Venezuela (Figure 18–12). American Indians are also high in Rh-positive, Duffy a, and Haptoglobin Hp[1]. The reasons for many of these blood-group patterns are not yet well understood.

**Asiatics**    The Asiatics, or Mongolians, occupy a large area of eastern Asia from Tibet and parts of central Siberia to the northwest, and south to Malaysia and Indonesia in the southeast. Today, they account for some 70 percent of the world's population. Asiatics are recognized by their small stature, straight black hair, yellowish to brown skin, flattish faces with prominent cheekbones, narrow noses, and broad lower jaws, shovel-shaped incisor teeth, and slanting eyes with epicanthic folds and brown irises (Figure 18–18). Their bodies are not hairy and their beards are scanty. Their hair turns gray only in old age. Like American Indians, they have relatively long trunks and small hands and feet; in these features they follow Allen's rule as cold-adapted groups. Although Asiatics' blood types vary locally, they have high frequencies of B, Rh-positive, and Duffy a, as shown in Figure 18–12.

In general, Asiatics' physical adaptations seem suitable for low mean temperatures and low humidity—the environment found in China and Siberia, where they probably originated. Today, however, Asiatics range southward into the hot, humid climates of Indonesia and Malaysia.

*FIGURE 18–18   The mainland Chinese are easily recognized by their wide, high cheekbones, straight black hair, and epicanthic eye folds. In most parts of their range, they are quite small in stature.*

They blend with Caucasians to the northwest and with aboriginal people of Australoid stock who live in southeast Asia. The populations of southeast Asia also blend with Arab, Spanish, and Indian colonists.

**Australians**   The aboriginal people of Australia have a peculiar combination of characteristics that separate them clearly from the Asiatic peoples who live to the north. Their dark skins, wavy hair, and rather Caucasian features suggest that they may have derived from an archaic Caucasian stock that occupied eastern Asia before the appearance of the true Asiatics. Other aboriginal peoples possibly related to them are found in southern India and Sri Lanka (Veddahs), the Malay Peninsula, and some islands of southeast Asia. A few of the groups have tightly curled hair reminiscent of the hair of Africans, but they probably evolved this feature independently. The physical characteristics of Australians suggest adaptation to high levels of sunlight and medium to low humidity.

The Australian Aborigines (Figure 18–19) vary a good deal in height, from fairly tall (five feet seven inches) to almost pygmy size. They have the largest teeth and jaws of any living race. The men generally have full beard growth and in the south they develop a good deal of body hair. Blond hair and light-brown skin is unusual but not rare. The percentage of whorls in their fingertips is the highest in the world. The Australian Aborigines have no blood type B (except where Asiatic contact has occurred in the north of the continent). Blood group N is the highest in the world at 70 percent, and so too is Rh-positive (up to 95 percent). Australians are also high in Duffy a and Haptoglobin Hp[1].

Many peoples of the islands of southeast Asia are related to the Australians, and are often called Australoids. The closest are probably the Papuans and Melanesians, who have woolly hair and brown skin.

FIGURE 18–19   *Australian Aborigines are usually recognizable by their wavy black hair, dark skin, and broad noses. They are not related to Africans, in spite of some superficial resemblance.*

**Caucasians**

The Caucasian peoples (Figure 18–20) include the so-called white races from northern Europe and northwestern Asia, the Arabs of the Middle East and Africa north of the Sahara, the Indians of the Indian subcontinent, and many other local races. Thus their homeland ranges east from Europe to meet the Asiatics' homeland in western Siberia and Burma. They have been minutely subdivided by anthropologists but generally have much in common. Their bodies are adapted broadly to temperature zones with lower insolation and some humidity. Skin color varies a good deal from light to dark, but is never black; its variations seem to reflect the level of insolation and mean temperature.

Caucasians are extremely hairy, though males often go bald. Hair varies from straight (in the north) to curly (in the south and east). Caucasians have high frequencies of blond hair and blue eyes, and the fairest skin of any peoples is found amongst the most northern Caucasians.

As with all other races, the blood groups are variable. Group $A_2$ is very common, and the northern Spanish Basques and Moroccan Berbers share a very high frequency (75 percent) of the Rh-negative gene. Caucasians also have uniquely low incidences of negative gamma globulins (see Figure 18–12).

There is some evidence of slower growth among Caucasian children than among children of some other races. Adaptations to malaria exist in the Mediterranean region and East to Iran, and these include genetic factors such as thalassemia, discussed earlier.

Caucasians now live in most parts of the world and in many places blend with local inhabitants, especially in the Americas.

FIGURE 18–20 *Caucasians occupy many different climates and are so highly variable in skin color, hair color, and hair form that they have been subdivided into numerous micro-races. However, they remain distinct from their neighbors in African and Asia.*

**Oceanics** The Oceanics are less homogeneous than the other racial groups; they are sometimes divided into three separate races, the Polynesians, Melanesians, and Micronesians (Figure 18–21). Some—such as Melanesians, Papuans, and New Guineans—seem closely related to Australians. Others, such as Polynesians, which include the Maoris of New Zealand, seem to bear a distant relationship with Asiatics. All peoples who may be classified as Oceanics have, however, been island dwellers long enough to become distinct from their parent groups. It is not possible in limited space to summarize the biological adaptations of such a far-ranging and variable group of peoples.

**Racial Differences** These units into which the human species may be classified are not clearly distinct. Contact between them has never been broken for long (if at all), and at present no racial groups are isolated. Indeed, interracial marriages are common and fertile, proving that the differences between the races are superficial. This statement is literally true: the surface of the body (skin and hair), which forms the barrier between organism and environment, is the first characteristic to respond to environmental peculiarities. The most obvious differences we see between the races are little more than skin deep and are an evolutionary response to the environments in which the various racial groups have lived and evolved. Furthermore, they are of recent origin: present-day racial dif-

FIGURE 18–21  *Oceanics are a very diverse group occupying a range of different island environments. This young man from the Fiji Islands is preparing for a ceremonial dance.*

ferences are all far less than the differences between modern human and their archaic forebears. This is not to say that racial diversity as such is something new, for it is not. It is the normal state of affairs in any widely dispersed animal species. But though there have always been races, they have not necessarily always had the form and distribution that we see today. Modern races were probably hardly recognizable more than 30,000 years ago.

One of the main reasons why racial differences introduce so many problems into our lives is that they are usually (but not necessarily, or invariably) accompanied by cultural differences, which include all-important language differences. Cultures, like characteristics of the body, consist in part of adaptations to environmental variables, such as the form of food resources and the climate, and they vary accordingly. In a very real sense, the so-called advanced civilizations developed in temperate rather than tropical zones simply because adaptations to temperate climates are necessarily more complex than adaptations to tropical ones. Fire seems to have been used in Eurasia long before it was used in the tropics: it simply was not necessary in the equatorial regions. Just as humans evolved physical characteristics in response to environmental stress, so they also developed the necessary culture. The function of culture and technology, however, is not only to protect against environmental stress (such as cold) but, equally important, to make the best use of available resources.

Because these cultural variations are added in many instances to the minor biological variations between races, they seem to emphasize racial differences. One day in the future, we may all share a culture and language. This condition would surely aid international understanding, but it would mean a sad loss of cultural variability, which makes travel so fascinating and human culture so rich. Similarly, extensive racial intermarrige would eventually lower racial tensions, but our species would ultimately lose in racial variability—a desirable prerequisite for further evolution.

**Racism and IQ**   *Racism,* the belief in the superiority of one or more races (and therefore all its members) over others, is, after even this short review, a meaningless concept. *Superior* is a word that says nothing until we know what quality it refers to: it could mean a thousand things, biological or cultural. If we are discussing athletics, we can reasonably expect to find the superior runners among the tallest, slimmest peoples; on the other hand, we might expect the pygmy peoples to do much better as gymnasts. If we are thinking of ability to survive in arctic conditions, then the Eskimo people are probably superior to other groups, just as black-skinned people are superior in their adaptations to sunny humid lands. If we consider the ability to write or communicate mechanically, then we refer to certain cultural developments, and the racial groups could be ranked differently in this respect.

But we are not really concerned with these things. Those who use the term superiority usually mean superior *intelligence*—that intellectual quality which we have elevated to an extraordinary height. But a number of things can be said on this point. First, those who care about these things do not agree fully in their definition of the characteristic they are attempting to measure. Second, all tests of so-called intelligence operate through linguistic and other cultural modes that are not shared by all races. No intelligence test devised is culture-free, and therefore none can be used cross-culturally. Third, it is now known that IQ (intelligence quotient) scores are altered by malnutrition of the mother, both before and after birth, and by malnutrition of the growing child. (About one third of peoples in the world today suffer from some malnutrition.) The IQ scores are also altered by psychological traumata during growth. In fact, almost any kind of stress can be shown to alter them. All this suggests that when we compare the IQ of two individuals, we are not learning anything of importance about the nature of our subjects beyond their individual ability to do IQ tests.

However, IQ scores are not without interest. They do correlate closely with success at school and college, and in the world of business. They seem to measure that aspect of general intelligence which is most highly rewarded in Western culture. Described by psychologists as analytic or abstract, this ability has made possible significant advances in science and technology and in resource extraction and productivity. The IQ scores of different racial groups of similar economic and educational background in the United States (e.g., Mexicans, Orientals, Blacks, and Europeans) do differ significantly, as do their scores in a host of other psychological tests (verbal ability, rote memory, and motor precision, for instance). Some racial groups score higher on some tests, others score higher on other tests. Although these tests have far to go in development and precision, they do highlight an area of racial differentiation, and this area is as yet poorly understood.

We may find that the small variations in intellect are important, because human societies are characterized by specialized activities of individuals with different aptitudes. Garn has suggested that beyond the anatomical differences, races may differ in form discrimination, color sense, tonal memory, mechanical reasoning, abstract reasoning, and many other aspects of intelligence. We may come to believe that it is a mistake to give people with different aptitudes a standardized form of education evolved over many centuries by Europeans to suit the aptitudes of Europeans. Indeed, our own traditional methods of education are at present being questioned by educators. Perhaps differences in aptitude will make it desirable for children to develop their own talents, of whatever kind, rather than be forced through a standard indoctrination to which they are not necessarily suited. The word "education" means to *draw out* inherent ability, not to attempt to force its expression in a predetermined form.

When we are considering the broad characteristics of racial groups, we are making no statement about particular individuals. There is no biological justification for racist behavior—for treating individuals in terms of some general aspect of their group rather than in terms of their manifest characteristics as distinct individuals. People should be treated solely according to their individual qualities.

Our discussion of human variability may seem to emphasize differences that at best are trivial (though in some cases obvious) and to overlook the broad similarities shared by all humans. It is extremely important to remember that we are closely related biologically (if diverse culturally) and share ancestry and history. Where cultural and linguistic barriers are dissolved, racial differences fade into complete insignificance. As one evolving species we became adapted to the hunting-and-gathering way of life for about 99 percent of the 2 million years of our existence, and today we all carry equally the imprints of our past.

## MODERN HUMANS: RELICS OF EARLY HUMANS

David Hamburg remarked that one of the best relics we have of early humans is modern humans. It is because we still have populations with relatively simple technologies that we are able to make so many deductions about the behavior of early humans. These living populations have in common with each other and with Paleolithic societies that their way of life is broadly based not on agriculture, but on hunting and gathering.

### Stress

But Hamburg's statement has more profound implications. The fact that he is a psychiatrist illustrates once again the eclecticism of modern anthropology, for it pulls together the fossil expert and the psychologist, each turning to the other to help bridge the gap that lies between their disciplines. Psychologists and physiologists are currently trying to learn more about the problems of stress and aggression in modern life and how these forces affect the physical and emotional health of people. In their search for causes they quickly find themselves talking to paleoanthropologists, sharing ideas and data in an effort to lay bare the origins of emotional patterns that are assumed to have arisen millions of years ago.

In the 1920s a great American physiologist, Walter Cannon, made a classic study of physiological changes that took place in cats and dogs during periods of excitement. He worked with the hormone adrenaline and investigated its effects on the nervous system. Cannon discovered that adrenaline acts like a shot in the arm at times of stress, calling forth carbohydrates from storage in the liver and pouring them into the bloodstream in the form of sugar for quick conversion to energy. He also found that it increases the flow of blood to the heart, lungs, central nervous system, and limbs, while decreasing the flow to the abdominal organs. These changes, as Cannon showed, help to mobilize the muscular, nutritional and nervous reserves of the individual, making it possible to withstand fatigue, move more speedily, and maintain activity longer.

Obviously adrenaline has great survival value for the individual in a "fight-or-flight" situation. But how is it released into the bloodstream? Cannon demonstrated that it is released during periods of intense emotion, whether or not they are followed by activity. Humans need only feel a rush of fright or anger and their system's emergency reaction will prepare them for what they have to do next. Fear does not always paralyze them; on the contrary, it usually keys them up and improves their chances of reacting in a crisis.

### San Bushmen and Stress

This reaction is confirmed by observing present-day hunter-gatherers. Anthropologists Irven De Vore and Richard Lee made a study of the San Bushmen in Botswana in southern Africa. The San in their daily lives are constantly confronted by situations that are greatly eased by adrenaline. Anticipation of the chase, the excitement of seeing and stalking an animal, trigger the hormonal response that will be needed to attack and kill the prey in a sudden burst of exertion. The interesting thing about San activities is that these bursts of exertion are only part of their hunting activity. Hunters often follow an animal's tracks for many miles before coming upon the animal. Then, tired as they may be, they must still summon the energy to sprint forward, in the hope of planting a poisoned arrow before the animal runs out of range. If it is a large animal, the poison will take effect slowly and the San may have to follow it doggedly for many more miles, and sometimes for several days, before they can close in and kill it. During this lengthy chase they may eat only a handful of food from time to time to sustain them as they run. Nevertheless, they have had the all-important stimulus at the crucial moment, and with the flow of adrenaline that has resulted, they can call on their bodies' resources to help them in this prolonged effort. Other materials, such as cholesterol and fatty acids, have also built up in the bloodstream in preparation for this need, to be worked off during the long tracking that is a constant part of a hunter-gatherer's life.

### Cholesterol and Life-Style

This discussion of adrenaline may appear to have taken us rather far from the behavior of ancient and modern humans, but that word cholesterol brings us back to Hamburg's studies in the field that might be called *stress biology*, the study of the effects of reactions to stress situations on the human body. Although readers of this book may no longer live a hunting life, they are still physically hunter-gatherers. The human body is still an efficient machine for facing daily perils, surviving long periods of deprivation while tracking prey, and mustering built-in energy reserves for sudden and unforeseen action. Our glands react as they have been reacting for hundreds of thousands of years. Unfortunately, most present-day humans do not have the chance to burn off the energy that once aided their ancestors; instead, most of us live sedentary lives, in an environment in which the stresses come one after another, releasing energy that inactivity never uses, leaving the carbohydrates and cholesterol to build up in our bodies and apparently do us harm. Many modern physiologists have addressed themselves to this problem. Recognizing that we are biologically equipped for one kind of life but live another, they ask: is there any connection between the primitive hunter-gatherer's emotional reaction under stress and the killing ailments of modern society, like heart disease?

Logically, there could be a connection. For example, modern medicine is extremely suspicious of the role cholesterol plays in heart disease. Strong emotions mobilize cholesterol, but if the Western way of life no longer provides an opportunity to dispose of built-up cholesterol, and if its buildup is bad for us, then the point is clear: people in Western society are not equipped for modern life but are still back in the Stone Age, emotionally and physiologically—and the strain is killing us.

## Adaptations to Modern Life

Odd as it may seem, there is practical value in learning as much as we can about the ways of hunter-gatherers. If we can find out what our systems were actually designed for, we may behave more in accordance with those systems and lead healthier lives. The solution cannot be as simple as taking a walk after a tension-building situation, but that might help. Many heart specialists advocate walking and cycling as beneficial exercise. Paleoanthropologists might have come to the same conclusion, but from an entirely different direction. They would have said that *Homo sapiens* is a creature whose evolutionary history as a hunter-gatherer required a great deal of steady walking and running. To ignore this way of life may well be dangerous—just as dangerous as keeping a hunting dog cooped up in a city apartment, or trying to adapt a lowland marsh plant to life on a mountaintop. Neither dog nor flower would do very well in its alien environment. The surprising thing about people is that we do as well as we do.

This is not to say that the human body is not changing in response to its new environment; the principles of natural selection certainly are still working as they always have. Therefore, if our environment were to stay as it is long enough, we could assume that the hormonal responses we have inherited form our ancestors—so inappropriate and so damaging to us—would be eliminated, as heart attacks and other natural ailments select against those of us who still express the traits. Certainly the modern world would be a healthier and safer place if its human inhabitants were gentler, more patient, and less neurotic than they are. We might even guess that the present very high rate of death from heart disease among men in the United States may be natural selection working in a part of the population that is well adapted to short-term success but poorly adapted to survival in our society.

The problem is that there is not enough time; the modern world does not stand still. Characteristic of human culture is the increasingly rapid rate of its development. It leaves us biologically far behind, tied to the ponderous machinery of natural selection, which, as we have seen, requires on the order of hundreds of thousands of years before it can produce significant differences in a species. As René Dubos said: "Even when man has become an urbane city dweller, the paleolithic bull which survives in his inner self still paws the earth whenever a threatening gesture is made on the social scene." Given emotionally archaic people such as we are and the fearsome power that modern technology has put in our hands, the situation may well become self-correcting, with archaic emotions bringing about destruction of our culture. Then, should we find ourselves running exhaustingly after our food once more, at least we could console ourselves that we were again doing what our bodies were designed for. We are not doing it now.

## SUCCESS OR FAILURE

### Population and Evolutionary Success

All this may convey the impression that something is necessarily damaging about culture, if all it can do is produce more heart attacks and worse wars. Nothing could be further from the truth. Evolutionary success, as we have seen, is measured not by the fates of individual members of a species but by the record of the species as a whole. As a species, *Homo sapiens* has to date been overwhelmingly successful. Our sheer numbers prove it. Edward S. Deevey estimates that the hominid population of the earth 2 million years ago was little more than 100,000 individuals. Three hundred thousand years ago, toward the end of *Homo erectus'* known tenancy, the human population had climbed to a million; and 25,000 years ago, during the time of the Cro-Magnon peoples, it had jumped to perhaps more than 3 million. It has risen at an increasingly steep pace since then (Figure 18–22). Deevey brings home the extraordinarily rapid mushrooming of today's human population when he shows that about 3 percent of humans who have ever lived are alive today.

The increase in population, according to Deevey, has not gone in a steady curve. Rather, the increase in the world's population has had a series of surges, reflecting the great cultural innovations associated with

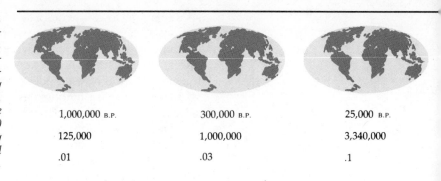

*FIGURE 18–22    Until about 25,000 B.P. humankind was a stable part of the equilibrium existing among animals and plants. With better hunting technology, animal domestication, and agriculture, humankind began to increase dramatically and to destroy the wilderness of which they had been a part. The figures given for the population of the past are of course estimates. That for 2000 A.D. is a projection that might be reduced by an effective, worldwide population-control policy or by extensive famines.*

| 1,000,000 B.P. | 300,000 B.P. | 25,000 B.P. |
| --- | --- | --- |
| 125,000 | 1,000,000 | 3,340,000 |
| .01 | .03 | .1 |

human evolution. The first cultural innovation, of course, was the development of stone tools. This advance allowed for population increase in two ways. Stone tools enabled hominids to venture out into a vast number of environments that people without such tools could not have survived in; it also made populations more efficient, enabling them to exploit those various environments more intensively. The population density of Africa 2 million years ago, in the days of the crude Oldowan industry, has been estimated at only one individual per hundred square miles. By the end of the Paleolithic, humans had spread throughout Europe and Asia as well as Africa, and their density had probably risen tenfold (Figure 18–22).

The second innovation was the double discovery of how to grow crops and how to domesticate animals. This event came about 10,000 years ago. This second innovation enabled people to settle permanently for the first time, and for the first time to live together in large numbers. Even nomads herding animals could exist in far greater concentrations on a given area of land than hunters could. The effect on world population was extraordinary. In 4,000 years it jumped from an estimated 5 million to 86 million.

The third innovation was the industrial age. It had its beginnings about 300 years ago, when the human population of the world was in the neighborhood of 550 million. World population has been ballooning ever since and today is more than 4 billion. If it continues at its present rate of increase it will double within fifty years.

Although these figures are impressive, even more impressive is the acceleration in the rate of population growth. It took a million years to get through the first phase; the second took only ten thousand years; and the third has been going on for only a few hundred. How long it will continue or what the human population of the earth ultimately will be is anybody's guess. But we can be sure that because the surface of the earth is finite, as are its resources, present rates of increase will bring us to the limit very soon.

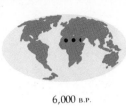

| 6,000 B.P. | 1750 A.D. | 1950 A.D. | 2000 A.D. | Year |
|---|---|---|---|---|
| 86,500,000 | 728,000,000 | 2,400,000,000 | 6,000,000,000 | Population |
| 2.6 | 12.7 | 42.5 | 120 | Persons per square mile |

**Limits to Growth**   It seems clear that the increase in our population is primarily due to making greater and greater use of available resources. When a forest is cleared and crops are grown in its place, all the sunlight in that area is contributing to synthesis of food for humans. When wild animals grazing in meadows and savanna grasslands are killed and replaced by cattle, sheep, and goats, conversion of plant energy into animal protein is turned to human benefit. In these cases we can see that the ultimate limitation is the amount of energy that can be delivered by the sun to the earth's surface and turned into carbohydrates by photosynthesis in green plants. Every green plant needs a place in the sun. Other limiting factors are the other requirements of plants: water, minerals, and appropriate soil. Lack of water in particular has long been a problem for farmers, though they have occasionally overcome it with irrigation. But even with advanced technology, we cannot obtain food from all the earth; the ultimate limits are firm both on land and in the oceans. Eventually, as Malthus predicted, these limits will indeed halt human population growth, if we do not bring about stabilization voluntarily.

In some parts of the world, famine is already becoming a normal condition, and malnutrition is found almost everywhere. People are dying of hunger by the tens of thousands, partly because the increase in population is due not merely to increased resources but also to advances in medicine. These have brought about an increased life expectancy. *Australopithecus* may have had an average life expectancy of fifteen to twenty years; *Homo erectus* lived for twenty to thirty years; today, a citizen of the United States can expect to live to seventy years (Figure 18–23). A doubling of life expectancy has brought a doubling of population without a corresponding increase in our efficiency at utilizing resources. Thus in many countries people live longer, but not enough food is grown to feed them all.

Large segments of human society have certainly come a long way: in life span, in efficiency at extracting resources, in population density, in technological complexity, and in increased physical comfort (Figure

FIGURE 18–23   *Since the time of the Cro-Magnons life expectancies have doubled in countries with modern medicine and technology. We probably live three to four times as long as* Australopithecus *did. The increased life span has made possible a rapid increase in cultural complexity, skill, and knowledge.*

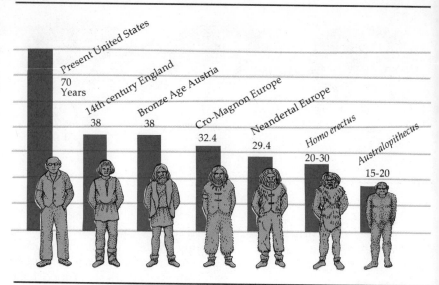

18–24). Whether we are really better off as a species, and whether our progress will continue, remains to be seen. Population size is certainly a measure of evolutionary success, but another measure that may be more significant is evolutionary longevity. Two million years is nothing in universal and geologic time, and a million species have evolved and gone extinct in earth history. Compared with most mammals, we are infants of evolution. From this point of view our apparent present success can continue only if we can achieve some sort of stability in our relationship with the earth's resources. Otherwise we shall surely perish.

**Survival**   Humankind is still evolving. Invisible and immeasurable changes are slowly taking place in the general and average characteristics of *Homo sapiens.* Evolution never stops but continues blindly, as our environment continues to select the fittest and destroy the unfit. Whereas in the past the selective agents were perhaps the rigors of climate and disease, today they may well be nitric oxide in the atmosphere or emotional stress.

Humankind, however, is undergoing evolution with a new twist. Among many animal species, the individuals that survive and breed are the stock selected by nature to continue the species. But *Homo sapiens* is a social and cultural species. Just as the infertile worker bees make an essential contribution to the survival of the bee colony, so too in our own society, all members contribute to the species' survival even if they bear no children. They do so all the more as our skills and roles in society become increasingly specialized (like the bees'). In the present state of human overpopulation, it is clear that those who do not reproduce are making a greater contribution to the species as a whole than

FIGURE 18–24   The combination of transport needs and the population explosion resulted in the development of the internal combustion engine; the effect on the environment is shown vividly in these pictures. Technological development and the high density of our population have profoundly altered the quality of the earth's surface and the air we breathe, thus bringing about the need for additional new technology, and for further cultural and biological adaptations.

those who do, because the stress of overdense populations is the greatest threat to our survival.

For a species like ours, whose survival depends on culture (which is based on knowledge), it is essential to use all available knowledge and understanding to achieve better adaptation to a changing environment. This is perhaps our most difficult problem: each new cultural adaptation we make alters the environment to which we are adapting. New adaptations increase population; greater population densities require further adaptations; new adaptations deplete world resources; resource depletion requires further adaptation. And so it goes on. We find ourselves in a vicious circle of ever-increasing instability (Figure 18–25). Essential now is an all-out attempt to break that accelerating positive feedback loop and bring about new stability in population size, in technological investment, in consumption.

## Prospect of Failure

How humanity will handle this critical problem is impossible to predict. The present—and projected—enormous number of people, together with the poverty and political instability that accompany those numbers in many parts of the world, are of great concern to economists and sociologists everywhere. It is all very well to talk about the success of the species as a whole, but if species success can be accomplished only with uncontrolled crowding and almost worldwide misery, then something is wrong. *Homo sapiens* is not just another species of animal. We are the first organisms to understand something of our place in the world and the laws that govern our activities here. This status makes us unique in having within our grasp the possibility of doing something sensible about the crushing problem of our numbers. But the mere fact that we have access to this kind of knowledge is no guarantee that we will use it. We have not always done so in the past; we do not seem to be doing so now. Not only do we damage ourselves individually through the stresses of our daily lives; we do even worse things to each other on a world scale, by our inability and unwillingness to control many of our actions.

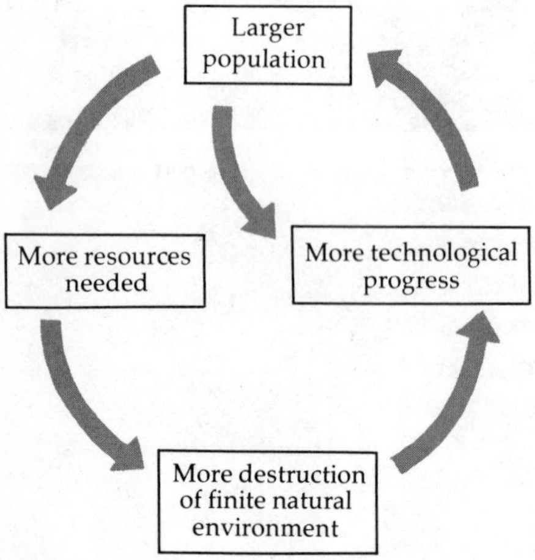

For all the surface glitter of our culture, the one thing of true value that humankind has achieved is a rather impressive amount of knowledge and understanding about ourselves and the world. Much of this knowledge is not yet widely available; sadly, it is rejected by many who do have access to it. Nevertheless it is there. The principles of evolution we have discussed in this book are true, and their truth can be demonstrated to any open-minded person. We ignore them at our peril. They have a direct bearing on our understanding of ourselves and thus they affect the future of all of us, for it is only a matter of time before we will have it in our power to direct the course of our own evolution. Here lies humankind's greatest challenge. For the first time in the 3.5-

FIGURE 18–25 *This positive feedback loop is the most dangerous to us, since it is accelerating very rapidly and involves environmental destruction. With the resource base of our livelihood seriously depleted, the survival of even our present number is threatened.*

billion-year history of life will come a chance to combine the good of the species with the good of the individual. This chance can be seized only by means of profound understanding of our place in nature. Let us see that our education and our comprehension of the human condition will make us equal to the challenge.

# Glossary

**Note:** Words in *italics*, excepting some Latin names, are defined elsewhere in the glossary.

**Absolute dating:** see *chronometric dating*.

**Acheulian industry:** method of making stone tools that first appeared about 1.4 million years ago in Africa. This style of toolmaking, which was used by *Homo erectus* and spread over Africa, Europe, and part of Asia, is distinguished from those preceding it by the bifacial technique (see also *biface*).

**Adaptation:** an evolutionary change, resulting from *natural selection*, which better suits a *population* to its environment, thus improving its chances for survival; a characteristic resulting from such a change.

*Aegyptopithecus:* fossil of the *Oligocene* epoch, found in Egypt in 1966. Although its skull was shaped like a monkey's, its jaws and teeth were apelike. Most primitive ape yet discovered.

**Agglutination:** the clumping of *red blood cells* as a result of reaction of *antibodies* to an *antigen*.

**Alleles:** *genes* occupying equivalent positions in paired *chromosomes* yet producing different effects in the *phenotype* when they are *homozygous*. They are alternative states of a gene, originally produced by *mutation*.

**Alloparent:** an individual that assists the parents in taking care of the young.

**Altruism:** behavior which is more or less self-destructive and which is done for the benefit of others.

*Amphipithecus:* a primate known only by fragments of fossil jaws found in Burma that date from the late *Eocene* epoch; possibly a very primitive monkey or ape.

**Angular gyrus:** part of the human *cerebral cortex* that allows information received from different senses to be associated (e.g., the sight of a cup to be associated with the feel of a cup and the sound of the word "cup").

**Anthropoid:** relating to humans, apes, and monkeys.

**Anthropology:** science of humankind; the systematic study of human evolution, human variability, and human behavior, past and present.

**Antibody:** a protein produced as a defense mechanism to attack a foreign substance invading the body.

**Antigen:** any organic substance, recognized by the body as foreign, which stimulates production of an *antibody*.

**Ape:** large, tailless, semierect mammal of the order *Primates*. Living genera are the *chimpanzee, gorilla, gibbon, siamang,* and *orangutan*.

**Aphasia:** loss or distortion of speech.

*Apidium:* primate of the late *Oligocene* epoch, found in Egypt; probably a primitive monkey.

**Arboreal:** adapted for living in or around trees, as are most monkeys and apes.

**Archaeology:** systematic study of prehistoric human cultures; finding and interpreting the cultural products of prehistoric people.

**Arcuate fasciculus:** bundle of nerve fibers in the human brain transmitting signals from *Wernicke's area* to *Broca's area*, making possible vocal repetition of words heard and memorized.

**Artifact:** a purposefully formed object.

**Aurignacian industry:** an *Upper Paleolithic* tool culture of early *Cro-Magnon* peoples in Europe that appeared from about 43,000 to 19,000 years ago, characterized by extensive use of bone, especially bone points, in addition to stone tools. Completely unlike earlier European styles, it seems to have originated elsewhere. Aurignacian culture included art and ritual.

*Australopithecus:* extinct hominid that walked erect and had humanlike teeth but apelike skull, jaw, and brain size. Evidence of four species—*afarensis, africanus, robustus,* and *boisei*—has been found in Africa, where *Australopithecus* is believed to have lived from about 6 million to 1 million years ago.

**Baboon:** large monkey with a long, doglike muzzle; most baboons have short tails and live on the ground in troops. They live close to the trees in East and Central Africa and in rocky desert in Ethiopia (see also *gelada* and *hamadryas*).

**Balanced polymorphism:** maintenance in a *population* of different *alleles* of a particular *gene* in proportion to the advantages offered by each (e.g., sickle-cell and normal *hemoglobin*).

**Band:** small, economically independent group of primates, smaller than a troop.

**Biface:** tool made by chipping flakes off both sides of a core, producing an edge straighter and sharper than those made in earlier cultures, which were chipped on one edge only. A common tool of the *Acheulian industry.*

**Bioaltruism:** behavior which appears altruistic but which in fact is believed to benefit the animal indirectly, by increasing its *inclusive fitness.*

**Biome:** area characterized by a broadly uniform climate and consisting of a distinctive combination of plants and animals.

**Bipedalism:** walking erect on the hind limbs only, which frees the hands for other uses.

**Blade tools:** *flake tools* at least twice as long as they are wide, common in *Upper Paleolithic* tool kits.

**Blending inheritance:** outmoded theory stating that offspring receive a combination of all characteristics of each parent through the mixture of their bloods; superseded by Mendelian genetics.

**Blood group:** group of individuals whose blood can be mixed without *agglutination* (e.g., groups A, B, O, or AB).

**Bolas:** two or more stones connected by thongs or a cord and used as a weapon.

**Brachiation:** locomotion in the trees in which the arms pull the body along. Characteristic of gibbons.

*Bramapithecus:* the name originally given to a fossil lower jaw, later determined to be identical with *Ramapithecus.*

**Branching:** splitting of a family tree into separate evolutionary lines: the monkeys, apes, and living prosimians diverged from a common prosimian ancestor; the hominid line diverged from the apes.

**Breccia:** fragments of rock consolidated and cemented by lime (calcium carbonate) in a fine matrix of soil, sand, or clay.

**Broca's area:** part of the human *cerebral cortex* that sends coded signals to the part of the brain controlling the muscles used in speaking.

**Brow ridge:** continuous ridge of bone in the skull, curving over each eye and connected across the bridge of the nose. An extremely prominent brow ridge is characteristic of *Homo neanderthalensis.*

**Budding:** gradual expansion of a species into new areas, accomplished by a group splitting off from a prospering *population* to set up in an unexploited area near the original territory.

**Burin:** chisellike *Upper Paleolithic* tool used to cut, incise, and shape other materials such as bone, antler, wood, and stone. A tool for making other tools, it is found frequently at *Cro-Magnon* sites and less frequently at *Neandertal* sites.

**Canines:** pointed teeth in the front of the mouth between the incisors and premolars. In monkeys and apes, canines are usually large, projecting beyond the other teeth, and are used for tearing up vegetation and for threats and fights. Hominid canines are much smaller.

**Carbon 14 (C¹⁴):** a radioactive element present in the atmosphere as $CO_2$ that disintegrates at a predictable rate. The amount of carbon 14 remaining in fossils indicates their age.

**Catastrophism:** Georges Cuvier's theory that vast floods wiped out ancient forms of life again and again, clearing the stage for new creations.

**Cenozoic:** geologic era that began about 65 million years ago.

**Centrioles:** minute granules present in many cells outside the nuclear membrane. The centriole divides in cell division (*mitosis*) and the parts move apart to form the poles of the spindle.

**Cerebral cortex:** gray, wrinkled outer layer of the brain. The largest part of the primate brain, it generates much of human reasoned behavior and abstract thought. It also records memory.

**Chain of Being:** pre-Darwinian theory of a hierarchy ranking all living things from lowest to highest, with humankind at the top; the chain was thought to have been fixed forever at the Creation, which meant that no species could change into other forms.

**Chemical signature:** unique nature of a volcanic eruption determined by analyzing its ash, lava, and so on.

**Chimpanzee:** social primate, least specialized of the great apes and thought to be the most like the ancestor from which apes and humans are descended. Lives in the trees of equatorial Africa. In the trees it climbs; on the ground it usually moves by *knuckle walking.*

**Chopper:** crude stone tool chipped from a pebble core to give a rough but serviceable cutting edge. Characteristic of the *Oldowan tool industry.*

**Chromosomes:** coiled, threadlike structures of *DNA,* bearing the *genes* and found in every living plant and animal cell (see also *meiosis* and *mitosis*).

**Chronometric dating:** estimating the age of geological deposits (and the fossils in them) by examining the chemical composition of rock fragments and organic remains containing radioactive substances such as uranium 238, potassium 40, and *carbon 14,* which decay at a known rate. Also known as *absolute dating.* Compare relative dating.

**Class:** a *taxonomic* rank in biology. Humans belong to the class *Mammalia.*

**Cleaver:** an *Acheulian* stone implement with a straight cutting edge at one end. It looks like a modern axehead and probably was used for heavy chopping or hacking.

**Cobble:** stone worn smooth by sand and water in running streams or on a rocky seashore. Often used as a core for making a stone tool.

**Coccyx:** the bones at the end of the human and ape spine, the remnants of an ancestral tail.

**Codon:** unit "word" of *genetic code* specified by three out of four possible nucleotide bases.

**Condyle:** part of a bone that fits into another bone, forming a movable, hingelike joint, like the part of the lower jaw that bears on the skull.

**Continental drift:** a theory proposed by Wegener in 1912 describing the movements of continental land masses over long periods.

**Core tool:** implement made by hitting a piece of stone with another to break off chips; the stone that remains becomes the tool. (Compare with *flake tool.*)

**Cranium:** the skull without the jaw.

**Cro-Magnon:** broadly, refers to the first modern humans, who lived between about 40,000 and 10,000 years ago. In strict usage, Cro-Magnon refers only to people living in southwestern France during that period.

**Cultural evolution:** changes in human *culture* resulting from the accumulated experience of humankind. Cultural evolution can produce *adaptations* to the environment faster than organic evolution can.

**Cultural swamping:** overwhelming of one *culture* by a technologically more powerful one, often leaving the culture with the weaker technology extinct or nearly so.

**Culture:** system of learned behaviors, symbols, customs, beliefs, institutions, artifacts, and technology characteristic of a group, transmitted by its members to their offspring.

**Cusps:** conical projections on the biting surfaces of teeth (see also *molars*).

**Darwinian fitness:** see *fitness.*

**Demography:** study of the size, density, distribution, and other vital statistics of *populations.*

**Denticulate tools:** *Mousterian* implements made with toothed or notched edges.

**Deoxyribonucleic acid:** see *DNA.*

**Diastema (pl. diastemata):** space between the upper incisors and canines of apes and some monkeys, which allows the upper and lower canines to interlock when the mouth is closed.

**Diploid:** having a full set of paired *chromosomes,* so that twice the *haploid* number is present; characteristic of all animal cells except *gametes.*

**Disk-core method:** toolmaking technique developed by the *Neandertals* in which a stone is trimmed to a diskshape,

numerous flakes are chipped off until the core is almost used up, and the flakes are then trimmed for use as tools.

**Diurnal:** active during the day, as apes, monkeys, and humans are.

**DNA (deoxyribonucleic acid):** chemical substance that makes up the *chromosomes,* reproduces itself, and carries the genetic code. It is found in every cell.

**Dominant:** type of *allele* expressed in the *phenotype* even when paired with a different allele (called *recessive*). If an allele is dominant, the phenotype is the same for both *heterozygotes* and *homozygotes.*

*Dryopithecus:* extinct primitive ape of the *Miocene* epoch found in Europe, China, and India.

**Ecosystem:** ecological system; the interacting community of all the organisms in an area and their physical environment, together with the flow of energy among its components.

**Encephalization quotient (EQ):** a number expressing the size of the brain of a species in relation to the size that would be predicted in an average mammal of the same body weight. The average mammal has an EQ of 1.0.

**Endogamy:** selecting a mate from inside one's own group.

*Eoanthropus dawsoni:* see *Piltdown man.*

**Eocene:** geologic epoch from about 58 million to 35 million years ago, during which the early *primates* evolved.

**Epicanthic fold:** protective fold of skin above the inner border of the eye, characteristic of Asiatic peoples.

**Estrus:** phase in the approximately four-week estrous cycle in female mammals that occurs around ovulation, during which the female is receptive to males and encourages copulation; also called "heat." The heat phase is not distinct in humans.

**Ethnographic analogy:** an analogy between the ethnography of a society and the supposed ethnography of a prehistoric one.

**Ethology:** study of the social behavior of animal species in the natural environment.

**Evolution:** cumulative changes in the average characteristics of *populations* that occur over many generations (see also *natural selection*).

**Exogamy:** mating between people of different social groups.

**Family:** in biology, a *taxonomic* rank. Humans belong to the family Hominidae (see also *hominid*).

**Fauna:** animal component of the ecosystem at a given place and time.

**Faunal correlation:** dating a site by the similarity of its fossil *fauna* to that of another site, which may carry a reliable absolute date.

**Fauresmith industry:** highly evolved version of the *Acheulian* *industry* found south of the Sahara, mostly in steppelike areas, from about 60,000 to 40,000 years ago. It included small hand-axes, scraping tools, and narrow flake knives.

**Feedback:** process by which a change in one component in a system affects other components, which in turn bring about changes in the first component.

**Femur (pl. femora):** the thighbone.

**Fish gorge:** device for catching fish on a line using a moving part that opens at right angles and sticks in the fish's mouth.

**Fission-track dating:** method of determining the age of rocks from tracks left by the spontaneous fission (that is, the splitting of the nucleus) of uranium 238. Because the rate of fission is known, the rock's age can be calculated by assessing the original quantity of uranium and the density of the tracks.

**Fitness, or Darwinian fitness:** contribution of an individual to the next and succeeding generations relative to the contribution of other individuals.

**Flake tool:** implement made by striking a chip or flake from a stone; the flake becomes the tool. (Compare with *core tool.*)

**Folivore:** a leaf-eating animal.

**Foramen magnum:** large opening at the base of the skull, through which the spinal cord passes to the brain.

**Fossil:** the remains of an organism, or direct evidence of its presence, preserved in rock. Generally only the hard parts of animals—teeth and bones—are preserved.

**Fossil magnetism:** naturally occurring property of rocks that indicates the polarity of the earth's magnetic field when they were laid down. By comparing the polarity of one layer with that of others, the age of a rock can, under certain conditions, be approximated.

**Founder effect:** genetic difference between a newly founded, separated *population* and its parent group. The founding population is usually different because its *gene pool* is only a segment of the parent group's.

**Frontal bone:** bone of the primate skull that constitutes the forehead and comes down around the eye sockets (orbits).

**Frugivore:** a fruit-eating animal.

**Gametes:** reproductive *haploid* sex cells generated by *meiosis,* which fuse with gametes of the opposite sex in fertilization. The female gamete is called the ovum, the male the sperm.

**Gelada:** species of terrestrial monkey related to the baboon, found in the mountains of Ethiopia.

**Gene:** a distinct unit of the *chromosomes* in cell nuclei, which controls the coding and inheritance of physical traits.

**Gene flow:** transmission of genes between *populations* through *exogamy,* which increases the variety of genes avail-

able to each and creates or maintains similarities in the genetic makeup of the populations.

**Gene frequency:** the number of times a gene occurs in proportion to the size of a *population.*

**Gene pool:** all the genes of a *population* at a given time.

**Genetic code:** chemical code based on four *nucleotides,* carried by *DNA* and *RNA,* which specifies amino acids in sequence for protein synthesis.

**Genetic drift:** random changes in a *gene pool* caused by such factors as differential reproduction rates, but not by *mutation* or *natural selection* or *gene flow.* Significant only in small, isolated populations.

**Genetic load:** *recessive* genes in a population that are harmful when expressed in the rare *homozygous* condition.

**Genetic swamping:** overrunning and absorption of a small *population* by a larger one; the *genes* of the minority are preserved but contribute little to their successors' physical characteristics.

**Genotype:** genetic makeup of a plant or animal; all information contained in the organism's *genes.* (Compare with *phenotype.*)

**Genus:** *taxonomic* category composed of a group of *species* that have more in common with each other than with other species.

**Geographical race:** a group of *populations* related to a distinct, major geographical area.

**Geology:** study of the earth's physical formation, its nature, and its continuing development.

**Gibbon:** small, long-armed, tree-dwelling, brachiating ape of Southeast Asia. Smaller than the other apes, and least like humans.

*Gigantopithecus:* extinct giant ape dating from the *Pliocene* and *Pleistocene* epochs, found in Asia.

**Gorilla:** the largest ape, a social, terrestrial, knuckle-walking vegetarian living in the rain forests and mountain forests of equatorial Africa.

**Gradualism:** hypothesis that *evolution* has consisted for the most part of gradual, steady change. (Compare *punctuated equilibrium.*)

**Group selection:** theoretical situation in which natural selection operates not on the individual animal but on a social group as a unit.

**Günz:** major period of glaciation in the Alps during the *Pleistocene* epoch, occurring from about 600,000 to 450,000 years ago.

**Half-life:** the time taken for half of any quantity of a radioactive element to decay to its fission products.

**Hamadryas:** species of baboon adapted to the desert regions of Ethiopia.

**Hand-axe:** typical stone implement of the *Acheulian industry.*

**Handedness:** the individual human's preference for using the right hand or the left, possibly connected with changes in the brain associated with the development of language.

**Haploid:** having a single set of unpaired *chromosomes* produced by *meiosis;* characteristic of *gametes.*

**Harem:** wives and concubines of a polygynous male, as among Muslim peoples; in zoology, a group of females guarded by a male that prevents other males from mating with them.

**Heidelberg man:** see *Homo heidelbergensis.*

**Hemoglobin:** red protein found in *red blood cells* that carries oxygen through the circulatory system of vertebrates and some other animals.

**Heterozygous:** controlled by nonidentical alleles. (Compare with *homozygous;* see also *dominant.*)

**Home range:** area of ground visited by a primate troop during one year of foraging. (Compare with *territory.*)

**Hominid:** a primate, of the family Hominidae, which includes *Homo sapiens,* earlier human species (like *Homo habilis*), and *Australopithecus.*

**Hominoid:** primate of the superfamily Hominoidea, including the great apes and humans.

**Homo erectus:** extinct human species that probably lived from about 1.3 million to 300,000 years ago.

**Homo habilis:** gracile, or delicate-boned toolmaker that probably lived from about 2 million to 1.3 million years ago. First discovered by Louis Leakey.

**Homo heidelbergensis:** a lower jaw (also called the Mauer jaw) about 500,000 years old, eventually identified as a fossil of *Homo erectus.* Also called Heidelberg man.

**Homo neanderthalensis:** early *Homo sapiens* fossils originally believed to be distinct species, but now considered a subspecies. Lived in Europe, Africa, and Asia from about 100,000 to 35,000 years ago. The name derives from a fossil skull found in Neandertal, Germany, in 1856.

**Homo sapiens:** most recent species of humans, believed to have first appeared about 300,000 years ago. A bipedal, culture-bearing, social, omnivorous primate.

**Homozygous:** controlled by identical alleles. (Compare with *heterozygous.*)

**Hybrid:** offspring of parents of different species or of distinct inbred populations.

**Ilium:** the hipbone, part of the *pelvis.*

**Inbreeding:** mating of related individuals within a closed *population;* in a small population, inbreeding sometimes causes *homozygous* pairing of harmful *recessive* genes, the *genetic load,* increasing disease and mortality rates. (Compare with *outbreeding.*)

**Incest:** copulation between closely related individuals, usually taboo. How closely related individuals must be before their mating is considered incestuous differs from culture to culture.

**Inclusive fitness:** sum of an individual's *Darwinian fitness* plus its influence on the fitness of its relatives.

**Infanticide:** practice of killing newborn infants; in zoology, any form of lethal curtailment of parental investment in offspring brought about by conspecifics (individuals of the same species).

**Interglacial:** a period in which glaciers retreat and the climate warms. The *Pleistocene* epoch had three major interglacials.

**Iron pyrite:** one of the few natural materials that, when struck with flint, makes sparks that can then be used to light a fire.

**Java man:** see *Pithecanthropus.*

**Kenyapithecus:** fossil ape found in Kenya, East Africa, by Louis Leakey.

**Knuckle walking:** *quadrupedal* walking on the knuckles of the hands and soles of the feet, used by chimpanzees and gorillas on the ground.

**Langur:** slender, long-tailed Asian monkey.

**Larynx:** the voice box; the organ in the throat containing vocal cords, important in human speech production.

**Laurel-leaf blade:** *Cro-Magnon* stone artifact so finely worked it may have had an esthetic or ritual function. Associated with *Solutrean* tool kits.

**Leister:** three-pronged spear used for fishing.

**Levallois technique:** toolmaking method in which a core stone is shaped and then a flake of predetermined size and shape is knocked off. This method is believed to have originated about 200,000 years ago in Southern Africa. Its use is characteristic of many *Mousterian* cultures.

**Limbic system:** the emotional brain; a group of structures in the brain important in regulating such behavior as eating, drinking, aggression, sexual activity, and expression of emotion. Proportionately smaller in humans than in other primates, it operates below the level of consciousness.

**Locus:** position of a *gene* on a *chromosome.* A locus can carry only one *allele* of a gene.

**Loris:** prosimian of India, Southeast Asia, and Africa that is small, solitary, quadrupedal, and slow-moving, with thick fur and a vestigial tail.

**Lothagam jaw:** a 5.5-million-year-old fossil jaw fragment of *Australopithecus.*

**Lower Paleolithic:** earliest part of the Old Stone Age, lasting from more than 2 million to about 100,000 years ago.

**Magdalenian industry:** *Upper Paleolithic* style of toolmaking used by the *Cro-Magnons* of Western Europe from about 20,000 to 10,000 years ago. It is distinguished by the prevalence of *blades* and the appearance of prototype harpoons.

**Mammalia:** the class of four-legged vertebrates—including humans—having hair or fur, milk glands for suckling their young, and warm blood.

**Mandible:** lower jaw.

**Manuport:** stone that could not have occurred naturally in an archaeological site and must have been carried there.

**Meiosis:** cell division resulting in formation of sex cells, each of which will have half the number of *chromosomes* present in the original cell. (Compare with *mitosis*.)

**Melanocyte:** kind of cell in the skin that produces pigment, giving skin color.

**Metabolic heat:** heat generated in the body, especially that produced by the musculature during exercise.

**Midden:** refuse heap or dunghill at an archaeological site in which artifacts and food remains may be preserved.

**Middle Paleolithic:** part of the Old Stone Age, from about 100,000 to 35,000 years ago (see also *Mousterian, Sangoan,* and *Fauresmith* industries).

**Mindel:** second major period of European glaciation of the *Pleistocene* epoch, occurring about 350,000 years ago.

**Miocene:** geologic period from about 25 million to 5 million years ago, during which the first hominids evolved.

**Mitosis:** cell division resulting in two cells that each have a full and identical set of *chromosomes*. (Compare with *meiosis*.)

**Molars:** grinding teeth, which bear many *cusps:* molars have four or five, depending on the animal; premolars normally have two.

**Monkey:** usually small or medium-sized, long-tailed, arboreal, quadrupedal, vegetarian primate. The two groups are: *New World monkeys* and *Old World monkeys*

**Morphological pattern:** the distinctive form of a species; those anatomical features common to members of a species, which as a group distinguish them from other animals.

**Mosaic evolution:** evolution of different parts of the body at different rates over long periods.

**Mousterian industry:** a *Middle Paleolithic* style of toolmaking associated with the Archaic humans of Europe, Asia, and Africa, employing both the *Levallois* and *disk-core* techniques, producing a number of *flake tools* from one core. Varieties of the Mousterian include *Mousterian of Acheulian Tradition, Denticulate Mousterian,* and *Quina-Ferrassie.*

**Mousterian of Acheulian Tradition (MAT):** industry that included very diverse tools, including numerous *hand-axes;* associated with *Neandertals* in Western Europe during the *Middle Paleolithic* period.

**Mutation:** change in a *gene* or *chromosome*. The accumulation of such changes may lead to *evolution* of a new *species* of animal or plant. See *point mutation.*

**Natural selection:** principal mechanism of *evolutionary* change, by which the individuals best adapted to the environment contribute more offspring to succeeding generations than others do. As more of such individuals' characteristics are incorporated into the *gene pool,* the characteristics of the *population* evolve.

**Neandertal:** *Homo sapiens neanderthalensis,* a subspecies of modern human beings living in Europe, Africa, and Asia from about 100,000 to 35,000 years ago (see also *Homo neanderthalensis*).

**Neuron:** nerve cell that transmits messages in the form of electrical impulses; the basic unit of the nervous system.

**New World monkeys:** members of the Primate order belonging to the superfamily Ceboidea, including marmosets and howler, spider, and squirrel monkeys, among other species. (Compare with *Old World monkeys.*)

**Niche:** precise environment and resource base of a *species* or *race.*

**Nonsense mutation:** a *mutation* affecting coding sequence in a *gene* where a "stop" *codon* replaces that for an amino acid. Such a mutation disrupts protein synthesis.

**Nuclear family:** family group of parents and their children.

**Nucleic acid:** long, chainlike compound formed from a large number of *nucleotides;* present in all organisms in one or both of two forms: *DNA* and *RNA.*

**Nucleotides:** organic compounds, consisting of bases, sugars, and phosphates; found in cells either free or as part of *nucleic acids.* Four nucleotide bases constitute the units of the *genetic code* in *DNA* and *RNA:* thymine (T) or uracil (U), cytosine (C), adenine (A), and guanine (G).

**Occlusal plane:** the plane lying parallel to the biting surfaces of the teeth.

**Occupation floor:** land surface occupied by prehistoric people.

**Oldowan tool industry:** earliest method of stone toolmaking, employed by *Homo habilis* as long as 2 million years ago. The products were very crude stone tools (see also *chopper*).

**Old World monkeys:** members of the Primate order belonging to the superfamily Cercopithecoidea, including langurs, baboons, and macaques, among other species. (Compare with *New World monkeys.*)

**Oligocene:** geologic epoch lasting from about 35 million to 25 million years ago, in which monkeys and most other modern mammals first appeared.

**Omnivore:** animal that eats both meat and vegetation.

**Open words:** words that can be used alone by children to convey meaning; i.e., nouns and some verbs. (Compare with *pivot words*.)

**Opposable thumb:** ability to hold thumb and finger together in opposition for grasping, giving hominids the *precision grip* that enables them to use tools.

**Orangutan:** tree-dwelling ape of Borneo and Sumatra. Has *prehensile* hands and feet for seizing and grasping; limbs articulated for reaching in any direction, and very long arms. Orangutans are on the ground rarely, but are then *quadrupedal*.

**Orbital closure:** protective bony ring around the eye socket, found in all living primates and most fossil ones, except for such primitive species as *Plesiadapis*.

**Order:** *taxonomic* rank. Humans belong to the order *Primates*.

**Outbreeding:** mating of unrelated individuals. (Compare with *inbreeding*.)

**Palate:** bony plate separating the mouth from the nasal cavity, which is arched in humans and flat in apes.

**Paleoanthropology:** study of the fossil and cultural remains and other evidence of the ancient forms of hominid life.

**Paleocene:** first epoch of the *Cenozoic* era, from about 65 to 58 million years ago, in which the first prosimians appeared.

**Paleolithic:** see *Stone Age*.

**Paleontology:** study of the fossil remains and biology of organisms that lived in the past.

**Parallel evolution:** evolution of similar but not identical adaptations in two or more lineages.

*Paranthropus robustus:* name originally given to a fossil now usually classified as *Australopithecus robustus*.

*Parapithecus:* a primate of the late *Oligocene* epoch, from Egypt; probably a primitive Old World monkey related to *Apidium*.

**Parental investment:** any behavior toward offspring that improves the likelihood of the offspring's survival.

**Particulate inheritance:** transmission of hereditary characteristics by discrete units of genetic material; first proposed by Gregor Mendel (see also *genes*).

**Peking man:** see *Sinanthropus*.

**Pelvis:** bony structure forming a basinlike ring at the base of the vertebral column with which the legs articulate.

**Perigordian tradition:** an *Upper Paleolithic* culture of Western Europe, largely contemporary with the *Aurignacian* culture. It seems to have grown out of the *Mousterian of Acheulian Tradition*.

**Persistence hunting:** hunting by chasing the prey until it stops, exhausted, when it can be killed.

**Pharynx:** the throat, above the *larynx*.

**Phenotype:** observable characteristics of a plant or an animal, the expression of the genotype. (Compare with *genotype*.)

**Phonemes:** smallest sound components of language.

**Phylogeny:** evolutionary lineage of organisms; their evolutionary history.

**Phylum:** a major *taxonomic* rank. Humans are in the phylum *Vertebrata*

**Piltdown man:** a ''doctored'' modern human skull and ape jaw ''discovered'' in 1911 that was supposed to represent a very primitive human, *Eoanthropus dawsoni*, but was exposed as a hoax in 1953.

*Pithecanthropus:* name originally given by Dubois to fossil hominids found in Java (*Pithecanthropus erectus*). Later the Peking fossils (*Sinanthropus pekinensis*) were also included in this genus. These forms are now known as *Homo erectus*.

**Pivot words:** words—like prepositions, adjectives, and some verbs—used by children to modify *open words* to make two-word sentences.

**Platelets:** minute bodies, formed by larger cells, found in mammalian blood and associated with clotting.

**Pleistocene:** geologic epoch that lasted from about 1.5 million to 10,000 years ago, in which *Homo sapiens* evolved.

**Pliocene:** geologic epoch lasting from about 5 million to 1.5 million years ago during which *Homo* evolved.

**Point mutation:** common type of *mutation* in a single *codon* causing substitution of one amino acid for another in a protein sequence; gene mutation.

**Polygenic:** trait that is determined by more than one *gene*.

**Polygyny:** having two or more wives; in zoology, the tendency for a male to mate with two or more females with whom he regularly associates.

**Polymorphism:** appearance of a gene in more than one form among individuals of a *population*.

**Population:** a local or breeding group; a group in which any two individuals have an equal probability of mating with each other.

**Positive feedback:** process in which a positive change in one component of a system brings about changes in other components, which in turn bring about further positive changes in the first component.

**Potassium-argon dating:** *chronometric dating* in which age is determined by measuring the decay of radioactive potassium 40.

**Power grip:** a grip involving all fingers of the hand equally, as a branch is gripped in climbing a tree. (Compare with *precision grip*.)

**Precision grip:** holding by opposing the tip of the thumb to the tips of other fingers, which allows firm and precise control of an object. Characteristic of the human hand. (Compare with *power grip*).

**Prehensile:** adapted for grasping.

**Primates:** *order* of placental mammals, mostly arboreal, with two suborders: the *anthropoids* and the *prosimians.*

**Proconsul:** apelike fossil of East Africa that somewhat resembles the chimpanzee but had some monkeylike characteristics; lived from 20 to 15 million years ago.

**Prognathous:** having the jaws projecting in front of the upper parts of the face.

*Propliopithecus:* Oligocene fossil from Egypt believed to be an ancestor of the apes and of humankind.

**Prosimians:** the "premonkeys," Old World arboreal mammals, including the small lemurs, lorises, and tarsiers. Less closely related to humans than other primates, they have survived with little change for nearly 50 million years. The descendants of extinct prosimians developed into today's monkeys and apes.

**Protein clock:** method for determining evolutionary relationships by using variations in the proteins of different living animal species to indicate the length of time since they diverged in their *evolution.* The method assumes a fairly constant rate of protein evolution, an assumption still open to some doubt.

**Punctuated equilibrium:** hypothesis that *evolution* has consisted of short periods of rapid change followed by long periods of relative stability; the "jump" theory. (Compare *gradualism.*)

**Quadrupedal:** walking on four feet.

**Quina-Ferrassie:** *Middle Paleolithic* toolmaking tradition associated with almost every *Neandertal* burial in Western Europe. It is characterized by a high proportion of *flake tools* used for scraping.

**Race:** a group of *populations* of a *species* distinct from other groups of the same species in at least a few characteristics.

**Racemization:** loss of left- or right-handedness (the ability to rotate polarized light) in the molecular structure of organic compounds, especially amino acids. By comparing the degree of racemization that has occurred since death with the racemization of a calibrated sample, the age of a bone can be established.

**Racism:** judgment and treatment of people in terms of some general aspect of their racial group, rather than in terms of their manifest characters as individuals.

*Ramapithecus:* an ape which lived from 14 to 6 million years ago and which may be an ancestor of the orangutan.

**Recessive:** *allele* that has no effect on the *phenotype* unless *homozygous.*

**Reciprocal altruism:** trading of apparently altruistic acts by different individuals at different times; a variety of *bioaltruism.*

**Red blood cells (corpuscles):** vertebrate blood cells without nuclei. Red blood cells contain *hemoglobin.*

**Relative dating:** estimating the age of geological deposits (and the fossils in them) by determining their stratigraphic level in relation to that of other deposits whose relative or chronometric age is known. (Compare with *chronometric dating.*)

**Replication:** capacity of *DNA* to generate copies of itself in the nucleus of a cell.

**Rhodesian man:** skeleton dated between 90,000 and 50,000 years ago, found at Broken Hill, Zambia, in southern Africa.

**Ribonucleic acid:** see *RNA*

**Riss:** third major glacial period of the *Pleistocene,* which covered 30 percent of the earth's surface with ice and lasted from about 200,000 to 125,000 years ago.

**RNA (ribonucleic acid):** found with *DNA* in the nucleus of almost every living cell and chemically close to DNA, RNA transmits the *genetic code* from DNA to direct the formation of protein.

**Sangoan:** tool tradition found in forests south of the Sahara from about 45,000 to 35,000 years ago, characterized by long, narrow, heavy stone tools (which may have served as combined machetes and stabbing weapons), hand-axes, and small scrapers.

**Savanna:** African tropical or subtropical grassland, often with scattered trees (woodland savanna).

**Scraper:** a stone or bone tool for preparing hides and leather, used to scrape the fat and other tissues from the inner surface of the skin

**Sectorial:** literally "cutting"; refers to the first lower premolar of apes and some monkeys, which acts as a cutting edge in moving against the upper canine.

**Selection:** see *natural selection.*

**Selective pressure:** influence exerted by the environment that promotes maintenance of traits that help a *population* survive in that environment and eliminates other, non-adaptive traits (see also *natural selection*).

**Serum (plasma):** a clear liquid component of blood that carries the *red blood cells, white blood cells,* and *platelets.*

**Sex-linked trait:** inherited characteristic coded on the sex chromosome, having a special distribution related to sex.

**Sexual dimorphism:** characteristic anatomical (and behavioral) differences between males and females of a species.

**Sexual selection:** effect of differences in sexual characteristics on rates of reproduction.

**Sickle-cell anemia:** genetically caused disease that can be fatal, in which the *red blood corpuscles* carry insufficient oxygen. Found in parts of West and Central Africa.

*Sinanthropus:* name originally given by Davidson Black to fossil hominids found at Choukoutien, near Peking. These fossils are now included in the species *Homo erectus* (see also *Pithecanthropus*).

*Sivapithecus:* extinct ape of the *Miocene* epoch, found in Africa and Asia, closely related to *Ramapithecus*.

**Sociobiology:** science of the biological basis of social behavior.

**Solo man:** skulls found in Java dated between 150,000 and 50,000 years ago.

**Solutrean:** an *Upper Paleolithic* culture occurring in Western Europe from about 19,000 to 15,000 years ago. Among its artifacts are the superb *laurel-leaf blades* and the first eyed needles.

**Speciation:** gradual separation of interbreeding *populations* into two or more groups that do not interbreed.

**Species:** a group of *populations* of organisms that are enough alike in structure and behavior that individuals can interbreed and produce fertile offspring if they have access to one another. Individuals from a species are reproductively isolated from other *species*.

**Spheroids:** spherical stone tools probably used as hammers or missiles or to pound food.

**Steatopygia:** development of extensive fat deposits on the buttocks in some human races.

**Steinheim man:** an early *Homo sapiens* skull, dated between 250,000 and 150,000 years ago, found in Germany near Steinheim.

**Stereoscopic vision:** vision produced by two eyes with overlapping fields, giving a sense of depth and distance; most highly evolved in carnivores and primates.

**Stone Age:** earliest period in cultural evolution, from more than 2 million to 5,000 years ago. Recognizable periods are Paleolithic, or Old Stone Age; Mesolithic, or Middle Stone Age; and Neolithic, or New Stone Age (see also *Lower Paleolithic, Middle Paleolithic, Upper Paleolithic*).

**Stratigraphy:** sequence of geologic strata or layers formed by materials deposited by water or wind; also, study of this sequence.

**Stress biology:** study of the way in which organisms respond to different kinds of adverse stimuli.

**Taiga:** northern coniferous forest bordering the *tundra*.

**Taphonomy:** scientific study of the conditions under which bones are preserved as fossils.

**Tarsier:** small East Indian *prosimian* with large eyes and a long tail.

**Taxonomy:** classification of plants or animals into groups according to their relationships, and the ordering of these groups into hierarchies.

**Terrestrial:** adapted to living on the ground.

**Territoriality:** an animal's distinctive behavior toward and tendency to defend a recognizable area of land.

**Territory:** area occupied and defended by a group of animals against others of their species. (Compare with *home range*.)

**Tool kit:** all the tools or implements used by a primitive culture; its technology. *Neandertals* had sixty or seventy kinds of known tools but *Cro-Magnons* had more than a hundred.

**True breeding (breeding true):** situation in which members of a genetic strain resemble each other in all important characters and show little variability.

**Tufa:** tuff; a rocklike substance formed from volcanic ash.

**Tundra:** treeless arctic or subarctic plain, swampy in summer, with permanently frozen soil just beneath the surface and low vegetation.

**"Unearned" resources:** prey with range larger than that of its predator; the predator benefits from the nutrients of that larger range while hunting its own smaller range.

**Uniformitarianism:** Charles Lyell's theory that the forces now affecting the earth—wind and flowing water, frost, volcanism—acted in a similar, or uniform way in the past.

**Upper Paleolithic:** most recent part of the Old Stone Age, from about 35,000 to 10,000 years ago. See *Aurignacian, Perigordian, Solutrean,* and *Magdalenian,* which were major cultures of this period.

**Veld (or veldt):** South Africa's open savanna grassland, which has few bushes or trees.

**Vertebrata:** major division of the animal kingdom containing all animals with backbones; comprising fishes, amphibians, reptiles, birds, and mammals.

**Weir:** barrier or dam made of stones or sticks set out in a stream or river and used as a fish trap.

**Wernicke's area:** part of the human *cerebral cortex* essential in comprehending and producing meaningful speech.

**White blood cells (leucocytes):** blood cells of vertebrates containing no respiratory pigment.

**Würm:** last major glacial period of the *Pleistocene* epoch, lasting from about 75,000 to 10,000 years ago.

*Zinjanthropus boisei:* fossil hominid found in Olduvai Gorge by Mary Leakey, now usually named *Australopithecus boisei*.

# Bibliography

## PART I EVOLUTION

*General References for Further Reading*

Campbell, Bernard. *Human Evolution,* 3rd ed. Aldine, 1985.

Dobzhansky, Theodosius. *Genetics and the Origin of Species.* Columbia University Press, 1969.

———. *Heredity and the Nature of Man.* New American Library, 1964.

———. *Mankind Evolving.* Yale University Press, 1962.

———, Francisco J. Ayala, G. Ledyard Stebbins, and James W. Valentine. *Evolution.* W. H. Freeman, 1977.

Ebert, James D., et al. *Science and Creationism: A View from the National Academy of Sciences.* National Academy Press, 1984.

Le Gros Clark, Wilfrid E. *The Antecedents of Man,* 3rd ed. Quadrangle Books, 1971.

———, and Bernard G. Campbell. *The Fossil Evidence for Human Evolution.* University of Chicago Press, 1978.

Mayr, Ernst. *Population, Species and Evolution.* Harvard University Press, 1970.

Sinnott, Edmund W., L. C. Dunn, and Theodosius Dobzhansky. *Principles of Genetics,* 5th ed. McGraw-Hill, 1958.

Stern, Curt. *Principles of Human Genetics,* 2nd ed. Freeman, 1960.

Wallace, Bruce, and Theodosius Dobzhansky. *Radiation, Genes and Man.* Methuen, 1960.

*Sources*

Ayala, Francisco J. "The Mechanisms of Evolution." *Scientific American,* 239, no. 3, 1978.

Brothwell Don, and Eric Higgs, eds. *Science in Archeology,* 2nd ed. Praeger, 1970.

Darwin, Charles. *On the Origin of Species* (facsimile of 1st ed.). Harvard University Press, 1966.

———, and Alfred R. Wallace. *Evolution by Natural Selection,* Cambridge University Press, 1958.

Darwin, Francis, ed. *The Life and Letters of Charles Darwin,* 2 vols. Basic Books, 1959.

———, and A. C. Seward, eds. *More Letters of Charles Darwin,* 2 vols. John Murray, 1903.

De Vries, Hugo. *The Mutation Theory,* 2 vols. Open Court, 1909–1910.

———. *Species and Varieties.* Open Court, 1905.

Eiseley, Loren. *Darwin's Century: Evolution and the Men Who Discovered It.* Doubleday, 1958.

Fisher, Sir Ronald Aylmer. *The Genetical Theory of Natural Selection.* Clarendon Press, 1930.

Haldane, J. B. S. *The Causes of Evolution.* Longmans, Green, 1932.

Hulse, S. F., and M. M. Firestone. "Blood-Type Frequencies among the Quinault Reservation Indians." *Proceedings of the Second International Conference of Human Genetics,* vol. 2, 1963.

Huxley, Sir Julian. *Evolution in Action.* Chatto & Windus, 1953.

———. *Evolution—The Modern Synthesis.* Allen & Unwin, 1942.

Huxley, Thomas Henry. *Man's Place in Nature.* University of Michigan Press, 1959.

Irvine, William. *Apes, Angels, and Victorians.* Weidenfeld & Nicolson, 1955.

Libby, Willard F. *Radiocarbon Dating,* 2nd ed. University of Chicago Press, 1955.

Moore, Ruth. *Charles Darwin: A Great Life in Brief.* Hutchinson, 1957.

Morgan, Thomas Hunt. *Evolution and Adaptation.* Macmillan, 1903.

———. *The Mechanism of Mendelian Heredity.* Constable, 1915.

———. *The Physical Basis of Heredity.* Lippincott, 1919.

Muller, Hermann J. *Genetics, Medicine and Men.* Cornell University Press; Oxford University Press, 1947.

Romer, Alfred S. *Man and the Vertebrates,* 2 vols. Penguin, 1954.

Simpson, George Gaylord. *The Major Features of Evolution.* Simon and Schuster, 1953.

———. *The Meaning of Evolution.* Oxford University Press, 1950.

Wallace, Alfred Russel. *My Life: A Record of Events and Opinions,* 2 vols. Chapman & Hall, 1905.

## PART II THE ORIGIN OF HUMANKIND

*General References for Further Reading*

Day, Michael. *Guide to Fossil Man.* 2nd ed. Meridian, 1977.

Hamburg, David A., and Elizabeth R. McCown. *The Great Apes.* Benjamin/Cummings, 1979.

Fossey, Dian, *Gorillas in the Mist.* Houghton Mifflin, 1983.

Le Gros Clark, Wilfred E. *Man-Apes or Ape-Men?* Holt, Rinehart and Winston, 1967.

———, and Bernard G. Campbell. *The Fossil Evidence for Human Evolution.* University of Chicago Press, 1978.

Szalay, Frederic S., and Eric Delson. *Evolutionary History of the Primates.* Academic Press, 1979.

van Lawick-Goodall, Jane. *In the Shadow of Man.* Houghton Mifflin, 1971.

Waal, Frans de. *Chimpanzee Politics: Power and Sex among Apes.* Harper & Row, 1982.

*Sources*

Broom, Robert. *Finding the Missing Link.* Watts, 1950.

Butzer, Karl W. *Environment and Archeology: An Ecological Approach to Prehistory.* Aldine-Atherton, 1971.

Ciochon, Russell L., and Robert S. Corrucini. *New Interpretations of Ape and Human Ancestry.* Plenum Press, 1983.

Clark, J. Desmond. *The Prehistory of Africa.* Praeger, 1970.

Coppens, Y., F. Clark Howell, G. L. Isaac, and Richard E. F. Leakey, eds. *Earliest Man and Environments in the Lake Rudolf Basin.* University of Chicago Press, 1976.

Dart, Raymond. *Adventures with the Missing Link.* Viking Press, 1959.

DeVore, Irven, ed. *Primate Behavior.* Holt, Rinehart and Winston, 1965.

Harris, Jack W. K. "Cultural Beginnings: Plio-Pleistocene Archaeological Occurrences from the Afar, Ethiopia." *African Archaeological Review,* 1, 1983, 3–31.

Hausfater, G., and Sarah Blaffer-Hrdy, (Eds.). *Infanticide: Comparative and Evolutionary Perspectives.* Aldine Publishing Co., 1984.

Howells, William W., ed. *Ideas on Human Evolution.* Atheneum, 1967.

Isaac, G. L., and Elizabeth R. McCown, eds. *Human Origins.* Staples Press, 1976.

Jay, Phyllis C. *Primates.* Holt, Rinehart and Winston, 1968.

Johanson, Donald C., and Maitland A. Edey. *Lucy: The Beginnings of Humankind.* Simon and Schuster, 1981.

———, and Tim D. White. "A Systematic Assessment of Early African Hominids." *Science,* 203, 1979, 321–330.

Jolly, Alison. *The Evolution of Primate Behavior.* Macmillan, 1972.

Jolly, Clifford. "The Seed-eaters." *Man,* 5, no. 1, March 1970.

Kummer, Hans. *Social Organization of Hamadryas Baboons.* University of Chicago Press, 1968.

Lancaster, Jane B., and C. S. Lancaster. "Parental Investment: The Hominid Adaptation," in D. J. Ortner, ed. *How Humans Adapt: A Biocultural Odyssey.* Smithsonian Institute Press, 1983.

Leakey, Mary D. *Olduvai Gorge,* vol. 3. Cambridge University Press, 1971.

Lovejoy, C. Owen. "The Origin of Man." *Science,* 211, no. 4480, 1981.

Napier, John, and P. H. Napier. *Handbook of Living Primates.* Academic Press, 1967.

Oakley, Kenneth, Bernard G. Campbell, and Theya I. Mollison, eds. *Catalogue of Fossil Hominids—Part I,* 2nd ed. Trustees of the British Museum (Natural History), 1977.

Schaller, George B. *Year of the Gorilla.* University of Chicago Press, 1964.

———, and Gordon Lowther. "The Relevance of Carnivore Behavior to the Study of Early Hominids." *Southwestern Journal of Anthropology,* 25, no. 4 (University of New Mexico Press).

Schultz, Adolph H. *The Life of Primates.* Universe Books, 1969.

Simons, Elwyn L. *Primate Evolution.* Macmillan, 1972.

Szalay, Frederic S., and Eric Delson. *Evolutionary History of the Primates.* Academic Press, 1979.

Tanner, Nancy M. *On Becoming Human.* Cambridge University Press, 1981.

Tobias, Phillip V. *The Brain in Hominid Evolution.* Columbia University Press, 1971.

Tuttle, Russell, ed. *The Functional and Evolutionary Biology of Primates.* Aldine-Atherton, 1972.

Washburn, Sherwood L. *Social Life of Early Man.* Aldine, 1961.

———, and Phyllis Dolhinow, eds. *Perspectives on Human Evolution,* 4 vols. Holt, Rinehart and Winston, 1968–1976.

White, Tim D., Donald C. Johanson, and William H. Kimbel. "*Australopithecus africanus:* Its Phyletic Position Reconsidered." *South African Journal of Science,* 77, 1981, 445–470.

## PART III THE EVOLUTION OF HUMANKIND

*General References for Further Reading*

Flint, Richard Foster. *Glacial and Quaternary Geology.* Wiley, 1971.

Howells, William W. "*Homo erectus*—Who, When and Where: A Survey." *Yearbook of Physical Anthropology,* 23. 1980.

Le Gros Clark, Wilfrid E., and Bernard G. Campbell. *The Fossil Evidence for Human Evolution.* University of Chicago Press, 1978.

Pilbeam, David. *The Ascent of Man.* Macmillan, 1972.

*Sources*

Butzer, Karl W. "Acheulian Occupation Sites at Torralba and Ambrona, Spain: Their Geology." *Science,* 150, no. 3704, 1965.

———, and G. L. Isaac, eds. *After the Australopithecines: Stratigraphy, Ecology, and Culture Change in the Middle Pleistocene.* Mouton, 1975.

Campbell, Bernard G., ed. *Sexual Selection and the Descent of Man, 1871–1971.* Aldine, 1972.

Chang, Kwang-chih. *The Archaeology of Ancient China.* Yale University Press, 1968.

Count, Earl W. "The Biological Basis of Human Sociality." *American Anthropologist,* 60, no. 6, 1958.

Covey, Curt. "Earth's Orbit and the Ice Ages." *Scientific American,* 250, 1984, 42–50.

de Lumley, Henry. "A Paleolithic Camp at Nice." *Scientific American,* 220, no. 5, 1969.

Gardner, R. Allen, and Beatrice T. Gardner. "Teaching Sign Language to a Chimpanzee." *Science,* 165, no. 3894, 1969.

Geschwind, Norman, "The Neural Basis of Language, in *Research in Verbal Behavior and Some Neurophysiological Implications,* ed. by K. Salzinger and S. Salzinger. Academic Press, 1967.

Hockett, Charles F. "The Origin of Speech." *Scientific American,* 203, no. 3, 1960.

Holloway, Ralph L. "The Evolution of the Primate Brain: Some Aspects of Quantitative Relations." *Brain Research,* 7, 1968, 121–172.

Hood, Dora. *Davidson Black: A Biography.* University of Toronto Press, 1971.

Howell, F. Clark. "Observations on the Earliest Phases of the European Lower Paleolithic." *American Anthropologist,* 68, no. 2, 1966.

Isaac, Glynn L. "The Diet of Early Man: Aspects of Archaeological

Evidence from Lower and Middle Pleistocene Sites in Africa." *World Archaeology*, 2, 3, 1971.

———. "Studies of Early Culture in East Africa." *World Archaeology*, 1, no. 1, 1969.

Jerison, Harry J. *Evolution of the Brain and Intelligence*. Academic Press, 1973.

Ju-kang, Woo. "The Skull of Lantian Man." *Current Anthropology*, 7, no. 1, 1966.

Krantz, Grover S. "Brain Size and Hunting Ability in Earliest Man." *Current Anthropology*, 9, no. 5, 1966.

Kurtén, Björn. *Pleistocene Mammals of Europe*, Aldine, 1968.

Lancaster, Jane B. "Primate Communication Systems and the Emergence of Human Language," in *Primates: Studies in Adaptation and Variability*, ed. by Phyllis C. Jay. Holt, Rinehart and Winston, 1968.

Lieberman, Philip, *On the Origins of Language*. Macmillan, 1975.

———, Edmund S. Crelin, and Dennis H. Klatt. "Phonetic Ability and Related Anatomy of the Newborn and Adult Human, Neanderthal Man, and the Chimpanzee." *American Anthropologist*, 74, no. 3, 1972.

Murrill, R. I. *Petralona Man*. Charles C. Thomas, 1981.

Napier, John. "The Evolution of the Hand." *Scientific American*, 207, no. 6, 1962.

Noback, Charles R. *The Human Nervous System: Basic Principles of Neurobiology*. McGraw-Hill, 1975.

Oakley, Kenneth P. *Frameworks for Dating Fossil Man*, rev. ed. Aldine, 1968.

———. *Man the Tool-Maker*, 6th ed. Trustees of the British Museum (Natural History), 1972.

Passingham, Richard L. *The Human Primate*. Freeman, 1982.

Semenov, S. A. *Prehistoric Technology*. Cory, Adams and Mackay, 1964.

Seyfarth, Robert M., Dorothy L. Cheney, and Peter Marler. "Monkey Responses to Three Different Alarm Calls: Evidence of Predator Classification and Semantic Communication." *Science*, 210, 1980, 801–803.

Shapiro, Harry L. *Peking Man*. Simon and Schuster, 1974.

Tobias, Phillip V. *The Brain in Hominid Evolution*. Columbia University Press, 1971.

van Lawick-Goodall, Jane. *In the Shadow of Man*. Houghton Mifflin, 1971.

von Koenigswald, G. H. R. *Meeting Prehistoric Man*. Harper and Brothers, 1956.

Washburn, Sherwood L. *Social Life of Early Man*. Aldine, 1961.

———, and Phyllis Dolhinow, eds. *Perspectives on Human Evolution*, 4 vols. Holt, Rinehart and Winston, 1968–1976.

Weidenreich, Franz. *Apes, Giants and Man*. University of Chicago Press, 1946.

Wolpoff, Milford H. *Paleoanthropology*. Knopf, 1980.

## PART IV MODERN HUMANITY

*General References for Further Reading*

Bordes, François. *The Old Stone Age*. McGraw-Hill, 1968.

Brues, Alice M. *People and Races*. Macmillan, 1977.

Campbell, Bernard G. *Human Ecology: The Story of Our Place in Nature from Prehistory to the Present*. Aldine, 1985.

Garn, Stanley M. *Human Races*, 3rd ed. Thomas, 1971.

———, ed. *Readings on Race*, 2nd ed. Thomas, 1968.

Leakey, L. S. B., and Vanne Morris Goodall. *Unveiling Man's Origins*. Schenkman, 1969.

Service, Elman R. *The Hunters*. Prentice-Hall, 1966.

Wilson, Edward O. *On Human Nature*. Harvard University Press, 1978.

*Sources*

Bordes, François. *A Tale of Two Caves*. Harper & Row, 1972.

Brace, C. Loring. "The Fate of the 'Classic' Neanderthals: A Consideration of Hominid Catastrophism." *Current Anthropology*, 5, no. 1, February 1964.

———. Ridiculed, Rejected, but Still Our Ancestor, Neanderthal." *Natural History*, May 1968.

Breuil, Abbé H. *Four Hundred Centuries of Cave Art*. Centre d'Études et de Documentation Préhistoriques, 1952.

Brose, David S., and Milford H. Wolpoff. "Early Upper Paleolithic Man and Late Middle Paleolithic Tools." *American Anthropologist*, 73, October 1971.

Chapman, Frank M. *Handbook of Birds of Eastern North America*. Dover, 1966.

Clark, J. Desmond. *The Prehistory of Africa*. Praeger, 1970.

Clark, J. Grahame D. *Prehistoric Europe: The Economic Basis*. Philosophical Library, 1952.

Cole, Sonia. *The Prehistory of East Africa*. New American Library, 1965.

Coon, Carleton S. *The Hunting Peoples*. Little, Brown, 1971.

———. *The Living Races of Man*. Knopf, 1965.

Daniel, Glyn A. *A Hundred and Fifty Years of Archaeology*. Duckworth, 1975.

Eiseley, Loren. "Neanderthal Man and the Dawn of Human Paleontology." *Quarterly Review of Biology*, 32, no. 4, December 1957.

Howell, F. Clark. "European and Northwest African Middle Pleistocene Hominids." *Current Anthropology*, 1, 1960.

———. "Recent Advances in Human Evolutionary Studies." *Quarterly Review of Biology*, 42, 1967.

Klein, Richard G. *Man and Culture in the Late Pleistocene*. Chandler, 1969.

Kranzberg, Melvin, and Carroll W. Pursell, Jr., eds. *Technology in Western Civilization*, vol. 1. Oxford University Press, 1967.

Kurtén, Björn. *The Ice Age*. Putnam's, 1972.

———. *Pleistocene Mammals of Europe*. Aldine, 1968.

Laming, Annette. *Lascaux*. Penguin, 1959.

Lee, Richard B., and Irven DeVore, eds. *Man the Hunter*, Aldine, 1968.

———. *Studies of the !Kung San and Their Neighbors*. Harvard University Press, 1976.

Leroi-Gourhan, André. *Treasures of Prehistoric Art*. Abrams, 1967.

Maringer, Johannes. *The Gods of Prehistoric Man*. Knopf, 1960.

———, and Hans-Georg Bandi. *Art in the Ice Age*. Praeger, 1953.

Marshack, Alexander. *The Roots of Civilization*. McGraw-Hill, 1972.

Mulvaney, D. J., and J. Gordon. *Aboriginal Man and Environment in Australia*. Australian National University Press, 1971.

Oakley, Kenneth P. *Frameworks for Dating Fossil Man*, rev. ed. Aldine, 1968.

————. *Man the Tool-Maker*, 6th ed. University of Chicago Press, 1972.

————, Bernard G. Campbell, and Theya I. Mollison. *Catalogue of Fossil Hominids*, 3 vols. Trustees of the British Museum (Natural History), 1967–1977.

Ovey, C. D., ed. "The Swanscombe Skull." *Occasional Papers of the Royal Anthropological Institute*, 20, London, 1964.

Semenov, S. A. *Prehistoric Technology*. Cory, Adams and Mackay, 1964.

Smith, G. Elliot. "Neanderthal Man Not Our Ancestor." *Scientific American*, August 1928.

Solecki, Ralph S. *Shanidar: The First Flower People*. Knopf, 1971.

Trinkhaus, Erik, and William W. Howells. "The Neanderthals." *Scientific American*, 241, no. 6, 1979.

Turnbull, Colin M. *The Forest People*. Simon and Schuster, 1962.

Ucko, Peter J., and Andrée Rosenfeld. *Palaeolithic Cave Art*. McGraw-Hill, 1967.

Van Doren Stern, Philip. *Prehistoric Europe*. Norton, 1969.

Wolpoff, Milford H. *Paleoanthropology*. Knopf, 1980.

# CREDITS

*The author acknowledges permission to use material from the following sources:*

**PART I** *Pages 4–5* Leonard Lee Rue/Monkmeyer Press Photo Services.

**Chapter 1** *Page 6* Neg. #329182, Courtesy of the American Museum of Natural History.
*Figure 1–1* The Bettmann Archive. *Figure 1–2* Buckland, *Reliquiae Diluvianae. Figure 1–3* Redrawn with permission from Tom Stalker-Miller map from *Darwin and the Beagle,* New York, Harper and Row, 1969, © 1969 by Alan Moorehead. *Figure 1–4* Illustration from *Journal of researches into the Natural History and Geology of the countries visited during the voyage of H.M.S. Beagle around the world,* by Charles Darwin, 1890. *Figure 1–5* The Bettmann Archive, Inc. *Figure 1–6* The Bettmann Archive. *Figure 1–7* Rainbird Publishing Group, Ltd. *Figure 1–8* T.H. Huxley, *Evidence as to Man's Place in Nature,* frontispiece, (London, 1863). *Figure 1–9* Photo Lennart Nilsson, *A Child is Born,* Dell Publishing Co., Inc., New York. *Figure 1–10* From *In the Shadow of Man,* by Jane van Lawick-Goodall. Copyright © 1971 by Hugo and Jane van Lawick-Goodall. Reprinted by permission of Houghton Mifflin Co. and Collins Publishers.

**Chapter 2** *Page 38* Jos. Bellinc, 15—, Musée Calvet, Avignon.
*Figure 2–2* Gibbs Gately. *Figure 2–3* © JoAnn Verburg. *Figure 2–5* top, Edna Bennett/Photo Researchers; bottom, Doug Fulton/Photo Researchers. *Figure 2–6* right, J.R. Napier and P.H. Napier, *A Handbook of Living Primates,* Academic Press, Inc. (London, Ltd.) © 1967 by Academic Press, Inc. (London, Ltd.) *Figure 2–7* (photo) Lester V. Bergman and Associates, Inc. *Figure 2–8* left, Andy Bernhaut/Photo Researchers; right, Jen and Des Bartlett, The National Audobon Society Collection/Photo Researchers.

**Chapter 3** *Page 56* The Picture Cube.
*Figure 3–1* The Bettmann Archive. *Figure 3–9* Brown Brothers. *Figure 3–10* Neg. #311414, Courtesy of the American Museum of Natural History. *Figure 3–11* Reproduced by permission from *The Sunday Times,* London.

**Chapter 4** *Page 72* Courtesy J.H. Tjio.
*Figure 4–1* Brookhaven National Laboratory. *Figure 4–4* Courtesy J.H. Tjio. *Figure 4–6* Courtesy of Boston Sickle Cell Center. *Figure 4–9* Data from *The Human Species: An Introduction to Physical Anthropology* by Frederick S. Hulse (New York: Random House, 1971).

**PART II** *Pages 92–93* Leonard Lee Rue/Animals, Animals.

**Chapter 5** *Page 94* M. Krishnah/Animals, Animals.
*Figure 5–2* Sarah Blaffer Hrdy/Anthro Photo. *Figure 5–3* New York Zoological Society. *Figure 5–4* Zoological Society of San Diego. *Figure 5–6* Redrawn from *The Antecedents of Man,* Le Gros Clark, 1971; © by Edinburgh University Press. *Figure 5–11* top, Irven DeVore/Anthro Photo; bottom, Ralph Morse, *The Primates,* courtesy of Animal Talent Scouts, Inc. and L. D'Essen and V. Phifer. *Figure 5–12* Fritz Goro. *Figure 5–13* E.L. Simons, Duke Primate Center. *Figure 5–14* E.L. Simons, Duke Primate Center. *Figure 5–15* E.L. Simons, Duke Primate Center. *Figure 5–16* Courtesy of the Trustees of the British Museum (Natural History). *Figure 5–17* Reproduced with permission from Day, Michael H., *The Fossil History of Man,* 3rd ed., 1984, Carolina Biology Reader Series. Copyright Carolina Biological Supply Co., Burlington, N.C.

**Chapter 6** *Page 118* Bellerose/Stock Boston
*Figure 6–1* New York Zoological Society. *Figure 6–2* top left, D.J. Chivers/Anthro Photo; top right, © Werner Muller/Peter Arnold, Inc.; bottom right, Nina Leen; bottom left, © Werner Muller/Peter Arnold, Inc. *Figure 6–4* Wolf Suschitzky. *Figure 6–5* left, Suzanne Ripley, *The Primates;* right, Steve Gaulin/Anthro Photo. *Figure 6–6* top left, Michael Rugier, *The Primates;* top right, Ralph Morse, *The Primates* and Animal Talent Scouts, Inc.; bottom right, Richard Wrangham/Anthro Photo; bottom left, New York Zoological Society. *Figure 6–7* Dr. Geza Teleki. *Figure 6–8* James Moore/Anthro Photo. *Figure 6–9* top, Sarah Blaffer Hrdy/Anthro Photo; bottom, Irven DeVore/Anthro Photo. *Figure 6–10* Irven DeVore/Anthro Photo. *Figure 6–11* Joseph Popp/Anthro Photo. *Figure 6–12* Irven DeVore/Anthro Photo. *Figure 6–13* Irven DeVore/Anthro Photo. *Figure 6–14* Stan Washburn/Anthro Photo. *Figure 6–15* Irven DeVore/Anthro Photo. *Figure 6–16* D.J. Chivers/Anthro Photo. *Figure 6–17* Irven DeVore/Anthro Photo. *Figure 6–18* Dian Fossey, courtesy of National Geographic Magazine. *Figure 6–19* Terrence Spencer, *The Primates. Figure 6–20* From *In the Shadow of Man* by Jane van Lawick-Goodall. Copyright © 1971 by Hugo and Jane van Lawick-Goodall. Reprinted by permission of Houghton-Mifflin Co. and Collins Publishers. *Figure 6–21* Dr. Geza Teleki. *Figure 6–22* Irven DeVore/Anthro Photo.

**Chapter 7** *Page 160* Photo A.R. Hughes, by permission of Dr. Phillip V. Tobias.
*Figure 7–2* Ernest Shirley. *Figure 7–4* William Terry. *Figure 7–5* top, Redrawn from *Man-Apes or Apes-Men,* 9th ed., Le Gros Clark, © Edinburgh University Press; bottom, Redrawn from *History of Primates,* 9th ed., Le Gros Clark, © British Museum (Natural History). *Figure 7–6* Transvaal Museum, D.C. Panagos. *Figure 7–8* Transvaal Museum, D.C. Panagos. *Figure 7–9* Transvaal Museum, D.C. Panagos. *Figure 7–10* Transvaal Museum, D.C. Panagos. *Figure 7–11* Kenneth MacLeish, *Early Man. Figure 7–12* Redrawn from the *South African Archaeological Bulletin,* Vol. 17, No. 66 (June 1962), p. 111.

**Chapter 8** *Page 180* Irven DeVore/Anthro Photo.
*Figure 8–2* UPI/Bettmann Archive. *Figure 8–3* Robert Campbell © National Geographic Society. *Figure 8–4* Gordon W. Gahan © National Geographic Society. Figure 8–5 Des Bartlett/Photo Researchers. *Figure 8–8* Redrawn and adapted by permission from Bernard Campbell, "Conceptual Progress in Physical Anthropology: Fossil Man", *Annual Review of Anthropology,* Vol. 1, 1972. *Figure 8–9* F. Clark Howell. *Figure 8–10* John Reader, *The Missing Link. Figure 8–11* National Museums of Kenya. *Figure 8–12* National Museums of Kenya. *Figure 8–13* The Cleveland Museum of Natural History. *Figure 8–14* top, The Cleveland Museum of Natural History; bottom, Redrawn from original drawings by Luba Dmytryk Gudz from *Lucy: The Beginnings of Humankind,* by Donald C. Johanson and Maitland Edey,

1981: Simon and Schuster. *Figure 8–15* Bobbie Brown. *Figure 8–16* The Cleveland Museum of Natural History. *Figure 8–17* Redrawn from original drawings by Luba Dmytryk Gudz from *Lucy: The Beginnings of Humankind* by Donald C. Johanson and Maitland Edey, 1981: Simon and Schuster. *Figure 8–18* Dr. Mary Leakey. *Figure 8–19* © National Geographic Magazine. *Figure 8–21* Jay Matternes, *Early Man*.

**Chapter 9** *Page 214* Irven DeVore/Anthro Photo.
*Figure 9–1* Reproduced with permission from Day, Michael H., *The Fossil History of Man*, 3rd ed., 1984. Carolina Biology Reader Series. Copyright Carolina Biological Supply Co., Burlington, N.C. *Figure 9–3* Redrawn by permission from R.H. Tuttle, "Knuckle Walking and the Problems of Human Origins", *Science*, vol. 166, pp. 953–961, Nov. 21, 1969, © 1969 AAAS. *Figure 9–5* Reprinted from LeGros Clark, *The Antecedents of Man*, 1959, © Edinburgh University Press. *Figure 9–6* National Museum of Kenya. *Figures 9–7, 9–8,* and *9–9* From *Olduvai Gorge*, vol. III, © 1971, by Mary Leakey; used with permission of the publisher, Cambridge University Press. *Figure 9–11* Painting by Burt Silberman, *The Missing Link*; background photo by J. Alex Langley/DPI. *Figure 9–12* George B. Schaller.

**PART III** *Pages 250–251* Andrew Hill/Anthro Photo.

**Chapter 10** *Page 252* Anthro Photo.
*Figure 10–1* From an unpublished manuscript: *Trinil, A Biography of Professor Dr. Eugene Dubois, the Discoverer of Pithecanthropus Erectus*, by Dubois' son, Jean M.F. Dubois. *Figure 10–2* Culver Pictures. *Figure 10–4* Neg. #298897, Courtesy of The American Museum of Natural History. *Figure 10–5* Courtesy of the Rijksmuseum van Natuurlijke Historie, Leiden. *Figures 10–6* and *10–7* From an unpublished manuscript: *Trinil, A Biography of Professor Dr. Eugene Dubois, the Discoverer of Pithecanthropus Erectus*, by Dubois' son, Jean M.F. Dubois. *Figure 10–9* Neg. #312823, Courtesy of The American Museum of Natural History. *Figure 10–10* Neg. #2A8657, Courtesy of The American Museum of Natural History. *Figure 10–11* UPI/Bettmann Archive. *Figure 10–12* Redrawn with permission from original drawings by Janis Cirulis from *Mankind in the Making* by William Howells © 1959, 1967. *Figure 10–13* Peabody Museum, Harvard University. *Figure 10–14* UPI/Bettmann Archive. *Figure 10–15* Neg. #333193, Courtesy of The American Museum of Natural History. *Figure 10–16* Courtesy of the Trustees of the British Museum (Natural History). *Figure 10–17* National Museums of Kenya. *Figure 10–20* From Mark L. Weiss and Alan E. Mann, *Human Biology and Behavior: An Anthropological Perspective*, 3rd ed., p. 318, copyright © 1981 by Mark L. Weiss and Alan E. Mann. Reprinted by permission of the publisher, Little, Brown and Company, Inc.

**Chapter 11** *Page 282* Irven DeVore/Anthro Photo.
*Figure 11–1* Courtesy of Henry de Lumley. *Figure 11–2* top, Redrawn with permission from "A Paleolithic Camp at Nice" by Henry de Lumley, *Scientific American* 220:5, © 1969 Scientific American, Inc.; bottom, Nina Leen. *Figure 11–3* Courtesy of Henry de Lumley. *Figure 11–4* Courtesy of Henry de Lumley. *Figure 11–8* M. Riboud/Magnum

Photos. *Figure 11–9* Redrawn by permission from *The Old Stone Age*, by Frances Bordes © Frances Bordes 1968, Weidenfield & Nicolson, publishers. *Figure 11–10*. M. Riboud/Magnum Photos. *Figure 11–11* Lee Boltin.

**Chapter 12** *Page 306* Marjorie Shostak/Anthro Photo.
*Figure 12–2* From *The Cry of the Fish Eagle* by Peter Molloy, published by Michael Joseph Ltd. *Figure 12–3* F. Clark Howell. *Figure 12–4* Nicolas Fasciano, *The First Men*. *Figure 12–5* F. Clark Howell. *Figure 12–6* Marjorie Shostak/Anthro Photo. *Figure 12–7* Irven DeVore/Anthro Photo. *Figure 12–8* From G.H.R. Koenigswald, *Begegnung mit dem Vormenschen* © 1956, Eugen Diederichs Verlag, Köln.

**Chapter 13** *Page 330* Richard Lee/Anthro Photo.
*Figure 13–1* top, Richard Wrangham, Richard Wrangham, Irven DeVore/all Anthro Photo; bottom, DeWys Inc., A. Borodulin, DeWys Inc. *Figures 13–2* and *13–3* From *In the Shadow of Man* by Jane van Lawick-Goodall, © 1971 by Hugo and Jane van Lawick-Goodall. Reprinted by permission of Houghton Mifflin Co. and Collins Publishers. *Figure 13–4* Nina Leen. *Figure 13–7* From Daniel E. Sheer, ed., *Electrical Stimulation of the Brain*, © 1961 by permission of The University of Texas Press. *Figure 13–8* Louis and Virginia Kay/DPI.

**PART IV** *Pages 352–353* Danile Nordi/FPG.

**Chapter 14** *Page 354* Ralph Solecki, Columbia University.
*Figure 14–1* Courtesy of the Rheinisches Landesmuseum, Bonn. *Figure 14–2* Neg. #27935, Courtesy of The American Museum of Natural History. *Figure 14–3* Collection Musée de l'Homme. *Figure 14–4* Collection Musée de l'Homme. *Figure 14–5* Courtesy Masson S.A. Editeur, Paris; from Boule and Vallois, *Les Hommes Fossiles*, 1952. *Figure 14–8* Courtesy of the Trustees of the British Museum (Natural History). *Figure 14–9* left, Courtesy of the Trustees of the British Museum (Natural History); right, Peabody Museum, Harvard University. *Figure 14–10* Redrawn with permission from original drawings by Janis Cirulis from *Mankind in the Making* by William Howells © 1959, 1967. *Figure 14–11* Courtesy of Henry de Lumley. *Figure 14–14* left, Peabody Museum, Harvard University; right, Collection Musée de l'Homme *Figure 14–15* Redrawn with permission from original drawings by Janis Cirulis from *Mankind in the Making* by William Howells, © 1959, 1967.

**Chapter 15** *Page 380* J. Kelley/Anthro Photo.
*Figure 15–2* Copyright © 1969 Scientific American, Inc. *Figure 15–5* Courtesy of the Field Museum of Natural History, Chicago. *Figure 15–6* Lee Boltin. *Figures 15–8, 15–9* and *15–10* Redrawn by permission from *The Old Stone Age* by Frances Bordes. © 1968 by Frances Bordes. Published by Weidenfeld & Nicolson. *Figures 15–11* and *15–12* Redrawn by permission from *Gods Of Prehistoric Man* by Johannes Maringer. © 1960 by Alfred A. Knopf, Inc. *Figure 15–13* Redrawn by permission from *The Old Stone Age* by Frances Bordes. © 1968 by Frances Bordes. Published by Weidenfeld and Nicolson. *Figure 15–14* Otto van Eersel, *Early Man*. *Figure 15–15* Redrawn by permission from *The Old Stone Age* by Frances Bordes. © 1968 by Frances Bordes. Published by Weidenfeld & Nicolson. *Figures 15–16* and *15–17* Ralph

Solecki, Columbia University. *Figure 15–18* Peabody Museum, Harvard University. *Figure 15–19* Collection Musée de l'Homme.

**Chapter 16** *Page 410* Novosti Press Agency, London, England. *Page 411* From "The chestnut casts his flambeaux," *The Collected Poems of A. E. Housman.* Copyright 1922 by Holt, Rinehart and Winston. Copyright 1950 by Barclays Bank Limited. Reprinted by permission of Holt, Rinehart and Winston, Publishers; The Society of Authors as the literary representative of the Estate of A. E. Housman; and Jonathan Cape Limited, publishers of A. E. Housman's *Collected Poems.*
*Figure 16–3* Peabody Museum, Harvard University. *Figure 16–4* Courtesy of the Trustees of the British Museum (Natural History). *Figures 16–5, 16–6* and *16–7* Redrawn by permission from *The Old Stone Age* by Frances Bordes. © 1968 by Frances Bordes. Published by Weidenfield & Nicolson. *Figure 16–8* Copyright © 1979 Scientific American, Inc. *Figure 16–9* top left, Courtesy of the Trustees of the British Museum (Natural History); top right, Courtesy of the Israel Department of Antiquities and Museums; bottom, Peabody Museum, Harvard University. *Figure 16–10* top left, Peabody Museum, Harvard University; top right, Collection Musée de l'Homme; lower left, Peabody Museum, Harvard University; lower right, Neg. #310724, Courtesy of the American Museum of Natural History.

**Chapter 17** *Page 434* FPG.
*Figure 17–1* Patrimoine de l'Institut Royal des Sciences Naturelles de Belgique. *Figure 17–2* Otto van Eersel, *Early Man. Figure 17–3* Pierre Boulat. *Figure 17–4* Richard Jeffery, courtesy of J. Tixier. *Figure 17–5* Pierre Boulat. *Figure 17–6* Axel Poignant. *Figure 17–7* Neg. #39686, Courtesy of The American Museum of Natural History. *Figure 17–8* Axel Poignant. *Figure 17–9* Enrico Ferorelli/Dot. *Figure 17–10* Neg. #273695, Courtesy of The American Museum of Natural History.

*Figure 17–11* © Alexander Marshack. *Figure 17–12* Ralph Morse, *Cro-Magnon Man. Figure 17–13* © Alexander Marshak. *Figure 17–14* Photo by Mamiya Press, Seker 1:35/100mm, F/11 material ORWO. *Figure 17–15* Gordon Tenney. *Figures 17–16* and *17–17* Novosti Press Agency, London, England.

**Chapter 18** *Page 460* NYT Pictures.
*Figure 18–4* David Rubinger. *Figure 18–7* From Mark L. Weiss and Alan E. Mann, *Human Biology and Behavior: An Anthropological Perspective,* 3rd ed., p. 421. Copyright © 1981 by Mark L. Weiss and Alan E. Mann. Redrawn by permission of the publisher, Little, Brown and Company, Inc. *Figure 18–9* From *The Living Races of Man,* by Carleton S. Coon, with Edward E. Hunt, Jr. Copyright © 1965 by Carleton S. Coon. Reprinted by permission of Alfred A. Knopf, Inc. *Figure 18–10* left, J.F.E. Bloss/Anthro Photo; right, Arktisk Intitut. *Figure 18–11* Adapted from *The Human Species: An Introduction to Physical Anthropology,* 2d ed. by Frederick S. Hulse. Copyright © 1963, 1971, by Random House, Inc. Adapted by permission of Random House, Inc. *Figure 18–12* From *The Living Races of Man,* by Carleton S. Coon, with Edward E. Hunt, Jr. Copyright © 1965 by Carleton S. Coon. Reprinted by permission of Alfred A. Knopf, Inc. *Figure 18–13* top left, Maxwell Coplan/DPI; top middle, J.I. Ferster/Anthro Photo; top right, Jerry Frank/DPI; lower left, Camera Hawaii/DPI; lower middle, Irven DeVore/Anthro Photo; lower right, Camera Hawaii/DPI. *Figure 18–14* J.F.E. Bloss/Anthro Photo. *Figure 18–15* Marjorie Shostak/Anthro Photo. *Figure 18–16* left, Natur-historisches Museum, Vienna; right, Jiro Tanaka/Anthro Photo. *Figure 18–17* Martin Etter/Anthro Photo. *Figure 18–18* Balzer/Stock Boston. *Figure 18–19* Smolan/Stock Boston. *Figure 18–20* Lejeune/Stock Boston. *Figure 18–21* Richard Katz/Anthro Photo. *Figure 18–24* Clockwise from upper left: The Bettmann Archive; Brown Bros.; Gatewood/Stock Boston; Herwig/Stock Boston; The Bettmann Archive.

# Index

Page numbers in italics refer to illustrations.

## DATE DUE

| | | | |
|---|---|---|---|
| COL JUL 22 1985 | | | |
| | | | |
| | | | |
| | | | |
| | | | |
| | | | |
| | | | |
| | | | |
| | | | |
| | | | |
| | | | |
| | | | |
| | | | |
| | | | |
| | | | |
| | | | |
| | 201-6503 | | Printed in USA |

LITTLE, BROWN AND COMPANY
BOSTON

ISBN 0-316-12553-9